LISTEN TO THIS!

LEADING MUSICIANS RECOMMEND
THEIR FAVORITE RECORDINGS

Alan Reder &
John Baxter

HYPERION

NEW YORK

Library of Congress Cataloging-in-Publication Data

Reder, Alan.
    Listen to this! : leading musicians recommend their
favorite artists and recordings / Alan Reder and John
Baxter.
        p. cm.
    ISBN 0-7868-8260-3
    1. Popular music—Discography. 2. Musicians—Biography.
I. Baxter, John. II. Title.
    ML156.4.P6B44   1999
016.78164—dc21   99–19504
                                                            CIP

FIRST EDITION
10 9 8 7 6 5 4 3 2

Book design by Richard Oriolo

To Hyiah, Ariel, Ajene,

Travis, and Jace

CONTENTS

ACKNOWLEDGMENTS

L isten to This! is the culmination of a nearly four-year-long project and a much longer dream. Hundreds of people have contributed to its realization along the way and if we fail to mention some of you in the following paragraphs, please forgive us.

First of all, we are grateful beyond words to all artists who were interviewed for the book. We would like to make special mention of a few, without whose early participation this book would not exist. We began this work long before we had a book contract, in the hopes that a publisher would recognize its worthiness. Many musicians shared that faith and agreed to be interviewed or otherwise associated with the project in this early stage. They include Charles McPherson, Jerry Harrison, David Grisman, Taj Mahal, Greg Brown, Pat Metheny, Doug Sahm, Andrew Hill, Graham Parker, Herbie Hancock, Bobby McFerrin, Laurie Lewis, and Michael Doucet. Please know that this book would not exist without you. We are also indebted to the various people who helped us make those early contacts, especially Gary Stewart and his assistant Christine Ostrander at Rhino Entertainment; Mike Kappus and his employees Margot Nassau, Becky Mussell, and Catherine Reid; Linda Goldstein; Michael Martin; Megan Rubiner-Zinn; Carey Williams; Pam Grisman; Eric Pederson; Eric Alan; and Herman Edel.

Several other musicians gave permission for future interviews during this preliminary stage. We had to finesse the book's concept in the process of pursuing a book contract and were not able to include these individuals, a painful exclusion for us both personally and artistically because those excluded are some of the finest in the world in their genre. Thank you for your generosity and we hope you understand.

In many cases, it was an artist's publicist or manager who first believed in this project and then convinced their client to take part. In nearly all cases, publicists, managers, or other contacts were crucial to making the interviews happen. We got to know many of you quite well over the phone and hope we get the chance to work together again. In addition to those named above, thank you Alexis Alexiades, Martha Baratz, April Biggs, Mike Cacia, Scott Cameron, Coran Capshaw, Melanie Ciccone, Millie Clements, Norman Cohen, Lance Cowan, Burrill Crohn, Jack Cruz, Chris Cuevas, Joanna Dean, Gregg DeMammos, Butch Denner, Bertis Downs, Gillian Durden-James, Alan Eichler, Jaime Farbstein, Kim Fuller, Rick Gershon, Joanna Gillespie, Dan Gillis, Verna Gillis, Mitch Goldstein, Laurie Gorman, Leigh Grinder, Ave Maria Hackett, Chris Harris, Danny Heaps, Stan Hertzmank, Matt Hickey, Tracy Hill, Peter Himberger, Keiko Jones, Leslie Jones, Melissa Jones, Danny Kahn, Kevin Kennedy, Jennifer Lasker, John Leal, Harold Levanthal, Mene Lopes, Sherry McAdams, Jennifer McMahon, Dennis McNally, Tony Margherita, Bob Merlis, George Michailow, Tracy Miller, Nikki Mitchell, Caroline Morgan, Miki Mulvihill, Kerry Murphy, Jessica Nathanson, Kymberlee Norsworthy, Shauna O'Brien, Thomas O'Keefe, Kevin O'Neal, Deborah Orr, Cynthia Parsons, Martin Pike, Clare Pritty, Mark Pucci, Patrick Robinson, Elisa Sanders, Susan Scofield, Wayne Sharp, Sheila Sheath, Laurie Stalter, Yvonne Staples, Julie Steeg, Antos Stella, Cece Stelljas, Susan Stewart, Ron Stone, Stan Strickland, Jeff Thompson, Chris Tobey, Sue Tropio, Chris Tuthill, Jill Ulrich, Linner Vasoll, Mark Williams, Shelly Wiseman, and Jill Wylly.

Promoters and concert presenters in our area were tremendously cooperative in helping us get access to musicians appearing locally. Thank you Melody Bynum of the Buffalo Music Hall, Ashland, Oregon; Mike Sturgill and Ron McUne of the Britt Festivals, Jacksonville, Oregon; and Tom Olbrich, Southern Oregon University Program Board, Ashland, Oregon.

For our agent/pal Laurie Fox, this project was as much a labor of love as it was for us. Without her support, this project, again, wouldn't have happened. And without the support of Linda Chester, Laurie doesn't happen. Thank you both. We really have it good with you and we never forget it.

Our editor, David Cashion, not only applied his considerable skills to hone this book into final form but helped us shape our artist list as well. Many friends offered their musical expertise in areas where we had holes (no, we have not listened to every record that was ever made), including Peter Gaulke, Kelly Minnis, Phil Catalfo, Gregg Arreguin, Keri Green, David Harrer, Eric Teel, Anna Beauchamp, George Collinet, and Ron Kramer.

Alan owes an unpayable debt to his wife, Hyiah, who knew what this book meant to him and never once complained that the considerable hardships (if you only knew!) she endured in its behalf were too much. Ariel and Ajene always understood what it meant when Daddy said, "I'm working right now," even though for months on end it seemed like he said little but.

John thanks family members John and Elizabeth Baxter, and Carol, Jerry, Griffin, Aishlin, and Dylan Harrison for their support and encouragement, which often included room and board; the entire staff of Jefferson Public Radio, who put their professional lives out of joint so he could work on this project; and his dear friends from the 'hood, Keri Green and Wilma Oksendahl, for their kind, patient spirits. Thanks also to Roger Stevenson for his friendship and skills as a translator; to our other translators, Celine and Vincent Anthonioz and Natalie Ruiz Jones; and to Kelly Weisheipl for inspiration as the deadline loomed.

Finally, we want to mention all the artists we hoped to include in this project but who "left town" before we could get to them, among them: Jerry Garcia, Carl Perkins, Don Cherry, Townes Van Zandt, Johnny Adams, and Betty Carter. They'd make a hell of a band.

LISTEN TO THIS!

INTRODUCTION

L isten to This! is the first guide to recorded music based on recommendations by musicians rather than critics. A large cross section of the world's leading popular musicians was approached to participate in *Listen to This!* All quoted material in this book is from original interviews conducted for this project unless otherwise indicated.

As you read interviewees' comments, you'll note that musicians tend to listen differently to music than do fans and critics. Fans and critics usually form their impressions of a record based on how they hear it as a whole. Musicians often look through the other end of the telescope, focusing on details such as how a particular instrumentalist is playing on the disc. This enables them to hear aspects of a record that others might miss. For example, many jazz critics and purist fans rejected the albums that guitarist Wes Montgomery made in the late 1960s because of their syrupy production values and orchestrations. But you'll see how Pat Metheny cuts right through the sugar-coating to acknowledge the quality of Montgomery's playing, which was superb on those albums.

How to Use This Book

The way an entry in *Listen to This!* appears depends on the information the interviewee gives about it. As general conventions, song titles appear in quotes—as in "A Day in the Life"—and album titles are in italics—as in *Sergeant Pepper's Lonely Hearts Club Band*. To help you find an album in the event you have to order it from a store or catalog, the record label is included in parentheses—as in (Rhino). If a single release includes several CDs, it is usually indicated with the label designation—as in (2 CDs: Rhino)—and occasionally within the text. The following examples explain other variations you will encounter:

EXAMPLE 1: The interviewee names a specific album by an artist.
> Listing: **Bob Dylan**—*Highway 61 Revisited* (Columbia).

EXAMPLE 2: The interviewee names favorite songs on an album as opposed to the album itself.
> Listing: **Bob Marley and the Wailers**—"Slave Driver" on *Catch a Fire* (Tuff Gong).

EXAMPLE 3: The interviewee names a favorite artist but doesn't select specific songs or albums. In this case, we, the authors, intervene—as designated by the symbol ◉—and suggest recordings that will introduce you to that artist, with emphasis on the qualities that the interviewee mentioned.
> Listing (from Pete Seeger's section): **Mississippi John Hurt**—Pete first heard Hurt in 1941. "I've never been expert enough to play Mississippi John Hurt stuff.... I admired him tremendously." ◉: *1928 Sessions* (Yazoo) captures the original recordings made of Hurt's music. *Memorial Anthology* (Adelphi), a two-CD set of Hurt's post-"rediscovery" performances in the mid-1960s, includes a 31-minute interview of Hurt by Pete Seeger.

EXAMPLE 4: The interviewee names a favorite song on an out-of-print or difficult-to-find album. The song is available on a current compilation.
> Listing: **Mary Wells**—"My Guy." ◉: *Mary Wells' Greatest Hits* (Motown).

If the interviewee does not emphasize particular aspects of a recommended artist, then we recommend recordings that are more generally introductory as well.

In those places where we make recommendations, we don't rely on our opinions alone. We have consulted various experts as well as such well-respected written guides as *The Rolling Stone Album Guide*, *The Penguin Guide to Jazz*, *The All Music Guide*, *The NPR Guide to Building a Classical CD Collection*, and a variety of Internet resources so that the recommendations represent a wide consensus of critical opinion.

Some albums mentioned may be out of print. We have indicated that in some places, but in general it's impossible to be current about a record's availability in the constantly shifting landscape of the recording business. See the appendix for help in finding obscure music, including out-of-print recordings.

Because our interviewees themselves represent a highly select group of musicians (see below), we asked them to name favorites among their own recordings as well. To give you a fuller sense of their work and so as not to neglect important records that they chose not to mention, we have supplemented their self-reviews in most cases with our own introduction to their discographies. These comments are also signified by the symbol .

ABOUT THE ARTISTS WHO APPEAR
IN *LISTEN TO THIS!*

How were the artists selected?

In compiling the list of artists we approached for *Listen to This!*, we sought to represent as many musical genres as possible, with certain restrictions. We didn't interview classical artists for the most part because classical music is a world of its own deserving its own book. However, many of those who appear in this book are classical music fans and recommend their favorite recordings in this genre. In addition, we weren't able to cover more than a sampling of world music artists—to do more would require a book devoted to world music exclusively. In fact, the scope of this book dictated that we limit ourselves to a select group of artists in each genre.

We only invited artists whom we considered artistically important or impressive—in other words, who had the depth and creative impact to make a contribution that readers would value. No artist was invited simply because of fame or number of record sales. There simply isn't the space in a book like this to include all members of a band, so we restricted ourselves to leaders, founders, key songwriters, and the like. We also limited ourselves to no more than two members from any one group.

Why isn't so-and-so included?

Obviously, not everyone invited to interview for this book was available to participate. Successful musicians have a great many demands on their time. Some have almost every spare moment booked years in advance. In addition, many musicians see their mission in life as making music, not talking about it. Some artists are extremely private and grant few interviews. Artists who are involved in making albums—and in pop, that process can last several years for a single record—often refuse to be interviewed while concentrating on their creative work. Many artists write their own books in which they talk about their favorite music, in which case participation in this project presents a competitive or contractual problem. Some reserve all their interview time for newspapers or magazines, not books, because they are mainly interested in promoting an upcoming concert or just-released record.

Fortunately, there are so many outstanding artists in popular music that we did not have to compromise with any of our choices. It would take several volumes this size to include every deserving musician, but if it becomes possible to make this an ongoing endeavor, we'll do our best to corral every great musician we missed the first time around.

How come the list of influences and favorite records by so-and-so is different from what I've seen in other publications?

Most musicians listen to such a vast quantity of music that not even a large book such as this one can begin to capture it. Their list of favorites and influences may also change from day to day depending on what mood they're in, what they've been listening to lately, or, especially in the case of records they last heard some time ago, what they remember. As such, any list of favorite recordings is necessarily incomplete and transitory. We've provided the date of the interview so you can place the interviewee's comments in the context of that period in his or her career.

HOW TO GET THE MOST OUT OF *LISTEN TO THIS!*

- To discover more excellent music, we suggest that you look beyond the recommendations made by your favorite artists to recommendations made by other interviewees in the book who create similar types of music or have similar musical interests.

- We also suggest that you look beyond the entries of the best-known artists to artists you may not know a great deal about. In our opinion, some of the most interesting lists and most knowledgeable artists we encountered during the course of this project were those who record for small, independent labels—for instance, Laurie Lewis, Robert Wyatt, Michael Doucet, Dave Alvin, and Peter Holsapple.

- In addition, use the index to see how many times an artist or album is recommended. That too may cue you to intriguing artists or albums you may not know about or have overlooked. For instance, Dave Matthews, Ani DiFranco, and Victoria Williams all rave about an obscure but very special album by Mary Margaret O'Hara called *Miss America*.

- To help lead you to other music you might enjoy, we have noted with an asterisk the name of any interviewee mentioned directly or indirectly by an interviewee. For instance, when Joey Spampinato of NRBQ talks about the Everly brothers, the Everlys are highlighted with an asterisk because Don Everly also has his own section in the book.

ARTIST
ENTRIES

R Y A N   A D A M S   (August 19, 1998)

The Ryan Adams now hailed as one of the bright young songwriters of the "New Depression" country-rock movement is not the same musician you would have projected from his youth. It's true that Ryan was raised in North Carolina, with Stanley Brothers and Louvin Brothers albums on the family's record shelves, and banjos and mandolins in the air. The music that first lit his wick, however, was more clang than twang—a Corrosion of Conformity record when he was 13, followed in short order by the Los Angeles hard core of Black Flag, the New York art noise of Sonic Youth, and the tunefulness-turned-up-to-ten of outfits like Social Distortion and Hüsker Dü. "Complete, unadulterated pain" is how Ryan describes Hüsker Dü's *New Day Rising* when we reach him by phone in New York, where he has just relocated. "I really absolutely knew I wanted to play when I heard that record. It's like, 'I wanna make somebody else feel like I just felt.' " Sonic Youth's *Sister*, same thing: "I thought, 'God, I'd love to feel like what that sounds like.' "

But the soil that you grow up in doesn't wash off, as Ryan noticed after he started a punk band called the Patty Duke Syndrome: "Everything I started to write at that time was on acoustic guitar, which turned into electric, but I always did these bends and stuff that wouldn't be any different from the Flying Burrito Brothers, except for mine would be really loud." Hearing X-offshoot the Knitters started rural-izing his musical ideas. The light came on full candlepower when he was spinning Gram Parson's *GP* with a musician friend, Eric "Skillet" Gilmore, after his band broke up: "We were listening to 'Streets of Baltimore' and I was like, 'Wow, this is great!' And we ended up listening to Merle Haggard and this rarities George Jones collection. And then it was weird. I mean, I knew all that music. I knew all the song titles and a lot of the words. I just didn't know [I knew]." Enter Whiskeytown, with Gilmore its sometimes drummer.

The Whiskeytown sound retains a vague punk echo—a howl in some vocals, some intentional instrumental slop. The country rock content, however, is 180-proof. With a little perspective, Ryan now understands the strange odyssey that carried him back to his Southern roots. When he was in the boonies, he tended to write things that were "metropolitan and busy—that way I didn't end up feeling bored in the middle of this country environment." When he moved to the city, he started writing country " 'cause I was like basically trying to beat the metropolitan environment and think my way back home." When Ryan's back in North Carolina, he pens material "that's really loud and it's the complete, unadulterated rock side of me. [And then our band will be in the city for a week] and I'll come to a sound check with this country song. I don't know where I've gotten it. I coulda sat four blocks down from the Empire State Building and written something that Gram woulda come up with."

RYAN ADAMS'S FAVORITE ARTISTS AND RECORDINGS

Black Flag—*Damaged* (SST). "It's like this violent street record, completely youth-oriented."

*Sonic Youth—*Sister* (SST) and *Daydream Nation* (DGC). Ryan says the former was "the most intensely beautiful music I'd ever heard" when he first encountered it. About the latter, he exclaims, "God, what a perfect double album."

Hüsker Dü—*New Day Rising* (SST). Ryan loved the band's *Zen Arcade* and *Flip Your Wig* (both SST), but "the record that I was looking for by them" was this one.

Social Distortion—*Mommy's Little Monster* (Triple X).

*X—*Under the Big Black Sun* (Elektra), *Los Angeles* (Slash), *See How We Are* (Elektra), and *Live at the Whiskey a-Go-Go* (Elektra). *Sun* is Ryan's favorite X record overall but the others spent plenty of time in his stereo, too: "Even though they're very much a Los Angeles band, I always felt kind of that X sounded like something lost somewhere out in the desert, or in the Midwest." : *Los Angeles*, X's debut, is available on a twofer CD with the group's second record, *Wild Gift* (Slash).

*The Knitters—*Poor Little Creatures in the Road* (Slash). This country rock sideband featured X's John Doe and Exene Cervenka plus the Blasters' *Dave Alvin, later to join X for *See How We Are*.

Gram Parsons—*GP/Grievous Angel* (Reprise). "We listened to that just about every day."

Stanley Brothers—*Stanley Brothers & Clinch Mountain Boys, 1953–58 & 59* (2 CDs: Bear Family).

George Jones—Ryan and his bandmates listened mainly to Jones's early singles. : See Master List.

Loretta Lynn—*Singin' with Feelin'* (Decca).

The Nitty Gritty Dirt Band—*Will the Circle Be Unbroken* (EMI America). "A huge, huge record for me. . . . That's pretty much where I learned most of my standards from."

*The Band—*Rock of Ages* (Capitol), *Music from Big Pink* (Capitol), and *The Last Waltz* (Warner Bros.). "I go back to The Band all the time, sort of like this centerpiece of what I would like consider to be the perfect mix. They use bluegrass instrumentation, R and B, soul."

The Rolling Stones—*Exile on Main Street* (Virgin). Songs such as "Torn and Frayed," "Sweet Black Angel," and "Sweet Virginia" on this album inspired Ryan's own electric country music: "That stuff really, really, really turned me on, 'cause I liked the fact that they were using electric guitars, almost predominantly, on stuff that you'd think of more in a country blues setting."

Merle Haggard—Ryan knows Haggard's music not so much through his albums but through covers by other artists and by taping Haggard tracks off compilation albums. : See Master List.

Tammy Wynette—*D-I-V-O-R-C-E* (Epic). "The production on that album, and her singing, and the arrangements—it's all perfect. It's so unadulterated. I think she wrote like two songs on that record but regardless, she owned all the versions."

Emmylou Harris—*Elite Motel* (Reprise) and *A Quarter Moon in a Ten Cent Town* (Warner Bros.). As with Tammy Wynette, Ryan is knocked out by how completely Harris owns the material she covers.

*Alejandro Escovedo—*Gravity* and *Thirteen Years* (both Watermelon). " 'By Eleven' on *Gravity*—that song is the most ridiculously heart-wrenching song in the world. . . . [When I play one of his records], I sort of sit in front of the stereo, absorbed by it. And that's when it really like opens up and you find out how huge what he's saying is."

*Lucinda Williams— : See the section on Lucinda and her recordings.

Fleetwood Mac—*Rumours* (Reprise), "Sara" on *Tusk* (Warner Bros.), and "Gypsy" on *Mirage* (Reprise). In addition to the Mac's widely lauded songcraft, Ryan loves how the band hints at its influences in traditional music while inventing its own sound. But except for the odd song, he hasn't liked the albums since *Rumours*.

Epic Soundtracks—*Change My Life* and *Rise Above* (both Bar/None). Ryan especially likes the song "She Sleeps Alone: Love Fucks You Up" on the latter album: "He's not a great singer but I like that. . . . He's just relaying the sentiment as good as he can."

Nikki Sudden—*The Jewel Thief* (U.F.O.) "It's the worst singing you ever fuckin' heard in your life, but he's trying to make a country record real bad. I mean, you can't listen to the thing unless you're bent backwards on bourbon. Then it makes sense [laughs]. . . . But dammit, he'll write a good song." Sudden was in Swell Maps with Epic Soundtracks (his brother).

Big Star—#1 *Record/Radio City* (Stax) and *Third/Sister Lovers* (Rykodisc). Ryan says Whiskeytown was especially influenced by this supremely talented but star-crossed group's ballads such as *Radio City's* "Back of a Car": "You can't come across better pop ballads than by those guys at that time."

Beer—"Probably our biggest influence of all, after we learned to play our instruments, was Miller Hi-Life. No shit. Just sittin' around with a beer, and ending up writing something."

RYAN ADAMS'S OWN RECORDINGS

"I love that record," Ryan says about Whiskeytown's debut, *Faithless Street*, originally released on the tiny independent label Mood Food, and re-released with twelve additional tracks by the band's current major label, Outpost. The basic album blends relatively straight country tracks with dirty electric rock, made dirtier still, Ryan notes, " 'cause I had a really crappy guitar, and I was playing my guitar through a bass amp." The added tracks include five from a project that was never released from what Ryan calls "a very Big-Star influenced time."

The Big-Star focus shows up again in the smart pop songcraft of tracks like the hit "16 Days" on *Strangers Almanac* (Outpost), the album that spurred the critics' excitement about Ryan. *Strangers* retains the dirty guitar sounds of *Faithless*—"We still let the guitars be out of tune, but that's just because to me a guitar is just supposed to make noise. It isn't supposed to be perfect," Ryan says. Despite that overlay of Gen-X attitude, the theme is pure country heartache. "We wanted to try to recreate the sound of one huge, terrible breakup," Ryan says. "And it worked, you know."

TERRY ADAMS (May 15, 1997)

For Terry Adams, NRBQ's untamed genius of the keyboards, even the greatest songs have always been more about the sounds than the words. "The first [music] I remember," he tells us, "is some four-record set on Merry-Go-Round Records by the Mother Goose All-Stars, and the reason I liked this so much was because of the organist on it. Very strange organist. I wish I knew who it was. I must have been three or somethin'. . . . To this day, sometimes when I'm playing organ, I try to get that sound."

Terry took the first Jimmy Reed record he heard as a youngster in much the same way. "What made this, besides how great the music was," he says, "was the fact that I couldn't understand what he was sayin'. My brother and I tried to figure it out, and the less we knew what he was sayin', the more I liked it." Elvis Presley, similar deal: "I think that once I found out what those lyrics were years later, it was a disappointment. It's not as much fun to hear it now."

"The reason for this," Terry explains, " is that I'm primarily and have always been interested in instrumental music. . . . I guess when vocalists would sing in a way that I couldn't understand what they were sayin', they became instrumentalists, too." And at least in this area, not much has changed over the years, he says: "When I hear music, I hear the band, and later on I start thinkin' about what the singer's talkin' about."

This same disposition that enables Terry to hear songs as instrumentals also enables him to hear all music as one. As "outside" a musician as you'll find in popular music, Terry sometimes plays as much with his palms and forearms as his fingers, splashing his solos with a discordant mishmash of notes. Even when he goes "linear," he often skews the lines a la Thelonious Monk, with impeccable hints of R&B or rockabilly dropped in like greeting cards from a long-absent friend. We ask Terry at what age free music started making sense to him: "I don't remember drawing any lines at any point," he says. "I was open to all music and still think music's all one thing. So as it came, whatever I heard, I learned from it. I didn't even understand what the fuss was about, about so-called far-out music. It sounded perfectly natural to me."

TERRY ADAMS'S FAVORITE ARTISTS AND RECORDINGS

Jimmy Smith—"Walk on the Wild Side." "I can remember my friends and I just rolling on the floor over that organ solo," Terry says about this famous Smith track. : *Verve Jazz Masters 29: Jimmy Smith* (Verve).

Sun Ra—*Secrets of the Sun* (Saturn) and *Fate in a Pleasant Mood* (Evidence). The former is the first Sun Ra record Terry bought, in the mid-1960s. The latter is an album he wore out in that same period: "When I first got to New York, I had to look him up immediately, so I guess around '67 I started seein' him live and he invited me to his apartment at one point at one of their rehearsals and he handed me a forty-five of 'Rocket 9' and he said 'This is especially for you.' " NRBQ recorded a version of the tune on their 1969 debut album and still play it today, often accompanied by horn players from Sun Ra's Arkestra who appear with the 'Q on occasion.

George Jones—"How Come It." Rockabilly music is one of the main ingredients in the eclectic stew that is NRBQ, but Terry took in this music more as a genre and style than by focusing on individual artists. Still, this single, from a brief period in Jones's career in the late 1950s when he recorded rockabilly singles as "Thumper Jones," is one that Terry recalls making a strong impression. ⬤: That track is included on the various artists compilation, *Rarest Rockabilly & Hillbilly Boogie: The Best of Ace Rockabilly* (Ace).

Thelonious Monk—*Monk's Dream* (Columbia), *Signals* (Savoy), *Criss Cross* (Columbia), and *Monk's Music* (Riverside). Terry discovered Monk's music in a record shop without ever being told about it: "The first thing I heard by him was 'Off Minor' by his septet [from *Monk's Music*]. He gave the tune a really pianistic arrangement, where he's got the trumpet playin' the crossover left-hand notes, really high, so it's seemingly random. That was the most beautiful music I'd ever heard, and still is." Another favorite Monk track is "Crepuscule with Nellie" from *Criss Cross*: "The first time I heard that one, it was richer than chocolate cake. There are no words for how beautiful the harmony is."

Paul Bley—*Footloose* (Savoy). Terry discovered Bley on a Sonny Rollins/Coleman Hawkins album and immediately sought out *Footloose*, the only album available by Bley at the time: "I ordered it by mail and heard all this beautiful piano playin' done on Carla's [Bley—see below] compositions, which were maybe what Ornette Coleman would've written had he been a piano player. I think that Paul Bley is brilliant and, of course, Carla Bley is a great composer. And I especially like that era [early 1960s]."

Carla Bley—Terry doesn't name particular albums, he just likes the songs by this noted avant garde jazz composer/pianist, formerly married to Paul Bley. "I always liked 'Vashkar.' Of course, we liked 'Ida Lupino.' We slaughtered that pretty good ourselves. She liked it, though." ⬤: Versions of "Ida Lupino" appear on Paul Bley's *Closer* (ESP) and Carla Bley's *Dinner Music* (ECM). A version of "Vashkar" appears on Paul Bley's *Footloose* (see above). By the way, Terry plays piano and organ on Carla's *Musique Mecanique* (Watt/9).

TV Theme Music—"A lot of the music I really loved came off of the TV. For example, 'Have Gun, Will Travel'—the opening theme for that was very powerful, written by Bernard Herrmann. Some songs on television were like in the opposite direction. There was a show called *Science Fiction Theater,* and every time I hear that I gotta laugh. It sorta sounds like somethin's gonna happen but nothin' ever does, sorta like the show itself."

John Cage—*Twenty-five Year Retrospective Concert of the Music of John Cage* (Wergo). Terry borrowed this multi-LP set so frequently from his public library that "I could've owned it."

Johann Sebastian Bach—Clavier-Übung (4 CDs: Music and Arts). Terry also used to check out this series of works from the library. These legendary recordings, played on the harpsichord by Ralph Kirkpatrick, were made by the Haydn Society in 1952. ⬤: Believe it or not, the anniversary edition of NRBQ's *Tap Dancin' Bats* (Rounder) includes an unrehearsed, loose version of "Capricio," a movement from this set.

Bunky and Jake—*LAMF* (Mercury). Jake later cut records with a group he called "Jake and the Family Jewels." Terry is a great admirer of his: "He has his own sound and is overlooked and not heard enough."

The Lovin' Spoonful—*Hums of the Lovin' Spoonful* (Kama Sutra). This record, the band's third, has been packaged on CD with the group's 1965 debut, *Do You Believe in Magic?*, as *Do You Believe in Magic?/Hums* (Kama Sutra). Terry's fans will hear the impact of this group on NRBQ instantly.

The Byrds—*Fifth Dimension* (Columbia). Terry says this album "used to bring me to tears."

The Beatles—*Revolver* (Capitol). "I think people have a long way to go before they catch up with this record. To me, that's the freshest, most original thing they ever did."

TERRY ADAMS'S OWN RECORDINGS

Terry says he can't really name a favorite NRBQ album but he knows what he's shooting for with the band's music: "When the band is being itself and when we play with each other with the real spirit that we have, unexpected things happen, and that's when I'm most delighted with the music. I don't really like to have things all planned out to the point where you're just filling in the spots correctly." Hopefully, he says, this sense of surprise is present in places in all the group's discs.

⬤: The most widely appreciated NRBQ album is 1978's *NRBQ at Yankee Stadium* (Mercury), a facetiously titled studio disc with a fabulous collection of songs by Terry, bassist *Joey Spampinato, and then-guitarist Al Anderson and some of the best playing the band has ever recorded. The album shows off the bard's remarkable range, which encompasses roots-conscious rock, McCartney-esque romantic confections, cracked pop, bent country, and all manners of jazz. The 1969 debut, *NRBQ* (Columbia), reveals just how consistent the group's delightfully unique vision has been throughout its three-decade-plus run. Other highlights in the group's extensive, joyous catalog include *Scraps/Workshop* (Annuit), a compilation of two early albums; 1979's *Kick Me Hard* (Rounder), a wilder and far more typical 'Q release than the more disciplined *Yankee Stadium*; 1980's *Tiddlywinks* (Rounder), much in the vein of *Yankee Stadium* in both attitude and quality; 1983's *Grooves in Orbit* (Rhino); 1994's *Message for the Mess Age* (Rhino); and the superb two-CD compilation, *Peek-A-Boo: Best of NRBQ (1969–1989)* (Rhino). In 1995, Terry cut a solo jazz instrumental album *Terrible* (New World), joined by NRBQ-mate *Joey Spampinato, Marshall Allen from Sun Ra's band, and trombonist Roswell Rudd. Terry has also produced three recordings of zydeco legend Boozoo Chavis including *Boozoo Chavis* (Nonesuch). The Neanderthals' *The Modern Stoneaged Family* (Sundazed) was produced by Terry as well. He plays on the disc, too, along with 'Q drummer Tom Ardolino. "You've heard of garage music—this is cave music." Terry chuckles.

LUTHER ALLISON (June 24, 1997)

Where it counted most, on disc and on stage, Luther Allison long ranked among the blues elite. But with the American public and media, Luther was a third-class citizen of electric blues guitar. *Buddy Guy could complain, legitimately, that he never got the attention of an Eric Clapton. Still, he, the late Albert Collins, and others—not to mention the "King of the Blues" B. B. King—cast a long shadow that obscured Luther's accomplishments. In frustration, Luther moved to France in 1984 to be closer to the French and German audiences that were his biggest fans. In the '90s, playing with the fire of a man half his age, he began to reclaim the land that was his by virtue of birth and talent. Unfortunately, death cut short his effort. A few days after our 1997 interview, he was diagnosed with lung cancer that had spread to his brain. The disease took his life six weeks later, just prior to his 58th birthday, abruptly ending one of the most tragically underpublicized careers in blues.

Born to a poor cotton plantation family in rural Arkansas, "next to the baby of fifteen children," as he put it, Luther moved with his family to Chicago when he was in his teens. He grew up without a record player at home, but made up for it with two important compensations—the family's "raggedy" radio and an older brother who played guitar. On WDIA out of Memphis he heard B. B. King, Robert Nighthawk, Joe Hill Louis, Muddy Waters, Howlin' Wolf, and Sonny Boy Williamson, star of the King Biscuit Time show. Luther was too young at first to take it all in, but his brother wasn't—he learned songs off the airwaves and played them for Luther. When little bro' was 18, he showed him the basic chords and scales so Luther could play the songs for himself and not just note-for-note but "our own way." A quick study, Luther was soon hanging out in Chicago blues clubs and sitting in with such royalty as Waters, Wolf, and Elmore James.

Getting to play with the legends was like a college education in the blues. The post-grad internship came when Luther went out on his own to compete for attention in the fertile Chicago blues scene. "As an entertainer, we knew what everybody else was doin'. For instance, Buddy Guy, Magic Sam, Freddie King, Otis Rush, Luther Allison, and more come up . . . at the same time. Our job was to respect [each other], stay out of each other's way, and outdo each other if we can, and every chance we got, to punch out each other's lights, right?" Luther said with a laugh. "That's the way it was. But it's the truth, man—one thing we had was respect for each other."

Luther made his debut recording in 1969 for Chicago's then-minor Delmark label. He promoted the record with annual performances at the nearby Ann Arbor Blues Festival and made such an impact that Motown signed him in 1972 as their first and only blues artist. He cut three albums for the giant label but the albums didn't sell. Touring for the records, however, enabled him to develop new audiences in Japan and Europe, leading to his migration to France. He continued to perform in the United States on occasion, however. In the 1990s, he proved at one blues festival after another that few on the circuit could match his inspired playing and soulful vocals. After signing with the American blues label Alligator, he released a string of typically impassioned albums that buoyed his street reputation even further. Whether those steps would ever have added up to the wider recognition he desperately sought will never be known. But his recorded legacy will document for all time that during his life, justice was not served.

LUTHER ALLISON'S FAVORITE ARTISTS AND RECORDINGS

B. B. King—Luther first heard B. B. playing on WDIA as "Blues Boy" and "Pep-ti-kon Boy" King (Pep-ti-kon was the commercial sponsor) when he was growing up. He told us with great pride that he once visited King backstage and found him in possession of Luther's own latest album. : See Master List.

Robert Nighthawk—Like Luther, an under-recognized player, Nighthawk was a key figure in the evolution of blues slide guitar. Born in the Mississippi Delta and transplanted to Chicago, he played acoustic and electric Chicago blues with a Delta edge. : Nighthawk recorded only sporadically, but with generally excellent results.

Check out *Robert Lee McCoy (Robert Nighthawk): The Bluebird Recordings 1937–1938* (RCA), *Bricks in My Pillow* (Delmark), or *Live on Maxwell Street* (Rounder).

Joe Hill Louis—Louis preceded B. B. King as WDIA's "Pep-ti-kon Boy." He also appeared on the station as "Be-bop Boy." ⦿: Louis can be heard on the anthology *Sun Records Harmonica Classics* (Rounder) and *Be-bop Boy with Walter Horton* (Bear Family).

Sam Cooke—"Little Red Rooster" and "Tennessee Waltz." "When he made ['Little Red Rooster'] all over again, it was beautiful, like a whole different sound. . . . Sam Cooke moved it up out of what we would call that low down, dirty blues trend up into that modern, beautiful sound that we all had to adapt to, too." ⦿: "Little Red Rooster" shows up on *Greatest Hits* (RCA) and *Rhythm & the Blues* (BMG). "Tennessee Waltz" appears on the live . . . *at the Copa* (Polygram) and *The Late & Great* . . . (RCA).

Otis Rush—"Once I got involved [in the blues], Otis Rush was my clearest figure," Luther said in tribute to the great Chicago guitarist. ⦿: *Door to Door* (MCA/Chess) devotes six of its smokingest tracks to Rush; the rest go to Albert King, who is pictured alone on the cover. Other releases with Rush in top form include 1976's *Right Place, Wrong Time* (Hightone), 1977's *Live in Europe* (Evidence), 1975's *So Many Roads: Live* (Delmark), 1991's *Lost in the Blues* (Alligator), and 1994's *Ain't Enough Comin' In* (This Way Up). *Cobra Recordings, 1956–1958* (Paula/Flyright) is a revelatory compilation.

Magic Sam—*West Side Soul* (Delmark).

Jimmy Dawkins—As a teenager, Luther played bass in Dawkins's band for a short time. He and Dawkins remained good friends (Luther lived next door to Dawkins's girlfriend). ⦿: *Kant Sheck Dees Bluze* (Earwig) and *Fast Fingers* (Delmark) are both fine examples of Dawkins's ultra-dirty style; despite the latter title, speed and flash are not his game.

Hubert Sumlin—"He was very close to me, coming up the ladder." ⦿: Sumlin's playing electrifies Howlin' Wolf's greatest recordings; under Wolf's name, see Master List. Sumlin's better solo efforts include *Blues Anytime!* (Evidence) and *Heart and Soul* (Blind Pig).

Willie James Lyon—⦿: This obscure Chicago blues artist can be heard on *Ghetto* (MCM), cataloged under the names W. J. Lyons & W. Kent.

Lefty Dizz—"He was another one with his own special way of doing things." ⦿: *Ain't It Nice to Be Loved* (JSP), *Lefty Dizz with Big Moose Walker* (Black and Blue), and *Somebody Stole My Christmas* (Isabel).

Eddie C. Campbell—Luther says he thought so highly of Campbell's playing that he'd listen even if Campbell "would play a guitar with his feet!" 💿: Campbell's better recordings include *King of the Jungle* (Rooster Blues), *Let's Pick It* (Evidence), and *That's When I Know* (Blind Pig).

Albert King—"To me, he was the ultimate genius of the new generation of the blues. B. B. is a lot different, but they have the same kind of mastery in their mind." 💿: See Master List.

Little Milton (Campbell)—"One of the greatest singers you'll want to hear when it comes to singing anything." 💿: See Master List.

T-Bone Walker—"He was a great rock'n'roller, a great soul man, a great funky R and B rhythm man, and a great bluesman." 💿: See Master List.

The Big Three Trio—"When I knew Willie Dixon in my first days [in Chicago], I knew him as the Big Three Trio, and they played swing jazz that you wouldn't believe. It was very hot, a very, very great group," Luther said. The trio, formed in 1946, also included pianist Leonard "Baby Doo" Caston and guitarists Bernardo Dennis and (beginning in 1947) Ollie Crawford. 💿: *The Big Three Trio* (Columbia).

Bernard Allison—Luther's son, Bernard, also a guitarist, has worked with both his dad and KoKo Taylor, among several others. 💿: Bernard's solo albums include *Hang On* (Peter Pan), *No Mercy* (Inakustik), *Keepin' the Blues Alive* (Cannonball), *Times Are Changing* (Ruf/Platinum), and *Next Generation* (Mondo). He also appears on Luther's *Reckless* (Alligator).

Lonnie Brooks—"He's comin' up there very strongly, a super guitar player." 💿: *Bayou Lightning* and *Hot Shot* (both Alligator); *The Crawl* (Charly).

Johnny Lang—"He is on fire right now and has the greatest playing that any blues guy can have coming up today, or any day," Luther said about the teenaged guitar phenom. "We have played together a number of times. He's gotten all the recognition at a very young age . . . and is going to bring a lot of young people back into the blues." 💿: See Master List.

Johnnie Taylor—"A great gospel singer, a great R and B singer. He's a decent blues singer when you look at the fact that he's around this music, lives this music." Taylor replaced Sam Cooke in the gospel group the Soul Stirrers before leaving for an R and B career. 💿: See Master List.

Freddie King—"Woman Across the River" and "Hide Away." About "Woman Across the River," Luther raved, "I think he just burns this song. Any song he really sings is a great song, but if he was right here, that would be one song I would love him to sing for me." "Hide Away" was King's signature tune. 💿:

The former song originally appeared on *Woman Across the River* (Capitol) and can be found as well on *King of the Blues* (2 CDs: Capitol), a compilation of the tracks King recorded for Shelter Records in the '70s. For the original "Hide Away" and other hot early King tracks, get *Hideway: The Best of Freddie King* (Rhino).

Otis Redding—"Try a Little Tenderness" and "These Arms of Mine." ●: Both songs are on *The Very Best of . . .* (Rhino), as well as more comprehensive compilations. For more Otis, see Master List.

Jimi Hendrix—*Are You Experienced?* (Reprise). Luther especially loved the tracks "Red House" (a blues tune) and "Purple Haze."

LUTHER ALLISON'S OWN RECORDINGS

Luther rated his catalog as follows: "Number one is *Bad News is Coming* [Gordy/Motown], then *Soul Fixin' Man* [Alligator], and then *Reckless* [Alligator]." He also mentioned his first recorded appearance, on the various artists' compilation *Sweet Home Chicago!* (Delmark). Delmark later released his first solo album, *Love Me Mama* in 1969.

●: Like many of his peers, Luther colored his blues with shades of soul, funk, and rock. In addition to the albums he named, you can hear his choice blend on such strong recordings as *Love Me Papa* (Evidence), *Serious* (Blind Pig), and *Blues Streak* (Alligator). Luther didn't often play acoustic so the album *Hand Me Down My Moonshine* (Ruf Records), self-produced and recorded in Luther's living room in St. Cloud, France, is well worth the search. It lacks the fire of his electric albums, but makes up for it in its relaxed warmth. *Ann Arbor Blues & Jazz Festival 1972* (2 LPs: Atlantic) features a ripping version of Percy Mayfield's "Please Send Me Someone to Love." *The Motown Years 1972–1976* (Motown) compiles Luther's work for that label and includes an unreleased track from one of Luther's Ann Arbor appearances.

GREGG ALLMAN (April 2, 1998)

Not too many kids have mapped their lives by the time they're nine years old, but Gregg Allman started the cartography soon after going to his first concert with ten-year-old brother Duane. "It was a black rhythm and blues review headlined by Jackie Wilson and second billing was Otis Redding," Gregg recalls. "Third was B. B. King, then Patti LaBelle and the Blue Belles [the name before the group changed it to LaBelle] and Johnny Taylor, a couple of others on there. Anyway, I saw my first Hammond organ and heard it and didn't have any idea what it was until the next time I went to church and saw it in there, and I said 'Man, they're playin' that thing and it's not supposed to sound like that.' "

When Greg was two, his father was murdered. The following year, his mother moved the family from their native Nashville to Daytona Beach. Shortly thereafter, Gregg was given a guitar as a gift and Duane a small motorcycle. One day, Duane brought what remained of his prized bike home in a sack—"he literally drove it till it just fell apart," says Gregg. "Then with his motorcycle in pieces in the garage, he was askin' me, 'Well, whatcha got there?' And we had more fights over that guitar, let me tell you. And my mother, to keep one of us from killin' the other, she had to get him one." Thus began a musical partnership that continued until Duane died, tragically and ironically, in a 1971 motorcycle accident at the age of 24.

The boys started learning tunes to play, but mostly white rock songs by artists like the Ventures and Duane Eddy until they met an African-American musician named Floyd Miles. Through Miles, the boys discovered the music that immediately became their obsession. For Duane, that meant the country blues of Lightnin' Hopkins. Gregg hooked into tight horn bands like James Brown's and B. B. King's, and then the blues-soul-R&B stew cooked up by Little Milton Campbell, who became one of Gregg's biggest vocal influences.

The rest of the story is better known. Growing up in the South and hanging with Miles and his buddies left a permanent stamp on the brothers. They soon displayed the ability to play and sing black music as if it was etched into their lives, not just the vinyl of their record collections. Gregg's vocals were astonishing in their blues authenticity, even when he was in his early 20s. Duane's soulful, biting guitar work would later earn him session work at Alabama's famed Muscle Shoals studio, where he would embellish tracks by Aretha Franklin, *Wilson Pickett, and King Curtis among others. After the usual hard times of playing in bands for little pay and less credit, they fell in with four like-minded and talented souls and formed The Allman Brothers Band, one of the most powerful musical units that rock has ever known. Looking back, Gregg notes with no small satisfaction, "When [Duane and I first] got a band together, our goal was to have the best band in Daytona Beach, and by God we made that goal. Far as I know, we still got the best band in Daytona Beach."

GREGG ALLMAN'S FAVORITE ARTISTS AND RECORDINGS

James Brown—*Live at the Apollo* (Polydor).

B. B. King—*Live at the Regal* (ABC/MCA). "I wore out more copies of that. Whoo!"

Little Milton (Campbell)—Gregg likes everything Campbell ever recorded: "I used to have his whole damn collection in my car." 🔘: See Master List.

Bobby "Blue" Bland—Gregg and his bands have performed a number of Bland's tunes. He likes all of Bland's recordings. 🔘: See Master List.

Ray Charles—"Good God. I'm sure he had a certain effect on shaping everybody that sang any kind of blues or rhythm and blues," notes Gregg, who loves all of Charles's classic recordings. 🔘: See Master List.

Otis Redding—"Can't Turn You Loose," "These Arms of Mine," and "I've Been Loving You Too Long." " I always liked the slow love songs, which you could really put a lot of power into." 🔘: *The Very Best of . . .* (Rhino) contains all three songs on one disc. For more Otis ballads, see Master List.

Sonny Boy Williamson ("Rice" Miller)—*The Real Folk Blues* (MCA/Chess). Early in his career, Gregg modeled himself after Williamson: "I never even gave it any thought that, you know, why don't you try and sound like yourself? because that's all you're ever gonna sound like is yourself."

James Carr—Gregg covered Carr's "Dark End of the Street" on his solo album *Searching for Simplicity.* "I did that because it was one of my brother's favorite songs, and he was always on me to learn that song and I just said, 'Man, nobody can sing like James Carr.' And then when he was on the staff at Muscle Shoals, he cut it with Clarence Carter. And I thought about all this stuff and I thought, 'My God, it might be a little late, but I'm sure he'll hear it wherever he is.' " 🔘: A treasure for soul music fans, *The Essential . . .* (Razor & Tie), surveys the career of the underappreciated soul greats who often sounded more than a little reminiscent of Otis Redding.

Etta James—"Oh, God, everything she sang she had such power. She'd get back about a yardstick away from the mike and just blow, man." 🔘: See Master List.

Jimmy Smith—*The Sermon* (Blue Note), *The Cat* (Verve), and *Bashin': The Unpredictable . . .* (Verve). "There's only ever been one B3 player," Gregg says of Smith.

Booker T. and the MGs—"Some people asked me how I would describe my style of organ playing. I said 'I just put the gravy on the meat.' And that's kinda what [Booker T. Jones] did, you know." 🔘: See Master List.

Throughout the Allman Brothers' run, as well as during its two acrimonious break-up periods in the 1970s and 1980s, Gregg has released a series of solo records. Typically, these spotlight his trademark vocals and Hammond B-3 organ playing on covers, original tunes, and re-cast Allman Brothers material. His favorite of those remains the first one, 1974's *Laid Back* (Capricorn). He also calls attention to two largely ignored efforts, 1977's *Playin' Up a Storm* (Capricorn) and 1988's *Just Before the Bullets Fly* (Epic). The former "got dropped on its butt" by the record company, Gregg says, "because the Brothers broke up." The latter suffered a similar fate, Gregg feels, in the record company's excitement over the Allman Brothers reforming. He's particularly proud of his orchestrated rendition of Ray Charles's "The Brightest Smile in Town" on *Playin'*.

From the Allman Brothers catalog, Gregg points first to the same record that almost any ABB fan would—*Live at Fillmore East* (Polydor). Truth be told, it's not a pure concert recording; it was seamlessly edited from a string of Fillmore East shows. But it still stands as one of rock's most potent live documents, with Gregg's vocals and B-3 work, the contrasting but equally impressive styles of guitarists Duane Allman and Dickey Betts, the muscular bass of Berry Oakley, and the polyrhythmic kick of the two drummers, Jaimoe and Butch Trucks, combining to make music with the pulling power of a locomotive. Gregg is also thrilled with the CD reissue package *The Fillmore Concerts* (Polydor), which presents the Fillmore tracks re-edited to their original length and includes additional songs from the same shows, all beautifully remastered. Finally, Gregg mentions 1979's *Enlightened Rogues* (Polydor), a gold record on which guitarist Dan Toler and bassist David Goldflies took the place of Duane and Oakley, the latter killed in a motorcycle wreck a year after Duane's.

: *Beginnings* (Polydor) packages the ABB's first two studio albums, 1969's *The Allman Brothers Band* and 1970's *Idlewild South*, together on one disc. Both records featured the original lineup, strong material, and stellar performances. The near-classic 1972 album *Eat a Peach* (Polydor) came out after Duane's death but he's there on several tracks, including the soaring "Mountain Jam," a live track from the Fillmore East shows. For another hit of the original group on stage, try *Live at Ludlow Garage: 1970* (Polydor), released in 1991.

The first Duane-and-Oakley-less album, 1973's *Brothers and Sisters* (Polydor), showcases a more country-flavored band, with Betts's guitar and vocals now the focus. After reforming in 1989, the group recorded *Seven Turns* and *Shades of Two Worlds* (both Epic) over the next two years. Both represent the group well, remarkable considering the tragedies, turmoil, and personnel shifts they had been through. The passing years and travails have wizened Gregg's vocals, already compellingly mature when he was still a young man. The ABB remain one of the country's hardest-working and biggest-grossing live acts, so expect many more recordings from this enduring blues-rock institution.

Gregg's solid 1998 solo disc, *Searching for Simplicity* (550 Music), includes warm, acoustic-accented reworking of ABB staple "Whippin' Post."

DAVE ALVIN (November 12, 1996)

From the moment he pounded his way into America's music consciousness with the Blasters, Dave Alvin has always sounded like the real deal. His blue-collar folk and blues, his dust-in-your-mouth trad-country, the turbo-charged rockabilly where they all meet—Dave executes all of them with the same wrenching authenticity as the roots music that inspires him. It's not what you'd expect from a beach boy raised in Southern California and fenced in by freeways instead of barbed wire—which only proves that when it comes to musical upbringing, what you stick in your ears matters much more than what you see out your window.

Early in his life, Dave's cousins supplied most of his crucial listening experiences. When he was four or five, Dave inherited prime doo-wop, R&B, and rockabilly 45s from his teenage cousin Donna. Cousin Mike turned Dave on to his bluesy folk idols a couple of years later. Meanwhile, cousin J. J. was growing up on a ranch and bathing Dave's ears in trad-country records.

Hearing so much great American roots music whetted Dave's appetite for more. By the time he was 12, Dave and his brother Phil were scavenging thrift stores for 78s, especially hard-core blues and R&B. But the Los Angeles area offered more than just cheap second-hand records. "In those days," Dave tells us from his Los Angeles home, "a lot of the blues greats were either living in L.A. or playing in L.A. a lot. We could sneak into bars or night clubs and see them at a real tender age. And because we were so young, some of the racial boundaries were down, and these guys like Joe Turner and Eddie 'Cleanhead' Vinson and T-Bone [Walker], or Lee Allen, they were all living in L.A. and we were just like cute, obnoxious little white kids that knew what record they made in 1941 [laughing]."

Turner and Allen, in fact, became close family friends. "I remember the first time I saw [Big Joe], at a club called the Ash Grove here in L.A.," Dave says. "Forget it, that was it. Everything in my life is graded on 'Well, that was good, but it wasn't like seein' Big Joe.' Or it wasn't like seeing Lightnin' Hopkins, who in those days was a pretty staple visitor to L.A."

In those years, Dave defined himself by the blues. The Ray Charles cutouts he bought at the corner Thrifti-Mart changed all that, with Charles singing, say, a bluesy Percy Mayfield tune followed by a Buck Owens song. "In the same way that Ray Charles combined blues and gospel, he was bringing a blues kind of approach to country music," Dave notes. "And that kind of turned me around, into seeing that there really was no difference."

That revelation has served Dave well from the beginning. At first, it helped him accept the paved-over landscape of his hometown as a viable musical environment, even seeing the surf music of his youth as a kind of SoCal folk music. In his professional career, it has enabled him to sound completely at home no matter what the stylistic leap—the Blasters rockabilly, X's poetic punk, the Knitters' country rock, or the various phases of his solo work.

"I'm a history buff of sorts," Dave says, "and to me, America's folk music— and I consider rockabilly folk music—is just the soundtrack to the history of the nation, even up to the writers of today. . . . There's a quote that I wish I had said originally, but it's Wynton Marsalis who said that America's music is where the actual dream [of a melting pot] came true."

DAVE ALVIN'S FAVORITE ARTISTS AND RECORDINGS

Big Joe Turner—*Big, Bad, and Blue: The Big Joe Turner Anthology* (Rhino). "Every American should be made to listen to Big Joe Turner."

Elmore James—*Let's Cut It: The Very Best of . . .* (Ace). This disc includes most of the tracks from *Legend of the Blues* (Kent), an album Dave bought when he was 13 that, more than any other, made him want to be a musician: "To me, it's the best Elmore stuff . . . It sounded like it had just come up from mud and mold and swamp root."

Lightnin' Hopkins—*Lightnin' Hopkins* (Smithsonian/Folkways). At one point early in his life, Dave wanted to *be* Hopkins.

Various artists (including Lightnin' Hopkins)—*The Blues: Smithsonian Collection of Classic Blues Singers* (4 CDs: Smithsonian/Folkways). In the original 3-LP set, one of the discs featured a Hopkins performance at the famed Ash Grove in Los Angeles.

Ray Charles—*Crying Time* (ABC). Dave collected most of Charles's ABC/Paramount records from the 1960s but this 1966 release was his favorite because of its blend of country-esque material with hard blues. ⬤ : *Greatest Hits, Vols. 1–2* (DCC, available separately) cover the ABC/Paramount period.

Elvis Presley—*The Sun Sessions CD* (RCA). "The Sun Elvis stuff to me is pretty magical."

Sunny Burgess—*We Wanna Boogie* (Rounder). This prime rockabilly record is effectively a Sun release. ⬤ : *The Classic Recordings 1956–1959* (2 CDs: Bear Family) includes Burgess's entire Sun output. Dave produced and played on Burgess's 1992 *Tennessee Border* (Hightone).

Junior Parker and His Blue Flames—The Blue Flames were Parker's band when he recorded the original, pre-Elvis version of "Mystery Train" and other tracks for Sun. ⬤ : *Mystery Train* (Rounder) contains at least one take of every song Parker cut at Sun.

Carl Perkins—About the rockabilly recordings of Perkins, Billy Lee Riley, Warren Smith, and Ray Smith (see below), Dave says "all those forty-fives influenced me a lot, because I could see this combination of R and B and country." ⬤ : See Master List.

Billy Lee Riley— ⬤ : See Master List.

Warren Smith— ⬤ : *The Classic Recordings: 1956–59* (Bear Family) includes all of Smith's rockabilly and country sides for Sun.

Ray Smith— ⬤ : *Ray Smith's Greatest Hits* (Columbia, out of print).

Howlin' Wolf—Dave likes the earliest material on Sun as well as Wolf's Chess sides: "Those early Howlin' Wolf records just had that wonderful edge to 'em." ⬤ : *Memphis Days: Definitive Edition, Vol. 1* (Bear Family) covers those raw Wolf sides for Sun that Dave loves. *Memphis Days . . . , Vol. 2* (Bear Family) includes Wolf's early 78s for Chess plus excellent unissued material. For Wolf's Chess albums and later singles, see Master List.

Frankie Lee Sims—Sims was Lightnin' Hopkins' cousin and purveyor of a hard, raw form of Texas blues. ⬤ : *Lucy Mae Blues* (Specialty) covers Sims's mid-1950s recordings for Specialty.

Lazy Lester—"Late, Late in the Evening" and "I'm a Lover, Not a Fighter." Dave says that Lester's mix of swampy, blues feelings with country melodies influenced his songwriting on tunes like "Marie Marie." ⬤ : *I Hear You Knockin': The Excello Singles* (Excello).

Slim Harpo—Like Lazy Lester, Harpo wove together blues, country, and swamp music threads in a way that powerfully impacted Dave. ⬤ : *Scratch My Back: The Best of Slim Harpo* (Rhino).

Lonnie Johnson—"If I could make everyone in America listen to Lonnie Johnson, I think America would just be a better place," enthuses Dave about this crucial link in the development of jazz and blues guitar. ●: *Stepping on the Blues* (Columbia/Legacy) features jazz/blues guitarist Johnson's legendary duets with jazz guitarist Eddie Lang, amazingly advanced considering they were recorded in the 1920s. The 1960 record *Blues and Ballads* (Bluesville), a wee-hours classic, pairs Johnson with jazz guitarist Elmer Snowden for a master course in playing slow with feeling.

Johnny "Guitar" Watson—Two decades before he reinvented himself as a funk-ster in the 1970s, Watson was a sizzling blues guitarist. "I'm kind of a sucker for anything Johnny 'Guitar' Watson did in his career, [including] the funk stuff later on," Dave says. ●: *Three Hours Past Midnight* (Ace) includes three of Dave's favorite tracks, "Too Tired," "Ruben," and "Three Hours Past Midnight." *Gangster of Love* (Charly) includes another Dave fave, "Space Guitar."

Tom Waits—*Closing Time* and *The Heart of Saturday Night* (both Asylum). Waits's first two records, Dave says, showed him that someone can hail from Southern California "and write great songs. And he was writing the kind of songs that I could see in my head. I could picture the diners he was talking about . . . If you want to see me cry, put on one of those."

Jim Ringer—"What I listen to more and more is songwriters," says Dave. "The older I get the more I realize that the song is everything." One songwriter he listens to often is the late Ringer. ●: *The Best of . . . : Band of Jesse James* (Philo).

Mary McCaslin—Married to Jim Ringer until their separation in 1989, McCaslin evolved from a cover artist to a major folk songwriter in the 1970s. Like Dave, she was raised in Southern California and her songs are replete with Western imagery writ large. ●: *Way Out West* (Philo) put McCaslin on the map as a songwriter. *The Best of . . .* (Philo) surveys her three solo albums for Philo in the 1970s, what most consider her peak work.

Tom Russell—A sometimes collaborator with Dave Alvin in recent years, Russell draws on both the cowboy and Latino heritages of the Southwest for his imagery and themes. His material is by turns folk, country, Tex-Mex, and rock. ●: Dave co-produced one of Russell's strongest albums, 1995's *The Rose of San Joaquin* (Hightone). Also try 1988's *Road to Bayamon* (Philo).

Guy Clark—*Dublin Blues* (Elektra). "Every note in every song that he writes and his presentation of his stuff—everything's in a perfect spot."

Robert Earl Keen—*A Bigger Piece of Sky* (Sugar Hill). Dave likes all Keen's records but this one the best: "I feel a lot of camaraderie with the Texas writers. Texas and California are dissimilar in a lot of ways, but in some more basic ways they're incredibly similar . . . I'd say the Hispanic influence had a big deal to do with that. You just had to be open to more diverse influences."

Bob Dylan—*Blood on the Tracks, Highway 61 Revisited, Blonde on Blonde, New Morning,* and *The Basement Tapes* (all Columbia). *Blood* . . . is Dave's favorite Dylan record "just because it's so damned big. It takes in so much, and in a way that only Dylan can get away with." It also includes one of his favorite songs, "You're A Big Girl Now." *The Basement Tapes* "was a big influence on me," Dave says, "because again, it was a seamless mixing of all these American musical forms. And they were doin' it so easily. It was like, 'Oh, we're just goofin' off,' which is why I think it worked so well." Dave also has a weakness for Dylan albums on which Al Kooper and Mike Bloomfield play. Both are on *Highway* . . . and *Blonde* . . . . Kooper returns on *New Morning.*

Merle Haggard— 🔘 : See Master List.

Percy Mayfield—This marvelous songwriter and smooth blues singer wrote many of Ray Charles's best tunes in the 1960s, including "Hit the Road, Jack." He scored a number one R&B hit with "Please Send Me Someone to Love" in 1950. 🔘 : The exceptional *Poet of the Blues* (Specialty) covers his prime material, including "Please Send Me," from 1950–54, the Specialty years. *My Jug and I* (Tangerine), from 1962, features Mayfield singing some of his best songs in front of Ray Charles's big band. The 1969 album *Bought Blues* (Tangerine) is another classy orchestral outing.

Curtis Mayfield— 🔘 : See Master List.

Woody Guthrie— 🔘 : See Master List.

Hank Williams— 🔘 : See Master List.

Iris Dement—"No Time to Cry" on *My Life* (Warner Bros.). "Just forget it. To me, that's the best song written in the nineties."

Billy Joe Shaver—Known more to musicians and critics than fans, outlaw country songwriter Shaver has authored outstanding material for artists such as *Waylon Jennings, Kris Kristofferson, Tom T. Hall, the Allman Brothers, and Elvis Presley. 🔘 : *Restless Wind: The Legendary* . . . *1973—1987* (Razor & Tie) will introduce you to some of Shaver's best material. The 1993 record *Tramp on Your Street* (Zoo) is a strong later record.

David Olney—"Another Place, Another Time" on *High, Wide, and Lonesome* (Philo). "He's a real word craftsman to me."

*Lucinda Williams—"A great craftsperson of words. She's incredible." ⬤ : See the section on Lucinda and her recordings.

Robbie Fulks—*Country Love Songs* (Bloodshot). "Witty, smart-ass country songs." ⬤ : 1997's *South Mouth* (Bloodshot), like *Love Songs*, features Fulks's lyrically clever, musically reverent takes on a variety of trad-country styles and sharp back-up from members of revered bar band the Skeletons. 1998's *Let's Kill Saturday Night* (Geffen) is Fulks's major-label debut.

*Taj Mahal—*Natch'l Blues* (Columbia). "That record had a very big influence on me when I was about eleven or twelve. The way he spanned from country blues to Memphis soul just made a lot of sense."

DAVE ALVIN'S OWN RECORDINGS

Dave finds it hard to choose between his recordings "because in a way I'm proud of everything," but certain albums and tracks do stand out for him, starting with the Blasters' debut, 1980's *American Music* (Hightone). Recorded for a tiny rock-abilly label called Rollin' Rock and long a valued collector's item, the album was reissued in 1997 with six additional tracks from the original sessions. "It really was a bunch of kids who didn't know anything about making a record," Dave laughs. "And I'm partial to that." He also calls attention to the Blasters' *Non-Fiction* (Slash/Warner Bros.) as the album "where I figured out that I could write songs."

From his solo catalog, Dave points to *King of California* (Hightone) as the record that marked his development as a compelling vocalist: "It was like, 'Oh, here's my instrument. Where'd this come from?' " He feels he did his best guitar playing on the overlooked *Museum of Heart* (Hightone). And he loves the medley of his own "Jubilee Train," Woody Guthrie's "Do Re Mi," and Chuck Berry's "Promised Land" on the live *Interstate City* (Hightone): "It kind of organically developed on stage without thinking about it, over the course of touring. But to me it's a way of trying to show what I was just saying, that this music is kind of the soundtrack of our country. . . . I might have said everything I'm ever gonna say in that medley."

⬤ : If you like what you hear on *American Music*, check the Blasters' albums that Dave doesn't mention above: 1981's eponymous major label debut, 1982's live EP *Over There*, 1985's *Hard Line*, or the compilation *The Blasters Collection* (all Slash/Warner Bros.). *See How We Care* (Elektra/Asylum) is the well-received X album featuring Dave's compositions and guitar playing. Dave was a prominent member of the Knitters with X's John Doe and Exene Cervenka; *Poor Little Creatures in the Road* (Slash) captured that music.

Dave's impressive solo catalog includes, besides those he discusses above, the eclectic *Romeo's Escape* (Epic), featuring remakes of tunes written for the Blasters and X as well as excellent new material; 1991's electric roots rock effort *Blue Boulevard* (Hightone); and 1998's largely acoustic, Guthrie-esque *Blackjack David* (Hightone). And don't overlook *Interstate City*, which is a kick-in-the-pants from cuffs to waistband. You won't hear many bands better than Dave's touring group at that time, the Guilty Men.

JOAN ARMATRADING (November 10, 1997)

In the battle for the pop world's attention, the musicians who stand out as originals always have the best chance for success. As a result, record companies will try to make familiar-sounding acts appear novel so they can dazzle the music market into buying something "new." Joan Armatrading's music has never needed that treatment.

None of the fin-de-siecle women singer/songwriters—not Shawn Colvin, not Alanis Morissette, and certainly not Tracy Chapman—would be possible without Armatrading. Back in 1976, when *Joan Armatrading* (actually Joan's third record) shot into the UK Top Twenty, nobody had ever heard anyone quite like her. Her brew was as appealing as it was unique—a combination of literate lyrics, subtly emotive vocals, and slapdash guitar rhythms as gentle as the waves lapping the shore of her native St. Kitts in the British West Indies.

Born in 1950, Joan emigrated with her family to the gritty English city of Birmingham when she was seven. She started making music at the age of 14—not, like so many others in 1964, because she heard the Beatles or the Stones, but because she came home one day and found that her mother had bought a piano. "I used to write funny little limericks and little funny stories and things like that," she tells us by phone from her English home. "And then when my mum got the piano, I started writing . . . and putting music to the lyrics. So there was no song or group or piece of music, really, that started me off."

In a few years, potential female role models began to emerge. Joni Mitchell in particular was stirring the waters. But that was in the United States and made little impact on Joan. "There weren't loads of women around," she points out.

"There wasn't a woman singing and playing the guitar for me to say 'Okay she's doing it, so I'll do it.' I was just doing what I was doing because I enjoyed it." To put it more plainly, she says, "I didn't follow anybody."

Then or since. Joan's music has changed over the years under the guidance of various star producers such as Glyn Johns and Steve Lillywhite. Starting with 1978's *To the Limit*, she began expanding beyond her folky beginnings with touches of rock, reggae, synth-pop, and jazz. She traded in her acoustic guitar for an electric and her playing grew crunchier as well as louder. But through it all, her songwriting approach has remained uniquely hers. As such, you don't get anywhere talking to Joan about her influences—there still aren't any. "Even now if you look in my [record] collection after all these years, it's sort of shameful really, not a lot of them there," she says sheepishly. "You'd actually find more classical recordings than contemporary pop."

JOAN ARMATRADING'S FAVORITE ARTISTS AND RECORDINGS

Muddy Waters—*Electric Mud* (Chess). Blues purists have long derided this record as a sell-out because Waters grafted psychedelia to his sound, but Joan, who first heard it in the late '60s, still plays it today: "He said that he was made to make that album because of Jimi Hendrix and the new young blood. . . . He didn't like the album, which I find incredible because I think it's the most amazing playing on it. So way out—more than Hendrix, to me. And his singing is so fantastic, and the songs are great."

Van Morrison—*Astral Weeks* (Warner Bros.). Joan credits the Van Morrison song "Madame George" from this 1968 album for turning her into a music consumer. "I was nineteen or twenty," she recalls, " I was in Newcastle, in Durham, under the bedclothes, listening to Radio Luxembourg, and I heard this brilliant, brilliant song, and had to wait to the end of it to hear what it was. I rushed out in the morning to buy this record."

George Frederick Handel—*Acis and Galatea*. Joan loves this Handel oratorio, but she also finds it profoundly funny. "It's not meant to be funny," she laughs, "but when you listen to some of the words and the way it's sung—singing 'Happy happy we'—it's so fantastic. . . . [English playwright] John Gay wrote the libretto. I have visions of Handel absolutely creasing up writing this stuff." ●: Recent critically acclaimed versions include those by the King's Consort (two CDs: Hyperion) and London Baroque (two CDs: Musique d'Abord).

Henry Purcell—*Dido and Aeneas*. Joan also enjoys this other vocal masterpiece of the English baroque, from a generation earlier than Handel's. This piece helped form the foundation of early opera. ⬤: Look for versions by the group Les Arts Flórissants with William Christie conducting (Harmonia Mundi) or The English Chamber Orchestra under Raymond Leppard (Philips). A nice budget disc features the Scholars Baroque Ensemble on period instruments (Naxos).

Johann Sebastian Bach—*Magnificat.* "Brilliant," Joan says of her favorite among Bach's compositions, a glorious work for soloists, chorus, and orchestra. ⬤: Try the English Baroque Soloists, conducted by John Eliot Gardiner (Philips), the Academy of St. Martin-in-the-Fields, conducted by Sir Neville Marriner (EMI/Angel), or a budget recording with Helmuth Rilling conducting the Bach Collegium, Stuttgart (Sony).

Wynton Marsalis—Trumpet concertos by Joseph Haydn and Leopold Mozart [Sony] and *In this House, on this Morning* (Columbia). Joan likes Marsalis both as a classical and jazz performer. About the Haydn/Mozart disc, she says, "He's just such a musician, anyway, and he's playing the work of such excellent composers you can't really go wrong." She describes *House*, an extended work by Marsalis portraying a church service, as "sort of gospely with very soulful playing from everybody. I got to see them perform this, and to hear that sort of thing live is very moving."

Mark Knopfler—"As a musician and a guitarist, I think he's one of the best around. If you listen to the guitar playing on 'Money for Nothing,' that riff—it's just fantastic." ⬤: The studio version of "Money" appears on two Dire Straits albums: *Brothers in Arms* (Warner Bros.) and the greatest-hits package *Money for Nothing* (Warner Bros.). There's also a live version on Dire Straits' *On the Night* (Warner Bros.). Knopfler contributed to Joan's album *The Shouting Stage* (A&M) as well, on the title song and "Did I Make You Up?" "It's an album that I produced, but it was fantastic for me to just sit and watch him and appreciate how clever he is," Joan says. "He's a fantastic chap, a very nice bloke, and that always helps as well. His guitar style just flows. It's so musical, so tuneful, and he seems to get just the perfect sound."

Steve Martland—*Patrol* (BMG/Catalyst). Joan recommends this British minimalist composer's title piece on this album. "If you like Michael Nyman and Philip Glass and the Piano Circus," she cautions. "When I listen to classical music, I seem to follow it up by listening to minimalist music."

JOAN ARMATRADING'S OWN RECORDINGS

Joan focuses more on particular tracks than entire albums when discussing her own work. She shares her fans' enthusiasm for "Love and Affection" [on *Joan*

Armatrading, A&M], a song that introduced her to millions of Americans when she performed it on "Saturday Night Live" in the mid-'70s. Beyond that one, she prefers tracks that feature her guitar playing: "Like Fire" on *Joan Armatrading*; "Killing Time" on *Secret Secrets* (A&M); "Sometimes I Don't Wanna Go Home" on *Square the Circle* (A&M); and "Lost the Love" on *What's Inside* (RCA). But her favorite of all is "Willow" on *Show Some Emotion* (A&M).

⊙: Other fine Armatrading albums include 1978's *To the Limit*, 1980's *Me, Myself, and I*, 1981's *Walk Under Ladders*, and 1985's *The Key*. A&M released a compilation in 1996 of Joan's best-known tracks for the label, called *Greatest Hits*.

S U S A N A   B A C A   (February 27, 1998)

Airy, mysterious melodies played on *zamponas* (pan pipes) over the strum of *charangos*—this is the sound of the folk music of the Andes, the first thing that comes to mind when most North Americans think of Peruvian music. But the hypnotic performances, and research, of singer/folklorist Susana Baca, have cued world music fans to another Peruvian sound that is no less compelling—a sound descended, like Baca, from mestizos (people of mixed blood) and born not on mountain peaks but in coastal barrios. It is a sound that has come to be called Afro-Peruvian music because unlike Andean folk, it includes the heritage of African slaves.

"In Peru, we can't separate the music according to cultures: they're all intertwined," explains Susana through a translator when we sit down with her prior to a concert in Medford, Oregon. The weave of Afro-Peruvian music includes elements of Spanish and Indian culture, as well as African strains. And she has woven yet more threads into her own repertoire. She draws on the African-influenced rhythms of Cuban music, the social urgency of the *nueva canción* movement (Latin America's protest music that arose in the 1960s), the improvisational license of jazz, and graceful, literate lyrics contributed by poets. When Susana performs, she is an artist, not a museum curator.

The fact that the various elements come together as gracefully as they do in Susana's music owes perhaps to a childhood "immersed in music," as Susana puts it. Her father was a guitarist and singer, her mother a singer and a beautiful dancer, she recalls. Her mother listened to Cuban music on the radio, where Susana first heard *salseros* like Ignacio Villa. But while their songs, along with those sung in her family, inspired her musically, she found the story they told wanting. "I [also] listened to a lot of creole [mestizo] music in my home," Susana adds, "and later I found that the lyrics in the music didn't say what I wanted to say. I started searching."

As a young woman, Susana pulled together a band that could help her realize her vision. Its combination of poetry and Afro-Peruvian sounds attracted the attention of Chabuca Granda, a noted singer/composer who also was championing Afro-Peruvian music. Susana ultimately moved into Chabuca's house for awhile. "She had a lot of albums," Susana recalls, "and I encountered in her house the works of Silvio Rodriguez, Pablo Milanes, Mercedes Sosa, Violeta Parra. She had all of this music and I was just fascinated by it." Most of these artists were giants in the *nueva canción* movement. Enthralled, Susana incorporated elements of what she heard into her developing style.

Chabuca died suddenly when she was in the process of helping Susana record her first record. The project collapsed but the tragedy only deepened Susana's resolve to unearth, document, and promote African-Peruvian culture with her husband Ricardo Pereira. Her efforts paid off when David Byrne's Luaka Bop label pulled together a compilation called *Afro-Peruvian Classics: The Soul of Black Peru*, with Susana's sinuous "Maria Lando" as its opening track. The song "broke" Susana to the world and paved the way for her Luaka Bop solo debut, co-produced by Byrne.

In describing the music she makes today, Susana makes clear that "the songs we sing are not the same songs that I heard from my parents, aunts, and uncles. We have these roots, but in our music the themes are contemporary. Also I have worked with poets of my generation who have written lyrics especially for me." The mission of celebrating Afro-Peruvian tradition remains but clearly the potential is now bigger than that. As a *New York Times* reviewer put it, "Ms. Baca . . . has the strength to create her own tradition."

SUSANA BACA'S FAVORITE ARTISTS AND RECORDINGS

Ignacio Villa— : Bola de Nieve (International).

Chabuca Granda—Chabuca, a powerful force in Susana's life, is renowned in Latin America. : The title track to the album *La Flor de la Canela* (ANS), Chabuca's best-loved song, gets performed all over the world and has been covered by many Latin artists. Look also for *Época de Oro* (BMG Latin). She is represented as well on the *Afro-Peruvian Classics* compilation mentioned above and below.

Silvio Rodriguez—Cuba's version of *nueva canción* is called *nueva trova*, and Rodriguez and Pablo Milanes (see below) are its leading exponents. Rodriguez supports his revolutionary lyrics with virtuoso guitar playing. : Compilations include the solid *Cuban Classics 1: Canciones Urgentes* (Luaka Bop) and *Dias y Flores* (Hannibal). Rodriguez and Pablo Milanes appear together on the live recording *Silvio Rodriguez y Pablo Milanes en vivo en Argentina* (Cubartista). Two recent releases are *Dominguez* and *Descartes* (both Fonedisc).

Mercedes Sosa—Another South American voice of political change, Sosa was exiled from her native Argentina during the country's "Dirty War." ⬤: Sosa's *Gracias a la Vida* (Philips, re-released by Tropical Music) is a *nueva canción* classic, but an extensive discography makes choosing a single best disc difficult. Other good bets: *30 Años* (Polygram), *Homenaje a Violeta Parra* (Musicrama—see below) and the compilation *Coleccion mi Historia* (Polygram).

Violeta Parra—Parra, a Chilean who died in 1967, helped lay the foundation of *nueva canción* with her folk-based songs of social change. She also introduced older South American songs, and traditional instruments, to young audiences. ⬤: Try *Canto a mi America* (Auvidis), *The Songs of Violeta Parra* (Last Call), or *La Jardinera* (Alerce).

Pablo Milanés—Milanés is Cuba's other main *nueva trova* star with Silvio Rodriguez. ⬤: *Cancionero* (World Pacific) is a Milanés compilation, drawing from Milanés's impressively long discography. If you want more, look for the three-volume *Colección para Vivir* (International), or *Clásicos de Cuba* (Simitar).

SUSANA BACA'S OWN RECORDINGS

⬤: Susana Baca's performance the evening following our interview revealed one of the most exciting, original talents we'd seen in a long time. Her coolly sensuous vocals floated with grace and elegance above the acoustic polyrhythms of her accomplished guitar-bass-percussion trio, like a Latina Billie Holiday accompanied by the musicians of the Buena Vista Social Club. Her eponymous debut record (Luaka Bop/Warner Bros.) captures the essence of what we heard that night to the extent that any studio recording can. In addition to *Afro-Peruvian Classics* (Luaka Bop/Warner Bros.), the track "Maria Lando" appears on the largely African/Latin American compilation *Music from the Coffee Lands* (Putamayo). If you search import sources, you'll also find Susana's *Vestida de Vida* (Kardu) and *Del Fuego y Del Agua* (Tonga). The latter disc also features her husband Ricardo Pereira and Francisco Basili and comes with an exhaustive 180-page book of Susana's research into the roots of Afro-Peruvian culture. But more is on the way in the States: "I have a contract to record four more records for Luaka Bop," Susana cheerfully reports to us.

LOU BARLOW (October 8, 1998)

Lou Barlow has astounded the pop underground with the casual regularity with which he turns out sharp, tuneful songs. Although many are cloaked in noisy, sonic gauze that blurs the edges almost beyond recognition, nothing can hide the craftsmanship underneath, which apparently comes as naturally to Lou as sleep. "I always loved music," he tells us in his shy voice when we reach him in Southern California. "I always wanted to sing. My sister and I used to put on shows for our parents when we were like six or seven, just making up songs. . . . I don't think there was ever a point when I decided [to make music my life]. It just sort of swept me away."

Born in 1966, Lou bought the Beatles' *Rubber Soul* and a greatest-hits package when he was in the sixth grade and "it just set my head on fire. There was just something so perfect about it." Although Lou was learning to play guitar in a school class at the time, "I didn't really think about how to play the music, or I didn't really necessarily want to be in a band. I just wanted to have the Beatles. I mean, they really helped me enjoy my life. You know, I didn't think about what I wanted to be, or what they were, necessarily. I just thought about how I felt listening to them."

Although no music has affected Lou the same way since, the stripped-down, revved-up records of the Ramones came close, and at a critical time. "Once I started going to middle school, everyone was talking about Pink Floyd, and *The Wall* was out at that time, and musicianship was such a huge deal, and I just felt like it was like sports, you know. I didn't want to be tested and I just kind of stopped playing. Until I really heard the Ramones, and I just started putting microphones inside of acoustic guitars and playing through a stereo."

After the Ramones revelation, Lou plunged headlong into the whole punk aesthetic and its most extreme expression, hard core. That led in short order to Lou and pal J. Mascis forming a hard-core band called Deep Wound while in high school in Amherst, Massachusetts; a reunion with Mascis in Dinosaur Jr., the pioneering alt-rockers; and an acrimonious departure after Dinosaur's third album. Lou swore to himself then that he would never again lock himself into any particular sound, and he's kept his word. Although he's become an underground legend with his plethora of concurrent low-fi, home-recorded projects (Sebadoh, the Folk Implosion, the mainly solo Sentridoh, and other solo permutations), nothing—not even Radio Shack production values—is set in stone. The only dependable quality of a Lou Barlow record is the quality of the material. "I don't believe you make great bands or great music by following the right steps," Lou says now. "It's about gaining the trust of the people around you in order for them to open up and for you to open up to them. Because I really believe that's all it's gonna take for a band someday to be better than the Beatles. I believe that can happen. You have to really start from scratch."

LOU BARLOW'S FAVORITE ARTISTS AND RECORDINGS

The Beatles—Early-, middle-, late-period records, it's all the same to Lou: "They're all just like hitting these very deep parts of my brain." ⬤: See Master List.

The Ramones—"I listened to them constantly, just the way that guitar sounded, that roaring guitar. . . . Just a very strange band. Nothing sounds anything like the Ramones, before the Ramones." ⬤: *All the Stuff & More, Vol. 1* (Sire) combines the group's first two albums, plus bonus tracks, on one CD. *All the Stuff & More, Vol. 2* (Sire) does the same for the third and fourth records. 1984's *Too Tough to Die* (Sire) was a late return to simple, blistering form.

Jimi Hendrix—*Are You Experienced?* (Reprise). "That was a pretty pivotal record, but it wasn't very inspiring. I was just totally awestruck. I was like, 'There's no way to do that, you know?' I thought people who tried to sound like Hendrix, it was an awful thing."

The Buzzcocks—*Singles Going Steady* (IRS). "They were a really amazing pop band. They were sort of taking that Ramones thing and totally gassing it even further. The songs were smarter."

Black Sabbath—*Paranoid.* (Warner Bros.). "Black Sabbath was a huge, huge influence to me. [*Paranoid*] was kinda like the Ramones. When I heard the Ramones, the only thing I could compare it to was Black Sabbath being sped up. I told some kids at school that and they threatened to beat me up."

The Dead Kennedys—*Fresh Fruit for Rotting Vegetables* (Alternative Tentacles).

Various artists—*Wanna Buy a Bridge?* (Rough Trade). "It was a compilation of singles that were released around England probably from like 1976 to 1978 or something. And it was bands like the Young Marble Giants, Cabaret Voltaire, Swell Maps, and Delta Five. That record was really influential to me. Very raw recording, but somehow more positive than punk rock."

Bush Tetras—At the time Lou bought Bush Tetras and Liquid Liquid singles, "I was just mail ordering records, like from the *Trouser Press* . . . I wasn't totally into hard core yet, and I wasn't only into new wave. I was into everything." 〔◉〕: See Master List.

Liquid Liquid— 〔◉〕: See Master List.

Young Marble Giants—*Colossal Youth* (Rough Trade). "[It's] really, really cool. It's a very quiet record. The songs are very short."

The Teen Idols—*Minor Disturbance* "I heard it on the college radio station and I couldn't even tell what the music was. It was so fast and it was so short that I had no idea what had happened and I was totally intrigued," says Lou about this hard-core band's EP.

Minor Threat—*Minor Threat* (Dischord). "It was the first time I heard their songs about how horrible it was to get drunk, and you need to keep your mind clear, and I thought that was pretty amazing, because I wasn't a stoner in high school."

The Meat Puppets—*In a Car* (World Imitation) and *Meat Puppets* (SST). Lou describes the EP *Car* as "just completely out of control. Like Minor Threat, they were tight. They sort of introduced tightness. Everyone who was in a hard-core band wanted to be tight after that."

Flipper—"I loved them. They were like really slow, and very messy, and incredibly emotional sounding, to me, and had nothing to do with rock." 〔◉〕: *Generic Flipper* and *American Grafishy* (both Def American) and *Public Flipper Limited* (Subterranean).

Various artists (early psychedelia and garage rock)—"I love sixties psychedelic music. Bands like the Creation. There's so many, like the Nuggets and Pebbles bands. There's a lot of totally unknown bands from England who were very influenced by like the Who and the Yardbirds and Hendrix, but some of it is just incredibly heavy." 〔◉〕: *Pebbles, Vols. 1–28* (AIP, available separately) compiles hundreds of regional hits by mid-'60s garage bands. Although most volumes don't have themes, Vol. 3 focuses on psychedelia. *Nuggets* (4 CDs: Rhino) expands upon the original 1972 collection compiled by Patty Smith Group guitarist Lenny Kaye. See also the Creation and Music Machine below.

The Zombies—*Odyssey and Oracle* (Rhino).

The Kinks—*The Village Green Preservation Society* (Reprise).

The Creation—*How Does It Feel to Feel* (Edsel). This disc compiles 1966–68 singles from this feedback-loving, Who-like group. The band was produced by early Who producer Shel Talmy and featured guitarist Eddie Phillips.

The Byrds—*Younger Than Yesterday* and *Fifth Dimension* (both Columbia). "Totally amazing records. I play those records for people now, and they're like 'Who is this?' David Crosby was truly amazing."

The Music Machine— ⬤: *Best of . . .* (Rhino) and *Beyond the Garage* (Sundazed), the latter a compilation of the group's later material for Warner Bros.

LOU BARLOW'S OWN RECORDINGS

With a catalog that expands almost by cell division, it may be hard to pick favorites, but Lou manages, starting with *The Asshole* (7-inch, Vertical) by Sebadoh, a side project he had formed during his Dinosaur Jr. run that became his main focus when he left Dinosaur in 1988. "When I first started recording and putting out singles, I think I was really interested in just totally freaking people out," Lou says. "I wanted to make music that nobody'd ever heard. Like, hard core had already happened. I didn't do that by being noisy. I wasn't going to be the angriest person alive or anything like that. I sort of developed this style of playing with my acoustic guitar, like with four strings, and I also had a ukulele, and I was just making up different tunings for every song. It was sort of hard core, like very short, and very personal lyrics, but sung like folk, sort of. I really felt as if I'd stumbled upon something pretty special. That got me through. I felt like I was doing something pretty important. I'll listen to that stuff now, it's funny how seriously I took myself. But I'm really glad I did, you know."

Also with Sebadoh, Lou points to the album *III* (Homestead), the track "Soul and Fire" from *Bubble and Scrape* (Sub Pop), and the group's latest album as of the interview date, *The Sebadoh* (Sub Pop). He's especially proud of the track "Flame" on the latter album.

Favorites from other involvements include *Winning Losers: A Collection of Home Recordings* (Smells Like), a solo project released under the name Sentridoh; the songs "Palm of My Hand" and "Electric Idiot" on *Ep* (Communion Table); and *Natural One* (EP, Polygram). The latter two discs are by the Folk Implosion, a home recording duo project with singer/songwriter John Davis. (The title song on *Natural One* was a Top 40 hit.) Finally, he mentions Dinosaur Jr.'s *You're Living All Over Me* (SST). "I didn't really write much of that record, but that's probably the greatest rock record that I'll ever play on," Lou opines. "J. was pretty much a genius back then. . . . He put a lot of pain and a lot of sonics on those records. It was pretty amazing to be a part of that."

⬤: Entering Lou's catalog can be an intimidating and confusing endeavor at first, but the following recordings are excellent places to start, along with those already brought up by Lou: *Collection of Home Recordings* (Smells Like) [under the name Lou Barlow]; *Another Collection of Home Recordings* (Mint) [under Lou Barlow and Friends]; and the self-titled release (City Slang) from "Lou Barlow and His Sentridoh."

Every member of Sebadoh writes. From that group, the most widely noted records are *Bubble and Scrape*, *Bakesale*, and *Harmacy* (all Sub Pop).

PAUL BARRERE (April 2, 1997)

When it came to joining the early Little Feat, all roads led through founder Lowell George but Paul Barrere traveled a shorter road than most. Paul's older brother had attended Hollywood High with George. "Lowell had his early band, the Factory, and I had my little garage bands, the names of which shouldn't be in print because they're probably too filthy," Paul chuckles. "And so we just kinda watched each other's careers grow." When he was forming Little Feat, George approached Paul about auditioning the next day as a bass player, a serious problem because Paul played guitar, not bass. A determined George brought Paul his bass to practice on overnight. Predictably, Paul flunked, but two years later was hired as a second guitarist, "so I was real flattered."

Paul came to Little Feat as a blues guy, although he would ultimately extend his reach in his new band's expansive company. The grandson of a well-known classical flautist and Juilliard professor, Paul started taking piano lessons at the age of five. But it wasn't his thing and by the time he was 11, he made that point clear to his parents. At a party, he watched a friend of his older brother playing Jimmy Reed tunes on guitar and thought the three chord progressions would be a painless transition from classical piano.

Paul sidetracked into rock'n'roll through the records of Chuck Berry, Fats Domino, and Little Richard. As a Southern Californian, he caught the surf music wave, too. But gradually, he was leaning toward the blues, first through the folkish blues of Mississippi John Hurt, then the early Bob Dylan, who was always a bluesman at heart. Next, he found out about Muddy Waters and Robert Johnson, and finally *John Lee Hooker. "And man, that turned me around," Paul says. "It was, like, 'wow.' Because quite frankly he's not the world's greatest guitar player, but [what other guys say] with a thousand notes, he can do with one."

Paul joined Little Feat at the same time as bassist Ken Gradney and percussionist Sam Clayton, which funked up the rhythms from the band's earlier Stones-ish style. "Those cats, believe me, when they were a quartet, they had everything going for them as far as the syncopation, the musicality, the notes, the space between the notes—all the things that I've learned from being a member of Little Feat. But what they didn't possess in some instances was a swing to it—that's almost for me what rock'n'roll's all about, where it gets your hips shakin' . . . ."

If Paul was teaching the group new rhythms, Bill Payne and George were showing him new songwriting tricks, beyond the three-chord blues formula. The instruction took so well that Paul was penning quintessential Feat fare almost from the start. "Back then there were six of us," Paul reflects, "and there were six different histories, six different viewpoints, and we all kind of bled them together, if you will, to make this sound. And even though the sound has evolved, it hasn't really changed from the original message."

PAUL BARRERE'S FAVORITE ARTISTS AND RECORDINGS

B. B. King—*Live at the Regal* (ABC/MCA). "When I heard [this record], I went 'Wow, now this is something you can do with an electric guitar.' "

*John Lee Hooker—*Boogie Chillun* (Charly). Paul calls "Solid Sender" on this disc "one of the downest blues tunes I've ever heard."

Howlin' Wolf—*Howlin' Wolf/Moaning in the Moonlight* (Chess). Paul loved Wolf's second album, paired with his debut recording (oddly, in reverse order) for one of the greatest twofer CDs in existence.

Albert King—*Born Under a Bad Sign* (Stax).

*Buddy Guy—*I Was Walkin' Through the Woods* (MCA/Chess). "An amazing record. It had a lot of that out-of-phase pickup position that a lot of Fender Stratocaster cats used, and I think we got it from Buddy."

Mississippi John Hurt—*1928 Sessions* (Yazoo) and *Memorial Anthology* (2 CDs: Adelphi). The former covers the original recordings made of Hurt's music. The latter surveys Hurt's post-"rediscovery" performances in the mid-1960s. It includes a 31-minute interview of Hurt by *Pete Seeger.

The Rolling Stones—*Beggar's Banquet* (ABKCO). "There's not a cut on that record that I don't like. I think it's just amazing, especially the techniques they used to record it. It's back when Brian Jones was alive. It has it all, from their humor to their Satanic wit."

The Yardbirds—"Over, Under, Sideways, Down" on *Roger the Engineer* (Edsel). This hit dates from Jeff Beck's brief but heavily influential period with the band. *Roger* is widely considered the greatest Yardbirds album.

Fleetwood Mac—Paul was a Mac fan back when they were a hard-edged blues band featuring guitarist Peter Green, not the mainstream popsters they would become: "Man, [Green] had a tone, and he had that thing that B. B. King and Albert King and Freddy King all had, where they make you feel the note. They put their emotions through that instrument." : *Peter Green's Fleetwood Mac* (Blue Horizon) was the group's 1968 debut. *English Row* (Epic) includes Green's "Black Magic Woman," later covered by Santana. *Then Play On* (Reprise), the last album with Green, features the hit "Oh, Well."

John Mayall and the Bluesbreakers—*Bluesbreakers with Eric Clapton* and *A Hard Road* (both Deram). The former, from 1966, features Clapton on some of the most unvarnished blues he's ever recorded. The latter, from 1967, features Peter Green on lead guitar.

The Paul Butterfield Blues Band—*East-West* (Elektra). On the groundbreaking title track, this 1966 record married electric Chicago blues to Indian raga-inspired extended improvisation, laying the foundation for psychedelic music. The outstanding band included Michael Bloomfield and Elvin Bishop on guitar, Butterfield on harmonica, and a rhythm section of Mark Naftalin, Jerome Arnold, and Sam Lay.

Jimi Hendrix—*Are You Experienced?*, *Axis Bold as Love*, and *Electric Ladyland* (all Reprise). "When I heard *Are You Experienced?*, I went 'Holy shit! How is this guy making the guitar sound like this?' "

*The Rising Sons—This legendary, albeit schizophrenic, band featured a young *Taj Mahal and even younger Ry Cooder (just 17 when he joined in 1964). Originally, the band included Ed Cassidy, later Spirit's drummer, as well. Paul caught them at the Teen Fair in the Hollywood Palladium in the mid-'60s: "Man, that stuff really knocked me out." : *Rising Sons* (Columbia/Legacy), produced by Terry Melcher of Byrds fame, features speedy but remarkably mature country blues for such young players—at least when Taj and Ry are up front. When Beatles wannabe Jesse Kincaid's songs are on tap, the British invade. Cassidy had been replaced by Kevin Kelley by this time.

*The Band—*Music from Big Pink* (Capitol). Paul calls this one of the albums he'd choose "if I was to have to pick a record to live with for the rest of my life, because here's something that encompasses all that funk and groove, yet it has more of that storytelling aspect of a song. . . . Really beautiful songs."

Steely Dan—*Aja* (MCA). Paul feels almost the same about this 1977 album as he does about *Big Pink*. This record fuses jazzish playing to rock songs much as Little Feat was also doing by this time.

Mahavishnu Orchestra—*Birds of Fire* (Columbia). This is Paul's favorite fusion album.

Miles Davis—*Kind of Blue* and *Bitches Brew* (both Columbia). "I think there's ways you can say things, you can understate them but still have the same impact," Paul says about the former record, a classic in that regard.

Charles Mingus—"Goodbye Porkpie Hat" and "Fables of Faubus." ⬤: Both of these tunes exist in live versions on various Mingus recordings but they appear together on the classic studio album *Mingus Ah Um* (Columbia).

The Modern Jazz Quartet—*Odds Against Tomorrow* (Blue Note).

Nina Simone—*Nina at Town Hall* (Colpix). Paul calls this "a great, great album" and says that it, like *Kind of Blue*, was a major influence on his approach to understating his music.

The Dixie Dregs—*What If* (Capricorn). ". . . like taking Mahavishnu and moving it more into a rock vein. And just some of the guitar tones that Steve Morse gets, I may have tried to borrow a little bit from that."

Alison Krauss—*Now That I've Found You: A Collection* (Rounder). Paul used to love country music when it was less glitzy and closer to its folk roots. Progressive bluegrass artist Krauss embodies those qualities. This outstanding 1995 compilation surveys her previous ten years on Rounder and was a major hit on both the country and pop charts.

Mary Black—Irish folk singer Black is adept at both traditional Irish and a wide range of contemporary popular music: "Those two women [Black and Alison Krauss—see above], just the sound of their voices gets to me." ⬤: 1986's *Collected* (Gifthorse) is a fine compilation that includes many traditional Irish tunes. Also check out *Babes in the Woods* (Gifthorse).

Sonny Landreth—*South of I-10* (Zoo). Paul lists Landreth, along with Dave Tronzo, Anders Osborne, Keb' Mo', and John Mooney, as five slide guitar brethren deserving of much wider attention.

David Tronzo—*Roots* (Knitting Factory Works). "He is one of the most outside slide guitar players you're ever gonna want to hear. I mean, he does tunes like 'Monk's Dream' on slide guitar and he's just ferocious," says Paul. Tronzo replaced Landreth in John Hiatt's band. He also records with avante garde New York players. Imagine country blues filtered through Ornette Coleman's brain.

Anders Osborne—*Which Way to Here* (Sony).

*Keb' Mo'—''Whew, another [great] young artist,'' says Paul. He knows Mo' from having shared a bill with him, not his records. : See the section on Keb' and his recordings.

John Mooney—*Against the Wall* (House of Blues). ''A real good friend of mine, who I think is just unbelievable . . . He lives in New Orleans and he's got that thing goin' for him, but he was kind of tutored by Son House when he was a kid. And I hear a lot of Son House in his stuff,'' says Paul.

Ry Cooder—*Get Rhythm* (Reprise). ''There's some things on slide guitar there that actually probably should be banned from the ears of young children, because they'll go out and do the boogaloo.''

*Dr. John—*Gris Gris* (Repertoire, out of print).

Various artists—*The Testament Records Sampler* (Testament). ''[It] has the original 'Cat's Squirrel' on it by Dr. Isiah Ross. It has the original 'Jesus Is on the Mainline' with Fred McDowell and the Hunter's Chapel Singers. It's got some J. B. Hutto and the Hawks on it. I mean, this is an amazing record for anybody who's into the blues, and especially anybody who's into the blues who listened to that [1960s] blues explosion—I'm the kind of guy when I hear a blues tune and I found out that the band doin' it isn't the band that wrote it, I like to go back and find out where did it come from. And this has a lot of that kind of stuff on it.''

PAUL BARRERE'S OWN RECORDINGS

Quite naturally, Paul is proudest of the Little Feat albums in which he's had the biggest roles, both in the original band and the group that reconstituted after Lowell George's death: ''I'll always be partial to *Time Loves A Hero* (Warner Bros.) because that was my first chance to step to the forefront and shine a lot. I enjoyed the making of that record. Lowell was very sick at the time [he died of a drug-and-obesity-related heart attack two years later, in 1979], and it was really left to Billy and me to kind of step forward and do a lot of work. I really liked a lot of stuff like 'Old Folks Boogie' on that record.''

From the re-formed band, Paul is thrilled with how 1995's *Ain't Had Enough Fun* (Zoo) turned out, both from the standpoint of its live-in-studio sound and the material. He likes the other post-reunion albums—*Let It Roll* (Warner Bros.), *Representing the Mambo* (Warner Bros.), and *Shake Me Up* (Morgan Creek), as well. From the earlier reunion efforts, he points especially to the songs ''Silver Screen'' and ''Ingenue'' on *Representing the Mambo*, ''where we liked to flash our cuffs. I mean, instrumentally we're a very great group of people because we know how to play ensemble . . . where all of a sudden we'll be jamming and we'll just take off into the Netherlands and by instinct we seem to cover each other's behinds."

Paul has made a few records in other shoes, as well. He recorded two solo efforts shortly after George passed away; of those, he prefers the first one, *On My Own Two Feet* (Mirage), because "it was funkier, it was more in line with what I'm all about." He also played in a band called the Bluesbusters with keyboardist T. Lavitz (ex–Dixie Dregs), Bonnie Raitt's ex-bassist Freebo, drummer Larry Zack, and blues singer Catfish Hodge. The group recorded two albums, *Accept No Substitutes* and *This Time* (both Landslide); Paul likes them both, "especially the second one."

●: For an overview of the Little Feat catalog, see the section on Bill Payne.

A D R I A N   B E L E W   (June 18, 1997)

In most ways, Adrian Belew's career has followed the classic baby boomer trajectory: kid joins the school band, hears Beatles, takes up guitar, starts teen band, becomes recording star. Like other boomer musicians, this virtuoso guitarist, studio wizard, producer, and songwriter also honed his craft singing in bars. But Adrian got this bit of woodshedding out of the way earlier than most—like, age five. "There was a little friendly neighborhood bar down the street from where my parents lived," he tells us, "and we used to go there on a Saturday, and people would give me money to put in the jukebox and stand there and sing along with the records. The adults got a big kick out of that. I think that's initially what gave me the impression that music was something I wanted to do—and I saw you could get a lot of attention that way."

Adrian absorbed more than beer breath and cigarette smoke at his folks' watering hole in Covington, Kentucky. The records he sang to exposed him to some of the best in early popular music—Hank Williams, Elvis, Dion, and Roy Orbison. Orbison is one of Adrian's favorites to this day. "There was just a certain tone to his voice and a certain emotional quality that no one else seemed to have and he was a remarkable singer as well," Adrian says. Even when he was just hamming it up for the grown-ups, singing to Orbison's "It's Over" "used to tear my heart out," he recalls.

Adrian's discovery of classical music, at age ten, proved more typically boomer-esque because, in addition to the school band, his other primary source was such movies as Disney's *Fantasia* and Stanley Kubrick's *2001*. Adrian's one problem with classical music, he says, was that he didn't have the skills to play it. But the British Invasion, headed up by the Beatles, made all that irrelevant. When the Beatles arrived, he recalls, "everything suddenly galvanized in my mind and I remember feeling 'That's what I want to do.' Some of it was because I wanted to be rich and famous, but I actually think it's because there was this mystery about recording, recording studios, making records." Adrian was a singing drummer in a teen band called the Denims when the Invasion started. He soon acquired a guitar, an instrument he would eventually all but reinvent.

Adrian has since fashioned one of pop music's most diverse careers. A widely acknowledged genius of exotic guitar sounds, he has graced some of the most seminal pop recordings of the last twenty years by such artists as the Talking Heads, David Bowie, and Paul Simon. He was a founder of cult faves The Bears, a group that specialized in catchy, crafty pop a la the Beatles and XTC. He spent a year touring and playing with Frank Zappa. With original member Robert Fripp, he co-anchored the second coming of King Crimson, one of the most artistically successful band resurrections ever. And his résumé also includes a string of distinctive solo albums and production projects that show off his mastery of melodic, technicolor pop.

With a past so straight from the '60s script, it's not surprising that Adrian would deliver the usual '60s generation boast—that his era's music was better than any that followed. But in the next breath, he offers a rationale: "I have a theory that most people just filter all the things they've heard and sort of stir it up in a new way and that's the soup they serve. That's true about me, too. I don't even try to hide my influences because I'm actually proud of them. The Stravinskys, the Gershwins, the Beatles—they're the people who made me want to do this, and so I don't mind paying tribute to them."

ADRIAN BELEW'S FAVORITE ARTISTS AND RECORDINGS

Roy Orbison—"It's Over." ⬤: *All-Time Greatest Hits of Roy Orbison* (Monument).

George Gershwin—*Rhapsody in Blue.* ⬤: Of the hundreds of versions available, look for the original version Gershwin himself recorded with the Paul Whiteman Orchestra, for whom it was written (Pearl). Not to be missed is Leonard Bernstein's wonderfully sympathetic 1959 recording with the New York Philharmonic (Sony). To hear Gershwin's solo piano roll version, obtain *Gershwin Plays Gershwin* (Nonesuch).

Maurice Ravel—*Bolero.* ⬤: With around 300 versions of this piece in print, try Pierre Boulez's version first (Deutsche Grammaphon).

Erik Satie—*Gymnopedies.* 🔘 : These three gorgeous and enduring miniatures for piano have been recorded countless times and transcribed for several different instruments. For the original solo piano treatment, try recordings by Aldo Ciccolini (EMI) and a recent set by Pascal Roge (London).

Igor Stravinsky—*The Rite of Spring.* 🔘 : You can get pretty close to the *Fantasia* film version with *The Stokowski Fantasia* (Pearl), which contains Leopold Stokowski's performances of all the music from the Disney film, including *The Rite of Spring.*

Various artists—*2001: A Space Odyssey* (Rhino). The original film soundtrack has been remastered. Khachaturian's *Gayne* Ballet Suite, from this soundtrack, made a particularly big impact on Adrian.

The Beatles—While Adrian likes everything the Beatles did, he says, "there were certain things by the Beatles that really thrilled me: when they started using classical instruments, and they did things like 'Yesterday,' 'Eleanor Rigby,' 'Strawberry Fields Forever,' and 'I Am The Walrus'; that's essentially my favorite style of theirs. I remember hearing the song 'I'm Only Sleeping' and hearing backward guitar for the first time—that sound just amazed me. Then there was the introduction of Indian music, which came through the Beatles in songs like 'The Inner Light,' 'Within You, Without You,' and 'Love You, Too,' and I've had a passion for that music ever since." 🔘 : To hear these songs, focus on the albums *Beatles '65*, *Yesterday and Today*, *Magical Mystery Tour*, *Revolver* and *Sgt. Pepper's Lonely Hearts Club Band* (all Capitol). However, some of the tracks Adrian mentions, like "The Inner Light," show up only on singles collections—in the case of "Light," *Past Masters, Volume 1* or on the big Beatles box set (both Capitol). Adrian also loved George Harrison's guitar work, so you might want to check out Harrison's solo recordings like *All Things Must Pass* and the *Best of George Harrison* (both Capitol).

Jimi Hendrix—"Purple Haze" on *Are You Experienced?* (Reprise). "The first time I heard 'Purple Haze' it changed my life. I think this is what really influenced me to play guitar."

Chet Atkins—Adrian says that Atkins, Les Paul, and Robert Fripp "are the guys whose records I figured out for hours and hours in order to develop my own mechanics, tastes, and sounds." 🔘 : Atkins, the Segovia of country guitar, has a discography that would fill a book by itself, but start with *The RCA Years* (RCA) or *The Essential Chet Atkins* (RCA). He also collaborated on a tasty set with Mark Knopfler called *Neck & Neck* (Columbia).

Les Paul—See Chet Atkins. ⬤: Les Paul, without whom the electric guitar would probably have been invented by the Soviet Union, made several classic pop recordings in the '50s with his wife Mary Ford. These are collected on *The Legend and the Legacy* (4 CDs: Capitol). For a distilled one-disc version, get *The Best of the Capitol Masters* (Capitol).

Robert Fripp—See Chet Atkins. ⬤: From Fripp's extensive discography, don't miss King Crimson's sensational 1969 debut, *In the Court of the Crimson King* (EG); Fripp's ambient collaborations with Brian Eno, *No Pussyfooting* and *Evening Star* (both EG); or his solo album *God Save the King* (EG) with the League of Gentlemen, a group he formed during King Crimson's hiatus. This record also features David Byrne and Eno.

Harry Nilsson—This master of pop songcraft was so loved by the Beatles that he was once rumored to be joining the band. He caught Adrian's ear, too: "His voice was remarkable, and he seemed to have the ability to sing all sorts of parts, all styles. His range was remarkable: he had a great, strong falsetto. But it was his writing too. He had a very unusual, quirky style of songwriting. The songs were a bit funny and a bit off. He was strongly influential on my songwriting." ⬤: Nilsson's best-known hits are collected on *All-Time Greatest Hits* (RCA). For a more comprehensive career survey, there's *Personal Best: The Harry Nilsson Anthology* (2 CDs: RCA). Nilsson died in 1994, and Adrian covered his song "Me and My Arrow" for a Nilsson tribute album, *For the Love of Harry: Everybody Sings Nilsson* (Music Masters).

Moby Grape—*Moby Grape* (San Francisco Sound) and *Wow/Grape Jam* (San Francisco Sound). "This is another band that was overlooked and forgotten. Their first two records were just sensational—five great players, great writers, great singers. They were a better version of the Eagles before the Eagles."

Jeff Beck—*Wired* and *Truth* (both Epic). "Along with Hendrix, I've always thought that Beck is the most lyrical, sensational guitarist of all. Even all the way back to the early Yardbirds records, his playing is great." ⬤: To hear Beck with the Yardbirds, check out *Greatest Hits, Vol. 1: 1964–1966* (Rhino) and *Roger the Engineer* (Edsel).

Frank Zappa—*Strictly Genteel* (Rykodisc). "This is an introduction to Zappa's more classical music. I had less of an appreciation for his actual songs—I liked the music. And his classical music is really remarkable. The year that I spent with Frank was very influential on me. It came at a time in my life when I really needed someone to show me how to make records, how to tour, how to be a professional musician. Frank did all that and more, and I owe him a great debt."

Beck—*Odelay* (Geffen). "My engineer brought this in, and that was fresh air to me."

BR5-49—Adrian loves this young band from Nashville, where he now lives: "Their self-described music is 'hillbilly-beatnik,' and they rely heavily on the Patsy Cline–Jim Reeves–Hank Williams era in music. . . . They do it very authentically, and they're very serious about it." ⦿: BR5-49's albums include the EP *Live at Robert's* and the full-length *BR5-49* and *Big Backyard Beat Show* (all Arista).

> NOTE: At the end of our interview, Adrian rattled off the names of a number of other artists who influenced him, without having time to elaborate. Those names are: David Bowie, XTC, Eurythmics, Bob Dylan, the Byrds, *Talking Heads, Crowded House, The Police, the Red Hot Chili Peppers, the Residents, *the Kronos Quartet, Frank Sinatra, Tony Bennett, and Louis Armstrong.

ADRIAN BELEW'S OWN RECORDINGS

Adrian's favorites from his own catalog are *Mr. Music Head* (Atlantic) and *Op Zop Too Wah* (Passenger): "They're very eclectic and they run through a lot of different styles, and I think if you listen to either of those records, you'll have a great understanding of all the different areas that I like and work in." With King Crimson, Adrian says "I can't get past the first [reunion] album, *Discipline* [EG], which some people point to as being pivotal for different musicians. It was the band's honeymoon record, and it's hard to beat that record."

Coming from one of the premier sidemen in the business, it's not surprising that Adrian cites some of his session stints among the work he likes best, starting with Paul Simon's *Graceland* (Warner Bros.). "I only played a minor part on *Graceland*," he acknowledges, "but it's almost an historic record." And with David Bowie, "my favorite record was a single we did that he wrote called 'Pretty Pink Rose,' which is also on my album *Young Lions* [Atlantic]. But I have the strongest memory of that because here I was in the studio standing next to David Bowie and singing into a microphone! I think David makes very innovative records. I liked *Lodger* [Ryko], and that had Brian Eno at the controls." Finally, Adrian speaks proudly of his work with Talking Heads on *Remain in Light* (Sire): "It captured that band at a certain time and place—just before they made it big—and that period where they did *Fear of Music* [Sire] and *Remain in Light*, I think was the essence of that band."

⬤ : Adrian made only two albums with the Bears, but it is during that period that he really honed his pop songcraft, much lauded by critics at the time. Check *The Bears* (Primitive Man), the group's debut, to sample this part of Adrian's career. *Lone Rhino* (Island) and *Inner Revolution* (Atlantic) are other widely loved albums from his solo catalog. For his 1999 release *Salad Days*, Adrian left the studio electronics on the shelf and performed acoustic versions of some of his best songs from earlier releases.

R A Y   B E N S O N   (March 10, 1998)

W e were sure it was Bob Wills records that inspired Ray Benson and Asleep at the Wheel to do their Western Swing thing. After all, Wills and his Texas Playboys were the most famous and able Western Swing band ever. But Ray admits that the record that rearranged their heads was a step removed from the source, Merle Haggard's 1970 salute to Wills called *A Tribute to the Best Damned Damn Fiddle Player in the World.*

"Actually, I had a couple of seventy-eights of Bob's," Ray says, "and I had a Kapp record of Bob's, but it wasn't very good, it was made in the sixties. His great stuff was the stuff made in the thirties, forties, fifties." In addition to being a joyous romp in its own right, *Tribute* enjoyed one big advantage over even the best Wills records, for the Wheel's purposes anyway. Its sonic superiority made it a far better record for the band's players to study, a vital consideration for a group that had decided on the basis of this record to devote itself to the western swing cause. "I could actually hear the rhythm guitar," Ray notes. "On seventy-eights, it was sometimes hard to discern the bass and the rhythm, although the spirit was great." Besides, Haggard had recruited a number of the original Play-boys to join his band, the Strangers, for the session so the Wheel was learning from the real deal, or at least a solid approximation.

Like Wills and his bandmates, Ray and the Wheel are an open-eared, highly skilled bunch with a genre-leaping repertoire and the chops to execute it for the folks. In Ray's case, the country spoke of the Wheel draws on a love formed when he heard Ferlin Husky's "On the Wings of a Dove" and Patsy Cline's "Crazy" as a child in the 1950s. The Crescent City spoke can be traced to his first hearing of Fats Domino's "Walkin' to New Orleans." And he was a rocker from the mo-ment he heard Jerry Lee Lewis's "Great Balls of Fire." As for the swing half of the Wheel equation, Ray discovered the incomparable pleasures of early Count Basie as a teenager in Pennsylvania. At the same time, he was jumping to the hits of Louis Jordan. Indeed, Asleep at the Wheel would have its first minor hit in 1974 with a Western Swing rendition of Jordan's "Choo Choo Ch'Boogie."

Thirty years on the Wheel job hasn't narrowed Ray's perspective in the least. "I'm just into music, you know, and I listen to everything that comes across my desk," he says. "I like classical music. I especially love Bach. I listen to jazz, of course. I like the classic stuff, obviously, the swing stuff, and be-bop. But in the modern vein, all the guitar players, I'm a fool for guitar players. I like pop music quite a bit. I listen to a little bit of rap music—my kids bring home stuff I dig. I like Prince's music quite a bit. I think he's a genius. I go the gamut, man. As Roland Kirk once said, it's just twelve notes, you know. We just re-arrange them differently."

RAY BENSON'S FAVORITE ARTISTS AND RECORDINGS

Merle Haggard—*A Tribute to the Best Damned Damn Fiddle Player in the World* (Capitol). Ray is hardly alone in considering this one of the better records ever cut. Ray also loves Haggard's work in general. ⊙: *Lonesome Fugitive: The Merle Haggard Anthology* (Razor & Tie) is a two-CD compilation that does a fine job of summarizing his peak years.

Count Basie—*Superchief* (Columbia). "I heard Count Basie when I was a teen-ager and fell in love with him," says Ray. About *Superchief*, he says, "It's all of the Okeh and Columbia recordings of Count Basie from the thirties. We wore that sucker out." ⊙: The original Columbia version of this record is out of print. Columbia has issued material from this Basie period, 1939–42, on its series *The Essential . . . , Vols. 1–3*. The Classics label has covered the same ground on a chronological series titled simply *Count Basie*. The sound quality varies from track to track but our sources tell us that it's better overall than on the Columbia discs.

Louis Jordan—*The Best of Louis Jordan* and *Five Guys Named Moe: Original Decca Recordings, Vol. 2* (both MCA). These two CDs cover Jordan's hits for Decca, the material that Ray and his mates in the original Wheel collected. Ray says that Jordan and Basie were the primary African-American influences on the band.

Hank Williams—*The Original Singles Collection* (Polygram). "That's everything that I had," Ray says about this set. "That's all in one box and it's all done perfect. I used to go anywhere—we'd go to junk stores, record stores, wherever, to find this stuff—because it was totally out of circulation."

The Byrds—*Sweetheart of the Rodeo* (Columbia). "That record really turned my head around a bit."

The Flying Burrito Brothers—*The Gilded Palace of Sin* (A&M). This was the first album Gram Parsons and Chris Hillman made with the Burritos, after leaving the Byrds in the wake of the groundbreaking *Sweetheart.* "I got to know the Burritos back then, when we first started Asleep at the Wheel and that was very cool," recalls Ray.

Moon Mullican—Ray says Mullican's piano-pounding honky tonk for King Records "is very important." And he's not alone. Mullican is said to be the predecessor to Jerry Lee Lewis. ⬤: *22 Greatest Hits* (Deluxe) includes "Cherokee Boogie," one of Ray's favorite tracks. *Seven Years to Rock: The King Years, 1946–56* (Western) may be the best Mullican compilation overall.

James Brown—Ray used to buy every Brown record when it came out during the years Brown recorded for King. "I used to love the el-cheapo kind of packaging," Ray laughs. "I remember it said 'Vivid Sound' on the bottom with these big arrows. Of course, James, was not only one of the great singers, screamers and dancers, but the band was so hot. To me it's the epitome of the tight band, whether or not they're playin' soul music, funk music, country music, jazz—it's so tight, everything's in place, everything's right." ⬤: *Star Time* (Polydor), the astoundingly good four-CD career overview, includes Brown's major hits for King. *Roots of a Revolution* (Polydor) is a two-CD set covering Brown's recordings from 1956–64. It includes many less-noticed hits and B-sides from that period that are equal in quality to the hits packaged in *Star Time.*

B. B. King—*Live at the Regal* (ABC/MCA). Ray notes that this album was a major influence on almost every electric guitar player alive, not just him, when it came out in the mid-1960s.

Emmett Miller—*Minstrel Man from Georgia* (Columbia/Legacy). Ray calls Miller, almost forgotten today, "the Rosetta Stone of country music" because of Miller's dramatic impact on so many of country's seminal figures. A white vaudeville singer who performed in blackface, Miller toured with minstrel shows for decades. His yodels, other vocal flourishes, joking asides, and song repertoire profoundly influenced three of country's seminal figures—Jimmie Rodgers, Hank Williams, and Bob Wills. Merle Haggard became a charter member of the Emmett Miller Secret Society when Wills told him that Miller was one of his greatest inspirations. In 1974, the baton was passed to Ray himself when Haggard gave a Miller bootleg to his fellow Wills acolyte. Ray couldn't help being obsessed with the man who had affected so many of his idols and ultimately would contribute liner notes to the above release. Note that the album features Miller with his band the Georgia Crackers, a stellar unit that included Tommy Dorsey, Jimmy Dorsey, Eddie Lang,

Jack Teagarden, and Gene Krupa—"a who's who of jazz in the twenties, thirties and forties," Ray observes.

Bob Wills—*The Tiffany Transcriptions, Vols. 1–9* (Rhino, available separately). "*The Tiffany Transcriptions* were radio shows that they did that never came out. They were recorded on these big acetate discs and they contain an incredibly wide range of material that was Bob's repertoire. Everything from 'In the Mood' to a fiddle breakdown."

Ernest Tubb—*Live at Cain's Ballroom* (Decca). "Incredible record—it's live and it showcases this place we still play, Cain's Ballroom in Tulsa, where Bob Wills started." ⬤: We don't doubt Ray, an inveterate record collector, about this disc, but we can't find it anywhere now. Most of Tubb's Decca output can be found on *Yellow Rose of Texas* (5 CDs: Bear Family). For more economical Tubb, see Master List.

Milton Brown—"I have all the Milton Brown stuff," Ray says about the man who rivaled Bob Wills's popularity in Western swing music until his untimely death in 1936. "I think Milton was incredible. He's obviously the father of Western swing. You know, I've been able to make this distinction that Milton Brown was the father of Western swing and Bob Wills was the king of Western swing. Because that's how it is. Milton got killed, and that was what happened." ⬤: *Pioneer Western Swing Band (1935–1936)* (MCA) and *With His Musical Brownies 1934* (Texas Rose) are the best introductions to Brown's music.

Speedy West and Jimmy Bryant—*Stratosphere Boogie* (Razor & Tie) and *Country Cabin Jazz* (Capitol, released under Jimmy Bryant's name). West was a pedal steel guitar virtuoso and premium session player who cut several albums of improvisatory country instrumentals with his partner, guitarist Bryant. "They were big influences on us," says Ray. "We all wanted to be like that."

Tony Bennett and Bill Evans—*The Tony Bennett/Bill Evans Album* (Original Jazz Classics). "It's just Bill Evans and Tony Bennett as a duo and it's one of the great performances of all time," Ray says about the 1975 pairing of the romantic vocalist with one of jazz's most sensitive pianists.

Tal Farlow—Ray says this jazz guitarist was one of his primary influences on guitar. ⬤: *First Set* (Xanadu), *Second Set* (Xanadu), and *The Return of Tal Farlow* (Original Jazz Classics). Much of Farlow's catalog is out of print but these trio and quartet outings are not and give a fine accounting of Farlow's fleet-but-gentle melodic style. *The Return*, from 1969, made after a long recording hiatus, is particularly intriguing because of its "pent-up demand" quality, with Farlow "spending" one rich melodic idea after another.

Ray Price—*Night Life* (CBS). *Willie Nelson wrote the title tune, which Ray loves, and Buddy Emmons contributes some sensational steel guitar playing. "That record would have to rate right up there with the ones that turned my head around and kept me out of medical school," Ray chuckles.

RAY BENSON'S OWN RECORDINGS

Ray can't really choose between his group's albums. "It's like kids," he says. "I don't have a favorite kid." He's not happy that some of the group's oldest albums are still unavailable in their original form, but he notes that the boxed set *Still Swingin'* (Liberty) contains most of the material from the 1970s.

●: One out-of-print AATW album worth a dedicated search is the group's debut, *Comin' Right at Ya* (EMI America), featuring the great original lineup with co-founder Leroy Preston and singer/guitarist Chris O'Connell. Also out of print and terrific is 1977's *The Wheel* (Capitol), featuring Preston's great song "My Baby Thinks He's a Train" (included on *Still Swingin'*). Sharp in-print releases include 1985's *Asleep at the Wheel* (Dot); 1985's *Western Standard Time* (Epic); *Live and Kickin': Greatest Hits* (Arista), an excellent live set; and *Tribute to the Music of Bob Wills & the Texas Playboys* (Liberty), an elegant celebration of Wills with guests such as Willie Nelson, Dolly Parton, Merle Haggard, Lyle Lovett, Garth Brooks, Vince Gill, Suzy Bogguss, and George Strait invited to the party.

GREG BROWN (1996)

His songs recall vintage country blues, especially when sung with his soothing rumble of a voice, but he's not just a white boy doing Lightnin' Hopkins. He often performs with just a guitar, but with that double-twinkle in his mind's eye, he just isn't *earnest* enough to be called a folksinger. His writing displays a keen-eyed regionalism from his small-town Midwestern roots, but he's also a world-wise universalist of high order. And although he recorded a winning kid's album called *Bathtub Blues*, you won't find his tunes on the playlist of the traditional family values set. So call Greg Brown a quintessentially American original and leave it at that.

Greg comes by his rootsy appeal honestly. Although his father eventually left the church (he now practices Baha'i), he was an evangelical preacher in the years Greg was growing up. The first music Greg remembers loving was the gospel he sang in church as a child, with his mother chording behind the choir on electric guitar. Kansas, where the family then lived, was still segregated in those days, but Greg heard African-American gospel too, drifting in from a black Baptist church down the street: "On summer evenings, the windows would be open and it was almost as close as the races got to dialogue in that town," Greg tells us by phone from his home in Iowa. "We would sing a song and down the block we'd hear the Baptists singing a song."

Greg heard wall-to-wall live music at home, too. "On my mother's side of the family, everybody played," he says. "My grandpa played banjo and I played with him my whole life and a pretty good chunk of his. It was just old hill music— stuff from the Appalachian Mountains and old country tunes. My grandmother on my mother's side was Irish and sang a lot of the old ballads." Greg also caught the fever of the early rock'n'roll he heard on the radio—Buddy Holly, Elvis, and, especially, Jerry Lee Lewis: "I was lucky in that even though my father was a preacher, there was never any music that was out of bounds in our house," he says.

The sound that would color Greg's future career grabbed him at a tender age. He was eight or nine, he recalls, when he chanced upon a 78 by Big Bill Broonzy at a fund-raising sale downtown and brought it home. "That was the first time I remember hearing country blues," he recalls. "I loved that." One of popular music's most skillful lyricists, Greg also tuned in to literary language early on. His mother read poetry to him and good literature lined the family book-shelves. Today, he notes that his lyric sensibility owes as much to poets Gary Snyder, Kenneth Rexroth, Robinson Jeffers, and Pablo Neruda as it does to other musicians.

In 1969, a year or so out of high school, Greg—who had been writing songs since childhood—won an audition contest to play an opening set for folksinger Eric Anderson in Iowa City. Afterward, Anderson suggested he bring his guitar to New York and Greg took the hint. He landed his first music job emceeing hootenannies at a noted folk club in Greenwich Village but got an even better musical education on the city's streets. When he wasn't working, he wandered the city's avenues with denizens of seemingly every other culture on earth. "You'd hear music coming out of a cafe or there would be an Italian street fair with accordion players or you'd be walking down the street and hear a reggae band," Greg remembers. All of it was a revelation to the preacher's kid from Iowa. The 1960s folk boom, which hadn't really affected him pre–Big Apple, won him over at this point, too—particularly the music of Tim Hardin and Bob Dylan.

Today, critics often compare Greg to Dylan because of his lyric intelligence, unblinking insights, and similar stew of influences, but he's a more intimate, quiet composer than Dylan has usually been. He prefers to paint sharply observed miniatures about everyday life, not the mythic allegories we've come to expect from Mr. Zimmerman. Like Dylan, Greg's lyrics can run dark, but his albums are always tempered with wry humor, poignant rumination, affectionate lust, and not a little sentimentality. On his album *Further In*, he sings "It's a messed-up world but I love it anyway." When we note that this seems to sum up the themes he covers, he laughs, "That's pretty much my philosophy if I could put it into a sentence."

GREG BROWN'S FAVORITE ARTISTS AND RECORDINGS

Jerry Lee Lewis—Of all the early rockers, Lewis made the biggest impression on Greg as a child in the first and second grade. ●: You'll get a liberal dose of the same piano pounders that rang in Brown's ears on the *Original Sun Greatest Hits* (Rhino).

Ray Charles—Greg doesn't remember the names of the Ray Charles and Harry Belafonte albums in his home as a child, although the early music of both artists "still really does it for me." ●: See Master List.

Harry Belafonte— ●: *All Time Greatest Hits, Vols. 1–3* (RCA)—each volume available separately—cover over 53 songs recorded from 1952 to 1973. *Calypso* (RCA), Belafonte's third, is the earliest Belafonte in print as of this writing; a huge hit in its day, it's probably one of those Greg's parents had at home. *Belafonte at Carnegie Hall* (RCA) captures a riveting live performance from 1959.

Tim Hardin— ●: See Master List.

Bob Dylan—*Another Side of Bob Dylan* (Columbia). Greg was a big fan of early Dylan. This album made the biggest impression.

Jimmie Rodgers—"The clarity of some of the early country lyrics by a Jimmie Rodgers or the Carter family—those were very important to me." Rodgers and the Carters were the first significant recording artists in what was then called hillbilly music, later to become today's country music. ●: Each of Rounder's reissues of Rodgers' music, all compelling listening, exposes a different side of his many-faceted career. On *First Sessions, 1927–1928*, Rodgers is accompanied by his own guitar and other strings. Although his performances are less polished on this disc, they are no less appealing than the later material. *The Early Years, 1928–1929* includes both solo guitar and small band tracks and such Rodgers classics (some co-written with Elsie McWilliams) as "Waiting for a Train," "My Little Lady," and "Any Old Time." *On the Way Up* features some great blues performances with a Texan backup band—the bawdy "Everybody Does It in Hawaii," other novelty numbers, cowboy tunes, railroad songs, and, of course, blue yodels galore. *Riding High, 1929–1930* (Rounder) and *America's Blue Yodeler, 1930–1931* catch Rodgers at his commercial peak. Both albums feature ground-breaking tracks with Lani McIntire's Hawaiians, revealing the bridge between country and Hawaiian music. *Down the Old Road, 1931–1932* stars the Carter family as guests on a few tracks but the most attractive cuts were made with the Louisville Jug Band, a black group led by a wonderful fiddler named Clifford Hayes. *No Hard Times, 1932* and *Last Sessions, 1933* wrap up Rodgers' brief but ever-forward-looking career; sick with tuberculosis most of his adult life, he died at 36, two days after recording "Years Ago" on *Last Sessions*. The former disc is highlighted by the title tune, "Blue Yodel No. 10," "Long Tall Mama Blues," and "Whippin' That Old TB," about the illness that was gaining on him. The emotionally haunting latter album is all the more gripping for Rodgers' weakened condition and drive to go out singing.

The Carter Family—The Carter Family's music hewed close to the Southern folk and spiritual music that flourished in their home region, Virginia's Clinch Mountains, but looked forward rhythmically, driven by Maybelle Carter's innovative guitar style. : See Master List.

Lightnin' Hopkins—Hopkins and the Reverend Gary Davis (see below) are Greg's favorite country blues artists. : See Master List.

Reverend Gary Davis— : *Harlem Street Singer* (Bluesville) includes such oft-covered songs as "Samson and Delilah," "Let Us Get Together Right Down Here," "Pure Religion," "Death Don't Have No Mercy," and "I Am the Light of This World." Other good choices include *Blues and Ragtime* (Shanachie); *Gospel, Blues, and Street Songs* (Fantasy), with Pink Anderson; and the live *At Newport* (Vanguard), a smooth performance from 1965.

Muddy Waters—Waters and Howlin' Wolf top Brown's list of favorite urban blues artists. : See Master List.

Howlin' Wolf— : See Master List.

***Taj Mahal**—When asked who influenced his guitar style most, Brown doesn't hesitate: Taj Mahal and Paul Geremia (see below). "I always just loved Taj's touch on the guitar," Greg says. : You can best focus in on Taj's style on *Giant Steps/De Old Folks at Home* (Columbia); for half its length, he's alone with his guitar and banjo.

Paul Geremia—"When I first went to New York, I saw him playing in a little joint. He's still out playing. . . . Paul's really the first young white guy I heard playing country blues that I found real satisfying." : *Gamblin' Woman Blues* (Red House).

Abdullah Ibrahim (aka Dollar Brand)—Brown especially loves the recordings the South African–born jazz pianist made with his band Ekaya ("home"). : Recordings by this unit include *Ekaya* (Ekapa), *Water from an Ancient Well* (Tiptoe), and *The Mountain* (Kaz), a live set.

D'Gary—*Malagasy Guitar* (Shanachie). "I love that record. I never get tired of that," says Greg about the debut recording by the guitar master from Madagascar.

Joseph Spence and the Pinder Family—*The Spring of Sixty-Five* (Rounder). Bahamanian Spence's recordings were passed around lovingly between many of the 1960s' most important folk and folk-influenced artists. Greg's choice among Spence's albums contains 13 performances, some with Spence alone on vocals and finger-style guitar and others with his sister and her family.

Eva Ivabittova—"Her records only come out in Czechoslovakia. I got them at the Vancouver Folk Festival five or six years ago, and I listen to her all the time." : We couldn't find her recordings in import sources.

Antonin Dvorak and Bela Bartok—Greg doesn't name specific pieces or recordings by these composers but notes that "stuff from that part of the world—Central Europe—has really grabbed me the most." One possible explanation: both Dvorak and Bartok drew heavily from folk music traditions in their countries and elsewhere. Interestingly, Dvorak summered in Spillville, Iowa (Greg's state) for several years. In fact, that's where he wrote both the Symphony No. 9 ("From the New World") and his American String Quartet.

GREG BROWN'S OWN RECORDINGS

Of his own releases, all of which are on the Red House label, Greg's favorites are *44 & 66*, which he recorded in four hours; *In the Dark With You*; *Down in There*, "although I'd like to remix that one—I've never been happy with the sound of that album"; and *The Poet Game*. "Those four albums are the ones where I got the closest to what I was after," he says.

: The 1996 album *Further In* hadn't yet come out when we spoke to Greg but many consider it his finest work. *Slant 6 Mind*, from 1997, continues the winning streak. And 1995's *A Live One* gives a good accounting of a Brown concert, including the hilarious asides and monologues that are a big part of the show.

R U T H   B R O W N   (February 18, 1997)

er smash hits for Atlantic Records came with such regularity from 1949 through the '50s that the label, a fledging when she started, became known as "the house that Ruth built." But little about Ruth Brown's upbringing predicted that she would become one of the first queens of R&B. Born in Virginia and raised in North Carolina as a sharecropper, Ruth grew up hearing mostly country & western music, which dominated the radio in her area. She sang in church, but couldn't even consider performing outside of it. "My father at that time had the rule that if you didn't sing in church, you didn't sing," Ruth chuckles when we call her at home in Las Vegas.

But Ruth had an ear for good music on Monday through Saturday, too. On a local radio station, she found an early morning program called *The Mail Bag* that reached beyond majority tastes. It was there that she discovered the rich baritone of jazz singer Billy Eckstine, the proto-R&B of Tiny Bradshaw, and the pioneering doo-wop of the Ink Spots. Then a music-loving uncle who visited every summer showed up one season with a stack of Ella Fitzgerald and Billie Holiday records in his bags. When she heard those, Ruth knew immediately what she wanted to do with her life; the only remaining question was how to tell Daddy.

In fact, in Holiday's case, Ruth liked her a little too much. In the early days of her career, Ruth says, "I sang everything that I heard by her. I even wore the gardenia in the hair, and the whole thing. And I phrased exactly like her." Which will only get you so far, as Holiday taught Ruth in person. One night while Ruth was working a club gig with folksinger Josh White, Holiday walked through the doors. "She sat in the audience and they told me she was there, and I did all the wrong things, like take out every song I was going to sing except Billie Holiday songs, and went out on the stage and began to sing in my best Billie Holiday voice," Ruth remembers. Holiday stormed away from her table and confronted Ruth later on her way to her dressing room. " 'You've got a great voice, you're a good singer,' she said, 'But as long as you go out on the stage and do what you just did, they'll call my name and never know yours. There's only one Lady Day and I'm it.' And years later I understood what she meant by that, and I'll be ever grateful to that advice that she gave me . . . Now, when I do these things, I do her song, dedicated to her, but I do it my way."

Ruth has done it her way for so long now that she has carried the title "Miss Rhythm," bestowed on her by Frankie Laine, since the '50s. But it's not as if she is simply rerunning her old hits. Even in her 70s, she continues to record new material and invests the older songs with new insights in every uniquely wrought phrase: "[I tell my audiences now] 'We're going to take a musical journey and just let's get inside of some of this music,' and it's the same music I sang forty years ago. But it's different now, 'cause I didn't just walk in the studio and they hand me a piece of music or a sheet of music and say 'Here, sing this lyric.' I have lived this lyric.''

RUTH BROWN'S FAVORITE ARTISTS AND RECORDINGS

Billy Eckstine—A fabulous ballad singer with a big, warm baritone voice, Eckstine is one of the most respected jazz vocalists ever. 💿: *I Want to Talk About You* (Xanadu) compiles key tracks with the Earl Hines Orchestra from 1940–41 and Eckstine's own big band from 1945. *Everything I Have is Yours* (2 CDs: Metro) is a fine compilation covering 1947–57. *No Cover, No Minimum* (Roulette) is a terrific live set from a Las Vegas nightclub date in 1960.

The Charioteers— 💿 : *Jesus Is A Rock In The Weary Land* (Gospel Jubilee).

Tiny Bradshaw—In the 1930s and '40s, bandleader/vocalist Bradshaw helped pioneer R&B with bands featuring such greats as saxophonist Sonny Stitt and vocalists Arthur Prysock and Roy Brown. 💿: *Breaking Up the House* (Charly) and *Great Composer* (King).

Lee Richardson—''He did a tune with Luis Russell's band 'The Very Thought of You' which was one of the first really great tunes that I heard by a male singer.'' 💿: We were unable to find recordings by this artist.

The Ink Spots—Led by tenor Bill Kenny, this group helped make possible the doo-wop classics of the 1950s. 💿: *The Greatest Hits 1939–46* (MCA).

Ella Fitzgerald—''There are some singers who at moments become so abstract you kinda get lost. But with Ella, you hardly ever missed melody even though she improvised.'' 💿: See Master List.

Billie Holiday—''I emulated her to the best of my ability. And I think that's the one thing that probably turned me around. But it did give me some insight into noticing the lyric, and giving attention to the lyric, and I think that's the criterion that you have to look for as a singer.'' 💿: See Master List.

Buddy Johnson—Johnson's popular jump blues band helped pave the way for rock'n'roll in the '40s and '50s. Johnson's wife Ella was the band's main vocalist. 💿: See Master List.

Lena Horne—''Stormy Weather'' and ''Good for Nuthin' Joe.'' ''Lena Horne just was the epitome of all that I saw and wished that I could ever be. I mean, everything: the looks, the gorgeous face, the classiness of this lady.'' 💿: *Stormy Weather: The Legendary Lena (1941–1958)* (Bluebird).

Carmen McRae—"I was in great awe of Carmen McRae, her phrasing, the clarity of the lyric." ⏺: *Here to Stay* (MCA) is a twofer from 1955–59 covering both small- and big-band sessions. *Any Old Time* (Denon), from 1986, captures McRae's late-career mastery.

Sarah Vaughan—"I'm Glad There Is You" and "Send in the Clowns." "Nobody did 'Send in the Clowns' the way she did. I've always wanted to do that song, but I haven't touched it as yet. I don't know if I've got the nerve, you know. Because there is such a thing as if it ain't broke, don't fix it." ⏺: "I'm Glad" is on *Complete Sarah Vaughan on Mercury, Vol. 1* (6 CDs: Polygram). "Clowns" is on *Send in the Clowns* (Pablo).

Dinah Washington—Ruth and Washington were once booked by the same agency and performed several times together. They also became fast friends: "Whatever it was that she took out and decided to do, she did it so well . . . A real showperson, you know what I'm sayin'? Stagewise, there are a lot of performers around, but not too many entertainers." ⏺: *The Dinah Washington Story* (2 CDs: Mercury) includes 40 prime tracks from 1943–59. *For Those in Love* (Emarcy), from 1955, presents Washington with a fine backing group including Clark Terry, Wynton Kelly, and Keter Betts.

Peggy Lee—"Peggy Lee was the first person that I heard sing that reminded me of Billie Holiday—a lot." ⏺: *Capitol Collector Series, Vol. 1: The Early Years* (Capitol) compiles Lee's jazz and blues hits before she crossed over in the 1960s.

Judy Garland—"Over the Rainbow," "A Star is Born," "The Man That Got Away," "Meet Me in St. Louis," and "Have Yourself a Merry Little Christmas." "She sang her life. She sang her pain. She sang her joy. And I was in awe of her." ⏺: No single compilation contains all these songs. Possible choices include *25th Anniversary Retrospective* (Capitol) ["Rainbow," "Christmas," "Man"], *The Best of Judy Garland* (EMI) ["Rainbow," "Man"], and *The Original Decca Cast Recordings* (MCA) ["St. Louis," "Christmas"]. The album *A Star Is Born* (Columbia) is still in print.

Mahalia Jackson—Jackson was gospel's greatest in the estimation of Ruth and many, many others. ⏺: See Master List.

Reverend James Cleveland—Known equally for his potent vocals, bluesy arrangements, and expressive songwriting, Cleveland was a trendsetter in the mass choir movement of the 1950s. ⏺: *Peace Be Still, . . . with the Gospel Chimes*, and *Touch Me (with the Charles Fold Singers)* (all Savoy).

Shirley Caesar—Another of Ruth's gospel favorites and one of the music's great shouting vocalists, Caesar started with the Caravans in the early '60s and then went solo in 1966. ⬤: *Her Very Best* (Word), *Sailin'* (Word), and *The Best of Shirley Caesar with the Caravans* (Savoy).

Aretha Franklin—"[I remember] when Aretha was called out by her father to sit down to the piano to play so I could hear her. And he said to me, 'What do you think?' and I said 'If I ever have to follow that girl, I'll break both of her legs.' I think that she is still the supreme being, musically. A gift's been handed to her, and she can sing gospel, spirituals, jazz, blues, torch, whatever there needs to be. But she's still in my mind one of the all-time great gospel singers. Incredible, incredible." ⬤: See Master List.

Oleta Adams—Adams is an R&B and contemporary gospel singer and a 1991 Grammy nominee. ⬤: *The Very Best of Oleta Adams* (Polygram).

Johnny Adams—"My goodness, I love him," Ruth says of the great New Orleans crooner who guested on her album *R+B=Ruth Brown*. Adams, known as "The Tan Canary," died in 1998, after this interview took place. ⬤: *Room with a View of the Blues* and *Walking on a Tightrope* (both Rounder) both feature Adams singing Percy Mayfield songs, accompanied by his long-time associate, guitarist *Walter "Wolfman" Washington, among others.

James Ingram—The career of the versatile Ingram has ranged from R&B to dance to MOR balladry. ⬤: *The Power of Great Music: Best of . . .* (Qwest).

Bonnie Raitt—"I Can't Make You Love Me" on *Luck of the Draw* (Capitol). "Ohhhhhhh, that's a great song . . . She's got a big voice. She's got a big heart more than that," Ruth says about her dear friend, who constantly reminds her audience about Ruth's influence on her.

RUTH BROWN'S OWN RECORDINGS

Ruth's favorites from her own catalog include several of her lesser-known works, starting with 1968's *The Big Band Sound of Thad Jones and Mel Lewis* (Solid State): "For whatever reason, it didn't get the airplay that it should have but musically it is one of the best albums." She's also proud of 1963's *Gospel Time* (Lection/Mercury), her one gospel record, made in Nashville with C&W session pros; 1962's *Along Comes Ruth* (Philips), "on which I covered some of the best R and B tunes out at that time"; 1993's *The Songs of My Life* (Fantasy), which included several standards; and 1959's *Late Date with . . .* (Atlantic). At the time we speak, she is in the midst of sessions for *Good Day for the Blues* (Bullseye, released in 1998), "I listen to the way I sound on this thing, I'm amazed that I'm that strong at this point."

: The excellent compilation *Miss Rhythm* (2 CDs: Rhino) covers all of Ruth's R&B hits for Atlantic from 1949–60, several lesser-known but worthy singles, and some unreleased material. If you want the hits only, go for the single disc *Rockin' in Rhythm: The Best of . . .* (Rhino). In either case, you'll be able to trace Ruth's transition from her lighter, swing-based early style to the husky-voiced blues belter she became. Just like her idols Billie Holiday and Judy Garland, Ruth in late career reflects a roller-coaster life in every earthy vocal nuance. *Have a Good Time*, *Blues on Broadway*, and *Fine and Mellow* (all Fantasy) are three rich albums from this period.

PETER BUCK (July 29, 1997)

REM hit the ground in the early 1980s, sounding both like the logical extension of the folk rock that had come before and a wholly new amalgam of popular music. Not coincidentally, that same fine line between the familiar and the exotic describes the listening habits of guitarist Peter Buck, a primary architect of the band's sound. Peter cut his musical teeth on records by the Rolling Stones, Led Zeppelin, the Beatles, Jimi Hendrix, and the Who, which dominated the non-commercial FM radio stations he listened to while growing up in California. But since his midteens, he's been conducting a dedicated search for unclaimed sonic territory and long-buried roots.

The head-stretching began in earnest when a teacher recommended John Coltrane's *A Love Supreme* to him. Peter bought the record when he was 15: "That was like a blast from another planet for me. . . . In retrospect, a lot of the sounds and ideas that come across in the music are almost philosophical in a sense. There are a lot of pictures of America in that thing, without him making any kind of conscious political statement."

Peter also learned a lot about music by reading music critics in the early 1970s. "There were still a fair amount of writers that were really good and had their ears to the ground," he says. "It was more of a free-form era. People would recommend in the same breath Bob Dylan and Sun Ra."

Of course, as nearly every REM fan would guess, it was the spacey folk rock of the Byrds and especially Roger McGuinn's guitar style that left the most audible stamp on Peter at this stage. "As a young, budding guitar player, all of a sudden it clicked—this makes sense, it's such a great way to play guitar. Nobody plays like this anymore. I didn't realize at the time that it was basically folk rock and folk picking, Roger McGuinn having been a folk musician for years. So

I immediately tried copying [McGuinn's] rhythm style. I had no idea he finger-picked. I played it with a flat pick. I got pretty good at copying the ideas he had by just flat-picking really, really fast. I can probably do that—arpeggiated chords—as fast as anyone in the world. It's the only way I'm a fast guitar player."

Punk—Athens, Georgia style (Peter moved to Athens after dropping out of college in 1978)—would also eventually influence the ideas he brought to REM and his outside projects. "Athens took punk rock in a wholly different way," says Peter. "In New York and Los Angeles, everyone got leather jackets and spiked up their hair . . . In Athens, everyone just kind of went, 'Gee, that means there aren't really any rules at all and you could do whatever you want to.' It was great, there were little scenes that didn't have anything to do with punk rock per se. Really weird and individual, a lot of kids in art school, and a lot of kids who had never picked up an instrument."

It wasn't until REM formed that Peter began to uncover the rural roots of the music he was now playing. Shortly after REM's recording debut in 1982, an alternative country scene sprang up led by the hard-rocking twang of Jason and the Scorchers. "I'd hear them and realize, you know, country sounds pretty darn good," Peter recalls. "I grew up in the South [Peter's family relocated from Oakland to Atlanta when he was a teenager] and automatically hated country music because my dad liked it. And it made me realize how cool some of those older songs were and some of the performers." Peter started investigating the music of Bill Monroe, the Louvin Brothers, and other musical heroes of his region. While traveling, the band would pick up truck-stop tapes. "What do you always get? Jerry Lee Lewis and Hank Williams . . . All that stuff filtered through," he says.

Peter is still digging out those roots today on Smithsonian/Folkways reissues, "the literal original ones that I'd find in junk shops or weird shops. That was my first introduction to stuff maybe fifteen or twenty years ago." As can be heard most obviously in his side band, Tuatara, he also keeps his ear peeled for intriguing ethnic sounds, from Jewish folk music to Indian sitar players to the Western African popular music made by such innovators as King Sunny Ade or Kanda Bongo Man. To Peter, it all relates. For instance, he points out that Ade devoured American music from James Brown to country, and then in turn influenced bands like REM. "King Sunny Ade has steel guitar because he loves Hank Williams. And you go, 'Well, that's just weird.' "

PETER BUCK'S FAVORITE ARTISTS AND RECORDINGS

John Coltrane—Peter loves anything the great Coltrane quartet with McCoy Tyner, Jimmy Garrison, and *Elvin Jones recorded. : See Master List.

Last Poets—"It was pre-rap but basically they were rapping. The music was all African based—a lot of percussion, and very little in the way of songs. Kind of fascinating stuff." ⬤: *The Last Poets* (Metrotone); *This is Madness* (Celluloid); *The Time Has Come* (Polygram); and *The Legend: The Best of the Last Poets* (M.I.L.).

Sun Ra—"I saw Sun Ra and the Art Ensemble of Chicago a lot and they were both really exciting because something's going on and they're acting out a world view without really telling you what it's about, which I found kind of exciting." ⬤: *The Solar Myth Approach* (Affinity) is a strong, well-recorded effort from 1970–71, near the time when Peter would have first caught Sun Ra and his Arkestra.

The Art Ensemble of Chicago—(See Sun Ra). ⬤: *Urban Bushmen* (ECM), a live disc from 1980, features the classic lineup that Peter probably saw—Roscoe Mitchell, Joseph Jarman, Malachai Favors, Lester Bowie, and Don Moye—and captures much of the musical dynamism, if not the visual theater, that makes an Art Ensemble concert special.

The Byrds—Peter first began to get into the Byrds after he picked up a copy of *The Byrds' Greatest Hits* at a garage sale for a quarter. ⬤: See Master List.

Velvet Underground—Peter bought *The Velvet Underground* (Verve), the group's third album, when he was 14 or 15 from a neighbor for 50 cents. The music inspired him to seek out the other albums, but only one was still in print at the time, *White Light/White Heat* (Verve), with its long, tortured improvisation, "Sister Ray." ⬤: See Master List.

Patti Smith—*Horses* (Arista). Peter read about Smith and the mid-1970s New York rock scene in *Stereo Review*, bought Smith's debut record, and then saw her perform in Atlanta in early 1976: "They were amazing shows, kind of redefined the idea of what rock performance could be for me."

Miles Davis—"I really like the Gil Evans, arranged stuff. I've gotten to appreciate more the *On the Corner* era, which I don't think I liked before because it sounded too much like all the stuff I hated on the radio." ⬤: *Miles Ahead* (Columbia), *Porgy and Bess* (Columbia), and *Sketches of Spain* (Columbia), the three classic Davis-Evans collaborations; *Miles Davis & Gil Evans: The Studio Sessions* (Columbia Legacy), which contains the three albums just mentioned plus much more; and *On the Corner* (Columbia), more electric funk than jazz and as loved by some as it is hated by jazz purists.

Laura Nyro—*More Than a New Discovery* (Verve/Forecast), *Eli and the 13th Confession* (Columbia), *New York Tendaberry* (Columbia), and *Gonna Take a Miracle* (Columbia). "I was obsessed with Laura Nyro when I was a teenager. Those first four records, no one's ever made music like that. The fact that she passed recently is really sad. I don't think she ever got the respect she really deserved."

Jason and the Scorchers—By the time the Scorchers debuted, Peter was too busy with REM to listen to records. By and large, he picked up on new music in clubs. : *Both Sides of the Line* (EMI) contains both essential Scorchers records—1983's debut EP *Fervor* and 1985's full-length *Lost and Found*—on one hell-bent-for-leather CD.

Vic Chesnutt—"That guy is really amazing and not a whole lot like anybody you've heard before." : *Drunk* (Caroline) and *About to Choke* (Capitol). REM contributed to the Chesnutt cover album *Sweet Relief II: The Gravity of the Situation: The Songs of Vic Chesnutt* (Sony), organized to raise money to pay medical bills for Chesnutt, who is paraplegic.

PETER BUCK'S OWN RECORDINGS

Peter's favorites in REM's catalog begin with the first full-length album, 1983's *Murmur* (IRS). "Considering how young we were and how naïve a record it was, it's actually kind of a cool record," he says. "It's not embarrassing and it doesn't sound hugely out of its time." He still feels strongly about 1987's *Document* (IRS), too, especially its first side: "It sounds like there's a flow all the way through, and the songs kind of related to each other. It's almost a mini-concept record."

From there, he skips to the group's 1990s output, *Out of Time*, *Automatic for the People*, *Monster*, and *New Adventures in Hi-Fi* (all Warner Bros.): "I think the *Hi-Fi* record is the strongest body of songs we've ever done. It doesn't have that really spooky air that *Automatic* does, which makes that a lot of people's favorite but I think the songs are stronger on this one. . . . *Out of Time* I think is kind of patchy but there's good stuff on it." The 1994 album *Monster* is the band's noisiest, "rock-iest" record, which Peter likes "for what it was."

Peter has produced a number of records as well, so we asked him which of those albums came closest to what he was seeking. First mention goes to the Feelies' *The Good Earth* (Coyote), although Peter deflects most of the credit for it: "Most of that was really their work. It was nice being involved. I love the Feelies and I think that's my favorite record of theirs."

Other favorite productions include *Uncle Tupelo's *March 16–20, 1992* (Gasatanka) and Kevn Kinney's *MacDougal Blues* (Island), both of which Peter likes because the records were made quickly, with an emphasis on spontaneity, a direction he's always wanted for REM as well. "I picked musicians to play, we cut it live, and that was really kind of a great experience. . . . I'm real proud of those records." He also names the Minus Five's *The Lonesome Death of Buck McCoy* (Hollywood), *Mark Eitzel's *West* (Warner Bros.), and Tuatara's *Trading With the Enemy* (Epic) "partly because I was involved in the writing of all those. I feel real strongly that that's really good work."

⬤: Real REM fans will want the spirited *Dead Letter Office* (IRS) which combines the group's excellent debut EP, *Chronic Town*, with B-sides and outtakes. Other excellent REM albums not mentioned by Peter include *Reckoning*, *Fables of the Reconstruction*, and *Life's Rich Pageant* (all IRS). The group's 1988 major-label debut, *Green* (Warner Bros.), may not be up to the standards of their best work but it's no slouch. On 1998's *Up* (Warner Bros.), REM uses the occasion of drummer Bill Berry's retirement to expand, not contract, its sound with electronica, strings, drum machines, and more on a set of mostly ballads. The band once swore to break up when any original member left; instead, they simply grow their sense of who they are.

R O S A N N E   C A S H   (March 11, 1997)

When country hitmaker Rosanne Cash declared herself a rocker in the mid-1980s, she was besieged with charges that she had snubbed her heritage. But the orange hair and pink nail polish she wore for the cover of 1985's *Rhythm and Romance* wasn't the makeover it seemed. Johnny Cash's daughter was only being true to her musical upbringing, which included not just hard-core country but Ray Charles and the Beatles.

Rosanne started down a country road as a child because the records her mother played at home "kind of went in as if I was branded with them," Rosanne tells us by phone from New York. Patsy Cline's vocal masterpieces, Marty Robbins's gunfighter ballads, the Collins Kids' rockabilly, Carl and Pearl Butler's and Johnny and Jonie Mosby's honky tonk, and, of course, the defiant country records made by her dad all left their stamp on her. But mom was also playing Ray Charles, albeit his country record. And once Rosanne got a taste of Brother Ray, she started digging his stuff with the backbeat, too. "I can remember running a path around my house listening to 'Hit the Road, Jack,' over and over and over," she says.

By the time Rosanne was eight, the Beatles had happened. It was soon clear to her, if not to everyone else, that she was going to walk a different musical path than Daddy's. "Once I heard the Beatles, it was like getting a DNA change operation," Rosanne recalls. "It was like being infused with this brand-new energy that could not have been foreseen in any way, and totally inspired me on every level. And that was it."

Although born in Memphis, Rosanne was growing up in Southern California. It was a post-Beatles world, and Rosanne was being pulled by the same gravity as everyone else her age. "I was listening to Crosby, Stills, Nash, and Young, and to Traffic—everything that was happening then," she says. "Early Elton John, early Fleetwood Mac, Buffalo Springfield, the Byrds—all those great, great bands. And Joni Mitchell. And I think that that's what had more of an influence later on."

When her first record, *Right or Wrong*, came out in 1983, it was marketed as a country album. But it was injected with rock-friendly production by then-husband Rodney Crowell and Rosanne's bold vocals pushed far beyond the polite bounds of the Grand Ole Opry. "I never considered that I was a pure country artist," Rosanne observes. "I was only marketed [by the] country division of the industry. It wasn't necessarily what the music was about. Because I knew from my childhood what real country music was, and I knew that I wasn't that."

By the time her second album, *Seven Year Ache* appeared, Rosanne was having another problem with the country crowd. As the new album hinted, she had the ambition and talent to write the kind of direct, confessional art songs that Joni Mitchell had pioneered. But the country music world did not look kindly on the sort of emotional and musical directness that Rosanne had in mind. "I found myself completely set up, you know," Rosanne says. "I was successful, I had a following, I could make hit records, and I was completely unhappy with it, with myself. I felt myself to be staring at a brick wall, artistically. So I had to pull the rug out from under myself and kind of dismantle it."

It was a high-risk move at the time, but the near-universal acclaim Rosanne received for 1990's startling *Interiors* established her as firmly in her new genre as she had been in the old one. "In retrospect," she says, "I'm glad I didn't know fully what I was doing [when I broke with country music]. Because I don't think I would've had the guts to do it." Although from another perspective, she notes, her background didn't give her much choice. "It was kind of out of respect that I made a statement that I know [country] is not what I'm doing. I'm a hybrid artist. There's no way I could be Patsy Cline or Loretta Lynn. I don't have that kind of purity. I'm polluted by my cultural influences, you know," she says, laughing.

ROSANNE CASH'S FAVORITE ARTISTS AND RECORDINGS

Ray Charles—*Modern Sounds in Country & Western Music* (Rhino). Ignore the overblown arrangements and just focus on Ray's masterful vocals.

Johnny Cash—*Ballads of the True West* (Columbia). Rosanne loved the linear momentum of her dad's concept album.

Johnny and Jonie Moseby—⬤: *Mr. and Mrs. Country Music* (Columbia).

The Collins Kids—Lawrence and Lawrencine Collins were a hot brother-sister country act by the time they were 11 and 13, respectively. Rockabilly lovers prize the Kids' hyper-charged performances in that genre. ⬤: *Hop, Skip, & Jump* (Bear Family) is a two-CD boxed set that covers their career.

Carl and Pearl Butler—"Don't Let Me Cross Over." ⬤: This song is available on *Don't Let Me Cross Over* (Columbia).

Patsy Cline—Rosanne loves all of Cline's classic material. ⬤: *Patsy Cline's Greatest Hits* (Decca), one of the biggest-selling albums ever, has only 12 tracks but covers several of her eight Top Ten country hits. *The Patsy Cline Collection* (MCA) is a four-CD boxed set with every hit and 16 previously unreleased cuts among its 104 tracks.

Marty Robbins—"Marty Robbins didn't make me want to play music as much as he gave me an appreciation for storyteller songs," Rosanne says. Her favorites included his movie-in-a-lyric hits "Streets of Laredo" and "El Paso" as well as the teen-pop smash, "A White Sport Coat." ⬤: To get all three songs, you'll have to buy both *All Time Greatest Hits* (Sony) and *16 Biggest Hits* (Sony/Legacy).

The Byrds—⬤: See Master List.

Neil Young—*After the Gold Rush* (Reprise) and *Harvest* (Reprise). Rosanne loves Neil Young's work in general and says the latter album in particular was "hugely important to me."

Cat Stevens—*Tea for the Tillerman* (A&M). "A really big record to me."

Big Brother and the Holding Company—*Cheap Thrills* (Columbia). Janis Joplin's major-label debut hit Rosanne as hard as it hit millions of others in the 1960s.

Tom Rush—"Driving Wheel" on *Tom Rush* (Columbia).

Eric Anderson—*Blue River* (Columbia). This was Anderson's commercial break-through record and a landmark album in the 1970s singer-songwriter movement.

Traffic—*Mr. Fantasy* (Island). Traffic's excellent debut still holds up over 30 years later, thanks to sharp collaborative songwriting.

Buffalo Springfield—*Buffalo Springfield* (Atco). The Springfield's first album included such memorable tracks as Stephen Stills's "For What It's Worth" and Neil Young's "Nowadays Clancy Can't Even Sing" among other memorable tunes.

Joni Mitchell—*Ladies of the Canyon* (Reprise) and *Blue* (Reprise). "She gave us all permission. Until Joni, I felt like all of those feelings and all of that artistic expression and working out your sexual selves and your emotional selves and your power selves in a public and a creative forum—I thought that was all the province of men until Joni did it. And then I saw how possible it was for a woman to explore herself in a public arena. And it was completely inspiring; it changed my world."

Fleetwood Mac—*Bare Trees* (Reprise). This fine record from the Mac's middle period, after their early blues-rock and before the poppier Buckingham-Nicks era, is all but forgotten, but not by Rosanne.

The Beatles—Rosanne loves it all. ⏺: See Master List.

Elton John—*Tumbleweed Connection* (MCA). This concept album, with its Old West themes, was "major to me," says Rosanne.

Miles Davis—*Kind of Blue* (Columbia) and *Sketches of Spain* (Columbia). At the time Rosanne was writing the bluntly emotional songs of her *Interiors*, she was drawing inspiration from several records, including this pair along with Peter Gabriel's *Passion*, Mark Knopfler's *Cal*, and Chopin's nocturnes. "Once you open up to Miles, everything changes," Rosanne says.

Peter Gabriel—*Passion: Music for "The Last Temptation of Christ"* (Geffen). "*Passion* just took me places. It really kind of unlocked some doors that I didn't even know were there. . . . It made me see how closed I had been."

Mark Knopfler—*Cal* (Mercury). This was Knopfler's soundtrack for a harrowing film about the Northern Ireland conflict.

Frederic Chopin—Nocturnes. "I've worn holes in those CDs. They're kind of essential to my record collection." The recording Rosanne has is with Elizabeth Leonskaja on piano (2 CDs: Teldec).

Ennio Morricone—*Mission* (Virgin). Rosanne is one of the many admirers of this widely praised soundtrack album to the 1986 Roland Joffe film that starred Robert De Niro and Jeremy Irons.

World Party—Rosanne likes all the work of this group, essentially Karl Wallinger plus backup musicians. ⏺: 1990's *Goodbye Jumbo* (Chrysalis) and *Egyptology* (Capitol) both feature Wallinger's cosmic lyrics and smart, Beatlesque melodies and production touches.

Crowded House—The clever pop songwriting of brothers Neil and Tim Finn was a great inspiration to Rosanne. ⬤: *Woodface* (Capitol) is the one album featuring both brothers, although the rest of the group's catalog, under Neil's leadership, is excellent, too. Also check out *Finn* (Parlophone) by the Finn Brothers, a duet record in which the Finns play all the instruments as well as write the songs.

June Tabor—Rosanne listens to a lot of Celtic music and this exceptional singer of traditional British folk songs ranks at the top of her list. ⬤: *Angel Tiger* (Green Linnet) features a mix of traditional and contemporary material with simple, graceful arrangements. *A Cut Above* (Topic) is more traditionally oriented.

Bob Dylan—*Highway 61 Revisited* (Columbia) and *Desire* (Columbia). Rosanne teaches songwriting and uses "Like a Rolling Stone" from *Highway* as a seminal example of a song that reinvented the craft.

Brian Eno—Rosanne describes Eno as someone "I listen to who's far removed from me. . . . I adore Brian Eno." ⬤: See Master List.

Elvis Costello—*King of America* (Rykodisc). "When I was younger, I used to copy down lyrics of songs I really liked, and really study them. I haven't done that since I was in my early twenties. But when I heard *King of America*, I went 'Man that's just fuckin' great! How did he do this?' "

John Leventhal—"I really admire him. He's incredibly inspiring to me," Rosanne says about her husband, a much-in-demand producer and multi-instrumental session player. ⬤: Leventhal produced Shawn Colvin's Grammy-winning album *A Few Small Repairs*. He has also produced albums by Marc Cohn, Patty Larkin, David Crosby, Rodney Crowell, and Kelly Willis, as well as Rosanne.

Lou Reed—*Magic and Loss* (Sire). "Ah, man, I adored that record, and then went to see him at Radio City, and he did the record sequentially in concert. That's one of the few times I've cried in concert. It was so beautiful."

Bruce Springsteen—*Nebraska* (Columbia) and *Tunnel of Love* (Columbia). Rosanne calls both these albums "brilliant pieces of work." "When *Nebraska* came out," she told us, "I sent it to my dad and said, 'Dad, this is where the real shit is. Listen to this record.' And he ended up recording 'Highway Patrolman.' "

Gillian Welch—*Revival* (Geffen). "That Gillian Welch record is so beautiful—really, really special," Rosanne said about the noteworthy debut from this young Los Angeles–raised singer songwriter, who sounds far more Appalachian than Angelino.

ROSANNE CASH'S OWN RECORDINGS

When picking favorites of her own work, Rosanne focuses on single tracks rather than entire albums. First mention goes to her rendition of Joni Mitchell's "River," which she contributed to *Spirit of '73: Rock for Choice* (Sony), a collection of songs by 14 women artists, including Cassandra Wilson, That Dog, and Babes in Toyland. (Proceeds benefited the organization Rock for Choice.) "It kind of sank without a trace," Rosanne says, "but I was so proud of it. I thought it was really pushing the envelope for me." The song "Paralyzed" on *Interiors* (Columbia) is a high point for her, too. "I think that's really raw, and it really conveys exactly what the song is," she states. Finally, she nominates "Bells and Roses" from *10 Song Demo* (Capitol). "I think that, for what it is, that song is conceptually kind of perfect—in a really ambiguous way," she laughs.

⊙: If Rosanne won't mention whole albums, we will, starting with 1981's superb *Seven Year Ache* (Columbia) from her more country-ish work. Although she performs mostly covers, the song selection is marvelous, and her own writing (the title tune and "Blue Moon with a Heartache") was formidable. The 1990 album *Interiors* is an open wound of a record in which Rosanne, writing all the songs for the first time, tells the story behind the breakup of her marriage to Rodney Crowell. Stark arrangements accent the material perfectly. The 1993 record *The Wheel* (Columbia), gorgeously co-produced by Rosanne and John Levanthal, is similarly confessional but is its own impassioned songwriting and musical statement, not an *Interiors* rehash. With these three discs on your shelf, fill in the gaps with Rosanne's strong 1979 debut, *Right or Wrong* (Columbia), 1982's *Somewhere in the Stars* (Columbia), 1985's *Rhythm and Romance* (Columbia), 1987's *King's Record Shop* (Columbia), and 1996's *10 Song Demo* (Capitol).

VASSAR CLEMENTS (March 31, 1997)

L ike a good tweed coat, the music of fiddler Vassar Clements goes with just about everything. Although best known as a bluegrass musician, his intuitive style of playing adapts itself to almost any setting, a fact that awes his peers but seems perfectly natural to Vassar. "If they're playin' those jazz chords and jazz beat, then that's what I try to make myself get into," he tells us from his home in Nashville. "I'll try to not think about anything else except that. And if they're playin' dyed-in-the-wool bluegrass and that real lonesome sound, well that's what I think about and that's what I try to get into."

Vassar has performed and recorded country, pop, and rock as a guest artist with scores of musicians from *Willie Nelson to Paul McCartney to the *Grateful Dead, but the styles that truly tickle his fancy are bluegrass, jazz, and swing. That seemingly stripes-and-plaid combination goes back to his days growing up in the Deep South in the 1930s and 40s and listening to the radio—the swing and jazz big bands of Benny Goodman, Glenn Miller, Tommy Dorsey, Harry James, and Artie Shaw on the one hand and then Bill Monroe on the other. Although he started off his professional career as a bluegrass fiddler—he joined his idol Monroe's band when he was only 14—the big band sound was always literally at his fingertips. "[Those bands were] still a big part of my thinkin'," Vassar acknowledges. "I was thinkin' about horn riffs and things like that."

Dissect that bluegrass/jazz/swing nexus of Vassar's playing and you'll find two more common denominators—all three forms of music feature improvisation and all three are based partly in the blues. Entirely self-taught, Vassar has always just felt his way around whatever musical form he was playing, but his unscrubbed, emotive tone and instinctive sense of rhythm have always made a perfect fit with blues-based, swinging music of any type. Explaining his versatility, Vassar notes, "I don't read or anything, and anything that I play is just all from feeling. And that's the only thing that I know of, because there's no set way for me to do anything. That's bad in a way and then sometimes I feel like I'm lucky in a way."

Perhaps the best-known phase of Vassar's career was also the shortest—his stint with Old and in the Way, the legendary "hippiegrass" band that was together for under a year in 1973. After being hired into the group, Vassar found himself in the friendly company of open-eared musicians—in particular Grateful Dead guitarist Jerry Garcia and string-music innovator David Grisman*—who combined his same love of bluegrass with the rhythmic feel of jazz and swing. This fortunate union of like-minded souls undoubtedly helped the band's remarkable chemistry. But as Grisman would later write, the real key was the inspiration of playing with Vassar, "like being a Yankee with Babe Ruth on the team."

VASSAR CLEMENTS' FAVORITE ARTISTS AND RECORDINGS

Glenn Miller—Vassar particularly enjoyed this immensely popular swing bandleader when his orchestra included saxophonist/vocalist Tex Beneke. ●: *The*

Essential . . . (2 CDs: Bluebird); *Legendary Performer* (Bluebird), covering well-known radio performances including a New Year's eve rendition of "In the Mood," a favorite of Vassar's.

Benny Goodman with Charlie Christian— ⦿: *Solo Flight (1939–1941)* (Vintage Jazz Classics), under Christian's name, features the guitarist live with the Benny Goodman Sextet, including a performance of Vassar fave "Airmail Special."

Benny Goodman with Ziggy Elman— ⦿: *Live at Carnegie Hall* (Columbia) is one of the pivotal live jazz recordings, with some outstanding soloing by trumpeter Elman.

Tommy Dorsey— ⦿: *Yes, Indeed!* (Bluebird) features great Dorsey recordings from 1939–1945, during which time the trombonist/leader's orchestra included Ziggy Elman. This set features "Well, Git It!" a tune Vassar loves.

Harry James— ⦿: *Snooty Fruity* (Columbia).

Artie Shaw with the Gramercy Five—"Cross Your Heart" and "Summit Ridge Drive." ⦿: *The Complete Gramercy Five Sessions* (Bluebird)—the Gramercy Five is what jazz clarinetist/bandleader Shaw called the small groups formed from his big band.

Bill Monroe with Chubby Wise—The great fiddler Wise was a featured member of Bill Monroe and the Blue Grass Boys' classic lineup, which also included guitarist/vocalist Lester Flatt, banjoist Earl Scruggs, and bassist Howard Watts. Wise "had the prettiest sound I ever heard," says Vassar. ⦿: See Master List under "Bill Monroe and the Bluegrass Boys (1945–47 version)."

Erskine Hawkins—Vassar especially enjoys "Tippin' In," a hit in 1945 for this trumpeter and his swing band. ⦿: *Erskine Hawkins (1941–1945)* (Classics).

Stephane Grappelli—"When I first heard Stephane Grappelli, shoot, it was somethin' out of the blue I never knew existed," recalls Vassar. He later recorded an album with Grappelli and remained great friends with him for the remainder of Grappelli's life. He loves everything Grappelli recorded with guitarist Django Reinhardt and the Quintet du Hot Club de France. "You could take one as much as the other, just any tune. It all sounded great to me." ⦿: See Master List.

Itzhak Perlman—"I never got to play with him but I thought the world of him and still do." ⦿: From Perlman's prolific recording career, get started with Beethoven: Violin Concerto in D, Op. 61, with Philharmonia Orchestra/Carlo Maria Giulini (EMI/Angel); Brahms: Sonatas Nos. 1–3 for Violin and Piano, with Vladimir Ashkenazy, piano (EMI/Angel); and Perlman's winning celebration of Klezmer music, *In the Fiddler's House* (Capitol), with Andy Statman, the Klezmatics, and the Klezmer Conservatory Band.

Ella Fitzgerald—"Such a range she had, plus the scat, I loved that. Oh, boy, she'd sound just like a horn." ⬤: See Master List.

Bob Wills and the Texas Playboys—"Tommy Duncan's singin' really stood out to me. And there was an instrumental called 'Silver Lake Blues' that I really loved. It was just a different kind of music and I loved it." ⬤: *The Tiffany Transcriptions, Vols. 1–9* (Rhino)—each volume is available singly, and all feature Tommy Duncan. "Silver Lake Blues" appears on *For the Last Time* (United Artists).

VASSAR CLEMENTS' OWN RECORDINGS

To celebrate his 50th year in professional music, Vassar recorded *Vassar's Jazz* (Winter Harvest), the first album he mentioned as a favorite among his own recordings. "There were some great musicians, there's some good music goin' on in that," says Vassar. "It was mostly my tunes that we rearranged and made 'em fit that category [jazz]." He also likes the way his two albums on Mercury, *Vassar* and *Superbow*, turned out.

As a rhythmically oriented player, Vassar has a special fondness for sessions where the musicians established a particularly deep groove. Along that line, he singles out his album with Stephane Grappelli, *Together At Last* (Flying Fish), which also features the exquisite guitarist Martin Taylor. Finally, there's the material with Old and in the Way. "Boy, it was great," Vassar sighs. "I enjoyed that to the utmost, believe me. And still do. [The surviving members still occasionally perform with replacements for Garcia and bassist John Kahn.] I'm sorry Jerry's not there, but when we play I still enjoy doin' those tunes. I can almost feel him on stage with us, really. Yeah, that was one of my high points." The classic initial release, *Old & in the Way* (re-released on CD by Rykodisc), was mostly recorded live during a run of shows at San Francisco's Boarding House in 1973. Vassar says "that really comes across the way it was." David Grisman subsequently culled two more Old and in the Way albums from unissued material from the same Boarding House shows. He released the discs, *That High Lonesome Sound* and *Breakdown*, on his own label, Acoustic Disc. Both feature outstanding soloing by Vassar.

⬤: Other notable recordings featuring Vassar include his own *Once In A While* (Flying Fish), the product of a jam session with Miles Davis alumni Dave Holland, John Abercrombie, and Jimmy Cobb; Bill Monroe's *In the Pines* (Rebel), a much overlooked record with Vassar in the fiddle chair on several tracks; *Hillbilly Jazz*

(Flying Fish), a classic of hip Western Swing recorded in 1975 with Doug Jernigan and David Bromberg; and the Nitty Gritty Dirt Band's *Will the Circle Be Unbroken* (2 CDs: EMI America), which joined the NGDB with such country and bluegrass stalwarts as Mother Maybelle Carter, Doc Watson, Merle Travis, and Earl Scruggs in addition to Vassar. This landmark recording introduced a young rock audience to real country music and re-kindled Vassar's career.

STEVE CROPPER (March 17, 1997)

The list of people influenced by Steve Cropper winds on nearly without end and will grow as long as soulful popular music is made. As guitar player first for the Mar-Keys and then Booker T. and the MGs, he invented many of the spare, slashing licks that became R&B staples. The entire era of 1960s and early '70s Memphis soul music—including classic records by Otis Redding, Sam and Dave, *Wilson Pickett, the *Staples Singers, and many others—bears his stamp as player and arranger with the MGs, the backing band of choice for the Stax/Volt label. He was also a key producer and engineer for the record company. As a songwriter, he co-wrote such powerhouse hits as Otis Redding's "Mr. Pitiful," "I Can't Turn You Loose," and "Sittin' on the Dock of the Bay"; Aretha Franklin's "See Saw"; Wilson Pickett's "In the Midnight Hour"; and Eddie Floyd's "Knock on Wood," "Water," and "Raise Your Hand."

The list of people who influenced Steve is much briefer. It starts with Bo Diddley, by way of future country music star Ed Bruce. Steve and Bruce, a few years Steve's senior, attended the same Nashville high school. At a monthly school talent show, Steve watched Bruce slap out Diddley's trademark rhythm on his guitar and was transfixed, he tells us by phone from Nashville: "I went backstage and I said 'Man, that's great. How do you learn how to play one of those?' And he said 'Oh, there's only one way to learn how to play guitar—you get one and learn how to play it.' " Which Steve did, in short order.

Steve drew more ideas from records by Jimmy Reed, Bill Doggett, Chuck Berry, and Hank Ballard and the Midnighters. Most of all, he studied the style of guitarist Lowman Pauling with the "5" Royales. "I got to hear these guys live one night," says Steve, "and got to see 'em perform ['Think'] and just the way that Lowman Pauling threw in those little stab licks—you know, little fills—just blew me away."

By and large, though, Steve plays Steve: "So as far as I can recall, after high school I don't think I ever sat down and listened to anybody's record and tried to learn it. . . . I didn't have time to do it. I was in the studio. And when the session was over, I was in there either mixing it, leading it, editing it, having it mastered or taking it to the plant and gettin' the records, or goin' out and seeing disc jockeys when I had time off." It's axiomatic in sports that superstars make poor coaches because they can't empathize with the struggles of mere mortal athletes. Something similar would seem to apply to Steve, who says he hasn't had time to practice for decades: "Guys say, 'Oh, you must sit at home and just play for hours,' and I go 'When I get home, that guitar sits in the corner and collects dust until I go out on the next gig.' And they don't believe me. Because most guys, they keep their chops up, and they play every day—you know, they never put it down. And I've never picked it up," he laughs.

STEVE CROPPER'S FAVORITE ARTISTS AND RECORDINGS

Bo Diddley—"Bo Diddley." : *Bo Diddley/Go Bo Diddley* (Chess) packs Diddley's first two records on one CD.

Ed Bruce—Bruce has had a diverse career that has included some acting (the "Maverick" TV series with James Garner), some radio stints in Nashville, and some jingle writing for major corporate commercials in addition to his run as a country music hitmaker. Bruce wrote "Mamas, Don't Let Your Babies Grow Up to Be Cowboys," made famous by *Willie Nelson and *Waylon Jennings. : *The Best of . . .* (Varese Sarabande) includes Bruce's 1975 version of "Mamas."

Jimmy Reed—"That had that real simple kind of boogie rhythm style," says Steve, who listened to Reed's records early on and performed such songs of his as "Take Out Some Insurance On Me Baby" and "Little Rain." : See Master List.

Bill Doggett—"Honky Tonk." Steve says that this 1956 instrumental hit was vitally important to guitar players in the South. It was the first tune he learned on guitar. : *Greatest Hits* (King).

Lowman Pauling with the "5" Royales— : *Monkey Hips and Rice: The "5" Royales Anthology* (2 CDs: Rhino).

Chuck Berry—"Maybellene." : See Master List.

Hank Ballard and the Midnighters—"Annie Had a Baby." : *Sexy Ways: The Best of . . .* (Rhino).

The Platters—When Steve was young, he and his friends loved to dance to this early doo-wop and R&B group's records. : *The Magic Touch: An Anthology* (2 CDs: Mercury).

Elvis Presley— : *The King of Rock'n'Roll: The Complete '50s Masters* (5 CDs: RCA), one of rock's best box sets, covers the Elvis era that got Steve excited. *The Complete Sun Sessions* and *Elvis' Golden Records, Vol. 1* (both RCA) are single-disc introductions to the same music.

Thomas Wayne—"Tragedy." : You can find this hit single on a budget collection called *Rock Stars on LP, Vol. 5* (Hollywood).

Otis Redding—In addition to being a soul singer for the ages and one of Steve's best songwriting partners, Redding had a major impact on the way Steve wrote horn arrangements. For more on this, see below. : See Master List.

Eddie Van Halen—Eddie is one of the contemporary guitarslingers Steve most admires. : The songs and vocals on *Van Halen* (Warner Bros.) may be massive pop overkill for all but the arena-rock set but Eddie's credentials as a legitimate guitar monster are established right here.

STEVE CROPPER'S OWN RECORDINGS

Steve has played, produced, or otherwise had a hand in so many records that he finds it hard to pick favorites. But he does have a special place in his heart for the Otis Redding music he worked on, even though he couldn't listen to most of it for years after Redding's 1967 death in a plane crash. "It would come on the radio and I'd switch stations," Steve says, his voice still catching with the memory. "It was very rough on me. But now, like things pass in time, the memories don't go away, but that other feeling has kind of faded out. And it's fun to listen to a lot of the uniqueness of those arrangements and stuff. We all did it together, but I think probably [MGs drummer] Al Jackson had a lot of influence in there as well as Otis [who] had his own groove and his own thing. And the way he approached horns and stuff was totally different. A lot of artists didn't even deal with horns. We always did it, you know. So Otis definitely influenced me in the way I did horn arrangements. . . . He used to wear the horns out. He used to try to stump 'em, just to see if he could come up with something they couldn't play. It was always fun and they all looked forward to having Otis come in." For a referral to Redding's recordings, see above.

From that same era, Steve also still listens to the work he did with Sam and Dave and recommends the set *Sweat 'n' Soul* (2 CDs: Rhino/Atlantic) as an entry to that music; in addition to backing up the duo with the MGs on many songs, he produced many of the tracks along with others on the Stax staff. He also speaks proudly of his production work on Jeff Beck's *The Jeff Beck Group* (Epic) and guitarist Robben Ford's *The Inside Story* (Elektra), as well as Tower of

Power's *Bump City* (Warner Bros.) ("probably one of the tightest bands and best productions I ever worked with.")

🔘 : *With a Little Help from My Friends* (Stax), Steve's 1971 solo album of rock, soul, and blues instrumentals with his guitar and arrangements at the center, is a tub of fun. To hear him with the Mar-Keys, get the twofer *Damifiknow/Memphis Experience* (Stax), which presents more succinct, punchy instrumental R&B that looks forward to the MGs. Be forewarned, however, that only the *Damnification* half features Steve and the rest of the original band, although that alone justifies the price of admission. Sample Booker T. and the MGs catalog via *Green Onions* (Atlantic) and *Very Best of . . .* (Rhino). It will set you back a car payment or two, but to get a comprehensive sense of Steve's contribution to the Stax soul sound, you should acquire the huge box sets *The Complete Stax-Volt Singles, Vols. 1–2* (both 9 CDs: Stax). Both are fabulous collections of music well worth the price although the first set, covering 1959–68, is more consistently rewarding than Vol. 2 (1968–71) since the classic Stax sound is best represented in the span it covers.

D M C   (December 4, 1998)

C rossover!" This single word embodies the hopes and dreams of ambitious musicians everywhere. When a record "crosses over" and becomes a hit outside its genre, sales skyrocket, often securing a lifetime's worth of fame, income, and other residuals. In 1986, rappers Run-DMC belted this industry grand slam with a cover of Aerosmith's "Walk This Way." The first single to ever grab rap and rock fans alike, it propelled the album *Raising Hell* to the top of the R&B charts, a Top Ten berth on the pop charts, and platinum status overall. The record, boosted by the contributions of Aerosmith's Steven Tyler and Joe Perry, seemed a master stroke of calculation, and the pop press has treated it as such ever since.

But there wasn't a premeditated note on it, says Darryl McDaniels, or DMC. From his standpoint, he was simply marrying two forms he had always loved— rap and '60s–'70s rock/pop. Darryl, who with friends Joseph Simmons (Run) and turntable scratcher Jason Mizell (Master Jay) forms the rap trio, had been a huge fan of an early rap group called the Cold Crush Brothers with a similar concept. "They would take melodies like [Harry Chapin's] 'The Cat's in the Cradle' and they used to change the lyrics but keep the melody," Darryl tells us. "Most of the black youth in the city didn't know where the Cold Crush was gettin' these melodies from. But since I was born in '64, these were the records that were playin' on the radio through like '69, '70, because they really didn't have no black urban stations."

Not that Darryl liked the radio music only by default. It still forms the core of what he listens to now. "I think the best music was made by groups like the Beatles, the Rolling Stones, Pink Floyd, and the Grateful Dead—that time period of music," Darryl says. "A lot of those rock groups, they wrote about life. They'd have songs about love, but they'd also have songs about war, Vietnam, drugs, the economy, and world affairs. That stuff really appealed to me." The rap groups he most appreciates today, such as *Public Enemy, are those that like Run-DMC use the music as a vehicle for delivering a social message. "I think there's something special when you can make music that really touches people," Darryl says. "To me, a lot of rap today is really selfish, meaning a lot of these rappers and producers are making the music just to get paid. So a lot of it looks alike and sounds alike."

That goes too for the groups following in Run-DMC's tracks. "After people heard us, people would set out to do what we would do," Darryl says. "Like they'd make it their goal—'We gotta make a crossover record so we get radio play.' No, not at all!" He points out that Run-DMC had flashed their love of rock from the get-go, long before "Rock This Way." Their first album featured a tune, "Rock Box," built up from a heavy metal guitar hook. Their second album was titled "King of Rock."

However, not even Run-DMC can take their music as far in this direction as Darryl would like, so at the time of our interview, he's wrapping up work on a solo album that samples his favorite music to the max: "I don't think my bandmates were—well, even to this day they tease me about the music I like. . . . I always wanted to do something in rap like what Bob Dylan did for rock, when he picked up the electric guitar and everybody booed him, and yet he just played on, and he broke down that barrier."

DMC'S FAVORITE ARTISTS AND RECORDINGS

The Cold Crush Brothers—"When they started making records, they didn't do what they were doing on the street. Their records didn't do well. But tapes of their live performances used to go for fifteen or twenty dollars [in New York City]," says Darryl, who as a rule prefers rap music from before the time it was put on records.

Elton John—Darryl got to know John's hits on the radio, without ever owning one of his albums. : 1974's *Greatest Hits* (MCA) is a collection of spectacular quality including "Benny and the Jets," one of Darryl's faves. *Greatest Hits, Vol. 2* (MCA), from 1977, and *Greatest Hits, Vol. 3 (1979–1987)* (Geffen) are other strong single-disc compilations but for the best overview, go for the boxed set *To Be Continued . . .* (4 CDs: MCA).

John Lennon—"Imagine." Lennon is Darryl's favorite artist ever, and while he loves all of Lennon's work, he calls *Imagine* "the greatest record ever made." ⬤: This song is on the album of the same name, one of Lennon's strongest, and also on the superb compilation, *The . . . Collection* (both Capitol).

The Beatles—*Sgt. Pepper's Lonely Hearts Club Band* (Capitol). This landmark record embodies all the qualities Darryl loves about the Beatles—their courage in challenging conventions, their topicality, their introduction of new musical textures such as their use of Indian instruments, and so on.

Pink Floyd—*Dark Side of the Moon* (Capitol). Darryl especially likes the track "Us and Them" with its portrayal of war as a contest between haves and have-nots.

The Rolling Stones—"Jumpin' Jack Flash" (single-only), "You Can't Always Get What You Want" on *Let It Bleed* (ABKCO), "Honky Tonk Woman" (single-only), and "Wild Horses" on *Sticky Fingers* (Virgin). "It sounds so beautiful, the music, the arrangement, Mick Jagger's singing, and the way they have the choir opening up," Darryl says about "You Can't Always . . ." He says "Wild Horses" "is like a hip-hop record to me, because when [Jagger] sings, and then drops the drum beat, and Keith Richards comes in there with the guitar." ⬤: All four tunes can be had on *Hot Rocks 1964–1971* (2 CDs: London).

*The Grateful Dead—"They didn't just make music, they were the music." ⬤: For a complete review of the Dead catalog, see the section on Phil Lesh.

Sheryl Crow—*Tuesday Night Music Club*, *Sheryl Crow*, and *The Globe Sessions* (all A&M).

Alanis Morissette—*Jagged Little Pill* and *Supposed Former Infatuation Junkie* (both Maverick).

Joan Osborne—"One of Us" and "Man in the Long Black Coat" on *Relish* (Polygram).

Sarah McLachlan—*Surfacing* (Arista). DMC especially likes the song "Building a Mystery" on this album.

Harry Chapin—"Cat's in the Cradle." ⬤: *Anthology of . . .* (Elektra).

The Doobie Brothers—*What Once Were Vices Are Now Habits* (Warner Bros.) Darryl loves the hit song "Black Water" on this disc.

Bad Company—⬤: See Master List.

Billy Joel—*Piano Man* (Columbia).

*Public Enemy—"I love everything that Public Enemy ever made. And that's because of the militancy of it, because of the way *Chuck D raps and the type of music he used." ⬤: See the section on Chuck D and his recordings.

Paula Cole—*This Fire* (Image/Warner Bros.).

Guns N' Roses—*Use Your Illusion II* (Geffen). Darryl liked the group's remake of Bob Dylan's "Knockin' on Heaven's Door."

Bob Dylan—*Oh Mercy!* (Columbia). "I had to buy a Dylan album because I listened to Joan Osborne's version of 'Man in a Long Black Coat.' I sat there and listened to Dylan and said he's like me. He don't care—he's writing what he feels and what needs to be said."

DMC'S OWN RECORDINGS

"I think the best album that we've done was definitely *Raising Hell* [Profile] in 1986," says DMC. "That was our most versatile prototype, authentic, pick-this-album-up-and-learn-about-hip-hop-and-rap album ever, you know what I'm sayin'? It was the full thing: rhymes, scratching, records with ideas, records with concepts, freestyle raps, the whole nine went into that album. But I think the most favorite record of mine of all time was a record called *Run-DMC Live at the Funhouse* (long out of print). That record was what used to go on in rap before rappers made rap records. And the reason why we used rock, James Brown, R and B, reggae, the reason why rappers rap over jazz is before we had a chance to go in the studio to make records, we had to find beats and stuff to rap over." To DMC, rap is, or was, primarily a performance art, created on the spot with MCs rapping over sounds created by DJs, not pre-recorded backgrounds, which is why few rap records make his list of faves: "[The live] record is what Run-DMC is all about and what hip-hop should be about. And it's not no more."

⬤: Despite its preference for live rap, Run-DMC helped elevate rap album production beyond its previous singles-plus-filler level. An essential Run-DMC collection would include *Raising Hell*'s two predecessors, *Run-DMC* and *King of Rock* (both Profile). *Tougher Than Leather* from 1988 and 1993's *Down with the King* (both Profile) are strong later records. *Together Forever: Greatest Hits 1983–1991* (Profile) includes some live tracks and the non-album song "Christmas in Hollis," besides all the expected tracks from the first five records (that is, through 1990's *Back from Hell* [Profile]).

CHUCK D (November 4, 1998)

As a teenager, Chuck D—then Carlton Ridenour—set his sights on a career in sportscasting, not hip-hop. But the accessibility of making music brought about by the rap revolution had definitely started him thinking. "The turntables, mixer, and microphone—that struck my curiosity," Chuck tells us from a hotel room in Michigan. "I was a fan of the music, pretty much, and didn't want to be an artist, but I was kind of upset at the people that was doin' it at the places I was going to, and I always thought it could be better. Like there was a party goin' and I didn't want to hear a guy get on the mike who didn't have a good voice. And I didn't want to hear a guy cuttin' on the turntable who didn't cut on beat."

Despite other intentions, Carlton was about to be drafted into the music business. While studying graphic design at Long Island's Adelphi University in the mid-1980s, he built a reputation as "Chuckie D" spinning rap and hip-hop as a DJ at the student radio station. Meanwhile, a friend he had met at the station, Hank Shocklee, had been making his own hip-hop demo tapes and Chuck ended up rapping over one of the tunes, "Public Enemy No. 1." Def Jam's Rick Rubin heard the tape and a contract offer soon followed. Initially reluctant, Chuck decided that this was his opportunity to implement a vision he'd been nurturing of a politically conscious rap that drew ideas from rock and rock-influenced rappers such as Run-DMC and the Beastie Boys. "We didn't just want to put together a rap album," Chuck recalls. "We wanted to put together a record similar to the rock boys, the way they put together concept records. One of the things that blew me and Hank away was Iron Maiden's projection of how they kept everything consistent from album to album, what the message was saying and also the artwork, you know. They were thorough. Musically, we drew from a whole bunch of different sources." (Shocklee is now a co-leader of Public Enemy's production team, the Bomb Squad.)

Despite a tumultuous history that threatened to bury the group at times, Public Enemy's basic vision hasn't changed. Still, as the music moves forward, Chuck and his bandmates move with it, checking out what's happening in electronica, drum-and-bass, and metal and extracting as necessary. Chuck is also mining the finer moments in rock history for choice samples. For instance, the title track from 1998's *He Got Game*, the soundtrack for Spike Lee's film, is built around the tremolo guitar intro to Buffalo Springfield's 1967 hit, "For What It's Worth" as well as samples from the Who's "Won't Get Fooled Again." More grist for the mill comes from the blues of Howlin' Wolf and Muddy Waters. Chuck also pours over seminal Motown soul by the Four Tops and Temptations; well-built pop by the Hollies and the Fifth Dimension; and even country crossover classics like Glen Campbell's "Wichita Lineman." "You know, you might ask me three years from now and I might add people like Little Willie John, but I'm not there yet. James Brown will be there until I die," he laughs. "If you ask anybody in rap, believe me, I got the most eclectic list [of influences]."

CHUCK D'S FAVORITE ARTISTS AND RECORDINGS

Grandmaster Flash and the Furious Five—In his early days of rap fandom, Chuck felt that Grandmaster Flash and his main MC Melle Mel, along with DJ Hollywood and Eddie Cheeba, were the models of how the music should be performed. "They blew me away the first time I checked them out," Chuck says about the former. : *The Message* (Sugar Hill) contains the groundbreaking title tune, which paved the way for more socially conscious rappers such as Public Enemy. *Message from Beat Street: Best of . . .* (Rhino) also contains "The Message" and ten other key tracks. *Adventures of . . . : More of the Best* (Rhino) completes the picture.

Eddie Cheeba—Cheeba was New York's leading DJ in the mid-'70s, earning $2,000 a night. : No recordings are available as of this writing.

DJ Hollywood—One of rap's first MCs, this important figure originated the idea of rhyming over recorded music and coined the term "hip-hop." In the prior disco era, he developed the technique of record mixing. His reputation was built primarily on live performances at the Apollo Theater, not recordings. : *Rarities* (Ol Skool Flava).

*Run-DMC—*Raising Hell* and "Rock Box" on *Run-DMC* (both Profile). In addition to the music itself, Chuck loved the production work of Larry Smith on these discs as well as the Whodini record cited below. "Rock Box" in particular was "a tremendous influence," says Chuck. "The greatest group of all time," he opines. : See the section on DMC of Run-DMC.

Whodini—*Escape* (Jive). These New York rappers helped set a new standard by basing their tunes in soul and R&B.

Beastie Boys—*Licensed to Ill* (Def Jam). "Inspirational in letting us know where we had to go with our music, and also just the sounds. Sounds and scrapes from everybody from James Brown to the *Meters to AC/DC. Not so much sampling, but arrangements," says Chuck about how this music, and especially the track "Hold It Now, Hit It" influenced him. He also studied the way producer Rick Rubin mixed rap and rock in the group's music.

Eric B. and Rakim—"I Know You Got Soul" on *Paid in Full* (4TH & Broadway). Chuck says that this and the Boogie Down Productions album cited below were important to Public Enemy as they planned their second album. "Turned our whole level of production around," he says.

Boogie Down Productions—*Criminal Minded* (Sugar Hill). Chuck especially likes the track "Poetry."

Doug E. Fresh and Slick Rick—"The Show." Chuck loves the arrangement on this single, under Fresh's name. 🔘: *Greatest Hits, Vol. 1* (BUS).

Fatboy Slim—Ex-Housemartins and Pizzaman member Norman Cook's latest project stands at the crossroads of hip-hop and electronica. Chuck likes Slim's work "across the board." 🔘: *Better Living Through Chemistry* and *You've Come A Long Way, Baby* (both Astralwerks).

DJ Shadow—Chuck also likes everything this furious sampler does. 🔘: *Pre-emptive Strike* (Mo Wax) collects his early singles. *Endtroducing* (Mo Wax) was his impressive 1996 debut.

Prodigy—With their techno beats and hooky, sample-filled tunes, this British band has created a huge dance following. 🔘: *Experience* (Elektra), *Music for the Jilted Generation* (Mute), and *The Fat of the Land* (XL Mute).

Chemical Brothers—🔘: *Exit Planet Dust, Dig Your Own Hole*, and *Brothers Gonna Work It Out* (all Astralwerks).

Korn—Chuck cites this group as a good example of the way that heavy metal and hip-hop music are coming together. 🔘: *Korn* (Immortal/Sony), *Life Is Peachy* (Sony), and *Follow the Leader* (Epic).

Cypress Hill—*Cypress Hill* (Ruffhouse) and "Riot Starter" on *IV* (Sony).

Sam and Dave—Chuck loves their vocal tradeoffs. 🔘: *The Very Best of . . .* (Rhino) covers all the essential tracks.

*Buddy Guy—"When My Left Eye Jumps" on *The Very Best of Buddy Guy* (Rhino). "Great arrangement."

Howlin' Wolf—Chuck likes the whole catalog. 🔘: See Master List.

Muddy Waters—*Electric Mud* (Chess/MCA). "Big influence. When I look back and I hear that critics smashed it or purists smashed it, I'm sayin' they didn't understand it. . . . Probably the album I've listened to the most in the last year."

Funkadelic—*Funkadelic* (Westbound). "I can't get enough of it."

Jimi Hendrix—"Voodoo Chile" and "All Along the Watchtower" on *Electric Ladyland* (Reprise).

Fifth Dimension—"One Less Bell to Answer." : *Greatest Hits on Earth* (Arista).

The Hollies—"He Ain't Heavy, He's My Brother." : *All-Time Greatest Hits* (Curb) covers 1964–75 but has only 12 tracks. *Epic Anthology* (Epic) has 20 tracks but starts in 1967, excluding such hits as 1966's "Bus Stop."

Ben E. King—"Stand By Me." : *Anthology* (2 CDs: Rhino) includes both solo hits and King's hits with the Drifters.

Moody Blues—"Go Now." This British group began life as an R&B quintet in 1965, topping both the U.K. and U.S. charts with this cover of an American R&B tune before reinventing itself as an orchestral progressive rock group. : *The Best of the Moody Blues* (Polygram).

Glen Campbell—"Wichita Lineman." This huge hit was one of many penned by superb songcrafter Jimmy Webb. : *The Very Best of . . .* (Liberty).

The Zombies—"Time of the Season" on *Odessey & Oracle* (Rhino).

The Temptations—"Don't Look Back" and "I Wish It Would Rain." Chuck is especially a fan of David Ruffin, the Temps' lead singer in their early years. "You can't overtop his vocal emotion," he says about "Rain." : *The Ultimate Collection* (Motown), an outstanding, single-disc compilation includes "Don't Look Back." . . . *at His Best* (Motown) features Ruffin's highlights with the Temps and as a solo artist, including "Rain."

James Brown—Chuck is crazy about the entire catalog and says that "Give It Up or Turnit a Loose" is "my all-time favorite song." : See Master List.

Redman—"He's my favorite rapper. I like Redman's phrasing. He uses words in such a big chunk, you know." : *Whut? Thee Album* (Chaos) is his highly regarded 1992 debut. Try also 1994's *Dare Iz a Darkside* (Ral) and *Muddy Waters* and *Doc's The Name* (both Def Jam).

The Four Tops—"Walk Away, Renee," "Ask the Lonely," and "Bernadette." Tops lead singer the late Levi Stubbs is one of Chuck's all-time favorite vocalists. : *Anthology* (2 CDs: Motown).

Isaac Hayes—*Hot Buttered Soul* (Stax). Another record that taught Chuck a lot about arrangements.

Dionne Warwick—"Walk On By." Chuck loved Warwick's graceful hit version of this Burt Bacharach/Hal David song. : *The . . . Collection: Her All-Time Greatest Hits* (Rhino) is packed with many other examples of the winning Warwick/Bacharach/David formula.

CHUCK D'S OWN RECORDINGS

"[Public Enemy's] *Muse Sick 'n' Hour Mess Age* (Def Jam) probably would be the favorite," Chuck says about his own records, "because in 1993 and 1994 we made a concentrated effort to make a record that would work in '99. And though critically bashed at that particular time, more people are picking it up and saying it fits more now than it did then. And in my liner notes I pretty much predicted it, and right now it's leading me to say I told you so. 'Welcome to the Terrordome' [on *Fear of a Black Planet* (Def Jam)] is my favorite single, not because of the song, how it sounds and all, but it signifies and reflects a period that I think came out in the song itself. You can hear it in the groove. I also had a good time making 'Give It Up' [EP: RAL], which was a totally different departure from 'Terrordome' [because of] the blues feeling. A lot of people in rap and hip-hop might be into jazz and reggae. I'm more into blues."

⦿ : Public Enemy built its reputation on *Yo! Bum Rush the Show*, their 1987 debut. From 1988, *It Takes a Nation of Millions to Hold Us Back* is regarded by many as the greatest hip-hop record ever made; 1990's *Fear of a Black Planet* and 1991's *Apocalypse '91 . . . The Enemy Strikes Black* (all Def Jam) continue the forward momentum, both musically and thematically. The 1998 record *He Got Game* (Def Jam) is ostensibly the soundtrack to Spike Lee's film of the same name, but in effect is a Public Enemy release after a four-year absence from recording. The Bomb Squad stripped the sound down to its basics for this effort, departing from their signature kaleidoscopic density.

GREGORY DAVIS (November 25, 1997)

I t's beside the point to ask Dirty Dozen trumpeter/vocalist Gregory Davis why he decided to make music his life. He didn't choose his career. It chose him. Gregory was raised in New Orleans, the party-down capital of the Western world, where music is the air that everyone breathes. In the years when he was growing up, his neighborhood was a living jukebox of New Orleans jazz, funk, R&B, and blues, Gregory says. Nearly every weekend, parades with bands blaring traditional New Orleans music would fill the streets, followed by a long column of people dancing the "second line." Bands played at ball games in the nearby park. Funeral processions led by brass bands passed by Gregory's kindergarten classroom in the Sixth Ward, where many of the traditional bands got their start.

From his front yard, he could hear bands starting up in the ballrooms—almost every neighborhood had one or two—just as evening fell and he was heading inside for dinner. When he would walk to school early in the morning, he'd hear some of the groups just finishing up. "And I'm talking about going to school about seven or eight in the morning, and the band's still playing!" Gregory says.

Of course, the streets could have gone dead silent and Gregory might not have noticed because the music was going almost nonstop at home, too. "Every holiday we had just lots and lots of people over. They'd just take out a bunch of records and start playing, then they would start the cooking." The atmosphere didn't change much on ordinary days: "My mother and my father, my grand-mother, aunts and uncles—we were a pretty close family—they would also just buy records and have records [playing] all the time."

In the notoriously liquor-friendly legal climate of the Crescent City, Gregory was able to earn regular money playing music when he was just 12 or 13. The R&B/funk group he formed with friends gigged in local bars under rules that permitted underage players to work as long as they walked through the doors with an adult. "From the time I was thirteen I never asked my parents or never expected an allowance, because I was able to earn twenty-five, forty, fifty bucks on the weekend. So that was a lot of money to me, and so that became the ticket for me. If you want to get this extra money, you gotta play in this band, and it all started to blossom from then."

Beginning with those first gigs, Gregory learned the First Commandment of New Orleans music—shake it or go home. Which explains how Dirty Dozen, which started life as the Dirty Dozen Brass Band with a traditional brass band lineup, has always gotten away with expanding the classic New Orleans sound. They know that the only real Crescent City tradition is to keep derrieres in motion. "Here in New Orleans it's okay to be the greatest musician in the world, but people here want to dance, they want to be a part of the show," Gregory notes. "They're not just content to sit down and listen. Like right now it's Thanksgiving and they're gonna show the Macy's parade and they got the one big grandstand in New York where people will stand and watch the parade. It's not like that here in New Orleans. The majority of the people want to follow the parade from the beginning to the end. They want to be part of it." In other words, when Dirty Dozen tours, it entertains, but when it plays at home, it simply performs its civic duty.

GREGORY DAVIS'S FAVORITE ARTISTS AND RECORDINGS

Ray Charles—Gregory remembers first digging Brother Ray's "I Got A Woman" when he was five or six years old and his father played it at home. ●: See Master List.

Fats Domino—Gregory prefers the New Orleans R&B music that Domino made with producer Dave Bartholomew before he crossed over as a pop act. ●: *They Call Me the Fat Man . . . : The Legendary Imperial Recordings* (4 CDs: EMI America) is the best compilation of this material. The single-disc *My Blue Heaven: Best of Fats Domino* (EMI America) has only two pre-crossover tracks.

James Brown—"Everything that James Brown did was happening here in New Orleans." ●: See Master List.

Earth, Wind & Fire—In classic brass band music, so many instruments improvise at once that the untrained ear can have trouble hearing the melody. EW&F's horn arrangements inspired DDBB to simplify and clarify its sound for popular consumption, Gregory says. ●: *The Best of . . . ,Vol. 1* (Columbia) contains most of the group's hits from the mid-'70s, its peak period of popularity and inspiration. *Open Your Eyes*, *That's the Way of the World*, *Gratitude*, and to a somewhat lesser extent, *Spirit* and *All 'n' All* (all Columbia) are well-received individual records from that time. *The Best of . . . , Vol. 2* (Columbia) covers all the essential tracks from their 1979 albums onward.

Louis Armstrong—Once Gregory began playing in his high school jazz band, he became interested in the great jazz players on his instrument, including Armstrong, the father of all jazz trumpeters. ●: See Master List.

Freddie Hubbard—*Red Clay* (CTI). "To me, it related to the music of New Orleans in that the music was danceable."

Art Blakey and the Jazz Messengers with Freddie Hubbard—Once Gregory got into Hubbard's records, he traced his career back to his early-1960s stint with Blakey's Jazz Messengers. ●: *Mosaic*, *Bahaina'a Delight*, and *Free for All* (all Blue Note) are outstanding albums featuring Hubbard.

Dizzy Gillespie—"I'm amazed at the facility that Dizzy had on his horn. I'm striving to get there, and I'll probably die without getting there, but it's something to shoot for," says Gregory, who also admires Gillespie's compositional innovations. ●: *Groovin' High* (Savoy), *Gillespiana/Carnegie Hall Concert* (Verve), *Dizzy's Diamonds: The Best of the Verve Years* (3 CDs: Verve), and *Verve Jazz Masters: . . .* (Verve), a solid, single-disc introduction to Dizzy's small- and big-band work as well as sessions with Charlie Parker.

Marvin Gaye—"Got To Give It Up." "That had this big bass line thing happening throughout the record. That influenced me and my playing and what I wanted to do with the Dirty Dozen." ⬤: *Every Great Motown Hit of . . .* (Motown).

Dinah Washington—"Nobody Knows The Way I Feel This Morning." Washington was a major influence on Dirty Dozen once the band started doing vocals. "I just love the way she phrased things," says Gregory. "It was not just a voice with her, it was also that she always had this very rhythmic background happening with her. Even if she was doing a slow ballad, there was some kind of driving beat." ⬤: *The Best of . . .* (Capitol).

Miles Davis—*Friday Night at the Blackhawk: Vol. 1, A Tribute to Jack Johnson*, and *Bitches Brew* (all Columbia). About *Blackhawk*, Gregory says, "That's when I really started to see where swing had its place with what we were doing here in New Orleans. . . . Boy, that had a big, big influence on what I thought the trumpet could do." The latter two records, savaged by jazz purists when they came out, confused Gregory at first, too. But they eventually taught him that music must be judged on its own terms, not by the criteria of what came before.

Lee Morgan—*The Sidewinder* (Blue Note). The funky title tune, a big hit, made a major impact on Gregory "for the soulful part of his playing."

Sidney Bechet—"[Before hearing Bechet], I had never heard any of the reed instruments played so fluently in the New Orleans traditional jazz genre of music." ⬤: *The Legendary . . .* (Bluebird) is a fine single-disc compilation culled from the excellent . . . , *1932–43: The Bluebird Sessions* (5 CDs: Bluebird). *Jazz Classics: Vol. 1* (Blue Note) samples sessions from 1939 and 1951.

Danny Barker—"Danny Barker was a person who was there at the beginning," Gregory says about this early New Orleans jazz musician, "and so his idea of music was not only that it should sound good, but that it should be entertaining. So that had an influence on my approach to what we were going to play or what I listened to." ⬤: *Save the Bones* (Orleans) is one of only two records Barker made as a leader. Barker, who died in 1994 at the age of 85, appears on the DDBB's *New Orleans Album*.

Jelly Roll Morton—The DDBB has performed New Orleans jazz pioneer Morton's suggestive "The Pearls" and uptempo dance number "Georgia Swing." ⬤: . . . , *Vols. 1–5* (JSP, available separately).

Professor Longhair—The DD honor Longhair with their rendition of his classic "Mardi Gras in New Orleans." ⬤: See Master List.

Duke Ellington—Gregory was greatly influenced by Ellington's chordal innovations, his use of unusual (for jazz at the time) instruments such as violin and conga drums, the alternating of dark and light colors in his music, and on and on. ●: See Master List.

GREGORY DAVIS'S OWN RECORDINGS

Gregory has special affection for his group's debut as the Dirty Dozen Brass Band, 1984's *My Feet Can't Fail Me Now* (Concord Jazz). But probably his proudest moment as a musician came when one of his idols, Dizzy Gillespie, appeared on the group's third effort, 1989's *Voodoo* (Columbia). In the same way Gregory, a student of the music he plays, was thrilled to work with Crescent City legends Dave Bartholomew and Danny Barker on *New Orleans Album* (Columbia). "Dave is a trumpet player and before Fats Domino, he had his own jazz big band. And I got to work with his band, in the mid-'70s and '80s. Danny Barker I would say would be the king as far as what I do and what we do with Dirty Dozen, because he was the connection, way back past Dizzy Gillespie and Louis Armstrong, to Buddy Bolden and Jelly Roll Morton and everybody who came after."

●: Other strong recordings not mentioned by Gregory include 1986's *Live: Mardi Gras in Montreux* (Rounder) and 1992's *Open Up: Watcha Gonna Do for the Rest of Your Life?* (Columbia). Note that Gregory's group underwent a transformation in the mid-'90s when its two drummers left for family-related reasons. One had played snare and the other bass drum in the traditional brass band style; the band was unable to find two replacements who could work together as well, so they hired a single drummer and filled the remaining open spot with a keyboard player. At about the same time, they decided to have sousaphone player Julius McKee, who had previously played all the bass parts on his horn, play an actual acoustic or electric bass on some tunes since he was adept on those instruments and the group wanted to expand its repertoire. The changes, accompanied by shortening the name to Dirty Dozen, were controversial with purists, although the brass band lineup never restricted itself to traditional material, either.

DR. JOHN (August 1, 1998)

Backstage before a show in southern Oregon, Mac Rebennack hobbles, his large frame leaning on an ornately carved walking stick. But once the concert starts and his band, the Lower 911, rolls out their party-in-the-streets New Orleans grooves, he is temporarily healed, rising from his piano bench time after time to dance for the people. This is no longer a strange venue in a strange town in the middle of a long road trip. It is home.

Few types of music anywhere are as closely tied to the ambiance of a place as the "second-line" strut of the Crescent City's players. In an interview before the performance, the man the world knows as "Dr. John" explains why. "All of New Orleans' music is connected to the Mardi Gras Indians or it's connected to the churches," he says. "[For instance], they had a beautiful church in New Orleans, the Guiding Light Spiritual Church, and it was like somethin' special, you know? A lotta good music came outta that church that influenced a lot of funk music later: Fran Lastie's drumming, Poppy Lastie's drumming, Melvin Lastie's trumpet, Jesse Hill—all of them came outta that church. There was somethin' about everybody that led to what became the *Meters' music, and led to a lot of other New Orleans music."

New Orleans music is a family thing, too, handed down through the generations like jewelry and fine china. "Whether it's the *Marsalis family, the *Nevilles, they all got that family thing happenin'," Mac says. "And then just among the musicians, we're a musical family. And it's somethin' that the old timers always pass down to the youngsters, and it's a good thing."

In Mac's case, the family connection was his father, who stocked in his appliance store the records of such New Orleans icons as Professor Longhair, Huey Smith, and Allen Toussaint, as well as Chicago blues and other so-called "race records." Those discs provided Mac an early schooling in the music that would become his life. But as an up-and-coming session pianist and guitarist in the 1950s, he got much of his education on the job. "I used to hang at the recordin' studio in New Orleans and a lot of the stuff that influenced me a lot never saw the light of day," he says.

The studio scene also helped broaden his pallette beyond New Orleans' musical borders. "A lot of people would come to New Orleans to record," Mac tells us, "like Ray Charles, Joe Turner. Even though Joe was from Kansas City, Ray was from Florida and all, that had a big influence on everything I was about. And workin' with a lot of different people that were heroes of mine, whether it was Little Willie John or Charles Brown or Amos Milburn. Workin' on their sessions, they all shifted some gear in me."

Like the international port he hails from, Mac welcomes whatever musical inputs come his way, from every corner of the world. He loves Afro-Cuban music, for instance, and the day before, he tells us, he was digging a record by the Trans-Global Underground, a U.K.-based band that creates pancultural dance music. To Dr. John, music is just food for the mood. "Some music has a certain effect on me at different times. It's there to use it for various purposes."

DR. JOHN'S FAVORITE ARTISTS AND RECORDINGS

Big Joe Turner—"I loved all of Joe Turner's stuff, whatever label he was with, all through the Atlantic days, too, but it was something about all the piano players that he had, whether it was Harry Van Walls, Pete Johnson, or Sammy Price, they all really accompanied him real good because he was a special cat." ◉: *The Complete 1940–1944* (Official) includes all of Turner's recordings for Decca. *Big, Bad, and Blue: The Big Joe Turner Anthology* (Rhino), is a three-CD career overview. *Greatest Hits* (Atlantic) includes 21 prime tracks recorded for Atlantic.

Huey "Piano" Smith—This wild vocalist and R&B pianist was one of Dr. John's favorite New Orleans musicians. ◉: See Master List.

Clarence "Gatemouth" Brown—"Okie Dokie Stomp." ◉: *The Original Peacock Recordings* (Rounder) includes the "Stomp" and is otherwise a fine introduction to this unique, Louisiana-born multi-instrumentalist.

Charles Brown—Dr. John ate up the easy-going blues of this pianist/vocalist on the latter's records for Aladdin and earlier labels. ◉: *Driftin' Blues: The Best of Charles Brown* (EMI America) is an excellent single-CD compilation of Brown's Aladdin material. *The Complete Aladdin Recordings of Charles Brown* (Mosaic), is a limited edition (still available as of summer '98) CD set available only by mail order. *Someone to Love* (Bullseye Blues) contains one of Dr. John's favorite songs by Brown, "Tell Me You'll Wait for Me," which the good doctor did a rendition of on his own *Afterglow* (Blue Thumb). *1944–1945* (Classics) is a pre-Aladdin compilation.

T-Bone Walker—"That was my hero when I was playing guitar as a kid." ◉: See Master List.

Micky Baker—Dr. John reveled in guitarist Baker's work backing up Big Maybelle on her Savoy recordings. ◉: *Candy* (Savoy Jazz).

Little Willie John—This R&B performer is still largely unknown to the listening public, but not to Dr. John and a host of other musicians who cite his influence. John's sidemen included guitarists Micky Baker and Billy Butler, both of whose licks Dr. John studied as a young guitarist. ◉: See Master List.

Miles Davis—*Sketches of Spain* and, probably, *Miles and Coltrane* (both Columbia). Dr. John couldn't remember the name of an album, which he called "a helluva record," that captured pianist Bill Evans first appearance with Davis's band. Evans worked with Davis in 1958 and recorded little with him then. The latter disc is the best known from that time and includes nearly all the personnel from Davis's landmark *Kind of Blue* session.

Thelonious Monk—"Bye-Ya" on *Thelonious Monk Trio* (Prestige).

Professor Longhair—Henry Roeland Byrd, aka Professor Longhair, cooked up a piano stew of rumba, boogie-woogie, blues, and calypso that became a foundation of the Crescent City R&B and rock and roll sound. ⬤: See Master List.

Allen Toussaint—Toussaint is not only one of the great New Orleans R&B songwriters and pianists but also an important producer, arranger, and all-around mover and shaker in the city's music scene. ⬤: *Allen Toussaint Collection* (Reprise).

Fats Domino—Dr. John loves the pre-crossover work this giant of New Orleans R&B recorded for Imperial records in the early 1950s with Dave Bartholomew at the console. ⬤: *They Call Me the Fat Man . . . : The Legendary Imperial Recordings* (EMI America) is a four-CD set. The single-disc alternative, *My Blue Heaven: Best of Fats Domino* (EMI America), includes only two of the pre-crossover tracks.

Smiley Lewis—Lewis never made it with the public the way his label-mate at Imperial, Fats Domino, did, but Dr. John and many others enjoy his work in the early 1950s (also produced by Dave Bartholomew) just as much. ⬤: *The Best of Smiley Lewis* (Capitol).

Muddy Waters—Dr. John prefers Waters' early records on Chess. ⬤: See Master List.

Howlin' Wolf—As with Muddy Waters, Dr. John goes for those early Chess classics. ⬤: See Master List.

Johnny Ace—Dr. John is a big fan of the output of Don Robey's Duke and Peacock labels in the 1950s and early '60s, starting with records by R&B pianist/vocalist Ace, who died at 25 playing Russian Roulette. ⬤: See Master List.

Bobby "Blue" Bland—As with Johnny Ace above and Junior Parker below, Dr. John likes the Duke recordings by this soul/blues vocalist best. ⬤: See Master List.

Junior Parker—Dr. John seems to have a weakness for velvet-voiced singers like Parker and Charles Brown, in contrast to his own gruff style. ⬤: See Master List.

Willie Mae "Big Mama" Thornton—Dr. John is a big fan of all the music blues belter Thornton recorded for Don Robey's Peacock records. ⬤: *Hound Dog: The Peacock Recordings* (MCA) is named for the title cut, a huge hit for Thornton before it became an even bigger one when Elvis covered it.

Lightnin' Hopkins—Dr. John likes Hopkins's early work on the Herald and Decca labels best. ⬤: *The Herald Material* and *The Herald Recordings, Vol. 2* (Collectibles). Also see Master List.

Ike Turner—"The records he made on The Kings of Rhythm, before he had the Ikettes, was some killer records." : *Rhythm Rockin' Blues* (Ace) includes 21 early hits by Ike Turner and His Kings of Rhythm.

Art Blakey and the Jazz Messengers—Dr. John prefers the Messengers' early recordings on Blue Note. Like many musicians, he flat-out likes the sound of Blue Notes records in the 1950s and '60s: "The way they backed up whoever the artist was, their records always had a certain sound that was another side of it." : *Moanin'* (Blue Note), features Lee Morgan on trumpet, a perfect soloist for Blakey's heated style, and Bennie Golson on tenor sax. *A Night in Tunisia* (Blue Note), with Morgan and Wayne Shorter in the front line, is a must buy for the volcanic title tune alone.

Horace Silver—Again, Dr. John likes this soulful jazz pianist's Blue Note recordings best. : *A Song for My Father* (Blue Note) is Silver's most famous record. *The Jody Grind* (Blue Note) is also widely admired.

Machito—Dr. John has a passion for Afro-Cuban music, and this bandleader's older records, especially those featuring vocals by Graciela and arrangements by Mario Bauza, are among his favorites. : *Mucho Macho* (Pablo) is a prized compilation from 1946 and '49 that features several of Machito's classic recordings and what many consider to be his finest band, including Graciela and Bauza.

Arsenio Rodriguez—Dr. John also loves the older recordings by this Afro-Cuban bandleader/composer, blinded at age three. : *Afro-Cuban Classic* (Ansonia).

Tito Puente—As with Machito and Rodriguez, Dr. John likes the older Puente albums best. : *Dance Mania* (BMG).

John Coltrane—*Giant Steps* (Atlantic), *My Favorite Things* (Atlantic), and *Ballads* (Impulse). Dr. John loves Coltrane in general but likes this period—1959–62—of his playing most of all.

DR. JOHN'S OWN RECORDINGS

When we asked Dr. John about favorites in his own catalog, he preferred to discuss his first projects as both an artist and a producer. "I just love that I got to record 'em with the studio cats and all of that, and the records when I started producin', back in the game, workin' with the guys like Joe Tex and stuff." Much of this material, including Dr. John's own 1957 track, "Storm Warning," is available on *The Ace Story, Vols. 1-4* (Ace). Of the records he is better known for, starting with *Gris Gris*, Dr. John says "my memories of things is dim on the level of I'm thinkin' about what I'm gonna do next already, and that's history, you know."

⬤: No Dr. John fan should be without a copy of *Gris Gris*, a mind-melting combination of Crescent City soul music, Creole patois, and voodoo weirdness. Intentionally or not, this is one of the more psychedelic records ever made. Dr. John, who debuted as "Dr. John Creaux, the Night Tripper" on that disc, says flatly, "Most of the gris-gris music that I recall in New Orleans never was recorded. That's why I recorded it, to try to keep somethin' of that alive." Unfortunately, *Gris Gris*, which last appeared on the Repertoire label, is currently out of print.

Another must-have is 1972's *Dr. John's Gumbo*, an updating of his New Orleans R&B roots with versions of "Iko Iko," "Junko Partner," and Professor Longhair's "Tipitina," plus a Huey Smith medley and the occasional dash of gris-gris. *In the Right Place* from 1973 (Atco) features the hit "Right Place Wrong Time" and backing by seminal New Orleans session band the Meters. If you like that one, the follow-up, *Desitively Bonaroo* (Atco), is in the same vein. 1981's *Dr. John Plays Mac Rebennak* and 1983's *The Brightest Smile in Town* (both on Clean Cuts) are both solo piano outings, focused on Dr. John's richly detailed command of New Orleans piano styles. The 1998 release *Anutha Zone* (Virgin) carries forward the Night-Tripper, voodoo sound with contributions by notables from the contemporary British pop, alt-rock, and trip-hop scenes. *Mos' Scocious: The Doctor John Anthology* (Rhino) is a two-CD career retrospective that includes "Storm Warning" and a few other early sides as well as the later material.

ANI DIFRANCO (May 18, 1998)

t seemed an oil-and-water booking, Ani DiFranco at Jacksonville, Oregon's Britt Festival. Britt's summer-long concert series draws largely affluent, aging boomers who picnic on their wine and focaccia bread before the outdoor shows, sit sedately, and applaud politely afterward, half-hoping there won't be an encore so they can get home earlier to pay the babysitter and put the kids to bed. Not the place for a punky-cum-hip-hoppy folksinger with (that night) green hair and lyrics that get in your face (though cheerfully) with every syllable.

Congratulations to the booker. From almost note one, Ani and her crack accompanists, bassist Jason Mercer and drummer Andy Stochansky, had the audience on their Birkenstock-shod feet shaking their Stairmaster-toned booties. Babysitters all over Jackson County scored heavily due to the lengthy encore and when it was done the audience stomped for more. We have it on good authority that not one middle-aged attendee groused about the current generation's music for at least a week afterward.

We were scheduled to interview Ani prior to that show but she canceled because she had been ill and needed to rest for the performance. She later completed her interview by correspondence, outlining her musical roots and tastes for us. "My parents' record player broke when I was very young and I wasn't really listening to recorded music until I bought my own cheap-ass cassette player in college," Ani wrote us. "Thing is, my childhood, while somewhat devoid of recorded music, was chock full of live, actual, happening-in-the-room music. I was always playing guitar and singin' with my friend Michael Meldrum (a Buffalo, NY singer/songwriter) and other local musicians, and I was also amongst a community of Greenwich Village songwriter types like Suzanne Vega, Rod MacDonald, Cliff Eberhardt, etc., so my early influences came not off tape, but from all around me."

But once the records listed below became part of her musical environment, they began to bend and shape her music in various ways. Ani has been, from the beginning, an original musical voice, a trend maker, not a follower. To underline her artistic independence, she heads her own record company, steadfastly refusing the millions that royalty such as David Geffen would swap for her signature on a contract. But as with any artist, she inevitably synthesizes those who tickle her ears. "I'm not sure how these records have affected my music specifically," Ani told us, "but I know they each expanded my sonic world immensely and impacted my life hard."

ANI DIFRANCO'S FAVORITE ARTISTS AND RECORDINGS

The Beatles—*The Beatles* (Capitol) [aka *The White Album*] and *Sergeant Pepper's Lonely Hearts Club Band* (Capitol). These are the first albums Ani can remember "rocking my world."

Joni Mitchell—*Blue* (Reprise) and *Mingus* (Asylum). *Blue* set the standard for unflinching autobiographical lyrics that have become Ani's signature as well. You'll hear a thread between *Blue*'s spare acoustic guitar textures and Ani's musical approach, too. *Mingus* is an ambitious tribute album, with Mitchell setting lyrics to the music of the great jazz composer, bassist, and bandleader Charles Mingus.

John Martyn—*Solid Air* (Island). This is one of the British singer/songwriter's best-loved albums.

Tom Waits—*Nighthawks at the Diner* (Asylum). Waits's third album, cut before a live in-studio audience with a jazzy back-up band, was another early favorite of Ani's.

Billy Bragg—*Back to Basics* (G0! Discs). This is actually a compilation that includes Bragg's first three releases, *Life's a Riot with Spy vs. Spy*, *Brewing Up with Billy Bragg*, and the EP *Between the Wars*.

Bruce Springsteen—*Nebraska* (Columbia). This was Springsteen's first acoustic folk record, as he stepped outside his superstar aura to offer almost unrelentingly despairing songs from the point-of-view of the lonely, the lost, the desperate, the down-on-their-luck, and the broken.

Baaba Maal, Mansour Seck, and Djam Leelii—*Baaba Maal, Mansour Seck, and Djam Leelii* (Mango). Ani's unique, highly percussive guitar-playing commands equal attention in her songs with her confrontational lyrics and are a much underappreciated aspect of her music. We asked Ani if any recordings influenced her approach to her instrument. She mentioned this mesmerizing disc, a return-to-roots by some well-known Senegalese Afro-pop stars, and the Ali Farka Toure album listed below.

Ali Farka Toure—*The Source* (World Circuit). This album features Toure in spacious, mostly acoustic settings with his usual bandmates plus a cameo by American fan *Taj Mahal.

Talk Talk—*Spirit of Eden* (EMI America) and *Laughing Stock* (Polydor). "Wanky eighties English pop band that had some kinda drastic musical revelation and made two mind-blowing records before being dropped from their label and breaking up."

Maceo Parker—*Life on the Planet Groove* (Verve). "Way killer live album by one of my favorite live performers."

Curtis Mayfield—*There's No Place Like America Today* (Curtom). "A fucking exquisite record by one of my heroes."

Mary Margaret O'Hara—*Miss America* (Koch). "The only solo album by a beautifully eccentric vocalist. It elevated my sense of my own vocal possibilities."

Various artists—*Earthrise.Ntone.1* (Instinct). "An excellent compilation of trip-hop/electronica that I had in heavy rotation for about a year of my life. I think it influenced my album *Dilate* a lot."

Massive Attack and Mad Professor—*No Protection* (Circa). This album is Mad Professor's remix of Massive Attack's 1994 release, *Protection* (Virgin) and widely considered a big improvement on the original. Ani's succinct review: "What re-mixes can be."

Stevie Wonder—*Fulfillingness' First Finale* (Motown). "Ahhh, Stevie."

Nusrat Fateh Ali Khan and Michael Brook—*Night Song* (Narada). "The second and most astounding of their collaborations."

*Greg Brown—*The Live One* (Red House) and *Further In* (Red House). The re-cordings listed prior to Brown's all influenced Ani in some significant way. Brown's two records and those on the remainder of the list "are albums made by my friends that I think kick ass," writes Ani. She calls Brown's releases "great folk albums by one of my favorite songwriters."

Utah Phillips—*Bound for Glory* (Independent cassette release: Utah Phillips, P.O. Box 1235, Nevada City, CA USA 95959). "Live radio show available on cassette—Utah in his element."

Sekou Sundiata—*The Blue Oneness of Dreams* (Mouth Almighty/Mercury). "Se-kou killer poetry in an R&B/jazz context."

Soul Coughing—*Irresistible Bliss* (Warner Bros.). "One of my favorite rhythm sec-tions ever in this band."

Dan Bern—*Fifty Eggs* (Sony). "Great songs."

Danielle Howle—*Live at the Kisswick Museum* (Daemon). "A great vocalist with a beautiful sense of melody."

ANI DIFRANCO'S OWN RECORDINGS

We were told by Ani's publicist that she welcomed this interview because it gave her the opportunity to focus attention on others rather than herself. And sure enough, when we asked her about her favorites in her own catalog, she focused on the one release where another artist takes center stage: Utah Phillips and Ani DiFranco, *The Past Didn't Go Anywhere* (Righteous Babe). "A collaborative pro-ject that I'm very proud of," Ani writes. "It's basically circular acoustic groves incorporating Utah's engrossing stories and poems. A journey into radical politics and heavy folk-hop." We'll add that, while Utah's populist raps are in the spot-light, Ani's musical settings and production touches accent and "contemporize" the proceedings perfectly.

●: Although Ani refrained from mentioning her solo work, allow us to introduce you to it if you haven't met her yet. 1995's *Not a Pretty Girl* is a great place to start, with a batch of strong material and a wider range of textures than on some of her records. *Dilate*, the follow-up, presents a slate of stark, biting songs built on percussive grooves, not melodies, established by Ani's slashing rhythm guitar. No disc could fully capture the experience of live Ani, who manages to shine incandescently while lyrically slapping you upside the head. Still, *Living in Clip*, a double-CD set, is a very representative concert album. The 1998 album *Little Plastic Castle* expands Ani's melodic palette and is probably the most musically advanced of her records, helped by a superb cast of backing musicians. *Up Up Up Up Up*, from 1999, continues the embrace of melody but the other conventions are Ani's own—agile vocals that by turns swoop and snarl, jagged rhythms, and words that aim between the head lamps. All her discs are released by Righteous Babe, her own company.

MICHAEL DOUCET (April 2, 1997)

Cajun music sounds like where it comes from—southwestern Louisiana—in the same way that gumbo captures that Louisiana taste. The music is its own kind of stew, combining "flavors" from each of its major cultures—Acadian, French, African-American, and Anglo-Saxon—which are then stirred up and heated for dancing. So it's only right that Michael Doucet, not some carpetbagger, should end up as Cajun's foremost advocate and exponent.

Michael was born to a French-speaking Acadian family in the heart of Cajun country. His family and their relatives all played music; before settling on the fiddle, Michael worked his way through banjo, guitar, drums, and trumpet. He played his first gigs in a swing band composed entirely of immediate and extended family members. Cajun music was in the air, especially in the bars, but it didn't do much for Michael. He came of age in the 1960s, and like much of his generation was a bug for authenticity. In his view, the dilute Cajun music of the time just didn't cut it.

"We wanted to get back to something," Michael remembers. "Something was missing for us . . . so we turned to the music of our grandparents, and kind of skipped a generation in Cajun music. Cajun music, what you would hear in bars, was very country and western influenced, and what we were looking for, what we missed, were the older songs we had grown up with, the really French songs of people who weren't performing, the back porch musicians. And that's what we started to do. We started to go and hang around with people who lived around our house, and just play that. You know, it was a young group of guys and it was very uncool, so we enjoyed it."

Michael elevated his reclamation project up another level when he entered college in 1969. Research in the archives of Louisiana State University led him to an article written in 1939 by one Irene Whitfield about Cajun and French folk songs in southwest Louisiana. "When I came back and told this to my great aunt," Michael tells us, "she said 'Oh, I know Irene. She lives right down the road.'" Whitfield gave Michael his first Amedee Ardoin (see below) records; she also encouraged him to call on the surviving Cajun legends who still lived in the area, just as she had done back in the 1930s. In 1974, Michael did Whitfield one better by journeying to France with his cousin Zachary Richard, where he traced back to the 16th and 17th centuries some of the French folk songs he'd learned as a child.

Having uncovered the roots of Cajun down to the nth degree, Michael concluded that the essence of the music was a mixture of French folk and the bluesy sensibility of French blacks like Amedee Ardoin. He now preserves the traditional sound in the Savoy-Doucet Cajun Band, with Marc and Ann Savoy. But in the much better known Beausoleil, he monkeys with the form, while always keeping that French/blues balance in mind. Jazz, blues, rock, and Caribbean sounds all get thrown in the pot, just as they have throughout Cajun's history. To Michael, it's still gumbo once you've cooked up the authentic base.

MICHAEL DOUCET'S FAVORITE ARTISTS AND RECORDINGS

Amedee Ardoin—"The greatest Cajun or Creole recordings, to me," Michael says about this black, French-speaking singer/accordionist. Ardoin may also be the founder of Zydeco, which combines Cajun with the blues and Creole dance rhythms. : *His Original Recordings* (Old Timey), *The Roots of Zydeco* (Arhoolie), *Louisiana Cajun Music, Vol. 6* (Old Timey), and *I'm Never Comin' Back* (Arhoolie).

Dennis McGee—This early Cajun fiddler played with Amedee Ardoin and thus contributed to the marriage of Cajun to the blues. : *Complete Recordings 1929–1930* (Yazoo/Shanachie), *Early Recordings of . . .* (Morningstar), and *Cajun and Creole Masters* (Music of the World), with McGee, Sady Courville, and Michael, too.

Fairport Convention—*Fairport Convention* (Polydor) and *Unhalfbricking* (Hannibal). *Unhalfbricking* in particular alerted Michael to the genius of Richard Thompson: "Richard is by far my favorite poet, musician, writer, and, you know, just kinda spiritual guy."

Nathan Abshire—Much of what Michael first learned about blues came from blues-oriented Cajun musicians such as this great accordionist. ●: *The Best of . . .* (Swallow), *French Blues* (Arhoolie), *The Good Times Are Killing Me, Pine Grove Blues* (both Swallow), and *A Cajun Tradition, Vol. 2* (La Louisienne).

Bebe Carriere—Fiddler Carriere, along with fiddler/accordionist Austin Pitre, Creole fiddler Canray Fontenot, and accordion legend Clifton Chenier were other bluesy Cajun and Zydeco artists who influenced Michael. ●: You can hear Bebe along with the Carriere Brothers on the anthologies *La La: Louisiana Black French Music* (Maison de Sol) and *Zodico: Louisiana Creole Music* (Rounder).

Austin Pitre— ●: *Opelousa Waltz* (Arhoolie) and *Cajun Legend* (Swallow). Pitre and his group the Evangeline Playboys also show up on the anthologies *Louisiana Cajun French Music from the Southwest Prairies, V. 1* (Rounder) and *Louisiana Cajun Music Special* (Swallow).

Canray Fontenot— ●: *Louisiana Hot Sauce, Creole Style* (Arhoolie) also features Michael, both in a supportive role and in duets with Fontenot.

Clifton Chenier—*Bogalusa Boogie, Out West,* and *Black Snake Blues* (all Arhoolie). Of these, *Snake* is Michael's favorite.

Harry Choates—Fiddler Choates blended Cajun with Western swing. A hard drinker and carouser, he died in jail at the age of 29. ●: *Fiddle King of Cajun Swing* (Arhoolie).

Doug Kershaw—"Mama Rita in Hollywood" on *Spanish Moss* (Warner Bros.). Michael prefers fiddler Kershaw's early work, when he was playing pure Cajun.

Jay Pelisa—This steel guitar player influenced Michael and Beausoleil in putting the steel guitar sound in their music.

Louis Armstrong—Michael's father was a big fan of Armstrong's early music so it was always around the house: "I guess that's why I played trumpet. . . . I don't really play like anybody, but I love that kind of music." ●: See Master List.

Bunk Johnson—"Because he really played the blues and he was around here in Louisiana. And he was that tie to the early jazz, the old Buddy Bolden era." ●: *. . . 1944, . . . 1944 (2nd Masters),* and *Bunk's Brass Band and Dance Band 1945* (all American Music).

Lester Young with Count Basie—"Lester Leaps In." ●: *The Essential Count Basie, Vol. 2* (Columbia).

Stuff Smith—"I think the first time I heard the jazz fiddler Stuff Smith play 'Cherokee,' I said, 'Hmmm.' So I changed my idea of approach to the fiddle, I tell you what.'' 🔘: *Stuff Smith Memorial Album* (Prestige) has "Cherokee" but is out-of-print as of this writing. As an alternative, try *The Chronological ... and his Onyx Club Boys* (Classics), from 1936.

Johann Sebastian Bach—Violin Sonatas and Partitas, BMV 1001-6, Nathan Milstein, violin (Deutsche Grammophon). Although elegantly virtuosic, Milstein plays with an edgy, emotional tone that greatly appeals to folk and blues fans like Michael.

Arcangelo Corelli—Sonatas for Violin and Continuo, Op. 5. Michael loves everything by this Italian violinist/composer but especially these works. 🔘: Locatelli Trio (2 CDs: Hyperion).

Patsy Cline—"Walkin' After Midnight." 🔘: *Patsy Cline's Greatest Hits* (Decca).

Peggy Lee—"Fever." Lee's interpretation of this Little Willie John tune is the signature performance of her career. 🔘: *All-Time Greatest Hits* (Curb).

Elvis Presley—Michael likes "Hound Dog" and the other early hits. 🔘: *Elvis' Golden Records, Vol. 1* (RCA).

Bobby Charles—"Bobby Charles is actually Bobby Charles Guidry. He's from Louisiana, right down the road. He taught our music, like 'See You Later, Alligator' was our music around here." 🔘: *The Chess Masters* (Chess) and *Bobby Charles* (Stony Plain), a CD reissue of a terrific Bearsville LP with *Dr. John and the *Band.

Om Kalsoum—"She was an incredible singer and she always had these great fiddle players in her band, and that definitely influenced my fiddle playing," Michael says about this Egyptian vocalist. 🔘: *Retrospective, Vols. 1–6* (Artists Arabes Associes), *Fakkarouni* (Sonodisc), *El Alb Yeshak Kol Gamil* (Sonodisc), and *Anta El Hob* (Sonodisc).

MICHAEL DOUCET'S OWN RECORDINGS

Michael's favorites from Beausoleil's extensive catalog begin with the band's 1976 debut *Arc de Triomphe Two-Step* (EMI), recorded in Paris after the president of EMI heard them playing on a boat on the Seine. Other Beausoleil faves include 1977's *The Spirit of Cajun Music* (Swallow) ("It was the first album of its kind that showed all the different types of French music from Southwest Louisiana, not just two-steps and waltzes, but we did ballads, blues, a lot of different things"); 1981's *Parlez-Nous a Boir* (Arhoolie), recorded in three hours, Michael says; 1986's *Bayou Boogie* (Rounder) ("That was before the whole Cajun thing really caught on, so it was still music just for people in Louisiana who liked to party and dance''); 1991's *Cajun Conja* (Rhino); and 1997's *L'Amour Ou La Folie* (Rhino), Michael's favorite Beausoleil record overall.

Michael also is extremely pleased with two records under his name, *The Mad Reel* and the film soundtrack *Belizaire the Cajun* (both Arhoolie). The former includes backing by Beausoleil and features several songs with Dennis McGee. The latter includes backing by Beausoleil members plus several electronic tracks by producer Howard Shore. Note that *The Mad Reel* includes all of Michael's tracks from *Belizaire* so there is little point in purchasing both.

: Beausoleil's *Hot Chili Mama* (Arhoolie) has been aptly compared to a Cajun *Los Lobos record—based in traditional music, it injects new vitality in the form with its bluesy rock kick. Michael's solo record *Beau Solo* (Arhoolie) is a wonderfully spirited traditional offering featuring Michael and brother David as a duo. The Savoy-Doucet Cajun Band, with outstanding accordionist Marc Savoy, can be heard to excellent effect on *Two-Step d' Amede*, *With Spirits*, the compilation *Home Music with Spirits*, and *Live! at the Dance* (all Arhoolie).

LUCKY DUBE (November 19, 1998)

Think it's tough to make it as a musician in America or Europe? Consider the struggles of Lucky Dube, growing up impoverished and black in segregated South Africa during the '60s and '70s. His family was too poor to even afford a radio, so the only recorded music he heard as a youngster was the English pop he overheard at the white household where he did garden work. When he and three friends first decided to form a band, they couldn't buy one guitar between them. Making his emergence even more improbable, politically conscious reggae, his eventual calling card, was virtually banned from the airwaves.

Lucky did eventually hear the music of Jimmy Cliff, a reggae artist whose records were getting played in South Africa because they were thought to be "safer." "Maybe his songs would sometimes just talk about love and stuff like that," Lucky explains when we reach him on a rainy day at home. "It wasn't like Bob Marley's and Peter Tosh's songs that were always hitting hard on the government . . . because during that era in South Africa if you got found with, say, a Peter Tosh or a Bob Marley tape by the police, they would confiscate the tape and they would sometimes kick the shit out of you or they would lock you up and no one would even know what happened to you."

Still, the music of Cliff, who also wrote some political songs, was inspiration enough to start Lucky down the reggae path. A little later, he was able to hear the records of Marley and Tosh and they became his greatest influences, not only musically but in the pointedness of their themes. Lucky went on to become the first South African black to have a song, "Together as One," played on white stations during the apartheid era, and the first South African reggae performer to become an international star. But not without resistance at home. While reggae has been freely available in South Africa for about a decade, Lucky says, repression—this time from the post-apartheid government—continues. Paraphrasing a South African DJ, Lucky observes "if you were against the past government you were seen as a terrorist, and if you are against this government, you are either seen as a racist or as someone who is nonpatriotic. So even now there are things that you can or cannot say."

Not that this has deterred Lucky in the least. On his most recent album as of this writing, *Taxman*, the title song confronts the government about alleged financial corruption much as Lucky raised other issues during the apartheid regime. Two weeks after the record came out, Lucky tells us, a cabinet minister phoned him to ask why he challenged a government that was on his side. Lucky was not intimidated, just disgusted. "As long as there's injustice, as long as there's lies and corruption, I will sing about those things," he asserts. "I don't look at it as politics, because I don't understand politics. I look at it as singing and telling the truth."

LUCKY DUBE'S FAVORITE ARTISTS AND RECORDINGS

Peter Tosh—*Mama Africa* (EMI America). "Songs like 'Glass Houses' are the ones that really got me."

Jimmy Cliff—"Many Rivers to Cross." Lucky loves much of Cliff's work but "that one, the way he did it, was killer. . . . I still think even today as far as I'm concerned that's his best recording." ⏺: You'll find this classic track on both *Reggae Greats* and the wonderful soundtrack, *The Harder They Come* (both Mango).

Bob Marley—"One Love" on *One Love* (Heartbeat). "That is what reggae music is about really."

Burning Spear—It wasn't until Lucky began touring in the United States that he first heard this Jamaican reggae icon. ⏺: Key albums include 1975's *Marcus Garvey*, 1976's *Man in the Hills*, 1977's *Dry and Heavy*, 1990's *Mek We Sweet*, 1992's *Jah Kingdom* (all Mango), 1982's *Far Over*, 1983's *Fittest of the Fittest*, 1984's *Resistance*, and 1993's *The World Should Know* (all Heartbeat). *Chant*

Down Babylon: The Island Anthology (2 CDs: Island) is a fine compilation with all the original hits plus dub versions and other rarities.

Eric Donaldson—"Freedom Street" (Black Art, out of print). ⚫: This 1977 single was a hit for this great Jamaican falsetto vocalist.

Culture—"Jah Rastafari." "When I did a show with them, that was the song I was really looking forward to hearing when they performed it." ⚫: Culture included the song on two different albums, both excellent: *International Herb* and *Nuff Crisis* (both Shanachie).

Israel Vibration—The three men in this soulful, rootsy reggae trio reunited after breaking up in the 1980s. ⚫: *Forever*, *Why You So Craven*, *Dub the Rock*, and *Freedom to Move* (all RAS).

*Aaron Neville—Lucky likes everything Aaron has done both in his solo career and with the Neville Brothers. He has special affection, though, for Aaron's rendition of "I Bid You Goodnight": "He's got this unique voice. Nobody in the world I know sings like him." ⚫: See the section on Aaron and his recordings. "I Bid You Goodnight" is on *Warm Your Heart* (A&M).

*Bruce Hornsby—"He's one of the people really that inspired me a lot. Bruce Hornsby is like Aaron Neville. Nobody copies him, nobody sounds like him." ⚫: See the section on Bruce and his recordings.

The Soul Brothers—"They sing *mbaqanga* music, which is basically Zulu traditional music here, Zulu soul music," says Lucky who performed mbaqanga as well as reggae when he first started, with the Soul Brothers as prime models. He likes the Brothers' entire catalog. ⚫: See Master List.

Foreigner—"Urgent" and "I Want To Know What Love Is." Jr. Walker plays a sax solo on the former track. Lucky covered the latter tune on *Taxman*. ⚫: "Urgent" is on *4* (Atlantic), a No. 1 album in 1981. "Love," with gospel vocals from Jennifer Holiday and the New Jersey Mass Choir, is on *Agent Provocateur* (Atlantic). For live versions of both songs, go for *Classics Hits Live* (Atlantic).

Beres Hammond—"He sings different stuff from like Jamaican stuff, because in Jamaica, everybody wants to sound like Bob [Marley] or Peter [Tosh]. Beres Hammond just sounds like Beres Hammond," says Lucky, who has toured with Hammond and loves all his work. ⚫: *Live & Learn Presents: . . . and Barrington Levy* (Live & Learn) is an eight-cut live recording with three excellent Hammond vocal performances. Also try 1996's *Putting Up Resistance* (RAS).

Bayete—*Mmalo-We* (Mango). Led by vocalist Jhabu Khanyile, Bayete is one of the most popular bands in South Africa. Khanyile has also performed with Sting and Phil Collins.

LUCKY DUBE'S OWN RECORDINGS

Lucky doesn't make a distinction between his releases "because all these songs have a special place in my heart."

🔘: *Slave, Prisoner, House of Exile, Victims, Captured Live,* and *Taxman* (all Shanachie) and *Trinity* (Motown/TABU) are all worthwhile purchases with the live recording an especially good example of Lucky's vocal powers and onstage chemistry with his audience. These are all reggae releases. *Serious Reggae Business* (Shanachie) is Lucky's greatest-hits package; it comes in CDE format with added graphics and video.

STEVE EARLE (January 7, 1999)

With a voice like rusted barbed wire and a personal history to match, Steve Earle has always seemed too dangerous for Nashville and just right for rock'n'roll. Like Hank Williams, Merle Haggard, and his own idol, Townes Van Zandt, Steve etches his songs and performances with the experience of a life lived on the rowdy edge. A tunesmith with enough imagination might be able to write material as strong as his, but the real test is do people believe him when he sings it? On every album Steve sells, it's clear who really paid the price.

Born in 1955 and raised in San Antonio, Texas, Steve exhibited an independent ear from the get-go. Dad was a fan of smooth vocal stylists like Nat King Cole and Jim Reeves. Dad's brother played piano and listened to swing and hillbilly tunes. But Steve's heart yearned for a bigger beat. "I heard the Grand Ole Opry and all that stuff when I was real little, but the first thing I sorta latched onto that felt like mine was Elvis," Steve tells us by phone from his management's office in Nashville. Steve was taking in a lot of country music from syndicated television programs like Buck Owens's, but another TV appearance, the Beatles on the *Ed Sullivan Show,* bored just as big a hole.

After an uncle got him started on the guitar, Steve started listening mainly to music he could play, he tells us: "For a lot of reasons, I never had an electric guitar when I lived at home, and it just sorta evolved that I couldn't make my guitar sound like Creedence Clearwater Revival or Jimi Hendrix, but I could make it sound like Bob Dylan or Tim Buckley or Tim Hardin, so I started gravitating toward that kind of acoustic stuff. I realized pretty early on that those guys could write their own songs, so I started trying to write songs."

It wasn't long, though, before Steve was being more heavily influenced by the people he was hanging with than what he was hearing on record and the radio. At the age of 17, he went AWOL from home to make a gig in Austin. While there, he got wind of a birthday party for Jerry Jeff Walker and crashed it, thereby meeting the late Van Zandt, who would become "pretty much the center of everything for a long, long time." "About halfway through the party, Townes walks in, and he had on this beautiful buckskin jacket that Jerry Jeff had given him for his birthday, which was only two weeks before . . . He started a crap game and lost every dime that he had and the jacket within fifteen minutes, and I thought 'My hero!' He was way, way, way bigger than life," Steve laughs.

By age 19, Steve had made his way to Nashville, where he met Guy Clark, Neil Young, Peter Rowan, Norman Blake, and John Prine, all of whom would make an impact on his work. Notes Steve, "Pretty quickly it stopped being about going and buying records and started being about being around 'em when they're made." But not exclusively. Steve had been a Bruce Springsteen fan from early in the latter's career. When he caught a show on the *Born in the USA* tour, it was only a couple years before the release of his own solo debut, *Guitar Town*, and that proved to be auspicious timing. "It was the first time I realized that band music could be played to where it was really huge, but it could also come down to a level where it could reach coffeehouse intimacy. I saw him do that in a fucking arena, and it was really impressive. I think it had a big influence on the way I ended up putting *Guitar Town* together."

Since that time, Steve has built a catalog of songs that span a Springsteen-ian range of moods, from back-porch blues folk to hard-bitten country to rousing, carousing rock'n'roll. His is one of the most admired careers in music, even with its oscillations and disruptions (in the early '90s, he did some hard time for hard drugs). But the experiential side of Steve's art, fundamental as it is, carries an unspoken warning—don't try this at home.

STEVE EARLE'S FAVORITE ARTISTS AND RECORDINGS

The Beatles—*Beatles for Sale* (Capitol). Steve says he's probably had six or seven favorite Beatles albums over the years, but this is his current fave: "That's the country Beatles record."

Bob Dylan—*The Freewheelin'* . . . , *Blonde on Blonde*, and *Blood on the Tracks* (Columbia). "That's the must-have Bob Dylan record to me," Steve says about *Freewheelin'*.

Tim Hardin— : See Master List.

Tim Buckley—*Tim Buckley* (Asylum).

The Rolling Stones—*Flowers* (ABKCO) and *Exile on Main Street* (Virgin). "I was into *Exile on Main Street* as much as anyone else. I think that's a great record and I listen to it a lot, but *Flowers* is my own favorite Stones record. And it's kinda their country record, too. It's got a lot of pseudo-country stuff on it, and that's maybe the reason I dig it," says Steve, who notes that "Mother's Little Helper" from that record was the first song he learned on guitar. "Never, ever allow your children to learn their first song in a minor key—it'll fuck 'em up forever."

Townes Van Zandt—*High, Low and In Between* (Rhino) and *The Late, Great* . . . (Tomato). : These two great albums have been combined on one CD called *High, Low and In Between* (Acoustic Highway).

Guy Clark—*The South Coast of Texas* (Warner Bros.). Steve also has affection for *Old #1* (Sugar Hill) because it was the first record he ever appeared on—he's one of the backing musicians. : *Old #1*, one of Clark's best song collections, is included in its entirety on the compilation *The Essential* . . . (RCA).

Norman Blake—*The Norman and Nancy Blake Compact Disc* (Rounder). "It's sort of an overview of the work they did together, and that's a record I listen to a lot."

Peter Rowan—*Dust Bowl Children* (Sugar Hill). "That record is shattering."

John Prine—*Bruised Orange* (Asylum). "It's a little later than the ones most people mention, but I love that record."

Neil Young—*Harvest* (Reprise). "Neil is pretty close to one of my biggest heroes, not only as a musician and a songwriter, but he's my role model as how one should carry oneself when dealing with the fucking music business," Steve laughs.

Bruce Springsteen—*Nebraska, Born in the USA, The River,* and *The Wild, the Innocent, and the E Street Shuffle* (all Columbia). "I like all of 'em to tell you the truth, and I'm a big, big fan, but those are my favorites."

The Pogues—*If I Should Fall From Grace With God* (Island). Steve says this band was his gateway to a lot of traditional Irish music and also "encouraged me to even push harder on combining acoustic and electric instruments because the Pogues did that really, really well. And I still think Shane MacGowan is one of the best songwriters alive." Steve has developed such a love affair with Ireland that he is buying a house in Galway and recording an album with accordionist Sharon Shannon, also from Galway. : The Pogues appear on Steve's album *Copperhead Road.*

*NRBQ— . . . *at Yankee Stadium* (Mercury). "The best white band in America. I want to make a record with them one of these days. We've talked about it, but we're both hard dogs to keep under the porch, and we haven't been able to figure out how to do it."

STEVE EARLE'S OWN RECORDINGS

"I like *Exit 0* [MCA] a lot. I've got some problems with the way it sounds, now. I've got problems with the way all my digital records sound now, but as a collection of songs, I really love *Exit 0.* It's funny, maybe because they're stepchildren in a certain sense, but I think *Exit 0* and *The Hard Way* are my two favorite records out of those first four that I made for MCA. And of these records that I've made in the last few years, *Train A Comin'* [Winter Harvest] is one of my favorite records and I like *El Corazon* [Warner Bros.] a lot, the last record. I'm proud of it."

: The 1980 record *Guitar Town* (MCA), much more acoustic-flavored than later records, is the edgy country album that started it all for Steve. His rock side really comes to the forefront on 1988's *Copperhead Road* (MCA), a snarling, defiant declaration of musical independence. *Shut Up and Die Like an Aviator* (MCA) is a strong live set from 1990. *I Feel Alright* (Warner Bros.), one of the toughest albums from an artist who is never less-than, was one of the most lavishly praised albums of 1996. *Essential . . .* (MCA) compiles standout tracks from Steve's first three MCA albums—*Guitar Town, Exit 0,* and *Copperhead Road.* The retrospective *Ain't Ever Satisfied* (2 CDs: HIPP), from 1996, includes highlights from all previous studio albums plus live Stones and Springsteen covers and other unreleased material. And don't miss Steve's single (E Squared), with the V-Roys, of the reggae classic "Johnny Too Bad," a song that tracks like it came straight from the Earle catalog. In 1999, Steve released a critically aclaimed bluegrass album, *The Mountain* (E-squared), with the Del McCoury Band, one of of bluegrass's most prized units.

MARK EITZEL (November 14, 1997)

A brief musical history of Mark Eitzel, related by phone from the offices of Matador Records: "When I was younger, at first I wanted to be like America and Crosby, Stills, Nash, and Young. And then I wanted to be Johnny Rotten. Then I wanted to be Ian Curtis [of Joy Division]. And then, I didn't want to be anyone but myself."

An army brat, Mark was born in 1959 in the San Francisco Bay Area but spent much of his early childhood in Taiwan, where he and his sister could buy bootleg versions of hit U.S. and U.K. albums for a quarter each. Then the family was transferred to England, plopping Mark directly in the path of the punk revolution. Punk rearranged everything he had ever thought about music, Mark says, "while everybody else in America was still listening to Foreigner and Heart. When I was eighteen, the Sex Pistols came out with 'God Save the Queen.' I remember listening to [influential British DJ] John Peel the day he played that, even though it was banned on the radio. Very exciting."

What made it even more exciting was the fact that the Pistols and other early punk lords were essentially Mark's age: "It was like 'Yeah, this is exactly right.' It's hard to describe. It did change my songwriting. It made me write better, instantly. It made me write more. . . . It was like, 'Okay, you can express yourself. You can say anything you want. You can be anything you want.' "

Not one to pick sides, Mark was also lapping up the more mainstream pop songcraft of such performers as Elton John, John Martyn, Joni Mitchell, and *Joan Armatrading. Still, after returning to America, he began his performing career punk to the max with the Naked Skinnies, who achieved the distinction of being so over-the-top that they were banned from San Francisco's supposed punk haven, Mubuhay Gardens. His next band, cult faves the American Music Club, also leaned that way. AMC blended a bucket of sounds—classic American rock, electronic machine music, depressive post-punk wailing, sheets of noise, vintage Americana—but drew its energy from a pure punk wall socket.

In 1991, AMC's *Everclear* was acclaimed by *Rolling Stone* as one of the year's best albums and Mark was named the year's best songwriter. The hoopla scored the band a major label deal with Reprise, but they remained cursed by the cult dichotomy—lavish critical praise, skinny sales. Mark now operates as a solo troubadour, dignifying the broken, the defeated, and the terminally sad who populate his stories and proclaiming solidarity with them via his own howling confessions. Wherever he goes, his AMC notoriety precedes him, but he's hardly sentimental about it: "The only time anything's a big deal, even when there's only five people in the audience, is when you get on stage and you kill that audience. Then it's a big deal no matter what. You're only as good as the work you put out. Legends should all be destroyed."

MARK EITZEL'S FAVORITE ARTISTS AND RECORDINGS

Elton John—*Madman Across the Water* (MCA). "It was such an ambitious songwriting album, and it really moved me that he could do so much with words."

Joni Mitchell— : *Ladies of the Canyon* (Reprise), *Blue* (Reprise), *For the Roses* (Asylum), and *Court and Spark* (Asylum) are all classic singer/songwriter fare, with *Blue* one of pop's most influential albums ever. *The Hissing of Summer Lawns* and *Hejira* (both Asylum) set the tone for the artier, more atmospheric music that Mitchell is still making today.

*Joan Armatrading—*Joan Armatrading* and *Show Some Emotion* (both A&M). "She was a huge influence . . . I read an interview with her and she said 'In songwriting I found the same five chords and I just play the same thing over and over until I find what I like to hear' and I was like 'Yeah, good! That's it!' "

John Martyn—When Mark started writing bluesier songs, it was primarily because of Martyn's influence, he says. : *London Conversation*, *The Tumbler*, *One World*, and *Grace and Danger* (all Island).

X-Ray Spex—This much-admired English punk band recorded only one album. : *Germ Free Adolescents* (Blue Plate), in its CD version, includes the great single "Oh, Bondage, Up Yours," not part of the original LP.

The Sex Pistols—Like everyone else caught up in England's nascent punk movement, Mark collected the Pistols' incendiary singles such as "God Save the Queen" and "Anarchy in the U.K." : *Never Mind the Bullocks* (Warner Bros.) includes both songs.

Wire—*154* (Restless). "It didn't hold up, but at the time it was really important to me."

The Specials—*The Specials* (2 Tone/Chrysalis). These punk-energized ska revivalists became one of Mark's favorite bands after he returned to America. This record, the group's 1979 debut, was produced by Elvis Costello.

The B-52's—*The B-52's* and *Wild Planet* (both Warner Bros.). "The first couple of albums were great. It's kind of embarrassing to reveal your New Wave loves, though, 'cause that music didn't last very well. A lot of it just seems real quirky and awful to me right now."

Kraftwerk—*Computer World* (Elektra). At the same time Mark was into punk, he was delving into the electronic experiments of Kraftwerk and Tangerine Dream: "It's funny listening to the ambient music now. It's really similar in a lot of ways." ⦿: Mark also loved Kraftwerk's earlier efforts, some of the best of which include *Autobahn* (Elektra), *Trans-Europe Express* (Capitol), and *The Man Machine* (Capitol).

Tangerine Dream—Mark bought every Dream album he could find. ⦿: *Phaedra* and *Rubycon* (Virgin) both rose high on the British charts during the group's mid-'70s peak. *Logos* from 1982 (Virgin) is a live recording.

Throbbing Gristle—*D.O.A.* (Mute).

Joy Division—*Unknown Pleasures* and *Closer* (both Qwest). Mark describes this gloomy post-punk band as one of his greatest influences.

Bob Dylan—"For me, the most exciting new artist is still Bob Dylan—the *Highway 61 Revisited* sort-of era. Because that's just fuckin' Shakespeare, I think. I'm a traditionalist in that way because that's really what's getting to me right now." ⦿: *Another Side of . . .* , *Bringing It All Back Home*, *Highway 61 Revisited*, and *Blonde on Blonde* (all Columbia), from 1964–66, comprise the output of the era Mark is referring to.

Nick Drake—*Pink Moon* (Hannibal). "That one is still so amazing, you know. Why? Because it's hard to describe. It's his guitar playing, in a big way. It's the way he delivers songs—sort of this ephemeral, point-of-disappearing way that he sings. The velvet hammer sort of thing."

The Replacements—*Let it Be* (Twin/Tone), *Tim* (Sire), and *Pleased to Meet Me* (Sire). "I think Paul Westerberg was, and still is, one of America's best songwriters. And also singers, a great fuckin' singer . . . That one song by Westerberg on *Tim*, 'Here Comes a Regular,' I love that fucking song. That song drives me nuts."

Paul Westerberg—*Fourteen Songs* (Sire). "There's at least five songs on that thing I wish I'd written."

Hüsker Dü—*Candy Apple Grey* (Warner Bros.). " 'Too Far Down' and 'Hardly Getting Over It'—two great songs, for me."

The Stooges—*The Stooges* (Elektra). "That record really changed my life at that early time."

Iggy Pop—*Lust for Life* (Virgin).

The Stranglers—*IV Rattus Norvegicus* (A&M). " 'Hanging Around'—what a great song."

Siouxsie and the Banshees—*The Peel Sessions* (Dutch East India). "I used to tape John Peel every week and listen to that over and over again."

Steve Hillage—*L* (Blue Plate). "I went to see Steve Hillage once and thought he was totally awesome. That was kind of a prog rock thing, but I also liked prog rock."

Boney M—: *Magic of . . .* (Atlantic/Hansa) collects 20 of the group's Euro-disco singles.

Sweet—: *Desolation Boulevard* (Capitol) includes "Ballroom Blitz," one of Mark's favorites by them. "Blitz" is also on *The Best of . . .* (Capitol), along with 15 other deliberately trashy teen hits.

Pink Floyd—*Meddle* and *Dark Side of the Moon* (Capitol). Mark loved both of these records as a kid: "It's so sad when I hear that on the radio nowadays and I'm like 'Come on, play something new!' "

Elvis Costello—*My Aim is True* and *Get Happy* (both Rykodisc). "I totally ate, breathed *Get Happy*."

LTJ Bukem—Mark likes to drive while listening to Bukem's innovative hardcore/breakbeat records. : *Demon's Theme* and *Apollo 2* (Looking Good).

*Talking Heads—*Fear of Music* and *Talking Heads '77* (both Sire).

Richard Hell and the Voidoids—*Blank Generation* (Sire). "That was huge for me, because he was American and I was American and I just thought 'Fuck, yeah.' And it was really poetic and kinda cool."

Belle and Sebastian—*If You're Feeling Sinister* (Enclave/Capitol).

Son Volt—*Trace* and *Straightaways* (both Warner Bros.). "I really love them."

Laika—*Sounds of the Satellite* (Too Pure).

Henryk Gorecki—Symphony No. 3, "Symphony of Sorrowful Songs" (Elektra/Nonesuch).

The Monkees—*Pisces, Aquarius, Capricorn and Jones Ltd.* (Rhino). "Really early on, I was a Monkees fan. I still love that record. It's beautiful songwriting. Totally changed my life."

MARK EITZEL'S OWN RECORDINGS

Mark doesn't have favorites per se among his records, although he's proud of the fact that they all contain songs that he's been able to perform year after year without growing tired of them. But other than that, the record that interests him most is whichever one he is making at the time.

He does talk at length about 1997's *West* (Warner Bros.), a project produced by REM's *Peter Buck, for which he and Buck wrote all the songs in a couple of days: "I was excited to work with him and he had only, like, three days. And I was like 'Okay, give them to me, and let's do it.' I'll do anything, you know. And it was inspiring, so I was inspired. I think that this album's going to be looked back on as a pretty great record in times to come." By the same token, Mark doesn't expect to work in such a free-form way again "because I really like music that you can tell somebody worked really hard on in a way . . . and there's things that I would change about the *West* album."

●: AMC's strong catalog includes its 1986 debut, *The Restless Stranger* (Grifter), which despite its rookie virtues was disavowed by the band; 1987's better-received *Engine* (Frontier); the spare, quartet-driven *California* (Frontier), from 1988; 1989's import-only *United Kingdom* (Demon), which strings together live and other unreleased material into a coherent, impressive whole; the densely arranged, song-cycle-ish *Everclear* (Alias), a critical favorite; 1993's major-label debut, the even bleaker than usual *Mercury* (Reprise); and 1994's, *San Francisco* (Reprise), which despite the signs of split-up-in-the-offing featured several more Eitzel gems.

Besides *West*, Mark's solo work includes the live *Songs of Love* (Demon), an evocative alone-with-my-guitar set performed in London while AMC was still together; 1996's atmospheric *60 Watt Silver Lining* (Warner Bros.); and 1998's *Caught in a Trap and I Can't Back Out 'Cause I Love You Too Much, Baby* (Matador), which gives most of its length to the stark acoustic music that has become his solo stock-in-trade but offers a few electric tracks for those that miss American Music Club. Mark's solo work reveals the strength of his songs and shows off his remarkably empathic vocals. But AMC is a no less effective forum, the instrumental treatments multiplying the possible meanings of his songs, like holding up a prism to the light.

ALEJANDRO ESCOVEDO (November 10, 1997)

I n the world of multinational entertainment companies and shopping mall music stores, the name Alejandro Escovedo barely registers. But put your ear to the ground and you'll hear it reverberating like a galloping herd of horses. For rockers drawn to both roots music and punk, Alejandro's indie-label albums are a major signpost. For producers hungry for new ideas, his arrangements are a prime model. For singers trying to wring more heartache from their vocals, his records represent an unscaleable peak.

The spaciousness of his music comes from living under the big skies in West Texas, Alejandro tells us by phone from his home in Austin. The pain embodied in his lyrics and vocals comes from hard living on rock's margins, an early marriage that produced two kids and then went bad, and the racism and intimidation his Latino family has endured. The rest—well, the last name hints at that. Brothers Pete and Coke Escovedo are well-known Latin musicians, the former a long-time percussionist with Santana. Pop star and former Prince drummer Sheila E. is his niece. In addition, Alejandro's Mexican-born father had been a vocalist in mariachi bands in the 1930s and '40s and later in jazz big bands around San Francisco.

Despite growing up in an incessantly musical home, Alejandro bounced around from scene to scene until he found his own voice in the 1980s. Born in 1951 and raised in San Antonio and Southern California, Alejandro caught the full brunt of the British Invasion and California surf music. From there, Alejandro's evolution more or less followed the evolution of rock itself, with landmark records becoming personal landmarks as well. When the first Velvet Underground album came out in 1967, Alejandro found its New York nihilism impossibly seductive. Same with Velvet John Cale's avant classical leanings, which spurred Alejandro to investigate composers such as John Cage. In the early '70s, the proto-punk of the Stooges and New York Dolls led then-aspiring filmmaker Alejandro and some cohorts to attempt a movie about a Stooges-like band; ultimately, they dropped the movie idea and became the act. That group was the San Francisco–based Nuns. As the Nuns flamed out, Alejandro helped form Rank and File, a country-punk band named for one of his songs, although brothers Tony and Chip Kinman would write most of its material.

Rank and File debuted with *Sundown* (Slash), one of the most highly acclaimed albums of 1982. But Alejandro was having a rotten time and split for Austin to form the True Believers with brother Javier, yet another musical Escovedo. That band, designed to evoke the wide open West Texas landscape, became a legendary live act. Gigging frequently in Austin and touring with *Los

Lobos, the Believers generated a buzz that resonated nationwide. "That was really my first experience at trying to sculpt my own sound and play my own songs," Alejandro says. "All that stuff I'd been listening to in the past, I was now technically capable of trying to create that stuff."

Unfortunately, the True Believers never happened on record the way they did on stage and ultimately broke up. But becoming a non-Believer has led to one of rock's most intriguing, although nearly underground, solo careers. Since the appearance of his much-praised *Gravity* in 1992, any number of rural rockers have been sparking off Alejandro's ideas and execution. Too bad such flattery don't pay the rent.

ALEJANDRO ESCOVEDO'S FAVORITE ARTISTS AND RECORDINGS

*The Everly Brothers—Alejandro loved their music as a kid, and still listens to it often. ⬤: See the section on Don Everly and his recordings.

Fats Domino—Alejandro likes the crossover tunes such as "Blueberry Hill" and "Walking to New Orleans" that were hits when he was a kid. ⬤: *My Blue Heaven: The Best of . . .* (EMI America) is a good single-disc introduction to Domino's crossover catalog including the songs Alejandro mentions.

Elvis Presley—*The Sun Sessions CD* (RCA).

The Rolling Stones—Alejandro started naming his favorite Stones' albums—*Sticky Fingers* (ABKCO), *Exile on Main Street* (Virgin), *Beggar's Banquet* (ABKCO), *Between the Buttons* (ABKCO)—and then gave up: "I've had this relationship with the Stones forever and it's only recently that I haven't been totally enamored with everything that they do. But for the most part I've always found something on each Stones album that was a killer."

The Beatles—*Rubber Soul, Revolver,* and *Abbey Road* (all Capitol). "What I love about the Beatles more than anything . . . was that their songs were just so positive. At the time I wasn't really ready for all that positivism, but now I really appreciate it, and their songs were just cool songs."

Gerry and the Pacemakers—"Don't Let the Sun Catch You Crying" and "Ferry Cross the Mersey." ⬤: *Best of . . . : The Definitive Collection* (EMI America).

Mickey and Sylvia—Alejandro not only loved the duo's hits as songs but also Mickey Baker's guitar tone. ⬤: *"Love is Strange" and Other Hits* (RCA).

The Zombies— ⬤: *Singles A's & B's* (See for Miles) covers many of the band's superb nonhit singles from 1964–67 as well as the hits "She's Not There" and "Tell Her No." *Odyssey & Oracle* (Rhino), released in 1968, was a fine, psychedelic-era effort that included "Time of the Season," one of Alejandro's favorites.

Them—*Them* (Polygram/London) and *Them Again* (Decca). Alejandro loved the first two albums by this soulful band, fronted by Van Morrison before he went solo.

Dick Dale—Dale fathered the surf guitar style that was so important to Alejandro when he first started playing. ⊙: *King of the Surf Guitar: Best of . . .* (Rhino).

The Chantays—This surf band played "Pipeline" and its other hits at Alejandro's junior high school when his family was living in Santa Ana. ⊙: *Two Sides Of The Chantays/Pipeline* (Repertoire).

The Challengers— ⊙: *Killer Surf: The Best of the Challengers* (GNP/Crescendo) or *The Best of the Challengers* (Rhino).

The Ventures—"Walk, Don't Run." ⊙: *Walk Don't Run: The Best of . . .* (EMI America).

Santo and Johnny—"Sleepwalk." "I still do that with my orchestra. It's such a beautiful song, a timeless piece." ⊙: This song is included on *Rock Instrumental Classics Volume 1: The Fifties* (Rhino).

The Velvet Underground—*The Velvet Underground & Nico* (Verve). "When that record came out, for some reason or another, in Huntington Beach, Fountain Valley, in that area, it was played at every party that we would go to. There was like this little pocket of Velvet Underground freaks, and that was it. That pretty much destroyed my life."

The Yardbirds—"You can't go wrong with the Yardbirds." ⊙: *Roger the Engineer* (Edsel) is this seminal group's most highly praised studio album. *Greatest Hits, Vol. 1: 1964–1966* (Rhino) is the best hits package.

Mott the Hoople—"Ian Hunter, obviously, just totally was a Dylan freak. And so his lyrics were a little more literate . . . and that really impressed me: the ability to have a killer rock'n'roll band and turn around and play a sensitive ballad that told a story. That's exactly what we tried to do in the True Believers." ⊙: *Mott the Hoople* (Atlantic), *Mad Shadows* (Atlantic), *Brain Capers* (Atlantic), *All the Young Dudes* (Columbia), *Mott* (Columbia), and *The Hoople* (Columbia) are all strong studio albums recorded from 1969–74. *The Ballad of Mott: A Retrospective* (2 CDs: Columbia) covers the Columbia period almost exclusively. *Backsliding Fearlessly: The Early Years* (Rhino) samples the first four albums, all on Atlantic, on one disc.

The Faces—"It was the Stones, Mott the Hoople, and the Faces that really influenced me as far as what I really wanted a band to sound like." ⬤: *First Step*, *Long Player*, and *A Nod is as Good as a Wink* (all Warner Bros.).

The Temptations—Alejandro loved the early Motown records of the Temps, the Four Tops, and Marvin Gaye. ⬤: *Anthology* (2 CDs: Motown). There are three versions of this set (1973, 1985, and 1995). All cover the 1960s hits and then some.

The Four Tops— ⬤: See Master List.

Marvin Gaye— ⬤: *Anthology* (2 CDs: Motown), a retrospective released in 1995 (more comprehensive than the 1974 set of the same name).

The Stooges—*Fun House* (Elektra).

The New York Dolls—*New York Dolls* (Mercury).

Brian Eno—*Here Come the Warm Jets*, *Taking Tiger Mountain (by Strategy)*, and *Another Green World* (all EG). "His whole philosophy about music for nonmusicians was real attractive to me."

Ronnie Lane's Slim Chance—"That band, in a way, helped model my orchestra, too. Because it was a bigger band, because he had more strings, more mandolins, banjos and dobroes—things like that," says Alejandro who sat in with Slim Chance when they came through Austin. ⬤: *Ronnie Lane's Slim Chance* (A&M) and *One for the Road* (Island).

Buffalo Springfield—"I loved that band," says Alejandro of the highly talented collective that included Stephen Stills, Neil Young, Richie Furay, and Jim Messina. ⬤: *Buffalo Springfield*, *Buffalo Springfield Again*, and *Last Time Around* (all Atco) comprise the band's entire studio output with the middle album one of the most impressive rock song collections ever.

Poco—*Pickin' Up the Pieces* (Epic). Richie Furay and Jim Messina founded this band as Buffalo Springfield was falling to pieces. This debut record displayed the Springfield's same aptitude for tuneful, tightly crafted country rock songs, although Poco was cleaner cut by far.

Jeff Beck—*Truth* and *Beck-Ola* (both Epic). "That was a killer band with Ronnie Wood on bass, Mickey Waller on drums, and Rod Stewart [vocalist]. Just monster records."

Lefty Frizell—Alejandro feels that Frizell's arrangements and use of elements outside of country demonstrated a musicality far more advanced than most country artists'. ⬤: See Master List.

*Willie Nelson—*Red Headed Stranger* (Columbia) and *Phases and Stages* (Atlantic). "They're concept records. They tell complete stories. I just love that."

*Waylon Jennings—Alejandro says that Jennings's records heavily influenced Rank and File, which found a way to blend reggae inflections with the cowboy beat on many of Jennings's tunes. ⏺: See the section on Waylon and his recordings.

Billy Joe Shaver—*Old Five and Dimers Like Me* (Monument). "I love him as a songwriter."

Townes Van Zandt—*The Late, Great . . .* (Tomato), *Live at the Old Quarter* (Tomato), and *Flyin' Shoes* (Rhino). "Lyrically, I thought he was the greatest songwriter. In hanging out with him, I felt that everything that came out of his mouth was like poetry. A really soulful person—maybe he just felt too much."

Leonard Cohen—Alejandro loves Cohen's poetry as well as his songwriting. ⏺: *The Songs of . . .*, *Songs from a Room*, and *Songs of Love and Hate* (all Columbia) are Cohen's first three records (1968–71). There are several more of similar quality right up into the 1990s.

Archie Shepp with Horace Parlan—*Goin' Home* and *Trouble in Mind* (both Steeplechase). "It's just saxophone and piano but it's so beautiful, so lush," Alejandro says of these two albums, the first the duo's take on a set of gospel tunes, the second their treatment of blues standards.

Neil Young—Alejandro prefers Young when he joins with raw rockers Crazy Horse. Together, they create music best described by their 1990 album title, Ragged Glory. ⏺: *Everyone Knows This is Nowhere*, *Zuma*, *Rust Never Sleeps*, *Live Rust*, *Ragged Glory*, and *Sleeps with Angels* (all Reprise) are the major albums issuing from this fruitful collaboration.

Lee "Scratch" Perry—*The Upsetter and the Beat* (Heartbeat).

Big Youth—*Screaming Target* (Trojan).

Doctor Alimantado— ⏺: *Born for a Purpose* (Greensleeves).

Joe Higgs—Higgs is one of reggae's father figures, with a career going back to the late 1950s. ⏺: *Life of Contradiction* (Vulcan), *Family* (Shanachie), and *Blackman Know Yourself* (Shanachie).

ALEJANDRO ESCOVEDO'S OWN RECORDINGS

Alejandro refers to *Gravity* (Watermelon) as "probably the most important record I've ever made." Its deeply pained writing was enhanced by what could best be described as a Texas rock orchestra. But Alejandro feels that his use of string arrangements didn't really blossom until 1994's *Thirteen Years* (Watermelon), his proudest accomplishment so far: "I'm proudest of it because I think it works as a story from beginning to end."

Alejandro occasionally performs with a side band called Buick MacKane, formed in 1989 after the True Believers broke up. "It was really a despised band in Austin, because it wasn't the True Believers," says Alejandro. "It was more about this nasty rock 'n' roll attitude. Austin has never really been a rock 'n' roll town." Austin be damned, Buick MacKane released an album anyway—*The Pawnshop Years* (Rykodisc)—with all original tunes by Alejandro. "It's a great rock 'n' roll record," Alejandro enthuses. "I really love that record, man."

With some reservations, he also feels good about the two True Believers albums, now available on one CD, *Hard Road* (Rykodisc). A tiny budget and inexperience in the studio hampered the first record, *True Believers*, but "I still think the songs were great songs," says Alejandro. "I know many people were disappointed because it wasn't like our live show, but it was still a good record." The second album "wasn't totally there, but it was closer," he feels.

⦿: 1996's *With These Hands* (Rykodisc) doesn't reach as far emotionally or artistically as Alejandro's previous two solo albums, but it is a passionate roots-rock record that may have wider audience appeal precisely because it is more conventional. *More Miles Than Money: Live 1994-96* (Bloodshot), as emotionally gripping a live disc as you'll find, shows off the strength of Alejandro's songs and haunted vocals by presenting them in settings as stark as a desert sunset, with violin and cello augmenting guitar, bass, and drums. A great-sounding rock record, *Bourbonitis Blues* (Bloodshot), from 1999, mixes a smattering of new songs and compelling covers of tunes by such Alejandro idols as Lou Reed, John Cale, and Ian Hunter. Alejandro's blend of strings with barbed-wire roots rock is masterful.

D O N   E V E R L Y (August 24, 1998)

The Everly Brothers literally constitute a central thread running through pop music history. Pull them out and the whole thing unravels. The Beatles, the Hollies, and Simon & Garfunkel looked directly to the Brothers' impeccable two-part harmonies for their vocal models. The Byrds were among the first of countless acts to pattern their vocal arrangements after the Beatles. Countless more emulated the Byrds. And so it goes. Almost any popular music that both rocks and employs harmonizing vocals probably carries an Everly "gene."

But the Everlys have their own roots, starting with a third Everly, their father. Don was only nine years old and Phil seven when Ike Everly, also a skilled guitarist, organized the family into a singing group in 1946. Dad taught the boys to sing in harmony, Don tells us by phone, drawing on his own models, the Mills Brothers, a jazzy black pop trio, and country duo the Delmore Brothers. Dad also introduced his sons to Hank Williams's tunes, which they performed on radio broadcasts in Iowa where the family then lived.

Born in Kentucky, the Everly Brothers evoked Appalachian folk, bluegrass, and traditional country when they sang. But Don notes that many of his most important influences and other favorites were black musicians, and not just the crossover Mills Brothers. In Chicago, where the family spent a lot of time when the brothers were growing up, "my father used to take me down to Maxwell Street, which was filled with old blues players from Mississippi and Alabama," Don recalls. "On the corners, they were playing. And it was wonderful, slide guitar and all that." Black gospel also caught Don's ears in Chicago "but then when I moved to Knoxville, Tennessee to finish up our radio career, I started really listening to the blues, and black music was really important. That was Bo Diddley and Little Richard, Chuck Berry—all that. *Ruth Brown, Etta James."

Diddley in particular left his mark on the Everly Brothers. Don had discovered Diddley's music in high school. "That rhythm moved me so much, and I said I'm never gonna be happy in just country music," Don remembers. The answer, of course, was to make Diddley part of the mix after the Everlys started their duo act in the mid-'50s. After a brief and unsuccessful stint on Columbia Records as a conventional Nashville act, the Brothers landed on Cadence Records. Don underpinned their first Cadence single, "Bye Bye Love," with Diddley's signature "shave-and-a-haircut-two-bits" rhythm. The song shot to Number Two on the pop charts in 1957, inaugurating a three-year streak of huge hits for the label and establishing the Everlys in the business.

Don still keeps his ears open for innovative sounds in popular music that will grab him the way Diddley did in the 1950s. "And I'll tell you that it pretty much goes around and around and around. I find that at this point in my life very little I hear sounds new. It's so rehashed now. It's a formula and it's a look, and actually I wonder sometimes if it would sell if they didn't see it." Of course, he can be excused for thinking he's heard it all before—since so much of today's music is Everly-bred.

DON EVERLY'S FAVORITE ARTISTS AND RECORDINGS

Hank Williams—Williams combined two of Don's primary musical loves, country and the blues. ⬤: See Master List.

Lefty Frizzell—When Don started working in country music as a teenager, he devoted himself to the music of Williams and Frizzell. The latter's smooth honky-tonk singing style set the tone for traditional country vocals ever after. ⬤: See Master List.

The Mills Brothers—"The first thing I ever learned how to sing was 'Paper Doll,' the Mills Brothers song, and my dad took me down to a little recording place where they used to do voice mails on little discs for the soldiers to send home. That was my first recording." ⬤: *The Anthology: (1931–1968)* (2 CDs: MCA) covers the group's entire landmark career, including "Paper Doll."

The Delmore Brothers—As with the Mills Brothers, Don and Phil learned the Delmores' songs second-hand through their father. Don didn't hear the originals by these early country harmonizers until later in life. ⬤: *When They Let the Hammer Fall* (Bear Family) and *Freight Train Boogie* (Ace) are two well-regarded compilations. There is considerable overlap between them, with the former delving deeper into the Brothers' bluesy, uptempo material and the latter giving a more complete overview.

Bo Diddley—Not only the Everlys but all of rock 'n' roll owe an unpayable debt to Diddley's rhythmic innovations and attitude. "No one's found a newer way to do Bo Diddley," notes Don. ⬤: *Bo Diddley/Go Bo Diddley* (Chess) combines Diddley's first two records on one outstanding CD. If that doesn't sate you, go for *The Chess Box* (2 CDs: MCA).

The Dixie Hummingbirds—"Very syncopated, wonderful stuff." ⬤: See Master List.

The Mighty Clouds of Joy— ⬤: See Master List.

Little Richard— ⬤: See Master List.

Chuck Berry— ⬤: See Master List.

*Ruth Brown— ⬤: See the section on Ruth and her recordings.

Etta James— ⬤: See Master List.

Ray Charles—"I used to listen to Ray Charles when I was young and I'd think 'God, I'll never, ever have any soul.' I think ultimately you get it if you sing from your heart and you stand there and you go to the blues and it comes out," Don says. His favorite Charles tracks are the 1950s recordings he made for Atlantic. ⬤:

The Birth of Soul: The Complete Atlantic Rhythm & Blues Recordings (1952–1959) (3 CDs: Rhino) includes "Leave My Woman Alone," a song the Everly Brothers used to perform.

The Beatles—It's well known that the Beatles studied the Everly Brothers' vocal harmonies, but the Everlys also incorporated a few tricks learned from their students, Don notes. ⬤: See Master List.

Sting—*Ten Summoner's Tales* and *Mercury Falling* (both A&M). "Sting writes great songs. I buy his albums before I even listen to them."

Don Henley—Don likes everything he's heard from the ex-Eagle: "You can just count on the quality of the material and the production, to my tastes, anyway." ⬤: Henley's solo albums are *I Can't Stand Still* (Asylum), *Building the Perfect Beast* (Geffen), and *The End of the Innocence* (Geffen).

Khaled—*Sahra* (Barclay). This Algerian *rai* legend is one of Don's recent favorites: "I saw him in London on television, playing Albert Hall with a show about music from North Africa and the Middle East, and I was astounded. It just blew me away, his vocal abilities and the way it came across."

Yehudi Menuhin and Stephane Grappelli—*Strictly for the Birds* (EMI/Angel). This release presents two great violin masters, jazzer Grappelli and classical virtuoso Menuhin, in a relaxed, lushly produced jazz setting with guitarist Martin Taylor on hand.

Roy Acuff—When Don buys CDs today, he's drawn mostly to older country records, including those by Acuff, whose publishing company hired Don and Phil as songwriters when they were still teenagers: "His early records are just extraordinary to me." ⬤: *The Essential . . .* (1936–49) (Columbia/Legacy) and *Columbia Historic Edition* (Columbia).

Alison Krauss—"I've listened to everything she's recorded at this point. I think she's given bluegrass a fresh appeal. She's a really great musician and a great singer." ⬤: 1995's *Now That I've Found You: A Collection* (Rounder), a compilation covering the previous ten years, was a hit in its own right and is a great introduction to this progressive bluegrass star. *I've Got That Old Feeling* and *Every Time You Say Good-bye* (both Rounder) are two of her strongest albums from that period, showcasing her agile, songbird-like vocals, award-winning fiddle playing, and forward-looking approach to the music. This is bluegrass with the radiance of prime singer-songwriter fare.

Luciano Pavarotti—*O Sole Mio* (London). "I call it my pasta record, to be perfectly honest. It's the old traditional Italian things that I remember from Chicago. I lived in an Italian neighborhood and I turned a little Italian."

DON EVERLY'S OWN RECORDINGS

Don's favorite Everly Brothers records are 1972's *Pass the Chicken and Listen* (One Way) and 1958's *Songs Our Daddy Taught Us* (Rhino). A country record, *Chicken* was done with Chet Atkins and a band of Nashville studio pros "and it's done pretty much the way we used to do records, live. So it's got some spontaneity to it." *Songs*, the brothers' second album, features spare arrangements and traditional songs like "Barbara Allen" and "Kentucky." "I think it might stand the test of time better than anything we've ever done," Don feels. *Heartaches and Harmonies* (4 CDs: Rhino) is a representative boxed set, in his opinion.

🔘: If you don't want to pop for the boxed set, you might start with *Cadence Classics: Their 20 Greatest Hits* (Rhino), which covers the late 1950s tracks the brothers are best known for. *Walk Right Back: . . . on Warner Bros.* (2 CDs: Warner Archives) collects their best-known 1960s material. *Hidden Gems from the Warner Years* (Ace) includes strong songs and performances that the public overlooked. Like *Songs Our Daddy Taught Us*, 1968's *Roots* (Warner Bros.) features the brothers covering songs that influenced them by such artists as Merle Haggard, Jimmie Rodgers, and Ron Elliot of the Beau Brummels as well as traditional material. Many regard this acoustic-textured record less innocent-sounding than the brothers' earlier work, an early country-rock classic.

BEN FOLDS (April 24, 1998)

The constant flood of new pop records hitting the stores in recent years means that more people than ever are writing songs. But not many write them like Ben Folds. The tunes that Folds writes are in the best rock tradition, but they also support their own weight without help from guitar noise, watery electronica, or attitude-soaked vocals. Perhaps to underline the point, he performs them relatively unadorned—with an acoustic piano trio, the Ben Folds Five (a name he chose, his website informs us, because "it sounded better than the Ben Folds Three").

"Yeah, I really dig classic song structure," acknowledges Ben when we ask him about the music that's most affected him. "There's only a few bands that I've listened to that I thought just basically jammed while the lead singer wrote lyrics over it."

But those influences aren't necessarily the ones you imagine. "Like, I never listened to the Beatles," says Ben. "Everyone thinks that's probably the biggest thing in my collection, but I don't have any of the Beatles' records. But I do have all of 10cc's records [he laughs]. And that's where I heard the Beatles from."

Originally, it was the living, booty-shaking stuff—not fussy, buffed and shined lyrics—that dominated Ben's musical world. Ben's father remodeled houses in low-income neighborhoods in Winston-Salem, North Carolina, where Ben grew up. Often Dad would enter a home that had been abandoned by its tenants and find stacks of records among the things left behind, which he would then cart home for his son. As it turned out, many of the records were R&B classics that thrilled Ben as a child. "I liked to put my parents' speakers on the floor and turn it up so I could feel the drums," Ben recalls. "There's something about black R&B music from that time, I think. It's so alive it makes kids think that the shit's alive in the speakers. It just really captures your imagination."

Slowly, Ben's focus in music changed from form to content. First, he honed in on the economical, emotionally direct songwriting of Otis Redding, a thrill quite apart from Redding's riveting performances. Many other musicians who impressed him worked right in Winston-Salem. "There was a band called the Other Mothers, and they were almost like a speed-punk band at the time," Ben remembers. "I loved that band, 'cause they played so fuckin' fast and they also had songs I could understand—about something." But he really began to feel like there might be a place for him in music when Mitch Easter's Let's Active and Winston-Salem natives the dB's began making their brainy power pop. "They brought in a sense of New Wave and England and New York—they brought all that to home where you could be involved with it. As opposed to being an extension of, like, Lynyrd Skynyrd," says Ben.

With the release of 1997's *Whatever and Ever Amen*, the Ben Folds Five, once known largely to locals and admiring musicians, became a hot national item. That sort of life change tends to sap all of a musician's attention and the consumption of new music stops. Not with Ben, who has never stopped enjoying being a fan. "I listen to so much music," he says. "I could be a critic instead."

BEN FOLDS'S FAVORITE ARTISTS AND RECORDINGS

Ike and Tina Turner—*Working Together* (Liberty). This is a favorite of Ben's from his childhood, for Tina's big voice and, again, the way the record was recorded. "That [drum] fill on 'Proud Mary,' I would play that over and over again."

Otis Redding—*In Person at the Whiskey a Go Go* (Rhino). "Otis Redding's songs were very concise and to the point. I mean, a little kid can understand 'Mr. Pitiful.' And 'Sittin' on the Dock of the Bay' or any of that stuff makes sense to a kid."

Earth, Wind & Fire—*Gratitude* (Columbia). "The music is so tight and so big. There's a lot to listen to in that record and it's still got the fun for a kid of being alive in the speakers."

Various artists—*Jesus Christ Superstar [Original Cast]* (MCA). "I didn't ever go to church, and I think it's kind of a pitiful way to have learned the Bible at all, but I think I learned some concepts from it and I really did dig that. I think I liked the way it captures your imagination that the person performing is theatrical about it. That's probably what I liked the most about it. I [also] like the fact that the voices are mixed at least twice as loud as the music behind. What I learned from that is that if the vocal is convincing, then you can mix it up as loud as you want to. I'm not a screamer, but I like to find out if I crank the vocals if it's still driving the band. If it's not, it needs to be sung better."

*REM—*Chronic Town* (IRS) and *Murmer* (IRS). Ben feels that REM's later albums were even better but these releases, REM's first two, have sentimental value for him because they were recorded in Winston-Salem and were a regional sensation when he was in high school. "Their music doesn't really fit in with the rest of what I listened to," Ben says. "Still, Michael Stipe's voice definitely drives things, and even though the songs don't have a ton of form, in a way, they've still got something that's grabbing you." ⬤: On CD, the whole of *Chronic Town* is on *Dead Letter Office* (IRS), along with a batch of early B-sides and outtakes.

*dB's—*Stands for Decibels* (IRS) and *Repercussion* (IRS). Like REM, the dB's were important to Ben for being a Southern band that put a premium on lyrical intelligence, an anomaly in the Southern rock scene of the time. But Ben prefers the band's first two albums, before Chris Stamey left the group.

Joni Mitchell—*Blue* (Reprise) and *Don Juan's Reckless Daughter* (Asylum). "When you've been listening to music that's all about the music and all of a sudden someone is basically writing music to their journal, then I think that kind of made me hip to the possibilities, taking all this boy stuff I knew about, kickin' ass, and making good songs [out of it]."

Nick Drake—*Five Leaves Left* (Hannibal) and *Bryter Later* (Hannibal). Ben says that Drake, like Joni Mitchell, inspired him to be more introspective and confessional in his lyrics. He also likes Drake's "below the radar" singing style. "It's like very compulsory now to scream in the third verse, or bring your third chorus up an octave and scream. Why does that have to happen? Dynamics are not just about getting loud at the peak of a song. Honestly, that's my theory as to why our song 'Brick' has done okay, because we never break the whisper.''

Elliott Smith—*Either/Or* (Kill Rock Stars). ''I really think he's the man. *Either/Or* is kind of the record of the year to me. And it's important. I know that years from now someone will be doing an interview with someone who's eight years old or ten years old now and they'll be talkin' about that album.''

The Flaming Lips—*Zaireeka* (Warner Bros.). This music comes packaged as four CDs that are to be played simultaneously. ''It's very organic,'' says Ben, ''but you have to have four CD players at your fingertips. It's a little prohibitive, but it's such a great album. It makes me proud to be in this era. There's some really great stuff going on.''

Elvis Costello—*Armed Forces* and *My Aim is True* (both Rykodisc). ''In the [New Wave] era, Elvis Costello was the man for me. It's probably the thread that makes me kinda know what I'm doing now. It like connects everything together, if I have to name one artist. Still, his quote 'new wave' sounds pretty relevant. It doesn't age. So much of that stuff ages so badly. You know what else, though, *Armed Forces* had a single in it with a live version of 'Alison' and 'Accidents Will Happen,' and the live version of 'Accidents Will Happen' was just piano and voice. It was included as a promotional single on the album depending on what pressing you bought. Man, I was lucky [it was in the copy I bought], because that was a big deal for me. Because you can hear how fucking good the song is.''

The Replacements—*Let It Be* (Twin/Tone). ''I listened to that until it turned white and I had to buy another one. 'Unsatisfied,' that's such a great song.''

Archers of Loaf—*Icky Mettle* (Alias). Ben says a couple of local bands, this one and Built to Spill, also made a big impact on the Ben Folds Five.

Built to Spill—*There's Nothing Wrong with Love* (UP). ''[That album] probably had something to do with the way this band went.''

Liz Phair—*Exile in Guyville* (Matador). ''Definitely, absolutely, completely. She doesn't have to be shocking, but with her sometimes it is. But each song has a definite, conversational effect on you, and I think I kept on checking what we were doing to make sure that it did that. And if it didn't do it as well as Liz Phair, then—like a song like 'A Song for the Dumped,' it's like 'Give me my black T-shirt back, you bitch.' It's almost embarrassingly influenced by Liz Phair.''

Elton John—*11-17-70* (MCA) and *Tumbleweed Connection* (MCA). John's song-writing with lyricist Bernie Taupin was a major influence on Ben. To Ben, John's individual songs stand up better than the albums as a whole do, but the albums mentioned contain, in his opinion, John's strongest group of songs. Ben prefers the live *11-17-70* overall, and is bugged by *Tumbleweed Connection*'s "Country Comfort" ("I guess because I'm from the South"), but says about the latter album, "there's so much on it, like 'Burn Down the Mission,' that's just a masterpiece."

Randy Newman—"Marie" on *Good Old Boys* (Reprise) and *Sail Away* (Reprise). Ben says about "Marie," "I can't think of a better song, really." And *Sail Away* "is a great album."

Rickie Lee Jones—*Pirates* (Warner Brothers). "It's just got a truth that rings through the whole thing. And even through what I'm almost politically and religiously opposed to—this huge production value with session men. That's what it is, but, God, she totally uses it to her advantage. That's the portrait of a sinking woman. Everything down to the cover is like that. There are certain songs on that album where the cadencing of the song stuck in my head so much that it's just like an institution. When I write songs, I emulate that."

Prefab Sprout—*Two Wheels Good* (Epic) [released overseas as *Steve McQueen*]: "That was a big album for me, too, I think just 'cause the guy's a literate songwriter and he kinda makes a stand—he's an island. There's never been anything cool about listening to Prefab Sprout and it's still something I listen to all the time and people are like 'You listen to that?' "

Steely Dan—*Pretzel Logic* (MCA). "That album's like a bunch of nerds wearing sunglasses, and I could relate to that. I couldn't quite put sunglasses on. They did more drugs than I could ever do. But it was kinda like someone with a brain can be cool, too."

BEN FOLDS'S OWN RECORDINGS

The Ben Folds Five, for which Ben writes almost all the material, had issued just two complete albums at the time of our interview. About those, Ben says, "I think our second album [*Whatever and Ever Amen* (550 Music)] is an improvement over the first album [*Ben Folds Five* (Passenger/Caroline Records)]. Generally I think the songs are better. But I think the first album has the earmarks of a record that could stick, even though it didn't sell much. I wouldn't dare compare it to *My Aim is True*, because I think that's one of the greatest albums, but it's in that category to me. I guess a lot of people's first albums are. I think the song 'Alice Childress' is good on the first album. And there's a song that was cut off the first album that was put on a B-side album [*Naked Baby Photos* (Caroline Records)] called 'Eddie Walker.' "

●: The title of Ben's 1998 solo project, *Fear of Pop Volume 1* (550 Music), speaks at least one volume about the music, an experimental, intentionally cheesy departure from the material he writes for the Ben Folds Five. William Shatner guests! The Five's latest, 1999's much-praised *The Unauthorized Biography of Rheinhold Meissner* (Sony) finds Ben's smart, sad pop freshened with lusher arrangements and more ambitious compositions.

TIM GANE (October 14, 1998)

I n a business class exercise at his school, Tim Gane, then 15, tipped his hand that he had career plans for which no school could—or would want to—prepare him. The assignment required students to send application letters to local businesses. Tim sent one of his to the grindingly intense industrial band, Throbbing Gristle: "They sent me back their big industrial newsletter full of all their lyrics—you know, 'Maggot Death' and so on—maybe thinking that it was going to frighten me away. But actually it attracted me to it much stronger."

To Tim, Throbbing Gristle offered the perfect alternative to his family's bland working class London existence: "They weren't people who put stage clothes on, got up on stage, and did an act. It was something they lived out . . . I really liked the idea of being different. I lived in the suburbs and it was kind of part of that, the sort of escape from suburban death, as I called it. And this music was completely exciting. For like five or six years, I listened to really nothing else, apart from basically electronic music or . . . what you call avant-garde rock music."

Tim had entered Throbbing Gristle's dark vision via the equally nightmarish Cabaret Voltaire. Although he was playing straight pop in the band that he formed in his school years, he had already started pulling away from the mainstream via the gloomy post-punk music he was hearing on the radio. But nothing prepared him for the electronic experimentalism of Cabaret Voltaire's "Nag Nag Nag" when he heard it in 1979: "Basically all the reference points were ones I had no understanding of, and so I spent . . . since then, my whole musical life trying to find out these kind of curiosities and kind of trying to get that feeling."

In the mid-1980s, Tim formed his first band, McCarthy, which recorded several albums and enjoyed some modest success. But Tim eventually lost interest in the band's "guitar-poppish" sound. He had already decided to break up the group when he met Parisian *Laetitia Sadier at a McCarthy gig. Laetitia would soon become both girlfriend and musical co-conspirator. A year later, they debuted Stereolab, which hit the ground with an already well-thought-out blend of harsh industrial noise, Krautrockish electronica, rock minimalism a la Velvet Underground and Jonathan Richman and the Modern Lovers, and sultry '60s-era French pop. The sound continues to morph and deepen as they add newer inspirations and recast older ones, and they document most of it as they go on not only conventional albums but also a steady stream of limited-edition releases of various forms. The changes keep fans and critics guessing, but one thing remains abundantly clear: Tim won't be sending Throbbing Gristle another job application anytime soon.

TIM GANE'S FAVORITE ARTISTS AND RECORDINGS

Cabaret Voltaire—"Nag Nag Nag" (Rough Trade). Tim admits this single sounds different to him now in his early thirties than when he was a teenager, but he says it still sounds fantastic and can put him back in his teenage head: "I was very attracted to it because it was just so strange and it really did seem the metaphor of beaming down from another planet or somewhere."

Throbbing Gristle—*DOA* and *Second Annual Report* (both Mute). "The overriding thing I had when I first listened to their records was fear, really—you know, what horrible things could be contained in their music?"

Faust—*Faust* (Recommended). When McCarthy broke up, Tim revisited the German electronic music that had intrigued him years earlier. He calls *Faust* "for me the number one record [of Krautrock]. It's the first record of all that lot that I heard and it's still the most strange and most difficult to get to grips with or understand."

Kraftwerk—*Kraftwerk 1* (Vertigo) and *Kraftwerk 2* (Philips). Describing these early '70s albums, Tim says, "the pre- really electronic stuff is full of strange melodies which kind of flick in and out of actually what is quite primitive music."

Neu—*Neu* (Billingsgate) and *Neu 2* (United Artists). This German electronic band's records provided another aesthetic cornerstone for Stereolab's sound.

Cluster—*Zuckerzeit* (Brain) and *Zwei Osterie* (Cleopatra). Cluster, another German electronic group, helped pioneer ambient music through their collaborations with Brian Eno and producer Conrad Plank.

Can—*Monster Movie*, *Deep End*, *Soundtracks*, *Tago Mago*, *Ege Bamyasi*, and *Future Days* (all Mute). : *Cannibalism 1* (Spoon) anthologizes these records.

Jonathan Richman and the Modern Lovers—*Modern Lovers* and *Live* (both Rhino). Tim says the former album gave him "this weird idea of what high school was like in America in the early '70s. It's pretty obvious that a lot of our early style was derived to a certain degree from the Modern Lovers, particularly 'Road-runner.' I mean, the simplicity and fluidness of it. It's just the pure sort of groove record.''

Silver Apples—*Silver Apples* (MCA) ''They're very hip again,'' Tim says. ''They're a very primitive electronic duo from late-'60s New York.'' The member known only as Simeon played an early synthesizer that he invented and named, yes, the Simeon. *Silver Apples* combines two albums on one disc.

My Bloody Valentine—*You Made Me Realize* (EP, Creation). ''The best band of the last fifteen years . . . Definitely a big influence on our earlier stuff.''

Tortoise—*Gamera* and *Vaus* (Duophonic). Tim numbers Tortoise among his favorite ''bands who are really investigating or exploring music.''

Pavement—*Slanted & Enchanted* (Matador) and *Perfect Sound Forever* (EP: Drag City). ''An absolutely brilliant and amazing record,'' Tim says of the former. : Tim likes all of Pavement's early singles and EPs, collected on *Westing (by Musket & Sextant)* (Drag City).

Dymaxion—This New York band is one of Tim's current favorites: ''They are a very primitive electronics and kind of a brash sort of '60s thing, but it's done in a very unique way.'' : Dymaxion has released a self-titled 7-inch on Stereolab's Duophonic label.

Serge Gainsbourg and Brigitte Bardot—''Bonnie & Clyde'' on *The Best of BB* (Polydor). Before starting Stereolab, Tim had Laetitia audition as a vocalist by singing this song and ''I'll Keep It with Mine'' (see below).

Nico—''I'll Keep It With Mine'' on *Chelsea Girl* (Polydor).

Mouse on Mars—*Iaora Tahiti* (Too Pure/American).

Harmonia—*Muzik von Harmonia* (Polydor).

The Plush—''No Education/Soaring and Boring'' (single, Fly Daddy).

TIM GANE'S OWN RECORDINGS

''I think if you wanted a summation of our earlier period, I would say the *Transient Random Noise Bursts* [Elektra] album. If you wanted a kind of most wide-ranging record, probably I'd say *Emperor Tomato Ketchup* [Elektra]. I think in many ways a big part of Stereolab, or real Stereolab in a sense, is all the records we recorded for small labels and just off-the-cuff things. They're gathered together on three compilations that we have, and I suppose *Refried Ectoplasm* [Duophonic], the second compilation, covers a very large area of all these off-cuts. And in a sense I think that's really as important as any of the albums because I think these sort of records are what make us a little distinct from other groups, the amount of things we do. These were things we made to just try something. My all-time favorite Stereolab record is a single we did called 'Farfisa' and 'Harmonium' [both available on *Refried Ectoplasm*], and that was our homage to the Silver Apples."

⬤: Other notable Stereolab releases include their 1992 debut *Switched On* (Slumberland), *Peng!* (WEA), *The Groop Played Space Age Bachelor Pad Music* (Too Pure/American), *Mars Audiac Quintet* (Elektra), the EP *Music for the Amorphous Body Center* (Duophonic), and the latest singles compilation, *Aluminum Tunes: Switched On, Vol. 3* (2 CDs: Drag City). Tim's previous band, McCarthy, released *I Am a Wallet* (Midnight), *The Enraged Will Inherit the Earth* (Cherry Red), *The Best of McCarthy* (Cherry Red), and *That's All Very Well, But* . . . (Cherry Red).

GILBERTO GIL (May 6, 1998)

ob Dylan, Joan Baez, Phil Ochs, the *Staple Singers, Buffy Saint-Marie—to any credible list of great protest singers of the 1960s must also be added the name Gilberto Gil. America was not the only place to spawn protest music in those seismic times. In the days before the Internet and fax machines, progressive culture still spread quickly in the ethers of the global underground. Thus it was that, inspired by social movements in the United States and elsewhere, the music called *tropicalia* flowered in Brazil, where its cries for emancipation and equity for the underclass recalled centuries of oppression. Gil co-led the movement and remains one of its most recognizable stars.

Because *tropicalia* arose from people with personal histories, not record company marketing departments, it can't be understood apart from the people who make it. Gilberto's history began in the city of Salvador in the northeastern state of Bahia, a region of Brazil steeped in African traditions that has produced some of Brazil's finest popular musicians. There, via the radio (his family didn't have a record player), he heard the two musicians who first inspired him: Luis Gonzaga and one Bob Nelson. Gonzaga popularized *forro*, a Brazilian dance music with folk roots that features the accordion, Gonzaga's instrument. Nelson? "[He] used to imitate Tyrolese music in a sense," Gilberto says, "and he used to dress himself as a cowboy, like Roy Rogers, and he used the Tyrolean yodeling."

Over the radio, Gilberto also fell in love with American big band music, especially Glenn Miller, and samba. But the music that most affected his career at that point was that of bossa nova legend Joao Gilberto. By now, Gilberto Gil had begun his musical life, as an accordionist playing in *forro* bands like his early idol Luis Gonzaga. Joao Gilberto inspired him to abandon the accordion for the guitar. And the impact only started there. Gilberto says that for him, bossa nova—especially Joao Gilberto's version of it—was "decisive" for his early songwriting, when he was 20. Gil was now stirring a pot that included an array of South and North American musical styles plus his own skills as writer, singer, and guitarist. In combination with other artists on a like-minded path, the result was *tropicalia*.

Although *tropicalia* was distinctive enough to be named, Gilberto has never considered it a true musical "style." "It was mostly an attitude," he explains. "We adopted electric guitars, we adopted long hair and a little drugs and rock 'n' roll [he laughs]. And we were sort of following the student movement, the Black Panthers movement, you know, all the social and political movements around the world. And, of course, changing a lot of the subject, the texts of the songs, writing about more up-to-date subjects, including nonconventional aspects of life. Musically, we were mixing bossa nova and rock 'n' roll, folk music, pop."

In 1971, the political component Gilberto speaks of won him and his friend and fellow *tropicalia* star, Caetano Veloso, a several-month stay in jail, courtesy of Brazil's repressive military government. Upon their release, the two were exiled to Britain, where they continued to experiment with incorporating rock and other popular elements into Brazilian music. Gilberto was now listening to the Beatles, Jimi Hendrix, and Miles Davis, and a little later, Stevie Wonder, Bob Marley, other Caribbean influences, and African pop. For all its worldly accents, though, his music remained rooted in the complex rhythms of Bahia.

Gilberto has since carried his politics from the stage to government chambers (he was elected to the Salvador city council). But with over 30 albums to his credit, he continues to make urgent and joyful music with Caetano Veloso and the other stars of *tropicalia*.

GILBERTO GIL'S FAVORITE ARTISTS AND RECORDINGS

Jorge Veiga—This vocalist was Gilberto's favorite samba artist when he was young. 🔘: *O Melhor de . . .* (Marcatu).

Luiz Gonzaga—This leading light of *forro* music from northeastern Brazil was not only a great accordionist but also a folklorist and champion of the country's roots music. Gilberto and the other *tropicalia* artists helped introduce Gonzaga to younger listeners in the '60s and '70s. 🔘: Gonzaga's only widely available recordings in the United States are collected on *Brazil Classics 3: Forro, etc.—Music of the Brazilian Northeast* (Luaka Bop); search import sources for the classic *Asa Branca* (RCA Brazil).

Glenn Miller—Gilberto loves big band music in general but Miller's most of all. ⦿: Good compilations include *Pure Gold* (Bluebird), a solid one-disc collection of Miller's immortal hits, and the two-disc set *The Essential . . .* (Bluebird), perhaps the best overview for fans who don't need every Miller track. Since Gilberto heard Miller on the radio, you might recreate the experience with *Legendary Performer* (Bluebird), a package of hits taken from Miller's radio broadcasts.

Joao Gilberto—"Chega de Saudade" on *The Legendary Joao Gilberto* (World Pacific). This single, written by Antonio Carlos Jobim, is widely credited as the ground-zero bossa nova song.

Caetano Veloso—"He is *tropicalia*, like myself," Gilberto says about the music's other most significant figure. A gifted singer, guitarist, and songwriter, Veloso is also a filmmaker and one of the most widely published poets writing in Portuguese. ⦿: Together, Gilberto and Veloso recorded *Tropicalia 2* (Elektra/Nonesuch), a critically acclaimed U.S. release, in 1994. As an introduction to Veloso's large catalog, also look for *Caetano Veloso* (Elektra/Nonesuch), an intimate collection with Veloso accompanying himself on acoustic guitar, or 1979's *Cinema Transcendental* (Verve).

Djavan—Gilberto describes his music as "a mix of bossa nova and northeastern folk music." ⦿: Djavan made some inroads to the North American scene with 1984's *Djavan* and 1988's *Bird of Paradise* (both Epic), both worth checking out for Djavan's gorgeous voice. Also seek out 1996's *Malasia* (Sony International).

Lulu Santos—"His origin is rock 'n' roll, but he's mixing music now." ⦿: *Toda Forma de Amor* (RCA) and the more recent *Assim Caminha a Humanidade* (BMG Brazil).

Gal Costa—Costa brings a bright, soaring vocal style to her version of *tropicalia*. ⦿: Start with either 1975's *Gal Canta Caymmi* (Verve), on which she covers tunes by Brazilian Dori Caymmi, or her more recent *Trilha Sonora Do Filme Gabriela* (RCA Brazil).

Maria Bethania—"She sings dramatic songs in the style of the divas, almost like Edith Piaf and Amalia Rodriguez," Gilberto says. Bethania, who is Caetano Veloso's sister, has been a major figure in *tropicalia* for over three decades. In recent years, she turned her attention to love songs on albums like 1997's highly produced *Ambar* (Capitol). ⦿: *Alibi* (Polygram) was Bethania's big breakthrough, selling over a million copies in Brazil. It's a collection of love ballads, on which she covers the Gilberto Gil/Chico Buarque song "Calice." If you're in the mood to torch it up, catch *Memoria de Pele/Memories of Skin* (Verve). You can hear her live on 1997's *Maria Bethania Au Vivo* (Polygram Brazil).

Bob Marley—*Catch a Fire* (Tuff Gong). Marley's first huge international hit, in 1973, really moved Gilberto. He has since covered several Marley tunes.

Stevie Wonder—*Songs in the Key of Life* (Motown). This and the following albums all influenced his songwriting and his particular version of *tropicalia*, Gilberto says.

Miles Davis—*Bitches Brew* (Columbia).

Jimi Hendrix—*Axis, Bold as Love* (Reprise).

The Beatles—*Sgt. Pepper's Lonely Hearts Club Band* (Capitol).

GILBERTO GIL'S OWN RECORDINGS

Gilberto suggests that those interested in his music start with his debut record, 1966's *Louvacao* (Philips). His other recommendations include *Refavela* (Philips), an album that wasn't released in the United States; *Nightingale* (Elektra), with several songs in English; *Live in Montreux* (WEA), recorded in '78; and 1997's *Quanta* (Mesa) "because of the quality of the songs and of the production." The Philips and WEA recordings will probably be available only through import sources.

: Gilberto mentions only one of his live albums, but several other strong live dates are available, particularly *Acoustic* (Atlantic) and the stunning *Quanta Live* (Mesa), recorded in Brazil in 1997. If you want to explore his back catalog, check import sources for 1972's *Expresso 2222* (Philips). The American release *Realce* (Elektra), recorded in the same period as *Nightingale*, includes a wonderful cover of Bob Marley's "No Woman, No Cry," a single that went platinum in Brazil. And the beautiful *Gil & Jorge* (Verve) pairs Gilberto with Brazilian singer/songwriter Jorge Ben—just the two of them with acoustic guitars, percussion, and a handful of their great songs.

DAVID GRISMAN (unknown date late in 1995)

What mandolinist David Grisman is doing for acoustic string music is only slightly less than what Noah did for biodiversity. The improvisatory "Dawg" music he established in the mid-1970s broke the bonds that bluegrass and folk held on acoustic string ensembles, pointing the way for such other progressive artists as *Tony Rice, Bela Fleck, The Turtle Island String Quartet,

Jerry Douglas, and Alison Brown. As owner/producer of his own record company, Acoustic Disc, he's shone a light on underappreciated current artists such as Argentinean guitarist Enrique Coria; reintroduced valuable recordings by such past masters, and key Grisman influences, as Oscar Aleman, Dave Apollon, Jethro Burns, Jacob do Bandolim, and David's old bandmates in the Kentuckians, Red Allen and Frank Wakefield; and issued a slew of other uncompromising yet accessible acoustic instrument recordings. Finally, he continues to stake out new acoustic ensemble territory as the leader of the ever-evolving David Grisman Quintet (DGQ).

Of course, the unpretentious Grisman deflects credit for most of this, in particular the direction that acoustic string music went after he first took dawg music public in 1974. Dawg music melds folk and bluegrass-type instrumentation, classical-like ensemble precision, jazzlike improvisation, and cultural accents from literally all over the map. The idea, first carried out by Grisman's The Great American Music Band (whose rotating lineup often included Jerry Garcia and *Taj Mahal) exploded the creative possibilities for acoustic artists who were feeling constricted by folk music. Yet looking back, David says, "I don't think any one person invents a great, universal idea . . . there's a point in time where that idea is right." He also acknowledges musicians such as mandolinists Burns and Apollon for originally taking folk instruments beyond bluegrass.

In the same vein, David discusses Acoustic Disc as if it was more of a happy accident than a realized vision. He started the label somewhat out of desperation after being dropped from his major-label recording contract in 1989. Like other corporately displaced Americans, David went the self-employment route. From the beginning, however, Acoustic Disc advanced causes besides David's own. After hitting the ground with DGQ and Garcia/Grisman projects, its third release featured *choro* mandolinist Jacob do Bandolim, dead for over 20 years and little known outside his native Brazil. The fifth release was a collection of solo avante-garde music by obscure Czech mandolinist Radim Zenkl. And so it has gone for Acoustic Disc, which seems to see itself as an acoustic music preservation society as much as a business. Yet, David told us, he is making more money now than at any time in his career.

Part of the success undoubtedly flows from Garcia's involvement. The projects featuring him sold predictably well, pumping cash through the fledgling company and alerting legions of Deadheads to Acoustic Disc's existence. But in an earlier interview, David gave us another insight into Acoustic Disc's seemingly paradoxical success. Commenting on a CNN business piece breaking down the previous year's music sales, he noted: "They said thirty-three percent of the sales were rock and roll, seventeen percent were rap and soul, and seventeen percent were country, and that's it. If you add that up, that's sixty-seven percent, and there's a whole thirty-three percent that's something else! That's as big a percentage of the pie as rock and roll. It's twice as big as country. It's twice as big as rap. But it doesn't even get a name. That's actually the real music out there."

DAVID GRISMAN'S FAVORITE ARTISTS AND RECORDINGS

Duke Ellington with Jimmy Blanton and Ben Webster—"I've always liked both composed and improvised music. To me, the best is someone like Duke Ellington, who's got it all," David says. He also finds himself drawn to great working bands that feature terrific ensemble interplay as well as individual brilliance. He calls the Blanton/Webster era the "quintessential" Ellington units in this regard. Individually, Blanton's bass playing with Ellington was a big influence on David's career, as was Webster's soloing on tenor sax. 💿: The three-disc set *The Blanton-Webster Years* (RCA/Bluebird) provides a superb overview of this Ellington period, which also heralded the arrival of pianist/composer/arranger Billy Strayhorn.

Ben Webster—*Plays Ballads* (Storyville). An all-around fan of the saxophonist, David especially loves this disc, which catches Webster in late career when his always personally affecting solos were at their peak of stripped-down elegance.

Bill Monroe—Few besides David could mention Ellington, Webster, and Blanton in one breath, Monroe in the next, and have it sound as natural as "peanut butter and jelly." David ate up mandolinist Monroe's recordings on Columbia and most of his Decca recordings early in his career. Monroe's Bluegrass Boys from the Columbia years, including guitarist Lester Flatt and banjo player Earl Scruggs, is one of those great working units that Grisman cherishes. 💿: A four-CD set, *Bill Monroe: Bluegrass 1959–1969* (Bear Family) chronicles the Decca years, including previously unissued material. For the band with Flatt and Scruggs, see Master List under "Bill Monroe and the Bluegrass Boys (1945–47 version)."

Flatt & Scruggs—*1949–1959* (4 CDs: Bear Family). "That's an incredible set of music," David says. About Scruggs, David adds, "The guy was like an encyclopedia of the banjo, what it could do by itself and in a band."

Django Reinhardt and Stephane Grappelli—David loves the entire recorded output from 1934–39 of the unmatched string band, the Quintette of the Hot Club of France, fronted by guitarist Reinhardt and violinist Grappelli. He's also a big fan of Grappelli and Reinhardt's final work together in Rome in 1949. 💿: *Souvenirs* (London) and *Swing from Paris* (ASV) provide solid, single-disc introductions to the Quintette. The 1949 period is captured on *Djangology* (Bluebird/BMG) when Grappelli and Reinhardt were being backed by a conventional jazz rhythm section instead of what David calls the "old chunka-chunka-chunka sound" of the Quintette. "You really don't hear the piano, bass, and drums," says David. "It's still dominated by Django and Stephane. In a way, this is their peak but those guys were always peaking."

Clarence Ashley and Doc Watson—*Old Time Music at Clarence Ashley's* (Smithsonian/Folkways). This is the record that introduced Watson to the world. Ralph Rinzler, whom David calls "my guru," recorded the tapes after rediscovering Ashley, an old-time banjo player and singer who had recorded in the 1920s, on a trip to North Carolina in 1960. "Doc Watson was playing in the local pub every Saturday night and he was one of the musicians who showed up on these recordings," David notes.

Neils-Henning Orsted-Pedersen and Oscar Pettiford—" I'll buy a record if Neils Pederson or Oscar Pettiford is playing bass." ●: David must buy a lot of records—both of these men have voluminous recording credits. For a taste of Orsted-Pedersen as a session leader, try *Dancing on the Tables* (Steeplechase); the group on this 1979 record includes *John Scofield and Dave Liebman. Coleman Hawkins's excellent *Hollywood Stampede* (Capitol) features Pettiford as a crucial element in the rhythm section.

John Coltrane—*Live at the Village Vanguard* (MCA), *Ballads* (Impulse), *Crescent* (Impulse), and *John Coltrane and Johnny Hartman* (Impulse). David says he'll listen to anything with Coltrane's famous quartet—with pianist McCoy Tyner, bassist Jimmy Garrison, drummer *Elvin Jones—but lists these albums first. All but *Live* feature that group. The last adds vocalist Johnny Hartman for a profound set of ballads. *Live* has Reggie Workman on bass in place of Garrison and Eric Dolphy on bass clarinet.

Oliver Nelson—*Blues and the Abstract Truth* (Impulse). This widely praised 1961 album exemplifies David's ideal—great compositions, arrangements, and ensemble play in addition to impressive soloing. The lineup for this date included reedman Eric Dolphy, pianist Bill Evans, trumpeter Freddie Hubbard, bassist Paul Chambers, and drummer Roy Haynes.

Ornette Coleman with Don Cherry, Charlie Haden, and Billy Higgins—Saxophonist Coleman's 1959–60 quartet exhibits the same all-around excellence as the Nelson unit above, albeit in a more "outside" context. ●: *The Shape of Jazz to Come* and *Change of the Century* (both Atlantic) both feature this group, absolutely as influential as the album titles boast.

Miles Davis—*Workin'* (Original Jazz Classics), *Steamin'* (Original Jazz Classics), and *Kind of Blue* (Columbia). The first two albums feature Davis's first great quintet, with Davis and John Coltrane plus pianist Red Garland's trio with bassist Paul Chambers and drummer Philly Joe Jones. *Kind of Blue*, of course, may be the most celebrated jazz album ever.

Cannonball Adderly—*Somethin' Else* (Blue Note). David especially admires Miles Davis's solos on this 1958 record.

The Beatles—*Revolver* (Capitol), *Sgt. Pepper's Lonely Hearts Club Band* (Capitol), and *Abbey Road* (Apple). David mentioned these albums first, but close behind is every other Beatles album from *Something New* (Capitol) on: "The whole is probably greater than the sum of the parts, but I give *George Martin a lot of credit. Even when it's just [the Beatles] playing, the parts are so well-conceived. It blew my mind, combining those elements—a lot of classical things, Indian stuff, Chuck Berry."

Jacob do Bandolim—*Original Classic Recordings, Vol. 1* and *Original Classic Recordings, Vol. 2* (both Acoustic Disc). These marvelous recordings of traditional *choro* music were never released in the United States until Grisman licensed them for his own label: "I was glad to make [this music] available because that was music I was listening to for years and years."

Red Allen and Frank Wakefield—*The Kitchen Tapes* (Acoustic Disc). When they were each 18, David and buddy Peter Siegel asked their bluegrass idols Red Allen and Frank Wakefield for permission to tape record them playing and singing together. After wearing his copy out studying it, David would ultimately join Allen's Kentuckians in the mid-1960s and produce three of their albums. In 1994, working from Siegel's surviving copy, he released the entire set on Acoustic Disc as a tribute to Allen, who had died a year earlier. Don't miss this one, an absolute treasure of unaffected mastery.

Charlie Parker—*The Quintet/Jazz at Massey Hall* (Original Jazz Classics). "A great band [alto sax player Parker, trumpeter Dizzy Gillespie, pianist Bud Powell, bassist Charles Mingus, and drummer Max Roach] in a live situation."

Charles Mingus—*Town Hall Concert 1964* (Original Jazz Classics). David is a great fan of Eric Dolphy, who's prominently featured on this record.

Bill Evans—*Sunday at the Village Vanguard* (Original Jazz Classics). This album stars another one of those great empathetic units that thrills David, with bassist Scott LaFaro and drummer Paul Motian joining pianist Evans for one of jazz's most storied live sets.

Jimmy Martin with J. D. Crowe and Paul Williams—These three formed a terrific overall band in the country vein, says David. ⬤: *You Don't Know My Mind: 1956–1966* (Rounder), a one-disc survey of the era in which Martin worked with Crowe and Williams, or the exhaustive box set *Jimmy Martin and the Sunny Mountain Boys* (5 CDs: Bear Family).

Harry Lookofsky—*Stringsville* (Atlantic). Lookofsky played under Arturo Toscanini in the New York NBC Orchestra. He was a virtuoso violinist but couldn't improvise, David tells us, so Quincy Jones reportedly wrote out his solos for this jazzlike recording. David says, "It comes off like the world's greatest jazz violin player—violin with [a tone like that of] Miles Davis and the technique of some incredibly heavy classical musician . . . about half the record's a little cornier than the other half but there are some cuts on there that are just amazing."

Various artists—*Mountain Music Bluegrass Style* (Smithsonian/Folkways). "Actually the first bluegrass album I ever heard, produced by Mike Seeger, who's now a friend of mine. It was mostly recorded in hotel rooms. Most of the bands on there are pretty obscure. There's some great stuff on there."

Ike and Tina Turner—*River Deep—Mountain High* (A&M). David liked it when it came out (1969), and still does.

Alan Hovhaness—*Mysterious Mountain*. This composition tops David's classical list. ⬤: The classic recording of this features the Chicago Symphony Orchestra conducted by Fritz Reiner (RCA). Another excellent version is with the Seattle Symphony/Gerard Schwarz (Delos).

DAVID GRISMAN'S OWN RECORDINGS

David focuses on albums on which he both played and served as producer when discussing his favorites among his own projects. First mention goes to *Tone Poems II* (Acoustic Disc), a duo album of vintage jazz standards with Martin Taylor, David's favorite jazz guitarist. He also takes pride in *Mandolin Abstractions* (Rounder), a duo mandolin recording with Andy Statman: "The very first piece was the first thing we played and the very last cut is the last thing we played . . . I was planning spontaneity. I didn't want to warm up or rehearse. It turned out pretty cool." Other favorites include Red Allen, Frank Wakefield, and the Kentuckians' *Bluegrass* (Folkways); Red Allen and the Kentuckians' *Bluegrass Country* (County) and *Red Allen* (County); Dave Apollon's *The Man with the Mandolin* (2 CDs: Acoustic Disc); Mandolinists Tiny Moore and Jethro Burns's *Back to Back* (Kaleidoscope); David's own *Home is Where the Heart Is* (2 CDs; Rounder); and David, Herb Pederson, Vince Gill, et al, *Here Today* (Rounder).

⊙: If the Dawg music idea appeals to you but you don't know which album to start with, start at the beginning: *David Grisman Quintet* (Rhino), the first full-blown Dawg music album. It features flatpicking guitar wizard Tony Rice and violinist Darol Anger, and sounds as fresh today as it did then. *Hot Dawg* (A&M) began David's major-label sojourn and includes Stephane Grappelli on several tunes. Must-purchase number three is *DGQ 20* (Acoustic Disc), a three-CD retrospective covering the DGQ's first 20 years. Unlike most such projects, all tracks are previously unreleased and of almost uniformly superb quality.

From there, take your pick—all the DGQ records are marked by tuneful Grisman compositions, a tasteful choice of outside material, graceful arrangements, and virtuoistic soloing—most compellingly, by David himself. Since 1990, his quintets have included a flute player—a controversial choice with string purists and other lovers of the old Dawg sound. But *Dawganova* (Acoustic Disc ACD-17), a Latin-flavored excursion, employs the flute to particularly good advantage and introduces the elegant Enrique Coria on guitar.

Grisman's collaborations with Garcia should not be missed. They matched two musicians with not only decades of shared personal history but also unusually compatible musical values. *Jerry Garcia/David Grisman/Shady Grove*; and *So What* (all Acoustic Disc) display, respectively, the eclectic, folk, and jazz sides of their extensive repertoire. Their first recorded efforts together were with the legendary "hippiegrass" band Old and in the Way in 1973. *Old and in the Way* (Rykodisc), *That High Lonesome Sound* (Acoustic Disc), and *Breakdown* (Acoustic), all live, capture the essence of this group's joyous, swinging brand of bluegrass.

BUDDY GUY (June 10, 1998)

Many of popular music's greatest instrumentalists first taught themselves to play. But Buddy Guy, who grew up the son of a poor sharecropper in Lettsworth, Louisiana, took the bootstrapping one major step further: he made his first guitar, with wire stripped from a window screen. "I would just stretch wires across a stick in a lighter fluid can," Buddy tells us by phone from Legends, the blues club he owns in Chicago. "You couldn't finger it with your left hand."

Struggling to make ends meet with his cotton and corn, Dad finally scraped together the money to buy Buddy a real guitar, but it only had two strings. Buddy banged away on it as best he could; when the strings broke, he spliced them.

One day, a man was walking by Buddy's home and saw him struggling to play on the front porch. Taking pity, he went out and bought Buddy his first full-fledged ax. "Later on that night, we went out to my Dad's house about sixty miles outside Baton Rouge and they started talkin' and they had grew up as little boys together," Buddy recalls. "Not knowin' that, he had bought me the guitar."

Buddy hadn't heard much music early in his life because at first his father couldn't afford a radio, much less a record player. It was when Dad was finally able to buy one that Buddy discovered the universe of blues guitar, and scrambled for the wire and lighter-fluid can. "Radio stations then would play anybody's music," Buddy recalls. "You would hear Frank Sinatra, Woody Herman, then Lightnin' Hopkins and Mahalia Jackson. Then you'd hear the Five Blind Boys [of Mississippi]. It wasn't separated like it is now, with the Top Ten, each disc jockey playin' the same thing over and over. Then finally there came along the Smokey Hogg, the Muddy Waters, the Howlin' Wolf and the B. B. King, and that was it: I just wanted to play."

Although long celebrated by guitar deities such as Jimi Hendrix, Eric Clapton, and Stevie Ray Vaughan, Buddy struggled for most of his career to make the same kind of impact on record companies and the public that his admirers had. Things turned around big time in 1991 when his album *Damn Right I Got the Blues* won a Grammy. His first domestic release in a decade, it not only marked his comeback but catapulted him to a new level in the business. He now sells out shows in major venues and lords over Chicago's historic blues scene. But Buddy still hopes to make that final leap to the status of the white players who built their careers playing black blues–based music, and is spiking his music with rock and R&B to make it happen. "I'm not exposed out there like an Eric Clapton or somebody," notes Buddy. "Anytime they go in the studio and put a record out, they gets on MTV and VH1 . . . My records get played at 3 and 4 o'clock in the morning if you play blues."

BUDDY GUY'S FAVORITE ARTISTS AND RECORDINGS

*John Lee Hooker—"Boogie Chillun," "Crawling Kingsnake," and "Weeping Willow Boogie." The former song was the first thing Buddy learned to play on guitar, he tells us. 🔘: *The Legendary Modern Records 1948–1954* (Virgin), an excellent anthology of the early recordings that established Hooker's career, includes all three of Buddy's favorite Hooker tracks.

Lightnin' Hopkins— 🔘: See Master List.

Muddy Waters—Buddy prefers the early material on Chess. 🔘: See Master List.

Howlin' Wolf— ●: See Master List.

Smokey Hogg— ●: See Master List.

Earl Hooker—"Hooker made all us cry with that slide." ●: *Blue Guitar* (Paula/Flyright).

Lonnie Johnson—"Tomorrow Night." "You could count the guitar players on one hand when I wanted to learn how to play that guitar, man. I think there was somebody like T-Bone [Walker], Lightnin' [Hopkins], and the ones that was available to me, that I heard on radio, Lonnie Johnson," Buddy recalls. The ballad "Tomorrow Night" was a huge R&B hit in 1948, when Buddy was 12. ●: "Tomorrow Night" on the compilation (with other artists) *Blues and Folk* (Rykodisc), or *Tomorrow Night* (Gusto), a two LP set that apparently has not been reissued on CD.

B. B. King—"Three O'Clock Blues," "Sweet Little Angel," "You Know I Love You," and "Crying Won't Help You." ●: *Singin' the Blues/The Blues* (Flair), an import twofer CD that combines two highly influential King albums from the 1950s, contains all four tracks.

T-Bone Walker—Buddy used to listen to Walker on a radio station out of New Orleans. ●: See Master List.

Clarence "Gatemouth" Brown—"Okie Dokie Stomp." "A lot of guitar players, including Ike Turner, fell in love with stuff like that." ●: *The Original Peacock Recordings* (Rounder) mostly showcases bluesman Brown's agile, sharply etched guitar work and raucous vocals but also gives a peek at his considerable violin prowess.

Louis Jordan—"Saturday Night Fish Fry." Buddy reminds readers, as the great blues guitarist Robert Lockwood once reminded him, that Jordan helped father rock 'n' roll. ●: *The Best of Louis Jordan* (MCA).

Big Joe Turner—"Honey, Hush." "People in the country didn't drink hardly anything . . . but on Christmas everybody's house would have a gallon of wine or a case of beer and they'd get a little high and you'd hear a lotta 'Honey, Hush.' " ●: See Master List. Both sets listed include this track.

Roy Brown—"Rockin' at Midnight." Like Louis Jordan, Brown was an innovator whose music was crucial to the development of rock 'n' roll. ●: *Good Rocking Tonight: The Best of . . .* (Rhino).

Guitar Slim—Buddy loves the material Slim recorded in New Orleans, with piano and arrangements by Ray Charles. ●: *Sufferin' Mind* (Specialty) includes four tracks from that October 1953 session, including the hit "The Things That I Used to Do."

Ray Charles—Buddy prefers Charles's work in the 1950s on Atlantic Records. ⦿: *The Best of . . . : The Atlantic Years* (Rhino) is a fine single-disc compilation of this music. But Ray never wears thin, so consider the whole shot, *The Birth of Soul: The Complete Atlantic Rhythm & Blues Recordings (1952–1959)* (3 CDs: Rhino).

The Five Blind Boys of Mississippi—Regarding the live music he heard while growing up in the South, Buddy says, "I never did see the B. B. Kings, and this guitar player and that guitar player. I saw a lot of spiritual groups comin' on one after the other." The Blind Boys, led by Archie Brownlee, influenced many secular artists, including Ray Charles. ⦿: See Master List.

Lou Rawls and the Pilgrim Travelers—Rawls led this group briefly before their breakup in 1956. ⦿: Two albums were issued under the title *Lou Rawls and the Pilgrim Travelers*, the first on Andex in 1957, the second on Capitol in the 1960s. Both are out of print.

Mahalia Jackson—"She would flip me out every time she would open her mouth." ⦿: See Master List.

Johnny Lang—We asked Buddy if he saw anyone on the horizon with the ability to carry on the blues guitar tradition. He named Lang without a moment's hesitation: "He's like the late Stevie Ray Vaughan. Those people comes along once in a lifetime." ⦿: See Master List.

Stevie Ray Vaughan—⦿: See Master List.

Louis Armstrong—"I tried to pick up something on the guitar from the way he played his trumpet." ⦿: See Master List.

BUDDY GUY'S OWN RECORDINGS

Buddy has long disparaged his earlier recordings, arguing that producers held him back. "I'm not goin' to name names, but [back then] I never got the freedom to say 'Well, let's turn Buddy Guy loose, let him play his own feelings.' And when I got the chance to do that I had my biggest record, which was *Damn Right I got the Blues* (Silvertone)." He's also proud of his most recent record as of this writing, *Heavy Love* (Silvertone), again because he was free to be himself on it: "Nobody's tellin' me nothin'. I'm playin' what I know and not what somebody's teachin' me as I'm recordin'." *Heavy Love* features both *Steve Cropper and Johnny Lang.

Buddy made a number of notable recordings with harmonica player Junior Wells. Of those, he singles out *Hoodoo Man Blues* (Delmark), widely viewed as a classic. "A guy just come got us early in the mornin' and said, 'I want you all to make a record,'" Buddy remembers. "We had no rehearsal or nothin'. We just got a bottle of wine and a couple of cans of beer and went in there and started playin'."

●: Although Buddy's views about his early work are well-known, many of those records are still prized by blues fans and guitarists who worship at Buddy's shrine. Some of the more widely appreciated releases are 1968's *A Man and His Blues* (Vanguard) with a crack back-up band led by pianist Otis Spann and loads of blues wattage even if Buddy's guitar amp is turned down to half-power; *I Was Walking Through the Woods* (MCA/Chess), a selection of early '60s tracks that is one of Buddy's few Chess records in stereo; and 1979's *Pleading the Blues* (Evidence), with Junior Wells. Good compilations include the single-disc *The Very Best of . . .* (Rhino), an 18-track summary of his pre-1990s Silvertone work, and *The Complete Chess Studio Sessions* (2 CDs: MCA/Chess). Since his resurrection on Silvertone, Buddy has frequently mixed in crowd-pleasing pop elements to broaden his appeal. *Slippin' In* and *Live* (both Silvertone) are more to the tastes of blues purists.

HERBIE HANCOCK (September 1, 1996)

When Herbie Hancock pulled away from the Miles Davis Quintet to lead his own groups in 1969, he effectively became the Miles Davis of keyboards. No other jazz artist except Miles navigated the treacherous electrified waters at the confluence of jazz and popular music in the late '60s and early '70s with more commercial and artistic success. And probably no other artist save Miles has endured as many accusations of selling out.

But unlike his former boss, Herbie didn't so much reinvent himself as start a parallel career. Influenced by Stravinsky and Ravel as well as Bill Evans and Sly Stone, he still straddles musical borders today, creating critically acclaimed acoustic jazz projects at the same time he releases albums aimed at the dance club. He may be the most commercially successful jazz artist since the big band era, yet his commitment to the subtler, and thus less popular, textures of acoustic jazz has never waned.

Herbie's first album for Blue Note, 1962's aptly titled *Takin' Off*, announced his arrival as a major composer and contained the soulful hit "Watermelon Man," still one of his most covered tunes. But the following year proved the real turning point. Not only did Herbie record two more outstanding Blue Note releases (*My Point of View* and *Inventions and Dimensions*), but he joined what would become one of the most celebrated and musically important units in jazz history—the Miles Davis Quintet with saxophonist Wayne Shorter, bassist Ron Carter, and drummer Tony Williams. Although he continued his own Blue Note projects during this period, his funk- and soul-inflected contributions to the Davis Quintet helped give birth to fusion on albums like Davis's transitional *Filles de Kilimanjaro* and the rocking *A Tribute to Jack Johnson* (Columbia).

Clearly, you don't work with Davis without learning from the master, but Herbie feels his most significant lesson came from the group's young drummer, Tony Williams, just 17 when he joined the quintet in 1963. "He got recognition sort of as a drummer's drummer," says Herbie, "but he really didn't get the recognition he deserved [for] his impact on the Miles Davis band I was in. The band was in many ways shaped around Tony Williams's style. He was such a great genius, not only of the drums but of music. He opened my eyes to the avant-garde in jazz and in contemporary classical music, too. I learned so much from him about rhythm and what I learned from him really shaped my style."

Herbie left Miles's band just before the fusion watershed record *Bitches Brew* and formed his own electric ensemble, releasing four albums of spacey, adventurous jazz for the Warner Brothers and Columbia labels. The challenging approach taken by the band met with public indifference, in part because of the enormous shadow cast by Davis in his own fusion projects. So Herbie broke the unit up in 1973, quickly forming the Headhunters group with an eye toward constructing a more poppish, funk-fired sound. Their 1973 debut, *Headhunters*, with its dance hit "Chameleon," went platinum, unheard-of territory for a jazz record at that time. While traditional jazz critics predictably savaged it, other music journalists hailed *Headhunters* as an artistic triumph and it remains a classic of its genre.

Herbie continued his two-headed adventures into the 1980s, releasing critically acclaimed acoustic jazz duo albums with Chick Corea and simultaneously assaulting the sales charts with hits like 1983's "Rockit," a dance record jazz fans met with chagrin but whose sonic jump cuts paved new paths in hip-hop. He also scored the Oscar-winning soundtrack to Bertrand Tavernier's 1986 film *Round Midnight* (Columbia) and flirted with world music on an album with Gambian Afropop star Foday Musa Suso. As the 1990s progressed, Herbie pushed his relationship with pop in new directions with a new Headhunters album. But the project that truly sums up Hancock's career is 1995's *The New Standard*. The album features a program of pop tunes written by artists such as Prince and Kurt Cobain, which Herbie morphs into fascinating jazz statements. It's as if he's answering his critics that the only barriers between types of music are the ones that listeners, and writers, choose to build.

HERBIE HANCOCK'S FAVORITE ARTISTS AND RECORDINGS

Miles Davis—*Kind of Blue* (Columbia) and *Miles Ahead* (Columbia). Modestly, Herbie's choices of the greatest Miles albums don't include those he contributed to, but rather a couple of Miles's classics from the late '50s. *Kind of Blue* (Columbia) is the storied session with Bill Evans, John Coltrane, and Cannonball Adderly. *Miles Ahead* is Davis's collaboration with arranger Gil Evans and a 19-piece orchestra.

John Coltrane—*Live at the Village Vanguard* (Impulse), *Giant Steps* (Atlantic), and *A Love Supreme* (Impulse). "*Giant Steps* was a cornerstone album at the time that turned me on a lot. But listening back to the whole repertoire of 'Trane, it sounded like something they did in the studio and only later on that they really developed. For some of the albums, like *Live at the Village Vanguard*, they were in the club, already on tour, and they just let it all hang out." About *A Love Supreme*, Herbie says simply "a very special album." Note that in 1997, Impulse issued a four-disc box of the Village Vanguard sessions that includes all of the material recorded during Coltrane's stint at the Vanguard in '61. The original single-disc release, with much less material, is also available for those on tighter budgets.

Bill Evans—*At the Village Vanguard* (Riverside). This album comprises ten tracks from *Sunday at the Village Vanguard* (Original Jazz Classics) and *Waltz for Debby* (Original Jazz Classics), two widely treasured albums recorded at the same live date. Both are more than worth owning in their own right if you can spring for two discs instead of one, as we're sure Herbie would agree.

Wayne Shorter—"He got recognition as being a master of the tenor saxophone, but he's one of my favorite composers, too," Herbie says of his former bandmate, although he doesn't name a favorite Shorter album. : Shorter's widely acknowledged classic '60s recordings on Blue Note are *JuJu* and *Speak No Evil*. Shorter also co-founded Weather Report; to hear what he's doing in the '90s, check out *High Life* (Verve), which, like Weather Report, emphasizes composition and arrangement over improvisation. Herbie released an introspective album of duets with Shorter, *1+1* (Verve), in 1997.

Weather Report—*Heavy Weather* (Columbia). Although Herbie named this album first, he says any one of this landmark fusion group's albums will do nicely.

Duke Ellington—" 'Diminuendo and Crescendo in Blue' from *Ellington at Newport* (Columbia) is fantastic. It's really a showcase for Paul Gonsalves, with a great live feel. But there are probably other things from Duke that really show off his mastery of orchestration and his own musicality. It's hard for me to pick one." No wonder, as most databases list between 500 and 600 Ellington albums currently available. ⏺: See Master List.

Bud Powell— ⏺ : See Master List.

Charlie Parker—"How am I going to pick one record?" Herbie laments. "*Charlie Parker with Strings* (Verve) is a great one for that kind of juxtaposition of instruments, that kind of setting. There's nothing like it: it's beautiful. It's sort of like a pop record of that era, with this incredible jazz mastery. But his other be-bop things are gorgeous, too." ⏺: See Master List.

Tony Williams— ⏺ : In addition to Williams's wave-making contributions to the Miles Davis Quintet, check out, under Williams's own name, the seminal fusion-fest *The Tony Williams Lifetime* (Polydor), with John McLaughlin, Larry Young, and Jack Bruce, and the two-CD set *Tokyo Live* (Blue Note), which presents Williams with a hard-driving young acoustic band, including pianist Mulgrew Miller and trumpeter Wallace Roney.

Manu Dibango—Herbie loves the songwriting of Cameroon's legendary saxophonist: "He always writes these little ditties that are really catchy." ⏺ : See Master List.

Toure Kunda— ⏺ : See Master List.

*Salif Keita— ⏺ : See the section on Salif and his recordings.

HERBIE HANCOCK'S OWN RECORDINGS

Herbie mentions 1964's *Maiden Voyage* (Blue Note) and 1968's *Speak Like a Child* (Blue Note) first as albums he's proudest of in his own catalog. About *Headhunters* (Columbia), he says, "We did that one right. The band got together, wrote the music together, and played some clubs for a few weeks, and then went into the studio to record. That was better: it got a chance to marinate a little bit, to develop beyond just the initial concepts."

He says *Dis Is Da Drum* (Mercury) "is interesting from a totally different perspective. It's not the perfect record. I think I could make that kind of record better now. I see what the weaknesses are. In spite of that, I think it's a real good record, but it never got much attention."

⊙: Anyone interested in Herbie's electric work should pick up *Mwandishi: The Complete Warner Bros. Recordings* (Warner Archives), which covers Herbie's intriguing pre-Headhunters material for that label. The well-received *New Standards* (Verve)—see description above—marks the continuing evolution of Herbie's jazz/pop synthesizing. On 1998's *Gershwin's World* (Verve), Herbie takes a typically expansive but reverent view of his subject, with vocal help from Stevie Wonder and Joni Mitchell; instrumental assistance from Wayne Shorter, Chick Corea, James Carter, Kenny Garrett, and the Orpheus Chamber Orchestra; and a nod to Duke Ellington and W. C. Handy. The release won two Grammys the following year.

DAVID HARRINGTON (September 30, 1997)

Most musicians trace their first inspiration to a song, the seismic ripple of giants like Elvis or the Beatles, or a powerful music teacher. For David Harrington, leader and first violinist of the Kronos Quartet, the spark was struck by a single note, played by legendary violinist Fritz Kreisler. When he was very young, David heard a record of Kreisler performing "Humoresque." From the vinyl moment when Kreisler first drew his bow across a string, David was so enchanted, he claims, that it not only shaped his approach to music, but to life. "I've even dreamt about that note," David says. "It feels like it's infinitely gentle and infinitely welcoming. It has such a beautiful smile."

In much the same way, David's passion for string quartets was ignited by hearing the series of E-flat major chords at the beginning of Beethoven's *E-flat String Quartet, Op. 127* on a recording by the Budapest Quartet. David says the idea for Kronos came to him in another one of those magic moments: around midnight in August of 1973, when he first heard George Crumb's string quartet composition "Black Angels" on the radio. The piece was "alarming, scary, wonderful, thrilling, and challenging all at once," he recalls. "I simply had to be involved in that."

David founded Kronos in Seattle in 1977. From the beginning, the quartet sought to establish itself as the leading chamber group devoted solely to present-day, forward-looking music. "Leading" turned out to be an understatement: Kronos redrew the classical map. The group has commissioned or inspired hundreds of pieces by contemporary composers, and it exploded the conventions of chamber music performance, often appearing in black leather instead of black tie. Electronics, African percussion, Tuvan throat singers—if the music demanded it, Kronos used it. Audiences quickly came to expect Jimi Hendrix and Terry Riley instead of Haydn and Mozart. And those audiences were sizable, another major surprise. Kronos shattered the notion that gnarly contemporary music couldn't be popular. In its wake, dozens of other ensembles committed to contemporary music have emerged, hoping for similar success.

It's no surprise that David's youthful musical taste extended well beyond Fritz Kreisler and Budapest Quartet records. He rattles off a string of major pop figures who captivated him in his teenage years, from the Beatles, Bob Dylan, Janis Joplin, and Jimi Hendrix to the vintage recordings of Bessie Smith and Billie Holiday. "I remember the girl across the street tried to teach me how to dance— to 'I Wanna Hold Your Hand'—when the Beatles first hit, and it just didn't quite work with me. But by the time I heard *Sgt. Pepper* and the White Album, they seemed like a great quartet," he says.

Kronos has recorded music by scores of contemporary composers, but David says the group's long relationship with minimalist pioneer Terry Riley is probably what shaped the quartet's sound most of all. Riley "enlarged our entire palette of what music is," he says. Working on Riley's music also honed Kronos' inimitable string sound. David's current listening, as any Kronos fan might expect, remains open to new ideas from all cultures. And he's always searching for new compositions for Kronos to tackle. "I spend every little tiny bit of energy I have and all the time I can muster to try to find the next great piece, the next person who might be able to lead all of us somewhere where we haven't been before in music," David says. "I wouldn't trade it for anything. I feel we're in a fortunate position to have a hand in discovering the music of the future."

DAVID HARRINGTON'S FAVORITE ARTISTS AND RECORDINGS

Ludwig van Beethoven—*String Quartet in E-flat, Op. 127.* 🔘: The Budapest Quartet's recordings of the Beethoven String Quartets has just been reissued by Enterprise.

George Crumb—*Black Angels.* 🔘: *The New York String Quartet* (CRI). Kronos also recorded the work (Elektra/ Nonesuch).

Fritz Kreisler—*The Complete Arrangements and Original Works (1903–1938)* (2 CDs: Enterprise) and . . . : *The Early Recordings* (Music & Arts). If you'd like to hear Kreisler's first note in "Humoresque"—and the rest of it—you'll find it on the former recording, a two-CD set. David also points to a number of other short Kreisler compositions, including the "Liebesfreud" and "Liebeslied," included in this package. From the latter disc, David especially loves Kreisler's recording of the Beethoven Violin Concerto in D, Op. 61.

Igor Stravinsky—*The Rite of Spring*, New York Philharmonic/Leonard Bernstein (Sony). "It shook me up," David says about this recording of the modernist classic. "It was the chords, it was the orchestration, it was the rhythmic quality, it was the urgency of that kind of music. Somehow it leapt out of the machine."

Charles Ives—Symphony No. 2, New York Philharmonic/Leonard Bernstein (Sony). "This was the first recording he made with the New York Philharmonic of this symphony. It's just such a marvelous, marvelous approach. Many years later I heard another performance he recorded with the Berlin Philharmonic and it simply wasn't the same at all. I remember that he tried to get Ives to come from Ives's home in Danbury, Connecticut to listen to the [New York Philharmonic's] performance, and Ives didn't do that. But I remember reading the story of Ives hearing it live on the radio, and I guess he danced around the kitchen when he heard it. It was the world premiere of the symphony more than fifty years after it had been written."

Bela Bartok—String Quartets/Juilliard Quartet (Sony) and *Contrasts*, for clarinet, piano and violin/Bartok, Benny Goodman, Joseph Szigeti (Sony). David's first contact with Bartok's six string quartets was the 1950 Juilliard recording; he points to the slow movement of the fifth quartet as particularly exciting. Bartok scored *Contrasts* for clarinet, violin, and piano, and David says don't miss the recording Bartok himself made as pianist, accompanied by violinist Szigeti and jazz clarinetist Goodman: "What an amazing piece, what an amazing group of people— so radically different from each other, and yet somehow they make that piece really work." : Kronos recorded the Quartet No. 3 on *White Man Sleeps* (Elektra/Nonesuch).

Jascha Heifetz—Stylistically poles apart from Fritz Kreisler, Heifetz nonetheless impressed David, and the Heifetz performances he recommends are of Sarasate's *Zigeunerweisen*, and Prokofiev's Second Violin Concerto (particularly the second movement). : Heifetz recorded *Zigeunerweisen* three times: in the acoustic era, with pianist Samuel Chotzinoff, in a version for violin and piano (RCA); with the London Symphony Orchestra conducted by Sir John Barbirolli (RCA); and with the RCA Victor Symphony Orchestra conducted by William Steinberg (RCA). He recorded the Prokofiev concerto twice: with the Boston Symphony under Serge Koussevitzky (RCA), and the Boston Symphony again, conducted by Charles

Munch (RCA). David says Heifetz's tone "sounded like the violin just couldn't play that high. There was something about the way he played those very high notes that made them sound even higher!"

Nusrat Fateh Ali Khan—*En concert a Paris* (Ocora). A friend recommended this three-CD set of the late Pakistani Qawalli singer to David, and he reports the first disc in the set to be "sensational—it changes your life."

Bob Dylan—*Highway 61 Revisited* (Columbia) and *Blonde on Blonde* (Columbia). David especially loves the earlier recordings, "when Dylan was really young and sounded ancient, like a Biblical prophet."

Astor Piazzolla—*Tango: Zero Hour* (American Clave). David calls this recording by the late Argentinean tango master "one of the great moments in ensemble playing. It's such a perfect vision of Piazzolla's music and a realization that is so passionate." : Kronos had a close relationship with Piazzolla. He wrote "Four for Tango" for the quartet (on *Winter Was Hard* [Elektra/ Nonesuch]), and played bandoneon with them on *Five Tango Sensations* (Elektra/Nonesuch).

Santo and Johnny—"Sleepwalk." "Yeah! For me that's right up there with Fritz Kreisler in the heart-on-the-sleeve department." : You'll find this packaged with many other jukebox faves on *Rock Instrumental Classics Volume 1: The Fifties* (Rhino).

Jimi Hendrix—"The Star Spangled Banner." David's introduction to Hendrix came via this legendary guitar meltdown of the National Anthem during his Woodstock appearance: "I don't know how I'd missed out until then. That was just shattering. It's an experience that redefines an instrument and takes it to a level that hadn't been thought of before." : Hear the National Anthem on the big festival four-CD box set, *Woodstock: 3 Days of Peace and Music* (Atlantic) or catch Hendrix's entire set on *Jimi Hendrix: Woodstock* (MCA).

*Pete Seeger—*We Shall Overcome* (Columbia). David finds Seeger "thrilling and inspiring" and calls him "one of my favorite vocalists and forces in music."

Inuit Throat Singers—"These women singers basically blow into each other's throats, and it creates this kind of bellowslike sound, but also just an amazing presence and feeling. At the end of the song, they keel over in this amazing laughter, and not only is the music great, the laughter is as great. It has a very earthy, even sexual sound." : Try *Katutjatut: Throat Singing* by Alacie Tullaugaq and Lucy Amarualik on Inukshuk Records, a label devoted to music by these indigenous people of the Far North.

Diamanda Galas—At the time of our interview, Diamanda Galas was writing a piece for Kronos, and David had just listened to a pre-release copy of her live recording, calling it "some of the highest, deepest, most astonishing singing that there is. Just truly inspiring." ⬤: One of her most powerful works is *Plague Mass* (Mute), about the suffering and tragic politics of the AIDS crisis.

Franz Schubert—"String Quintet in C Major." The first recording of this David remembers included cellist Pablo Casals (Sony), and he says everyone should hear the slow movement of this piece at least once in their lives. Don't procrastinate.

Various artists—*Musique Centrafricaine* (Auvidis). This music, played on horns, comes from the Banda and Linda tribes. "In this particular ensemble there are about eighteen players, and each horn plays just one note," David explains. "And so the music is all interlocking hocketing, and it's just fantastic. And the harmonies! It sounds to me like Schoenberg learned everything he knew from the Banda and Linda people!"

Terry Riley—David speaks enthusiastically about Riley's latest piece for Kronos, a three-quartet work called *Three Requiems*. Riley's seminal minimalist piece, In C, was first recorded, with the composer conducting, in 1968 (CBS). Riley made a later version with the Shanghai Film Orchestra in 1989 (Celestial Harmonies). The Kronos Quartet also appeared on *In C: The 25th Anniversary Concert* (New Albion). Kronos has recorded his *Salome Dances for Peace* (Elektra/Nonesuch) and an excerpt from it, "Half-Wolf Dances Mad in Moonlight," appears on their release *Winter Was Hard* (Elektra/Nonesuch). The group also recorded Riley's "Cadenza on the Night Plain" (Gramavision) on an album of the same name.

Korean Sinawi music— ⬤: *Sinawi Music of Korea* (King).

The Stanley Brothers—"Amazing Grace." ⬤: David heard a live version of this on a friend's tape and doesn't remember the title, but we believe it came from The Stanley Brothers' *Live At the Old Home Place* (Rebel).

Taraf de Haidouks—*Taraf de Haidouks* (Cram World). Taraf is a Rumanian gypsy band.

Bessie Smith with Louis Armstrong—"St. Louis Blues." ⬤: *Essential Bessie Smith* (Sony).

Janis Joplin with Big Brother and the Holding Company—"Ball and Chain" on *Cheap Thrills* (Sony).

Billie Holiday—"Gloomy Sunday." ⬤: *Essence of Billie Holiday* (Sony).

Patsy Cline—"The Wayward Wind." ⬤: *The Patsy Cline Story* (MCA).

The Ink Spots—"I'll Get By As Long As I Have You." ⬤: *Songs That Got Us Through WWII* (Rhino).

Artur Rubinstein playing Chopin— ⬤: *Chopin Favorites* (BMG).

Johann Sebastian Bach—*The Well-Tempered Clavier BMV 846-893*, Glenn Gould (Sony).

Duke Ellington—"East St. Louis Toodle-oo." 🔘: *Okeh Ellington* (Sony).

Thomas Mapfumo—*Corruption* (Mango).

Dick Dale—David loves Dale's surf music in general. 🔘: Catch the big wave on *King of the Surf Guitar: Best of Dick Dale* (Rhino).

DAVID HARRINGTON'S OWN RECORDINGS

True to Kronos's relentless pursuit of the new, David maintains that his favorite Kronos CDs are those they haven't made yet. But he speaks proudly of their recording, with Klezmer clarinetist David Krakauer, of *The Dreams and Prayers of Isaac the Blind* by the Argentinean composer Osvaldo Golijov (Elektra/Nonesuch). He also mentions *Early Music* (Elektra/Nonesuch), a collection of miniatures ranging from the middle ages through contemporary composers like John Cage, Arvo Part, and Moondog.

Looking toward Kronos records yet to be made, David recommends that readers watch out for albums featuring the works of younger composers like Guo Wen-jing from China, Vietnamese-American P. Q. Phan, Aleksandra Vrebelov from Yugoslavia, and, from Mexico, Gabriela Ortiz, of whom David says, "There have been very few people who have ever written a first quartet piece as strong as Gabriela's."

🔘: For a jazzier side of Kronos, listen to their collections of the music of Bill Evans and Thelonious Monk, which were originally issued as separate albums, but now live together on one reissue, the *Complete Landmark Sessions* (2 CDs: 32 Jazz). In 1998, Kronos released *25 Years* (10 CDs: Nonesuch), a chronicle of the group's extraordinary career. The set includes both previously released recordings and nearly a dozen new pieces.

JERRY HARRISON (June 15, 1996)

n popular music, "cutting-edge" usually means "short-lived." But Jerry Harrison has managed to thrive on the edge for over two decades—and from both sides of the mixing console. As a member of Jonathan Richman and the Modern Lovers, he helped shape *The Modern Lovers*, the band's only album and a true cult classic revered by musicians, critics, and the band's fans alike. He played guitar and keyboards for the Talking Heads, one of the most influential bands of the '70s and '80s; in fact, *Rolling Stone*'s Mark Coleman has called him the group's secret weapon. Today, he makes his mark primarily as an in-demand producer, having crafted albums for some of the most highly regarded acts in mainstream and alternative rock.

Jerry grew up in Milwaukee, Wisconsin, a blue collar city that launched the careers of such diverse acts as proto-punks the Skunks, alternative folk-pop faves the Violent Femmes, and Liberace. In the 1960s, Jerry played in local Milwaukee rock bands and, like legions of American rockers, was introduced to American blues music by such British Invaders as the Yardbirds, John Mayall and the Blues Breakers, and Eric Clapton. "There was a cool record called *What's Happenin'* in the 1960s," he recalls. "It was an anthology of English blues-based rock and hard to find. And that, of course, led me to listen to [these musicians'] sources, John Lee Hooker and Robert Johnson, who are fantastic."

Jerry needed no introduction to blues' poppier offspring, R&B. Even before the garage band explosion of the mid-1960s, Jerry was schooling himself in Milwaukee's rich music scene. He started off in R&B groups—"We did James Brown, Rufus Thomas, Major Lance, The Impressions—really wonderful music." But when he landed in Jonathan Richman and the Modern Lovers, he had to reconstitute his musical core. "Jonathan really got me into the Velvet Underground [whose John Cale would produce *The Modern Lovers* album] and the Stooges," Jerry remembers, "and with Jonathan, like with all new bands, much of our focus was rejecting things, saying, 'This is what we're about and these are the only influences we allow and everything else is garbage.' And a large part of what Jonathan was about was rejecting anything that was blues-based."

Blotting out the blues, Jerry believes, made the Modern Lovers one of the principal progenitors of punk: "Punk stylistically had really nothing to do with blues, even though it would use [standard blues] changes. There were no licks in the same way [as blues]. And there was this other core of music that came along that Bo Diddley [really impacted], because he played rhythms and not phrases so much. The Velvet Underground were obviously very influenced by him. Basically, [punk] was very white music. Even though it was into syncopation, it wasn't really connected to black rock 'n' roll. The lyrics were very important, very direct—and sometimes very depressing. You know, 'I'm sitting in my room, there's nothing to do, no fun.' " He laughs, "It really caught a mood."

When Richman's band blew apart, Jerry attended Harvard for awhile before auditioning for the then three-member Talking Heads, who hired him because he could play both rhythm guitar and keyboards. First misunderstood as a punk band, Talking Heads quickly established a reputation as its own one-band category with its odd rhythms, minimalist sound, pure pop instincts, and arty overlay. But the band's name always belied the body music that inspired it, Jerry notes: "Talking Heads started really with R&B, with Al Green, James Brown, and Funkadelic—American music. And then around the time of *Fear of Music*, we picked up some records by Manu Dibango and particularly Fela Kuti . . . We had that song on *Fear of Music*, 'I Zimbra,' and we weren't even going to put it on the record, but we were listening to mixes just before we went on tour, and I said, 'We've got to finish this.' David [Byrne] and I actually flew back from Australia on our way to Europe to finish it. I think we all knew that was the course we were going to take, that the next record [*Remain in Light*] would be more of that. We felt we were going from R&B back to its roots."

Jerry was also going back to his roots in African-based music. With funk and African pop rhythms now part of the weave, Talking Heads began augmenting their roster with African-American musicians like Steve Scales, Alex Weir, and Funkadelic veteran Bernie Worrell. Their final studio release, *Naked*, was made in Paris with a cast of African players.

Parallel to his involvement with Talking Heads, Jerry released three solo albums, one under his own name and two with his side band, the Casual Gods. The records showed off the production skills that would become his primary occupation when Talking Heads disbanded after *Naked*. In his second career, he's demonstrated the same stylistic open-mindedness he displayed as a player. Among the growing list of releases bearing his widely admired stamp are discs by such disparate acts as the Violent Femmes, the BoDeans, Poi Dog Pondering, Crash Test Dummies, General Public, the Bogmen, the Verve Pipe, Black 47, Rusted Root, the Mayfield Four, Kenny Wayne Shepherd, and *Live. "It's odd that after I've done all this world music, I've ended up producing more straight-ahead rock bands," he says. "Now that I've had success with Live, people see I can do that kind of music." As if his versatility was ever in question.

JERRY HARRISON'S FAVORITE ARTISTS AND RECORDINGS

Velvet Underground—*The Velvet Underground & Nico* (Verve), *White Light/White Heat* (Verve), *The Velvet Underground* (Verve), and *Loaded* (Warner Bros.). "The first three albums are just fantastic. And *Loaded* is great. But most of *Loaded* is Doug Ewell singing, rather than Lou Reed. Only 'Sweet Jane' and 'Rock and Roll' are Lou singing. And even though they're Lou's songs and it's a very well-made album that sounds in some ways better than their other records, it lacks the poignancy of having the person who wrote the songs singing." ●: See Master List.

Lou Reed—*New York* (Sire). "For me, Lou wasn't ever as consistently great in his solo albums until *New York* and some of the most recent things, where he has had a great rebirth. He stripped his band down and he found the right production technique to get him really excited."

The Stooges—*Stooges* (Elektra) and *Fun House* (Elektra). Jerry prefers the first two Stooges albums, when the original lineup was intact, although he also loves the songs "Raw Power" and "Search and Destroy" on the third album *Raw Power* (Columbia): "What nobody ever talks about with the Stooges is that they were really kind of polyrhythmic and very syncopated in the Bo Diddley school. And in that way they were a very advanced band, almost sort of a world-beat sound ...I think that when David Bowie started working with Iggy [Pop] [after *Fun House*], even though there were some really great songs, [the music] didn't have that kind of propulsive syncopation that the first two Stooges albums had."

Jimi Hendrix—*Are You Experienced?* (MCA) and *Axis Bold As Love* (MCA). Hendrix's first two records were important influences on Jerry.

*The Soft Machine—*Volumes 1 and 2* (Big Beat). "They became [jazz-rock] fusion after the first record, but their first record sounded kind of demonic—music based on fourths rather than thirds—and it was very frightening, whereas their music got softer after that. I've never been a huge fan of fusion. It seems to me like the worst of both worlds." The above CD combines the Soft's first two records on one disc.

Buddy Holly—*The Buddy Holly Story* (Showpieces). Jerry listened to this album "over and over as a kid."

Fela Kuti—"I've found that of the ethnic music, African music is still what I gravitate to, far more than Brazilian music, which David [Byrne]'s gone off on. It's more direct. And Fela is more aggressive than most of the African music. I mean, I love King Sunny Ade with that sort of light beat, but Fela is more like rock 'n' roll to me, more American-sounding." ●: See Master List.

Manu Dibango—●: See Master List.

JERRY HARRISON'S OWN RECORDINGS

Among records made by bands he's played with, Jerry particularly likes the album with Jonathan Richman, *The Modern Lovers* (Rhino), and two Talking Heads albums, *Fear of Music* and *Remain in Light* (both Sire). About the latter two, he says, "They represent sort of the two periods [of Talking Heads]. I'd say probably my least favorite is *True Stories*, although there are some great songs on it, like 'City of Dreams' and 'Papa Legba.' " Of the records he's produced, Jerry is especially fond of two of the more obscure releases: "Billy Goat's *Bush Roaming Mammals* (Third Rail) is a great record that probably nobody's ever heard of. They're incredibly irreverent. One of their songs is called 'Fuck More, Bitch Less.' I think that's pretty good advice. Another band, Fatima Mansions [*Lost in the Former West* (UNI/MCA)], no one in the United States knows much about. Fatima Mansions takes its name from a particularly odious public housing project in Dublin."

⬤: Jerry's most commercially successful productions so far are the first two multi-platinum albums by *Live, *Mental Jewelry* and *Throwing Copper* (both Radioactive). In 1996, he joined former Talking Heads Chris Frantz and Tina Weymouth to form The Heads, a Byrne-less project that featured lead vocal contributions by Concrete Blonde's Johnette Napolitano, the late Michael Hutchence of INXS, Deborah Harry of Blondie, Ed Kowalczyk of Live, and others. They made one album, *No Talking Just Head* (MCA/Radioactive).

L E V O N   H E L M (December 12 and 14, 1998)

The Band has always been considered remarkable for the way this mostly Canadian group nailed the spirit of Americana. Both lyrically and instrumentally, the group worked in sepia, portraying a largely Southern past when most people made their livings from the land, when a whole town turned out for the carnival rolling through, when King Harvest, not holiday sales, marked the change of a season. But as impressive as the music is, it was never as imagined as legend had it, thanks to the presence of the group's lone American, Levon Helm. In his drum chair, Levon sat both literally and symbolically at the music's center, for many of the songs' images were drawn straight from his childhood in Phillips County, Arkansas.

Levon's father raised cotton; Levon joined the operation in 1949 when he was nine years old, driving a tractor. He got his first guitar the same year. Levon's was a musical family in a musical region, the Mississippi Delta, where blues, R&B, and country songs fueled the hard work necessary to make even a meager living. At high noon, the Helms would tune in radio station KFFA out of nearby Helena to catch Sonny Boy Williamson II (Rice Miller) on the *King Biscuit Time* show. Whenever traveling music shows came through town, the family attended faithfully. Their favorite act in those years was F. S. Walcott Rabbits Foot Minstrels, later evoked in the Band's "W. S. Walcott Medicine Show." When Levon was 10 or 11, he used to hop a ride on a farm truck into Helena to see the *King Biscuit* show live, where he stared drop-mouthed at Williamson's outstanding drummer, Peck Curtis. "That lit the fuse fairly early for me, as far as wantin' to play music, and especially to play drums, them crashes on the cymbals and just the rhythm itself," Levon tells us by phone from his home in Woodstock, New York. "It always looked to me like Peck Curtis was havin' more fun than anybody."

Phillips County produced another notable musician in those years; Harold Jenkins, known later as Conway Twitty. At the Delta Supper Club in Helena, a teenage Levon studied the technique of Jenkins's drummers, Jack Nance and Jimmy "Pork Chop" Markham. He also watched up close the moves of D. J. Fontana in Elvis Presley's band and Carl Perkins's guy, W. S. Holland. He took note of how other excellent bands worked—Muddy Waters's superb units, rockabilly ace Billy Lee Riley's thundering group. Rock 'n' roll was just emerging in those years and Levon attended the birth.

Fast forward several years and Levon is now a crack drummer himself, first in rockabilly singer Ronnie Hawkins's backup group, then in its eventual permutations as Bob Dylan's band, and finally, *the* Band (where he also plays mandolin). But he's still in school in his own mind, learning from records featuring such drum legends as Al Jackson with Booker T. and the MGs and New Orleans session stud Earl Palmer. As the Band gets its sound together, the whole group is marveling at the vocals of the Staple Singers, arranged by Levon's fellow Mississippi Deltian, *Roebuck "Pop" Staples. "Those were our heroes, was the Staple Singers," Levon recalls. "We thought they were the best. Richard [Manuel], Rick [Danko], and myself, we'd swap verses and then the rest of us would do the background, like the Staple Singers. Probably not as good, but we was aimin' at it, anyway," Levon laughs.

Today, a new generation of musicians listens to Levon and the Band as faithfully and awestruck as he once did his own idols. He feels plenty flattered but a bit too far up the lineage. "Tell any of the younger players that think that this is gonna be their life to not pay any attention to me, to go straight to the horse's mouth and listen to it themselves—hear it the way I heard it," he says to us. The horse is hitched immediately below.

LEVON HELM'S FAVORITE ARTISTS AND RECORDINGS

Sonny Boy Williamson II— 🔘 : See Master List.

Muddy Waters—Late in his life, Waters cut an album in Woodstock with Levon, the Band's Garth Hudson, and Paul Butterfield contributing alongside Muddy, Pinetop Perkins, and Bob Margolin. Levon called it "a dream come true." 🔘 : See Master List. The album with Levon is called *The . . . Woodstock Album* (Chess).

Conway Twitty—"In my own humble opinion, Conway Twitty had one of the best bands in the Memphis area during that early fifties period." 🔘 : *The Rock 'n' Roll Years* (8 CDs: Bear Family) provides an exhaustive collection of Twitty's rockabilly years from 1956 through the early '60s. For a single-disc sampler, go for *Rockin' Conway: The Best of the MGM Years* (Mercury).

Elvis Presley—Levon liked Presley's band best after drummer D. J. Fontana joined, but one of his favorite Presley tracks is "Milkcow Blues Boogie" from before Fontana's tenure: "Damned if Bill Black doesn't slap that bass fiddle in such a way that he's playin' the bass and drum backbeat part. And with Scottie Moore usin' that echo on his guitar and playin' the style that he plays, plus Elvis's six-string Martin. It wasn't no damn prop back then for Elvis. Elvis played the shit out of that guitar." 🔘 : "Milkcow" is on *The Complete Sun Sessions* (RCA). You can hear Fontana's work on *The King of Rock 'n' Roll: The Complete '50s Masters* (5 CDs: RCA) or such classic early albums as *Elvis* and *Elvis Presley* (both RCA).

Little Richard—Richard's singles were "some of the first of what I called jukebox hits. They had to be good if you heard them on the radio or on the jukebox." 🔘 : See Master List.

Carl Perkins—Levon loved the sound of Perkins's early bands. 🔘 : See Master List.

Billy Lee Riley— 🔘 : See Master List.

*Booker T. and the MGs—"American heroes to me. They could make their own records or they could help you make the best one you ever made." 🔘 : See the section on Steve Cropper and his recordings.

Otis Redding— 🔘 : See Master List.

*The Staple Singers—Levon and the Band kept up with all the Staple's recordings, but "Respect Yourself" topped Levon's list: "Boy, does *Pop and *Mavis sing that damn thing." 🔘 : See the sections on Roebuck "Pop" Staples and Mavis Staples and their recordings.

Jimmy Reed— 🔘 : See Master List.

Chuck Berry—"Deep Feeling" on *After School Sessions* (Chess). "A slow blues instrumental that's beautiful," Levon comments about this obscure track on Berry's debut album.

Bobby "Blue" Bland—Levon happened to be upstairs making a record with Ronnie Hawkins at the same studio where Bland was making his classic "Turn on Your Lovelight" downstairs: "I couldn't stay on the floor when that band was cuttin' that day. Wasn't that a righteous record, man?" 🔘 : See Master List.

Junior Parker— 🔘 : See Master List.

Jimmy McCracklin—"I always thought that Otis and the whole Stax company really took a page from Jimmy McCracklin, because Jimmy McCracklin had that Memphis sound, with horns and a good rhythm section at least ten or twelve years before that." 🔘 : *I Just Gotta Know* (Imperial), . . . : *The Mercury Recordings* (Bear Family), and *Blast 'Em Dead* (Ace) all feature some top sides from the late '50s to give you a feel for what Levon is saying.

Tina Turner—*Wildest Dreams* (Virgin). "Tina Turner keeps cuttin' better and better records. *Wildest Dreams* is just a whole brand new flavor of rock 'n' roll. You know, Tina's all-American, and she's cuttin' with all these European cats [including Sting]. It sounds like they're playin' their hearts out on some very good damn rock 'n' roll, man. It obviously ain't from Memphis, but damn, that don't hurt it none."

***Little Feat—**"Still one of the best bands goin'." 🔘 : See the sections on Paul Barrere and Bill Payne and their recordings.

***Los Lobos—**"There's no better singer anywhere than the guy [David Hidalgo] with Los Lobos. I love them guys," says Levon, who appears on the group's *The Neighborhood* (Slash). 🔘 : See the sections on David Hidalgo and Louie Perez and their recordings.

Bob Dylan—*Nashville Skyline* and *Pat Garrett and Billy the Kid [soundtrack]* (both Columbia). "He's turned himself into a decent bandleader. He don't strum no more. Bobby plays an electric guitar. He plays like [*Steve] Cropper plays. He's really part of the rhythm section. Oh man, I love the way Bob has led his band."

LEVON HELM'S OWN RECORDINGS

In his 1993 book, *This Wheel's on Fire* (Morrow), Levon detailed how acrimony, greed, and music-business politics destroyed the Band's music at its creative peak. When we speak, he repeats the charge, first made there, that the Band's songs, almost universally credited to Robbie Robertson alone, were often collaboratively composed: "I'll tell you who's got the best punch lines outa all of them, lyric-wise, was Richard [Manuel]. Robbie and Richard were probably the best lyricists, but that doesn't mean that somebody else don't think of something every now and then. And everybody put the music together. We'd cut one and tear it up and go back and start all over. We had to do it like that a lot of times because you gotta find out where the tune lives, you know, if you gonna bring it to life."

To Levon's mind, the group made two excellent albums, 1968's *Music from Big Pink* and 1969's *The Band*, and half of a third, *Stage Fright* (all Capitol) before conflicts over publishing rights diluted the spirit of the music. But if the communal vigor of their best songs had been destroyed, they could still make good live discs—and needed to, because they still owed Capitol a bunch of albums. Levon likes the results on *Rock of Ages* (2 CDs: Capitol), recorded on New Year's Eve 1971, with horn arrangements by Allen Toussaint.

Levon also loves all the records the Band made with Dylan: the gloriously frivolous *The Basement Tapes*, *Planet Waves*, and the live *Before the Flood* (all except *Planet* 2 CDs: all Columbia). He's always enjoyed Dylan's ad hoc recording and performing style: "I like to go like that, just no plan, and play it all by ear. He's as good at it as anybody I know."

⦿ : It's hard to argue with Levon that the Band's first two studio albums present the group at its all-too-brief peak. But *Stage Fright*, while more fragmented, is also a thrilling listen from start to finish. True Band fans will also want the better of the albums that followed, despite the reduced candlepower. Those include *Moondog Matinee*, a set of early rock 'n' roll covers; *Northern Lights Southern Cross*; and, of course, *The Last Waltz* (2 CDs), which documents the group's farewell concert with an all-star roster of guest participants, including Dylan, Joni Mitchell, Eric Clapton, Muddy Waters, Van Morrison, Paul Butterfield, and Neil Young. All of the foregoing are on Capitol. Levon, Hudson, and Danko plus some new sidekicks began playing together again under the name the Band in the early '90s. Their releases include *Jericho* and *High on the Hog* (both Rhino) and *Jubilation* (River North).

The Band had a different character—looser, edgier, harder rocking—when working with Dylan. You can hear that difference to superb effect on *The Basement Tapes* and *Bob Dylan Live 1966* (2 CDs: Columbia). Note however, that Levon is not the drummer on the latter set. He had returned home during the leg of Dylan's tour when this show was recorded. Micky Jones is the drummer for this gig.

"TOOTS" HIBBERT (November 24, 1997)

Nearly everyone who hears the gritty, soulful singing of reggae legend Frederick "Toots" Hibbert gets the same thrilling impression—Otis Redding-plus-patois. But while the resemblance is unmistakable, it isn't so much a case of one man reflecting his idol as two trees growing in the same soil. Like Redding, Toots's youth was steeped in African-American gospel music. "My mother and father took me to the Seventh Day Adventist Church," Toots tells us when we reach him with a wee-hours phone call to Jamaica. "I listened to Mahalia Jackson when I was small, about eight, nine, ten. I grew up listening to gospel." The churchy soul music of Ray Charles also made a huge impression on him, Toots says. By the same token, Toots also grew up loving the crooning country hits of Jim Reeves, a sure stumper for anyone trying to guess his influences.

Toots spent his early boyhood in the Jamaican countryside but hit funky Kingston at age 11, in the pre-reggae days. There he became a fan of eventual reggae superstars Jimmy Cliff and Bob Marley as well as Owen Grey and Alton Ellis, pioneers of rock steady, reggae's immediate predecessor. In the early 1960s, he formed the Maytals with Nathaniel "Jerry" Mathias and Raleigh Gordon. The vocal trio then surfed the changes of the evolving Jamaican pop scene as the music morphed from jittery ska to the more loping rock steady and finally to the ganja grooves of reggae. The group scored with the public from the beginning and Toots soon took his place alongside his heroes as one of the stars of Jamaican music. "In those days it was just Wailers and Maytals. Then it was *Bob Marley* and the Wailers and *Toots* and the Maytals," he laughs.

Not only was Toots on the scene when the music was born but he seems to have given it its name. The term "reggae" apparently sprung from the Maytals' late-1960s single "Do the Reggay," penned by Toots. "People who were listening to the reggae beat didn't know what to call it," he notes. "Some people called it blue beat, some called it boogie beat, some called it all different kind of names." Still, he claims his only design with "Reggay" was to make a hit record: "People told me that they saw it that I was the inventor of the word 'reggae.' I was shocked with that."

In an effort to take control of his music from the notoriously rapacious Jamaican studio system, Toots now produces his own recordings and has started his own record label. Our interview with him occurred during a break from recording a new album, and just after the release of the album *Recoup* (Artists Only/Allason). He also plans to search for new talent for his company. "I want to sign real artists who make good lyrics and make sure that the songs are really intelligent," he says, true to the model he's established with his own music. He plans for *Recoup* to be the first in a series of both old Maytals material and new songs. "There's goin' to be a whole lot of recoupin' going on," he assures us.

TOOTS HIBBERT'S FAVORITE ARTISTS AND RECORDINGS

Mahalia Jackson— 🔘 : See Master List.

Ray Charles—Toots recommends "all of his songs, really. I'm just a Ray Charles fan!" 🔘 : See Master List.

Jim Reeves—Reeves may be a surprise choice to Maytals fans, but the country-pop sensation, one of the first of Nashville's lush-sounding crossover stars, enjoyed massive worldwide popularity in the '50s and '60s (he died in a plane crash in 1964 at the age of 39). 🔘 : You can sample Reeves's biggest hits on *He'll Have to Go & Other Hits* (RCA) or catch a more complete career retrospective on the two-disc *Welcome to My World: The Essential Jim Reeves Collection* (RCA).

Jimmy Cliff—"Hurricane Hattie" and "Lie and See." 🔘 : "Hurricane Hattie" was Cliff's first hit single, in 1962, but neither this nor "Lie," the two Cliff ska songs Toots heard when he first arrived in Kingston, appear to have been reissued yet. Cliff subsequently scored many enormously popular hits. You can hear several of his best performances—"Sitting in Limbo," "You Can Get It If You Really Want It," "Many Rivers to Cross," and the title song—on the fabulous soundtrack to the film *The Harder They Come* (Mango), which starred Cliff. (Toots and the Maytals's great song "Pressure Drop" also appears on the album.) Many later hits, plus these songs, are collected on *Reggae Greats* (Mango).

Bob Marley and the Wailers— 🔘 : The best single-disc compilation is *Legend* (Island), but to hear some of the Wailers earlier songs from the 1960s, when Toots would have first heard the group, *One Love at Studio One* (Heartbeat) is the album to buy. The four-CD box set *Songs of Freedom* (Tuff Gong) contains a rich collection of unusual Marley recordings. *Catch a Fire*, *Burnin'*, *Natty Dread*, and *Live* (all Tuff Gong) are crucial albums from the mid-'70s.

Judy Mowatt, Rita Marley, and Marcia Griffiths (The I-Threes)—Mowatt, Marley, and Griffiths formed the I-Threes in 1974 and did back-up vocals on Bob Marley's concert tours. But all three had successful solo careers independent of Marley, and Toots loves their work. 🔘 : Judy Mowatt's strong debut *Black Woman* (Shanachie) remains her best. Rita Marley's *Who Feels It Knows It* and *We Must Carry On* (both Shanachie), the latter recorded with former Wailers As-ton Barrett and Tyrone Downie, give a good accounting of her recent work. Of the three women, Marcia Griffiths has the biggest profile in Jamaican music, her string of hits extending back to her teen years. Her early hits are collected on *Naturally* (Shanachie), and her big '80s hit "Electric Boogie" is on *Carousel* (Mango). Also check out *Marcia* (RAS), which features members of Third World.

Alton Ellis—Ellis's career dates back to the late '50s, but his main contribution to the evolution of Jamaican music came in the '60s. As the frenetic beat of ska decelerated to rock steady, Ellis drove the bus. ⬤: *Cry Tough* (Heartbeat) is the Ellis collection to buy.

Owen Grey—Grey is another rock steady pioneer who inspired the young Toots Hibbert. ⬤: To sample Grey's music, try the two-CD collection *Ska Bonanza: The Studio One Years* (Heartbeat), which features tracks by Grey, Alton Ellis, and others.

TOOTS HIBBERT'S OWN RECORDINGS

Toots says he still enjoys most of his songs, but especially recommends his albums *Pass the Pipe* (Mango) and *Reggae Got Soul* (Mango).

⬤: For a comprehensive listen to Toots's years with the Maytals, the two-CD set *Time Tough: Anthology* (Island) contains material from every phase of the band's career. The Maytals's first major-label U.S. release, *Funky Kingston* (Mango), is one of the greatest reggae albums ever. *Ska Father* (Artists Only), from 1999, including a ska rendition of the Kinks's "You Really Got Me," shows that Toots remains one of the most tastefully soulful vocalists in popular music. And not to be missed is *Toots in Memphis* (Mango), an album of classic American soul tunes that Toots cut with a group of elite reggae and Memphis studio pros. His natural affinity with American R&B yields some marvelous performances and the grooves are state-of-the-art.

DAVID HIDALGO (May 28, 1997)

Los Lobos may be one of the more unpredictable bands in American music, but you never needed tea leaves to tell the future of key Lobo David Hidalgo. From an early age, blues and rock guitar instrumentals knocked David sideways: the hits "Cannonball" and "Rebel Rouser" by rock trailblazer Duane Eddy, later, the hit blues singles "Hide Away" by Freddie King and "Frosty" by Albert

Collins, not to mention such other extended guitar workouts as B. B. King's paean to his guitar, "Lucille," and Albert King's crowd-stroking "Blues Power."

David's family also filled his ears with other roots-based music that would later surface in Los Lobos. One older brother was a jazzbo—"I would sit with him and his buddies. They would drink beer and they'd give me ginger ale," David recalls. "He was into Miles [Davis], Dizzy Gillespie, and the Jazz Crusaders and Coltrane, too." Another older brother was listening to Dinah Washington and David's parents were spinning discs by colorful bandleader Louis Prima. "All that stuff stayed with me and helped develop my taste in music," David says.

In the early 1960s, the youngest of David's three older brothers joined a band. "The way the bands were in East L.A. at the time, they played everything. They played the hits of the day, and they would play Mexican music—the ballads, the *cumbias*, the *rancheras*, the polkas." They also played a little swing and Chuck Berry, but "James Brown was the main thing," says David. "That was tops of the pops in those days. So when I first got a guitar, I'd sit in my bedroom with the door closed and the guitar unplugged. They'd be playing in the front room and I'd be playing along, trying to figure out what they were doing. They were playing 'Prisoner of Love,' 'Out of Sight,' 'Poppa's Got a Brand New Bag,' 'Try Me'—all that great James Brown stuff . . . Before the Beatles, James Brown was *it*."

Not that Beatlemania passed David by. Around 1965, he bought a Beatles songbook, *The Golden Beatles*, and began trying to learn the songs—discovering, of course, the pop-songbook curse: Most of the chords were wrong. The country influence that would express itself so affectingly on songs like Hidalgo/Perez's "One Time, One Night" had sunk in by this time, too. A number of country stars, including Ernest Tubb and Buck Owens, hosted their own shows on Los Angeles's Channel 13. "I used to watch Ernest Tubb and Buck Owens every Saturday," says David. "Me and my brothers would be sitting there in our pajamas eating cereal and watching Buck Owens. That's when I first learned to love country music . . . I just liked the guitar playing and got into it from there."

The blues also won over David, via the tube. David was watching Steve Allen's talk show one afternoon when guest B. B. King performed "Sweet Little Angel." "When he shook the strings, the lights hitting his palm would flash, and I thought, 'Wow!' I'd never seen anybody shake a string like that. The whole package just hit me, what the band was wearing, everything. It was just too cool." English blues rockers like Eric Clapton and John Mayall provided another education about the homegrown music that most American players had ignored. "In interviews, they would mention people like Otis Rush, Slim Harpo, Muddy

Waters, Buddy Guy, Albert King, Freddie King," David remembers. "So I started looking into those records and really getting into it."

In 1967, one of David's brothers brought home a couple of new albums, including Canned Heat's first, which gave David another course in the blues. But it was the other record in the bag—Jimi Hendrix's *Are You Experienced*—that made the biggest dent, fracturing everything David had concluded about music until then. "Nothing was as strong as Hendrix," says David. "There's no end to what he had inside of him that he had to get out."

Ironically, it was a Jewish guy from Southern California who led David back to the popular music of his own culture. Frank Zappa, who began his career as a doo-wop producer in a small studio in Cucamonga, was also lacing his Mothers of Invention records with doo-wop. "He was using all this slang . . . , this mixture of English and Spanish and made-up words that were characteristic of the East Side and it was like, 'Wow, man, somebody else knows what's going on over here,'" says David. "It made me feel proud and appreciate my own neighborhood more than before. I started paying attention to early-'50s doo-wop and stuff like that, songs like 'Cherry Pie,' 'Night Owl,' 'Eddie, My Love,' the typical R&B ballads, 'Daddy's Home,' 'A Thousand Miles Away,' that kind of stuff." It would take another 15 years of woodshedding and low-rent gigging, but eventually millions who never before realized they loved Mexican-American music would be lavishing the same kind of attention on David and Los Lobos.

DAVID HIDALGO'S FAVORITE ARTISTS AND RECORDINGS

The Yardbirds—"It was the first psychedelic stuff I heard even before it was called psychedelic . . . I would buy the Yardbirds' singles . . . the B sides were always better than the A sides. Jeff Beck did some stuff that nobody had done." : *Roger the Engineer* (Edsel) and *Greatest Hits, Vol. I (1964–1966)* (Rhino). The latter features both Beck and Eric Clapton on guitars, the former Beck only.

Music Machine—"Talk Talk." "That was a big one for me," says David about this early psychedelic hit song. : *Best of the Music Machine* (Rhino) contains "Talk Talk," more highlights from the band's first LP, and other well-chosen sides, some previously unreleased.

James Brown—See above. : See Master List.

Canned Heat—*Canned Heat* (Liberty). David loves Henry Vestine's guitar playing for the band.

Jimi Hendrix—*Axis Bold as Love* (Reprise). David finds something of value in everything Hendrix recorded but this album tops his list.

Jethro Tull—*This Was* (Chrysalis). The jazz and folk textures of this debut album contrast mightily with the arena-rock of later releases.

Cream—*Fresh Cream, Disraeli Gears, Wheels of Fire* (all Polydor). Cream's three primary albums before the inevitable slide downhill are all favorites of David's.

Frank Zappa—*Freak Out* (Rykodisc) and *Cruising with Reuben and the Jets* (Rykodisc).

Thee Midnighters—Like his buddy Louie Perez and countless other aspiring musicians in East L.A., David looked to this local band and their lead singer, crooner Little Willie G., for inspiration. Listening to Thee Midnighters as well as the records of Richie Valens and fellow East L.A.-ers Cannibal and the Headhunters helped nudge the then-acoustic Lobos towards rock and roll. 🎵: See Master List.

Stevie Wonder—*Music of My Mind* (Motown). "It had that free spirit. He was having a great time and you could hear it. He was liberated. He had to wait until he was twenty-one to have full control of his music and he went wild, and you could feel it. The spirit of that record has a lot to do with how I try to look at music now. You 'play' music. It's not work . . . If you can keep that going, the music will stay fresh."

Marvin Gaye—*What's Going On* (Motown). "That first side, I couldn't listen to it without crying," says David, whose voice breaks a little while recalling the music.

Richie Valens—"When I was a kid, his music was around. He'd already died by the time I was old enough to pay attention but 'La Bamba' was at every wedding and 'Donna' and 'Let's Go' you heard all the time. I took it for granted, but it wasn't until later on that we realized how important he was. There wouldn't have been any 'Twist and Shout' or [a number of other songs] without 'La Bamba.' " 🎵: *The Very Best of Richie Valens* (Del Fi).

*The Blasters—*American Music* (Hightone). "It was just ballsy, in-your-face. And great songs, too," says David. Like Louie Perez, David acknowledges the Lobos' huge debt to the Blasters for helping to put them in the national spotlight and for an enduring friendship that included many late nights marinating in Phil and *Dave Alvin's collection of blues 78s.

Ernest Tubb—David liked Tubb, an early popularizer of the electric guitar, for his outstanding band and humorous personality. 🎵: See Master List.

Buck Owens—David loved the twin Fender Telecaster attack of Buck and lead guitarist Don Rich, who also played fiddle. ⬤: *Live at Carnegie Hall* (Country Music Foundation) captures a lively show from 1966, just past David's pj's-and-cereal years. *The Buck Owens Collection (1959–90)* (Rhino) is a comprehensive three-disc set. Either volume of *Very Best of . . . , Vols. 1–2* (Rhino) provides a good single-disc introduction.

B. B. King—*Lucille* (MCA). This late-'60s release includes B.B's eight-minute tribute to his guitar.

Otis Rush—*Door to Door (with Albert King)* (Chess). This compilation features King on more than half the tracks, but includes some powerful Rush sides as well.

Slim Harpo—*Scratch My Back: The Best of Slim Harpo* (Rhino). David first became acquainted with this blues guitarist and harmonica player through his hit singles but praises the quality of the Rhino compilation, which contains all of Harpo's hits, with improved sound.

Albert King—*Live Wire/Blues Power* (Stax). This classic was recorded live at San Francisco's Fillmore Auditorium in 1968. "We could listen to 'Blues Power' and do the rap with him, the whole dialogue," recalls David.

Freddie King—"Hide Away" on *Let's Hide Away and Dance Away* (King). "Hide Away" was one of King's first hit singles and became his signature piece. ⬤: The song also appears on *Hide Away: The Best of Freddie King* (Rhino).

Muddy Waters—*Folk Singer* (MCA/Chess). David enjoys nearly everything Muddy Waters ever recorded but likes this one, an acoustic trio album with Willie Dixon and a teenage Buddy Guy, the best.

Albert Collins—"Frosty." "That song really knocked me out." ⬤: *Truckin' with Albert Collins* (MCA) includes "Frosty," a million-selling single for Collins in 1962, and other early work.

Clifton Chenier—*Louisiana Blues and Zydeco* (Arhoolie). David hadn't heard of Chenier when he first spotted this 1965 release at a used record store in Santa Monica. "I said, 'Whoa, blues on accordion—that sounds good to me!' "

*Dr. John—*Gris Gris* (Repertoire, out of print). Deep Louisiana voodoo mysticism, New Orleans R&B, and '60's psychedelia find a wonderfully eerie meeting place.

Fairport Convention—*Full House* (Hannibal). "It had a bigger influence on the Lobos than we would have thought. The whole idea of mixing the folk music with rock and really doing it. The Byrds kind of did that but it was more like a singer/songwriter sort of thing. But doing jigs and reels with electric instruments, that had a big impact on me."

Harry Partch—David was as affected by a film about Partch on PBS as his various recordings. A true American original, Partch created unique tonal systems, performed on his beautiful homemade instruments. : See Master List.

Ornette Coleman—*Dancing in Your Head* (A&M). *Dancing* was Coleman's first recording with his electric band, Prime Time. David said Prime Time was even more powerful when seen live: "Prime Time was two drummers, two bass players, two electric guitarists and he had them set up like two trios with him in the middle. It was amazing. It was this free-for-all, free-spirited thing. And it wasn't scary, either. It was like 'Check this out. You might dig this.' "

Incredible String Band—*The Incredible String Band* (Elektra) and *Earth Span* (Island). David liked their early albums in general but mentioned these two, from 1966 and 1972 respectively, first: "They influenced us in their do-it-yourself attitude. They wanted to hear a sitar so they went out and got one. A flute, recorder, [same thing]."

Thelonious Monk—*Thelonious Alone in San Francisco* (Original Jazz Classics), *Solo Monk* (Columbia), *Underground* (Columbia), and *The Thelonious Monk Orchestra at Town Hall* (Original Jazz Classics). "Again [like Ornette], he heard things differently from everyone else but he was friendly about it. He was having a good time."

Duke Ellington—: David was unsure of the title of his favorite Ellington disc, but we believe from the way he described it that it was *Early Ellington (1927–1934)* (RCA Bluebird).

Rafael Cortijo—*Sabor Boricua* (RCA). David found this record from the early 1960s in a bin at a used record store in East L.A. "The pop music of Puerto Rico from the sixties. It had the Puerto Rican rhythms—like the *plena* and the *bomba*. That stuff really hit me." : We could not find an in-print version of this LP, which David says was on RCA. The current version of Cortijo's original band is called El Gran Combo and is led by pianist/composer/arranger Rafael Ilthier. For a strong sample of its work, start with *Nuestra Música* (Combo).

Andres Huesca—Huesca is a harp player from Veracruz, says David. "His were some of the earliest recordings of that style of music, from the 1940s. He was amazing." : We could not find available recordings by Huesca.

Lino Chavez—Chavez played a style of music known as *son jarocho*, from Veracruz, Mexico. : He can be heard on the compilation *Colección del siglo* (RCA International)

DAVID HIDALGO'S OWN RECORDINGS

David has special affection for all the Los Lobos albums, starting with *Just Another Band from East L.A.*, produced on a shoestring budget and released by tiny New Vista Records. (Three vibrant tracks, all acoustic traditional Mexican music, appear on *Just Another Band from East L.A.—A Collection* [Slash/Warner Bros.], a marvelous compilation that samples all the group's albums through *Kiko*.) About *How Will the Wolf Survive?*, David says, "That was the first complete record. We'd started to get more into songwriting, and the song 'Will the Wolf Survive?' was the last song we wrote for the album. It was the bridge to [the next album], *By the Light of the Moon*."

Los Lobos then contributed several tracks, including the title song, to the soundtrack of the Richie Valens bio-flick, *La Bamba,* released in 1987. The *La Bamba* record became a monster success. David describes the period of that album through 1990's *The Neighborhood* as "a blur" but it also resulted in *La Pistola y El Corazon*, a delightful return to acoustic Mexican folkloric music. Critics branded the move commercial suicide, not without reason considering it was the follow-up to *La Bamba*. However, it convinced any remaining doubters that Los Lobos' integrity was incorruptible. Hidalgo says simply, "That was something we had to do at the time."

In spite of their mighty efforts to resist commercial pressures, Hidalgo acknowledges the band took years to recover its sense of purpose after *La Bamba*. But "*Kiko* did that. We started working with Mitchell [Froom] and Tchad [Blake]. They reminded us you can be a kid, you can have fun. If you want to take it a little further than most people would, that's okay. That helped us get fired up again." David describes *The Latin Playboys*, his side project with Louie Perez that followed *Kiko*, as "another big step in just letting go and letting the music happen. That was done at home on a four-track cassette. The music had no intention of being the next record or demo for Los Lobos. It was just putting the ideas down as they come and not worry about it and that's why the record has the feeling it does." He feels just as strongly about *Colossal Head*, the band's 1996 release that continues the sonic experiments on *Kiko* and *The Latin Playboys*. "I think [all three are] big steps for us," he states.

⏺: Los Lobos has never made a weak record. Complete your set. (All Los Lobos albums except the 1983 EP *And a Time to Dance* (Slash) are mentioned by David above.)

A N D R E W   H I L L   (October 5, 1997)

Perhaps someone with a weird shoe size would understand. Jazz writers have divided the music into at least 20 subgenres to accommodate all its styles, and Andrew Hill doesn't really fit in any of them. Andrew's unique harmonic language and rhythmic innovations earned him the mantle of the avant-garde—indeed, his Blue Note recordings from the '60s sound cutting-edge 30 years later. But his melodic gifts clearly set him apart from the iconoclastic free playing of the '60s and '70s. With such an unusual mix of attributes, Andrew confused critics—one prominent jazz scribe labeled Andrew as "alternative avant-garde"—and defied jazz conventions and fashions. He still does.

Born in Chicago in 1937, Andrew grew up in one of the country's richest musical environments. However, in the Windy City of the 1940s, an exploding urban blues scene overshadowed jazz. Andrew remembers his birthplace as home to a number of startling jazz musicians, but their music was poorly documented. "A lot of the players I would recommend from my days in Chicago never recorded!" he says. "I came up in an era when everybody in my high school had some type of horn—so many people played. And a lot of them struck on very unique, individual styles."

Because his own style was equally original, Andrew didn't turn to records for inspiration. Instead, he used them more as tools, "just to identify and research a certain type of sound," he says. He mined the works of earlier piano giants like Fats Waller, Erroll Garner, and Earl Hines (a dominant figure in Chicago in the '30s and '40s), and made sure to include the requisite Thelonious Monk and Bud Powell. He fell in love with be-bop, and the blowing of saxophonists Charlie Parker and Wardell Gray and trumpeter Clifford Brown in particular. He learned blues changes from Pat Patrick, the long-time Sun Ra sideman. But most of Andrew's musical education came via his fellow musicians as he gigged around Chicago, and from an inner harmonic vocabulary completely his own.

The one notable exception to this rule came from another musical galaxy. In a Chicago hotel lobby, Andrew chanced upon the neo-classical German composer Paul Hindemith. The conversation they struck up led to Hindemith tutoring Andrew in formal composition. To this day Andrew finds their relationship curious. He remembers Hindemith as "a kind, gentle person. I don't know what attracted him to me, or vice versa, where he could recognize my talent and I would feel comfortable letting him into my world." But Hindemith taught the young jazz pianist valuable lessons about "harmony and a combination of sounds. And he respected my idea of approaching music as a rhythm, with melody and harmony being rhythm. He showed me in a sense how to write music, create melodies and stuff, away from the piano."

Andrew continues to explore music with a harmonic and rhythmic vision that remains fresh, so he finds the interest that the current jazz generation takes in his older work somewhat ironic. Oddly conservative, they seem far more intrigued by his Blue Note recordings from 30 and more years ago than anything he's done since. "In my time, the people who were sterile, to a certain extent, were the older musicians because people were holding on to past styles," Andrew notes. He needn't add that now that he's one of those older musicians, the stereotype no longer applies.

ANDREW HILL'S FAVORITE ARTISTS AND RECORDINGS

Earl "Fatha" Hines—*Earl Hines: Solo Piano* (Laserlight). You normally find releases from Laserlight, a budget CD label, in discount department stores, but this bargain is worth the search, says Andrew, who calls the disc the best Hines CD he's encountered. Of "Fatha" Hines, he says simply, "He will always be in my house."

Charlie Parker—*Now's the Time* (Verve). Andrew sat in with Parker in the 1950s, and he loves this 1957 Bird quartet recording.

Thomas "Fats" Waller—Although their styles differ radically from each other, Andrew groups pianists Waller, Thelonious Monk, and Bud Powell together because they formed part of his self-education. "By the time I heard them I was already playing," he notes. "I had already developed some type of formula so I could play. They weren't part of my reference because there were so many people around me in Chicago who were playing. [They] became important to me after I became more literate, in a sense." 🔘: See Master List.

Thelonious Monk— 🔘: *Brilliant Corners* (Riverside), *Thelonious Monk with John Coltrane*, *Monk's Music*, *Thelonious Himself*, and *Alone in San Francisco* are some of Monk's best-loved records for Riverside. *The Complete Blue Note Recordings* (Blue Note), a four-CD set, presents an earlier look at this giant, with his remarkable compositional abilities already fully mature. *At the Five Spot* (Milestone) features one of Monk's better quartets with saxophonist Johnny Griffin.

Bud Powell— 🔘: See Master List.

Paul Hindemith—"I really didn't know who he was, or his music, until maybe ten years after [I met him]," Andrew admits. "I listened to his music later because I appreciated his attention." 🔘: Andrew doesn't recommend specific Hindemith compositions, but the Symphony: *Mathis der Maler* probably remains his most often-performed work. Look for Claudio Abbado's version with the Berlin Philharmonic (Deutsche Grammaphon) or Leonard Bernstein with the Israel Philharmonic (Deutsche Grammaphon). Also try the tenderly elegaic *Trauermusik* for viola and orchestra with Hindemith himself as the viola soloist (Biddulph). And if you want to try to tease out any influence the composer had on Andrew's music, explore the small group *Kleine Kammermuzik* in versions with the Bergen Wind Quintet (BIS) or the Swiss Wind Quintet (Discover International), and Hindemith's solo piano music, including his three piano sonatas performed by Glenn Gould (Sony).

Erroll Garner—"I just liked the sound, the fullness he got out of playing the piano. I had heard other people around Chicago, like Earl 'Fatha' Hines, play stride piano. But the way Garner approached the piano, it wasn't stride. He would play countermelodies and counterrhythms in both hands." ●: Garner's discography would stretch to the moon, but for a first listen, look for *The Original Misty* (Emarcy) or *Concert by the Sea* (Columbia).

Clifford Brown—This important be-bop trumpeter made a big impression on Andrew early in the latter's development. ●: See Master List.

Wardell Gray—Gray, a tenor saxophonist with an affectingly personal sound, played for a while in Earl Hines's band. He died in 1955 at the age of 34, leaving behind a considerable legend but relatively few recordings. ●: If you can find it, start with *Central Ave.* (Prestige, out of print), a compilation that includes representative Gray sessions from the early '50s, about when Andrew heard him. From the same period, easier to find, and also excellent are *Memorial, Vols. 1–2* (Prestige, available separately).

Mulgrew Miller—Andrew finds few younger players who interest him, something he attributes to the fact that more players are being cookie-cuttered in music schools rather than learning by trial-and-error as they did in earlier times. But Andrew praises Miller, whom he caught live at a jazz piano festival in New York. ●: *Hand in Hand* (Novus) presents Miller with a frontline of Joe Henderson, Eddie Henderson, and Kenny Garrett, plus Steve Nelson on vibes. *Work!* (Landmark) is a fine trio date.

Greg Osby—*Further Ado* (Blue Note). Andrew's two Blue Note "comeback" albums in the late '80s featured this young alto saxophonist, and Andrew says this album shows "he's really living up to the potential I saw in him."

ANDREW HILL'S OWN RECORDINGS

Paradoxically, considering his views about them, Andrew sides with the younger players in effect when he encourages readers to first seek out his Blue Note material from the 1960s: "I like basically all of it because it was pure. I like it more now than I did when I recorded it. And all of a sudden they have become the standard for a certain type [of my] sound. One of the challenges I'm faced with is that people want me to sound like I sounded thirty years ago, which is impossible!"

⊙: If you want to hear why so many loved Andrew during that period, start with *Point of Departure* (Blue Note), widely considered to be one of the classic jazz recordings of the '60s. The group he gathered for this album included Eric Dolphy, Joe Henderson, and Freddie Hubbard. Other outstanding albums from Andrew's Blue Note years include *Smokestack*, *Black Fire*, and *Judgment*.

In the late '80s, Andrew rejoined Blue Note for a couple of notable releases, *Eternal Spirit* and *But Not Farewell*, both featuring Greg Osby on saxophone. To sample other post-'60s recordings, look for two albums Andrew cut in just two days for the Italian label Soul Note, *Shades* and the solo piano recording *Verona Rag*.

TISH HINOJOSA (November 12, 1996)

For Tish Hinojosa, born in San Antonio, Texas, to Mexican immigrant parents, music has always been a magical vehicle not bounded by the rules of ordinary reality. Her mother turned the kitchen radio on early in the morning and it played all day, tuned mostly to Spanish-language stations that spun Mexican romantic records. Many of the songs hailed from earlier decades, even as far back as the 1920s. "Hearing Agustin Lara and Mexico's other songwriters—those [tunes] were already twenty or thirty years old when I heard them but they would transport me to another time and place," Tish tells us by phone from Austin, where she now lives. "That's where it started for me."

Tish always loved music but the idea of making her own seemed a remote fantasy until her high school years in the early '70s, when singer/songwriters were—gently, of course—storming popular music's gates. "It was people like Jim Croce, James Taylor, Paul Simon, even John Denver for what it was worth at the time," Tish recalls. "The whole focus on folk music, taking a turn for storytelling and listening to something simple like a voice and a guitar—that's where things began to seem possible to me."

Although both mainly performed songs by other writers, Joan Baez and Linda Ronstadt inspired Tish in another way because both were Mexican-Americans striving to express their whole selves on record. Even more than those early idols, Tish has gone on to fashion a career that honors both sides of her border heritage. By turns, her songs evoke her family's often difficult past in Mexico, the big skies and rugged beauty of her home state, the injustices suffered by Mexican-born people in this country, the forget-your-troubles-for-a-night exuberance of border dance music, and, of course, her own life and loves. Defying pop marketing wisdom, her albums and concerts often pair English and Spanish lyrics. She has performed at numerous benefits for migrant farmworkers and wrote a song, "Something in the Rain" on *Culture Swing*, exposing the dangers the workers face in pesticide-drenched fields. She has even carried her social mission beyond the stage, penning a passionate editorial on behalf of bilingual public education that ran in the *Los Angeles Times* during California's fierce battles over the issue in the late 1990s.

In 1996, Tish sought to extend her reach with her album *Dreaming from the Labyrinth (Sohar del Laberinto)*. Recorded in a 170-year-old former chapel on the San Antonio River near where she attended parochial school, its poetic lyrics and folk-pop melodies are designed to transport listeners much as her mother's radio did with her. But though ambitious and panoramic, it is still just another step on her journey to explore the truths of her life and heritage. "I've got songs that haven't gotten on a record yet," she says, looking forward to the next project. "They're like special children I'm having to keep in the closet, to find the right moment for them."

TISH HINOJOSA'S FAVORITE ARTISTS AND RECORDINGS

Raphael—*Digan Lo Que Digan* (Capitol Mexico). Tish was really struck by this Mexican artist when she was 10 or 11: "He was like a cross between a flamenco singer and a crooner so the passion was just incredible."

Agustin Lara—*Homenaje a Lara* (Discos Musart).

Jose Feliciano—*Mas Exitos* (RCA).

The Hollies—"Bus Stop." : *All-Time Greatest Hits* (Curb).

Stevie Wonder—"Blame It on the Sun" on *Talking Book* (Motown).

John Denver—*Rhymes and Reasons* (RCA). "That was a real important one to me," says Tish, who liked the record because "it was playful and real tender."

Denver made the idea of performing her own songs seem accessible and she also loved his ability to mix entertainment with a social message.

Joan Baez—*Gracias a la Vida (Here's to Life)* (A&M). "She was connecting the American audience to the South American protest music that remains kind of an underground thing. It was wonderful to hear her pay tribute to that."

Violetta Parra—*Las Ultimas Composiciones de . . .* (RCA).

Ataltualpa Yupanque—*La Mejor de . . .* (RCA).

Roberto Carlos—*En Castellano* (Columbia).

Neil Young—*Harvest* (Reprise).

Uncle Walt's Band—*An American in Texas Revisited* (Sugar Hill).

Linda Ronstadt—*Heart Like a Wheel* (Capitol) and *Get Closer* (Asylum). "I think I learned every single song on that," Tish says about *Heart*. "It was always reviewed kind of strangely," she notes about the latter. "Linda I listen to as a singer, not a writer, but she sure can pick songs."

Karla Bonoff—*Karla Bonoff* (Asylum).

*Los Lobos—*And a Time to Dance* (Slash).

Emmylou Harris—*A Quarter Moon in a Ten Cent Town* (Elektra).

Shawn Colvin—*Steady On* and *Fat City* (both Columbia). Like Ronstadt, Colvin is one of Tish's primary influences as a singer. "There's something very clean and melodic about her voice," Tish says, who likes how Colvin adds nuance with her vocals beyond the words she is singing.

Juan Luis Guerra—*Areito* (BMG).

Maldita Vecindad—*Circo* (Polygram International).

Nancy Griffith—*Once in a Very Blue Moon* (Rounder/Philo).

Jimmie Dale Gilmore—*Fair & Square* (Hightone).

Loreena McKennitt—*The Mask and the Mirror* (Warner Bros.). Tish picked up this record at a time when she was looking to move beyond her roots/country-based work into more poppish territory, but without pandering: "Loreena's music did that. It brought what I like about instrumental music—the etherealism, the enjoyment of just hearing the sounds."

Butch Hancock—*No Two Alike* (14-tape series, available by subscription only from Rainlight Records, Box 468, Terlingua, Texas 79852). This series of tapes captures six nights of performances at the Cactus Café, during which the Texas songwriter appeared with several notable guests.

*Steve Earle—*Guitar Town* (MCA). "I don't expect I'm going to hear an incredible vocal performance by Steve Earle. I'm going to hear a really strong song."

Paul Simon—*Graceland* (Warner Bros.). Tish says Simon's music helped show her how to incorporate a social purpose elegantly and artfully: "*Graceland* has elements of [a social statement] but it's also real listenable and rhythmic, which I think is real important."

Ruben Blades—*The Best of Ruben Blades* (Sony).

Guardabarranco—*Dias de Amar* (Redwood).

TISH HINOJOSA'S OWN RECORDINGS

Fronm 1995, the extroverted *Frontejas* (Rounder), Tish's exploration of Mexican-American border music, remains a favorite of hers. "It kind of surprised me in its own development," Tish says. "I learned a lot and therefore I was hopefully able to broaden people's perspective on how they see the border culture."

In contrast, *Dreaming from the Labyrinth* (Warner Bros.) is an introspective, layered work that universalizes the biculturalism of *Frontejas*. Its poetic lyrics address questions of love and spirit and hint of mysteries etched into the landscape and carried by the elements. Tish acknowledges that she was heavily influenced by Loreena McKennitt's literate, worldly songs while making the record.

She names three other favorite projects: *Cada Niño (Every Child)* (Rounder), a children's album; *Memorabilia Navidad* (Watermelon), a Christmas record; and Robert Skiles and Beto and the Fairlanes's *Salsafied* (Dos), on which she sings two songs. About the latter, she notes, "That's a different side of Tish. He isn't the bona fide schooled musician so his melodies are quite complex and of a whole different nature than what I strum on a guitar."

: The 1987 record *Taos to Tennessee* (Watermelon) is Tish's true debut, and an impressive one. She released it independently on cassette; Watermelon issued it on CD in 1992. 1989's *Homeland* (A&M), produced by Los Lobos' Steve Berlin, first brought her to the attention of critics and musicians; Linda Ronstadt, renowned for her taste in material, covered its "Donde Voy (Where I Go)." The 1992 album *Culture Swing* (Rounder) was named Folk Album of the Year by the National Association of Independent Record Distributors (NAIRD).

PETER HOLSAPPLE (April 29, 1997)

lthough he harbors few regrets, Peter Holsapple has been bloodied by one double-edged sword after another in the music biz. The artful tunes he's crafted for the dB's and Continental Drifters have earned him a glittering reputation with other musicians—and neglect from an industry that would prefer another Spice Girls. His talent for concise pop songs has resulted in some of the most tasteful popular music of the last 20 years. But "tasteful" also means "sans bombast," which disqualifies him for the star-making machine.

And then there's the older brother problem. Curtis, 11 years Peter's senior, turned him on to his first major influences, the 1960s British Invasion records that were rocking Curtis's world. Unfortunately, Curtis got Peter so hooked on the stuff that he ended up making records that were out-of-step, albeit brilliantly, with his age group. Peter was also both saved and done in by his contrarian nature and like-minded friends. "I was hangin' around with a kind of articulate bunch of obscurists like Mitch Easter and Chris Stamey and Will Rigby and a buncha other people that I'm still friends with today," Peter, 41, tells us by phone from his home in Louisiana. "You know, if you're growing up in North Carolina in the sixties and seventies and you're just inundated with Marshall Tucker and the Allman Brothers, it kind of turns you against that in a way, so we went for some of the most tweedy, twinkly British pop I could find, and really obscure blues, and things like that."

Stamey, Rigby, and Gene Holder started the dB's in 1978 in New York. Peter, who had known the trio since elementary school, joined them two months later. The dB's combined Brit-like songwriting smarts, psychedelic quirkiness, punky energy (especially on the first record), and garage band frivolity. Not nearly raw or dark enough for punks and post-punks and too young for most boomers, the dB's made four terrific albums and then went the way of their idols Big Star, another ingenious, weak-selling pop band with its head hooked into the British Invasion.

Peter says he doesn't care that the spotlight has passed him by. "That stuff is kind of a younger man's game now," he shrugs. To underscore his point, he has committed himself to another talent-laden outfit operating well out of the public eye, the Continental Drifters, who include Vicki Peterson (Bangles), Mark Walton (Dream Syndicate), and Peter's wife, Susan Cowsill, among other skilled music vets. "Our pedigrees are fairly immaculate," Peter says proudly, "but the great thing is we just like each other's songs so much. We just want to have a good time, and drink a beer and eat some food and do it for the right reasons. . . . To actually have a band like the Continental Drifters now, this is my reward for stickin' it out."

PETER HOLSAPPLE'S FAVORITE ARTISTS AND RECORDINGS

The Beatles—Peter ate up all the Beatles albums through *Revolver*, with special mention of that album, *Meet the Beatles*, *Beatles '65*, *Rubber Soul*, and *Yesterday . . . and Today* (all Capitol): "They basically reinvented everything, didn't they? Since then, I've conceded that the Beatles' mistakes are sort of our vocabulary. There are a lot of wonderful errors on those Beatles records."

The Kinks—*Lola vs. the Powerman & the Money-Go-Round, Part One* (Reprise). "That's just such a completely successful and wonderful record," Peter says. With the exception of *Lola*, Peter was more into Kinks' singles than albums. ⏺: 1972's *The Kink Kronikles* (Reprise) is the best compilation of early Kinks tracks.

The Lovin' Spoonful—*Daydream* (One Way), *Hums* (Pair), and *Everything Playing* (Kama Sutra). In addition to loving the Spoonful for their own material, Peter appreciated them as a gateway to other jug band music. *Hums* has been packaged with *Do You Believe in Magic?* on a single CD (Kama Sutra).

Jim Kweskin and His Jug Band—*Greatest Hits* (Vanguard). "What an amazing little band."

Koerner, Ray & Glover—*Blues, Rags, and Hollers* (Red House), *Lots More Blues, Rags and Hollers* (Elektra), and *The Return of . . .* (Elektra). Peter's brother turned him on to these records by three folkies from the University of Minnesota, thereby introducing him to the country blues.

The Beach Boys—*Wild Honey, Smiley Smile*, and *Friends* (all Capitol). More treasures via big brother.

Michael Bloomfield—with the Electric Flag, *A Long Time Comin'* (Columbia); with Al Kooper and Stephen Stills, *Supersession* (Columbia); and with Kooper, *The Live Adventures of Mike Bloomfield and Al Kooper* (Columbia). "Most people were into Clapton. I was really into Mike Bloomfield."

Paul Butterfield Blues Band—*The Resurrection of Pigboy Crabshaw, In My Own Dream*, and *East West* (all Elektra). Peter first preferred the post-Bloomfield records *Crabshaw* and *Dream* because he liked Bloomfield's solo efforts better than his work with Butterfield. He now also enjoys the original Butterfield Band records with Bloomfield and Elvin Bishop sharing guitar duties: "I really liked Elvin Bishop's sense of humor on guitar. He seemed like such a weird, funny cat."

The Move—*Shazam* (A&M), *Message from the Country* (One Way), and *The BBC Sessions* (IMC). "My high school rock band with Chris [Stamey] and Mitch [Easter] did I would probably say seven or eight Move songs note for note, and it was pretty fascinating."

The Idle Race—*The Birthday Party* (Sunset) and *Impostors of Life's Magazine* (A&M). The Race was the band Jeff Lynne inhabited before joining the Move. "This is the old days of Jeff Lynne when his writing style was more that arcane British music hall thing the Kinks did so well, the 'When I'm Sixty-four' New Vaudeville band sort of sound," says Peter.

Electric Light Orchestra—*No Answer* (Jet). "ELO kinda lost its sheen after the first record for me."

MC5—*Kick Out the Jams* (Elektra), *Back in the U.S.A.* (Rhino), and *High Time* (Rhino). "In a way, *High Time* is a kind of neglected record. There's a little more of the jamminess that I don't really care for, but there's also some bursts of power, like 'Miss X' and Dennis Thompson's song, 'Gotta Keep Movin On,' was just spectacular."

Mott the Hoople—*Mott the Hoople* (Atlantic), *Mad Shadows* (Atlantic), *Wildlife* (Atlantic), *Brain Capers* (Atlantic), *Mott* (Columbia), and *All the Young Dudes* (Columbia). Peter says that to catch his ear back then, bands "basically needed guitars, keyboards, bass, and drums, and it didn't matter whether the vocalist was any good or not. It had to have energy and it had to have conciseness." With those essentials in place, "Mott the Hoople was huge in my life," Peter says.

Big Star—*#1 Record/Radio City* (Stax). "If you can build a better Beatles, the world will beat a path to your door, and for my money they just embodied every bit of melody, harmony, off-the-wall production sounds, draggy drums where they were needed, and strange lyrics that didn't have a lyric sheet. And it was bliss for a teenage boy, you know."

Chris Bell—*I Am the Cosmos* (Rykodisc). Distraught by Big Star's commercial failure, Bell left the band to work on a solo record. He was killed in a car wreck before its release. *Cosmos* compiles his solo tracks. "I got to meet Chris right before he died," Peter says. "That's the Big Star record that never was. That's just beautiful, sad, stately music."

The New York Dolls—*New York Dolls* (Mercury). "Guys drinkin' beer through straws in full drag, excuse me? North Carolina, I don't think so."

The Velvet Underground—*Loaded* (Warner Bros.). "Definitely my high school record."

*Grateful Dead—*Live Dead* (Warner Bros.). "I wasn't big into the jammy stuff but I listened to 'Turn On Your Love Light' fifteen times in a row once in prep school."

Blodwyn Pig—*Ahead Rings Out* and *Getting to This* (both A&M). Peter still listens often to the records of this late-'60s British blues-rock group that featured guitarist Mick Abrahams.

The Yardbirds—*Live at the BBC* (Warner Bros.) "It will just blow your mind. . . . It's especially nice to see that these groups that did such wonderful albums were able to pull it off live."

Fairport Convention—*Heyday* (Hannibal). "Believe me, if you like Fairport, that is totally worth your while. It's so beautiful and so good," Peter enthuses about this collection of BBC performances from 1968 and 1969.

Various artists—*Troubadours of British Folk, Vols. 1–3* (Rhino, available separately). "An absolute, essential must-have. That is something I would give to every newborn baby if I possibly could."

Nic Jones—*Penguin Eggs* (Shanachie). "He uses this very obscure tuning for his guitar. He's got a beautiful voice. *Penguin Eggs* is eight or nine, like, seafaring songs. But as dry as that may sound, this is just like living music . . . The songs are breathtaking."

Blue Mountain—*Dog Days* (Roadrunner). "A three-piece band and for my money they really got it all just right. The songwriting is real pure and real unaffected. The performances are all just meticulous and lively and real."

Peter Blegvad—*Just Woke Up* (East Side Digital), *Knights Like This* (Virgin), and *The Naked Shakespeare* (Virgin). See below for more on Blegvad.

The Bulgarian Radio Women's Chorus—*Le Mistere des Voix Bulgaire, Vols. 1 & 2* (Elektra/ Nonesuch). "The first two volumes of that have been constant traveling companions with me for years. And there's a lot of other stuff out there by the Bulgarian ladies that is just extraordinary."

Various artists—*Music from the Morning of the World* (Nonesuch). "It's Balinese gamelan music. And it is stunning—just beautiful, beautiful stuff."

The Drummers of Burundi—*Live at Real World* (Real World). "I love good drums like that."

The Nitty Gritty Dirt Band—*Will the Circle Be Unbroken* (EMI America) and *Will the Circle Be Unbroken, Vol. 2* (Universal). "Those ought to be placed in the National Registry for Great Musical Events. I have a tremendous fondness for the second one, especially. Some of the stuff on there is just blinding. . . . *Levon Helm singing 'When I Get My Rewards.' Oh, God, I'm just getting goose bumps thinking about that.''

The Louvin Brothers—*Tragic Songs of Life* (Capitol), *Satan is Real* (Capitol), *A Tribute to the Delmore Brothers* (Capitol), and *When I Stop Dreaming: The Best of* . . . (Razor & Tie).

The Stanley Brothers—*Angel Band: The Classic Mercury Recordings* (Mercury Nashville).

Ella Fitzgerald—*The Complete Ella in Berlin* (Verve). This famous live record includes a version of "Mack the Knife" where Fitzgerald forgets the words and improvises substitute lyrics that work just fine. "Oh, what a powerful record!" says Peter. "I don't have a tremendous working knowledge or great fondness for jazz, but I know what I like when I hear it.''

Judy Collins—*Baby's Bedtime* and *Baby's Morningtime* (Lightyear). Peter heartily recommends these children's records to parents and music lovers in general: "That's a voice we've all grown up with and it's sung so beautifully. . . . My daughter and her mother and I all kind of bonded over that record. *Baby's Bedtime*, I practically stole that from my daughter to take on the Hootie [and the Blowfish (Peter was hired as a sideman for that tour.)] trip so I could go to sleep at night.''

The Grease Band—*The Grease Band* (Shelter). "Some wonderful guitar playing and songwriting by Henry McCullough . . . the Grease Band record was this wonderful, sloppy, great, funny, silly record. A lot more laid back than whatever they did with Joe Cocker.'' : *Chronicles* (Line), a CD reissue, combines this album with the Grease Band's second release, *Amazing Grease*.

Judee Sill—*Heart Food* (Asylum). "The lyrics are allegorical in that there's a certain Christian tinge to the lyrics . . . but the songs are just beautiful. Her voice—I've never heard anybody sound like that, and I don't know much about her story but I think it's a pretty sad one.''

Norma Waterson—*Norma Waterson* (Hannibal). "She is one of the sisters from the group the Watersons, who were the first family of British folk music. And this is a more casual affair. It's got Richard Thompson, Danny Thompson, and her husband, Martin Carthy, playing on it. It's got her daughter Eliza Carthy, who is the new leading light of British fiddle. She's astounding. But the record is great . . . Her voice is a beacon.''

Linda Thompson—*Dreams Fly Away* (Hannibal). "There's not a dud track on that. Oh, it's beautiful.''

Maddy Prior and June Tabor—*Silly Sisters* (Shanachie). "It's a great collection of British songs from over the ages. It's really beautifully handled, and the singing voices are so pure and offset each other so well."

Richard Thompson—*Starring as Henry the Human Fly!* (Hannibal). "That's a good place for anybody to start with Richard Thompson."

Gene Clark—*Echoes* (Columbia). "Man, that guy—some fine songwriting and some beautiful singing and some just wickedly intriguing arranging."

*The Band—*Stage Fright* (Capitol). "I love all the Band records, but that one in particular is kind of a great audio treat for me."

Coulson, Dean, McGuiness, Flint—*Lo and Behold* (Raven). "It's a great, low-key, cool, successful Dylan cover record," Peter says about this 1996 release. "It's got a nice vibe to it that just works from the minute that the needle goes into the groove."

Eddie Hinton—*Very Extremely Dangerous* (Capricorn) and *Cry and Moan* (Bulls-eye Blues). "What a rockin' fuckin' record that is," Peter says about *Dangerous*, by the late Muscle Shoals session guitarist and occasional solo artist. And Peter loves the songwriting on *Cry and Moan*.

Freddie Roulette—*Sweet, Funky Steel* (Janus). "Freddie Roulette is a black Ha-waiian steel guitar player. He is the proto–David Lindley in my book. All those weird drops that Lindley does with the bar on the steel, banging the steel, and zipping over the top of the pick-up and stuff like that—that's Freddie Roulette, right there. . . . You've not heard steel guitar playing like this. It just defies all boundaries I can think of."

PETER HOLSAPPLE'S OWN RECORDINGS

"I'm proud of every single dB's album," says Peter. "Those I call the legitimate four: *Stands for Decibels* (I.R.S.), *Repercussion* (I.R.S.), *Like This* (Rhino/Bearsville), and *The Sound of Music* (I.R.S.). And my favorite among those four I think is still *Like This*, just because that was a very difficult time in the development of the band. Chris had left and suddenly the mantle was foisted upon me to lead the band, to write the songs, and by jingo, I did it. . . . That's a real consistent album to me and sonically it's still pleasing."

Peter also takes pride in his 1997 solo record *Out of My Way* (Monkey Hill), 1991's *Mavericks* (Rhino), a duo project with Chris Stamey, and the Continental Drifters's self-titled debut (Monkey Hill). "It's great to be able to look at your curriculum vitae and say 'I've never really worked on a record that I'm not proud of my work on,'" he notes. In that vein, he points to an album he appeared on as a session player, avant-garde rocker/songwriter/cartoonist Peter Blegvad's *King Strut and Other Stories* (Silvertone). "Peter is a paragon among human beings. A more talented person I don't think I know. . . . It's really thrilling, that record. That's one of those things that the family puts on for comfort music around here. When you hear the first notes of the first song, you just sink into the goodness."

⊙: Note that the character of the dB's inevitably changed after Stamey left the group. The albums under Peter's helm are less frivolous, less edgy, more melodic, and more polished. Also, Peter points out, his country influences assert themselves on the latter two albums. True dB's fans will enjoy *The dB's Ride the Wild TomTom* (Rhino), a collection as Peter puts it in his liner notes, of dB's "home and field recordings," most of which predate the group's debut album by several years. The furious creativity and aura of wild fun are infectious.

JOHN LEE HOOKER (December 6, 1996)

Of all the great blues players never captured on record, Will Moore may have been the best, if his effect on another legend, his stepson John Lee Hooker, is any measure. John Lee notes, "All of the musicians you can see who've heard my music [say], 'Nobody's guitar sounds like John Lee Hooker's guitar.' That was my stepfather's sound."

Moore's playing so completely captivated the young John Lee that no other musician has substantially affected him since (the list below of John Lee's favorite artists are truly favorites, not influences). Such blues immortals as Blind Blake, Charlie Patton, and Blind Lemon Jefferson used to drop in on Moore at the family home near Clarksdale, Mississippi, when John Lee was in his teens. But though he was suitably impressed, he had already committed himself to the guitar approach he would make his own.

Since the late 1940s when John Lee made his recording debut, that approach has been one of the strongest, most recognizable signatures in music— dark, droning, percussive grooves, each based on a single chord that stretches out the tension like a 60-minute man. Ultimately, he would develop a matching vocal style that seems to warn of danger around the bend. It's a sound that has influenced legions of blues-based rockers even as it sets John Lee's music apart.

Born in 1917, John Lee is now blues' reigning elder statesman, a role he bears proudly and actively. Still a prolific recording artist in his eighth decade, he has recorded five albums in the 1990s alone and *The Healer*, released in 1989 when he was 72, became one of the best-selling blues albums of all time. When listening to music for his own enjoyment, he turns—where else?—to the blues, and also to rock that still displays its blues heritage. "I like good, deep-down funk rock," he tells us, "not sophisticated rock." Deep-down, funky, and stripped to the fundamentals—John Lee could just as easily be describing himself.

JOHN LEE HOOKER'S FAVORITE ARTISTS AND RECORDINGS

Tony Hollins—This obscure bluesman from Hooker's hometown of Clarksdale, Mississippi, was the first name John Lee mentioned to us as a favorite. Hollins made the original recording of "Crawling Kingsnake" (for Okeh), the model for John Lee's later version. ⬤: Hollins recorded sporadically; a few sides show up on compilations, especially *The Retrospective* (Columbia/Legacy).

T-Bone Walker—"Stormy Monday" and "Bobbie Sox Baby." John Lee says that while he didn't play Walker's style, this Texas-born guitarist made a major impression on him. ⬤: *The Complete Capitol/Black & White Recordings* (2 CDs: Capitol).

Muddy Waters—"Hootchie Coochie Man." ⬤: You'll find a superb live version of this classic Waters song on *Muddy Waters at Newport* (MCA/Chess). The original studio version appears on *The Best of Muddy Waters* (MCA/Chess).

Lightnin' Hopkins—"Ida Mae" on *Smokes Like Lightnin'* (Original Blues Classics). John Lee loves this song so much he didn't just mention it, he sang part of it over the phone for us.

Stevie Ray Vaughan—We asked John Lee if there were any contemporary blues musicians who impressed him. "There are quite a few of them, but my main man, he's gone," he replied, referring to Vaughan. "He was something . . . He was so sincere." ⬤: See Master List.

Charley Patton—Patton dropped in regularly on Will Moore and played the blues with him, much to John Lee's delight and edification. ⬤: See Master List.

Tower of Power—"They play *good* funk," says John Lee with a knowing laugh. He likes everything the band has recorded. ⬤: *Tower of Power*, *Back to Oakland*, and *Urban Renewal* (all Warner Bros.), featured the band's best-ever lead singer, Lenny Williams, in front of the band's master-blaster five-piece horn section.

Eric Clapton—"He's got such a neat style and he really plays the blues, he doesn't fake the blues." ⬤: *Money and Cigarettes* and *Unplugged* (both Reprise) show off some of Clapton's better blues playing. You'll find a rawer, less-pop-influenced Clapton on the seminal John Mayall album from 1966, *Bluesbreakers with Eric Clapton* (Deram). This was Clapton post-Yardbirds and pre-Cream.

Albert Collins—"He backed me up on some of my recordings. Everything he did, he comes from his heart." ◉: 1969's *Truckin' with . . .* (MCA) and 1978's *Ice Pickin'* (Alligator) together provide a great introduction to the "Master of the Telecaster."

Albert King—"Big Albert—oh boy, the man could play some guitar!" ◉: See Master List.

Little Walter (Jacobs)—"He was the king of the harmonica. Everybody today tries to copy him. He was a complete harmonica player." ◉: See Master List.

Jimmy Reed—"He was an old buddy of mine. Everything he did in music, he did [great]. He was nice, but he was into kicking people's asses all the time. He liked to drink." ◉: See Master List.

Bobby "Blue" Bland—"Farther Up the Road," "Stormy Monday," and "Turn on Your Lovelight." "Everything he did, the man came from his heart and soul." ◉: *The Best of Bobby Blue Bland* (MCA) contains all of the aforementioned songs. For more by this blues/R&B great, see Master List.

JOHN LEE HOOKER'S OWN RECORDINGS

When we asked him to name favorites in his own catalog, John Lee stuck to songs, not albums, including "Boogie Chillun," his hit for Modern Records that topped the R&B charts in 1948; "Boom Boom," a mid-1950s hit on Vee-Jay Records; and "It's You I Love, Baby."

◉: *The Ultimate Collection (1948-1990)* (Rhino) is a fine two-CD career overview that includes "Boogie Chillun" and "Boom Boom." *The Legendary Modern Records 1948–1954* (Virgin) contains "Boogie Chillun," of course, and may be the best single anthology of the early recordings that established his career. From the same period, *Graveyard Blues* (Specialty) presents John Lee in primarily solo settings, where his ominous style comes through loudest and clearest. *Boogie Chillun* (Fantasy), from 1962, includes "It's You I Love, Baby" plus the driving title cut. John Lee is alone with his guitar throughout, and more subdued on many tracks than is typical.

BRUCE HORNSBY (November 22, 1996)

e careful what you wish for, the saying goes, 'cause you might just get it. Bruce Hornsby has probably posted that statement all over his house by now because his wishes have a way of turning into substantial professional entanglements. Not that he's complaining because the potent combination of his talent and his fancy has led to a distinctly charmed life.

Take for instance Bruce's ties with the Nitty Gritty Dirt Band. Bruce grew up in Williamsburg, Virginia, just two hours from the Motherland of American rural music, the Appalachian mountains. But Bruce's fascination with old-time country tunes really exploded when older brother John turned him on to the Dirt Band's landmark record project, 1972's *Will the Circle Be Unbroken*. The introduction eventually turned to prophecy. After Bruce proved himself with a Grammy-winning start to his career, the Dirt Band recruited him to appear on 1989's *Will the Circle Be Unbroken, Volume 2*. (Bruce contributed a bluegrass version of his "The Valley Road.")

John Hornsby—later Bruce's songwriting partner—also catalyzed Bruce's second wish come true: the ultimate Deadhead fantasy of playing in the band. It was John who first exposed Bruce to the Grateful Dead's music. Bruce then joined his older brother's Grateful Dead cover band when he was a freshman in college. Sitting in the middle of it, he gained an even greater appreciation for the Dead's sonic poetry. "The Dead have fifty or sixty great songs," Bruce asserts, "and they're not given enough credit as songwriters. And the music would evolve. They were not set in their way of playing a song. Their arrangements would change and it would allow the music to breathe and develop. That combination of elements was what drew me to them."

The Dead, in turn, were drawn to Bruce because of his own attributes. After Bruce rose to national prominence with his bright, country-tinged pop, the Dead recognized a kindred spirit. They invited him and his band the Range to open for a number of their shows; when the Dead's keyboardist Brent Mydland suffered an untimely death, Bruce got the call to fill in, happily setting aside his own gigs until the Dead found a permanent replacement. In addition, Jerry Garcia began appearing on Bruce's solo albums, beginning with 1990's *A Night on the Town* and continuing through *Hot House* in 1995, the year he died.

Turnabout III in what was now clearly a pattern, not just coincidence, occurred in 1992. That year, Bruce was called in to produce Leon Russell's "comeback" album, *Anything Can Happen*. Russell's pounding, gospel-inflected style had been one of Bruce's earliest and strongest influences; if you listen closely, you can hear the impact of Russell's playing in Bruce's propulsive left hand.

Finally, in 1991, Bruce got the opportunity to give a high-level salute to an even earlier influence, Elton John. It was John's 1971 record, *Tumbleweed Connection*, that Bruce says sparked his infatuation with rock piano. When Polydor pulled together the Elton John tribute album *Two Rooms: Celebrating the Songs of Elton John & Bernie Taupin*, Bruce answered the bell by contributing a rendition of "Madman Across the Water." Predictable? By now, yes. Boring? We haven't heard Bruce complain.

BRUCE HORNSBY'S FAVORITE ARTISTS AND RECORDINGS

Charles Ives—*Concord Sonata*, John Kirkpatrick, pianist, (Columbia, out of print). "Ives's music had a certain spirit, a certain earthy spirituality. I know that sounds a little cosmic, but that's basically how I feel about it. It always moved me in a soulful, deep way. It is alternately very dark and dissonant, and then comedic. It runs the gamut of musical emotions." : This record was issued in 1949. Kirkpatrick was a noted Ives scholar.

Nitty Gritty Dirt Band—*Will the Circle Be Unbroken* (EMI America). This set of traditional country and bluegrass tunes, performed by the Dirt Band and a stellar cast of country and bluegrass greats from Earl Scruggs and Merle Travis to Doc Watson and Mother Maybelle Carter, opened the ears of countless musicians and fans to America's rural music heritage, transforming popular music in the process.

Miles Davis—*Kind of Blue* (Columbia). "I have about twenty Miles Davis albums, and that's still my favorite one."

Frank Sinatra—*A Man and His Music* (Reprise). Sinatra recorded this hits compendium in the mid-'60s, and accompanied it with his own narration and anecdotes. According to Bruce, "Everything on this is just amazing."

John Coltrane—*A Love Supreme* (Impulse). "I could say the same thing about [this record] that I said about Ives: a real earthiness and spirituality that got under my skin."

Chick Corea—*Now He Sings, Now He Sobs* (Blue Note). "Some people say that, of modern jazz piano since about 1960, this is one of the five classics. This is a trio with Roy Haynes and Miroslav Vitous. To me the playing is truly amazing and this record has been transcribed like crazy in the jazz schools for years."

*The Band—*Rock of Ages* (Capitol). "I always loved Robbie Robertson's writing. I'm a terrible accordion player, an old bootleg player. I don't really practice it a lot: it's just something I like to do. But I got into playing the accordion because of Garth Hudson's playing—not so much on this record, but on some of their other records."

Grateful Dead—*Europe '72* (Warner Bros). This live release, a two-CD set, displays both the evocative songwriting and intricate group interplay that first attracted Bruce to their music.

Leon Russell—*Leon Live* (Cema/Capitol) and *Leon Russell and the New Grass Revival* (Paradise). Bruce names Russell as one of his biggest heroes, but singles out Sam Bush's mandolin playing on the relatively obscure collaboration between Russell and the New Grass Revival. As for *Leon Live*, Bruce says, "A lot of people have slagged that record for years, but I love it!"

Bill Evans—*Sunday at the Village Vanguard* (Original Jazz Classics), *Waltz for Debby* (Original Jazz Classics), *Since We Met* (Original Jazz Classics), and *The Tony Bennett/Bill Evans Album* (Original Jazz Classics). Bruce says he can name many, many more marvelous Evans albums, but these are the must-haves, he feels.

Bud Powell—*The Amazing Bud Powell, Vols. I and II* (Blue Note, available separately).

George Jones—"His voice is the great country voice. He's the singer that moves me the most in country music," Bruce says, adding that a greatest hits package is as good a way as any to discover his music. ⬤: See Master List.

Joni Mitchell—*Hejira* (Asylum). Bruce says this 1976 release "creates a mood that's alluring. It's very sensual, draws you in, and stays there for the whole record."

Sam Cooke—*A Man and His Music* (RCA). Most critics consider this one of the most essential greatest-hits packages in popular music. Bruce agrees.

The Soul Stirrers with Sam Cooke—*The Soul Stirrers* (Specialty). "This was Sam Cooke's gospel group, where he was the lead singer in the fifties. A truly incredible record."

Ravel—The Complete Piano Music. "I think Bill Evans got a lot of his concept of voicing chords from Ravel," Bruce says. He prefers the version by French pianist and composer Robert Casadesus. Unfortunately the recording, originally issued on Columbia, is out of print and hasn't been reissued on CD. Bruce's copy is on vinyl so you'll either have to listen to it at his house or check specialty vinyl retailers. ⬤: Another highly acclaimed set of the complete Ravel piano music has been recorded by a younger Frenchman, Jean-Yves Thibaudet (London).

Bob Dylan—*Biograph* (3 CDs: Columbia) and *The Bootleg Series* (3 CDs: Columbia). The former is a retrospective covering the first 20 years of Dylan's career. The latter features outtakes and unreleased material of prime-Dylan quality.

Keith Jarrett—*Facing You* (ECM) and *Tribute* (ECM).

Marvin Gaye—*Anthology* (2 CDs: Motown).

Aretha Franklin—*Amazing Grace* (Atlantic).

Elton John—*Tumbleweed Connection* (MCA).

The Beatles—*The Beatles* (aka the White Album, Capitol).

Wes Montgomery—*Smokin' at the Half Note* (Verve).

Muddy Waters—*The Chess Box* (3 CDs: Chess).

James Brown—*Star Time* (4 CDs: Polydor).

Joe Cocker—*Mad Dogs and Englishmen* (A&M).

Various artists—*Atlantic Rhythm & Blues, Vol. 6* (Atlantic).

BRUCE HORNSBY'S OWN RECORDINGS

Speaking about his solo albums and work with the Range, Bruce says, "*Scenes from the Southside* (RCA) and *Harbor Lights* (RCA) are my favorites. They're both really solid collections of songs. I can tell this [by] how many songs from each record we continue to play live, and those two records seem to be the ones we keep going back to. I also like certain tracks from *Hot House* (RCA)."

Bruce's favorites among his contributions to outside projects include "The Valley Road" on *Will the Circle Be Unbroken, Vol. 2* (Universal, filed under Nitty Gritty Dirt Band). "I felt we captured a certain moment, a certain feeling," Bruce tells us. He also still enjoys his cut on *Two Rooms: Celebrating the Songs of Elton John & Bernie Taupin* (Polydor). Bruce played keyboards on one of Bonnie Raitt's most memorable songs ever, "I Can't Make You Love Me" on her *Luck of the Draw* (Capitol). "I was proud to be a part of that," Bruce says. Another proud moment: the title track he wrote for Don Henley's *The End of the Innocence* (Geffen). He mentions, too, what had to be one of his most poignant performances, a version of "I Know You Rider" that he and his band did as a tribute to Jerry Garcia for *Rock 'n' Roll Hall of Fame* (Sony) shortly after Garcia passed away.

⊙: The album that started it all for Bruce was *The Way It Is* (RCA), more rural- and acoustic-shaded than his later records and packed with memorable melodies and vibrant, impressive musicianship. The 1990 release *A Night on the Town* (RCA) was also well-received and featured, besides Garcia, saxophonist Wayne Shorter. The 1998 album *Spirit Trail* (2 CDs: RCA), showcasing Bruce's most adventurous solos yet recorded, is one of the most highly praised albums of his career.

GEORGIA HUBLEY (August 11, 1997)

Yo La Tengo sits atop a bohemian New York rock scene in which the social pressures to be hipper-and-more-off-putting-than-thou seem almost impossible to resist. But resist the band has, making its own, friendlier rules with a crafty mix of tuneful pop, folky roots, ambient gauze, and high-rise-construction-zone noise. The distortion always lets you know what time it is, but the warm song frames and often beguiling vocals welcome you inside.

We can only speculate but the crucible for this unlikely outcome seems to be a marriage that works between founding members Georgia Hubley, the group's drummer, and guitarist *Ira Kaplan. And in Georgia's case, a complete lack of pretense about her artistic destiny, despite auspicious background credentials. Georgia's parents are Oscar-winning animators (her father created Mr. Magoo) who worked closely and socialized with jazz musicians like Dizzy Gillespie and Ray Brown. Her mother played cello and sent her children to Mannes music school. But in spite of all that, "I sort of had the typical early teenage music taste that's mostly embarrassing," laughs Georgia shyly.

The shift that would culminate in Yo La Tengo started in Georgia's late teens, although she seems slightly embarrassed about that, too: "I can't quite remember what really made me want to start playing. I'm sure it was something much more mundane than my love for music, almost from a social point of view, from going out and seeing bands. I guess I was about eighteen or nineteen and was getting really interested in going to clubs and seeing kind of obscure bands and falling into that . . . I think at that point I kind of developed taste in music that might have resulted in what's come out now, for Yo La Tengo."

And not in the way some would expect. Hearing her limitations, she was looking beyond the obvious spit-shined bands and discs for inspiration. "I was finding sounds that were rawer and even spastic or whatever, as appealing," says Georgia, "and then I'd start hearing that in records and enjoying it. But I'm sure that came from playing and being in that boat." Rock wildmen like Roky Erickson and Syd Barrett, eons removed from Georgia's teenage radio days not to mention ordinary reality, exuded a tragic thrill. The stumbling but no-holds-barred excursions of the Velvet Underground suddenly sounded like envelope-pushing of the highest order because she was hearing the intention as well as the result.

Georgia met Ira during her forays to CBGB's and Max's Kansas City in the early 1980s. They started Yo La Tengo in 1985. When the group's music is at its most inviting, it is generally her vocals delivering the invitation, which reaches its most direct expression on 1997's *I Can Hear Your Heart Beating as One*. The album closes with a cover of Anita Bryant's 1960 hit, "My Little Corner of the World," Georgia sweetly cooing from the open doors of Yo-La-Tengo land, "We always knew we'd find someone like you/So welcome . . ."

GEORGIA HUBLEY'S FAVORITE ARTISTS AND RECORDINGS

The Rolling Stones—*Between the Buttons* (ABKCO). "I think right when I was starting to play drums I used to play along with that," Georgia says about her favorite Stones album.

Gram Parsons—*G.P./Grievous Angel* (Reprise). "We've tried to cover some of his songs. . . . It's inconceivable how many sections and chords [there are] and yet when you listen to the whole thing, it doesn't come across as convoluted, it just sounds so natural . . ." Parsons's two major solo works have been packaged on a single, stunning CD.

The Flying Burrito Brothers—*The Gilded Palace of Sin* (A&M) and *Burrito Deluxe* (A&M). As with Gram Parsons, "I really don't think that led to very much in terms of Yo La Tengo, but I really loved the Flying Burrito Brothers," says Georgia. Naturally, she prefers the albums that feature Parsons before he quit the band he co-founded.

The Byrds—Although a devoted Byrds fan, Georgia appreciates their body of work more as a collection of great songs than as a series of albums, and feels the better compilations are a good way to approach the music. ⬤: See Master List.

The Velvet Underground—"It's hard to separate your feelings about it from hearing about how much you sound like them for the last ten years. But that's a band I don't think either of us would ever get sick of listening to. . . . I think some of the bootlegs where you're hearing them droning away for twenty or thirty minutes, that has at least as strong an impact for me as say 'Femme Fatale' or something like that." ⬤: See Master List.

Mission of Burma—This early 1980s Boston band inspired many groups besides Yo La Tengo. Their intense volume proved to be their undoing, severely damaging guitarist Roger Miller's hearing. Georgia says she and Ira often saw them perform. "It was one whole package, the live show, the records, the whole thing." ⬤:

Mission of Burma (Rykodisc) contains the band's total studio output, plus two live tracks, on one long CD.

Television—*Marquee Moon* (Elektra) and *Adventure* (Elektra). "Television is another band that I never saw, but I loved the two records."

Fairport Convention—*What We Did on Our Holidays* (Hannibal). Georgia loves Richard Thompson's playing and writing on this 1969 record, the band's second.

Richard and Linda Thompson—*Pour Down Like Silver* (Hannibal/Rykodisc). "The way Richard and Linda sang together—the impact of that is so strong, and those songs are so sad."

Pink Floyd—*The Piper at the Gates of Dawn* (Capitol). Georgia searched out this album, the band's 1967 debut, after first thrilling to the solo work of Syd Barrett, Pink Floyd's original singer, songwriter, and lead guitarist. Heavy psychedelic drug use unhinged this already unstable artist and early in 1968, he left the group he started.

Syd Barrett—*The Madcap Laughs* (Capitol) and *Barrett* (Capitol). Georgia describes Barrett's music as "eerie and sad and deranged, but really beautiful, too."

Roky Erickson—"Two-Headed Dog." Erickson, like Syd Barrett a talented acid casualty, more than satisfies Georgia's taste for raw, messy rock, particularly on this track. "It's all over the place," says Georgia, "and it's so great." ●: *You're Gonna Miss Me* (Restless).

Pere Ubu—*The Modern Dance* (Blank) and *Datapanik in the Year Zero* (DGC). *Dance* was this dada rock band's potent although difficult 1978 debut. *Datapanik* is a five-CD boxed set comprising nearly every thing the band released from 1978–82 and then some.

My Bloody Valentine—"We did a tour with My Bloody Valentine. I think that really we had such a great time and love that band so much. I'm sure that has trickled down into certain things that we've done, and certain attitudes about sound and recording and instrumentation." ●: The 1991 release *Loveless* (Sire) is a good introduction to the band's sound sandwich—pure, melodic pop between slices of assaultingly loud but still engaging noise. Also try 1988's *Isn't Anything* (Creation/Sire).

Sleater-Kinney—*Dig Me Out* (Kill Rock Star). "I love that record. Actually, I didn't love the record until I saw them . . . and I just thought that they were amazing."

The High Llamas—*Gideon Gaye* (Alpaca Park/Epic). "It's very Brian Wilsony in a way I don't think anyone is—even him."

Brian Wilson and The Beach Boys—"We keep acquiring more and more. They keep coming out with these collections of stuff so I got that *Smile* bootleg. That music is amazing." ●: *Good Vibrations: Thirty Years of the Beach Boys* (Capitol) is a five-CD, 142-cut boxed set that may still seem insufficient to Brian Wilson fanatics. The set includes almost an album's worth of tracks from the legendary, unreleased *Smile* sessions.

GEORGIA HUBLEY'S OWN RECORDINGS

Georgia doesn't often listen to Yo La Tengo's discs, so she finds it hard to talk about her own work. But she singles out the 1993 album *Painful* (Matador): "I think that we really extended ourselves in a big way when we made that record. I don't know if it's my favorite record, but clearly it was a big step for us to make that record. And some of the songs on it—'Big Day Coming,' there's two versions of that—I'm proud that we were able to go from where we were before to that." She also has grown to appreciate the 1993 single *Shaker* (Matador): "There are a lot of instruments on it and it kinda seems like a big mishmash of stuff. At the time I didn't know if it worked out. But then I heard it a couple of years later and I thought 'Well, that sounds pretty good.'"

●: All Yo La Tengo albums are worth your attention. Since this is still very much a growing and not declining or static band, 1997's *I Can Hear the Heart Beating as One* (Matador) is a great place to start with this group, in addition to the records mentioned by Georgia. Other albums in the group's impressive discography include the 1986 debut, *Ride the Tiger* (Coyote); *President Yo La Tengo/ New Wave Hot Dogs* (Matador), two records combined on a single CD; 1992's *May I Sing with Me* (Alias); and 1995's *Electr-O-Pura* (Matador). Finally, check out 1990's *Fakebook* (Bar/None), an infectious, mostly acoustic set of covers (Peter Stampfel, the Kinks, Flaming Groovies, Daniel Johnston, and more). It doesn't sound much like the band's atmospheric electric records but is a widely loved side trip.

CHARLIE HUNTER (December 5, 1998)

n the conservative era that now grips jazz, with overly schooled young players emulating past greats almost note for note, Charlie Hunter continues to carve out his own niche. One of the few young artists daring to urge the music forward, he creates a bubbling, funk-charged jazz hybrid on a custom instrument as unique as he is—an eight-stringed guitar keyed to sound like a Hammond B-3 organ whenever he flips the switch, which is often. Not that Charlie has cut all ties to the past—the soul-jazz of the '50s and '60s echoes in every set he plays. But so do some striking non-jazz influences. On one record, he does a Nirvana tune; on another he covers an entire Bob Marley disc. His defunct (but never de-*funked*) side band, TJ Kirk, postulated common ground between Thelonious Monk, Rahsaan Roland Kirk, and James Brown.

None of this is quite so surprising, though, when you know that Charlie grew up in Berkeley, California, a university town brimming with musicheads and connoisseur record stores that can scratch almost any itch. Charlie got his musical baptism at home with Mom's typical Berkeleyite record collection, brimming with choice blues and folk from the likes of Robert Johnson and Leadbelly. He also found Jimi Hendrix and Beatles records lying around the house, and "as a guitar player that's kinda how you get into it," he says.

However, as a young musician, Charlie was moving too fast to fall into any bag. "I just went through a phase a week. I was actually pretty hip for my age, when I was like fifteen or sixteen," he says plaintively, citing a string of early faves: Hendrix, Ry Cooder, David Lindley, Guitar Slim, Stevie Ray Vaughan, rock-abilly, Chet Atkins. "I also listened to a lot of stuff that was going on at the time, like the soul, and the R&B, and the hip-hop. I mean, me and my friends, we had the first Grandmaster Flash record, and we learned every single line on the record," he laughs.

With his restless head, it soon became clear to Charlie that the standard tools of the trade weren't going to get him where he wanted to go. Hence the custom guitar, fitted with three strings tuned to the lower three strings from a bass, and five more tuned to the higher five of a regular guitar. Not finding many eight-string players to emulate, he searched elsewhere for models and found them in jazz organists such as Big John Patton, Larry Young, and Jimmy Smith. "What they had going was . . . the left-hand bass—or the foot pedals, in Jimmy Smith's case—and they would do that and the melodies and the chords at the same time," Charlie says. "I had pretty much the same range on my eight-string guitar. I wanted to try to duplicate that on my instrument and it was just a great template to try to figure that stuff out."

Charlie found the other main musical inspiration of his adult life in a bargain record bin, where he snagged his first Rahsaan Roland Kirk album. Kirk played oddball instruments like the stritch and manzello and often blew two or three horns simultaneously. His feats were so analogous to Charlie's own that the younger musician bonded on the spot. In fact, Charlie is such a Kirk devotee that he views his own innovations far more modestly than others do: "I feel like all I'm trying to do is to be Roland Kirk on the eight-string guitar."

CHARLIE HUNTER'S FAVORITE ARTISTS AND RECORDINGS

Elvis Presley—*The Sun Sessions CD* (RCA) Charlie loves guitarist Scotty Moore's playing on these seminal rock classics.

Jimi Hendrix—*Band of Gypsys* (Capitol). Charlie says all of Hendrix's recordings are important to him, although this live date is his favorite. "Pretty much anything by him rocks," Charlie says. In fact, he adds, nobody has ever rocked as much since because Hendrix broke the mold. But then he corrects himself: "Well, nobody rocks and *rolls*. They just rock. And that's not as interesting to me."

Thelonious Monk—"Thelonious Monk is as original as it gets: he's the franchise. I particularly like the records on Columbia with [tenor saxophonist] Charlie Rouse, because I just loved how Charlie Rouse played his tunes, and the chemistry between them. Rouse is the unsung hero [in that music]." : *I Like Jazz: The Essence of Thelonious Monk* and *Standards* (both Columbia) anthologize Monk's Columbia recordings

James Brown—*Funk Power 1970—A Brand New Thang* and *Motherlode* (both Polydor). "The seventies band, all the stuff with [bassist] Bootsy [Collins] . . . I think is the funkiest stuff," Charlie says. " 'Sex Machine,' 'Super Bad,' 'Soul Power,'—all the classic stuff is on there," Charlie notes about the former disc.

Rahsaan Roland Kirk—"It's not just that he played three horns at once, or two horns at once, but the way that he would switch between those horns during a solo, to make it sound like a few people were playing. He would play different licks, too, when he would play the different horns," says Charlie, who raves about the entire Kirk catalog. : You might begin with one of the recent CD compilations like *Does Your House Have Lions?* (2 CDs: Rhino) or *The Vibration Continues* (Atlantic). If you've got the Kirk jones as badly as Charlie does, go for *The Complete Recordings of Roland Kirk* (10 CDs: Mercury). A widely loved individual album is *The Inflated Tear* (Atlantic).

Magic Sam—*West Side Soul* (Delmark). "He's just amazing, his guitar playing and his singing—another one of those things that will never be replicated," Charlie says. Of Sam's remarkable voice, Charlie notes, "He had a really big range. And his pitch was right on, like within a millimeter of the note."

Julian "Cannonball" Adderly—*Nancy Wilson/Cannonball Adderly* and *Country Preacher* (both Capitol). Charlie calls Adderly's album with Nancy Wilson "one of the great vocal records—the early version of his band, with Joe Zawinul, completely getting down and her just singing beautifully." He taps *Preacher* for a lot of the ideas he's worked out with his own bands.

John Coltrane—*Transition* (Impulse), *Dear Old Stockholm* (Impulse), . . . *and Johnny Hartman* (Impulse), *Giant Steps* (Atlantic), and *My Favorite Things* (Atlantic). "You can't go wrong with any Coltrane, but this is fabulous," Charlie says about *Transition*. "I think that's one of his most spiritual records. He does that 'A Love Supreme' thing but takes it a step further."

Ornette Coleman—*Twins* (Atlantic). "I really like the early Ornette stuff, when he had his first group. All those tunes [are] like clever little pop songs. They kind of feel the same way to me, but through a very distorted, funk-ified lens."

Ry Cooder—*Chicken Skin Music* and *Paradise and Lunch* (both Reprise). "At the time when I was learning guitar—the late seventies, early eighties—everyone wanted the thin string sound. . . . But Ry Cooder had this fat, heavy, tremoloed-out sound, and I just loved it."

Larry Young—Charlie recommends any of Young's '60s Blue Note recordings. : *The Art of . . .* , *Into Somethin'*, and *Unity* (all Blue Note).

Jimmy Smith—From this organist's voluminous catalog, Charlie picks any of the albums Smith made with drummer Donald Bailey. : Start with *Back at The Chicken Shack*, *The Sermon*, or *Crazy Baby* (all Blue Note).

Big John Patton—*Understanding*, *Boogaloo*, and *Let it Roll* (all Blue Note).

Miles Davis—*Miles Smiles* and *Filles de Kilimanjaro* (both Columbia). Charlie loves all of the records Davis made with Tony Williams, Wayne Shorter, *Herbie Hancock and Ron Carter, but named these two because he knows them best: "[All those records] have a great vibe. It's all incredible stuff that will never be done again. I mean, how many jazz music students try?" Note that *Filles* is a transitional album, albeit a great one, with Chick Corea and Dave Holland on board for two tracks and the quintet playing its swan song.

Bill Evans—*New Jazz Conceptions* (Original Jazz Classics). "That's just great group chemistry, with [bassist] Scott LaFaro and [drummer] Paul Motion."

Donny Hathaway—*Live* (Atlantic). "[It's] just soul city, unbelievable singing. He's a great piano player, band leader, and performer. You can hear him really connecting with the crowd. Also, that's one of my favorite electric bass records of all time," he adds, raving about Willie Weeks's performance.

Dave Douglas—*The Tiny Bell Trio* (Songlines). "He's got this group called the Tiny Bell Trio, which is some original music, man; [Douglas] on trumpet, a drummer, and a guitar player. It sounds like it wouldn't work, but it works brilliantly and it's a different, great sound." : Douglas records with several different ensembles, but the trio also appears on *Live in Europe* (Arabesque).

Kurt Elling—"He's really taken his stuff to a much more original level than most other singers out there." : *Close Your Eyes* and *This Time It's Love* (both Blue Note), and *The Messenger* (Capitol).

Cassandra Wilson—Charlie loves Wilson's entire body of work. : *New Moon Daughter* and *Blue Light 'Til Dawn* (both Blue Note) are the best introductions to Wilson's more contemporary sound. She sings standards on *Blue Skies* (JMT) and, with pianist Jacky Terrason, *Rendezvous* (Blue Note). Also recommended: *She Who Weeps* and *After the Beginning Again* (both JMT).

D'Gary—Like many other guitar players, Charlie is blown away by the mastery demonstrated by this guitarist from Madagascar. : *Malagasy Guitar/Music from Madagascar* (Shanachie); *Mbo Loza* (Indigo).

Robert Johnson—*The Complete Recordings* (2CDs: Columbia). Charlie calls this box set of the Delta blues legend's music a must-have.

Leon Parker—"His records are so original and bear repeated listening." : *Above & Below* (Epicure); *Belief* and *Awakening* (both Columbia).

Wes Montgomery—*Boss Guitar* (Original Jazz Classics). "You mention jazz guitar playing and that's what comes to mind. He's the cornerstone."

Various Artists—*Get Your Ass in the Water and Swim Like Me* (Arhoolie). "It's early rap. It's all prison poetry, basically signifying kind of stuff from the twenties and thirties. Just amazing rhymes."

Pat Martino—*We'll Be Together Again* (Muse). "He plays with Gil Goldstein, who plays Fender Rhodes. Pat Martino was a big influence. I mean, I can't play all those fast runs, but I transcribed a lot of his stuff."

True to his eclectic nature, Charlie also recommends the following diverse titles: **Horace Silver**—*Blowin' our Blues Away*, *Song for My Father*, and *Cape Verdean Blues* (all Blue Note); **Eddie Harris**—*All the Way Live* (Milestone), with Jimmy Smith, and *Mean Greens* (Atlantic); **The World Saxophone Quartet**—*Rhythm and Blues* (Elektra/Musician); **The Leaders**—*Out Here Like This* (Black Saint); **Stevie Wonder**—*Fullfillingness' First Finale* and *Songs in the Key of Life* (both Motown); **Astor Piazzolla**—*Tango: Zero Hour* (American Clave/Pangaea); **Little Walter Jacobs**—*The Best of Little Walter, Vols. 1–2* (MCA/Chess, available separately); ***Buddy Guy and Junior Wells**—*Hoodoo Man Blues* (Delmark); and **Albert King**—*Wednesday Night in San Francisco* and *Thursday Night in San Francisco* (both Stax).

CHARLIE HUNTER'S OWN RECORDINGS

Charlie prefers not to name favorites from the Charlie Hunter Quartet catalog but notes that *Ready, Set, Shango* and *Natty Dread* (both Blue Note), the latter his Bob Marley cover record, are cited most often by his fans. Of his work with TJ Kirk, Charlie calls the second album, *If Four Was One* (Reprise), the better of the two. He's especially proud of *Duo* (Blue Note), his 1999 project with drummer Leon Parker: "This is the most excited I've ever been about any record I've done. I don't know how I'm ever gonna play with another drummer again. It's serious."

⦿: Charlie's debut, *The Charlie Hunter Trio* (Mammoth) garnered much critical acclaim and still sounds fresh. For a sample of his live sound from the early '90s, search for the two volumes of *Up & Down Club Sessions* (Mammoth), recorded at San Francisco's Up & Down Club. Also check out Charlie's other Blue Note albums: *Bing Bing Bing* (with its winning cover of Nirvana's "Come as You Are") and *Return of the Candyman*.

M A R K   I S H A M (September 1, 1996)

I love records and music that cross genre lines," trumpeter/composer Mark Isham tells us as he relaxes backstage before a late summer performance at the Britt music festival in Jacksonville, Oregon. Clearly, Mark knows how to get what he wants because he has made genre-melding his career whether with his innovative jazz and New Age recordings, his many notable film scores, or his innovative children's albums.

Mark was leading a more mundane musical life, however, until one of those border-leaping recordings he likes turned his life around. Classically trained, Mark had played in the Oakland and San Francisco Symphonies and the San Francisco Opera Orchestra. He had also landed some intriguing side jobs, in jazz with Pharoah Sanders among others, and in rock with the Beach Boys. But that was still in the subservient role of helping others follow *their* muse. The turnaround began when he stopped by the house of a high school pal, Peter Maunu, who played him a record—the first Weather Report album—that had opened eyes all over the music world. "I said, 'God, this is great,' " Mark recalls, "so on my way home I stopped by the record store to buy it. They didn't have it, but the second one [*I Sing the Body Electric*] had just come out. So I took that home and didn't get past side one for two weeks. To this day, side one of that album is a masterpiece [to me] and it really helped shape my musical interests. If I had to pick one moment, that moment that I heard the opening bars of that record—it was as if all the ideas that I had been playing around with in my head but had never really figured out how to do, all of a sudden, [Joe] Zawinul and Wayne [Shorter] showed me 'yes, it can be done and this is how to do it.' "

With Weather Report as a signpost, Mark focused on jazz to express his now unleashed creativity. In the late 1970s, he joined Art Lande's Rubisa Patrol, writing several impressive themes for the band's two adventurous chamber jazz albums on ECM. In 1979, while still with Rubisa, he started his own fusion quartet, Group 87, with Maunu on guitar. He hadn't left the side gigs behind just yet—his 1970s résumé also included some time in the horn section of rock 'n' soul masters The Sons of Champlin and six years as part of Van Morrison's touring band. But he was on the verge of bigger things.

It all began to fall in place for Mark with his 1983 debut solo release, *Vapor Drawings* (Windham Hill), which helped define the cutting edge of the exploding New Age music scene. The movie industry came calling, attracted by Mark's ability to create unique musical atmospheres, and he's never looked back. While he's continued to record occasional jazz dates (he was touring with a jazz group supporting his *Blue Sun* album when we talked with him), Mark's career as a film music composer (nearly 50 scores and counting) and children's music producer has hit the stratosphere. The simplest explanation is that the latter projects draw on an obvious talent for mixing and matching sounds as few others can.

"I never aspired to it," Mark notes about his serendipitous relationship to film music, "and never really paid particular attention to the music in films. Really just out of the blue I got offered the opportunity to score a film and I said, 'Why not,' and just tried it. . . . I just applied my interest in music and musicians that crossed boundaries to making music I thought worked well with the pictures. For some reason, it worked out very well."

MARK ISHAM'S FAVORITE ARTISTS AND RECORDINGS

Miles Davis—*Sketches of Spain* (Columbia) and *On the Corner* (Columbia). Mark calls *Sketches* "a major influence on me and a major influence on music in the latter half of the twentieth century. It's not always a successful thing, to take classical music and bring it across into jazz, but I think this is one hundred percent successful." Mark also loves Miles's work in the years beginning with *Corner* "when he went to his most avant-garde, in the 1970s. Actually, the live records were the ones that were more whacked-out, because he would play, and Chick [Corea] would do his John Cage stuff, these sheets of electronic sound. A lot of those records are very self-indulgent and I can't recommend them to be-ginners coming into jazz, but they're great documents of a very historic time in jazz, one that I miss." ⬤: For an example of live '70s Miles, try *Pangaea* (2 CDs: Columbia).

Weather Report—*I Sing the Body Electric* (Columbia). "Weather Report came along and were obviously masters of the jazz vocabulary, but brought an intense interest in lots of different ethnic musics and in classical music. They created their own unrivaled blend of those various influences in a sound that was very unique and very, very powerful."

Sam Rivers—*Point of Many Returns* (Blue Note). "That was a big hit for me: Sam Rivers and Freddie Hubbard. Sam never broke through the way I thought he would. He's an amazing tenor player. And Freddie on there is just unbelievable, and this was at the height of his prowess. From a technical point of view, he's got to be one of the greatest trumpet players ever . . . for me, there was a period in those days when he was just untouchable."

John Coltrane—*Live at the Village Vanguard* (Impulse) and *Live at the Village Vanguard Again!* (Impulse). "Those records are seminal to me. *Live at the Village Vanguard*: I could practically sing every solo on that record. That redefined jazz in the early sixties." ⬤: The first Village Vanguard disc is from 1961, the second from 1966. *The Complete 1961 Village Vanguard Recordings* (4 CDs: Impulse) includes the performances from the first date plus much more from that run of performances.

Don Ellis—"He's somebody who has probably gotten lost," Mark says about the trumpeter/ bandleader. "At the time I think people knew about this guy, but now I don't think anybody does. He was a big influence on me. He got popular right when I was in high school, and yeah, Miles was starting to get electric but Don was already electric. He had a big band where everybody was electric. It had the wah-wah pedals and the Echoplexes and was doing this really wild stuff. That was what really pushed me into thinking of the trumpet not just as a be-bop instrument, but as something that could really move into the future." ⬤: *Electric Bath* (Sony) and *Tears of Joy* (Columbia, out of print).

Brian Eno—Mark admires Eno "as a philosopher of music. His whole rap is that he's not a musician. He's a lot more of a musician than he'd like to admit. But I know what he means: He's not a virtuoso on any instrument, never studied to be a performer . . . but what makes him really a tremendous force in music is as a conceptualist and as a producer. He has really changed the shape of popular music to a great degree." ⬤: See Master List.

John Hassell—*Power Spot* (ECM). Trumpeter Hassell's album, says Mark, is "one of the most cohesive things that he's done. Beautifully recorded. The thing about John is that he sort of has his one thing and has worked diligently over the years to try to place it in different sort of mediums: with Africans, then with hip-hop guys. The thing that's nice about *Power Spot* is within one record it's placed in a very wide variety of settings."

Nusrat Fateh Ali Khan—"Not his crossover records," Mark insists, "the real stuff." ●: *Devotional Songs* (Real World) and *Traditional Sufi Qawwalis* (Navras), which comes in four volumes available separately and is "the real stuff."

*Talking Heads—"Especially the records that Eno was involved in. I thought they were some of the most creative records of that period." ●: *More Songs About Buildings and Food, Fear of Music*, and *Remain in Light!* (all Sire).

Gustav Mahler—"I went through a period when I listened to the symphonies every day. When I was young, I actually worked in various symphony orchestras and played associate principal in one Mahler symphony." ●: See Master List.

Johann Sebastian Bach—The *Brandenburg* Concertos. Mark calls the six *Brandenburgs* "a sublime wrapping-up of baroque culture. As a trumpet player, one big area that I love is baroque music, and for a brief period I really had the ambition to be a baroque trumpet specialist." ●: Of the hundreds of *Brandenburg* recordings, try either Boston Baroque/Martin Pearlman (2 CDs released as separate titles: Telarc) or, Munich Bach Orchestra/Karl Richter (2 CDs: Archiv).

Vaughan Williams—*The Lark Ascending*. ●: Kennedy/Rattle/Birmingham Symphony Orchestra (EMI/Angel).

Samuel Barber—Adagio for Strings. ●: New York Philharmonic/Leonard Bernstein (Sony).

MARK ISHAM'S OWN RECORDINGS

"My point of view of my records is going to be a little different from an audience's," Mark notes. "I look at my records as the producer of the record." From that standpoint, he is happiest with *Blue Sun* (Columbia), an acoustic jazz date in the spirit of *Kind of Blue*–era Miles Davis, because "I don't see any mistakes on it."

Some of his favorite writing was done for film scores, including *Romeo is Bleeding* (Verve). "It was a dark little thriller—you know, no money," he explains. "So I just threw together this score with some of the guys from the [*Blue Sun*] band. I don't know if I'd recommend that record to someone who doesn't know much about jazz—a steep gradient, there," he laughs. But he would suggest "to just about anybody *A River Runs Through It* [Milan America], which couldn't be more different. It's a really well-written, beautifully melodic orchestral film music. I'm really proud of that."

Among his many children's recordings, Mark feels strongly about *The Firebird* (BMG Kidz), a daring project given the long shadow cast by Stravinsky's ballet. "That was of course exceedingly intimidating when I started. So I refused to listen to Stravinsky for a long time. I finally did it sort of as ancient Russian music, for percussion, cathedral organ, trumpets, balalaikas, and handbells—stuff you might find in an old Orthodox church." He's also fond of his work on *The Emperor and the Nightingale* (BMG Kidz), "which is a Chinese story narrated by Glenn Close. I really enjoy those [sorts of] projects because I force myself to come up with a really unique little ensemble, which is always the most fun."

⬤: Mark's lyrical *Vapor Drawings* (Windham Hill) remains a major achievement, in many ways the zenith of the Windham Hill jazz/New Age aesthetic, and it stands the test of time. So does the meditative, ambient *Tibet* (Windham Hill). Fans of Mark's jazzier playing on *Blue Sun* should also look for his 1990 Grammy-winning album *Mark Isham* (Virgin). Mark's latest is *The Silent Way Project—Miles Remembered* (Columbia), a tribute to his main man, Miles Davis. Some of his better-known film scores, besides those already mentioned, are *Trouble in Mind* (Island Visual), *Little Man Tate* (Varese Saraban), *The Hitcher* (Silva America), and *The Education of Little Tree* (Sony).

WAYLON JENNINGS   (December 10, 1998)

The industry branded Waylon Jennings an Outlaw for the way he cut against the buffed-up Nashville grain, and as with his buddy and sometimes partner *Willie Nelson, he was able to ride that Old West image to superstardom. But while that may have been savvy marketing, it's not as if the public was being sold an outright lie. Born in Littlefield, Texas, in 1937, Waylon was at odds with the Nashville system from the beginning with his weathered voice, cowpuncher appearance, and shoot-from-the-hip lyrics.

Plus, Waylon was as much rocker as country troubadour. He was nuts for Elvis Presley's music from the moment he first heard it on Littlefield's KVOW in 1954, and a few years later got fired from his own KVOW show for playing Little Richard. While in Lubbock, he became friends with Buddy Holly, then plotting to be the new Elvis. Holly later produced Waylon's debut single, "Jolie Blond," while

Waylon played bass on Holly's final tour. (He wasn't on the plane that went down with Holly on board only because he had given up his seat to the Big Bopper.) The rocking beat he played with Holly survived in his own music and was part of what made Nashville execs shake in their $400 boots.

Waylon chose many of his other models like a rocker, too. He had idolized rough-cut honky tonker Ernest Tubb since childhood, an influence that colored his music from the beginning. But he was getting other ideas from a Saturday night radio show on KWKI out of Shreveport, Louisiana. "They played B. B. King, Bobby 'Blue' Bland, and Fats Domino," Waylon writes us while vacationing in Arizona. "In those days, that music was called 'no-name jive.' That definitely had an influence on my music."

Touring less heavily these days than in the past, Waylon has created a legacy of defiant artistry. When current independent-minded country artists look for inspiration, the stripped-down sound Waylon created in the early '70s and the emotional honesty of his lyrics still light the way. And another musical Jennings may soon be holding the torch. We asked Waylon if there were any newer artists he wanted to turn the world onto, and he replied: "My son Shooter—you will have to wait a little while, but trust me it will happen."

WAYLON JENNINGS'S FAVORITE ARTISTS AND RECORDINGS

Ernest Tubb—"Walking the Floor Over You." Tubb's first major hit, in 1941, made him a star not only in country music but also the movies. In fact, that's how Waylon first encountered him, at the drive-in theater behind his house when he was growing up in Littlefield. : See Master List.

Buddy Holly—"Buddy Holly had a big influence on me—his in-the-pocket rhythm and straight-eight beats," Waylon writes. : *From the Original Master Takes* (MCA) presents 20 of Holly's biggest hits.

Hank Williams, Sr.—In his autobiography, published in 1996, Waylon notes about Williams: "I always wanted to be singer, but he etched it in stone." He also says that "If I had an Outlaw hero, someone to set my standard and measure my progress, it was Hank Williams." : See Master List.

Carl Smith—Waylon met Smith, a huge country star in the '50s and an early hero of his, when he first went to Nashville. He writes in his book that "I tried my damnedest to look like him and sing like him; I even combed my hair like his, and I didn't want him to notice." : *The Essential . . .* (Columbia/Legacy).

Elvis Presley—"I was crazy about Elvis. I loved that churning rhythm on the bottom. He didn't even have his drums yet, but the rock 'n' roll part was unmistakable" 🔘 : To hear Presley the way Waylon did, pick up on songs like "That's All Right, Mama" or "Blue Moon of Kentucky" on *The Complete Sun Sessions* (RCA). You can hear Elvis soon after he added a drummer on *The King of Rock 'n' Roll: The Complete '50s Masters* (5 CDs: RCA) or classic early albums like *Elvis* and *Elvis Presley* (both RCA).

Fats Domino— 🔘 : *They Call Me the Fat Man . . . : The Legendary Imperial Recordings* (4 CDs: EMI America) may be more than casual fans want. Keep in mind, though, that the single-disc alternative, *My Blue Heaven: Best of Fats Domino* (EMI America) includes only two of Domino's early New Orleans R&B tracks from before he crossed over to the pop charts.

B. B. King— 🔘 : See Master List.

Bobby "Blue" Bland— 🔘 : See Master List.

WAYLON JENNINGS'S OWN RECORDINGS

"I think the album I did with Don Was [1994's *Waymore's Blues (Part II)* (RCA)] has some of my best work on it," writes Waylon, choosing to highlight this record alone.

🔘 : *Early Years* (RCA) captures Waylon in the pre-Outlaw period, although "Only Daddy That'll Walk the Line" was a harbinger of things to come. *Honky Tonk Heroes* (Pair), released in 1973, features nine songs by Billy Joe Shaver. Other winning albums from the 1970s include *This Time*, *Dreamin' My Dreams*, and *I've Always Been Crazy* (all RCA), the latter with a Buddy Holly medley. 1985's *Will the Wolf Survive* (MCA) includes simpatico covers of *Los Lobos' title tune and *Steve Earle's "The Devil's Right Hand." The 1996 album *Right for the Time* (Justice) is a strong late-career effort. *Only Daddy That'll Walk the Line: The RCA Years* (2 CDs: Camden) is the best compilation, but if you can only spring for one disc, go for *Essential . . .* (RCA).

E L V I N   J O N E S   (March 18, 1998)

By the time Elvin Jones hit his teens, older brothers Hank and Thad were already up-and-coming players on the national jazz scene. But Elvin had plotted a different course for his life until a record changed everything. Elvin had joined the Army Air Corps and was playing percussion in the Air Corps Band.

He planned to make the military his career. Although most of his friends and acquaintances were either jazz musicians or fans, Elvin was only vaguely interested in the music. Through Hank, who was touring with Norman Granz's Jazz at the Philharmonic, Elvin had met the likes of Coleman Hawkins, Lester Young, and Charlie Parker and seen Hank's concerts when the tour came through Columbus, Ohio, where Elvin was stationed. "You can enjoy the music without really understanding it," notes Elvin, whose unpretentious, almost shy demeanor belies his assertive playing. "It didn't motivate me in any way. I said, 'Oh, this is nice entertainment.' I enjoyed meeting colleagues of my brother and I was impressed and all that, but I didn't think that was the life for me."

Then someone played a Dizzy Gillespie record for him and the Army Air Corps Band lost a drum major. The tune was "Salt Peanuts," Elvin recalls, but it was Sid Catlett's work on the drums that nailed his attention. Elvin had never heard anyone use wire brushes the way Catlett did on the intro to that tune: "After I heard that music, it changed my mind completely. [I thought] 'This is what I want to do.' "

From that point on, Elvin began listening hard to every outstanding example of jazz drumming he could find—at first, records featuring Kenny Clarke or Max Roach, later, the explosive work of Art Blakey. Some of his most useful lessons came not from a musician but from an engineering student friend who happened to also be an ardent jazz fan. "He could hear somebody play something and he could tell you exactly what they were doing," Elvin says. "So, he gave me a deep insight into what it was that I needed to study in order to bring myself up to speed. I already knew how to play the drums. That wasn't the problem. The thing was how to use that knowledge to play this new music that I was listening to."

As for the African feel of Elvin's drumming, so big a part of his work with John Coltrane, that too came via a friend, but this time a player—pianist Bobby Timmons, who would later serve in some of Blakey's most memorable units. Timmons lived across the street from Elvin, who had moved to New York from Detroit, and turned him onto some anthropological field recordings that he had picked up at the United Nations record store. "[There were] tribal celebrations, funerals, and things like that. And then there was another collection, a series about pygmies," Elvin says. "And that was before I played with Coltrane. I was so fascinated by it, just the spirit of the music. I couldn't get enough of it. I guess that music became part of me at that time."

Perhaps the greatest teaching Elvin received in jazz came from John Coltrane, with whom Elvin began working in 1959. 'Trane pushed the spontaneity at the heart of jazz about as far as it could go. Although it seems impossible to comprehend given the power and empathy of the music they created, Elvin confirms what we'd heard about the great Coltrane quartet (Jones, Coltrane, McCoy Tyner, and Jimmy Garrison): that in their entire six years together, they never rehearsed. "When we went on stage, Coltrane would just start playing and we'd pick it up," Elvin says. Why did 'Trane work that way? "I think he did it like that because he felt we were capable [because of] the kind of chemistry and rapport that existed between us . . . It's just a matter of listening. . . . If the rapport is such that you don't have to worry about what the rest of the group [will do], you flow just like a river flowin' down. When it comes to a bend, the current goes with the course of the river, so it's no problem." No problem, that is, for a perhaps never-equaled quartet anchored by a drummer named Jones.

ELVIN JONES'S FAVORITE ARTISTS AND RECORDINGS

Kenny Clarke—Clarke made only a few albums as a leader, but Elvin says you can appreciate him just as well as a sideman. ⬤: Outstanding jazz records featuring Clarke on drums include Miles Davis's *Walkin'* (Original Jazz Classics), Dexter Gordon's *Our Man in Paris* (Blue Note), J. J. Johnson's *The Eminent J. J. Johnson, Vol. 2* (Blue Note), and Hank Jones's *The Jazz Trio of Hank Jones* (Savoy).

Max Roach—Elvin points to the recordings Roach made with the group he coled with Clifford Brown and his sessions with Charlie Parker and *Sonny Rollins. "They were all young then, and the music was new and fresh. That was some of the most beautiful music I ever heard in my life." ⬤: Start with *Clifford Brown & Max Roach* (Polygram), Sonny Rollins's *Saxophone Colossus* (Original Jazz Classics), and *The Charlie Parker Story* (Savoy).

Big Bill Broonzy—Elvin liked Broonzy's blues guitar playing. ⬤: See Master List.

Huddie Ledbetter ("Leadbelly")—As a kid, Elvin had a copy of Leadbelly's "How Long Blues," which he wore out on the family's wind-up Victrola. ⬤: "How Long Blues" is on *Leadbelly—Vol. 3—Shout On* (Smithsonian/Folkways). See also Master List.

***Pete Seeger**—"They called it folk music, but to me it was just beautiful music." ⬤: See the section on Pete and his recordings.

Thelonious Monk—"I thought Thelonious Monk's music was so advanced, for lack of a better word. Not particularly complex, if you listen very closely, but it just came from another direction completely." Elvin greatly prefers Monk's records that feature either Art Blakey, Max Roach, Roy Haynes, or Frankie Dunlop, among the very few drummers, he feels, who really understood Monk's aesthetic. ⏺: *Thelonious Monk with John Coltrane* (Original Jazz Classics) and *Monk's Music* (Original Jazz Classics) are superior records with Art Blakey on traps. Roach is the drummer on the classic *Brilliant Corners* (Original Jazz Classics).

Art Blakey—"I liked Art Blakey because of the passion he put into the way he played. Art Blakey was one of the very few drummers I thought that could play with [Thelonious] Monk and enhance and make what Monk was doing even more significant." ⏺: *Art Blakey's Jazz Messengers with Thelonious Monk* (Atlantic), from 1957.

Duke Ellington—*Black, Brown, and Beige* (Sony). For Elvin, Ellington's music ranks with the best classical music in its sophistication and beauty. He likes the entire catalog but makes special mention of the above album, which Ellington recorded with gospel singer Mahalia Jackson. About her performance of Ellington's song "Come Sunday" Elvin says, "When I heard that record, tears were in my eyes." ⏺: Excerpts from the Ellington suite appear on the superb *The Duke Ellington Carnegie Hall Concerts, December 1944* and *The Duke Ellington Carnegie Hall Concerts, January 1943* (both 2 CDs: Prestige). *The Blanton-Webster Band* (Bluebird), a three-CD set of wonderfully accomplished music, is from the early 1940s.

Dinah Washington—"Harbor Lights." "Dinah Washington's recording is straight to your heart, it's so beautiful." ⏺: *The Complete Dinah Washington on Mercury, Vol. 2 (1950–52)* (Mercury).

Al Hibbler—"One of my all-time favorite vocalists . . . and the perfect background for him was Duke Ellington's orchestra. I don't think it could have been better if it was with the Metropolitan Opera or the New York Philharmonic." ⏺: Again, Ellington's *Carnegie Hall Concerts, December 1944* (2 CDs: Prestige) and *Sophisticated Lady* (Bluebird.)

John Coltrane—In Elvin's opinion, his former boss was the greatest musician in the world. ⏺: See below.

ELVIN JONES'S OWN RECORDINGS

Of his recordings under his own leadership, Elvin singles out 1968's *Puttin' It Together* (Blue Note) and 1993's *It Don't Mean a Thing* (Enja). The former is a trio outing with Joe Farrell on reeds, about whom Elvin says, "Joe Farrell was one of these guys. I don't think there's anything that he couldn't do with a woodwind or a reed instrument. He was phenomenal." The latter album features vocalist Kevin Mahogany, whose voice Elvin loves, along with trumpeter Nicholas

Payton, reedman Sonny Fortune, trombonist Delfeayo Marsalis, pianist Willie Pickens, and bassist Cecil McBee.

His favorites with other groups include *Illumination* (Impulse), by the Elvin Jones/Jimmy Garrison Sextet, featuring McCoy Tyner. "I've always had a special place in my heart for that because it was Jimmy [Garrison] and I," Elvin says. "You know, he died so prematurely. He just never had an opportunity to develop." Elvin also mentions the atmospheric *John Coltrane and Johnny Hartman* (Impulse), with the classic Coltrane quartet backing the aptly named Hartman, one of Elvin's favorite singers.

⊙: Elvin is the drummer on almost all the greatest Coltrane records, including *My Favorite Things* (Atlantic), *Live at the Village Vanguard* (Impulse), *Afro-Blue Impressions* (2 CDs: Pablo), *A Love Supreme* (Impulse), and many others. *The Classic Quartet: Complete Impulse! Studio Recordings* (8 CDs: Impulse) is a gold mine for devotees of this music. Elvin also contributed to many landmark albums by other artists, notable among them Wayne Shorter's *Speak No Evil* (Blue Note).

IRA KAPLAN (August 6, 1997)

Yo La Tengo's Ira Kaplan knows pop music history well enough to have been a rock critic in his pre-YLT days. But he prefers not to play the writer's game of dissecting how a group's "influences" show up in its music—at least when it's his group that's being dissected. "I mean I can mention records that were important to me and I can sort of by inference assume they're important to the band," he tells us. "But I'm not always that sure or even that interested in what the connection is."

And then in the next breath, we find ourselves talking about those connections—sort of—starting with the Kinks. Ira listened to this band more than any other when he was growing up in the early 1970s. While he doesn't hear the musical link to YLT, he notes that neither band was a dedicated follower of fashion: "Those records—not the early 'You Really Got Me' and 'All Day and All of the Night' records but the ones like 'Sunny Afternoon'—it was just a sound unlike anyone else and so personal that I think in some way that must have registered as a good idea [to me]."

Then there's the matter of the Velvet Underground, a group that nearly everyone assumes Yo La Tengo idolized, and not just because both bands are from New York, feature women drummers, and have curly-haired Jewish guys singing and playing guitar. In the music, where it counts, one can't help noticing some similarities—the juxtaposition of fragile prettiness and defiant ugliness, the blend of classic pop songcraft and sonic chaos. Ira has been hearing the comparison for over a decade, and he wants to make clear that he's no longer fighting it. "If I had to pick one band, after resisting picking one band, the Velvet Underground would be as good a choice as any," he says with only a trace of weariness. "The cliché aspect of it makes that hard to say, particularly with the number of times that they're invoked with our group. I try not to get defensive about it, with varying degrees of success, but I'm staring at a record shelf filled with their albums and bootlegs, you know, so their importance to me is huge."

Not by any means exclusive, though, as the list below reveals. (Ira even did his time as a Deadhead, although "I never joined the caravan," he laughs.) Nevertheless, Ira asserts again that YLT ultimately looks inside, not out, for inspiration. "The fact is, the three of us do listen to a wide variety of music," he acknowledges, "and so I think that ends up reflecting itself." But only, he suggests, because evolving tastes reflect evolving people: "As you change from year to year and record to record, if you allow your music to change along with yourself, that is what I hope is going on."

IRA KAPLAN'S FAVORITE ARTISTS AND RECORDINGS

The Kinks—Ira saw them play in 1972 and raced to a local department store the next day to buy *The Kinks Kronikles*, an early best-of package. He quickly acquired the rest of their catalog, not an easy task then because several of their discs were out of print. ⬤: Great Kinks albums from the prime of their career include *Face to Face* (Reprise), *Something Else By the Kinks* (Reprise), *The Village Green Preservation Society* (Reprise), *Arthur* (Reprise), *Lola vs. The Powerman and the Money-Go-Round, Part One* (Reprise), and *Muswell Hillbillies* (Rhino). *The Kinks Kronikles* (Reprise) samples their best songs for Reprise, where they did their most notable work.

*The Grateful Dead—*Anthem of the Sun, Aoxomoxoa* (Warner Bros.), *Live Dead* (Warner Bros.), *Workingman's Dead* (Warner Bros.), *American Beauty* (Warner Bros.), *The Grateful Dead* (Warner Bros.), and *Europe '72* (2 CDs: Warner Bros.). Ira listened primarily to their albums through *Europe '72*. We've listed them all except the less-distinguished debut, *Grateful Dead* (not to be confused with the 1970 live release *The Grateful Dead*). "As that became more and more kind of a cross to bear [to have] been such a fan of them, it's kind of interesting sometimes to think of what they meant to me and what that represents. But you know the way I grew up was definitely a very hippie town, so they were really in the air, much more than the Kinks were. The Kinks were more of a private discovery. Grateful Dead was more of a rite of passage."

The Jefferson Airplane—*After Bathing at Baxter's* (RCA). When he was young, Ira was attracted to the Summer of Love aura radiated by the early San Francisco groups like the Dead and the Airplane. "I had to be much older before the concurrent New York, Velvet Underground anti-community had its appeal," he recalls. About *Baxter's*, he says, "That was a record that kinda kept changing shape in front of me, which I appreciated."

The Velvet Underground—See above. ⬤: See Master List.

The Byrds—*Fifth Dimension* (Columbia), *Younger Than Yesterday* (Columbia), *The Notorious Byrd Brothers* (Columbia), and *Sweetheart of the Rodeo* (Columbia). The Byrds prove, Ira says, that organic growth isn't the only way to improve your music. The Byrds "somehow got such strength from inner turmoil and constant changes."

Sun Ra—*The Singles* (2 CDs: Evidence). Ira loves Sun Ra's work in general but found this collection of early singles "astonishing." "It begins as a doo-wop record, and then goes in almost every direction. I mean, there's blues stuff, there's the space stuff he's more notorious for, different singers. This guy Yochanon . . . might be the most way-out R&B singer of all."

Eleventh Dream Day—*Ursa Major* (Atavistic) and *Eighth* (Thrill Jockey). "When a band becomes a hobby, you could argue persuasively that that's a bad thing for a band, but I think in this case it's completely re-energized them. And the last two records they've made since they've almost ceased to exist are the two best records they've ever made."

*NRBQ—*Kick me Hard* (Rounder). Like the ex-critic and true Q-head that he is, Ira says that *At Yankee Stadium* (Mercury) may be a better record in the traditional sense "but if I had to pick one record, I guess it might be *Kick me Hard*. That's just one of the records that kind of captures what's unique about them."

Half Japanese—*½ Gentleman/Not Beasts* (Armageddon). "Their first album was a triple album and was one of the most amazing records, and most amazing debut records I can imagine." Ira says his favorite guitar players include this group's infamous primitives Jad and David Fair. (Other fave stringbenders are all New Yorkers: Jody Harris, Robert Quine, and the ex-Television pair, Tom Verlaine and Richard Lloyd.) ⬤: Yo La Tengo and Jad Fair collaborated on 1998's *Strange But True* (Matador).

The Monkees—The Monkees were formed to star in a "Hard Day's Night"-ish TV series for the kiddies. The secret of this manufactured band's musical success was its catalog of impossibly hooky songs, written by such pros as Carol King, Neil Diamond, Barry Mann, Tommy Boyce, and Bobby Hart. "It's nothing I'm capable of doing," says Ira, "but I really admire the way they just turn out those songs like an assembly line." ⏺: *Greatest Hits* (Rhino) contains all the big hits plus several much-loved album tracks such as "Mary, Mary."

David Kilgour—*David Kilgour and Heavy Eights* (Flying Nun). "He was in the band the Clean, which was one of the important bands in underground New Zealand music, and their records were some of my favorites. He continues to make really good records."

Tara Key—Key records both solo and with the band Antietam. "I think the records only tell half the story and probably a misleading story as well," says Ira. "She's just an amazing guitar player and one I've learned a lot from watching and being friends with." ⏺: Hear Tara with Antietam on *Burgoo* (Triple X) and *Rope-a-Dope* (Homestead). Tara's solo albums include *Bourbon County* and *Ear & Echo* (both Homestead).

Peter Stampfel—*Have Moicy!* (Rounder). "That's sort of a special record where really just about every song is great. As Stampfel himself writes in various liner notes, his approaches to recordings over the years have been a little haphazard and on that one, everything just worked." Note that this record is credited to Michael Hurley, the Unholy Modal Rounders, and Frederick and the Clamtones, even though it was Stampfel's idea, and is a project of his then-group, the Holy Modal Rounders, which frequently adopted other guises.

Lambchop—"Lambchop is a current band that I think is just amazing." ⏺: See Master List.

IRA KAPLAN'S OWN RECORDINGS

Like many of our interviewees, Ira was reluctant to rank YLT's output. "I hope the new one [at the time, *I Hear the Heart Beating as One* (Matador)] is the freshest to us, the one we have the most emotion invested in right now. I certainly don't react to our records the way I react to other people's records, having favorites. You know, they kind of represent snapshots. I don't know, do you have a favorite old picture of yourself? Or does it represent the time?"

: For recommended YLT releases, see Georgia Hubley's entry.

SALIF KEITA (March 26, 1996)

Literally a son of Mali, Salif Keita can trace his family's roots hundreds of years back to Soundjata Keita, who founded the Empire of Mali in the 13th Century. But Salif was also a disowned son. He was born an albino, a bad omen to his people, which made him an outcast. The screws tightened when he chose a career in music. His disapproving father cast him out of the family, abandoning him to the streets of Bamako, Mali's capitol.

Undaunted, or perhaps because he had no choice, Salif supported himself for years by performing for passersby. He also sang in the Bamako clubs and eventually landed a vocalist gig with the Super Rail Band, a fast-rising group aided by government support. The Rail Band played a blend of traditional and Western styles, with an undercurrent of Cuban music. In 1973, Salif and Rail Band guitarist Kante Manfila moved over to Les Ambassadeurs Internationaux, another important Malian pop band. With their new group, they installed a pop blend of traditional Malian music, Zairian and South African Afropop, and Cuban salsa. Their vision proved itself by helping to propel Les Ambassadeurs to international stardom.

Salif left Les Ambassadeurs in 1987 to launch a solo career, relocating, like so many African musicians, to Paris, the Afropop capitol of the world. His solo debut, *Soro* (Mango), released later that year, became an immediate international hit and ultimately one of the best-selling world music albums ever. It also revealed a new Salif, updating the traditional sound of his sweeping, acrobatic Malian vocals with a hip world pop approach.

As Salif's celebrity has grown, he has displayed a generosity to match. Exploiting the spotlight of his stardom, he has helped bring attention, and some measure of relief, to the plight of Africa's often-oppressed albino population. In addition, he has introduced the world to lesser-known but remarkable vocalists from his native country, several of whom he records in his new studio in Bamako. Clearly, Mali's rejected son has welcomed himself home, and come laden with gifts.

SALIF KEITA'S FAVORITE ARTISTS AND RECORDINGS

Orquesta Aragon—When we reached Salif one evening in Mali, he discussed a dizzying array of influences and other favorites, beginning with this group. Hybridized Cuban music shows up all over Africa, from Mali to Mozambique. Orquesta Aragon, which caught fire in the '50s, augmented the traditional sounds of the Cuban *son* bands with violins and woodwinds in a style called *charanga*.

The band also toured Africa frequently. ⦿: *That Cuban Cha-Cha-Cha* (BMG) or *Danzones* (Discuba).

Irakere—One of the few Cuban bands to have a significant profile in the United States during the long cultural embargo against Castro's country, Irakere became an international sensation in the early '70s. ⦿: *The Best of Irakere* (Columbia/ Sony) or *Misa Negra* (Messidor).

Celia Cruz and Johnny Pacheco—"I have listened to this music a lot. I still listen to it. It never ages, and I love that about it. It's really great music." Johnny Pacheco is another Cuban bandleader whose groups toured Africa. ⦿: See Master List.

Bryan Adams—"I really like his melodies," Salif says. He likes every record Adams has made. ⦿: *Cuts Like a Knife* and *So Far So Good* (both A&M).

Pink Floyd—"I listened to *beaucoup, beaucoup, beaucoup* Pink Floyd," Salif says about his favorite Western rock band. ⦿: *Meddle*, *Dark Side of the Moon*, *Wish You Were Here* (all Capitol), and *The Wall* (Columbia) represent the band at its commercial zenith in the 1970s, but if you want to transcend into true *beaucoup* territory, also grab Pink Floyd's 1967 debut *The Piper at the Gates of Dawn* (Capitol), the only full Pink Floyd album to feature the erratic psychedelic visionary Syd Barrett, and the 1969 live opus *Ummagumma* (Capitol).

James Brown— ⦿: See Master List.

Otis Redding— ⦿: See Master List.

Rod Stewart— ⦿: *Gasoline Alley*, released in 1970, and 1971's *Every Picture Tells a Story* (both Mercury) are two of his most memorable records. *Best of Rod Stewart* (Mercury) contains classic early Stewart, including some tracks with the Faces and Stewart's early solo hits, like "Maggie May." *Downtown Train* (Warner Bros.) collects tracks from the Stewart box set, concentrating on the '80s hits.

Bad Company— ⦿: See Master List.

Fantani Touré—*N'Tin Naari* (Stern's Africa). Salif produced this album in his new studio. "It's great, pure music," he tells us. "It is almost totally acoustic, and she sings so well."

Fela Kuti—Fela's pointed political messages coupled with his long, groove-charged songs won him huge audiences in West Africa. For his efforts, Fela was jailed and tortured by Nigeria's military government. ⦿: See Master List.

Oumou Sangaré— ⦿: Her spectacular voice shines on *Ko Sira* (World Circuit).

Ali Farka Toure—People who listen to this Malian guitarist's music for the first time marvel at its resemblance to American delta blues. ⏺: Start with *The Source* (World Circuit).

Issaka Luli—"Issaka plays some really great stuff. He plays a traditional Goni and is a wassoulu singer. He is a super musician, and I know that I'm going to like him a lot." ⏺: As of this writing, his debut album was yet to be released.

Sory Kandia Kouyate— ⏺: To hear perhaps the most important living exponent of traditional Malian music, check out *Tara* and *Doua* (both Sonodisc).

Camara Demba--Demba was the lead singer at Bembeya Jazz National from Guinea. ⏺: *Bembeya, Jazz National* (Sonodisc) is a solid introduction to the group's work.

Siramory Diabate— ⏺: Her recordings are extremely hard to come by outside of Mali, but search for a French release called *Sira Mory* (Syllart).

Miriam Makeba—Makeba's anti-apartheid activism got her exiled from South Africa in the 1960s; Harry Belafonte helped her career continue in the United States. However, her Black Nationalist positions and marriage to Black Panther leader Stokely Carmichael bought her harassment from the government and she wound up in Ghana. Her music continues to inspire. ⏺: *Pata Pata* (Sonodisc), *Sangoma* (Warner Bros.), and *The Click Song* (Esperance), and her early vocal ensemble work with the Skylarks on *The Best of Miriam Makeba and the Skylarks* (Camden).

Hugh Masakela—South Africa's leading jazz trumpeter also pioneered what some now call world music with his transcultural fusion of South African rhythms, jazz, and R&B. ⏺: See Master List.

Penny Penny—South African Penny Penny is renowned for his infectious Afro-disco dance rhythms. ⏺: *Shaka Bundu*, *Yogo Yogo*, and *La Finda Ishangaane* (all Shandel).

SALIF KEITA'S OWN RECORDINGS

Like so many artists, Salif's favorite record is the one he just finished. At the time of our interview, that was *Folon . . . The Past* (Mango).

⏺: The 1991 release *Amen*, produced by Joe Zawinul with cameos from Carlos Santana and Wayne Shorter, may be Salif's most accessible disc for Western ears. And *Soro* (Mango), his 1987 breakout album, probably belongs in any collection of African pop music. For a sample of Salif's earlier career, check the collection

Les Ambassadeurs Internationales Featuring Salif Keita (Rounder). Salif's latest as of this writing is *Sasie* (Stern's Africa).

EDWARD KOWALCZYK (November 13, 1998)

The Live story is not the usual dues-paying epic. The first album by vocalist/ songwriter Edward Kowalczyk and friends, 1991's *Mental Jewelry*, made them stars in both the alternative and mainstream rock worlds. Their second, 1994's *Throwing Copper*, shot them into the rock elite with over four million copies sold in its first year. So Edward tries hard to keep the whole thing in perspective: "You have to remember that [our fans] are relating to it in the way that I related to U2 when I was seventeen or eighteen. It was my religion at the time, rock 'n' roll. I was just waiting on pins and needles until the next thing came out. So I just always remember that feeling and try to turn it in on myself and say 'hey, we're lucky enough to be doing that for some people out there, too, and it's just fun.' My job is to feel it in the deepest place I possibly can and go give it to those people."

Live fans are well aware that Edward based the group's sound on an amalgam of his favorite bands, U2 and *REM. But he makes clear to us that the Beatles played a big part in his thinking, too. While he was growing up in York, Pennsylvania, Mom pampered his ears with her Beatles and John Lennon albums. For him, the Beatles are "sort of a base ground of melody and sense of structure and phrasing." And he says he listens to Lennon's records today even more than the Beatles.

In high school, while still searching for his musical comfort zone, Edward passed through a heavy metal stage, too, although he'd rather not call it that: "To me heavy metal was the stuff that I didn't like, like Twisted Sister and Ratt. But I really remember being into Led Zeppelin and Black Sabbath. So I was doing my early experimentation with pot and partying and letting loose and listening to stuff that made my mom mad. That was the gist of it. I always loved Ozzy Osborne's voice. I thought he was such a great singer, and just so bizarre, but also such a really cool lyricist and vocalist and melody writer. Some of [Live's] harder edge came from the fact that I wasn't afraid of big loud guitars. In fact, I like them quite a bit."

Still, as he contemplated starting his own band, Edward hoped to sing about something more elevating than the demon spawn of Satan. He began turning away from Ledfoot rock and discovered U2 and REM. "I was sort of sick of hard rock and growing out of that rebellious stage at that point, I think," Edward says. "There was something about REM and U2 . . . [They had] this beautiful sense of songwriting, and also very intelligent, sensitive, expressive lyrics."

While still in high school, Edward formed the band that ultimately became Live, with a vision that looked beyond sold-out sports arenas. "My other interest in life at that point was a sort of burgeoning interest in spiritual literature and teachers," he says. "So they kind of came together at this interesting moment. I was becoming the singer/songwriter of this fledgling new band and then also getting into my spiritual interests, and also being totally heart-moved by these bands' [R.E.M. and U2] records."

Edward's spirituality is quickly moving to center stage in Live's current shows. The group's 1997 document, *Secret Samadhi,* introduced sitars and hinted at Indian musical structures. On his upcoming album (untitled and still in production as of this writing but due on Radioactive/MCA), the sound expands to incorporates several new musical sources, including Edward's fascination, encouraged by his spiritual teacher, with Indian devotional music. The new album, he says, "has the energy of faith . . . rather than being angst driven, like a lot of our music has been in the past. There are songs on this record that are happy from start to finish."

EDWARD KOWALCZYK'S FAVORITE ARTISTS AND RECORDINGS

John Lennon—*Imagine* (Capitol). Edward feels that this classic album comes from "a period of John Lennon's work where I think he was absolutely tapped into something really profound and wonderful, and it was cut short too early." He particularly likes the song "How Do You Sleep?" on this record.

The Beatles—*The Beatles* (a.k.a. the White Album, Capitol). "I definitely remember the White Album as something my mom played a lot. I think more than anything, because I didn't understand the lyrics, the melodies seeped into . . . my cerebrum way back when and became the foundation for everything I'm doing now."

Led Zeppelin— ⬤: *Led Zeppelin, . . . II, . . . III, . . . IV, Houses of the Holy,* and *Physical Graffiti* (all Swan Song) are the prime releases in the catalog. The entire heavy metal genre in essence sprang from Zeppelin's 1969 debut.

Black Sabbath—"Ozzy's vocal had this very haunting quality, which nobody could really write off. It's also the band forging new ground with guitar sound and just their overall thing." ⬤: The signal Sabbath releases of the Ozzy Osborne years are *Paranoid* and *Masters of Reality* (both Warner Bros.). The compilation *We Sold Our Soul for Rock and Roll* (Warner Bros.) samples the group's heyday of heaviness.

*REM—*Lifes Rich Pageant* (IRS). "I had to buy two of those cassettes because I wore one of them out in my Walkman in my senior year in high school. I just couldn't get enough of REM."

U2—*War* and *Joshua Tree* (both Island). "My very first concert that I actually paid for was U2 on their *Joshua Tree* tour in 1987. That was a pretty important moment, just because I remember watching them and thinking very forcefully, 'This is where I wanna take my band,' this kind of communal experience they were giving people with the music and their performance and their passion . . . Bands like U2, it was like, 'Man, this opens my heart, this makes me feel good, I gotta get more of this!' "

The Smiths—*The Queen Is Dead* (Sire). Edward groups this with the above-mentioned albums as "absolute inspirations of that mid-'80s era, that fortified me and made me really want to be in the band."

The Psychedelic Furs—*Forever Now* (Columbia).

Hari Om Sharan—Sharan, from India, specializes in the bhajan, a kind of light classical Hindu religious song form. ●: *The Best of . . .* (T Series: contact Khazana India Arts Online: www.khazana.com) and *Memorable Bhajans* (EMI India).

Nusrat Fateh Ali Khan—Edward's love of devotional music extends beyond India to the late Pakistani qawalli singer. "His devotional music is like singing to the Lord of the Universe, the Source," says Edward. ●: See Master List.

EDWARD KOWALCZYK'S OWN RECORDINGS

Rather than pick favorite albums per se, Edward picks favorites songs on each Live album—"Mother Earth is a Vicious Crowd" on *Mental Jewelry*, "Lightning Crashes" on *Throwing Copper*, "Lakini's Juice" from *Secret Samadhi*, and "I Stood Up For Love" on the upcoming release (all Radioactive). "Lightning" may seem a no-brainer choice to the band's fans, because it was a hugely successful single but Edward says it was far from a sure thing. The first two singles released off *Copper* had already soared up the charts when Edward asked Radioactive to release "Lightning," calling it the most important song he'd written to date: "And the record company said, 'There's no freakin' way it'll ever be a hit. It takes three and a half minutes to get to the first chorus! What are you, crazy?' " It became the biggest-selling single in the band's history.

About the new album, Edward says, "I really think that we're in the midst of making our greatest record yet." He comments that "I Stood Up For Love" "is as simple and straightforward as you get. But it's [a song] that I think if people come to it, it'll do something special. You hope and pray for those moments as a rock band that you really nail it, you really get something that is just going to be around forever, and always have the same depth."

JON LANGFORD (May 22, 1998)

The closest pop culture analogue to the Mekons isn't another band, it's cable TV with its gazillion channels. Since their birth in the late-'70s British punk scene, the Mekons have careened, in every sense of the word, across the musical landscape, snatching up hunks of punk, British folk, pop, and even American country to create music that drops hints everywhere but sounds mainly like itself. With this group, only a few things ever stay the same—critical raves, the wild devotion of its fans, and guitarist/vocalists Jon Langford and Tom Greenhalgh, the band's only consistent members.

The band's name was lifted from a British comic book of the 1950s in which "evil, intelligent aliens with little green heads and stout bodies—the Mekons— zipped around in flying saucers and fought the ultraconservative 'heroes,' " Greenhalgh once explained to an interviewer. When we contact Jon Langford, he informs us that he has drawn on roots that were just about as mobile as the group's namesake. "The first thing that inspired me was the first thing that I tried to play, and that was a Johnny Cash song, 'Folsom Prison Blues,' which is really quite funny, because we still play that song now," Jon says. But his interest in Cash got short-circuited by the reigning pop of the early '70s: "That's what I was into, very much what was on the charts that week. So the glam thing was very big. . . . Rod Stewart and the Faces, Slade, T Rex, David Bowie, the kind of music people who like football liked. . . . It was a strange combination, kind of a precursor to punk, and a lot of the people in punk bands had that sort of background.

"Then I sort of grew up," Jon adds, "and got more maudlin, and listened to stuff like Procol Harum, Hawkwind, and Black Sabbath. We had a band [then and the singer] had the first Black Sabbath album, which had the ghostly woman standing in some ruins on the front. We used to listen to that with the lights off and just the little red light on the stereo on, and then he would like move the cover from one side of the room to another and swear it had levitated. I knew he was moving it, but it was still really scary when I had to walk home. I'd walk home down the middle of the road."

Jon survived those nervous late night strolls, and by the time the Mekons formed was listening, like so many of his peers then, to the Velvet Underground, Velvet member John Cale's early solo work, *Graham Parker and the Rumour, and the punchy pub rock of Dr. Feelgood. His band, though, was drawing more directly from the work of groups like the Buzzcocks, the Sex Pistols, and the Clash, purveyors of the short, aggressive pop song. Then punk's initial wave lost force and the Mekons moved on.

"We started thinking about what we were doing a little bit more," Jon says. "It wasn't like 'Let's do a three chord bash with sort of screaming political lyrics.' We saw there were connections to blues and reggae, and country in the end, you know, when we finally heard some decent country. I got tapes and records from friends in the States when we first came over here, in like '85, and started getting into Merle Haggard and Ernest Tubb, George Jones. We really didn't hear that much in England." That phase led to three albums' worth of ragged country/punk, beginning with 1985's *Fear and Whiskey* (Sin).

By 1988, the Mekons' saucer had relocated again, this time with *So Good It Hurts* (Twin/Tone), which owed as much to Fairport Convention and the Pogues as it did to rural Americana. A year later, they were back with raw punk on *The Mekons Rock 'n' Roll* (A&M). "We were trying to tell stories in the music," Jon explains, "so the music we were attracted to was reggae, country and folk, or folk-dance music, which was very simple, music that was there for people to dance to."

The mainstream continues to ignore the Mekons and the band's problems with major record companies have become legendary, but an adoring cult still follows them through every morph and label switch. Returning the favor, the Mekons have stayed true to their inner, albeit manic, muse. "We started seeing ourselves more in a tradition of folk music, even though what we were doing was fairly weird, avant-garde," says Jon, trying to put a handle to it. "We were [interested in making] music that *had* to be made, rather than a lot of the pop music in the '80s, which seemed pretty rootless." No one, even the band itself, can predict where it will light next. But wherever that is, true Mekonphiles will be waiting for them, salivating.

JON LANGFORD'S FAVORITE ARTISTS AND RECORDINGS

Slade— : *Slade Smashes* (Polydor) has all the band's '70s heavies like "Cum on Feel the Noize," and "Look Wot You Dun," the latter one of the first singles Jon ever bought.

Black Sabbath—*Black Sabbath* (Warner Bros.). It wasn't just this album's ability to levitate that captivated the young Mr. Langford: "They were *the* heavy metal band, as far as I was concerned. They were actually heavy. A lot of these heavy metal bands now are not heavy at all. I don't think they were heavy as individuals—they were three beery blokes from Wolverhampton—but the chords they used: there was something really dark about that music that I liked."

Buzzcocks—*Singles Going Steady* (IRS). "The early Buzzcocks singles were great, well designed little records, classic A-B sides," says John. This hot compilation collects 16 prime tracks.

Roxy Music—*Roxy Music* (Reprise). "I think just their image was very powerful. It was sort of scary art-rock stuff. That's why I liked it. It didn't sound like anything else, even though they were using soul music a lot, stuff like that. Good songs, good strange songs."

*Graham Parker & The Rumour—*Heat Treatment* and *Howlin'Wind* (both Mercury) "are just classic records that we used to listen to—*Heat Treatment*, mainly. I was really into them, although they don't have much to do with the way the Mekons ended up sounding."

Lee "Scratch" Perry—Wildman producer Perry's anarchic records completely won Jon over when he started listening to a lot of reggae. ⏺: *Some of the Best* (HeartBeat), with Bob Marley; the mid-'60s Studio One singles collection *Chicken Scratch* (Heartbeat); and the 1991 Channel One opus *Lord God Muzick* (Heartbeat).

Prince Far I—*Dubwise* (Caroline/Plan 9). This album by the late dub master contains the track "No More War," which Jon says "is a single that John Peel played on the radio sort of around the time punk was happening. That's a classic record. Just in terms of sound, a lot of dub stuff is really important to me."

The Congos—*Heart of the Congos* (2 CDs: Blood & Fire)."The best reggae album you could ever imagine—really great singing, really great dub, beautiful harmonies."

Bob Wills & His Texas Playboys—*The Tiffany Transcriptions, Vols. 1–9* (Rhino, available singly). "At the moment I find those fairly inspirational, just the fact that they would be on tour, like seven hundred nights a year, and then find time to go into the studio on their day off and record fifty tracks. It's quite ridiculous. [The transcriptions] were just for radio. I think they are very cool recordings, very casual." These recordings, considered by many to be the best way to hear the Playboys, cover a phenomenal range of music. Every volume is superb, although Vol. 2 contains more of the hits the band was known for. ⏺: See also the Pine Valley Cosmonauts' tribute to Wills below.

John Cale—*Vintage Violence* (Sony) and *Paris, 1919* (Warner/ADA). *Vintage*, released in 1970, was Cale's solo debut. The orchestral *Paris* features help from members of *Little Feat.

Nick Drake—"He seems to be very fashionable at the moment, but all of his albums are really kind of strange, timeless. Although he's so '60s and kind of nostalgic, still the recordings are just so beautiful, so fresh and of now." ●: See Master List.

Captain Beefheart—*Clear Spot* (Reprise). "You don't feel like you're listening to something that happened a long time ago. It's really fresh." ●: A Reprise CD reissue pairs 1973's *Clear Spot* with 1972's *The Spotlight Kid* on a single CD—double your pleasure!

The Handsome Family—*Through the Trees* (Carrot Top). "They do this sort of gothic country thing. Kind of maudlin, atmospheric stuff. Very amazing album."

***Alejandro Escovedo**—*More Miles Than Money: Live 1994-96* (Bloodshot). "I've been listening to that nonstop as well. Really stripped down, but just beautiful singing, great songs."

JON LANGFORD'S OWN RECORDINGS

Jon doesn't hesitate in naming his favorite of his own discs: the Mekons' *Fear and Whiskey* (Sin), which Twin/Tone reissued, with bonus tracks, in the States in 1989 as *Original Sin*. "I'm really fond of it. It incorporates a lot of the country sort of thing, in terms of the songwriting, but sonically there's quite a lot of playing around in the studio, thinking about reggae. Not trying to replicate it, but being open to the sound that a reggae producer would bring." He also recommends *Curse of the Mekons* (Blast First), "which is possibly the best album we did," although the machinations of the music business have kept the album from release in the United States.

●: The 1986 album *Edge of the World* (Sin) and 1987's *Honky Tonkin'* (Loud) are the two country-punk follow-ups to *Fear and Whiskey*, both excellent. The 1989 release, *The Mekons Rock 'n' Roll* (A&M)—loud, punky, pissed-off—and 1998's *Me* (Quarterstick), washed clean of country/punk dust but brimming with the group's trademark Lefty social critiques, are highly recommended as well. Look also for Jon's 1998 solo release, *Skull Orchard* (Sugar Free). The Mekons played a large role in *Commemorative: A Tribute to Gram Parsons* (Rhino), a 1993 tribute to the country-rock legend, where they were joined by *Uncle Tupelo, Vic Chesnutt, Bob Mould, *Victoria Williams, *Peter Holsapple, and a cast of thousands. And Jon is the commander of the Pine Valley Cosmonauts, whose joyous . . . *Salute the Majesty of Bob Wills* (Bloodshot) roughs up Wills's western swing songbook a little with some alt-country/blues rowdiness. The music is expertly and lovingly executed by the Cosmonauts and their long list of tasty guest vocalists, who are reverent, but, thankfully, never polite.

D A N I E L   L A N O I S   (August 28, 1998)

D aniel Lanois's handprint on popular music has grown so large that it has altered the form. As a producer, he has helped shape some of the most captivating rock and pop albums ever made: Peter Gabriel's *So*, U2's *The Unforgettable Fire*, *Achtung, Baby* and *The Joshua Tree*, Robbie Robertson's eponymous solo debut, the Neville Brothers' *Yellow Moon*, and Bob Dylan's *Oh, Mercy* and *Time Out of Mind* among them. A virtual band member on many of his productions, he often contributes songwriting and guitar-playing as well as behind-the-console artistry. More quietly, Daniel has also left his imprint as a performer, recording one of the better-received albums of the last ten years, 1989's *Acadie*, plus a well-regarded follow-up, 1993's *For the Beauty of Wynona*.

Up-and-coming producers now study Daniel's works as if they were sacred texts, but Daniel got his own music education on the streets, or more accurately, the fortunate intersection of geography and cultural history that was Hamilton, Canada in the 1960s. Located on the road from Buffalo, New York to Toronto, Hamilton was a popular tour stop for a number of R&B and blues acts. "Sly and the Family Stone were playing down the street at the community hall, so if you can imagine hearing something that potent when you're a young teenager, that's like a year of university right there," Daniel tells us by phone from Los Angeles. "And you know, other really great folks like Wilson Pickett*, James Cotton, Howlin' Wolf."

Daniel did more "coursework" in Toronto where he was working as a guitarist at the Brown Derby hotel, down the road from the Edison, where top-flight country acts such as George Jones and Ray Price would play. "I would swing by the Edison and hear my country and go to Le Coq D'Or and hear the R&B," Daniel recalls, "so there was this active little strip that allowed me to hear a lot of really great American music . . . and Joni Mitchell would be playing Toronto coffeehouses, and Leonard Cohen would be hanging around. It was kind of a hotbed of great music culture."

The late 1960s were also the heyday of underground radio, with one landmark album after another appearing on the airwaves and in the record stores. "There was a lot of really amazing music being played on radio which could actually change your life if you were interested in it," Daniel notes. "I was very much glued to radio through the whole psychedelic era." Jimi Hendrix's brief but stunning recording career, Miles Davis's *Bitches Brew*, the Sly and the Family Stone discs—"all these records add up to my university," Daniel says. "You put those on and you can't believe it actually happened."

The graduate degree came at the side of Brian Eno, who had heard an innovative tape that Daniel made in 1979 and came to Hamilton to work with him. "That's what I'm calling the ambient chapter," Daniel says, "and what was interesting about that relationship was to go into the studio with somebody as bright and inventive as Brian and work on music that at that time I regarded as totally esoteric and to the left, records that I thought may never get a chance to be heard. But to see somebody of his caliber absolutely dedicated to this quite obscure corner of things was really touching for me. I realized at that point that one must make a decision to go after what one loves. . . . I just stayed with those lessons, and to this day I will only work on things that I'm highly moved by." Of course, it is the contagious nature of Daniel's esoterica that when he's moved, hundreds of thousands, even millions, move with him.

DANIEL LANOIS'S FAVORITE ARTISTS AND RECORDINGS

Sly and the Family Stone—Daniel loves all the classic tracks plus one semi-obscure one, "In Time": "If you were to line them all up and you said, 'okay, we're putting a time capsule together here, and what is *the* funkiest track on the planet?' The answer is 'In Time'. . . ." : *Anthology* (Epic) is the most complete hits package. "In Time" is on the group's last successful record, *Fresh* (Epic).

*Wilson Pickett—"Mustang Sally." "I'm sure I wore it out in my bedroom as a kid. That's an amazing record."

James Cotton—Daniel prefers the blues harmonica great's work in the 1960s. : *Best of the Verve Years* (Verve) includes Cotton's entire 1967 eponymous debut album for the label plus other well-chosen tracks from his succeeding two records.

Sonny Boy Williamson—As with James Cotton, Daniel likes the 1960s recordings. : *The Real Folk Blues*, *More Real Folk Blues*, *One Way Out*, and *Bummer Road* (all MCA/Chess) are prime albums from this decade. As an alternative, try the compilation *The Essential . . .* (2 CDs: MCA/Chess) that surveys Williamson's recordings for Chess from 1955 until his death in 1965.

Howlin' Wolf— 🔘 : See Master List.

*The Band—_Music from Big Pink_ (Capitol). "A classic . . . when everybody else was running away from the Establishment, they were embracing it."

Joni Mitchell—_Don Juan's Reckless Daughter_ (Asylum). "I think it's a really great record because it's epic and it's not so fragmented. . . . I love her more popular songs, of course, like everybody, but there's something special about that record."

Leonard Cohen—"Stranger Song" and "Suzanne" on _The Songs of . . ._ (Columbia). " 'Suzanne' does it for me every time."

Jimi Hendrix—_Are You Experienced?_ (Reprise). "Jimi Hendrix played a really big part in my life as a guitar player and to this day I put on my Hendrix records and they give me the same thrill. It's amazing, actually, that those records have the power that they have."

Miles Davis—_Bitches Brew_ (Columbia). "I refer to that record as 'the sound of speed.' It's almost like you can see the lamp posts flying by when you listen to that record. It automatically puts you on some kind of a mysterious highway."

Kraftwerk—_The Man Machine_ (Capitol). "Even though it's all seemingly electronic, that's a very heartfelt record with a lot of organics in it. I like it when technology disintegrates into organics."

Sam Cooke and the Soul Stirrers—In addition to loving the music, Daniel likes the ambiance of some of the group's records "where they sound like church performances . . . where everything has a natural placement and you get a sense that some people are further back in the room and other people are closer to you. It's a nice feeling on records, and I think we got that feeling on the new _Time Out Of Mind_ record, Bob Dylan." 🔘: _The Original Soul Stirrers Featuring Sam Cooke_ or _The Gospel Soul of Sam Cooke, Vol 2_ (both Specialty).

James Brown—_Star Time_ (4 CDs: Polydor). "That's an amazing compilation and definitely a desert island package."

Nino Rota—_The Symphonic Fellini_ (Silva American). This recording contains symphonic renderings of many of Rota's classic scores for Fellini films, including _La Dolce Vita, La Strada_, and _Amarcord_. "This is a really great record. This ranks up there with Jimi and Sam Cooke, on a very different level. It has a lot of humor in it, which really works for the Italians, you know [laughs]."

Jeff Buckley—_Sketches for My Sweetheart the Drunk_ (2 CDs: Sony). "I don't hear that many current records that really change my life. . . . I've found it in Jeff Buckley and I find it in Bjork on occasion." The first disc of this posthumous set contains material drawn from sessions for what would have been Buckley's second album, produced by Tom Verlaine. The second CD contains Buckley's four-track home recordings of works-in-progress, plus material recorded from the studio of alternative station WFMU.

Bjork—"Hunter" on *Homogenic* (Elektra). "[This track] really does it for me every time."

Bob Dylan—*Blonde on Blonde* (Columbia). Daniel especially revels in the track "Sad Eyed Lady of the Lowlands" on this landmark record.

National Radio and Television Chorus plus various artists—*La Mystere des Voix Bulgares* (Nonesuch) and *La Mystere des Voix Bulgares, Vols. 2–3* (Nonesuch—Vol. 2, Polygram—Vol. 3) . "Spine-chilling great singing."

Nat King Cole—"China Gate" and "Route 66." : Daniel remembers being enthralled with a "wildly rhythmic" version of "China Gate" featuring Cole accompanied only by a guitar. He believes it was produced for inclusion in a film. We could not find a recording of it. You'll find "Route 66" on *The Best of the Trio (Vocal '42–'46)* (Capitol).

DANIEL LANOIS'S OWN RECORDINGS

Daniel is quite pleased with how *Acadie* (Opal/Warner Bros.) turned out and has worn: "I think *Acadie* is a little bit of a classic for those who like me. . . . I listen to that record and I'm quite touched by its innocence." He's less satisfied with *For the Beauty of Wynona* (Warner Bros.) "because I think that it sounds more labored, although I think it has some great moments on it. I really believe in that song 'The Collection of Marie Claire,' which is a story about an abduction and a kind of demented, passionate love, not unlike that classic story 'The Collector.' And then there's another song on there called 'The Unbreakable Chain,' which is a true story about my cousin giving her baby up for adoption and then meeting her son thirty years later. So there's those gems in there that aside from anything else are true, and resonate some kind of reason to be." Another Lanois solo record is in the works as of this writing.

Of the albums he's worked on as a producer, he first spotlights *So* (Geffen): "There's a track on there called 'Mercy Street,' which I think is kind of a classic. And another called 'Don't Give Up,' which I think is a highly innovative song-writing angle, one of Peter's great ones." *Achtung, Baby* (Island) is another favorite "because I think it strikes a very interesting balance between technology and organics. It's a very good use of available tools of the time, and yet hangs onto the integrity of what U2 is about at its core." He also singles out *Time Out of Mind* (Columbia), perhaps the consensus record of the year for 1997, and intriguing for its blend of Daniel's input and Dylan's make-it-up-as-you-go-along working style. "You can't project innocence," Daniel points out. "You can't project naivete. You can't project soul. You could make the greatest blueprint ever, and it would not work. You can only look at it after the fact. So all that stuff with Bob, it's all true and it's all instinctive. You go into a project and you've just gotta be smart enough to accept what comes your way and that's really the brilliance of record production when you get it right."

Finally, Daniel calls attention to some obscure records he worked on with Eno: avant-garde composer Harold Budd's *The Pearl* and *Ambient 2: The Plateaux of Mirror A* (both EG) and Eno's *Apollo: Atmospheres & Soundtracks* and *Ambient 4: On Land* (both EG). These four albums well represent Daniel's ambient period, he says, which he regards as the most important time of his artistic life: "At the time nobody was paying much attention to that stuff, but when ambient became hip, I think those records became references for those people."

●: Check out Daniel's contributions to Emmylou Harris's *Wrecking Ball* (Elektra/Asylum), on which Harris successfully transitions to ambient rock. In addition to producing, Daniel wrote two songs for the record, including the lovely opening track, and plays lead guitar.

PHIL LESH (November 1, 1996)

t was a classic case of synchronicity that formed the Grateful Dead in 1965—the perfect people coming together at the perfect place at the perfect moment in cultural history. But this was a strange kind of perfection. In its first incarnation, as the Warlocks, the band brought together five people of starkly different musical goals, backgrounds, and abilities. Indeed, at the beginning, a couple of the players didn't even have the chops for the gig.

One of the latter was Phil Lesh, a classical music student and trumpeter in a college jazz band who had only recently begun to dig rock 'n' roll and who had never touched a bass guitar until his friend Jerry Garcia invited him to join the band. The Warlocks' previous bassist was having trouble making rehearsals and jobs and needed to be replaced. Garcia nominated Lesh for the role on the pure faith that his musical knowledge and talent would see him through. It was a faith that would be paid back in spades.

While Phil had first closed his ears to the Beatles and the Rolling Stones, he'd laid them wide open to other artists whose music would become vital to the Dead's evolution—John Coltrane, for one. Phil turned his bandmates on to Coltrane's *Africa Brass* early in their relationship together. "Coltrane's work, not only on this record but later, when he evolved a modal approach, was very influential on us, because we saw how it was possible for jazz players to improvise endlessly on one chord," Phil tells us by phone from the Grateful Dead office. "And we took that to our hearts and started doing it ourselves, and it became the basis for some of our wilder extemporizations, like 'Dark Star.'"

Phil had been listening to Indian music in the early 1960s as well—he had seen Ravi Shankar perform in San Francisco several times and was delving into sitar and Indian drum records. The Indian players operated from radically different harmonic and rhythmic ideas but in their own way knew all about tripping. That opened doors in the Dead's work, too, when Phil brought the concepts to his band: "We tried to superimpose different rhythms on top of one another. Four bars of five equaled five bars of four—that kind of thing. We had one song called 'The Eleven' which used eleven and twelve rotating simultaneously, which got to be pretty interesting."

The preeminent psychedelic band of the 1960s, the Dead became adept at creating synesthesia—"seeing" sound, "hearing" color. Although drugs provided the main inspiration, Phil's background helped the visual aspect of the Dead's sound, too. Long a devotee of difficult classical music, he introduced his pals to the works of Charles Ives, renowned for his sound "movies," and avant-garde composer Karlheinz Stockhausen. Speaking about the latter's "Kontakte," Phil notes, "Stockhausen went through WWII in Germany in various camps and was bombed and so on. He was in his teens at the time and it must have made a huge impression on him, because you can almost see the searchlights sweeping the sky, the planes droning over, the bombs exploding."

One crucial aspect of the Dead's music that didn't come out of Phil's background or anyone else's was his approach to playing bass. The Dead's music at its best was a free-flowing, endlessly transforming vehicle that didn't want an anchor. Accordingly, Phil abandoned the bass' standard role of providing one. As his abilities grew, the way his linear, melodic style intertwined with Garcia's probing guitar leads became crucial to the band's approach. "I really never thought of it as 'The Bass,'" says Phil now. "I perceived the music of the band as a web, and everybody was making an equal contribution to it."

With the Dead's touring days behind him, Phil is now spending much of his time doing something he largely abandoned when he joined the band—composing formal music. "Right now I'm working on a Grateful Dead song symphony," he says. "I'm using motifs from Grateful Dead songs and I'm going to weave them together somewhat in the spirit of Ives on the basis of three layers:

a space layer, a kind of motif-jam layer, and an actual song layer, where the melodies will float to the surface, and recede again and morph together . . . I have many projects, so I'm just going to continue to compose music and rear my children and stay healthy. That's my desire. I don't have any desire to get a band together and be a rock star or anything like that."

Of course, by 1998, he had relented on playing live Grateful Dead music again and began touring with former bandmates *Bob Weir and Mickey Hart, sometimes band member *Bruce Hornsby, and three added musicians as The Other Ones. Although Garcia is irreplaceable, the alchemy survives—the music the new group makes conveys much of the power sparked three decades before.

PHIL LESH'S FAVORITE ARTISTS AND RECORDINGS

Miles Davis and Gil Evans—*Miles Ahead* (Columbia) and *Miles Davis & Gil Evans: The Studio Sessions* (Columbia Legacy). About the former, Phil says, "It's really a landmark in the use of a big band and even in the treatment of the big band. The arrangements are considered absolute classics of their kind. Miles's improvisations in and around these arrangements are also classics of their kind." Phil finds all of Davis's work with Evans astounding and highly recommends the *Studio Sessions* box set, which collects all the Davis/Evans studio recordings including *Miles Ahead*.

The John Coltrane Quartet—*The Complete Africa Brass Sessions* (Impulse). "A very, very important album for me," says Phil about 1961's original *Africa Brass*, released in this two-CD version with alternate takes in 1995. "There are a couple of tunes besides the title tune which are really dynamite: 'The Song of the Underground Railroad,' 'Greensleeves,' and a really swinging thing called 'Blues Minor,' which is just about my favorite thing on the album because Coltrane really explodes on that one. There's a drum solo in [the tune] 'Africa Brass' that I played for one of our drummers, and it changed his life—*Elvin Jones playing the long drum solo where he plays melodically and twists the rhythm around. Really wonderful."

Ravi Shankar—Phil's favorite albums with Shankar pair him with the renowned tabla drummer, Alla Rakha, whom Phil calls "amazing." : Try *Ravi Shankar in New York* (BGO), *Sound of the Sitar* (BGO), and *Ravi Shankar in San Francisco* (BGO).

Chatur Lal—*Drums of North & South India* (World Pacific). Phil played this album for Dead drummer Mickey Hart and "that was definitely influential on him, not only in his work with the Grateful Dead, but in his interest in world music in general."

Charles Ives—Symphony No. 4, American Symphony Orchestra conducted by Leopold Stokowski (Columbia). "In terms of the music we called 'space music,' the first recording of Charles Ives's Fourth Symphony was very important to all of us. In fact, in sixty-seven or sixty-eight, when we were in New York City, the same forces who recorded the Ives's Fourth on Columbia performed it again at Carnegie Hall for two nights, and the entire band was there for both nights—even Pig Pen. Even Pig Pen liked Ives."

Bob Dylan—*Highway 61 Revisited* (Columbia) and *Blonde on Blonde* (Columbia). "His delivery is so unique, and I don't think any of the guys in the band ever tried to imitate him—that would be impossible—but surely the way his songs scan, their rhythm and their meter [affected us]."

*Youssou N'Dour—*Set* (Virgin), *Eyes Open* (40 Acres & a Mule), and *The Guide (Wommat)* (Columbia). Phil calls Senegalese star N'Dour's work "state-of-the-art in African pop music because he takes some of the most interesting and complicated rhythms and puts them into a context where you can still dance to them. . . . And he's such a wonderful singer, and his band is absolutely crackling. I would recommend that music to anyone who wants to dance down the street, or through life."

Karlheinz Stockhausen—*Stockhausen Verlag* (Wergo). Several versions of this piece are available but this is the original recording with Stockhausen himself and electronic performance pioneer David Tudor. "This disc had two electronic pieces on it," says Phil. One was called 'Gesang der junglinge' (Song of the Youth) and the other was called 'Kontakte.' 'Gesang' is based on a text from the Book of Daniel—Shadrach, Meshach and Abed-nego, and the fiery furnace, that kind of thing—and it's the first really aesthetically mature electronic composition that was ever composed. This was fifty-four or fifty-five, I think. It was also one of the first compositions that used space as an element . . . the antiphony of the voices, which goes back to sixteenth-century Venice, where they had antiphonal choirs and brass instruments on either side of the church. That sort of fell into disfavor when music moved out of the church, and it waited for electronics to resurrect it. Part of the interest is in the treatment of the voices. The voices are being manipulated electronically as well as being allowed to sing out. It's a wonderful piece and very colorful. 'Kontakte' is a longer electronic piece [that is] maybe the most advanced version of what you can do with cutting up tape, speeding sounds up, slowing them down, and putting them through revolving loudspeakers and re-recording them. It's really the definitive tape manipulation piece, and it's also very dramatic."

Havergal Brian—Symphony No. 3, BBC Symphony Orchestra/Lionel Friend (Hyperion), Symphony No. 7 Royal Liverpool Philharmonic/Sir Charles Mackerras (paired with the Symphony No. 31, EMI), and the Symphony No. 1, "Gothic" and Slovak Philharmonic Orchestra/Ondrej Lenard (2 CDs: Marco Polo). At Phil's suggestion, the Grateful Dead's charitable arm, the Rex Foundation, sponsored recordings of several obscure classical music works, including Brian's. "He wrote thirty-two symphonies, the last of them at the age of ninety-two, and he composed his whole life in a complete absolute vacuum of neglect," Phil says. "Yet his music is so amazing and interesting." Rex sponsored the recordings of Brian's Third and Seventh symphonies. Phil also recommends the recordings of his other symphonies on the Marco Polo label.

Robert Simpson—"He's another British composer who probably writes some of the most energetic music since Beethoven, but in a completely modern context and idiom. We sponsored his Symphony Number Nine [Bournemouth Symphony Orchestra/Vernon Handley (Hyperion)]. You could almost call it a cathedral in sound, a majestic and numinous work I highly recommend to anyone. Also his Symphony No. 5 [(paired on the same CD with the symphony No. 3: Royal Philharmonic Orchestra/Vernon Handley (Hyperion)]—in fact, anything the man wrote is worth hearing." : Hyperion offers recordings of Simpson's Symphonies 1–10 as well as many volumes of his chamber music.

James Dillon—*helle Nacht* and *ignis noster*, BBC Symphony Orchestra, London/Artutro Tamayo (Montaigne Auvidis). "Two big orchestral pieces by one of the most hallucinatory composers you could imagine. I can only give this the highest possible recommendation: turn out the lights, turn the stuff up, and just go with it."

Robin Holloway—Concerto No. 2 for Orchestra, London Symphony Orchestra/Michael Tilson Thomas (NMC). "His music really is like an encyclopedia of the Twentieth Century. It is so rich and tuneful, but similar in some ways to James Dillon. It is truly fascinating."

PHIL LESH'S OWN RECORDINGS

When we asked Phil what his favorites of his own work were, he replied, "The stuff that I haven't done yet. My function in the Grateful Dead was not such that I felt compelled to write a lot of songs for the band. Having a team like Garcia and Hunter was exciting enough and the songs they created were stimulating enough that for most of the time I didn't feel like writing songs. The few [of my songs] that have come out I am perfectly happy with and wouldn't change any of them. There are three new ones that never got out on record that I was pretty proud of, but those will be out eventually."

⬤: Phil has only released one solo album in his career, 1975's highly experimental *Seastones* (Round), a collaboration with keyboardist Ned Lagin. But he personally chose the material that appears on *From the Phil Zone* (2 CDs: Grateful Dead), a potpourri of concert tracks from throughout the band's history that on several selections rival the best live music released by the group to date. As far as choosing your own Grateful Dead music, if you don't already know the voluminous catalog, the best way to appreciate it is to understand a few things about the band beforehand:

First, because of its almost religious dedication to improvisation, the Dead only rarely captured on studio recordings the qualities its fans love most about it. Most of the band's truly magical moments are on live releases. Fortunately, almost every concert the band performed was taped and several of those are released on CD every year. Most go from tape box to CD with minimal production and are released, warts and all, in a sort of authorized bootleg series called Dick's Picks. Although far from state-of-the-art in recording quality, the Dick's Picks series contains some spectacular music. (If your local record store does not carry Dick's Picks, call Grateful Dead Mercantile Co. [800/225-3323] to order and log on to www.dead.net for information about future releases.) A smaller number of live shows have been fully produced up to contemporary professional standards and are available on major labels or Grateful Dead records—in the latter case, as part of a series called From the Vault.

Second, the band and its music underwent some significant changes in its 30-year history that will affect which part of its catalog is for you. Its pre-1967 output is primitive musically and of interest to completists only. From 1968 through 1969, the band's music was the apex of California psychedelia, as perfect an evocation of a sunny acid meltdown as exists on record. Recordings from this period have an edgy energy and reckless improvisatory spirit that the band would rarely equal again. For many fans, the band's peak—from a pure musical, not cultural, standpoint—came in the mid-1970s. By now, individual members had grown enough as musicians to give the jams a sophistication that could approach chamber musiclike delicacy. The energy level, while usually more laid-back, still served the music. Garcia was still singing well at this point—his voice never fully recovered after his 1986 diabetic coma. The Dead played many superb shows after 1974 and any performance deemed worthy of release by the Dead's organization is worth your consideration. But shows were gradually becoming more formalized and less exploratory, so the 1968–74 material is a richer vein to tap when collecting multiple live CDs from a single period.

With the above in mind, we recommend the following recordings as introductions to this problematic but frequently stunning body of recorded work. Of the studio releases, 1970's *Workingman's Dead* and *American Beauty* (both Warner Bros.) are the classics in the traditional sense of songcraft and performance, although as *Bob Weir points out, they don't sound much like the band on stage. Since the Dead weren't a traditional band, though, true Deadheads tend to select other favorites—1968's *Anthem of the Sun* and 1969's *Aoxomoxoa* (both Warner Bros.), which are essentially aural LSD; 1973's *Wake of the Flood* (Grateful Dead), oddly produced but packed with material that became concert standbys; 1974's *. . . from the Mars Hotel* (Grateful Dead); 1973's *Blues for Allah* (Grateful Dead), which sounds on most tracks like the live band at the time; 1977's *Terrapin Station* (Arista), with creamy pop production that is all wrong for the band but, again, much strong material and playing; and 1987's *In the Dark* (Arista), on which the band finally discovers a recording style that captures its essence.

Of the fully produced (and sometimes retouched) live recordings, 1969's *Live/Dead* (Warner Bros.) still offers the best evidence of the band's performance power; by itself, it probably made dazed acolytes of millions of once-ordinary citizens. Other worthwhile purchases in this category include 1971's *Grateful Dead* (Warner Bros.); 1972's *Europe '72* (2 CDs: Warner Bros.); 1981's *Reckoning* (Arista), a warm, intimate mostly acoustic performance that draws material from both the band's folk beginnings and the *Workingman . . . /American Beauty* period; and 1990's *Without a Net* (2 CDs: Arista), a strong document of the band's denser, more synthesized sound in its last years. On the Dead's own label, go for *One* (1975) and *Two from the Vault* (1968); *Hundred Year Hall* (1972); and *Fillmore East 2-11-69* (all 2 CDs).

Unlike the fully produced live albums, Dick's Picks usually cover entire shows, meaning that lesser material—and the Dead often rode the brakes until the second set—has not been edited out. That said, the collections with the highest proportion of first-rate performances include Volumes 1 (2 CDs: 1973); 2 (1971), a butter-smooth example of the band's ability to morph one song into another; 3 (2 CDs: 1977), featuring exceptional soloing and ensemble interplay in what was a spotty year for the group; the justly revered 4 (3 CDs: 1970), the most energized Dick's Picks release so far; 5 (3 CDs: 1979), with spirited, soulful playing by then-new keyboardist Brent Mydland, who would rarely sound this spunky again; 8 (3 CDs: 1970), with some excellent acoustic Dead on Disc 1, a terrific semi-electric "Cumberland Blues," and a white hot "Good Lovin' " mid-way through the second set that ignites the rest of the show; 10 (3 CDs: 1977), with a first set that rocks harder than most and a closing set that displays the silky transitions the band was managing by the mid-'70s; and 12 (3 CDs: 1974), which blends highlights from two shows in late June. Of course, the true Deadhead will tolerate considerable mortal musicianship for those moments of transcendance that the band was capable of at any moment. Such moments exist in enough abundance on Volumes 7 (3 CDs: 1974); 6 (3 CDs: 1983); and 11 (3 CDs: 1972) to make them worthwhile secondary purchases.

LAURIE LEWIS (August 5, 1997)

In 1986, the small Chicago label Flying Fish quietly released a record of old timey/country/bluegrass tunes called *Restless Rambling Heart* by an unknown artist named Laurie Lewis. The album's striking songwriting, singing, and fiddle playing rang with such rustic authenticity that it became a guessing game as to where Lewis, who had no discernible regional accent, hailed from. Kentucky, Tennessee, old Virginny? Try Berkeley, California, land of haute cuisine, progressive politics, and gun control—on the surface, worlds apart from the rural America about which Lewis sang.

Berkeley's saving grace, of course, was that like many college towns, it also embraced the traditional acoustic music that would become Laurie's life. When Laurie was a teenager, every summer brought the Berkeley Folk Festival, which she flocked to faithfully from the age of 14. "They'd have Doc Watson and Mississippi John Hurt, Jesse Fuller and Joan Baez, Phil Ochs and just the gamut of acoustic music at the time," Laurie tells us by phone from her Berkeley home.

Laurie had grown up around folk music—her mother's family included several traditional Norwegian folk musicians. Dad's musical background was more formal, but that ended up boosting her career, too. Laurie's father, a physician, was an amateur classical flautist who had played in the Dallas Symphony while in medical school. Laurie began studying classical violin as a child. When she started playing bluegrass in her early 20s, "I was actually pretty good right off the bat because I had this classical technique," Laurie says. "And I had a good ear." Far from discouraging his daughter, Dad bought Laurie some of the key recordings that influenced her development as a folk artist, including an album by the immortal Chubby Wise and a live record from the Newport Folk Festival.

Although folk music had captured her soul in her early teens, Laurie didn't really think much about making a career of it until some 20 years later. She was running a violin sales-and-repair shop and writing the occasional tune when she got the bug to make a record—"you know, sort of a vanity recording thing, just because I had faith in these songs I was writing," she says. "During that recording process I just knew beyond a shadow of a doubt that what I wanted to do was play music. And I knew at that point that the stuff I was doing was good enough."

Good enough indeed—the record was *Restless Rambling Heart*. With a confidence born in the sessions, Laurie sold the violin shop, committed herself to playing music, and has never looked back. "It's like making the conscious decision, the commitment to myself, just opened up all kinds of doors immediately for me," says Laurie, only now sounding Berkeleyite to the max.

LAURIE LEWIS'S FAVORITE ARTISTS AND RECORDINGS

Bob Dylan—*Nashville Skyline* (Columbia). Laurie listened heavily to all of Dylan's albums through *John Wesley Harding*, but Dylan's country record was particularly important to her: "And I don't know really why that sound grabbed me. It was not in my background."

Chubby Wise—*Chubby Wise and the Rainbow Ranch Boys* (Star Day). Of the many albums the great fiddler Wise made after leaving Bill Monroe's Bluegrass Boys, Laurie says this one, with Hank Snow's band, "is by far the best one."

Clarence Ashley and Doc Watson—*Old Time Music at Clarence Ashley's* (Smithsonian/Folkways). Watson's appearance on this seminal record began his long career.

Various artists—*Folk Music of the Newport Folk Festival 1959–60, Vol. 1* (Folkways, out of print). Although this album features such well-known folkies as Mike Seeger, it was the tracks with the obscure Willie Thomas and Butch Cage that caught Laurie's attention: "It was just the rawest, roughest stuff. And when I first heard it, it was shocking to my ears. I just didn't know if it was a joke, or just really bad, but I kept going back to it. Now I listen to it and I just love it. They're so good. The blues fiddle just knocks me out. It's not technically much of anything. It's just groove and feel. So, those guys pried open my ears in some way. It's like I didn't even want them to but they did."

Various artists—*The World Library of Folk and Primitive Music Vol. 2: Ireland* (Rounder). These songs were collected in Ireland by folk archivist Alan Lomax. "It's all field stuff, and it's really great," enthuses Laurie.

Benny Thomasson—*Country Fiddling from the Big State* (County). "I listen to this stuff a lot."

Various artists—*Texas Farewell: Texas Fiddlers Recorded 1922–1930* (County). "Another truly great fiddle record."

Kenny Baker—*Portrait of a Bluegrass Fiddler* and *A Baker's Dozen: Country Fiddle Tunes* (both County) and *Kenny Baker Country* (Dormouse). "I got to see him at festivals down in Southern California, with Bill Monroe, of course, and he was always out jamming. And I got to play with him, and he scared me to death. It was just myself, because I was so scared to play in front of him, and he was really supportive, because he would just stand and play stuff with you."

Ray Park and Vern Williams—Park, whom Laurie calls "a great, great fiddle player," and mandolinist/vocalist Williams, a major influence on her singing, have often worked together in country/bluegrass groups but Laurie doesn't feel they have ever been captured well on record. Laurie saw them perform many times when they had a bluegrass band together. "Unfortunately, people will just have to take my word for it that they were great," she says.

Billie Holiday—"She completely opened up my ears in terms of phrasing and listening to her made me a much better singer." (●): See Master List.

Terry Garthwaite—When Laurie was in her 20s, she played bass and sang in a traditional jazz band in which Garthwaite, known for her work with the Berkeley-based Joy of Cooking, was the chanteuse. "Her sense of phrasing and playing with the beat, and her playfulness with vocal tones really opened my ears to the possibilities of what you can do with your voice—you know, that you can play," Laurie says. (●): *Hand in Glove* (Fantasy).

LAURIE LEWIS'S OWN RECORDINGS

Laurie doesn't choose between her albums: "I think that they're all sort of different aspects of me, so there's something I like about all those aspects or I wouldn't have put 'em down."

(●): Although it was her first record, *Restless Rambling Heart* is still the place to start with Laurie's discography. Another winner in a similar vein is 1989's *Love Chooses You* (Flying Fish), featuring one of her signature tunes, the Bob Wills- and Flaco Jimenez-influenced two-step, "Texas Bluebonnets." The 1995 release *The Oak and the Laurel* (Rounder) is a sweet duo album with life-and-musical partner Tom Rozum. Highlights include the title tune, a Lewis original; "My Baby Came Back," a Louvin Brothers cover; and the Everly Brothers' "So Sad (To Watch Good Love Go Bad)." And don't miss Laurie and Tom's outstanding seasonal record, 1999's *Winter's Grace* (Signature Sounds).

Not all of Laurie's work is folk purist in nature. Over the years, she has written several songs in the sensitive singer-songwriter vein. "I'm a complex person who's been influenced by all kinds of different music in my life and it just keeps coming out in different ways and I don't want to be pigeonholed as just a bluegrass musician, or specifically a traditional musician," Laurie asserts. "I'm a musician who works with traditional music forms, which I love, but I bend 'em and I intend to continue to do that." The 1993 album *True Stories* (Rounder) shows this side of Laurie. The compilation *Earth and Sky* (Rounder) shows Laurie's full range, with songs from all three of her Flying Fish albums (including some of the most shining moments from *Restless Rambling Heart*) plus some previously unissued tracks.

BOBBY McFERRIN (September 28, 1998)

I t was a Keith Jarrett piano record, not a songfest in the shower or even his opera singer parents, that inspired Bobby McFerrin to begin his career as a vocal performer. By telephone from his home, Bobby tells us about the first time he heard 1971's *Facing You*, Jarrett's inaugural recording of solo piano improvisations: "I hadn't heard music like that before, someone simply sitting at the piano and just playing it. . . . At the time, I was convinced I was a piano player, but I always had a nagging suspicion that the piano wasn't my instrument. So when I shifted to voice, and I discovered that I was a vocalist, the whole concept of solo anything at that point was really fascinating to me. You know, the fact that someone would just go to trudge that path alone, that they would do it by themselves—I found that really very intriguing. So that record turned me in that direction."

As crucial as Jarrett's album was to Bobby, it also initiated a period of not listening to recorded music—by singers, that is. Twenty-two at that time, Bobby purposefully avoided buying records by vocalists for a couple of years because, he explains, "I really wanted to find out what singing meant to me, personally, and I wanted to find a style that spoke to me. I was afraid that if I started collecting a lot of [records by] singers that it would be difficult for me to decipher who I was, or the process would have taken longer."

Obviously, Bobby's strategy worked. His "package" of musicality, jazzlike inventiveness, vocal gymnastics, and entertainment ability stands alone. There are no Bobby pretenders or challengers—apparently, no one dares. But mastery only seems to interest Bobby for the moment that it is first achieved. As if seeking new arenas where the competition intimidates *him*, Bobby has for the last several years devoted much of his time to conducting classical orchestras.

When Bobby does perform or record vocally, he leans, Jarrettlike, toward pure improvisation, not repeating his hits or traveling any other comfortable path. Like the jazz artist that he once was, he lives for performances that are intimately shared, and co-created, with audiences and that are more accurately recorded in hearts and minds than on acetate. "I find that extraordinarily beautiful, when someone comes up to me and says 'You know, there was this chord that your group did that I'll never forget,'" Bobby says. "It's inside their head and they can hear it, and it's theirs. That's my favorite kind of music making."

BOBBY McFERRIN'S FAVORITE ARTISTS AND RECORDINGS

Keith Jarrett—*Facing You* (ECM). See above.

Sergei Rachmaninov—Rhapsody on a Theme of Paganini, Op. 43, Artur Rubenstein, piano; Chicago Symphony/Fritz Reiner (RCA). "The first music that made me cry—I was about five or six."

George Gershwin—*Porgy and Bess*. Bobby's father sang the voice of Sidney Poitier in the 1959 Otto Preminger film adaptation, which won an Academy Award for Andre Previn's score, Bobby tells us. He has started conducting the opera and dreams of one day manning the baton with the New York Metropolitan Opera: "That music's in my bones. I've been loving that music since I was eight years old." : Leona Mitchell, Florence Quivar, Willard White, McHenry Boatwright, Barbara Hendricks, Francois Clemmons, Cleveland Orchestra/Lorin Maazel (3 CDs: London).

Sergio Mendes—"I really loved the work that Sergio Mendes was doing in the sixties . . . I also loved the arrangements that Dave Grusin was doing for him." : *Four-Sider* (A&M) includes one of Bobby's favorite tracks, the hit "Mas Que Nada." *Look Around* (A&M, out of print) has another, "The Frog."

Weather Report—*Mysterious Traveler* (Columbia). Bobby loves their entire catalog but this album completely knocked him out.

Charles Ives—*Calcium Light Night*, Orchestra of New England/James Sinclair (Koch International). "That album just really opened my ears to the possibility of consonance and dissonance actually working together in such a way that it makes musical sense. . . . It was so close to life, you know, like you're standing on the street and a car goes by and you hear its music. At the same time there's a guy on the street corner playing solo saxophone or something. And it doesn't bother you because somehow it's in the mix of life." : The version Bobby first heard of this music is no longer in print, but the above rendition is highly praised.

Henry Mancini—*Mr. Lucky* (RCA). Bobby liked Mancini's music, especially this TV soundtrack album, when he was in high school.

Johann Sebastian Bach—*Goldberg Variations, BWV 988* (Sony Classical), Glenn Gould, piano. "That had a profound effect on me because his sound, his touch, his sensitivity to that music was absolutely extraordinary. Dense, subtle. I've never heard piano played that softly. And I don't mean *pianissimo*, necessarily. I don't mean quiet, I mean soft."

Herbie Hancock—*Mwandishi* (Warner Bros.) and *Sunlight* (Columbia). "Great bass player, goodness gracious," Bobby says about Paul Jackson's work on the latter album.

Miles Davis—*Live: Evil* (Columbia). "Completely messed up my head. Incredible. The bass player would just hang, you know. Everything around him was just completely disruptive, and completely disengaging and engaging and foolin' around and messin' around and jumpin' up and down and stompin' and yellin' and screamin'. And at the same time, he's just holding down this groove."

Gabriel Faure—Requiem. Barbara Bonney, Thomas Hampson, Ambrosian Singers/Philharmonia Orchestra/ Michel Legrand (Teldec). "Even though some of the tempos I think are a little on the slow side, still, [Legrand] found some stuff there that's very interesting."

Stevie Wonder—*Music of My Mind*, *Talking Book*, and *Fullfillingness' First Finale* (all Motown).

Joni Mitchell—*Hejira* (Asylum) and *Night Ride Home* (Geffen).

Paul Simon—*Rhythm of the Saints* (Warner Bros.). Simon was working on this record at the Hit Factory studios in New York at the same time Bobby was recording his own album, so he sent word that Bobby was welcome to come by and say hi: "So, I dropped in on one of his sessions. And all the rhythm tracks were done, he was laying down his vocals, and he asked if I wanted to hear something. And I said 'Well, sure,' not knowing what to expect, and they started playing the rhythm track, and he got down at my ear level and sang in my left ear. And I'll never forget that, that he actually sang to me, rather than just listening to something on tape. And I found that just very kind, somehow, that he would sort of let me in on what he was doing, and I got a chance to hear a live vocal version of it, so I felt really special."

Ludwig van Beethoven—Symphony No. 7 in A, Op. 92 (no recording specified) and Symphony No. 9, in D Minor, Op. 125, *Chorale*, Vienna Philharmonic/Leonard Bernstein (Deutsche Grammaphon). ⏺: Symphony No. 7: Orchestre Revolutionaire et Romantique/John Eliot Gardiner (Archiv) or Berlin Philharmonic/Herbert von Karajan (Deutsche Grammaphon).

James Brown—Bobby loves all of Brown's records. ⏺: See Master List.

BOBBY McFERRIN'S OWN RECORDINGS

Bobby is reluctant to name *favorites* among his records but he does feel that 1997's *Circlesongs* (Sony) "seemed like my truest self, because they were completely, spontaneously created pieces, you know, just on the spot." This unique record features the first recorded appearance of his Voicestra, the a cappella vocal ensemble that improvises with him on the album's eight selections.

Bobby does have favorite moments on all of his records, though, including his favorite song that he's written and recorded, "A Sightless Bird" on his debut album, 1982's *Bobby McFerrin* (Elektra). He likes nearly every moment on 1984's *The Voice* (Elektra). The tunes "Baby" and "Angry"—the latter for the background voices—get the nod on 1990's *Medicine Music* (EMI), although he is critical of his lyric-writing, something he hopes to work on intensively in the future. On 1995's *Bang! Zoom* (Blue Note), he is especially fond of "Friend": "I just wanted to capture the essence of having good friends and what that meant to me."

He is less enamored than his fans of 1988's *Simple Pleasures* (EMI) and its huge hit "Don't Worry, Be Happy." Although it was his greatest commercial success, his subsequent career moves have demonstrated how little that meant to him. He loved doing the album, he says, but didn't think that multi-tracking his voice was as interesting as multi-tracking other singers would have been, and much prefers the freshness of *Circle Songs*.

⏺: Bobby did not mention three other fine efforts. The 1985 release *Spontaneous Inventions* (Blue Note) features witty interactions with *Herbie Hancock, Wayne Shorter, *Manhattan Transfer, Jon Hendricks, and Robin Williams! *Play* (Blue Note), from 1990, is a live collaboration with jazz pianist Chick Corea. On 1991's *Hush* (Columbia), Bobby and cellist Yo Yo Ma do their respective things on a series of jazz compositions.

ANNA McGARRIGLE (June 15, 1998)

Anna McGarrigle can't remember the moment when the music bug first bit because she can't remember a moment without music. "There were always people singing in our house—parents, sister, uncles, etcetera," she writes us. But she does know the first record that knocked her silly—Hoagy Carmichael's rendition of his song "Old Music Master," back before she started school. "Because I couldn't read, I pasted a green metallic star on the label of the seventy-eight so I could recognize it. It was about a little black boy appearing to an old white music master and telling him to get with it or his stuff wouldn't get played on the 'Happy Cat Hit Parade.' The rhymes were way over my head. 'You'd better tell your friend Beethoven and Mr. Reginald B. Koven' Who were these people?"

Many ask the same question when they first trip upon the engaging, thoughtful music Anna makes with her sister Kate. *Rolling Stone* has described the McGarrigles as "probably the finest singer-songwriter team to go ignored by the American public." Brought up in a small, mostly French village above Montreal, the McGarrigles began their career in attention-getting fashion—in 1974, Linda Ronstadt named her album *Heart Like a Wheel* for the title song by Anna. Kate and Anna's self-titled debut album the next year, featuring their own rendition of that tune, was named Record of the Year by *Melody Maker*. But their closely observed lyrics, home-and-hearth modesty, delicately woven vocals, and elegant arrangements make their music a refined pleasure, like a savory meal prepared for a few dear friends. Which may also explain why their fan base—one of the most passionate in popular music—remains considerably below Golden Arches level.

In the early 1960s, Anna and Kate were teenage folksinger wannabes who had their ears to the ground of the emerging musical culture. They got an early graduate course in folk music after meeting Peter Weldon and Jack Nissenson, who were both folk performers and graduate students. Weldon and Nissenson took the same scholarly approach to their avocation that they did in university. They convinced the sisters that the real folk music wasn't in the campfire songs that everyone knew but in roots and field recordings, many of which could be accessed through a record-lending library in Montreal. Acting on that tip, Anna discovered Doc Watson's first recording, with Clarence Ashley; the Bahamian guitarist/singer Joseph Spence; and the sacred harp singers tracks on the *Anthology of American Folk Music*—all music that was changing the lives of a generation of budding folkies and folk rockers on both sides of the Canadian-American border.

The records of two other soon-to-be folk icons, Joan Baez and Bob Dylan, were also planting ideas in the McGarrigles' brains. "I think Joan Baez had a huge effect on every teenage girl in the early sixties including this one," says Anna. "I think people realized you could do something not at all 'poppy' and have mass appeal." Shortly on Baez's heels came Bob Dylan, the man she introduced to nearly the entire world except for Anna and Kate, who discovered him through another connection. "Peter had an old girlfriend who was married to one of Bob Dylan's first producers," Anna tells us. "She brought Dylan's first record to Montreal just before it was released. What an eye opener!"

Anna and Kate later took in more classic '60s folk/pop influences. At a Montreal club called Harlem Paradise, they caught a number of leading African-American performers. They bought the requisite Beatles and Stones albums and danced to the radio hits of the day. But that really is the McGarrigles' secret—from ingredients that rarely surprise, they make music that rarely fails to. (For Kate's side of the story, see her section immediately following this one.)

ANNA McGARRIGLE'S FAVORITE ARTISTS AND RECORDINGS

Joan Baez—*Joan Baez* (Vanguard). "Her first record was great. So dramatic and beautiful."

Clarence Ashley and Doc Watson—*Old Time Music at Clarence Ashley's* (Smithsonian/Folkways).

Various artists—*Sacred Harp Singing. The Library of Congress: Archive of Folk Culture* (Rounder). "So gothic and weird," Anna comments about these recordings made by folklorist Alan Lomax in 1942.

Various artists—*The Bahamas: Islands of Song* (Smithsonian /Folkways). Anna especially loved Joseph Spence's tracks on this album. ●: For Spence alone on this label, try under his name *The Complete Folkways Recordings (1958)* (Smithsonian/Folkways).

Bob Dylan—"Went to See the Gypsy" on *New Morning* (Columbia).

Jussi Bjorling—"I have loved Jussi Bjorling ever since hearing his records for the first time thirty years ago. He's understated but still very powerful." ●: Bjorling stars in a version of Puccini's opera, *La Boheme*, with Victoria de los Angeles, Robert Merrill, Lucino Amara, and the RCA Victor Symphony Orchestra & Chorus/ Sir Thomas Beecham (2 CDs: EMI); and in Puccini's *Madama Butterfly* with Victoria de los Angeles, Miriam Pirazzini, Mario Sereni and Rome Opera House Orchestra/Gabriele Santini (2 CDs: EMI). For a single disc introduction to Bjorling, try *The Pearl Fishers* (RCA), a collection of duets and scenes with Bjorling, Robert

Merrill, Licia Albanese, Zinka Milanov, and Renata Tebaldi. . . . *Edition* (4 CDs: EMI) collects 89 tracks of arias, duets, and songs from the tenor's peak years.

The Beatles—When the Beatles and Stones hit, Anna writes, "all the serious folkies started to dance." ⬤: See Master List.

John Lennon—"Instant Karma." ⬤: This track from a superseded compilation, *Shaved Fish*, appears on the current package, the terrific *The John Lennon Collection* (Capitol).

The Rolling Stones—"Sympathy for the Devil" on *Beggar's Banquet* (ABKCO). Although this is Anna's favorite Stones' song, she loved all their early records.

Junior Walker & the All-Stars—"Roadrunner." (Motown). Anna says this bar-band classic is "my favorite single of all time." ⬤: *The Ultimate Collection* (Motown).

Bobbie Gentry—"Ode to Billy Joe" on *Ode to Billy Joe* (Capitol). Anna is a fan of pop music in general and finds this huge 1967 hit "very interesting. Sort of a melding of jazz, folk, and country."

Norman Greenbaum—"Spirit in the Sky" on *Spirit in the Sky* (Reprise). "Amazing."

*Taj Mahal—"Corinna" on *Natch'l Blues* (Columbia).

Bruce Springsteen—"Dancing in the Dark" on *Born in the U.S.A.* (Columbia). "So poetic, sexy, and danceable."

A Flock of Seagulls—"Wishing (If I Had a Photograph of You)" on *Listen* (Jive). Anna says she likes "some of those early synthesizer groups that used the tone bender," especially this track.

ANNA McGARRIGLE'S OWN RECORDINGS

Anna is happy with all of the McGarrigles' albums.

⬤: Anna's not bragging. The magic never runs out in the McGarrigles' catalog. That being the case, you might as well start at the beginning with their strong 1976 debut, *Kate and Anna McGarrigle* (Hannibal). Of special note because of their uniqueness are 1981's widely loved *French Record* (Hannibal), which is sung entirely in French but is a melodic and vocal feast that makes understanding irrelevant, and 1998's *The McGarrigle Hour* (Hannibal). The latter features Anna and Kate and an informal, intimate gathering of family members and friends including Kate's ex-husband *Loudon Wainwright III, Kate and Loudon's son Rufus Wainwright (whose own 1998 debut was a critical favorite), Anna and Kate's other children, and guests Emmylou Harris and Linda Rondstadt. The captivating set mixes old-time family favorites, McGarrigle originals, standards, and other well-chosen material; although recorded in studios, the ambiance—and concept— makes it sound so living-room cozy that you can nearly feel the heat from the fireplace. Other albums in the McGarrigles' cedar chest include 1977's *Dancer with Bruised Knees* (Hannibal), a record brimming with inviting melodies, insightful poetic lyrics, and lovely vocal harmonies; 1978's *Pronto Monto* (Warner Bros.); 1983's *Love Over and Over* (Polydor); 1990's *Heartbeats Accelerating* (Private Music), with some tasteful electronic textures accenting the conventional instruments on another excellent collection of McGarrigle miniatures; and 1996's *Matapedia* (Hannibal), whose centerpiece is an absolute giant of a song, Anna's "Goin' Back to Harlan."

KATE McGARRIGLE (May 5, 1998)

When an 11-year-old Kate McGarrigle first imagined herself as a singer, it was as a dramatic, continental stylist like Edith Piaf, whom she'd caught on the *Ed Sullivan Show*. But it was seeing *Pete Seeger perform a few years later that made her think that it just might be possible to make her own music. "He even made mistakes," Kate chuckles. "He'd laugh at mistakes and correct them. Before that, the only kind of performing I'd ever done was playing some little piano recitals. Of course, you got a note wrong, you'd get your fingers rapped, and you weren't allowed to forget it. . . . Pete was having fun with the audience and with everything."

Kate also liked the idea of accompanying herself on guitar or banjo, just as she'd seen Pete do. It wasn't long after that she and her older sister Anna began singing folk songs and listening to folk records with another girl in the French Canadian village where they lived. But things really started cooking after they met studious folksingers Peter Weldon and Jack Nissenson. The two men exploded the sisters' musical world by exposing them to the roots of folk on field recordings. And their influence only began there. "Peter would have like Verdi's Requiem blasting, so it was a real mixture," Kate recalls. "I mean, suddenly music was not just what you heard on the radio. It was enormous in scope."

Other elements of what would become the McGarrigle sisters' signature sound were more or less absorbed from their environment. There wasn't much of a folk music scene in their town but "just like a mile or two over the mountain, out of the valley, there were people who looked like those people in those songs, the Appalachian stuff," says Kate. "There were people in unpainted houses, and real poverty, and they were like hillbillies. . . . I think when I heard that music it reminded me of those faces, those people." At the French Catholic school they attended as girls, Kate and Anna learned centuries-old—albeit sanitized, Kate laughs—French folk songs taught casually to the children by the nuns to accompany their playground games. At home, they marinated in their parents' connoisseur-ish record collection. Mom loved Gershwin, Dad "liked people like Al Hibbler when everybody else liked Frank Sinatra. He was daring in his taste," Kate remembers.

When Kate and Anna began performing as a duo, after starting separate songwriting careers, they learned just how well their background had prepared them for that moment. "When the [debut] record came out and everybody said 'My God, this is brilliant, this is new, this is innovative,' I mean, we didn't think it was innovative or not innovative," says Kate. "It never occurred to us. We hadn't tried for that sound. It was just the sound that came out of working together."

KATE McGARRIGLE'S FAVORITE ARTISTS AND RECORDINGS

Joseph Spence—*The Complete Folkways Recordings (1958)* (Smithsonian/Folkways) and *The Real Bahamas, Vols. 1–2* (Nonesuch).

Leroy Carr—When Kate started playing piano seriously, she liked to play the music of Carr and other blues pianists such as Memphis Slim and Walter Roland. Carr was a top blues star in the 1920s and '30s before he died at 30, his health ruined by alcoholism. 🔘: *Blues Before Sunrise* (Portrait) includes one of Kate's favorite songs of his, "Midnight Hour Blues," and features duo tracks with Carr's frequent partner, guitarist Scrapper Blackwell, as does *Naptown Blues (1929–1934)* (Yazoo).

Memphis Slim (Peter Chatman)—Slim's polish and professionalism, along with rousing, commanding style, made for consistently engaging records. 🔘: *Rockin' the Blues* (Charly) features Slim performing his classic songs in the late 1950s, backed by an excellent band that stars guitarist Matt Murphy.

Walter Roland—Roland was a semi-obscure blues singer and pianist who recorded little but is much admired by those who know his work. 🔘: *Vol. 1 (1933)* and *Vol. 2 (1934–35)* (both Document).

Wade Ward—Ward was a banjo player in the old-timey style. 🔘: Ward appears on *Ballads and Songs of the Blue Ridge Mountains* (Smithsonian/Folkways) and *Southern Journey Vol. 2: Ballads and Breakdowns—Songs from the Southern*

Mountains (Rounder), from Alan Lomax's late 1950s recordings, and on *High Atmosphere: Ballads and Banjo Tunes from Virginia and North Carolina Collected by John Cohen in November of 1965* (Rounder).

Clarence Ashley with the Carolina Tar Heels—"I liked his style," Kate says about another one of her favorite banjo players. "Kind of a clawhammer style. Not smooth, very rhythmic. And I tried to imitate that." The music overall, Kate notes, "really had that kind of Appalachian, almost kind of a religiosity to it. I don't know what it is, fear of God more than anything else. You hear it in Bill Monroe's music. I like that." : Very little of Ashley's or the Carolina Tar Heels' music is currently available. Ashley can be heard on the in-print *Doc Watson and Clarence Ashley: The Original Folkways Recordings 1960–1962* (2 CDs: Smithsonian/Folkways) and the out-of-print *Tennessee Strings* (Rounder).

*The Everly Brothers—This was one of Kate's favorite groups when she was still a child. : See the section on Don Everly and his recordings.

Jean Carignan—"In the world of fiddlers, he's sometimes considered the best," notes Kate, who likes his whole body of work. "He would sit and clog with his feet while he played . . . It's as powerful as that Irish dancing you see. I mean, it's really hitting the floor with incredible force. There's nothing polite about it. And incredibly rhythmic." : *French Canadian, Irish, and Scottish Fiddle Music* (Legacy); *Old Time Fiddle* (Smithsonian/Folkways), with *Pete Seeger; and *Jean Carignan* and *Homage a Joseph Allard* (both Philo, both out of print).

Galt MacDermot—*Fergus macRoy at the Homestead Upright* (Kilmarnock) MacDermot, who wrote the score to the musical *Hair* with Gerome Ragni and James Rado, is from French Canada, like the McGarrigle sisters. "This record is so unusual," enthuses Kate. "He didn't write the lyrics. There was a poet from Vancouver who did. They're always about someone going to jail. They're kind of silly. But the songs have twists and turns that you just never heard anywhere else."

John Herald & The Greenbrier Boys—*Better Late Than Never* (Vanguard, long out of print). Kate enjoyed this Cajun-inflected folk group's electric recording. : *The Best of . . .* (Vanguard), including Kate fave "Alligator Man" from *Better Late Than Never*, is the only current album in the Vanguard catalog.

The Rolling Stones—Kate was a big Stones fan in the mid-'60s. : There are no weak Stones albums in this period, but *12 x 5*, *Aftermath*, and *Between the Buttons* (all ABKCO) are widely considered a cut above the rest.

The Beatles—*Revolver* (Capitol).

Bob Dylan—*Blonde on Blonde* (Capitol). "I liked Bob Dylan, because I found him so interesting. He had the great capacity to throw off one skin and put on another one," says Kate, who learned about Dylan through her folk music gurus Peter Weldon and Jack Nissenson and with them and Anna attended Dylan's first concert in New York in 1962 when she was 16.

Modest Mussorgsky—*Boris Godunov.* : National Symphony Orchestra/Matilslav Rostropovich with Ruggero Raimondi, Nicolai Gedda, Paul Plishka, Kenneth Riegel, Galina Vishnevskaya, the Choral Arts Society of Washington, and the Oratorio Society of Washington (3 CDs: Erato) or Vienna Philharmonic/Herbert von Karajan with Nicolai Ghiaurov, Aleksei Maslennikov, Martti Talvela, Ludovic Spless, Galina Vishnevskaya, the Sofia Radio Chorus, and the Vienna State Opera Chorus.

Leos Janacek—*Jenufa.* : Soderstrom, Popp, Randova, Dvorsky, Sir Charles Mackerras/Vienna Philharmonic Orchestra & State Opera Chorus (London).

Johann Sebastian Bach—6 Sonatas for Violin and Harpsichord, Jaime Laredo and Glenn Gould (Sony).

Franz Schmidt—Intermezzo from *Notre Dame* Berlin Phillharmonic-Herbert von Karajan / *The SuperConcert, Volume III* (DGG). "One day I was listening to the radio and they played this lovely piece and I drove right to the record store and bought it."

KATE McGARRIGLE'S OWN RECORDINGS

Like Anna, Kate is quite pleased with the entire McGarrigles' catalog.

: See the preceding section on Anna McGarrigle.

CHARLES McPHERSON (1996)

To hear jazz alto saxophonist Charles McPherson is to wonder if this is the body where Charlie "Bird" Parker's soul came to rest. Parker's charismatic brilliance spawned a generation of Bird-loving emulators, most of whom brought little to the party but a skill for mimicry. Charles has always approached Parker's bebop more as a base language through which to express his own distinctive musical imagination. In his words, bebop is "the avenue that leads to other avenues." Those other avenues have included such disparate influences as

Ellington, Gershwin, Bartok, and Rachmaninoff. Charles also stands apart from Parker in his tone, a sweet, inviting voice distinctly more intimate than Bird's.

Still, the effect is undeniably Parkeresque. As Jimmy Heath has said of Charles, "The stuff just bubbles out of the saxophone. I've never heard anybody else who came that close to the explosive quality of that surprise and feeling . . ." Which is why when Clint Eastwood and his musical supervisor Lennie Niehaus went hunting for a saxophonist to evoke Parker in Eastwood's reverent film biography "Bird," all paths led to Charles's door.

The first time he heard Parker, Charles was, appropriately, a kid in a candy store. As a 14-year-old in Detroit in 1953, he had been learning to play the saxophone in the school marching band. He was listening to records by masters like Johnny Hodges on the side when his boyhood pal, the late trumpeter Lonnie Hillyer, insisted that he couldn't go on living without checking out Parker. While in the neighborhood sweet shop, Charles spotted a Parker record, the Latin tune "Tico, Tico," on the store's jukebox. He slipped in his dime, the needle dropped on the record, and his future came into instant focus. "I knew then that I wanted to play music as a livelihood," Charles says by phone from his San Diego home. "It affected even the way I looked at marches in the school band. I started to get serious about the whole thing."

"Tico, Tico," from a series of recordings called *South of the Border*, wasn't the bebop that Parker co-pioneered in the early 1940s. But his fascination with his new idol soon led Charles to the real deal. He then discovered that some of the hottest bebop in the country was being played at the Bluebird, a club down the street from his home. The Bluebird's house rhythm section included locals *Elvin Jones on drums and Barry Harris on piano. Such other Detroiters as trumpeters Thad Jones and Donald Byrd and baritone saxman Pepper Adams headlined along with national and international stars traveling through the area. The underage Charles began spending his summers lingering in front of the club, listening through the open doors. When the weather cooled, he'd stand outside the window behind the bandstand and tap on the glass; the pre-arranged signal cued Elvin Jones to adjust the blinds so the kid could see inside. "I couldn't believe the virtuosity of these musicians," Charles recalls. "That just sealed it for me."

Another chance meeting at the Bluebird hooked Charles up with Harris, who also lived in this musical mecca of a neighborhood. Charles was soon spending every afternoon in Harris's living room, studying music theory and jazz soloing. By age 19, he and Hillyer were playing professionally in New York, where a year later a massive goateed man named Charles Mingus would hear them and hire them for his band (replacing multi-woodwindist Eric Dolphy and trumpeter

Ted Curson, who had just given their notices). Charles would work with Mingus on and off for the next dozen years, until 1972.

The spotlight has only occasionally shone on Charles in his post-Mingus phase. He maintains devout followings of fans and writers in sophisticated jazz centers like New York and Chicago as well as in Europe and Japan, where he frequently tours. The media outside those areas pay scant attention, but his peers and critics know. In an era when most players of Charles's generation have lost their passionate edge and most younger players have yet to demonstrate one, Charles stands nearly alone as a master of the alto, like his main man decades before.

CHARLES McPHERSON'S FAVORITE ARTISTS AND RECORDINGS

Charlie Parker—Not surprisingly, Charles recommends every note the matchless altoist ever played. But if you're just dipping into the Parker catalog, he says, don't neglect Bird's Latin-style recordings with Afro-Cuban jazz maestro Machito and others or his records with string arrangements—in particular, the tune "Just Friends." About the string sessions, which some jazz fans resist, Charles says, "Bird was the greatest melody player I ever heard in terms of playing the melody and the little ad libs around the melodic statement. No one does that better— bar none. Why wouldn't the world want to hear the greatest ballad player play ballads?" ●: If you're flush with cash, the 10-CD set *Bird: The Complete Charlie Parker on Verve* (Verve) covers the string and Latin sessions and loads of seminal bebop besides. *Charlie Parker with Strings: the Master Takes* (Verve) covers the strings sessions in isolation; *South of the Border* (Verve) does the same for Parker's Latin side, including essential sessions with Machito. For a less pricey intro to the Verve material, try either of the following, which sample the 10-CD set: *Bird: The Original Recordings of Charlie Parker* (Verve), which includes "Just Friends," or *Verve Jazz Masters: Charlie Parker* (Verve). Among many other worthy purchases, *The Complete Dial Sessions 1946–47* (Stash) is a four-CD set of astounding musical quality. *Charlie Parker Memorial, Vol. 1* (Savoy) contains some of his best work for Savoy in the late 1940s.

Duke Ellington, Cole Porter, Thelonious Monk, and George Gershwin—"There are certain tunes that taught me something about music when I played them. ['Embraceable You' by Gershwin] is one of them. [The same goes for] certain tunes that Cole Porter wrote—even obscure ones like 'All Through the Night.' Almost anything that Duke Ellington wrote, there's a lesson. Anything that Thelonious Monk or Gershwin wrote, you learn more than just the tune." ●: For pleasant entries to the Porter and Gershwin song catalogs, check out Charlie

Parker—*The Cole Porter Songbook*, a beautiful ballad record, and by Ella Fitzgerald with Nelson Riddle's orchestra, the three-CD set *The George and Ira Gershwin Songbook* and *The Cole Porter Songbook, Vols. 1–2*. All the preceding are on Verve. One of Charles's favorites by Ellington is his *Far East Suite* (Bluebird) from 1966—"The band's sound, the tunes, the arrangements by Strayhorn—all great." For prime Monk, see Master List.

Billie Holiday—*Lady in Satin* (Columbia). "I learned a lot from that one, too," says Charles. Among Holiday's last recordings, it's not for all tastes. Her voice is nearly shot, but the poignancy of her art is at its tragic peak.

James Brown—Charles doesn't mention specific recordings; he just likes Brown's whole concept. 💿: See Master List.

Igor Stravinsky—*The Firebird* and *The Rite of Spring*. "I listen to as much European classical—especially modern classical—as jazz, actually." 💿: You can hear Stravinsky himself conducting the entire *Firebird* ballet with the Columbia Chamber Ensemble (Sony) and the ROS with the Columbia Symphony (Sony). Another recommended version of the ballet is by the London Symphony Orchestra/Antal Dorati (Philips). For the ROS, try the New York Philharmonic/ Leonard Bernstein (Sony). For a strong recording that includes both ROS and the Firebird Suite, try the London Symphony, Gennadi Rozhdestvensky (Nimbus).

Bela Bartok—Concerto for Orchestra. 💿: See Master List.

Nikolai Rimsky-Korsakov—*Scheherazade, Op. 35*. "That opened a door for me." 💿: Try either Royal Concertgebouw Orchestra/Kirill Kondrashin (Philips) or Royal Philharmonic Orchestra/Sir Thomas Beecham.

Sergei Rachmaninoff—Prelude in C Sharp Minor, Op. 5, No. 2. 💿: This favorite of the romantic piano repertoire has been recorded countless times, including by Rachmaninoff himself (RCA). For contemporary interpretations, look to Howard Shelley (Hyperion) or Alexis Weissenberg (BMG). Another intriguing version was released on the first volume of *A Window in Time* (Telarc), which features state-of-the-art digital reproductions of player piano rolls Rachmaninoff cut in 1911.

Stevie Wonder—*Journey Through the Secret Life of Plants* (Motown). "It didn't sell at all, but it's the most gorgeous thing you ever heard."

Sade—"I don't like a lot of people today, jazz or otherwise. But she's one I'll listen to." Sade was born in Nigeria as Helen Folasade Adu but was heavily influenced by American singers Billie Holiday and Nina Simone. 💿: *Best of Sade* (Epic).

CHARLES McPHERSON'S OWN RECORDINGS

Charles's favorites among his own releases include *Live in Tokyo* (Xanadu), *From This Moment On* (Prestige), *Horizons* (Prestige), *First Flight Out* (Arabesque), and the self-produced *Illusions in Blue* (Chazz Jazz). The latter shows off five excellent McPherson compositions and offers a powerhouse live performance to boot, with a tight working group of largely unknown players including son Charles Jr. on drums. *From This Moment On* is an overlooked classic of more accessible, and often dance-able, jazz with two soul-jazz-ish tunes by Charles that should have been hits. We know from a subsequent conversation with Charles that he also is quite satisfied with 1996's *Come Play with Me* (Arabesque)—in particular, he was happy with the empathy that emerged between the players (pianist Mulgrew Miller, bassist Santi Debriano, and drummer Lewis Nash) gathered for that session.

⊙: Also revealing is *Live At the Five Spot* (Prestige), a 1966 club date with Hillyer, Harris, and the inestimable drummer Billy Higgins on board. Then only 27, Charles was already plumbing emotional depths beyond most seasoned players' reach. For a sample of Charles's work with Mingus, try *Live in Chateauvallon, 1972* (France's Concert). His latest release as of this writing is 1998's *Manhattan Nocturne* (Arabesque), his finest yet for his current label. *Nocturne* features several strong McPherson compositions, tight ensemble work, and inspired soloing from both Charles and Mulgrew Miller, who form as complementary a pairing of top-tier improvisers as exists in jazz today.

TAJ MAHAL

Every wind in the river finds its way to the sea, Taj Mahal sings on his 1991 album, *Like Never Before*. He could say much the same about his music. In a recording career winding its way back to the mid-1960s, Taj has performed rural blues, reggae, calypso, rock 'n' roll, and big-city R&B, in each case drawing from his far-flung cultural roots.

Taj was born in Harlem to a South Carolinian mother whose parents were of African and Native American descent and a father of African heritage whose parents came from the West Indies. He grew up in Springfield, Massachusetts, but came of age tending crops, cattle, and chickens on a farm in nearby Palmer, fulfilling a dream he'd had since childhood. As he says, "My background gave me a lot of different options."

"I grew up listening to what my parents played," Taj adds, "and the early music I heard from them [included] classical, gospel, spiritual music, and jazz—lots of jazz, lots of different styles of jazz . . ." His folks listened to calypso, opera, and jump blues, too, and when he went to Aunt Bessie's house to mow her lawn, he heard her spinning James Brown and the Chicago blues of Muddy Waters and Jimmy Reed. "[To me, it was all] just The Music," he says. "It wasn't all these different categories." But while he loved the urban music, especially jazz, that suffused his life, he hadn't yet heard the music he wanted to make.

The 1960s blues revival exposed Taj to Son House, Mance Lipscomb, Sleepy John Estes, Big Mama Thornton, and others, and the circle suddenly felt complete—thanks also to the fact that he was driving tractors, harvesting corn, and milking cows in those days. "The music from the city just didn't cut it when I was working on a farm," Taj recalls. "I remember saying to myself, 'I've never heard this music before yet I understand it perfectly . . . Is this stuff in my DNA or part of culture?' "

Country blues, with folk and rock accents, dominated Taj's first few albums. Subsequent records found him delving into his Caribbean and African sides with reggae riddims, steel drums, and chiming West African tones on his National steel-bodied guitar. In recent years, he's even returned to the brassy urban sound that had stopped making sense to him down on the farm.

Of course, no matter how much musical territory he covers, he never strays too far from the blues. He sympathizes with Eric Clapton, Van Morrison, Jimmie Vaughan, and the late Stevie Ray Vaughan—all true bluesmen to his mind who've been criticized for copping from an outside culture: "We were all out of context in the sense that we were no longer picking cotton in the South. But who's running with Emiliano Zapata? Does that mean you don't play Mexican music anymore? So I didn't see a reason to leave the blues behind."

TAJ MAHAL'S FAVORITE ARTISTS AND RECORDINGS

Nat King Cole with Oscar Moore—Taj first knew the music of this compelling vocalist/pianist before he became a pop sensation, when he recorded in a jazz trio format with the great Oscar Moore on guitar: "In fact, that's where I first started hearing guitar that I liked." : *The Best of the Nat King Cole Trio* (Capitol).

S. E. Rogie—Few guitar players make a note or chord resonate like Taj. He says he got that sound from this musician from Sierra Leone: "There's a ring on African guitars that American guitar players don't get. When you hear five guitarists playing on the stage, you'll hear each one individually from the other [because] they've got this beautiful, sustaining ring. It's a part of the ancient culture and the music, so I've always tried to maintain that." ●: *The Palm Wine Sounds of S. E. Rogie* (Stern's).

Louis Jordan—"I just adored Louis Jordan. He ultimately said the same thing that I said. A lot of people got on him because he wasn't playing this radical, scream-through-your-horn music with weird harmonies. Louis said, 'I want people to come and hear the music and forget about their troubles.' The songs are so funny, they've got catchy lyrics, and the arrangements are great." ●: See Master List.

*Sonny Rollins—*Way Out West* (Original Jazz Classics). "I listened to that until I wore it out."

Miles Davis—*Sketches of Spain* (Columbia) and *Kind of Blue* (Columbia). *Kind of Blue* also comes in an audiophile version (Columbia MasterSound Collector's Edition). Taj was about to drive to Portland, Oregon, for a concert when we interviewed him and had a copy, which he says puts him "right in the rhythm section with those guys," primed for his car stereo.

Sonny Boy Williamson II (Rice Miller)—*Down and Out Blues* (Chess), *The Real Folk Blues* (Chess), and *More Real Folk Blues* (Chess). Taj says these three albums (the latter two are compilations) are the best place to start with Miller, the most prominent of the two Delta bluesmen to go by the performing name of Sonny Boy Williamson.

Howlin' Wolf—*Howlin' Wolf/Moaning in the Moonlight* (Chess). This budget-priced CD includes Burnett's first two classic albums for Chess and is Taj's choice for your first taste of Wolf. But everything the man laid down on tape is worth your attention, says Taj who confesses, "I'm a Howlin' Wolf nut!"

*John Lee Hooker—Taj prefers Hooker's earlier works. ●: *The Legendary Modern Recordings, 1948–1954* (Virgin) contains 24 tracks on the Modern label, including "Boogie Chillen," "I'm in the Mood," and "Crawling Kingsnake." *The Early Years* (Tomato) covers 51 tracks recorded for Vee Jay from the mid-'50s to mid-'60s.

Muddy Waters—The impact of Waters's style, bred in the Mississippi Delta and electrified in Chicago, can be heard in Taj's early bands. ●: See Master List.

Smokey Hogg—A skilled, melodic singer (although primitive guitarist), this potent bluesman may not be as well known as his cousin Lightnin' Hopkins, but he's a hero to Taj. ●: See Master List.

Lightnin' Hopkins—Hopkins is a giant of the country blues that was Taj's preferred style when he started out. ⬤: See Master List.

Coleman Hawkins—"From the time I was six or seven until the time I was twelve or thirteen, my favorite song was 'Body and Soul' [performed] by Coleman Hawkins." ⬤: *Body and Soul* (RCA Bluebird) contains a classic performance of the title song and a variety of other performances from 1939 to '56. The schmaltzy string arrangements from 1956 are distracting but Hawk is magnificent throughout. His many excellent smaller group recordings include *The High and Mighty Hawk* (London), . . . *Encounters Ben Webster* (Verve), and *The Hawk Flies High* (Original Jazz Classics).

Ella Fitzgerald—Taj recommends anything and everything by this immortal vocalist. ⬤: See Master List.

Count Basie—As with Ella, Taj finds something to like in all of the Count's recordings. But most jazz fans agree that the place to start with Basie is his early bands that featured Lester Young, Walter Page, Freddie Green, Jo Jones, and an army of other immortals including the incomparable Jimmy Rushing on vocals. ⬤: See Master List.

Dakota Staton—*Late, Late, Show* (Collectibles), *Crazy He Calls Me* (Capitol), and *Dynamic!* (Capitol). "I absolutely adored her. Jeez, she could sing," Taj gushed about this jazz vocalist, whom he's performed with on a couple of occasions.

Ray Charles—*Ray Charles Live (1958–59)* (Atlantic), *Genius + Soul = Jazz* (DCC) and *Ray Charles and Betty Carter* (DCC). Taj loves Charles's entire catalog but these three titles rolled right off his tongue. For other great Charles recordings, see Master List.

Ahmad Jamal—*At the Pershing* (UNI/MCA). Taj relived fond memories about this jazz pianist's disc after picking up a CD reissue: "I can remember I would hear it in my head and I would come home and wouldn't be satisfied until I heard it through at least two times."

Jimmy Reed—Taj's first blues albums were by songwriter/guitarist Reed. He says the entire Reed catalog is vital: "That was some of the best music ever put together, for taking a simple way of doing something and putting it out there." ⬤: See Master List.

Bullmoose Jackson and His Buffalo Bearcats—A fabulous shouter in his own right, Taj points to this early R&B bandleader/shouter as a big influence. ⬤: Try *Big Fat Mamas Are Back in Style Again* (Route 66), *Badman Jackson, That's Me* (Charly), and *Sings His All-Time Hits* (King).

Buddy Johnson—Jump blues bandleader Johnson's records were some of Taj's favorites when he was growing up. ◉: See Master List.

Slim (Gaillard) and Slam (Stewart)—They were dismissed by some as a hipster novelty act, but guitarist/pianist/vocalist Slim and bassist/vocalist Slam could also flat-out play. ◉: Under Gaillard's name, *Original 1938 Recordings—Volume 1* (Tax) and *Original 1938–9 Recordings—Volume 2* (Tax) cover the original Slim and Slam records that Taj remembers.

Charles Mingus—*The Clown* (Atlantic). Taj loves this album's "Haitian Fight Song": "By [the time I first heard this], I was starting to make up my mind about what instrument I wanted to play, and I wanted to play the bass. I heard Charles Mingus and I thought, '*What* is the use?' "

Milt Jackson—*Bags and Flute* (Atlantic). "Bags" is the nickname of MJQ vibraphonist Milt Jackson, and the flute on this 1958 album is played by Bobby Jaspar.

Lee Morgan—*The Sidewinder* (Blue Note). Taj especially likes the trumpeter's title cut, a rare jazz hit in its day.

Thelonious Monk—Taj credits Monk's solo piano recordings with helping him develop his own solo playing style. ◉: *Thelonious Alone in San Francisco* and *Thelonius Himself* (both Original Jazz Classics)

Horace Silver—*Song for My Father* (Blue Note). *Song* is a certified jazz classic by this consistently uplifting pianist.

Donald Byrd—Taj likes the early Byrd before he achieved his first crossover success in the 1970s, but he also enjoys the jazz trumpeter's 1990s work with Jazzmatazz. ◉: *Early Byrd* (Blue Note), which covers the years 1960 to '72; *Jazzmatazz* (EMI).

Marv Johnson—"He was one of the first guys to have hits for [Motown founder] Berry Gordy when he started out. Love Marv Johnson's work." ◉: See Master List.

Digible Planets—*Reachin'* (Pendulum). "I'm sitting in a van and I hear like *doom, doom, doom* . . . and I think 'Wait a minute, this is a contemporary thing and that's an upright bass? And these cats come in there, and I'm going 'OOOOOO, that's great!' "

Joseph Spence—"You're talking about somebody who really inspired a lot of things. I had never heard any music in the U.S. that sounded like my grandparents. Certain people, there's music coming out of them. Old people had music coming out of them, just the way they moved, the tones that [came out in their language]." This Bahamanian guitarist/singer, who had a profound effect on Taj's old partner Ry Cooder and many other prominent musicians in the 1960s, including *Pete Seeger, had an orchestra in his fingertips and angels in his heart. ⏺: See Master List.

Ali Farka Toure—Taj recorded a few sides with the mesmerizing guitarist from Mali in the early 1990s, but he'd been listening to him for 25 years: "There was something I heard in old blues music that was expressively African . . . That's why when I got together with Ali Farka Toure, we were like bookends." ⏺: The Farka Toure album with Taj, *The Source* (World Circuit), is a fine introduction to the former's music.

TAJ MAHAL'S OWN RECORDINGS

When we asked Taj which of his albums he was proudest of, he replied, "The whole works. I just didn't put songs on a record that I wouldn't like to do. I didn't want to have people call up requests for songs I didn't like."

⏺: Ideally, the best way to start collecting Taj would be at the beginning, with his first three releases—*Taj Mahal*, *Giant Step/De Ole Folks at Home*, and *Natch'l Blues* (all Columbia). Taj's much-admired roots-rock band in those days included the late Jesse Ed Davis on guitar, and the music was simultaneously exuberant, relaxed, and sweet. Unfortunately, only *Giant Step* is on CD as of this writing. The 1974 record *Mo' Roots* (Columbia) seamlessly pulled in reggae accents from Taj's Caribbean heritage. In the 1990s, Taj released a series of albums—*Like Never Before*, *Dancing the Blues*, *Phantom Blues*, and the Grammy-winning *Señor Blues*, all on the Private Music label—that proclaimed his reconnection with urban music. While largely a cover artist at this stage of his career, his interpretations of Chicago blues, R&B, jump jive, and hip-hop shake and shimmy with the usual Taj verve and his original tunes, although few and far between, are as infectious as ever. The 1998 release *Sacred Island* (Private Music) finds Taj, who has lived in Hawaii for years, mixing his original country blues sound with Hawaiian music—a mellow, inviting blend that should delight those who loved his early records. *In Progress and in Motion (1965–1998)* (3 CDs: Columbia/Legacy) is a substantial, much-praised compilation.

Long-time fans of both Taj and Ry Cooder should also check out *Rising Sons* (Columbia/Legacy), Taj and Ry's first recorded effort, circa 1964 (although not released until 1992). Stylistically, it bounces from the Mississippi Delta to Liverpool, thanks to bandmate Jesse Lee Kincaid's Beatlesque leanings, but Taj's winning approach to country blues, in liberal evidence on this disc, was already fully formed.

Finally, readers with children should investigate Taj's recordings on the Music for Little People and Rabbit Ears labels. Taj helped pioneer the concept of making parent-friendly children's music. His adult musical values stay absolutely intact on his family recordings; besides, we can't think of a better grown-up buddy for kids.

BRANFORD MARSALIS (August 28, 1997)

He grew up in an African-American neighborhood in New Orleans, in what would become this country's pre-eminent jazz family, but a walk down the train tracks to his Catholic school transported the young Branford Marsalis into an entirely different musical world. The jukebox in the room where his Catholic Youth Organization meetings were held was stuffed with white pop like Elton John's hits and the "progressive rock" of Yes and Emerson, Lake & Palmer. "The first record I ever fell in love with was an Elton John record called *Honky Chateau*," he recalls. "This was some very interesting music to me, being a black kid living in a black neighborhood in Louisiana and growing up to the sounds of Aretha Franklin, James Brown, the Bar-Kays, and the Isley Brothers."

That jukebox and the highly produced English pop it spun gave Branford an eclectic perspective on music that persists to this day. "I had the best of both worlds," he explains, "because none of the friends in my 'hood knew about Yes or Led Zeppelin or Procol Harum. And none of the white kids in my school knew about Donny Hathaway or Stevie Wonder or Marvin Gaye and Tammi Terrell. It was everybody's loss. And they continue to lose to this day as our airways get more and more fragmented and chopped up by race and age and every sort of ridiculous demographic that you can conjure up."

Branford took up keyboards as his first instrument, then switched to clarinet at age 7, and alto sax at age 15. During his high school years, he played in a band that covered Top 40 hits, Parliment/Funkadelic tunes, and the like. But with a jazz pianist for a father and the emerging jazz superstar, trumpeter Wynton Marsalis, as a younger brother, Branford eventually came to grips with his family's main musical tradition. "I was sixteen when I first heard Charlie Parker," he remembers. "I had been playing the piano but I decided I wanted to play the saxophone. I had been listening mainly to Grover Washington, Jr. My father played me this record *Charlie Parker With Strings* and the first song I heard was 'April in Paris.' I heard this cat playing this fucking saxophone, and two things struck me. First was I'd never heard a saxophone sound like that in my life. The other was, jazz was not a music I wanted to play at that time in my life, but if I ever did, the stuff I was listening to at the time was not good enough to get me there."

Hearing Wayne Shorter on record changed all of that. "The first time I heard Miles Davis's *Nefertiti* and heard Wayne Shorter's approach to playing, then I realized that I had found a way that I could play jazz and enjoy it and be intellectually challenged by it," Branford says. "It blew my head wide open, and I started buying everything I could of Wayne Shorter's. He became my guru." Twenty at the time and an obvious quick study, he followed Wynton into Art Blakey's Jazz Messengers a year later, in 1981.

Shorter, of course, had also starred in an earlier edition of the Messengers. Branford later established himself on tenor and soprano saxes, Shorter's primary instruments, and followed Shorter's lead in another way, playing with sophisticated pop stars. Shorter had recorded with Joni Mitchell, Steely Dan, and Santana; Branford frequently sat in with the *Grateful Dead and *Bruce Hornsby and recorded and toured with Sting. He even repeated Shorter's role with Miles, playing soprano sax on Miles Davis's funk-charged 1984 album *Decoy*.

In the '90s, Branford has created his own irrepressible identity not only musically but in the media as host of NPR's *Jazzset* and in his stint as leader of the *Tonight Show* band. Through it all, he displays a versatility that springs mostly from a staggering amount of talent but owes just a little to a honky jukebox.

BRANFORD MARSALIS'S FAVORITE ARTISTS AND RECORDINGS

Charlie Parker—*Charlie Parker With Strings: The Master Takes* (Verve). "At the time that he made that record, people considered it a sell-out. Charlie wanted his music to be heard on a larger level and he wanted to make some money, but the thing they didn't understand is that at no point on that record did Charlie Parker ever compromise himself. . . . He was playing his shit on these songs, and, man, that record messed me up."

Wayne Shorter—*Juju, Speak No Evil,* and *Supernova* (Blue Note); on Miles Davis's *Nefertiti, Miles Smiles* and *E.S.P.* (all Columbia); and with Art Blakey's Jazz Messengers on *A Night in Tunisia* (Blue Note). Branford says he learned a lot from Shorter's playing on his solo records and the Davis albums: "Those are all very seminal, important records for me," he reports. About Shorter's stint with Blakey, he says, "That was interesting hearing Wayne play in a more conventional, bebop sense. It's amazing . . . because if you'd only heard him play with Art Blakey, you would never even think that that was the same guy who was playing with Miles Davis, because the harmonic approach was so dramatically different."

John Coltrane—*Coltrane* (Impulse). Branford says that he avoided listening to John Coltrane for years because he didn't want to end up sounding like him, as nearly every young tenorman of Branford's generation did. He credits saxophonist Billy Pierce, a bandmate of his in Art Blakey's group, with directing him to the correct Coltrane records. "I told him I don't want to sound like a Coltrane clone," Branford says, "and he says 'Man, those cats are listening to the wrong stuff. They're spending their time listening to those Atlantic records. What you need to do is go listen to those Impulse records.' "

Ludwig van Beethoven—Symphonies Nos. 3, 5, 6 and 9. Branford credits Wynton for his love of European classical music. When the brothers were teenagers, Branford overheard Wynton, who was playing in an orchestra, listening to the trumpet parts in Beethoven's Symphony No. 3. "And," he laughs, "I did what any self-respecting black child from America would do: I said 'What is this crap you're listening to?' and turned up my Isley Brothers records louder. But then a strange thing happened. With quality music, if you spend any time being exposed to it, it kind of creeps inside you and doesn't let go. Then I would find myself walking around the house whistling the Third Symphony and thinking 'What in the hell are you doing? You don't like that! Don't whistle that!' " ⬤: Although Branford doesn't mention specific recordings, many consider the versions conducted by Herbert von Karajan (Deutsche Grammophon) to be seminal. And John Eliot Gardiner's recent collection on original instruments (Archiv) gives the symphonies a fresh perspective.

Gustav Mahler—Symphonies Nos. 1, 3, 4, and 5. A confessed Mahler fanatic, Branford also confesses to snitching one of his Mahler albums from Wynton: "When I went to college I just stole this record. It was Mahler's Third with Claudio Abbado conducting [Fonit-Cetra Diamante]." ⬤: See Master List.

Giacomo Puccini—*Madame Butterfly*. Just as Wynton turned him on to Beethoven, a housepainter spurred Branford's love for opera. When he was in his 20s, Branford was visiting jazz bassist Ron Carter, whose house painter was listening to 'Madame Butterfly' as he worked. Branford confronted the painter about his choice of music: "I was like 'What are you listening to that b.s. for?' He says 'Man, I've heard you play before. If you start listening to opera it will become like a disease. You won't be able to turn it off.' I was on the road with Sting a year later. We were in London, and I went to the Tower Records in Picadilly Circus, and there sitting on the counter was a discounted, newly released version of 'Butterfly' with Luciano [Pavarotti] singing, and I said 'What the hell.' " After buying the set, Branford says, "the disease spread very quickly." ⬤: The version with Luciano Pavarotti, Mirella Freni, and Christa Ludwig in the cast and Herbert von Karajan conducting the Vienna Opera Orchestra and Chorus was released on London (3 CDs).

Giuseppe Verdi—Branford loves Italian opera. In addition to Puccini, he names all of the Verdi operas, and Bellini's, too. ⬤: With Verdi, start with the operas *Aida* and *La Traviata*. Try a version of *Aida* with Placido Domingo, Katia Ricciarelli, the La Scala Chorus and Orchestra, conducted by Claudio Abbado (2 CDs: Deutsche Grammophon). With *La Traviata*, try the recording with Joan Sutherland, Luciano Pavarotti, and the National Philharmonic and London Opera Chorus, conducted by Richard Bonynge (3 CDs: London).

Vincenzo Bellini—⬤: Bellini's opera *Norma* has been recorded dozens of times: check out a performance with Joan Sutherland, Luciano Pavarotti, Montserrat Caballe, and Samuel Ramey, the National Symphony Orchestra, Richard Bonynge, conductor (3 CDs: London). Another popular opera, *La Sonnambula*, in an excellent rendition with Maria Callas and the La Scala Opera, is on EMI/Angel.

Richard Strauss—*Der Rosenkavalier, Salome.* "Some guy told me 'Man you gotta graduate to German opera. Once you do, that Italian stuff will seem really trite,' and I'm like, 'Whatever.' So then one day when I was on the *Tonight Show*, Wynton called me and said 'Man, I've just come back from seeing the Ring Cycle,' so I bought that, and I graduated! Now I've been listening almost exclusively to German operas. I'm knee deep in this Wagner, Strauss stuff . . . I can't get rid of it." ⬤: For *Der Rosenkavalier*, look for Herbert von Karajan conducting the Vienna Philharmonic with Anna Tomowa-Sintow, Agnes Baltsa, and others (3 CDs: Deutsche Grammophon). A classic version of *Salome* is one conducted by Eric Leinsdorf, with Montserrat Caballe and Sherrill Milnes (2 CDs: RCA).

Richard Wagner—*The Ring of the Nibelung, Parsifal,* and *The Flying Dutchman.* ⬤: If you want to buy the complete *Ring* cycle, first stop by your nearest financial institution for a low-interest loan. Once sufficiently flush, buy Karl Böhm's live 1967 Bayreuth Festival performance, with Birgit Nilsson, Leone Rysanek, and others (14 CDs: Philips). For a smaller, more economical sampling, try the two-disc set of excerpts from the same performance (Philips), or one disc of highlights with Sir Georg Solti conducting the Vienna Philharmonic, and Birgit Nilsson, among other singers (London). For *Parsifal*, we suggest a version with Solti and the Vienna Philharmonic, Christa Ludwig, and Dietrich Fischer-Dieskau (4 CDs: London). For the *Flying Dutchman*, try Sir Georg Solti again, this time with the Chicago Symphony, Rene Kollo, and Martti Talvela (2 CDs: London). You can find single-disc excerpt collections of all of Wagner's operas if you'd rather dip a toe into the deep Wagnerian waters.

*Herbie Hancock—*Headhunters* and *Thrust (both Columbia). Branford was there when his father opened for Herbie Hancock's Headhunters-era band at a gig in New Orleans. "I remember Herbie was really skinny, with a huge Afro," he laughs, "It was a great band—Bennie Maupin, Mike Clark, Paul Jackson, and Wah-Wah Watson—sort of an experimental funk band."*

Parliament/Funkadelic—"They was my boys," Branford says. ⬤: *One Nation Under a Groove* (Priority), *Tales of Kidd Funkadelic* (Westbound), and *Live: 1976–93* (4 CDs: AEM).

Bob Marley—"No Woman, No Cry" and "Natty Dread" on *Natty Dread* (Tuff Gong), and "Crazy Bald Head" on *Rastaman Vibration* (Tuff Gong). Branford first heard Marley at the age of 16 when "a friend of mine convinced me to listen to a college radio station instead of the usual pop garbage I was used to."

*Los Lobos—Although this band's wide-ranging music defies categorization, Branford calls Los Lobos the best blues band in America because they understand the blues in a deeper sense: "If you're a good enough musician to hear the blues in its extended form and its melodic influence, then it will be plainly obvious. Of course, they're not a band that plays dum-da-dum-da-dum [hums] song after song after song—you know, the generic college stuff." ⬤: See the sections on David Hidalgo and Louis Perez and their recordings.

Keith Jarrett—*Changes*, *Standards, Vol. 1*, and *Standards, Vol. 2* (all ECM). Branford calls *Changes* "a phenomenal record." The same trio—with bassist Gary Peacock and drummer Jack DeJohnette—played on the *Standards* records. Of the second one, Branford says, "Keith plays these introductions to songs that are out of this world." ⬤: Branford also loved both of the bands Jarrett led in the 1970s and early '80s: his European quartet with Palle Danielsen, Jan Garbarek, and Jon Christensen and the American quartet of Dewey Redman, Charlie Haden and Jack DeJohnette. *Belonging* is one of the best of the European quartet's fine recordings for ECM. *Death and the Flower* is a much-loved disc from the American quartet's catalog on Impulse.

The Police—*Zenyatta Mondatta* (A&M). "I went out and bought all their records and loved them, and then a year later Sting calls me and asks me to play in his band. It was hilarious."

Peter Gabriel—Branford says his reaction to Genesis was only lukewarm, "but when Peter Gabriel started coming out with his solo stuff, like the record *Security*

[Geffen], with 'San Jacinto' and 'Shock the Monkey,' I became a huge Peter Gabriel fan. I have all his records and listen to them incessantly." ⬤: For an avenue into Gabriel's catalog, start with 1980's *Peter Gabriel* and *So* (both Geffen). Note that the former disc is the third of three self-titled albums. Gabriel co-produced the latter with ambient ace *Daniel Lanois.

Joni Mitchell—*Mingus* (Asylum). "It is funny that people consider it a jazz record, and nothing could be further from jazz. But it is a great record."

The Blue Nile—*Peace at Last* (Warner Bros.) and *Hats* (A&M). Branford says of this obscure choice, "It is really strange, kind of like the first Scritti Politi record. It is machine oriented, but it's more passive. It's this guy meandering about life— all the lyrics are about hopelessness and being lost in the world. But it's this really spacey, ethereal music that I found quite enjoyable and couldn't stop listening to."

Huun-Huur-Tu: The Throat Singers of Tuva—⬤: *50 Horses in My Herd* (Shanachie).

***Youssou N'Dour**—See the section on Youssou and his recordings..

***Salif Keita**—See the section on Salif and his recordings.

Reddy Amisi—Amisi is a soukous artist from Zaire who has often been associated with African music legend Papa Wemba ⬤: *The Best of Reddy Amisi* (Sonodisc).

M'bilia Bel—Bel, another Zairean soukous singer, got her start with Tabu Ley. ⬤: *Bameli Soy* (Shanachie) and *Phenomene* (Melodie Makers).

Elton John—*Honky Chateau* (MCA).

BRANFORD MARSALIS'S OWN RECORDINGS

When asked to name favorites of his own music, Branford answers at first, "None of it. I don't think about that." Pressed further, though, he identifies *The Beautiful Ones Are Not Yet Born*, *The Dark Keys*, and *Bloomington* (all Columbia). "That's where everybody is talking to one another on their instruments, learning and sharing ideas and moving in a specific direction, versus what I feel is the corny be-bop way of playing these solos where people are most concerned with how good their solo sounds rather than a group improvisation."

⬤: Also check out Branford's *Trio Jeepy* (Columbia), which he recorded with one of jazz's great elder statesmen, bassist Milt Hinton. He has experimented with a jazz/hip-hop marriage with his Buckshot LeFonque recordings, the eponymous debut and a second release called *Music Evolution* (both Sony). Branford's classical side comes out on *Romances for Saxophone* (CBS), a collection of impressionistic arrangements of works by Debussy, Ravel, Stravinsky, and others. His latest jazz album is 1999's *Requiem* (Sony), another inspired quartet date of mature, progressive improvisation.

SIR GEORGE MARTIN (October 31, 1996)

I f he hadn't produced all those Beatles albums, hadn't contributed so much to a canon that irrevocably altered the sound and direction of popular music, hadn't revolutionized the way that records are made, Sir George Martin could still boast of an amazing career. He not only signed the Beatles to their first record contract, an act of seismic significance still rumbling through the music industry, but also produced scores of notable albums by the likes of Jeff Beck, John McLaughlin, Stan Getz, Kate Bush, Cleo Laine, America, and Gerry and the Pacemakers, not to mention the still beloved comedy albums of Peter Sellers.

Nevertheless, it's the magic that happened when Sir George and the Fab Four put their furiously creative heads together that will always define him in the public's eyes. The debate about whether Sir George was actually "The Fifth Beatle" will probably rage forever, but his association with the group makes him to this day the best-known record producer ever and the first one to become as widely recognized as a star musician.

Sir George was born in London and received conservatory training at the Guildhall School of Music. He began his career in the record business in the A&R department of record giant EMI, and was later chosen to head up EMI's Parlophone label, where he worked with British pop stars like Shirley Bassey, produced the milestone Peter Sellers comedy albums that laid the foundation for Monty Python and Firesign Theater, and in 1962 signed the Beatles. He started sculpting the group's sound almost immediately, by suggesting the band dump their drummer at the time, Peter Best, and hire EMI studio cat Ringo Starr.

Dramatic as Sir George's personnel proposal was, it proved to be relatively minor compared to the impact he would make on the group's recorded sound. His love and knowledge of classical music helped the Beatles give form to their expansive ideas as they were moving beyond the live-in-the-studio quartet style of their earlier records. When the group's experimentalism exploded during the making of *Revolver* and *Sgt. Pepper's Lonely Hearts Club Band*, Sir George invented multi-tracking, tape-looping, and other studio techniques that turned raw creativity into revolutionary recordings.

Now in his seventh decade and knighted, Sir George retired from the music business with the release of *In My Life*, an album of Beatles song renditions with cameos from such musical luminaries as Phil Collins, *Bobby McFerrin, Jeff Beck, and Celine Dion, plus film stars Robin Williams, Goldie Hawn, Sean Connery, and Jim Carrey. We reached Sir George at his London studio during the production of this record, and the conversation quickly turned to his favorite Beatles tracks. But he spoke with equal passion about his favorite works of classical music. When speaking about more contemporary music, Sir George became philosophical: "Being an old man, I'm liking older men now, like Elton John and Sting and Eric Clapton and Phil Collins. They're very much middle-of-the-road people now, but I prefer them to the younger people who are coming along. It's very difficult to put the young talents up with the big ones. It's like saying 'Is George Michael the equivalent of George Gershwin?' Well, he's not. But then you say who is the equivalent of Elton John? Is it Oasis? No, it's not Oasis. They write good songs. They're all good, but they're not yet giants, and whether they will be, only time can tell." The question about who will be the next Beatles needn't be asked.

SIR GEORGE MARTIN'S FAVORITE ARTISTS AND RECORDINGS

The Beatles—"There were well over two hundred [songs]. It's very difficult to give a particular favorite," Sir George says. But he gives it a whirl, picking according to authorship:

"From a recording point of view, one of my favorites [of Paul McCartney's] is one of the last tracks we ever did—the end of *Abbey Road* [Capitol], which is 'Golden Slumbers,' 'Carry that Weight' and 'The End.' To me, it's still one of the best pieces of almost near-symphonic writing that you can get. It's the kind of thing that Queen would have been able to do. It's a terrific song. More than a song—it's a work, really. On a simpler scale, a very simple song like 'Here, There and Everywhere' [on *Revolver* (Capitol)] is one of my favorites. It's such a gentle, unadulterated song that it goes right to the heart. The melody is very easy, and very original, the lyrics very simple.

"In the case of John [Lennon], the equivalent of 'Here, There and Everywhere' with John was 'In My Life' [on *Rubber Soul* (Capitol)]. Again, a very simple song with a most beautiful lyric which comes from the heart, where he talks about all the friends he's known and loved in the first verse, and in the second verse compares them with his love for his love. It's very effective, very simple, and a very nice recording. And of course, particularly poignant for me because I wrote the middle bit, which is a keyboard solo. . . . Of the more complicated songs of John's, it has to be 'Strawberry Fields Forever' [on *Magical Mystery Tour* (Capitol)] because that was a kind of watershed in John's writing, and in recording in a way. It was a preface, if you'd like, to the whole *Sgt. Pepper* album. It was intended to be on the *Sgt. Pepper* album, and it was excluded because it was issued as a single. I suppose people look back on 'Strawberry Fields' as being a drug-oriented song. I didn't think of it that way: I thought of it as being comparable to the best of the impressionist writers. . . . It was post-Debussy, post-Ravel, a very evocative piece of writing that you could virtually smell what he was talking about when you listened to the thing. It led us into a dream world. But also musically, it was very, very interesting indeed—different sounds and different harmonies.

"George [Harrison] wasn't all that prolific . . . but [from *Abbey Road*] I have always liked 'Here Comes the Sun' and of course 'Something' is one of the big hit records of all time. That has a great simplicity about it, too."

The Beach Boys—*Pet Sounds* (Capitol). "They come high on my list, and 'God Only Knows' I think is my favorite track."

Johann Sebastian Bach—*Easter Oratorio*, *St. Matthew's Passion*, and Mass in B Minor. "There's a lovely little sequence from the *Easter Oratorio*, a little prelude with oboe and strings which is one of my favorite pieces of music. But anything of Bach's is a favorite of mine. I think his *St. Matthew's Passion* and Mass in B Minor are wonderful pieces of writing." 🔘: For the *Easter Oratorio*, check out the rendition by the Collegium Vocale/Phillippe Herreweghe (Harmonia Mundi) or the budget-priced version by Philadelphia Orchestra/Eugene Ormandy (with the Magnificat in D, Sony). The recording of the Mass in B Minor by the New Philharmonia Orchestra/Otto Klemperer features vocalists Nicolai Gedda and Hermann Prey (2 CDs: Angel). The version by the English Baroque Soloists/John Eliot Gardiner, with the Monteverdi Choir (2 CDs: Archiv) is also very fine. For *St. Matthew's Passion*, try again the Philharmonia Orchestra/Otto Klemperer, with superb soloists Elizabeth Schwarzkopf, Christa Ludwig, Nicolai Gedda, and Dietrich Fischer-Dieskau (3 CDs: Angel) or the English Baroque Soloists/John Eliot Gardiner and Monteverdi Choir with Anne-Sophie von Otter (3 CDs: Archiv).

Wolfgang Amadeus Mozart—Piano Concerto No. 21 and the String Quartets. Other than the piano concertos, Sir George prefers Mozart's chamber music. 🔘: For the Concerto No. 21, good choices include the versions with pianist Mitsuko Uchida and Geoffrey Tate conducting the English Chamber Orchestra (Philips) and pianist Murray Perahia performing as soloist and conductor with the Chamber Orchestra of Europe (Sony). Mozart composed 23 string quartets, and Sir George doesn't specify favorites. For a good sampling, we suggest the Juilliard Quartet's collection of Mozart's six "Haydn" Quartets (Nos. 14–19) (3 CDs: Sony) or the Budapest Quartet's recording of the same six quartets (2 CDs: Sony). The next step up is the budget-priced *The 10 Celebrated String Quartets* with the Franz Schubert Quartet of Vienna (5 CDs: Nimbus), but if you want to go all the way, look for the Quartetto Italiano's complete quartets box (8 CDs: Philips).

Piotr Ilvich Tchaikovsky—*Romeo and Juliet* Fantasy Overture. "Much maligned," Sir George says of Tchaikovsy, "but I think his handling of orchestration was fantastic. A work like *Romeo and Juliet* was film music, really. I mean, he orchestrated the first sexual climax I've ever heard! A fantastic writer." 🔴: There are countless recordings of this Tchaikovsky warhorse; start with the New York Philarmonic/Leonard Bernstein (with the *Marche Slave*, Sony) or the Berlin Philharmonic/Herbert von Karajan (with the *Nutcracker* Suite, Deutsche Grammophon).

Claude Debussy—*Prélude à l'après-midi d'un faune* (Prelude to the Afternoon of a Faun). Sir George calls this piece "a lovely tone poem in which you can literally be transported into a wonderfully natural scene of a deer on the edge of a wood. You can actually see it in its pastoral color. It's what I was talking about with Lennon, with his imagery. In listening to the music, you see things, things come to life in three dimensions. You're seeing with your ears rather than your eyes." 🔴: See Master List.

SIR GEORGE MARTIN'S OWN RECORDINGS

In addition to the Beatles recordings discussed above, Sir George speaks proudly of his album, *In My Life*. He has also been involved in numerous soundtracks, including the much-maligned film version of *Sgt. Pepper's Lonely Hearts Club Band* (Polygram); from that recording, he is especially pleased with the BeeGees' version of "Being for the Benefit of Mr. Kite."

🔴: Relatively few recordings, other than soundtracks, have been released under Sir George's name. Most were orchestral rearrangements of Beatles songs, released in the 1960s at the height of Beatlemania—for example, *George Martin Plays 'Help'* (United Artists) and *Instrumentally Salutes the Beatles* and *Off the Beatle Track* (both One Way). Soundtracks on which he worked include *Yellow Submarine* (Capitol), *Live and Let Die* (United Artists) and *Ferry Cross the Mersey* (United Artists).

DAVE MATTHEWS (January 30, 1997)

t was thirty years ago today that Sergeant Pepper taught the band to play, but the Beatles' song-cycle continues to transform pop music around the world. Prime example: Dave Matthews. As a seven-year-old growing up in South Africa, Dave happened upon the album in his parents' collection. It zapped him like lightning. "If not for that album, I don't think I'd be doing what I'm doing now," Dave says. "It just completely flipped me out. I found this interesting-looking cover, put the album on, and fell madly in love. . . . Still today, that album is like the smell of Play-Doh to me, it's so familiar."

During his high school years, Dave encountered the music of Bob Marley and, later, the adventurous African jazz of Abdullah Ibrahim. With idols like Marley, Ibrahim, and the Beatles, the building blocks of what eventually became Dave Matthews Band music were now in place, and Dave began writing songs while tending bar in a jazz club in the university town of Charlottesville, Virginia. It was also in Charlottesville that he met the other founding members of the band, many of whom brought their own strong jazz backgrounds to the project.

With his new mates, Dave crafted a unique sound that is equal parts jazzy polyrhythms, woody folk rock, appealing pop, and global village. As diverse as these roots may be, they've evolved into a pop music force so powerful that the group's 1998 release *Before These Crowded Streets* rose to Number 1 on the *Billboard* charts, displacing the soundtrack to the film *Titanic,* which had been a fixture there for months. Just prior to that, the 1997 concert album *Live at Red Rocks 8.15.95* sold over a million copies. It was the kind of multi-album sales performance only rarely seen since, well, Dave's original inspiration, the Beatles.

DAVE MATTHEWS'S FAVORITE ARTISTS AND RECORDINGS

The Beatles—*Sgt. Pepper's Lonely Hearts Club Band* and *Magical Mystery Tour* (both Capitol). "It really was like getting new eyes for me, when I was little. There was some click, like from joy to some very serious passion, that happened to me listening to *Sgt. Pepper.* All the simple tricks they did, and the real awareness of sounds, just a really creative way of using sounds. The Beatles were real inventors."

Bob Marley—*Uprising* (Tuff Gong). "There was a live quality to his studio albums—you feel so much in the room. And his just phenomenal arrangements. It has 'Redemption Song' on it, which I think is one of the greatest songs. And he knew it, because something made him put it on the album in such a simple form. To have such confidence in a song! It seems like everyone was trying to make pop music slicker and slicker and slicker around that time, and he was definitely [following] a different spirit.''

Abdullah Ibrahim—*Zimbabwe* (Enja) and *Water from an Ancient Well* (Tiptoe). Ironically, this legendary South African jazz pianist didn't come to Dave's attention until after Dave had returned to the States. ''There's a spine in the music that is very particular to South Africa,'' Dave says. ''The whole treatment, the way they move, it's sort of trancelike. It comes from somewhere deeper—it doesn't come in your ears and land right on your brain, it comes in your ears and makes a detour to someplace a lot older.''

Tom Waits—*The Black Rider* (Island) and *Blue Valentine* (Asylum). ''He's almost like performance art on a recording. There's something about his music that has so much character and so much playfulness that it's sort of storylike. *Black Rider* is a perfect example: there's so much comedy and so much melancholy, too.''

Ben Harper—''He has just the sweetest voice in the world, and the way it comes out of his mouth, it's almost like the word of God when he sings live. He's not earnest in a soppy way. He's very serious, but it doesn't come from a false or learned goodness—he's very genuine. We toured with him some and I never missed one of his shows.'' ⬤: See Master List.

Keith Jarrett—*The Koln Concert* (ECM). ''I listen to this all the time. . . . It calms me down, like watching windshield wipers. It goes through light rain and stormy weather.''

Led Zeppelin—*In Through the Out Door* (Swan Song). ''Lots of perfect songs on this album. It was a nice swan song for them.''

Leonard Bernstein—*West Side Story* (CBS). ''I take it with me everywhere. I saw the movie when I was a kid. Also, I was in love with Natalie Wood. God, she was beautiful! I had it start going through my head a while ago, bought it, and I can't turn it off. God, he could write strange music.''

Bob Dylan—''It wouldn't be fair if I didn't name every Dylan record. It almost makes me furious sometimes, how good his lyrics are. You know, you aspire to things. I'm trying and trying [to write a song], and I'll get something and say 'That's pretty good,' and then I'll listen to *Blood On The Tracks* [Columbia] and think 'Who the hell am I kidding? What the hell am I talking about?' 'Come in, she said/I'll give you/shelter from the storm.' Asshole!''

Neil Young—*After the Gold Rush* (Reprise). ''There's not a dud on that album.''

Mary Margaret O'Hara—*Miss America* (Koch International). ''She came out with this one album and it's definitely one of the best albums I've heard. It's really spare, not a lot of different sounds. There's a guitarist with a delay pedal, maybe an amp, and a straightforward drummer, but really beautiful. She stutters through the most beautiful melodies. I haven't been able to find it for a while. I keep buying it and giving it away."

African Jazz Pioneers—"Awesome! I guarantee everything you buy of theirs is gonna be good. They have a real specific kind of African jazz sound. It's upbeat and just moves—it's a storm. The original members that are still in the band are from the same school as Hugh Masakela and Abdullah Ibrahim, that same time." : *Live at Montreux* (Intuition).

David Gray—*A Century Ends* (Caroline) and *Flesh* (Vernon Yard). "He's a Welsh guy. These are both beautiful albums. He has a lovely presence in his music. It's sort of folk music, but a little heavier."

XTC—*English Settlement* (Geffen). Calling this "one of my favorite albums of all time," Dave adds, "It's a little out. It's full of angst, and there's a lot of direct accusations against government, no attempt to edit themselves to sound slick. There's music that crosses paths with them that I can't stand, but everything they've done I've liked."

Soul Coughing—*Ruby Vroom* (Slash/Warner Bros.). "It's almost like poetry. The lead singer, M Doughty, comes up with some great images, and in a way reminds me of Tom Waits . . ."

Johann Sebastian Bach—*Goldberg Variations* (Sony). Dave insists on versions by pianist Glenn Gould, but he can't decide between Gould's electrifying 1955 debut recording or his grand 1981 reprise. "Which version did he moan the loudest on? I kind of feel that it makes it better, hearing him there. When Glenn Gould does it, it feels like he's channeling, he's so lost in it. Makes you tired!"

Claude Bolling—*Suite for Flute and Jazz Piano Trio* (Sony). "That's good music to do things by, to turn up loud because it can't cause damage and the neighbors won't complain."

Jethro Tull—*This Was, Stand Up*, and *Too Old to Rock 'n' Roll, Too Young to Die* (all Chrysalis). Dave recommends all the stuff Jethro Tull did in the late '60s and early '70s. *Too Old* is from 1976.

Phish—*Billy Breathes* (Elektra).

*Daniel Lanois—*Acadie* (Opal/Warner Bros.).

Steeleye Span—"King Henry" on *Below the Salt* (Shanachie).

DAVE MATTHEWS'S OWN RECORDINGS

Given that his group had only recorded a couple of albums at the time of our interview, Dave chose to focus on favorite songs rather than entire discs, starting with "I'll Back You Up" from the group's independently released debut, *Remember Two Things* (Bama Rags). "[That] is the first song I ever wrote," Dave says. "It's just a real young song that hit the nail on the head of what I was feeling at the time." He states that "I'm sort of laden with ambiguity in my songs, because I don't know what the hell I'm talking about, but there are a few that have some clarity to them. I think I like 'Pay for What You Get' [*Under the Table and Dreaming* (RCA)] and 'Let You Down' [*Crash* (RCA)] because the lyrics are real simple. Those are the ones I'm most happy with today. Who knows about tomorrow?"

⬤: *Under the Table and Dreaming* was the album that first brought the DMB into public focus, garnering excellent reviews and spawning a Deadheadish following. *Crash* displays the considerable instrumental prowess of the band and the energy level at least partly explains why some young people quit their jobs and follow the band around. *Before These Crowded Streets* (RCA) shows off the increasing "clarity" in Dave's songwriting on such songs as "Don't Drink the Water" and "Pig."

PAT METHENY (July 30, 1996)

His warm, lyrical approach and peerless musicianship have made Pat Metheny the most successful jazz guitarist of the last two decades, but Pat "blames" it all on his brother Mike. In 1966, when Pat was 12 years old, Mike walked into the family home in Lee's Summit, Missouri, with the record *Four and More* by Miles Davis under his arm. Pat still remembers the moment Mike placed it on the turntable: "Some people talk about how jazz is this thing that you're supposed to advance to. You start out with rock or folk, and eventually you move toward jazz. But for me, after about thirty seconds of *Four and More*, the zone that I'm still in, which is being completely fascinated by the whole idea of people improvising music, was placed and fully formed. I had just never heard anything that exciting. And that's still true."

The next records to scorch Pat's ears featured Gary Burton's innovative jazz-rock unit. Pat points out that Burton, not Miles Davis as most people think, was the first to fully utilize electric instruments in jazz and the first to feature electric guitar in the front line rather than back in the rhythm section: "In fact, it was that group—whether with Larry Coryell or Jerry Hahn, Roy Haynes, Steve Swallow, and Bob Moses—that I dreamt about playing in. If I had done nothing but play in that group, that would [fulfill] every dream I had." Powerful dreamer—at the age of 18, Pat made his national debut in Burton's band.

However, not even this achievement could contain Pat's outsize talent. Following his recording debut as a leader, 1975's *Bright Size Life*, he set off on a solo career that has been as triumphant artistically as it has been popular with the public. Pat has also distinguished himself with his ear for talent. Like his early mentor, Burton, and other great bandleaders, Pat has discovered and hired a succession of outstanding young players, including Jaco Pastorius (who, like a bright comet, was spotted by nearly everyone), Dan Gottlieb, Mark Egan, and Lyle Mays.

Pat's pioneering use of open tunings and guitar-driven synthesizers and his integration of Brazilian pop give him an instantly recognizable sound, which first showed up on his commercial breakthrough, the 1978 ECM release *The Pat Metheny Group*. But Pat has also recorded several notable adventures outside his usual, more tranquil, context, including *Song X* with Ornette Coleman and the noisy solo guitar ramble *Zero Tolerance for Silence*.

You may not detect the impact on his playing, but Pat's listening habits extend far beyond jazz to include the Beatles and even Dolly Parton. "I will say that most of the best music I've heard has been jazz, but that's not just automatic," Pat asserts. "Some of the most boring music I've ever heard is bad jazz. Part of the reason jazz isn't more popular is because most of what people hear under the name of jazz is, in fact, not very fun to listen to.

"I love any kind of music where it sounds like the people playing it have to play that way or they're not going to be happy. And that includes everything from Albert Ayler to the Carpenters. Style has never had much to do with it. It's much more about spirit and intent and resonance and truth."

PAT METHENY'S FAVORITE ARTISTS AND RECORDINGS

Miles Davis—*Four and More, My Funny Valentine, Miles Smiles, Nefertiti, Miles in the Sky, Filles de Kilimanjaro,* and *Bitches Brew* (all Columbia). "Whenever I meet anybody who I'm trying to interest in music, I always buy them a bunch of Miles records. Prior to the time he sort of retired in the mid-seventies, he just didn't make a bad record." About the celebrated group that appears on the third-through-sixth titles above, Pat says, "For anybody who's a jazz fan, the Miles Davis quintet that included Wayne Shorter is like the Beatles, and for so many people I know, that was the ultimate band. And of course anything by those musicians on their own I'll always be interested in hearing.''

Miles Davis and Gil Evans—*Miles Davis & Gil Evans: The Complete Columbia Studio Recordings* (6 CDs: Sony). Pat loves all the material Miles collaborated on with arranger Gil Evans, especially the material from the album *Miles Ahead* (Columbia), a great starter purchase if you don't want to pop for the above boxed set.

Wes Montgomery—*Smokin' at the Half Note* (Verve), *Wes Montgomery Trio* (Original Jazz Classics), *Guitar on the Go* (Original Jazz Classics), *A Dynamic New Jazz Sound* (Original Jazz Classics), *A Day in the Life* (A&M), *Down Here on the Ground* (A&M), and *Road Song* (A&M). "He's sort of like Miles in that you can't find a bad Wes Montgomery record," says Pat, although he likes *Smokin'* most of all. His favorite Montgomery track, 'If You Could See Me Now," is on that album: "That's the greatest guitar solo recorded, period." A close second, Pat says, would be Montgomery's solo on "Down Here on the Ground," which appears on one of those ultra-lush Creed Taylor–produced projects that Montgomery did in late-career: "Wes's solo on that tune is just unbelievably insightful about life and wisdom and music and everything—it's all there. Also, the way *Herbie Hancock and Ron Carter play behind him on that track just kills me . . . People often put down his late A&M records but some of my favorite Wes playing is on those records [the last three albums listed above].''

Gary Burton—*Gary Burton Quartet in Concert* (RCA). "He's one of the most eloquent improvisers of all. Gary, to me, is one of the musicians who understood the harmonic breakthroughs of [jazz pianist] Bill Evans and applied them to his instrument in a way that very few people have managed to do. The sheer amount of knowledge he has about improvisation, about how to get from point A to point B—he's like an encyclopedia." About the album cited above, Pat says, "I still listen to it all the time, particularly to the way Larry Coryell played—some of the best, freshest guitar playing I've ever heard.''

John Coltrane—*Coltrane Jazz* (Atlantic), *Blue Trane* (Blue Note), and *Crescent* (Impulse).

*Sonny Rollins—*A Night at the Village Vanguard, Vols.1-2* (Blue Note). "Absolute essentials for me. I listen to these at least once a month.''

Joe Henderson—*Black Narcissus* and *Power to the People* (both Milestone). "Almost anything he's playing on is good. I'm endlessly fascinated by him and he's a constant source of inspiration," says Pat about this jazz tenorman, who has emerged in recent years from the shadow of Coltrane and Rollins to take his place among the immortals.

Freddie Hubbard—*Red Clay* (CTI/CBS), *The Night of the Cookers* (Blue Note), and "Moment to Moment" on *First Light* (CTI/CBS). "I can't think of another musician who's on more important records and has consistently played so well and gotten no credit for it," says Pat of this noted jazz trumpeter. "He's beyond masterful when it comes to telling a story, being creative, having a fantastic sound, and particularly playing with a rhythm section. There's no living trumpet player who's even in the ballpark with this guy." *First Light* is a high-gloss Don Sebesky/Creed Taylor job, but Pat approaches this disc like he does the orchestrated Wes Montgomery records—forget the background, dig the foreground. Hubbard "plays unbelievably" on this disc, says Pat.

Brad Mehldau—"The way he plays on [*Joshua Redman's *Mood Swing* (Warner Bros.)] is so advanced. . . . It's rare that anybody shows up already so fully formed. Jaco Pastorius was that way." : Jazz pianist Meldhau hadn't yet cut his own records when we spoke to Pat. He has since. Check out *Introducing Brad Mehldau* and the three volumes released under the overall title of *The Art of the Trio* (all Warner Bros.).

Joe Lovano—"In the last ten years, he's become really great," Pat says about this jazz tenor saxophonist. : *Live at the Village Vanguard* (Blue Note).

Clifford Brown—"I listen to him all the time," Pat says about the influential jazz trumpeter, who died at 26 in a car crash, "particularly the records with [drummer] Max Roach. In terms of phrasing and how to make a line come alive with a rhythm section, he's a real model." : See Master List.

Jim Hall—*Undercurrent* (Blue Note) and *Sonny Rollins's *The Bridge* (Bluebird). "The father of modern jazz guitar—by that I mean myself, Mick Goodrick, Bill Frisell, *John Scofield, John Abercrombie. All of us are directly descended from the way Jim figured out how to make the instrument work, around the time he was playing on *The Bridge* with Sonny Rollins. His record *Undercurrent* with [pianist] Bill Evans was a real watershed in terms of rhythm section playing and just understanding how to imply time in a way that hadn't been done before."

Billy Bean—"This guitarist is largely unknown. He was probably the best pre–Wes Montgomery bebop player I've heard, if not the best bebop guitar player ever. He only made one record in the nineteen-fifties, but he was incredibly fluent and really, really, really out there in the best sense of the term. I've never even heard the actual record he made," says Pat. "Mostly what I base my opinion on is a cassette some guy in France gave me of Bean practicing, and it's beyond anything I've heard." ⬤: Bean appears on Herbie Mann's *Copacabana* (Saludos Amigos), Buddy DeFranco's *Cross-Country Suite* (Dot, out of print), and the compilation *Guitar Player Presents: Jazz Guitar Classics* (Original Jazz Classics). Under his own name, he made *Makin' It* (Decca/Brunswick, out of print), *Take Your Pick* (Decca), and *The Trio* (Riverside). The small label String Jazz has recently unearthed some duo tapes of Bean with guitarist John Pisano and is releasing them as *Makin' It Again* and *Vol. 2: Rare Sessions*.

Weather Report—*Heavy Weather* and *I Sing the Body Electric* (both Columbia). The former, Pat says, "is a real strong piece of evidence of what electric instruments can do. And my favorite synthesizer solo ever is on *I Sing the Body Electric*, the tune 'Unknown Soldier.' "

Keith Jarrett—*Backhand* and *Shades* (both Impulse). Pat calls these "records of just great compositions for small groups there that nobody ever plays." The group on both is Jarrett's American Quartet—Dewey Redman, Charlie Haden, and Paul Motian, plus percussionist Guillherme Franco.

*Branford Marsalis—*Bloomington* (Columbia).

Chick Corea—*Now He Sings, Now He Sobs* (Blue Note). This is one of jazz's most prized piano trio albums, with bassist Miroslav Vitous and drummer Roy Haynes.

Paul Bley—*Footloose* (Savoy). This too is a widely loved piano trio record, with bassist Steve Swallow and drummer Pete LaRoca supporting the adventurous Bley.

Dolly Parton—"I'm a huge fan. She's one of the best singers around." ⬤: *The Essential . . .* (RCA) is a solid single-disc introduction to both Parton's early and later hits. *The RCA Years 1967–86* (RCA) is a two-disc set that is more comprehensive than *The Essential*. It's still sketchy, especially with her earlier work, but was the best overview available as of this writing.

The Beatles—Every Beatles album is great, says Pat.

Jimmy Raney, Kenny Burrell, *Joshua Redman, Igor Stravinsky, Claude Debussy, Maurice Ravel, John Adams, and Steve Reich. We interviewed Pat just prior to a sound check for a performance in Jacksonville, Oregon. He rattled off the above names, without mentioning specific albums or compositions, just as our time with him ran out. Of the lesser-known names, Raney is a jazz guitarist and Adams and Reich contemporary minimalists in the classical vein.

PAT METHENY'S OWN RECORDINGS

Pat finds it difficult to single out a favorite among his own releases. "I'm very critical of my own stuff," he says. "Usually there are just a couple of tracks on each record that I really love. In terms of an overall record, *Secret Story* (Geffen) is a very complete picture of a bunch of things about music and personal issues that coalesced pretty close to the way I imagined it. I like the live records *The Road to You* (Geffen) and *Travels* (ECM). *Question and Answer* (Geffen) is a pretty good reflection of that way of playing, and Dave [Holland, bassist] and Roy [Haynes, drummer] sound so great together. They had never played together before. [Drummer] Jack DeJohnette and [bassist] Charlie Haden had never played together before we made *80/81* (ECM) either, so I feel good about bringing them together. I like 'Endangered Species' from *Song X* (Geffen). I like the title tune on *New Chautauqua* (ECM), and the first track on *Zero Tolerance for Silence* (Geffen).

"In general, all the Geffen records are solid for me, but the ECM records are much spottier because of the way we did them—sometimes under really bad conditions. But *First Circle* (ECM) is a good record, I think. And *Bright Size Life* (ECM) holds up pretty well. Especially with Jaco [Pastorious, bassist] having left town [i.e. died], that has special meaning for me. That was a record that for about ten years I couldn't listen to because I felt I didn't play well on it—we did it in one day. But about ten years later I could say, 'I can see why other people like it.' It took me that long to hear it."

●: *The Pat Metheny Group* (ECM) was the breakout record that made Pat a jazz star. Pat's most recent disc, 1997's *Imaginary Day* (Warner Bros.), departs from the usual but remains accessible, leaving Brazil behind for other global textures (including Balinese gamelon), adding dense and exotic electronic touches, and even rocking on "The Roots of Coincidence."

K E B ' M O ' (December 21, 1998)

Keb' Mo' happened upon the blues the same way he now performs them—easy as you please. Born Kevin Moore in Los Angeles, he'd been puttering along in a musical career that he'd always viewed as just a temporary job until "I buckled down and got serious." Almost in spite of himself, he was making progress. An R&B band he joined when he was 21 was hired to back Papa John

Creach for a tour. Keb' ended up playing on three of Creach's albums and was at his side when Creach opened for such big-time acts as Mahavishnu Orchestra, Jefferson Starship, and Loggins & Messina. But just when it seemed luck might be turning in his direction, it would spin away on its heels. In 1980, for instance, he cut a record for Casablanca in the pop/R&B vein, but the label folded soon afterward and his album died a quiet death.

Professionally and personally frustrated, Keb' joined a blues band as a guitarist when he was 35 and began studying the music of Robert Johnson, Son House, Charlie Patton, Bukka White, the Reverend Gary Davis, and other old-time country bluesmen. In his mind, he was just doing the "buckling down" he should have begun much earlier. "I always had the notion that I love to play, so I want to keep playing 'til I'm old," he tells us from his motel room in L.A. "So I said, 'Well, if I start playing the blues and I just play by myself, then I can play longer, because the older you get, the more authentic you get.' " But the music itself took over and all that calculation was soon beside the point. The country blues awakened memories of the music he'd heard in church as a child. "If you're listening to the old spirituals, they're just like the brother and the sister of the blues," he notes. "There was no not goin' to church. So you got a built-in saturation of your roots right there."

A man with a plan now, Keb' started working low-rent club gigs around Los Angeles as a country blues act and then landed a role as a Delta bluesman in a local theater production. The theater's dramaturg put together cassette tapes of obscure Delta musicians to help him prepare for the role. Keb's music was already sounding like the genuine article; listening to the tapes added even more seasoning. When Keb' made a self-titled record in 1994, the excited reception it received confirmed just how far he had come. Critic after critic wrote that there hadn't been such an appealing rural blues debut since another former city boy, *Taj Mahal, cut his first records in the 1960s.

Much like Taj, Keb' seems determined to not get stuck in the revivalist bag. On subsequent albums, he has spiked his music with dashes of urban R&B and funk. But what does remain constant is the temperature—never too hot to touch. "I guess my personality is kind of mild and even tempered," says Keb', "so I like my music to be even-tempered, too."

KEB' MO'S FAVORITE ARTISTS AND RECORDINGS

Mongo Santamaria—*Watermelon Man* (Milestone). Just like his career, Keb's listening preferences divide neatly into two phases. Early on, he played pop, R&B,

and light jazz and listened to the same. Later, he plunged with both feet into the country blues. This album by the popular Cuban percussionist/bandleader was a key one for Keb' during the first period.

David T. Walker—*Sidewalk* (Revue). This was another Phase 1 favorite.

Marvin Gaye—*What's Going On* (Motown). Keb' has always preferred albums he can listen to front-to-back, over and over, and just soak in the feeling. This classic, plus the Beatles, Led Zeppelin, Taj Mahal, Jimi Hendrix, James Taylor, and Brasil '66 albums mentioned below, top his list in that regard.

The Beatles—*Abbey Road* (Capitol).

Led Zeppelin—*Led Zeppelin II* (Swan Song).

*Taj Mahal—*Natch'l Blues* (Columbia).

Jimi Hendrix—*Electric Ladyland* (2 CDs: MCA).

James Taylor—*Mud Slide Slim and the Blue Horizon* (Warner Bros.) and *Hour Glass* (Sony). Keb' speaks with more passion about the latter album than any other he mentions: "I could listen to that record all day every day."

Sergio Mendes and Brasil '66—*Four Sider* (A&M).

Nat King Cole—"What always amazed me about him was that his pitch, sense of timing, and diction were impeccable. . . . He had skill, musicianship, feeling, charisma, the whole deal." : See Master List.

Big Bill Broonzy— *. . . Sings Folk Songs* (Smithsonian/Folkways).

Muddy Waters—*The Complete Plantation Recordings* (MCA) and *The Chess Box* (3 CDs: MCA/Chess). The former contains field recordings from 1941–42 including interview segments. Keb' especially likes Waters's renditions of "I Can't Be Satisfied" and "Goin' Home," included in the Chess set.

Son House—"Preachin' Blues." House's gripping slide guitar style was a major influence on two of Keb's other heroes, Robert Johnson and Muddy Waters. : *Original Delta Blues* (Columbia/Legacy).

Charley Patton— : See Master List.

Reverend Gary Davis—"Samson and Delilah." Davis's irresistible treatment of this tune makes it one of the jumpingest acoustic blues songs ever recorded. : *Harlem Street Singer* (Prestige/Bluesville) contains this song and a mix of other great blues and religious tunes such as "Let Us Get Together Right Down Here," "Pure Religion," and "Death Don't Have No Mercy."

Robert Johnson—Johnson is probably the most storied blues performer ever, and an inestimable influence on blues rockers such as Eric Clapton and the Rolling

Stones. : *The Complete Recordings* (2 CDs: Columbia/Legacy), one of the seminal collections in blues.

Bukka White—B. B. King's cousin and early mentor was also one of country blues' most rhythmically compelling artists. : *The Complete . . .* (Columbia).

Babe "Black Ace" Turner—"I Am the Black Ace" on *I'm the Boss Card in Your Hand 1937–1960* (Arhoolie). This self-taught blues guitarist and singer from Texas, who took his name from this song, recorded in the 1930s and 1940s, then mostly dropped out of music until a 1960 recording for Arhoolie.

KEB' MO'S OWN RECORDINGS

Keb' doesn't feel qualified to rate his own albums: "I'm so critical of myself [because] I know my flaws so well, and I hear them and I go 'hmmmmm,' you know? It's hard for me to enjoy it maybe like someone who's not so close." But he does feel that his third blues album, 1998's *Slow Down* (Okeh/550), nearly achieves his goal of a record that is a solid, durable listen through every track. Note that *Slow Down* was rated one of 1998's "albums that mattered" by *Rolling Stone*.

: Keb's other two albums of his country blues career, the self-titled debut and *Just Like You* (both Okeh/550), have also been widely praised. In fact, Keb' is one of the few performers in any genre who gets high marks from commentators on all counts—songwriting, vocals, guitar work, and ability to tweak the form without harming its essence.

M O B Y (July 30, 1998)

The corporations that rule the pop music airwaves rate lower than pond scum to rock critics, cult band lovers, and musicians who don't make the play lists. But to the musical chameleon known as Moby, they provide the very breath of life. "What I'm most excited about now is whatever song I've just heard on the radio," he admits to us when we reach him by phone at his place in New York.

As his animated stage shows attest, music sets Moby in motion and where it stops, nobody knows. As a teenage guitar player in the New York punk scene of the early 1980s, he didn't so much play in bands as light on them momentarily like a hummingbird on a nectar frenzy. He seemed to settle into the dance scene only because its ever-splintering, frantically evolving spirit matched his own.

Within a few years, Moby was dominating dance music as one of its biggest international stars. But he eventually grew restless again, finding the dance world too insular—socially, artistically, and intellectually. As he exited, he did the musician's equivalent of kicking over the furniture, issuing an album—1997's *Animal Rights*—that was a loud, guitar-driven protest against dance music myopia.

He's come back to dance music recently, realizing that despite whatever objections he may have about the scene itself, good records are still being made. In fact, he feels that way now about popular music in general: "I think music right now is as good or better than it's ever been. What I mainly listen to these days is a lot of hip-hop and sort of Top 40. I think it's a delightful time for that."

MOBY'S FAVORITE ARTISTS AND RECORDINGS

Donna Summer—"I Feel Love" and "Love to Love You, Baby." "I just think they were really, really wonderful records. I think 'I Feel Love' is possibly one of my all-time favorite pieces of music." ●: *Endless Summer* (Casablanca) contains these two and all the other major hits.

Maxine Nightingale—"Right Back Where We Started From." "On the one hand it was a disco record, but it was very unconventional. It had live strings, and sort of borrowed from Motown production value. And it just had this really joyful quality to it." ●: The compilation *Mighty Real: Dance Classics* (EMI) contains this song along with hits by Donna Summer, Thelma Houston, the O'Jays, Brothers Johnson, Sister Sledge, and several others.

Harold Melvin and the Blue Notes—"Bad Luck" and "Don't Leave Me This Way." Moby loves both the songwriting and vocals on these tracks: "Teddy Pendergrass was their singer and has one of the best voices of anyone I've ever heard." ●: *If You Don't Know Me By Now: The Best of Harold Melvin and The Blue Notes* (Sony) features the group's hits during the Pendergrass era.

Bad Brains—*Bad Brains* (ROIR) and *Rock for Light* (Plan 9/Caroline). "Of the early eighties period in general, of the hard-core punk stuff, I'd say Bad Brains were far and away the best hard-core band. Their first couple of records are just unbelievable."

Black Flag—*Damaged* (SST). Moby likes all their early records but this one he feels is the best.

Television—*Marquee Moon* (Elektra). "It's got this epic scope. It's sort of pretentious but reserved at the same time. The songwriting is outstanding. I don't really care about performances but the musical performances are great. It's just got this emotional quality that very few records have."

Grandmaster Melle Mel—"New York, New York." "A beautiful record." ⬤: Grandmaster Flash, Melle Mel, and The Fabulous Five, *Message From Beat Street* (Rhino).

Grandmaster Flash—*The Message* (Sugar Hill). "Obviously."

Schoolly D—"PSK—What Does It Mean?" on *Schoolly D* (Jive). "An early wonderful hip-hop record," Moby says about this chilling gangsta track.

Afrika Bambaataa—"Renegades of Funk." "It was just a really aggressive, funky hip-hop record. Just amazingly well put-together." ⬤: *Planet Rock—The Album* (Tommy Boy).

Liquid Liquid—"There was this period from seventy-nine to about eighty-four in New York, when there were a lot of really sorta like underground rhythmic bands, like Liquid Liquid, Esg, the Bush Tetras, Medium Medium, Suicide. It was this genre of music, I guess you could call it No Wave: that's what they sort of called it back then. And it's kinda been passed over. You know, people will get all rapturous talking about a lot of the guitar bands of the era, but a lot of this stuff was really great." ⬤: See Master List.

Esg— ⬤: *Esg, Esg Says Dance to the Beat of Moody*, and *Come Away with Esg* (99). The first two are EPs, the latter is an LP; all are out of print. Their 1998 comeback, *Return of the Living Dead* (Blackhearted) was well-received.

Bush Tetras— ⬤: See Master List.

Medium Medium— ⬤: *The Glitterhouse* (Cherry Red).

Suicide— ⬤: *Half Alive* (ROIR).

Echo and the Bunnymen—*Heaven Up Here* (Sire). This 1981 release was the group's first Top Ten hit in the UK.

Simple Minds—*Empires and Dance* (Virgin). This 1980 record was the Scottish art-pop band's third release.

Roxy Music—"I think every record they ever made is outstanding. Strangely enough, it's the only band that I have every record they ever made. On one hand there's this real degenerate quality to them, but on the other hand there's this very sincere, emotional side. And it's got this sort of campy, theatrical side, but a very earnest side as well. And that really appeals to me." ⬤: See Master List.

Daf—*Alles ist Gut* (Virgin). This German electro-dance band is one of Moby's all-time favorites and he likes this album of theirs best. "It's really, really minimal," he says. "Similar to Suicide in that sense. You know, early electronic stuff where it's just a drummer, a synth, and vocals. I still to this day don't know what they're saying because they're speaking in German, but very guttural, really wonderful stuff."

Joy Division—*Closer* (Qwest). "The production on it is really beautiful. It's just really stunning and lyrically, one of the nicest records ever made."

Todd Terry—*A Day in The Life of Todd Terry* (Ministry of Sound) and "Royal Pulse." Brooklyn-based Terry made some of the most arresting house music around. Moby likes much of his early work.

Marshall Jefferson—"Move Your Body: The House Music Anthem." Anyone who's been remotely near a dance club in recent years knows this famous 12-inch that was a fave of the Chicago acid house scene.

JVC Force—"Strong Island." This hip-hop record is out of Long Island. ⬤: *Doin' Damage* (MIL Multimedia) and *Force Field* (Warlock).

Eric B. and Rakim—*Paid in Full* (4th and Broadway) and *Follow the Leader* (UNI). Moby says the early work by this duo was "one of hip-hop's finest moments." His favorite tracks include "Eric B. Is President" and "Move the Crowd" on the former album and "Microphone Fiend" on the latter.

Acen—"Trip II the Moon." *75 Minutes* (Profile). This is one of Moby's favorite recordings from the rave scene. "I never took drugs during this period," he notes, "but I remember being out dancing at five in the morning and some of these records would come on, and even if you were completely straight, it just made you feel totally fucked up. You felt like someone had, I don't know, just filled your brain with drugs."

Liquid—"Sweet Harmony." This record, another Moby rave fave, was recorded for under $1000 but became a Top Twenty hit. ⬤: "Sweet Harmony" appears on *Best of House Music, Vol. 7: Funky Breaks* (Sm:)le).

Prodigy—"Your Love" on *Experience* (Elektra). "Liam Howlett's sort of one and only foray into the world of really melodic, beautiful dance music, the B-side to 'Charlie,' their second single. And it's really just break beats and really nice piano stuff going on top of it."

Julee Cruise—*Floating Into the Night* (Warner Bros.). "I thought that was just beautiful, as far as maintaining this really perfect atmosphere throughout the course of the album," opines Moby. A Cruise song in the vein of this record underpins a disturbing scene in the David Lynch film, "Blue Velvet."

Ron Trent—"Altered States." "That was a really, really wonderful twelve-inch." ⬤: If you can't locate the 12-inch, look for the compilation *Formule Techno, Vol. 3* (Wotre, France).

Rozalla—"Everybody's Free (To Feel Good)" (Epic). This dance-oriented pop single includes a variety of mixes.

Notorious B.I.G.—"Mo' Money, Mo' Problems." "I thought that was a wonderful, wonderful pop record, the irony being that hip-hop is oftentimes rampantly homophobic and the biggest hip-hip song of the year samples from a gay disco anthem." : *Life After Death* (Bad Boy).

Sepultura—*Roots* (Roadrunner). "It's just remarkable, almost in a genre of its own. It's sort of speed metal, but it's not—just a rich, organic, wonderful album," says Moby about this Brazilian band.

The Spice Girls—*Spice* and *Spice World* (both Virgin). "I'm a huge Spice Girls fan. I think both of their albums are pretty stellar—maybe not as albums, but the pop singles are great. I had to do a Top Ten list of music of the 20th Century for *Harper's* magazine and Spice Girls' 'Spice Up Your Life' was on there, right next to George Gershwin."

MOBY'S OWN RECORDINGS

"I think that my favorite album of anything I've ever done is an album under the pseudonym of Voodoo Child, called *The End of Everything* (Mute/Elektra)," says Moby in review of his own work. "It came out about two years ago with no fanfare. There were no videos from it, no singles, no promotion done. But I think honestly it was one of the most beautiful records ever made. And I think everyone should own one just because it improves the quality of your life."

Moby takes a similarly unabashed stand for the American version of 1997's *Animal Rights* (Mute/Elektra): "Although it's a really difficult record, I don't want to sound arrogant, but I think it's one of the better records made in the last ten years. It antagonized a lot of people, but as a sixty-five-minute album, I think it's pretty remarkable. I'm impressed that I made it." He also looks back proudly on 1995's *Everything Is Wrong* (Mute/Elektra): "That was a really interesting, nice album. It had some beautiful, beautiful moments on it. I think if someone was to go out and buy or steal three of my albums, I would point to those three I've just mentioned."

Of his soundtrack work, Moby points first to the song "God Moving Over the Face of the Waters" which was embellished for the movie *Heat* but originally appeared on *Everything Is Wrong*. "That's a classical piece. I think that's one of the nicer things I've ever written," he says.

⬤ : To hear more of what Moby is doing in the movie music vein, check out *I Like to Score* (Mute/Elektra), a collection of his film and soundtrack creations.

T H U R S T O N   M O O R E   (May 22, 1997)

More than just a band, Sonic Youth is a point of demarcation in rock history. Much as Ornette Coleman and John Coltrane did for jazz, SY in its early years exploded the head space of rock. Musically, they created a new world with their innovative use of guitar noise, discordant tunings, and utter abandonment of pop song structures. Culturally, they split the difference between the punk and New York avante-garde art scenes and became heroes to both.

When SY guitarist Thurston Moore was a little punk, though, he didn't know anything about art. He just knew what he liked. "I remember going to Woolworth as a little kid, and I had an older brother and I remember him pleading with my mom to buy certain albums. . . . The first record he brought home and played incessantly was 'Louie, Louie,' backed with 'Haunted Castle,' which is even cooler in a way. He would play that record over and over on my father's stereo, and he would mouth along with it and he would tell me that he made that record, that it was him. And being so young and impressionable, I believed him," Thurston laughs. "That's an incredibly seminal rock 'n' roll single, an American garage classic, so it's kind of cool that it was that song and not Bobby Rydell or something."

Although Sonic Youth pushed electronic noise to the outer limits, they were—like all innovators—building on what had come before. In his pre-teen years, Thurston absorbed the sonic experiments of the psychedelic 1960s by osmosis. Still under the sway of his older brother's record collection, Thurston was enveloped in the music of Jimi Hendrix and especially the Jefferson Airplane, whom his brother had adopted as "his" band. (On the opposite coast, some other guitar-noise pioneers, the Velvet Underground, were recording their own droning, feedback-wrapped improvisations. Thurston didn't discover their albums until much later, but the VU would become one of SY's primary models.)

By the time he was about 14, Thurston was buying his own records with money earned from lawnmowing gigs. First purchase: the self-titled second record by critics pariah Grand Funk Railroad. Next obsession: shock-rock pioneer Alice Cooper. To stretch his limited buying power, Thurston frequented the cut-out bins at Woolworth, where 49-cent specials abounded. That's where he found the first Stooges album and Can's *Ege Bamyasi*, two albums he bought just because the covers intrigued him. Both became pillars, along with the Velvets, of the eventual Sonic Youth.

To Thurston, Woolworth represented an enticing underground of commercially failed but creatively thrilling rock. Then the Sex Pistols broke up, transforming punk from a Pistols wannabe frenzy to rock's creative edge. The furious inventiveness and underground appeal of the music made Thurston an instant convert—apparently for life. By the early 1980s, Sonic Youth had formed. The band, sounding like nothing that had come before, was exerting its own influence but still being affected by other bands as well—the near-secret world of American hardcore punk and SY's adventurous labelmates on SST such as Black Flag, the Butthole Surfers, Saccharine Trust, the Minuteman, and the Meat Puppets.

"I remember going home to my mom's house in rural Connecticut—I was living in New York—and finding a crate of my old albums," says Thurston, recalling the turning point in the late 1970s. "And there were all the Zeppelin and Floyd records and I remember staring at them and I had completely crossed them out of my life and I had almost forgotten about them . . . I remember looking at them and thinking, 'These are just grotesque and bloated and weird-looking.' I'll never forget that impression, being eighteen or nineteen and seeing those after such a long time and knowing that my life had completely been altered by punk rock." Legions of rockers since then have testified just as reverently about Sonic Youth.

THURSTON MOORE'S FAVORITE ARTISTS AND RECORDINGS

The Kingsmen—"Louie, Louie" and "Haunted Castle." "It's still one of the most brutally cool singles ever. . . . Iggy did that incredible nasty version of ["Louie, Louie"] The song is so loaded it's unbelievable." ⬤: *Best of . . .* (Rhino) includes both tracks.

The Rolling Stones—*Their Satanic Majesties Request* (ABKCO). "That record used to sort of scare me."

The Beatles—*Abbey Road* and *The Beatles* [aka the White Album] (both Capitol).

Grand Funk Railroad—*Grand Funk Railroad* (Capitol). "I would listen to records when my parents would go out at night and I would play that record. There's one song that starts off with a crying baby, and it used to freak me out."

Alice Cooper—*Killer* (Warner Bros.) "[I loved] the songwriting style, the approach, the sense of humor, and the complete mystery. The sound that they were going after and the dynamics really appealed to me."

The Stooges—"They were just sort of treated like these morons in the Midwest playing one note. . . . [Iggy's] whole perception of himself in the music business was that he was like a joke but there were people out there like myself who were completely drawn to what he was doing," says Thurston, who loves the band's entire output. ⬤: *The Stooges* (Elektra), *Fun House* (Elektra), and *Raw Power* (Columbia) are the three studio albums. *Metallic K.O.* (Skydog) captures the group's last furious concert, in 1974. It includes the above-mentioned version of "Louie, Louie."

Can—*Ege Bamyasi* (Mute). "There's no record past the age of sixteen or seventeen that has such importance [to me]," Thurston says about this together with the first Stooges record.

Amon Duul, II—*Phallus Dei* (Repertoire). Thurston bought this one on a lark at Woolworth and got lucky.

Velvet Underground—"It's great how these records that never sold such as Velvet Underground and Stooges records became the most important records for the late 20th century. It's really artistic justice in a way," Thurston comments. As with the Stooges, he likes everything the band did. ⬤: See Master List.

Saccharine Trust—*Pagan Icons* (SST).

The Minutemen—*Paranoid Time* (SST). "It was just amazing," Thurston says about the group's debut EP. "It was unlike anything else. The music was like this really fast, spindly, haywire music."

Meat Puppets—*Meat Puppets* and *Up On the Sun* (both SST). Thurston found the Puppets debut "just mind-boggling. Everything on it was like this thirty-second, jabbering, speed-noise thing." Their third record, *Sun*, was to Thurston "the culmination of everything that was great about the Meat Puppets."

Black Flag—*Damaged* (SST). "I remember thinking it was really atonal and unlistenable when we first heard it. It's a pretty early document of that period. But the arrangements and the guitar playing and the lyrics and the way that Henry [Rollins] was singing them—that record is just phenomenal."

Redd Kross—*Born Innocent* (Frontier).

Various artists—*Flex Your Head* (Dischord). "That was the first overview of the whole D.C. scene of straight-edged hardcore and Minor Threat and Henry's first band before Black Flag, SOA [State of Alert]. . . . That was really important because it denoted a stylistic way of playing for these kids that was influenced as well by Black Flag, etcetera, but it was a much more strict set of rules in a way."

Dinosaur Jr.—*Dinosaur* (Positive) and *You're Living All Over Me* (SST).

THURSTON MOORE'S OWN RECORDINGS

Our interview with Thurston ended abruptly when he had to unexpectedly run an errand. When we contacted him subsequently, he decided to not comment on his recordings with Sonic Youth or as a solo artist.

⬤: *Bad Moon Rising* (DGC), from 1985, and 1986's *EVOL* (SST) find the group getting its sound together as it transitions from an arty free-noise group to an arty pop band. Noisy experimentation still rules, but pop melody and rhythms and hard-rocking energy are becoming crucial elements of the band's appeal. For most Sonic Youth fans, 1987's *Sister* and, especially, 1988's *Daydream Nation* (both SST) are high-water marks both for the group and for indie-rock in general. The 1990 release *Goo* and 1992's *Dirty* (both DGC) are strong 1990s efforts but their best-received album of the decade is 1995's *Washing Machine* (DGC), on which the group gets its point across in real songs that never pretend to be otherwise, even while maintaining their exploratory edge. *Rolling Stone* rated *A Thousand Leaves* (DGC) one of 1998's "albums that mattered." Thurston's solo efforts include 1995's critically praised *Psychic Hearts* (DGC), with some of the more pop-ish tracks he's ever recorded, and 1996's *Just Leave Me* (Pure). Also in 1996, he released the experimental instrumental *Piece for Jetsun Dolma* (Victo), recorded live at the always adventurous Victoriaville Music festival in Quebec. And in 1998: *Not Me* (FTD).

CHARLIE MUSSELWHITE (April 15 and 16, 1997)

n certain places at certain times, the elements come together just right to create a bubbling crucible of great art. Such was Memphis in the 1950s, where seminal gospel, R&B, blues, rockabilly, and country music coursed from the radio, garages, dancehalls, and bars. Memphis attracted many rural poor from Mississippi, among them the family of one Charlie Musselwhite, a kid from Kosciusko who would become one of the greatest harmonica players in blues.

Being able to claim Elvis Presley, another poor Mississippi transplant, as part of your local scene wasn't a bad start for a young guy interested in music, but Charlie says some of the most impressive sounds he heard came right out of the neighborhood because rockabilly legend Johnny Burnette lived just across the street. "Jimmy Griffin lived next door to me—he had that band Bread and later The Remingtons," Charlie says. "He and I used to go over to Johnny Burnette's and hang out and watch them have jam sessions. We were just kids then. We saw Johnny on the *Ed Sullivan Show* and we thought that was really something. It gave you the feeling that there was more to life than just working in a factory."

Although at a distance, Presley inspired Charlie in much the same way. "Here was this poor kid from Mississippi, and that really meant something to all of us, because a lot of Memphis was poor kids from Mississippi," Charlie notes. "He was like one of us, and it meant that we had something going, too, and it was a way out."

Still, blues was just a thread in the sound of Presley and Burnette. It was Southern radio that first exposed Charlie to the music that would become his life. "I listened to WDIA, a black station that played gospel, blues, and R&B, and WLAC out of Nashville," he recalls. "There were some hillbilly stations I used to listen to, too—I really dug them. The people I heard were all the regular people, like John Lee Hooker, Muddy [Waters], [Howlin'] Wolf, also Johnny Cash, the Wilburn Brothers, Johnny and Jack, Hank Williams—all those people." WDIA introduced Charlie to one of his earliest harmonica heroes, Sonny Terry, too. "Every night, Rufus Thomas would come on with his radio show, and his theme song was 'Hootin' Blues' by Sonny Terry," he says, "and it was great to be out ridin' around in your car and turn that up full blast out of your radio. Going down the street with Sonny Terry hootin' and hollerin'."

As he started to do his own hootin' and hollerin', Charlie began scouring junk stores for vintage 78s—"anything that said 'blues' on it," he says. Obscure 78s of rural, southern blues harmonica players (some of whom remain total mysteries even to blues scholars) became some of his favorite records. He encountered urban blues players like Little Walter on 78s too but found it tough to digest their harder sound at first. "I thought they were interesting," he remembers, "but in the beginning they sounded too modern to me. Too much like rock 'n' roll or something—not bluesy enough. Now, I can't understand why I ever thought that, because I really love those tunes. Stuff like 'Boom, Boom, Out Go the Lights,' I thought was the dumbest thing I ever heard," he laughs.

Charlie understood the citified sound much better after he moved to Chicago, ground zero for urban blues, in 1962. There, he hung out with all the great harmonica players, Little Walter and James Cotton among them, gigged in bands led by Michael Bloomfield and J. B. Hutto, and released his own first album in 1966. The Windy City player who really shook his tree was Walter "Shakey" Horton, aka "Big Walter." Charlie claims no record ever captured the real Horton: "It seems like he was savin' it up, he wouldn't play that stuff on a record. It's the same kind of attitude that [blues guitarist] Earl Hooker had. He'd say 'Don't ever record your good stuff. That's just for dummies.' Because then other people would steal it. So you'd see [Hooker] in a club just screaming this wild stuff, and then on records there's good playing, but it's just the tip of the iceberg. That's the way it was with Walter, too. Even with the kind of audience it would change drastically. I'd see Walter in front of a college crowd, and he'd be holdin' way back. Then I'd see him in the alley drinkin' wine with his friends, and he'd be playing incredible things.''

It may surprise most of his fans that Charlie maintains a passionate interest in world artists, but he hears blues echoes in music without a single root in the American South. From trips to Brazil, he is incorporating the rhythms of *forró*. And he feels right at home with Middle Eastern sounds that others find exotic and strange. "I was in Turkey and I was at a flea market," he tells us. "I saw a crowd of men standing around, and I went over to look at what they were lookin' at. There were these two blind guys sitting there. One of them was playing a kind of stringed instrument and the other guy was playing some kind of a drum; and they were just staring up into the sky with their blind eyes, playing this gut-wrenching—I don't know what it was, but man it sounded like blues to me! They were really singing from their hearts and playing to be damned. I [played with] some Turkish musicians and at first they weren't too impressed until they could hear me bending notes, and they told me the microtones in the bent notes were in their music. So there's that thread throughout the world, I believe, that comes from the heart: Hard-living-trying-to-make-the-best-of-the-situation kind of music.''

CHARLIE MUSSELWHITE'S FAVORITE ARTISTS AND RECORDINGS

Sonny Terry—"Hoootin' Blues.'' 🔘: Renditions of this tune appear on *Hootin' and Hollerin'* (Choice) and *Hootin'* (Muse).

Sonny Boy Williamson I and II—Two vital blues harmonica players adopted this moniker and Charlie loved both of them: "I got a lot of the first Sonny Boy's (John Lee Williamson) seventy-eights, and they really knocked me out. And then I would hear Sonny Boy Two (Rice Miller) on the radio and he really knocked me out. It was really confusing to me how this one guy (I thought) could sound so different. I didn't know there were two Sonny Boys.'' 🔘: From Sonny Boy I's catalog, *Sugar Mama* (Indigo) is a fine compilation of Williamson's Bluebird years from 1937 to '42. *Complete Recorded Work, Vols. 1–5* (Document) covers chronologically recordings from 1937 to '47. For Sonny Boy II, the better-known of the two, see Master List.

Will Shade with the Memphis Jug Band—Charlie first heaerd Shade on a 78 of the Memphis Jug Band doing "Kansas City Blues,'' which featured him on harmonica. Later, he says, "I got to know Will Shade, and that was a big influence. He also taught Walter Horton." ⊙: "Kansas City Blues" is available on the Memphis Jug Band's *Complete Recorded Works, Vol. 1: 1927–1928* (Document). For a more exhaustive listen to this seminal band, pick up Vols. 2 and 3 as well.

Elvis Presley—Charlie loves the early Elvis records, especially "That's All Right, Mama," and "Baby, Let's Play House." ⊙: Both songs are on *The Complete Sun Sessions* (RCA), the starting place for any good Presley collection. *King of Rock 'n' Roll: Complete '50s Masters* (5 CDs: RCA) is an essential summary of his early work.

Johnny Cash—Charlie likes "all of those old, sad Johnny Cash tunes, like 'Home of the Blues.' " ⊙: *The Essential Johnny Cash 1955–1983* (3 CDs: Columbia/ Legacy).

Lightnin' Hopkins—"Lonesome Dog Blues" and "Santa Fe Blues." ⊙: You'll find the former song on *Blue Lightning* (Paula/Flyright), the latter on *Golden Classics, Pt. 4* (Collectibles).

*John Lee Hooker—"He sounded so eerie and sinister, like on 'Hobo Blues' and 'Crawlin' Kingsnake.' Those tunes just killed me. They still do. There was no sound like that, ever." ⊙: Both tunes are on *The Best of* . . . (GNP).

Little Walter— ⊙: See Master List.

Bullet Williams—"He was an amazing player, just a wild harp player." ⊙: *Alabama Blue 1927–1931* (Yazoo) or *The Great Harp Players 1927–1936* (Document).

Palmer McAbee—"Lost Boy Blues" and "Railroad Piece." "These were two sides of a seventy-eight I had, and I just played them over and over and over. Just totally solo harmonica playing, no singin', no other instrument. I've never been able to find anybody who knows anything about the guy. They don't know where he was from, or if he was black or white, young or old." ⊙: Both named tunes are available on *The Great Harp Players 1927–1936* (Document).

Rabih Abou-Khalil—*Sultan's Picnic* (Enja). "He's a Lebanese oud player. Howard Levy plays harmonica on this record. Kahlil has about eight or ten CDs out. And I like all that stuff, it's kind of a mixture of jazz and Middle Eastern scales, which I think are really bluesy."

Various artists—*Septetos Cubanos: Sones de Cuba* (2 CDs: Corason). The *son* form, which this set is devoted to, underlies the primary song and dance music of Cuba.

Ry Cooder/V. S. Bhat—*A Meeting by the River* (Water Lily). "The whole thing really creates a nice mood."

The Blues Etilicos—*Salamandra* and *Buena Sorte* (both Natasha). "They're from Rio. Flavio Guimaraes is the leader of the band and he's a tremendous harmonica player. They play straight-ahead blues, and they're mixing up some of the local Brazilian folk styles of music." ⬤: Also check out *Dente de Ouro* (Polygram), but their albums are only available through import sources.

Teo Azevedo—"He is a Brazilian *forro* player and he gave me a lot of records to listen to and he wrote a tune that I adapted to the blues, so we split the writer's royalties on it. Instead of hearing harmonicas in *forro* music, you hear accordions, so they're interchangeable. There are great melodies and riffs [in *forro* music] and it's really all in the blues scale. It's a new place to explore. And it all has the same influences—there's the European and black influences coming together to make this new music, just like what happened with blues. So it produces to my ears a similar music, and certainly from the heart it feels the same to me, the same spirit in the music, the same subjects in the lyrics. *Forro* has the same parents [as blues], but it's a different child." ⬤: We cannot locate any Azevedo recordings, but you can hear "Feel It In Your Heart," the song he composed with Charlie, on Charlie's *Rough News* (see below).

Various artists—*From the Heart* (Corason). "This compilation has a lot of Cuban and Mexican stuff. Latin music has heart, and I can feel it when I hear it. It makes me feel good the same way as when I hear good blues. It has a genuineness about it, a real human quality. I've got a lot of material combining blues and Latin music."

Arsenio Rodriguez—*Como Se Goza en el Barrio* (Tubao). This Cuban *tres* player (the *tres* is the guitarlike instrument characteristic of cuban *son* music) "really kills me," says Charlie.

Rembetika—No, not a band, but a whole style of music, says Charlie: "It's the real low-life music of Greece, the back-in-the-alley stuff. It's pretty raunchy, all about smoking hashish and whores and getting murdered. The scales are real similar to blues." ⬤: Various artists, *Greek Oriental Rembetika 1911–37* (Arhoolie) and Stratos Xarhakos and Nikos Gatsos, *Rembetika* (CBS).

El Camaron de la Isla—*Autorretrato* (Philips). "Man, it really swings," Charlie says about the late Spanish flamenco singer's music. "[El Camaron] could belt it out like nobody's business. He was a real hard liver and died young. I look at the picture on the album, and he has a pompadour, long sideburns, and a sharkskin suit on. Man, he's lookin' cool. He sings as tough as any Howlin' Wolf tune."

The Five Blind Boys of Alabama—"I Could See Everybody's Mother" on *True Convictions* (Vee Jay). "That just killed me."

CHARLIE MUSSELWHITE'S OWN RECORDINGS

Charlie feels that his latest recording, *Continental Drifter* (Pointblank), is also his best album. *Drifter* is divided jinto three sections. The first features his touring band, a skilled, versatile unit that "can play whatever I have in mind to play." The second section focuses on the Delta sounds Charlie was raised around, with Charlie performing solo. The third Charlie named "The Cuban Sessions"; it is comprised of four tracks Charlie recorded with his Cuban pal and associate Eliades Ochoa and his group Cuarteto Patria. Several other tracks also include accents from the Cuban and Brazilian music that has enthralled Charlie over the years. Charlie also recommends the albums *Rough News* (Pointblank), with the *forro*-influenced tune "Feel It in Your Heart," and *In My Time* (Alligator).

: Not-to-be-missed albums from Charlie's earlier work include his debut (when he was 22) *Stand Back! Here Comes Charlie Musselwhite's Southside Band!* (Vanguard), *Tennessee Woman* (Vanguard), and the audiophile reissue of *Memphis, Tennessee* (Mobile Fidelity), which features the extraordinary steel guitarist Freddy Roulette.

YOUSSOU N'DOUR (November 3, 1997)

The term "Afropop" which drapes the rich popular music pouring out of Africa conceals as much as it reveals. Afropop is not just traditional African folk music played on electric guitars and saxophones. In many cases, it bears a complex relationship to African history, in particular the history of colonization and slavery. These two forces savaged West African cultures for hundreds of years and did the same in slave economies in the New World. In the wake of this exploitation, new cultures sprang from the dislocated seeds of the old. They then began "talking" to each other about their common roots. For instance, Afro-Cuban music has migrated back to Africa in recent decades and found new ears among West African popular musicians. So has other music with African roots such as North American rock and R&B, which fills the record shelves of many of Africa's top musical performers today.

Case in point: Youssou N'Dour, probably the most celebrated African singer alive. Youssou is both inventor and leading light of *mbalax*, a lively mix of African, Caribbean, and pop sounds. Raised in the crowded Medina section of Dakar, Senegal, Youssou was born with music coursing in his blood. His mother, herself a well-known singer and composer, came from a lineage of *griots*, the West African singers who are also part bard, tribune, newscaster, and storyteller. But Youssou began his own climb to international stardom singing Afro-Cuban tunes with the Star Band of Dakar, one of the leading Senegalese bands of its type. Like many African musicians of his generation, he was also listening to R&B giants from the States. "The first music that really impressed me was the music of the sixties—soul—and at the same time I was a great fan of Latin American–Cuban music, which has always been my favorite music right up to the present day," Youssou tells us by phone from his home in Dakar.

Still, Youssou draws a careful line between artists he likes and the music he makes. "I don't think the word 'influence' is the word for me," he asserts. "They are the people who made me love music, but they didn't influence me. I have been influenced by my environment, by what I experience here. . . . [I loved] things from the music of James Brown to Marvin Gaye or from Manu Dibango to Fela Kuti, people whose names I heard, but their kind of music didn't necessarily make me play the same thing. I walked a different path. I tried to make music that was close to the people who were close to me, the Senegalese people."

In so doing, though, Youssou has ignited yet another round of cultural exchange. Impressed by his *mbalax* singing, Peter Gabriel featured Youssou on the song "In Your Eyes" on his album *So*; "Eyes" became one of several hit singles from the record. *So* proved to be a turning point for both men. It boosted Gabriel's audience significantly and introduced Youssou to Western music fans, who have faithfully followed his career ever since. His earnings have enabled Youssou to open his own recording studio in Dakar, Studio Xippi, which has begun introducing the world to other outstanding Senegalese musicians like Cheikh Lo, Youssou's sister Abibatou N'Dour, and Manel Diop. Youssou may have been careful to protect himself from influences, but his own influence is spreading to many corners of the globe.

YOUSSOU N'DOUR'S FAVORITE ARTISTS AND RECORDINGS

Johnny Pacheco and Celia Cruz—Pacheco, who moved to New York from the Dominican Republic in the late '40s, and from Cuba, Cruz made their reputations separately but have also performed together. The two salsa stars toured West Africa often. ⏺ : See Master List.

Marvin Gaye—"I'm a big fan of Marvin Gaye, and everything he has done." ●: See Master List.

James Brown—As with Gaye, Youssou recommends anything by the Godfather of Soul. ●: See Master List.

The Artist Formerly Known as Prince—Youssou recommends everything Prince has done. ●: In chronological order, the classic TAFKAP albums are 1980's *Dirty Mind*, 1982's *1999* (2 CDs), and 1984's *Purple Rain* (all Warner Bros.), and 1987's *Sign o' the Times* (2 CDs: Paisley Park), although striking moments abound in the rest of the catalog.

Cheikh Lo—*Ne La Thiass* (Atlantic). "I think that he is someone who ought to eventually be much better known throughout the world and that his music is very interesting," says Youssou, who produced this Senegalese singer's impressive, folkish album.

Fela Kuti—Nigerian Kuti's music and fearless political stance influenced an entire generation of African musicians. ●: See Master List.

Manu Dibango—The Cameroonian Makossa man, with his blend of jazz and African pop, is one of Afropop's true superstars. ●: See Master List.

U2—Youssou says it may surprise his fans that this is one of his favorite groups. ●: This group's enormous talent is sometimes undermined by its even larger ambitions, but not on *War*, *The Joshua Tree*, and *Achtung, Baby* (all Island), the latter two produced by *Daniel Lanois, who also produced Peter Gabriel's *So*.

YOUSSOU N'DOUR'S OWN RECORDINGS

"I like all my songs, but it's the moment that is the most important. I accept my albums as they are at the time when I make them," says Youssou. After some reflection, though, he acknowledges that the track "Africa Remembers" from *Eyes Open* (40 Acres & a Mule/Sony) "really worked for me."

●: Youssou's early solo work on *Nelson Mandela* (Verve) and the unfortunately brief *Immigres* (Earthworks) lets you hear him as he breaks onto the international scene, as does the 1991 collection of previously unreleased '80s tracks, *Djamil* (Celluloid). To go back even further, investigate the ten (!) volumes of Etoile de Dakar reissues on the Stern's Africa label; Etoile de Dakar, which later evolved into the group Super Etoile, is the band Youssou founded after leaving the Star Band. The 1990 record *Set* (Virgin), which introduces Western crossover elements drawn from funk and Western pop, is widely considered Youssou's strongest. From 1992, *Eyes Open* continues the crossover direction. His more recent *The*

Guide (Wommat) (Chaos/Sony) features collaborations with Neneh Cherry, his partner on the hit single "7 Seconds," and *Branford Marsalis.

WILLIE NELSON (November 23, 1998)

It isn't often that an artist gets the four-star treatment from the recording industry's hype machine and still emerges underappreciated. But that just may be the case with Willie Nelson. Despite his superstar status, few have really considered the full breadth of his talent, which runs as wide as Texas, his native state. Consider that if he'd never sung a dang note, he'd still be hailed as one of country's greatest songwriters ever; his catalog lists hundreds of top-shelf tunes going back to "Night Life" (a smash for Ray Price in the early '60s), "Crazy" and "Funny How Time Slips Away" (two of Patsy Cline's most memorable hits), "Hello Walls" (a chartbuster for Faron Young), "On the Road Again," "Blue Eyes Crying in the Rain," and on and on. By the same token, if Willie had never written a line, he'd be celebrated as one of the great song interpreters, a Sinatra of country music. In fact, calling him a fabulous country singer doesn't quite cut it either, because like one of his idols, Ray Charles, he can apply his skills to almost any tune in the American canon and make it his own.

When Willie talks about his own musical heroes, it becomes clear that no matter how hard the music industry tries to pigeonhole him, he's never restricted himself to any genre. In Willie's book, Sinatra and Charles have always ranked up there with such early country icons as Ernest Tubb, Hank Williams, Roy Acuff, and Bob Wills. "I loved it all and just started learning what I could," Willie tells us by phone. In songwriting, he admires Hoagy Carmichael and Johnny Mercer as much as Williams and Kris Kristofferson. And when it comes to playing guitar, his greatest idol isn't a rural picker but a European jazzman, the Belgian-born gypsy Django Reinhardt. "I'm probably Django Reinhardt's biggest fan," Willie says, "and I would turn every guitar player in the world onto Django if he hadn't already got all his stuff."

Despite his outsized abilities, Willie didn't really catch on as a performer until he abandoned Nashville's Music Row and came home to Texas. "I think I instinctively knew that back in Texas I could do better, whatever better it was, because I was from there," Willie recalls. "I had relatives, fans, and a whole lot of people and a whole lotta places to play." Settling into progressive Austin in the early '70s, Willie mingled with the college students and hippies, started listening to the same singer/songwriters they were into, and grew his hair long.

But it was a two-way cultural exchange. Young Austinites were also getting into traditional country music so "I could also introduce them to other music that I knew about. Again, if you like Hank Williams, wait until you hear Hoagy Carmichael." It's a lesson Willie's still teaching, for anyone who cares to really listen.

WILLIE NELSON'S FAVORITE ARTISTS AND RECORDINGS

Frank Sinatra— 🔘 : The strong compilation of Sinatra's hits for Reprise *The Very Best of Sinatra* (2 CDs: Warner Bros.) includes two of Willie's favorite songs, "My Way" and "Foggy Day."

Ray Charles—Willie loves the material from the late 1950s and early '60s—for instance, 1959's "What'd I Say" and Hoagy Carmichael's "Georgia on My Mind" (1960)—plus Ray's country tracks. 🔘 : For Ray's Atlantic recordings from the 1950s, go for either the single-disc *The Best of . . . : The Atlantic Years* (Rhino) or the more comprehensive *. . . : The Birth of Soul* (3 CDs: Rhino). For the 1960s material on ABC/Paramount, the choice is *Greatest Hits, Vols. 1–2* (DCC, available separately); "Georgia" is on Vol. 1. Ray recorded two volumes titled *Modern Sounds in Country & Western Music* (both Rhino). To ride that horse 'til it drops, go for the boxed set *Complete Country & Western Recordings 1959–1986* (4 CDs: Rhino), which Willie also heartily endorses.

Bob Wills—Willie loves the whole catalog. 🔘 : *. . . Anthology* (Columbia) covers 24 tracks from the '30s and '40s, a prime period for the band. *Anthology (1935–73)* (2 CDs: Rhino) comprehensively and superbly covers the band's entire history. The stunning *The Tiffany Transcriptions, Vols. 1–9* (Rhino, available separately) were recorded between 1946 and '47; they approximate the group's live sound, replete with instrumental solos, and span almost every conceivable musical genre.

Ernest Tubb— 🔘 : See Master List.

Roy Acuff— 🔘 : *Columbia Historic Edition* (Columbia) covers important recordings from early in Acuff's career. *The Essential . . . (1936–1949)* (Columbia/Legacy) includes 20 tracks from Acuff's prime years.

Johnny Mercer—Willie says he never really studied songwriters but "I listened a lot, so it's probably the same thing." Mercer, who wrote or co-wrote over 1000 songs, was one he listened to most. 🔘 : *Johnny Mercer Sings . . .* (Everest) and Ella Fitzgerald's *The Johnny Mercer Songbook* (Verve).

Hoagy Carmichael— 🔘 : *Classic . . .* (3 CDs: Smithsonian) presents notable performers, and in some instances the man himself, singing and playing Carmichael's classic songs.

Hank Williams—"Everything he wrote was great. 'Your Cheatin' Heart,' 'Jambalaya,' 'I Saw the Light'—great songs." ⏺: See Master List.

Leon Payne—Payne was a blind, Texas-born multi-instrumentalist and songwriter who composed over a thousand songs during his long career, part of which he spent with Bob Wills and the Texas Playboys. ⏺: *Leon Payne* and *Americana* (both Starday).

Floyd Tillman—Tillman was a traditional country and honky tonk performer as well as a country composer but it's the latter ability that Willie paid most attention to. ⏺: *Columbia Historic Edition* (Columbia) and *Country Music Hall of Fame Series* (MCA).

Roger Miller—Miller may be best-known for country novelty fare like "King of the Road," but he was one of the genre's craftiest all-around songwriters. ⏺: *Best of . . . , Vol. 1: Country Tunesmith* (PolyGram) and *Best of . . . , Vol. 2: King of the Road* (Mercury).

Kris Kristofferson—"Help Me Make It Through the Night" and "Sunday Mornin' Comin' Down." A rebel after Willie's heart, Kristofferson shook up Nashville with his anti-Establishment image but wrote some of his genre's best material, including the two Willie mentions. ⏺: *Me and Bobby McGee* (Monument) features Kristofferson singing his own songs, including Willie's two favorites and the title tune.

Django Reinhardt and Stephane Grappelli—"Two of the greatest musicians that ever, ever played. If you're going to be in music, you should know these guys." ⏺: See Master List.

WILLIE NELSON'S OWN RECORDINGS

Willie's favorites from his large catalog begin with the influential narrative concept albums, 1975's *The Red-Headed Stranger* (Columbia) and its 1974 predecessor, *Phases and Stages* (Atlantic). He also lists 1996's *Spirit* (Island), bare-bones acoustic treatments of 13 original songs; 1980's *Honeysuckle Rose* (Columbia), a film soundtrack that introduced his classic "On the Road Again"; and 1978's *Stardust* (Columbia), a set of standards (including "All of Me," "Georgia on My Mind," and "Sunny Side of the Street") with Booker T. Jones arranging and Willie's rugged band at the time playing. *Stardust* proved to be another intuitive triumph. Willie's label didn't like his concept for the record, but this is the album that made him a superstar. Willie's final mention goes to 1998's *Teatro* (Island), a mix of old and new originals plus covers, with atmospheric rock producer *Daniel Lanois at the console.

: On 1977's *To Lefty from Willie* (Columbia), Willie honors troubled crooner Lefty Frizzel with covers that explore both the blue and upbeat sides of his honky tonk songs. The excellent *Me and Paul* (Columbia), from 1985, is currently out of print but certainly worth the search. The 1995 album *Just One Love* (Transatlantic) is another strong set of cover tunes. The 1992 record *Who'll Buy My Memories?* (Columbia), originally sold through TV ads to bail Willie out of his notorious IRS troubles, presents him alone with his beat-to-hell guitar on a collection of demos, outtakes, and other rarities plus some well-known numbers. Excellent compilations include 1981's *Greatest Hits (& Some That Will Be)* (Columbia), which summarizes the previous five years; *Nite Life: Greatest Hits and Rare Tracks, 1959–1971* (Rhino), which focuses on Willie's early songwriting career and features his versions of hits by others ("Crazy," "Hello Walls," etc.); *The Early Years: The Complete Liberty Recordings Plus More* (2 CDs: Liberty), which surveys his first recordings as a performer; *Revolutions of Time: The Journey 1975–1993* (3 CDs: Columbia), which covers his most popular recording period but includes obscure material, too; and *The Essential . . .* (RCA), a summary of his work for RCA.

AARON NEVILLE (April 17, 1998)

He was blessed with one of the most striking singing voices ever heard and was raised in New Orleans, where music is the unofficial language. But as a youngster, Aaron Neville wasn't dreaming of stardom. He just liked to sing. "When I was a little boy," Aaron remembers, "my mom and dad had all the Nat King Cole songs. I used to try to sing like him. I'd sing 'Mona Lisa' and 'Pretend' and 'Nature Boy' and all that stuff." At night, he would hear older brother Art and his doo-wop group working on their repertoire on a park bench. They may have been imagining record deals and radio play but all Aaron wanted was to join in the harmonies.

All of which says something about the strength of passion. Through all of Aaron's successes—his 1966 solo hit, "Tell It Like It Is," his lead vocals with the Neville Brothers band, and his current solo career, reignited in the 1990s—his major influences remain the music he loved as a child. The list includes Nat Cole, of course, as well as the doowop and R&B tunes he pined to sing with his brother's group (especially the songs of Sonny Til [Tillotson] and the Orioles, Pookie Hudson and the Spaniels, the Flamingos, and Clyde McPhatter).

None of those artists, though, account for the single most notable aspect of Aaron's style, a vocal waver so pronounced you find yourself wondering about studio trickery, although there isn't any. "That was just something that was in me," Aaron explains. "I also liked the cowboys. I could yodel. I'd go to the movies and see Roy Rogers and Gene Autry and Riders of the Purple Sage, and I'd come outta those movies, and I was a cowboy, you know, and I'd sing like them. I was a big Hank Williams fan, too. . . . I was all just a mixture of that, too, you know—the cowboys, and the yodeling, and then my voice just was like that. They used to try to stop me from doing different things. They just wanted me to sing straight and I couldn't do that. I mean, hey, that's the way I sing."

AARON NEVILLE'S FAVORITE ARTISTS AND RECORDINGS

Nat King Cole—Aaron enjoys Cole's earlier jazz trio recordings, but the music that really affected him was that of Cole's second career, as an ultra-smooth pop singer. ⬤: *Greatest Hits* (Capitol) includes three of Aaron's favorite tracks, "Mona Lisa," "Too Young," and "Pretend."

The Flamingos—"I Only Have Eyes For You" and "I'll Be Home." Prime doo-wop favorites of Aaron's, by one of the great vocal groups of their era. ⬤: *The Doo Bop She Bop: Best of . . .* (Rhino).

Pookie Hudson and the Spaniels—"Goodnight, Sweetheart, Goodnight." "I used to try to sing like him . . . We'd be in the boys' bathroom at school, you know, with the good acoustics—because it had a nice echo." ⬤: *Goodnight, Sweetheart, Goodnight* (Vee Jay).

Clyde McPhatter—Aaron was a fan of McPhatter's from the time the latter was one of Billy Ward's Dominoes. ⬤: See Master List.

The Orioles—This gospel-influenced vocal group, with lead vocalist Sonny Til, helped pave the way in the late '40s and early '50s for the doo-wop that would follow. ⬤: *. . . Sing Their Greatest Hits* (Collectibles) is a decent introduction. *Jubilee Sides* (Bear Family) is a six-CD box set that gives the complete picture of this important group.

The Heartbeats—"A Thousand Miles Away" and "Daddy's Home." Both songs were huge hits, the latter in this doo-wop group's incarnation as Shep and the Limelites, when Aaron was in junior high school. ⬤: *The Best of . . .* (Rhino).

The Penguins—"Earth Angel." This classic doo-wop hit sold five million copies worldwide. ⬤: *Best of the Mercury Years* (Polygram) is a comprehensive anthology that includes, besides "Earth Angel," singles, album tracks, and B-sides.

The Clovers—"Blue Velvet" and "Devil or Angel." "The Clovers did all this stuff back in the early fifties—'52, '53, and '54. And Bobby Vinton came along in the seventies, or late sixties and got hits with it." ⬤: *Down in the Alley: Best of . . .* (Rhino).

Bobby "Blue" Bland—Aaron likes everything Bobby "Blue" Bland did; "He had the growl in his voice, you know." ⬤: See Master List.

Larry Williams—Aaron also likes virtually everything this fellow New Orleans R&B and rock 'n' roll singer recorded. ⬤:The exceptional *Bad Boy* (Specialty) features 23 tracks by this engagingly rowdy-voiced vocalist and some first-rate backing from New Orleans and Los Angeles session musicians. Williams was groomed by his label to be the successor to Little Richard after the latter left secular music for the ministry.

Little Willie John—"He was one of the best singers of all time, as far as I'm concerned. He was the first one that sang 'Fever.' Everybody thinks Peggy Lee did that first, but Little Willie John was the first." ⬤: See Master List.

Sam Cooke and the Soul Stirrers—Aaron says that hearing Cooke sing "Any Day Now" over the radio is what made him want to sing spirituals: "When I was a kid I used to rock on my grandmother's lap and she'd be listenin' to the gospel station . . . Sam came through with his smooth voice, and it was sort of like my voice, and it just turned me on." ⬤: See Master List.

Ray Charles—"Oh man, I got his albums downstairs and I listen to him all the time. . . . I like anything Ray Charles did, even when he went to the country stuff." ⬤: See Master List.

Hank Williams—"I liked all his stuff. I used to do 'Lovesick Blues,' 'Hey Good Lookin.' " ⬤: See Master List.

Junior Parker—"Me and the brothers, when we first started we used to do his songs. And I got to go to one of his sessions a long time ago when I was on the road with Larry Williams. Got to meet him." ⬤: See Master List.

Ted Taylor—"Be Ever Wonderful" and "Need You Home." "He had one of those real high voices." ⬤: *Greatest Hits* (Collectibles).

Marvin Gaye—Aaron likes all of Gaye's work, but especially the records he made after he convinced Motown's Berry Gordy to give him more creative control over his music. ⬤: The landmark *What's Goin' On* (Motown) was the first album in this period. Other memorable records from that time include the erotically charged *Let's Get It On* (Motown) and *Midnight Love* (Motown), weaker overall than the others but containing the sensational "Sexual Healing."

The Impressions—"The Gypsy Woman" and "Your Precious Love." Curtis Mayfield sang lead on the former, the group's first hit in 1961. Jerry Butler sang lead on the latter, then promptly headed for a solo career when the single charted. ⏺: . . . *Greatest Hits* (MCA) contains both songs and many other sweet soul classics.

Johnny Ace—Aaron loved everything by this vocalist/pianist, who died at 25 after losing a game of Russian roulette before a Christmas Day show in 1954. ⏺: See Master List.

Frankie Lymon and the Teenagers—This doo-wop favorite of Aaron's was one of the primary inspirations of Berry Gordy's Motown sound. ⏺: *The Best of Frankie Lymon and the Teenagers* (Rhino) includes all their best-known tracks, including their first big hit, "Why Do Fools Fall in Love?"

Gene Allison— ⏺: This now obscure R&B singer's hits appear along with other singles from the '50s on *The Vee Jay Story, Vol. 1* (Vee Jay).

Linda Jones—"Hypnotized." "I used to love her voice." ⏺: *Hypnotized: 20 Golden Classics* (Collectibles).

Aretha Franklin—If Aretha sings it, Aaron likes it. ⏺: See Master List.

The Chantels—"Maybe." "Maybe" was this early female vocal group's biggest hit. ⏺: *The Best of . . .* (Rhino).

The Swan Silvertones—Aaron especially loved the work of tenor Claude Jeter. ⏺: See Master List.

The Brooklyn All-Stars—Aaron told us he used to warm up for gigs with this gospel group's hit, "When I Stood On the Banks of Jordan." ⏺: *Our Greatest Hits* (Nashboro).

Art Neville—"He was one of my first influences," Aaron says of the first Neville sibling to become a professional musician. "Art still inspires me." ⏺: *Art Neville: His Specialty Recordings: 1956–58* (Specialty) includes tracks with such New Orleans session players as Earl Palmer, Lee Allen, Roy Montrell, and Allen Toussaint. No introduction to Art Neville is complete without checking out the Meters, the seminal New Orleans funk/R&B band that he co-founded. See Master List.

Cyril Neville—"Cyril's got something in his voice, you know, [like] no singer I've heard. . . . He's one of the soulfulest cats in the world. He needs to be heard. He does a great version of Bob Dylan's 'The Times They Are a-Changin' " that gives me chills." ⏺: See the section on Cyril and his recordings.

Charles Neville—"Charles inspires me the way he blows," Aaron says about the Neville Brothers' saxophonist. "I try to imitate some of the stuff he does on his horn, which is hard, because he sounds like he's in Arabia sometimes, or China, or India." ⬤ : *Charles Neville and Diversity* (Laserlight), his only solo album, focuses on jazz.

AARON NEVILLE'S OWN RECORDINGS

Aaron's favorite tracks from early in his career, including "Tell It Like It Is," his unforgettable ballad hit from 1966; "Waitin' at the Station"; "Let's Live"; "Hercules"; and "The Greatest Love" can all be found on the Neville Brothers compilation *Treacherous* (Rhino). In 1985, Aaron recorded an EP of ballads, *Orchid in the Storm*, now available from Rhino. When we spoke, Aaron fondly recalled this recording, which contains covers of many of his favorite doo-wop and sweet-soul songs including the Penguins' "Earth Angel," Jerry Butler's "Your Precious Love," and Johnny Ace's "Pledging My Love."

In 1991, Linda Ronstadt, with whom Aaron had recorded several duets, including the Grammy-winning "Don't Know Much" for her *Cry Like a Rainstorm—Howl Like the Wind* (Elektra), produced the critically well-received solo album *Warm Your Heart* (A&M). "On that album, 'Ave Maria' was my favorite song," says Aaron. "We put something spiritual on each album, and that was the spiritual on that one, that and the [Joseph Spence] song called 'I Bid You Goodnight.' " Aaron is justly proud of the latter track, too.

When we spoke about his subsequent solo works, Aaron also focused his remarks primarily on favorite tracks rather than albums. Those tracks include "Don't Take Away My Heaven," "I Owe You One," "Betcha By Golly Wow," and Aretha Franklin's "Ain't No Way," on *The Grand Tour* (A&M) and "Some Days Were Made for Rain" and "Every Day of My Life" on *Tattooed Heart* (A&M). He's particularly enamored of the material on his latest album as of this writing, *To Make Me Who I Am* (A&M), including the title song, "Say What's In My Heart," "What Did I Do (To Deserve You)," "The First Time Ever I Saw Your Face" (a duet with Linda Ronstadt), and "Please Remember Me."

Aaron called our attention to spiritually oriented projects, too—*Aaron Neville's Soulful Christmas* (A&M) and *Doing It Their Own Way*, a meditation tape he recorded with a priest from Baton Rouge, Father M. Jeffrey Bayhi. "He's doin' the stations of the cross in his own words of today, and I'm singin' in between each verse. We get letters from people from all over [about this one]." To find it, visit the website www.Nevilles.com.

Of the Neville Brothers' records, Aaron defies the critics in singling out the band's first recording, 1978's *The Neville Brothers* (Capitol). He notes that Keith Richards said in *Rolling Stone* that the group's second release, 1981's *Fiyo on the Bayou* (A&M) should have been named album of the year. Other favorites include, in chronological order, *Live at Tipitina's* (Spindletop) from 1985, the *Daniel Lanois-produced *Yellow Moon* (A&M), its same-vein follow-up *My Brothers Keeper* (A&M) from 1990, and 1994's *Live on Planet Earth* (A&M). Aaron also feels strongly about the 1986 compilation *Treacherous* (2 CDs: Rhino). Besides Neville Brothers tracks, this well-conceived package includes samples of the siblings' various solo and group projects over the previous three decades.

⬤: For more on the Neville's catalog, see Cyril Neville's section immediately below.

CYRIL NEVILLE (July 21, 1996)

The brothers Neville—Cyril, Art, *Aaron, and Charles—may hail from New Orleans but the tale of how they became the Neville Brothers band would make a Russian novel. Here's the Cliff Notes version: Over the years, various brothers had played with various other brothers in various configurations—the Neville Sounds, the Soul Machine, and most notably, Art's band the Meters, which included Cyril in its final years in the mid-'70s. The brothers' alliances warmed their parents' hearts but Mom and Dad hoped for more—all four brothers in the same group. If the boys could be brought together under some pretense, they reasoned, they'd find a way to make the arrangement permanent. The reunion was engineered by the brothers' uncle, Mardi Gras Indian George (Chief Jolly) Landry, who convinced the four to join him and some buddies for a recording date. The sessions took place in 1975—unfortunately one year after Mrs. Neville had passed away—and resulted in the legendary *The Wild Tchoupitoulas* album. Sure enough, as Mom and Dad Neville had predicted, the Neville Brothers debuted on record three years later and are now one of popular music's most treasured institutions.

Although Aaron, with his linebackerlike profile and unique singing style, is the band's most visible member and eldest bro' Art, with a recording career stretching back to the mid-'50s, its most storied, Cyril is the quintessential secret weapon. His smoky vocals are one of the pillars on which the band's soulful reputation is built. He also writes or co-writes much of its material and his percussion touches are a prime ingredient in the band's vaunted rhythmic drive. As Cyril tells us on the Nevilles' tour bus before a show in Southern Oregon, Mr. and Mrs. Neville gave their sons more than just the concept of a family band. They also trained their ears with the tasty music they played at home. Some of Cyril's favorite artists to this day—Nat King Cole, Louis Jordan, Big Maybelle, Jimmy

Reed, and gospel queen Mahalia Jackson—are those he first heard on his parent's record player.

When Cyril grew old enough to pick his own music, he grooved on ultimate groovemeister James Brown, an adopted hero in the Crescent City. He was a teen during the Motown era of the '60s and loved that music, too. But in his view, New Orleans was still the capital of Planet Soul. "There was this other thing happenin' in New Orleans at the same time that the Motown thing was goin' on that was churnin' out just as many hits," points out Cyril, who had been a fan of homegrown stars like Ernie K-Doe, Huey "Piano" Smith, and James Booker long before '60s soul music descended on his town.

Eventually, Cyril began digging below the surface to the roots of the music he loved—the blues he'd first heard at home; the Caribbean sources of New Orleans' "second line" rhythm; and, of course, Mother Africa, including the music of worldbeat artists like South Africa's Mahlathini and Hugh Masakela and Senegal's Toure Kunda. Those explorations helped deepen the Nevilles' sound, which now embodies almost the entire history, including ancient African history, of funk and soul.

For several years now, Cyril has branched out into solo projects, too. Since 1986, he has been a member of the Uptown All-Stars, which plays a New Orleans/Caribbean hybrid called "second-line reggae." He also heads his own record label, Endangered Species. But none of that threatens his commitment to his primary gig, the Neville Brothers. Mom and Dad were right about that band, and the boys ain't fightin' it.

CYRIL NEVILLE'S FAVORITE ARTISTS AND RECORDINGS

Nat King Cole— 🔘 : See Master List.

Louis Jordan— 🔘 : See Master List.

Mahalia Jackson—Jackson is one of New Orleans own, born there in 1911 before moving to Chicago with her family at age 14. Cyril cites her as probably his greatest influence, along with James Brown. 🔘 : See Master List.

James Brown— 🔘 : See Master List.

Ernie K-Doe—Most people think of K-Doe as a one-hit wonder ("Mother-in-Law") but folks in New Orleans know differently. He may not have had another national hit, but he cut some fabulous New Orleans R&B sides. 🔘 : *Burn! K-Doe, Burn!* (Charly) contains 24 K-Doe singles.

Huey "Piano" Smith—Cyril especially liked Smith's hits with his band, the Clowns, in the 1950s. 🔘 : See Master List.

James Booker—Cyril highly recommends "anything you can find" by this New Orleans R&B/boogie-woogie pianist to aspiring piano players: "He was one of the greatest piano geniuses that ever lived." ●: Rounder has released a number of excellent Booker recordings, including *New Orleans Piano Wizard: Live!, Classified, Spiders on the Keys*, and *Resurrection of the Bayou Maharajah*. Also look for *King of the New Orleans Keyboard, Vols. 1 & 2* (JSP), *The Lost Paramount Tapes* (DJM), and *Junco Partners* (Hannibal).

Jimmy Reed—"Honest I Do," "Big Boss Man," and "Ain't That Lovin' You Baby." "He was one of my momma's favorite people, so I picked up on him from her." ●: *Speak the Lyrics to Me Mama Reed* (Vee Jay) includes all three of Cyril's favorite songs and is otherwise an excellent introduction to Reed's work.

Ivory Joe Hunter—"Since I Met You Baby." Another pianist Cyril loves, Hunter was a smooth R&B singer and songwriter who composed over 7,000 songs including "Baby," a big hit in the mid-'50s. ●: *Since I Met You Baby: The Best of . . .* (Razor & Tie).

Big Maybelle—Huge in stature with a voice to match, Maybelle recorded some prime R&B and jump blues before dying at 47. ●: *Big Maybelle* (Savoy) or *The Complete Okeh Sessions 1952–55* (Epic/ Legacy) are both good collections from Maybelle's best period.

Tony Bennett—"A lot of people don't think that would be somebody that I would check out." ●: Bennett's long career has yielded a raft of compilation albums. Start with *Tony's Greatest Hits, Vol. 3* (Columbia). He's recorded with a number of jazz greats; to sample that work, try *Jazz* (Columbia), a compilation, and especially the exquisite *The Tony Bennett/Bill Evans Album* (Fantasy). 1962's *I Left My Heart in San Francisco* (Columbia) is the album that launched Bennett's career into the stratosphere, where it's stayed.

Curtis Mayfield—Cyril says that Mayfield and Willie Dixon are his two favorite songwriters. ●: See Master List.

Willie Dixon—Bassist/composer/producer/arranger Dixon wrote a string of Chicago blues classics including "Hoochie Coochie Man," "Wang Dang Doodle," "Spoonful," and "Little Red Rooster." ●: *The Chess Box* (2 CDs: Chess) is an excellent compilation. The otherwise solid 1959 recording *Willie's Blues*, with pianist Memphis Slim, is worth it for the track "Sittin' and Cryin' the Blues" alone. *I Am the Blues* (Columbia) features Dixon interpreting nine of his best songs with a terrific session band.

Randy Newman—Cyril is among the legions who worship the songwriting talents of this other son of New Orleans. ●: Aaron Neville covered Newman's "Louisiana 1927." You can hear that song on the superb *Good Old Boys* (Reprise). Other Newman classics include *Sail Away* (Reprise) and *12 Songs* (Reprise).

Diamonds—*Solemnly Yours* (Endangered Species). This gospel group includes Cyril's wife, Gaynielle. "That's another group from New Orleans that deserves more national recognition," says Cyril.

Lois Dejean and the Dejean Family—"Three generations of singers singing great gospel music," Cyril comments. The various Dejeans have also made their marks in R&B and jazz. : Lois and the Dejeans haven't recorded much, but Lois can be heard leading the Youth Inspirational Choir on the live compilation *10th Anniversary New Orleans Jazz & Heritage Festival* (Flying Fish). She regularly performs around New Orleans leading the gospel group The Johnson Extension. Lois's son, Eddie, released an independent album, *Jesus is the Man* (http://www.satchmo.com/dejean/), in 1998.

Raymond Myles and the Rams—"They got some of the baddest gospel groups in the country in New Orleans," Cyril says, citing Myles, the son of gospel queen Christine Myles, and his Rams as a prime example. : The group's only CD currently available is *Heaven is the Place* (Honey Darling). You might be able to find an older release on vinyl called *New Orleans Gospel Genius* (Great Southern). Myles also appears on Allen Toussaint's *New Orleans Christmas* (NYNO).

***Lucky Dube**— : See the section on Lucky and his recordings.

Toure Kunda—This Senegalese band lit a fire in Europe in the early '80s that's still burning. : See Master List.

Mahlathini—"The Lion of Soweto!" : See Master List.

Hugh Masakela— : See Master List.

Mickey Hart—*Mickey Hart's Mystery Box* (Rykodisc). "That's an international thing right there, an experience in itself," Cyril says of this album by the former Grateful Dead percussionist.

Fela Kuti—Cyril recommends Fela's entire catalog. : See Master List.

CYRIL NEVILLE'S OWN RECORDINGS

Cyril is pleased with the Neville Brothers' entire catalog and doesn't pick favorites.

: Start your Nevilles collection with three studio albums, 1981's *Fiyo on the Biyou,* the *Daniel Lanois-produced *Yellow Moon* from 1989, and 1990's *Brothers Keeper* (all A&M). Fans are still waiting for the live album that captures the experience of a great Nevilles show. In the meantime, *Neville-ization* (Black Top); *Live at Tipatina's* (Spindletop), from the same mid-1980s performance; and 1994's *Live on Planet Earth* (A&M) at least hint of the group's cooking ability. *Treacherous: A History of the . . .* and *Treacherous Too!* (both Rhino, the former 2 CDs) are more than just good Neville Brothers compilations. They also survey three decades worth of solo and group recordings by the various brothers for a revealing insight into the band's genesis and chemistry. And don't overlook *The Wild Tchoupitoulas* (Antilles), which features George Landry and his Mardi Gras Indian pals plus instrumental support by all four Nevilles and members of the Meters. Vocally, it's pretty rough, but the material and band sound make it a true, funkified classic. Cyril wrote the album's opener, the infectious "Brother John," and co-wrote with Landry the double-funky closer, "Hey, Hey."

To hear Cyril's work with the Meters, search for the out-of-print but muchprized *Cabbage Alley* (Reprise). He's also represented on the Meters compilation *Funkify Your Life* (2 CDs: Rhino). Cyril has also recorded two albums with the Uptown All-Stars, *Fire This Time* and *Soulo* (both Endangered Species).

GRAHAM PARKER (December 9, 1996)

Rock's fogged memory forgets easily but Graham Parker was once It. In 1976, before the Sex Pistols and the Clash, Graham and his ripping band the Rumour awakened rock from its post-psychedelic stupor with their debut album *Howlin' Wind*. Graham's lyrics burned not unlike Dylan's; his music by turns strutted and bounced with Stonesish snarl, Jamaican riddim, and Stax soul. Punk followed his lead two years later, and though it was less poetic, utterly white, and infinitely louder, Graham understood entirely. "I felt exactly the same way two years before," Graham tells us from his home in New York state. "Why are they still sitting there pretending we're still hippies? It's over. . . . Let's rock for the revolution instead of laying around. Let's get out of our spiritual thing and make it physical again."

None of this was calculated. In jolting rock back to its earthy roots, Graham was just hailing back to his own. The first music he remembers mattering to him during his East London youth was on a British television show in the early '60s. On a set evoking a railroad station was "this large black woman with a square guitar, like one of those electric guitars that maybe Bo Diddley or somebody played. And she was singing and playing. It was the rawest, most amazing thing that I'd heard. And it was the first time I think I'd really gotten a visceral feel from music.''

Enter 1963 and in quick succession, the Beatles, Stones, and Kinks. Graham, born in 1950, followed the generational road map: someone gave him a guitar and he started a band. But he started to pull away from the flock after coming across some Little Richard 45s. ''We figured out pretty quickly, me and my friends, that the Beatles and the Stones were copping this from black American music,'' Graham remembers. ''So that was the next stage, to find out who the originals were.'' In the mid-'60s, Graham plunged into American soul music and Jamaican ska and a tough proto-skinhead scene that went against the flower-power grain. ''Basically, anybody who wasn't black and didn't play a saxophone I thought was square,'' he says.

Graham next phased through British blues and singer-songwriter music, and then, belatedly, psychedelia in the early '70s. But he was still searching for an identity of his own until he glimpsed his musical future while listening to Van Morrison's *Astral Weeks* one night. ''I'd be sitting there around people's pads, we'd all be wiped out, and I'd sort of rather hear something like Pink Floyd,'' he recalls. ''Then I got it for some reason. It dug in and it was like this total record. It was all the influences that I'd had, in a way. It was very spacey, very metaphysical, very ethereal. But blues at the same time. 'Madame George' is a three-chord blues song, taken to outrageous limits.''

Astral Weeks led Graham to other Morrison records that were even more firmly based in blues and soul. He discovered a lyric style that made sense for him as well in Bob Dylan's *Blood on the Tracks*. He reconnected with the Stones in their peak *Exile on Main Street* period. He tripped upon reggae, which rewired him to Jamaican rhythms. ''This is just before I stared really writing songs that became my first album,'' he notes. ''So I'd gone full circle back into the early roots of things again.''

And that's pretty much where it's stayed since. ''I still pick up things,'' Graham says. ''But [no music since] has gone where it makes me want to sit in a room and shed tears like Otis Redding did.''

GRAHAM PARKER'S FAVORITE ARTISTS AND RECORDINGS

Little Richard—In the mid-'60s, someone gave Graham some Little Richard 45s ''and I just thought this was so much better than Cliff Richard.'' : See Master List.

Otis Redding—*Otis Blue* (Atco). A cousin gave Graham this record when it came out in 1966: ''I remember sitting in my front room in my house, like tears welling up. And *Steve Cropper's guitaring on that record was also one of the most influential things to me."

*Wilson Pickett—"In the Midnight Hour." "Incredibly influential single [for me]."

The Four Tops—*The Four Tops* (Motown). "This record pre-dated the Motown sound . . . it wasn't that raucous tambourine on the snare drum thing as 'Reach Out, I'll Be There.' It was a very lush record with strings."

Aretha Franklin—Graham's swipe at contemporary Aretha on his *Acid Bubble-gum* was also a celebration of her earlier greatness. ⬤: *30 Greatest Hits* (Atlantic) is the Aretha Graham loved in the 1960s.

Jackie Wilson— ⬤ : *The Very Best of . . .* (Ace) covers all the big hits Graham and his fellow toughs danced to in the 1960s.

Prince Buster—Graham got into ska through the records of this outrageous artist, along with the incomparable Skatalites. ⬤: *Fabulous Greatest Hits* (Melodisc).

The Skatalites— ⬤ : See Master List.

Desmond Dekker—"007 (Shantytown)." This early rock-steady tune by one of reggae's godfathers was one of the first things Graham learned on electric guitar. ⬤: *Rockin' Steady: The Best of . . .* (Rhino).

Fleetwood Mac—*Then Play On* (Reprise). "That really opened me up to the realization that you didn't just have to play twelve-bar blues, you know, to have the feeling."

James Taylor—*Sweet Baby James* (Warner Bros.) As the 1970s dawned, Graham stopped trying to play like the Mac's Peter Green and bought an acoustic guitar because of records like this one.

John Prine—*Diamonds in the Rough* (Atlantic). "That was another influential record, but you know, he's really so much like Dylan, you can barely tell the difference."

King Crimson—*In the Court of the Crimson King* (EG). Graham abandoned his street tough scene for the hippie thing in the early '70s, with this album part of the sonic landscape.

Pink Floyd—*The Piper at the Gates of Dawn* and *Ummagumma* (both Capitol). These early Floyd albums were two more psychedelic favorites of Graham's.

The Beatles—*Sergeant Pepper's Lonely Hearts Club Band* (Capitol). Graham turned his back on the Beatles as a teenager infatuated with black music. But when he turned on to hippiness, he discovered the genius of this album, several years after its release.

David Bowie—*Hunky Dory* and *The Rise and Fall of Ziggy Stardust and the Spiders From Mars* (both Rykodisc). "It was campy, but you could tell he had roots in the Stones and in Dylan. . . . So that opened up a whole other new door: you could apply something new to the roots of stuff that went way back to the folk music and R&B."

Roxy Music—Graham loved this talented assemblage's music in the early-to-mid- '70s. ⊙: See Master List.

Bob Marley and the Wailers—*Catch a Fire* (Tuff Gong). Graham bought this album when it came out in 1973, "so suddenly I'm back into Jamaican music again. Everyone was still listening to the Eagles and Pink Floyd in the suburbs of England, and I was listening to reggae."

Van Morrison—*Astral Weeks, St. Dominic's Preview,* and *Hard Nose the Highway* (all Warner Bros.). After finally understanding *Astral Weeks,* Graham picked up on *Preview* and *Highway.* "They were much less ethereal than *Astral Weeks,* much more blues- and soul-oriented. . . . That set my course in a way."

Bob Dylan—*Blood on the Tracks* (Columbia). "I don't think anybody has made a record as good as that. Same with *Astral Weeks.* You know, we're all trying, but we ain't getting there, pal."

The Rolling Stones—*12 x 5* (ABKCO), *Got Live If You Want It* (ABKCO), *Out of Our Heads* (ABKCO), *Sticky Fingers* (Virgin), and *Exile on Main Street* (Virgin). Graham loved the Stones when they broke in the early '60s, abandoned them for awhile, and then came back to them: "After all that seventies psychedelic thing, I wanted to rock again."

Gladys Knight and the Pips—"The Way We Were," "Midnight Train to Georgia," and "Best Thing That Ever Happened to Me." Graham says that hearing the live version of "The Way We Were" "made my hair stand on end." ⊙: *Soul Survivor: The Best of . . .* (Rhino) contains all three songs listed above.

The Jackson Five—"Those hits by the Jackson Five, I was getting tapes of that and driving around and playing that stuff [in my mid-twenties]. Which really confused my friends, because they were still into Pink Floyd." ⊙: *The Ultimate Collection* (Motown) has all the major hits.

Steely Dan—*The Royal Scam* (MCA).

Eddie Cochran—Graham didn't buy the records, he just dug Cochran and Gene Vincent oldies on the radio in the early '70s. ⊙: *Legendary Masters* (EMI America) contains all the hits.

Gene Vincent— : *Capitol Collectors Series* (Capitol) includes the one major hit, "Be Bop a Lula," plus 20 other prime tracks.

The Happy Mondays—*Pills 'n' Thrills and Bellyaches* (Elektra). Graham hasn't been excited by much new music since about 1975. This 1990 album was an exception.

GRAHAM PARKER'S OWN RECORDINGS

"I'm proud of every song I've ever released," Graham says. "There's nothing that I've done that I've compromised in a way that sells my soul." But he does have favorite albums in his catalog, starting with the debut, *Howlin' Wind* (Mercury), which he points out is ironically sort of a career summary: "There's a song 'Between You and Me'—we're talking singer-songwriter stuff here. 'Gypsy Blood,' a mixture of Van Morrison and the singer-songwriter thing. 'White Honey' has the swing of Van Morrison and early soul music, and the horn sections. 'You Gotta Be Kidding' is Dylan. 'Soul Shoes' is the Stones, right? Those influences are all over that. Really, that kind of music powers me still." If he could change the vocal performances on *Wind*, though, he would in a breeze: "The singing I think is awful, but at least I meant it."

He perhaps feels most strongly about 1979's *Squeezing Out Sparks* (Arista) "which is really me, and that's it. . . . Nobody is that unique, but I really was writing my own stuff, and it was new." This album, one of rock's most prized, has been re-issued, packaged with a strong live set of the same material that was originally distributed as a promotional-only release. His other favorites— 1988's *The Mona Lisa's Sister* (RCA), 1991's *Struck by Lightning* (RCA), and 1995's *Twelve Haunted Episodes* (Razor & Tie)—come from the latter stages of his career, and particularly in the latter two cases, the instrumentation is primarily acoustic, not electric—to great effect, we'll add. He is especially proud of *Episodes*, on which the lower volume pushes some of the most intimate lyrics he's ever written to the foreground, where they belong.

: The restless attention spans of the public and mainstream rock press have forced Graham to labor in semi-obscurity for many years, a tragedy because he is still writing and performing some of the most bitingly effective material around. For evidence, check out "Obsessing with Aretha" and "Character Assassination" on *Acid Bubblegum* (Razor & Tie). In 1999, Razor & Tic released *Loose Monkeys*, a collection of "spare tracks and lost demos." As of this writing, it was only available through the 'Net at www.razorandtie.com.

ALEX PATERSON (February 17, 1998)

While Alex Paterson was attending boarding school in his native England, he experienced recorded music in a way that oddly predicted his musical future. The school was divided into seven houses, each with its own music room. "We had a certain hour or two allocated every night where we could go in and play music," he tells us. "And it was a real mishmash with different people playing music—Roxy Music in one house, Jethro Tull and Rush in another, Led Zeppelin and Pink Floyd in another house. Other groups like Tangerine Dream— all sorts of things. It was quite bizarre." Popular music today stands divided into at least as many "listening rooms" as that boarding school and Alex, as the creative force behind ambient innovators The Orb, helped build one of them.

After boarding school, Alex entered art school in Bromley at a time, 1976, when the reigning rock orthodoxies of Rush and Led Zeppelin were crumbling under the onslaught of punk. "I became a punk rocker, really, sort of following a trend," he says. "There was this Bromley contingent, a sort of group of eccentric punks that were following the [Sex] Pistols. Siouxise and the Banshees formed out of it and Generation X formed out of it as well. Some of them used to go to my art school and it was really quite bizarre . . . having clownlike figures walking around, avant-garde arty people who were so far ahead of what anyone else was thinking about then. Then [punk] sort of got eaten up by the media, and they made it accessible, sort of like fashion by 1979, unfortunately." The Orb's radiations may sound galaxies removed from the original punk but for Alex, the attitude is the message: "I'd like to think I've always been on that edge of music, as opposed to trying to make real popular anthems with The Orb."

Alex's ambient ascent began when a stint as a roadie for the band Killing Joke led to a gig doing A&R for Brian Eno's EG records, Killing Joke's label at the time. At EG, he came into contact with many of the pioneering lights of ambient music, including Eno, Cluster, and the prolific German producer Conrad Plank. Another artistic jolt came by mail from across the pond. "I heard abstract, really mad DJ sessions from New York," Alex recalls, "[and that] was really the way into dance music for me, listening to the dance mixes coming out of KISS-FM and 92KTU in New York. I had some friends in New York who were recording them and sending us these tapes. . . . I'd never heard two records being mixed together before. It was phenomenal."

Alex had already been conducting audio experiments in the Killing Joke days, and had even formed a band to record a bizarre sort of dub music, but to no productive end. The New York tapes inspired a trip to America where he spent a couple of weeks taping sets from radio stations, which he then sliced and diced into his 1989 EP release *The Kiss* (EP: WAU! Mr. Modo). Shortly thereafter, he joined with Jimi Cauty to create the sample-laden ambient house collages that ultimately formed the framework of The Orb.

"Jimi would come along with all these effects and I'd be DJing and we'd do these six hour or ten hour sessions at house clubs and chill everybody out. And then the word 'chill-out band' came out. It was quite bizarre. We were just turning out something experimental," he claims. Cauty left to join KLF after The Orb's debut 1989 recording *A Huge Ever-Growing Pulsating Brain that Rules from the Centre of the Ultraworld* (Big Life), beginning a long string of Orb personnel shifts with Alex the only constant.

Like the band's electro/ambient precursors Cluster and the Can, the Orb's success in Europe and the U.K. hasn't repeated itself in the United States. But Alex says he and his Orb-mates don't really care. What really matters to them is their commitment to keep experimenting. The group has already made its mark, helping to define a genre that has grown dominant in popular music. Alex admits, "we sort of coined a phrase and that's how we became popular in that sense. It was part of a cult thing more than a pop star thing. We never wanted to be pop stars."

ALEX PATERSON'S FAVORITE ARTISTS AND RECORDINGS

Joe Gibbs and Studio One—*African Dub, Chapter 3* (Lightning) and *Majestic Dub* (Laser). Alex fell in love with reggae during his boarding school days, and he says that "we should go and do some dub tracks because I don't think a lot of people are actually seeing the connection [in our music]." Many of his dub favorites come from rock steady star-turned-producer Joe Gibbs and his Studio One productions.

Prince Far I—This growling DJ offers a voice straight from the Howlin' Wolf–Mahlathini continuum. 🔘: The Prince rules on *Dubwise* or the compilation *Black Man Land* (both Plan 9/Caroline).

U Roy—U Roy is one of the pioneers of Jamaican DJ rap along with mixmaster partner King Tubby. 🔘: Check out *Dread in Babylon* (Frontline) and *Natty Rebel* (Plan 9/Caroline).

I Roy—I Roy is one of the great Jamaican toasters. 🔘: *Don't Check Me With No Lightweight Stuff* (1972–1975) (Blood & Fire), a compilation of I-Roy singles, features mixes by King Tubby.

Mikey Dread—Mikey Dread is a premiere toaster, known for his musically revolutionary radio and topical commentaries, particularly in the late '70s to early

'80s. : Mikey's edgy 1981 *Beyond World War 3* (Heartbeat) fused his toasting with a near-punk feel. His more recent *Obsession* (Rkyodisc) offers a softer, almost pop approach.

Cluster—Alex sings the praises of Moebius and Roedelius, who together comprise Cluster, and their work with Brian Eno and Conrad Plank. : Try *Begegnungen* (Sky), which was released not as a Cluster album but as Eno, Moebius, Rodelius, Plank, and the two Cluster and Eno collaborations, *Cluster & Eno* (Sky) and *Old Land* (Gyroscope), both co-produced by Plank.

Killing Joke—*Revelations* (EG). Conrad Plank produced this album during Alex's tenure as A&R man for EG records. "There's some stunning stuff on there," Alex says of this third Killing Joke release.

The Can—Along with Cluster, Alex names this seminal German electronic band as one of the Orb's artistic forebears. : A comprehensive collection from the band's long career has been released as *1968–1993: Anthology* (Mute [A.D.A.]).

Witchman—Alex had just been to see Witchman at a London club several days before our interview, and he insists Witchman "is going to be really, really, really big. . . . He's a really big drum and bass man. He has the most amazing sound, sort of industrial sounding as well. We had him on tour with The Orb in Britain, and he's phenomenal." : As of this writing, Witchman's two available CDs are *Explorimenting Beats* (Deviant) and *Heavy Traffic* (Deviant).

ALEX PATERSON'S OWN RECORDINGS

"I think some people when they do their fifth or sixth album either they're fully on or they're not there," Alex observes. "I've just gone past that point. I almost lost it with *Pomme Fritz* [Island] and *Orbvs Terrarvm* [Island], but *Orblivion* [Island], I think, put us back on the track. We've got our sound back again." Still, Alex strongly recommends The Orb's first album, *Adventures Beyond the Ultraworld* (Big Life), as the best introduction to the band. "It's a pretty timeless album. I mean, a lot of people said that to me at the time and it still continues to sell in dribs and drabs, by word of mouth, and it's doing really well." After that, he says, the best Orb album may depend on who you are: "I met a complete psychopath cab driver the other night, and he was a real fascist, and he loved Prodigy, and he was really into dance music. So I said 'I've got to give you something' so I gave him *Pomme Fritz*. I told him to park the car and ran in and gave him the CD."

: If you want to approximate the feel of a live Orb experience, look for the two-disc *Orb—Live 93* (Island). The 1992 album *U.F.Orb* (Big Life) hit number one on the UK charts. A collection of remixes of *Adventures Beyond the Ultra-world* has been released in the *Peel Sessions* series of BBC studio performances (DEI).

B I L L   P A Y N E   (April 4, 1997)

f you want to know all the ingredients in Little Feat's sonic gumbo, just hone in on a Bill Payne keyboard solo. If it goes long enough, he may cover every influence in the group's flavorful mix—blues, country, jazz, and New Orleans–flavored rock and R&B, one melding into another like a two-minute course in American roots music. "Yeah, it's a lot of fun," Bill laughs about his improvisation style when we reach him by phone in Los Angeles. "And in a sense it's a real curse—just trying to figure out where to land sometimes." Bill has never taken the easy way out with the songs he writes, either. His classical training, rock 'n' roll heart, and love of verbal tricksters like Lenny Bruce meet in tunes that make the usual pop three-chorder seem like a nursery rhyme.

Credit for this Mixmaster style of his, Bill says, begins with a rock-loving older sister and an open-minded piano teacher. Through sis, he discovered Elvis Presley and rock 'n' roll radio. Once he was wired in, he turned onto Little Rich-ard, the Olympics, and Fats Domino and started figuring out rock 'n' roll piano licks on his own. When he tried a couple on his classical piano teacher, she encouraged him to keep playing by ear, as long as he continued to learn how to read music.

Bill started playing in rock bands at about age 15 in Santa Maria, California, and eventually developed new fascinations with country and New Orleans music. The problem was how to put all these seemingly random parts together, but he began to sort that out after hearing the eccentric orchestrated pop of Van Dyke Parks and, especially, Frank Zappa's irreverent but virtuosic Mothers of Invention. "Zappa would stretch the boundaries of songs and the idiom to include jazz, classical, country, and humorous records that I grew up listening to," Bill says. "It was all in this one ball of wax, but in his own style, which was truly amazing."

Bill was so taken with the Mothers' *Uncle Meat* that he moved to Los Angeles to audition for the band, setting in motion the chain of events that would lead to his joining Little Feat. Although he failed the Mothers' tryout—"I didn't have the chops then," he admits—he met ex-Zappa cohort Lowell George, who was following Zappa's advice to start his own band. A magnetic figure—"the best singer, songwriter, and guitar player I have ever heard, hands down," George acolyte Bonnie Raitt once called him—George showed Bill the roots of much of the music he enjoyed including the Southern folk roots of the music he was planning for Little Feat.

Little Feat went on to create such a persuasive blend of American roots styles that countless bands now play in the Feat mold. Others—Bonnie Raitt, Travis Tritt, John Cale, and Robert Palmer among them—have just hired the whole band to play behind them and Bill in particular has been one of the most in-demand session keyboardists for decades. "It blows me away," Bill says, "because whether we've gotten recognition or not in the sense of awards or massive record sales or anything else, I know what this band has done and meant to other players."

BILL PAYNE'S FAVORITE ARTISTS AND RECORDINGS

Elvis Presley— ●: The excellent hits packages *Elvis' Golden Records, Vol. 1–2* (RCA, available separately) cover the period when Bill was digging Elvis on the radio.

Little Richard—"I think our records like 'Let It Roll' [on *Let It Roll* (Warner Bros.)], 'Oh, Atlanta' [on *Feats Don't Fail Me Now* (Warner Bros.)]—that type of stuff, that's the nerve we're trying to hit." ●: See Master List.

The Olympics—"Big Boy Pete." "That kind of style is almost a New Orleans–type of thing in a way, particularly with the piano, the way it bounces from the one to the five chord." ●: *The Olympics Meet the Marathons* (Collectibles).

Fats Domino—Domino's music helped introduce Bill to New Orleans R&B. The hard core Crescent City material with the city's premiere session players, before Domino crossed over to the pop charts, was done for Imperial Records in the 1950s. ●: *They Call Me the Fat Man . . . : The Legendary Imperial Recordings* (EMI America) is a four-CD set. The single-disc alternative, *My Blue Heaven: Best of Fats Domino* (EMI America), includes only two of the pre-crossover tracks.

Professor Longhair—"When I met him, I said, 'You know what? I've sort of inadvertently lifted every lick you've ever played, but through other artists.' And I mentioned Fats Domino and Dr. John, and folks like that." ●: See Master List.

*Dr. John— ●: See the section on Dr. John and his recordings.

Frank Zappa and the Mothers of Invention—*Uncle Meat* (Rykodisc). This instrumental album, cut as the soundtrack for a movie that was never completed, includes Zappa's noteworthy composition "King Kong." : Other great albums from the "Meat" period in the mid-late 1960s include *Freak Out*, which introduces the Mothers' blend of irreverent theater and brilliant avant rock and jazz; *Absolutely Free*, which continues the satiric assault on dumb rock lyrics and all conventions, both hip and straight, and lets the talented band father out of the bag; and *We're Only In It for the Money* (all Rykodisc), widely considered the Mothers' masterwork. Under Zappa's name, don't-miss records from this era include *Lumpy Gravy* (Verve), whose basic elements were a 50-piece orchestra and Zappa's John Cage-ish tape experiments; *Hot Rats*, a mostly instrumental album with both jazz-rock workouts and neo-classical compositions such as the tasty "Peaches En Regalia"; *Weasels Ripped My Flesh*, a mix of studio and live tracks that showcases the instrumental talents of Zappa's group; and *Burnt Weenie Sandwich* (all Rykodisc).

Various artists—*Sounds of the South* (4 CDs: Atlantic). Lowell George introduced Bill to this seminal collection of Southern folk music field recordings made by Alan Lomax in 1959.

Lenny Bruce—*The Berkeley Concert* (Rhino). "There's a lot of humor running throughout Little Feat and there's very little compromise in what we do. Certainly people like Lenny Bruce are a part of that type of edge that our band has in a lyrical sense."

Charles Mingus—"Goodbye Porkpie Hat." "The tempo thing that folks like he and Ray Charles get into is so slow you just think 'How the hell could anybody play like that?' I mean, they are on another planet when it comes to tempo." : The best-known version of this tune is on the classic album *Mingus Ah Um* (Columbia).

Leon Russell—*Leon Russell* (Capitol). "I liked the way the guy sang. I liked the music. I loved the players on it, 'cause a lot of those players were the same people who worked with Joe Cocker, as did he," says Bill about Russell's 1970 debut.

*The Band—*Music from Big Pink* (Capitol). Bill especially loves the poetic sweep, narrative power, and deep sense of rural American heritage in the songwriting, and also "Garth Hudson playing the organ unlike anything I'd ever heard in my life."

Bob Dylan—"Subterranean Homesick Blues" on *Bringing It All Back Home* (Columbia). Bill says "the freedom and style" of this track, including the sound of the "raging organ," was a direct influence on such Little Feat songs as "Oh, Atlanta" and "Shake Me Up."

Miles Davis—*Bitches Brew* (Columbia). Jazz-rock fusion's rock beat but sophisticated chops attracted Little Feat in a big way. The group put its own distinctive stamp on the music on such tracks as "Day at the Dog Races" (on *Time Loves a Hero* [Warner Bros.]). Bill says this is the album that set them off in that direction.

Joe Zawinul with Julian "Cannonball" Adderly—*Preacher Man* (Blue Note). "That is just some soulful, soulful stuff."

Weather Report—"Birdland" on *Heavy Weather* (Columbia). Bill sides with the masses in naming his favorite tune by this innovative fusion group, spawned by Miles Davis's *Bitches Brew*–era bands and another major influence on Little Feat's own fusion efforts.

Randy Newman—*Randy Newman* (Reprise). "There are so many [great] songs on that. But the one that just tore me up and still does is 'I Think It's Gonna Rain Today,' from the lyrical standpoint, and the way he plays, which is just beautiful."

Van Dyke Parks—*Song Cycle* (Warner Bros.). Bill especially loves the song "Palm Beach" on this storied disc, the composer/arranger's 1968 solo debut. Bill says Parks's music also helps him counter his own tendency to crowd too many notes in musical space: "He just has such an unusual way of orchestrating things. . . . Just his sense of humor when it comes to writing songs is ten feet over my head."

Steely Dan—*Gaucho* (MCA). This group's Donald Fagen and Walter Becker are two of Bill's favorite songwriters. The title song and especially "Babylon Sisters" on this 1980 record amazed Bill, and as a whole the album was "encouragement, because I already was into that kind of thing."

Charles Ives—*Three Places in New England.* "My way of thinking about composing and writing is born out of listening to Charles Ives," Bill says. About this piece, he adds, " I love movies and I love cinematic music and music that creates a mood. And I listened to his music watching a snowstorm once in New England, and it just captured everything about the beauty of the way the snow falls and the way the wind catches it and swirls it back up, and it falls down silently." ⬤: See Master List.

Johannes Brahms—Piano Concerto No. 2 in B Flat, Opus. 83, John Lill, piano; BBC National Orchestra of Wales/Tadaaki Otaka (Nimbus).

Bela Bartok—Concerto for Orchestra. ". . . wonderful in my mind because of the orchestral properties in it, with the specific use of the woodwinds. And also the [way] that he and Stravinsky and others like him would [use] folk music. I guess when you really sum up what most of us do in popular music, or not-so-popular music, is we are dealing with folk music." ⬤: See Master List.

Maurice Ravel—Concerto for Left Hand: Alicia de Larrocha, piano; St. Louis Symphony/Leonard Slatkin (RCA). "I think she's absolutely brilliant."

Glenn Gould—*Images* (2 CDs: Sony). Bill has been listening to recordings by this reclusive pianist, who helped to popularize Bach, since he was a child. This set samples Gould's brilliant recording career for Columbia and Masterworks.

Aaron Copland—Billy the Kid Suite, New York Philharmonic/Leonard Bernstein (Sony Classical) [Four Dance Episodes from *Rodeo*, with *Billy the Kid* Suite].

Conway Twitty— . . . *Sings* (Decca). Bill especially likes the song "Honky Tonk Man" on this disc.

George Jones—Bill was turned on to country music when he was in high school by his girlfriend's Uncle Billy: "I think it was in seventy-two or seventy-three, Bonnie Raitt came over to the house and she said 'Who're you listening to?' and I said 'Oh, some George Jones,' and she goes 'Who's that?' 'You don't know George Jones?' I go, 'Get in here.' I felt rather honored to at least have introduced her to that music." ⬤: See Master List.

Porter Wagoner and Dolly Parton—"The Dark End of the Street" on *Just the Two of Us* (RCA). ⬤: *The Essential Porter Wagoner and Dolly Parton* (RCA) compiles all of the duo's hits plus more on a single disc.

BILL PAYNE'S OWN RECORDINGS

Little Feat disbanded in 1979 and Lowell George died a few months later from a heart attack while pursuing a solo career; even before this time, George's presence in the band had diminished, with Bill's and *Paul Barrere's writing coming to the fore. The band reunited in 1988. Bill's favorite Little Feat albums honor both the pre- and post-reunion periods, starting with the two live records, 1979's *Waiting for Columbus* (Warner Bros.) and 1996's *Live from Neon Park* (Zoo). The former features a classically kaleidoscopic Payne keyboard break on "Dixie Chicken," which Bill is thrilled was captured on disc: "I thought that was a pretty wild solo and it kind of showed [better than I can describe] my stream of consciousness when I play, just how quickly I'll move in and out of idioms, and then how they all seem to flow into one another. That's a real trick—it's like a card trick, one that's taken me a long time to feel comfortable with and also to be able to sit back and listen to it and really be able to feel good about."

Bill also looks proudly on his song "Gringo," a sophisticated Payne masterpiece that appears only on *Hoy, Hoy* (Warner Bros.), a compilation of unreleased tracks that yields an intimate view of the band's creative process. Bill co-produced the two-record set, which includes a version of "Rocket in My

Pocket" with just Lowell George and an acoustic guitar: "I did it to show the purity of Lowell without the band . . . This beauty that the guy had as a writer, and the simple soulfulness that he possessed in music that was quite extraordinary in terms of his phrasing." Bill also co-produced *Let It Roll* (Warner Bros.) and likes how that turned out, too—"as an album I think it's really, really solid."

⦿: Little Feat's eponymous 1971 debut could have been titled *Roots and Quirks*—both are on display in abundance on a record that subverts traditional pop structures with a vengeance. George and Payne wrote most of the album's strong, Beat-ish songs either separately or in collaboration. The 1972 classic *Sailin' Shoes* is hardly conventional but most of its melodies and rhythms are more straight-ahead, with a strong echo in places of the Rolling Stones. Paul Barrere joins the band along with bassist Ken Gradney and percussionist Sam Clayton for 1973's triumphant *Dixie Chicken*. Like an engine after a tune-up, the band's rhythms grow slicker and funkier and Barrere adds yet another strong songwriting voice to George's and Payne's, making the band's lineup as talent-laden, and its sonic signature as distinctive, as any in rock. The 1974 album *Feats Don't Fail Me Now* is another winner, introducing several of the best-formed songs in the group's catalog. By the time of 1975's *The Last Record Album*, the dissipated George is fading from view as a songwriter, but Payne and Barrere come to the rescue. George's odd production touches yield a twisted, disorienting ambiance that recalls the group's debut. *Time Loves a Hero*, from 1977, anticipates in many ways the denser, fusion-influenced sound of the reunited group 11 years later. When the band reformed, Pure Prairie League founder Craig Russell was hired to fill George's songwriting and vocal shoes. His considerable but mainstream skills took away from the band's edge, in the opinion of many fans. However, the songs by Payne and Barrere on records from this period (*Let It Roll*, *Representing the Mambo*, and *Shake It Up*) not only were in the classic Little Feat vein but showed continued growth from an already lofty level. Brassy, bluesy Shaun Murphy replaced Russell starting with 1995's *Ain't Had Enough Fun* (Zoo) and the band started sounding like its old rambunctious self again. The 1998 release *Under the Radar* (CMC) adds a few new sonic touches but otherwise stays the course. The gang ain't getting any younger, but you'd never know it from the turbo-charged grooves. Finally, fans of the band's instrumental abilities should track down Chico Hamilton's 1973 album, *The Master* (Stax [UK]), on which the jazz drummer is joined by Little Feat members Payne, Barrere, George, Gradney, and Clayton for a soul-jazz workout.

LOUIE PEREZ (March 21, 1997)

The tunes that Louie Perez, Los Lobos' drummer and primary lyricist, brews for his band started percolating, appropriately enough, in the kitchen of the East Los Angeles home where he grew up. His mother, who had sung in her own groups when growing up, played music around the house almost every waking hour. "From a very young age, the morning would be waking up to Mexican radio and the smell of coffee," remembers Louie. On the family's big, brown Admiral record player, she would spin *rancheras* and other Mexican folkloric songs.

Louie's mother would also haul the kids down to Mexican variety shows at the Million Dollar theater in Los Angeles. His favorite part of the performance came when the main attraction, a Mexican star vocalist, would enter the stage in a flashy embroidered outfit on silver-bedecked horses in front of a large *mariachi* band. Microphone in hand, he would begin to sing. "As a little kid, I'm thinking, man this is incredible!" Louie remembers.

One of the biggest of those stars was Miguel Aceves Mejia. When he appeared, Mom—who also played his records at home—dragged the kids backstage with her to get his autograph. Mejia's music would later profoundly influence Los Lobos, who first formed in 1973 as an acoustic outfit playing mostly Mexican folkloric music. The Lobos prepared by studying their families' record collections, and Mejia's music was a key, Louie says.

But a dramatically different cultural heritage was also finding its way to Perez's ears then via the streets and airwaves. "By the time I got tall enough to start flipping that radio knob, I discovered I actually had a choice and started discovering a lot of stuff—Ray Charles, a lot of R & B and other stuff going on in the early sixties," Louie says. By his mid-teens, he was deep into Motown sounds: "All that stuff was really big in East L.A. The East L.A. sound was really R & B distilled through the Mexican-American sensibility."

In 1972, shortly before Los Lobos first got together, Perez began hanging out with *David Hidalgo, a multi-instrumental wizard, to listen to music and write songs. Ears wide open, they took in everything from early English folk rock to classical and avant-garde iconoclasts like Charles Ives, Harry Partch, and John Cage to seminal performers in the regional styles of old Mexico. The result, eventually, was a group that although often typecast as a *Mexican*-American rock band, is probably the most comprehensively American band extant. Cultures may clash on the streets and in the legislatures, but in Los Lobos' music, roots rock, *norteño, rancheras* (Mexican country music), American country, R&B, cajun, and Anglo folk music live together in exquisitely balanced harmony.

Louie doesn't listen to new music with the same veracity any more: "When a record came out [when I was growing up], it was a big event. Now when you go to a record store, it's floor-to-ceiling new releases . . . There's too much for me to want or even have time to digest. So I kind of pick up on stuff almost by osmosis. Dave will turn me on to something new, or if we're on the road, Steve Berlin will throw on something that I'll listen to. That's how I maintain 'the big event'—when I hear something that really jumps out at me."

LOUIE PEREZ'S FAVORITE ARTISTS AND RECORDINGS

Ruben Fuentes/Miguel Aceves Mejia—15 Los Huapangos de Oro (BMG/US Latin). Huapango is a traditional Mexican folk style and Fuentes is a classical composer interested in pre-Columbian music. For this record, Fuentes arranged and adapted old folk songs and Miguel Aceves Mejia sang them. "He combined mariachi with orchestra, Vera Cruz harp with classical harp. It's the most amazing thing you'd want to hear," Louie gushes.

Ray Charles—The first non-Mexican record Louie saw played on a turntable was Charles's "Hit the Road Jack": "My older sister had a cousin come over with her little burgundy and gray-speckled record player, put this record on, and I'm watching this thing go around and I thought it was the craziest, wildest thing I'd heard in my life." 🔴: See Master List.

Smoky Robinson and Miracles—"The emotional thing was incredible. I'd always play both sides of the record because there was always a really cool thing off the album on the B side." 🔴: Anthology (2 CDs: Motown).

The Four Tops—Another of Louie's Motown faves. 🔴: See Master List.

Thee Midniters—As the first successful band out of East L.A., this outfit made a big impression on all the guys who later formed Los Lobos. "They opened for the Beatles at the Hollywood Bowl," recalls Louie. "They brought Beatlemania very close to home. Those guys would get chased down the street just like the Beatles in 'Hard Day's Night.' " 🔴: See Master List.

Stevie Wonder—Music of My Mind (Motown). After winning creative control in a new contract with Motown, Wonder produced this visionary work, his first break from the Motown formula in which an album was just a collection of hits and B-sides. This was one of the primary albums Perez and Hidalgo listened to together.

Randy Newman—Sail Away (Reprise). "That really brought into focus how song-writing was done. Early on, we were just listening to musicianship—guitar players because we played guitar. But the songwriting connection really came from people like Randy Newman, Joni Mitchell, Bob Dylan."

Joni Mitchell—*Blue* (Reprise). "I always found great songs on all her records, but *Blue* is the one that from beginning to end, there isn't one miss for me as a songwriter."

Bob Dylan—Louie loves all Dylan's classic songs. ●: . . . *Greatest Hits, Vols. 1–3* (Columbia, available separately) are all excellent compilations, but the most essential classics are on Vol. 1.

Merle Haggard—Haggard is one of the prime sources of the country thread in Los Lobos' sound, says Louie. ●: See Master List.

George Jones—With Haggard, Jones is the other main country influence on Los Lobos. ●: See Master List.

Fairport Convention—*Full House* (Hannibal). "At one point we put away the electric instruments and devoted ourselves to acoustic folkloric music of our culture. Fairport Convention was the bridge for us because they took traditional English folk music and adapted it and interpreted it in a modern way with electric guitars."

Incredible String Band—"The arrangements, the soundscapes of different instrumentation and songs worked in—it was stretching what Fairport Convention did. Probably everything they did we just devoured." ●: See Master List.

Laura Nyro—*Eli and the Thirteenth Confession* (Columbia). "Just an incredible record—again, the songwriting is the part that really connected with me."

Ry Cooder—*Boomer's Story* (Reprise). Louie especially likes the rendition of "Dark End of the Street." "Dave turned me on to Ry Cooder," says Louie. "His musicianship and songwriting sensibility were really impressive."

Leo Kottke—*6- and 12-String Guitar* (Takoma). This all-instrumental album made Kottke a star.

Jimi Hendrix—*Are You Experienced* (Reprise), *Axis Bold as Love* (Reprise), and *Electric Ladyland* (Reprise). Louie went to see Hendrix when he played the Hollywood Bowl on his *Axis Bold as Love* tour: "I was like fourteen or fifteen, sitting down in that audience. He came out and went right into 'Spanish Castle Magic' and I was never the same after that. It changed me completely inside and out."

Marvin Gaye—*What's Going On* (Motown). Prior to Los Lobos recording *Kiko*, Perez and David Hidalgo sat down with Lenny Waronker, the president of Warner Brothers records, to discuss album ideas, Louie remembers: "I said, 'I want to do a *What's Going On*. That record will stay with me forever because it's so powerful.'"

John Coltrane—*Ballads* (Impulse). Listening to Coltrane and Roland Kirk first inspired Perez and Hidalgo to try the odd harmonies and other musical experiments that began showing up on Los Lobos albums starting with *The Neighborhood* and in their Latin Playboys side project: "I've always loved Coltrane for his experimentation but the guy can play the shit out of ballads. The economy of notes and the phrasing is beautiful."

Rahsaan Roland Kirk—*The Inflated Tear* (Atlantic). "Still one of my Desert Island favorites."

Cornershop—*When I Was Born for the Seventh Time* (Luaka Bop/Warner Bros.) We asked Louie which newer albums had impressed him and this was the first one he mentioned. "Sitar, guitar, drums, and tabla—a whole convolution of musical and cultural sensibilities."

Medeski, Martin, and Wood—Los Lobos selected this psychedelic jazz-rock-funk trio to open for them on one of their tours. "I couldn't believe what these young guys were doing," says Louie. "They sound like they have these old souls." : *Notes from the Underground* (Accurate), from 1991, finds MMW as an acoustic jazz trio but with hip-hop in its pocket. *It's A Jungle In Here* (Gramavision), is an impressive, forward-looking jazz record, although still not signature MMW because of the horns and guitar augmenting the trio. *Shack Man* (Gramavision) establishes the band's current identity as a spacey, funky, jam-bandish organ trio. *Combustication* (Blue Note) adds some turntable scratching but is otherwise in the current vein.

Ornette Coleman—*Dancing in Your Head* (A&M). Coleman is another important influence on Los Lobos' experimentalism. The band members met Coleman after going to see him and have maintained an ongoing conversation about music.

Harry Partch—Perez and Hidalgo listened to this avante-garde composer, who made many of his own instruments, back in the 1970s. : See Master List.

John Cage—*Interdeterminancy* (Smithsonian/Folkways). This disc features Cage telling stories, many from his own life, over experimental piano and electronic music.

Erik Satie—*Satie: L'Oeuvre pour piano, vol. 1–3; Angel Cicollini, piano* (EMI).

Maurice Ravel—Boléro. Berlin Philharmonic/Herbert von Karajan (Deutsche Grammaphon).

Charles Ives—*Three Places in New England.* This composition, also known as First Orchestral Set, vividly illustrates Ives's remarkable ability to paint pictures with sound. "Early on, this was the stuff that told me that there was more to music than a major or minor scale," Louie says. "Atonality, dissonance—something really resonated in my bones about that." ⬤: See Master List.

Charles Ives—Songs. Louie recommends a recording featuring vocalist Cleo Laine and her husband, pianist/arranger John Dankworth (RCA), which also includes Arnold Schoenberg's *Pierrot Lunaire*: "When I first got introduced to them, they were on Johnny Carson all the time. But not until that record came out was I able to appreciate what she does."

The Germs—*GI* (Slash). During the time when Los Lobos was making the transition from playing Mexican music to rock 'n' roll, "it was the punk thing that drove us back to the clubs," Louie say. "Something very exciting was going on over there and that hadn't happened [in a while]." The Germs were labelmates of Los Lobos on Slash records.

Social Distortion—*White Light White Heat White Trash* (Sony). Louie loves the songwriting on this newer album by a seminal L.A. punk band.

Circle Jerks—"Their early records impressed the heck out of me." ⬤: *Group Sex* (Epitaph), *Wild in the Streets* (Epitaph), and *Golden Shower of Hits* (Rhino).

Gears—*Rockin' at Ground Zero* (Iloki). This L.A. punk band included some Latino members, Louie notes.

The Blasters—*American Music* (Hightone). A crucial band for Los Lobos, both musically and otherwise, the Blasters' blend of punk energy, accomplished musicianship, and rootsy revivalism helped give the Lobos confidence in their own musical instincts. The Blasters ultimately befriended the Lobos and, appreciating their talent, invited them to open for them one night during a high-visibility, five-night run at the Los Angeles club The Whiskey. That gig created a buzz about Los Lobos, leading to more desirable gigs, a record deal with Slash, and commercial success that eventually eclipsed the Blasters' own. The Hightone reissue of the original *American Music* on Rollin' Rock Records includes six previously unissued tracks.

The Last Poets—*The Last Poets* (Metrotone). This trio, formed in 1969, rapped before there was rap. Their aggressive social and political consciousness landed them simultaneously in the music industry's Top 10 and on Richard Nixon's COINTELPRO list.

Jack Kerouac—*The Jack Kerouac Collection* (Rhino). This set includes three albums released during the Beat icon's lifetime plus unreleased recordings. "What's really cool about that is it's the real shit," Louie says. "The stuff that Kerouac did with [jazz saxophonist] Zoot Sims. And of all people, when he got together with Steve Allen doing that stuff. The image I get in my head is Steve Allen and

Kerouac sharing a bottle of cheap wine in a paper sack in the studio, making this record."

Allen Ginsberg—Louie appreciates how Ginsberg brought poetry down from its elevated literary standing to a grassroots level. : *Holy Soul Jelly Roll—Poems and Songs (1949–1993)* (Rhino), a four-CD set that includes Ginsberg's first complete reading of "Howl" and musical collaborations with Bob Dylan, Elvin Jones, Bill Frisell, the Clash, and others.

Tom Waits—*Swordfishtrombones* and *Frank's Wild Years* (both Island). Not hard to find the parallels between these records and the Lobos' own dissonant song treatments.

LOUIE PEREZ'S OWN RECORDINGS

For many fans and critics, *Kiko* is the ultimate Los Lobos album and Louie seems to agree: "*Kiko* was the record I had been wanting to make forever. Not by design. You get to a point that's a crossroads, you know [you've got to go somewhere new]. Without even thinking, you're led down a certain path and that path led us to *Kiko*." *Latin Playboys* was another step along that path, Louie adds: "It was really kind of going back to stuff we were tuning into in the early seventies when we were just going over to Dave's house and listening to music, and writing songs, and coming up with different ideas and concepts." Louie describes it as a Zen-sensibility, "first-thought, best-thought" effort. "I'm really proud of that record."

How Will the Wolf Survive? is another personal favorite: "There are songs like 'A Matter of Time' and 'How Will the Wolf Survive?' that will always be very special." And like David Hidalgo, he stresses the importance of *La Pistola y El Corazon* for the band: "We had reached that point in our careers where we could either sell Doritos for the rest of our lives or take this focus and attention and do something responsible with it, and that's why we did *La Pistola* . . . It was our opportunity to . . . redirect that limelight to music that was really important to us, to expose folkloric Mexican music, and also to lay it to rest to a certain extent. We're not trying to change the world here. We're a band. The myths and stereotypes people have about Mexican music—yeh, you go to El Torito and listen to the *mariachi* band. But there's so much more to it than that . . . We took that record and put examples on it of all the different folkloric styles coming out of Mexico."

Louie says the band took a similar approach with their children's album, *Papa's Dream* (Music for Little People). "It's essentially *La Pistola* for kids . . .

Children are so pure. They don't see color or gender. Life gets more complicated as you get older. And I think it's important to let kids know at a young age, and in our case through music, that this is something we can use to bring people together."

: A second Latin Playboys album, *Dose* (Atlantic), highly experimental like the first, came out in 1999 to excellent reviews. Also see David Hidalgo.

WILSON PICKETT (December 14, 1998)

When he dubbed himself "the Wicked Pickett" in the 1960s, Wilson Pickett seemed to be advertising himself as King of the Night. But talking to Wilson today puts a more confessional slant on the matter. Born in Prattville, Alabama, and raised there and Detroit, Wilson started singing in church when he was a child. He was still a teenager when gospel stars like Sam Cooke were moving over to secular pop with spectacular success. It was a temptation that Wilson couldn't resist, either, but "you have to understand that we was told that if we started singing this kind of stuff, it was the Devil's stuff," he notes.

Even after Wilson began making his own waves in the pop world, first with proto-soul group the Falcons (he was the lead singer on the 1962 hit "I Found a Love," a song he wrote) and later as one of the true titans of Memphis soul, he listened mainly to gospel music. "My collection of gospel albums was huge," Wilson remembers. "I had just about everybody."

Wilson came to personify deep soul music in the mid-1960s along with James Brown and Wilson's labelmates on Atlantic Records, Otis Redding and Aretha Franklin. And the word "soul" seemed a perfect fit, because when any of the four sang, they seemed to tap resources not accessible in the ordinary physical world. At the time, many treated '60s soul as a whole new thing but stars like Wilson knew from whence it came. "Listen now to Patti LaBelle, you know what I mean? You can tell that gospel stuff had a great influence," Wilson points out. "Aretha Franklin, now everything she sings sounds like she's singin' in the church."

In Wilson's case, though, he wasn't just bringing his heaven-raising style over from the sanctuary. He was also beseeching the heavens, literally. Wilson expanded the soul music genre by writing or co-writing outstanding original tunes such as "In the Midnight Hour," "Don't Fight It," "Mustang Sally," "She's

Looking Good," and "I'm a Midnight Mover." But he also made it a habit to include a gospel number on some of his albums. "It seems like it was luck for us sometimes, just to put a gospel [tune] in there, you know?" Wilson says.

At the time we spoke, Wilson had just finished a pop album, but he hasn't stopped thinking about returning to his first, and still biggest, musical love. "If it's push come to shove, I can go and make a gospel CD tomorrow," Wilson asserts. And a whole bunch of Wicked Pickett fans would rush to nab it as soon as it hit the retail racks.

WILSON PICKETT'S FAVORITE ARTISTS AND RECORDINGS

The Five Blind Boys of Alabama—Formed in 1937 at the Talladega Institute for the Deaf and Blind, the Blind Boys became one of gospel's most popular acts during the music's Golden Age in the '50s. As of this writing, they are still touring, led as they were then by potent shouter Clarence Fountain. ⬤: *The Sermon* (Specialty) contains 27 prime Golden Age sides. *Oh Lord Stand by Me/Marching Up to Zion* (Specialty) is an outstanding twofer from the same period.

Inez Andrews—Andrews possessed one of gospel's most powerful voices, and started with the Caravans in the late '50s. ⬤: 1972's *Lord Don't Move the Mountain* (MCA) is an excellent crossover gospel effort. The 1988 release *If Jesus Came to Your Town Today* (Miracle) and 1991's *Raise Up a Nation* (Word) are more traditional religious records; the former includes a churchy version of Curtis Mayfield's "People Get Ready." Also check out *Two Sides of Inez Andrews* (Shanachie).

Sam Cooke—"When Sam Cooke left the gospel and went to singin' pop, his first single was 'You Send Me' and I thought that was the most beautiful song I'd ever heard in my life. And I said 'Ohhhhhh-oh. I gotta get me some of this.' " ⬤: See Master List.

Nina Simone—"I love the way she sings, the way she conducts her piano, and everything the way she do it." ⬤: *Folksy Nina* (Collectables) includes one of Wilson's favorite performances, "Chain Gang." For an overall introduction to this unique performer, try *In Concert/I Put a Spell on You* (Mercury), which combines two albums from the '60s on a CD reissue. *In Concert* in particular captures the essence of her styles, which combines jazz, blues, gospel, and soul with Broadway dramatics.

Joe Cocker—"Joe could sing anything and it was all right with me. And I used to love to hear him sing 'With a Little Help From My Friends'—he leans back and seems like he's straining every vessel in his body. Man, he delivers a ballad!"

⦿: The great individual albums are his star-making 1969 debut, *With a Little Help from My Friends*, 1969's follow-up *Joe Cocker!*, and 1970's live *Mad Dogs and Englishman* (all A&M). The best-known hits are on *Classics, Vol. 4* (A&M). Outstanding tracks from his Capitol career are compiled on *The Best of . . .* (Capitol). The most comprehensive compilation is *Long Voyage Home: The Silver Anniversary Collection* (4 CDs: A&M).

The O'Jays—"You can put any song in there, any song that the O'Jays did and that would be my favorite." ⦿: *Back Stabbers* and *Skip Ahoy* (both Philadelphia International) are the top single albums and better bets than the haphazard compilations as of this writing.

Aretha Franklin—Like nearly every Aretha fan, Wilson feels Franklin's greatest work came after she moved over to Atlantic Records from Columbia and began recording in the Muscle Shoals studios where Wilson was also recording his biggest hits. ⦿: See Master List.

The Temptations—"They was a unique, unique, unique group. I remember in Detroit, Michigan, we used to sing in the alleys." ⦿: As with most singles-oriented soul groups, compilations are the way to go. *The Ultimate Collection* (Motown) is an outstanding, single-disc introduction. *Anthology* (2 CDs: Motown) includes all the major hits plus other well-selected singles and album tracks.

The Stylistics—⦿: See Master List.

The Five Blind Boys of Mississippi—⦿: See Master List.

The Swan Silvertones—⦿: See Master List.

The Dixie Hummingbirds—⦿: See Master List.

The Pilgrim Travelers—⦿: See Master List.

Albertina Walker and the Caravans—⦿: See Master List.

The Meditation Singers—The foremost female gospel group in Detroit when Wilson was there, the Meditation Singers launched the career of Della Reese. ⦿: *Good News* (Specialty).

The Davis Sisters—⦿: See Master List.

WILSON PICKETT'S OWN RECORDINGS

"My whole thing is I like to deliver ballads," Wilson says about his own catalog. "I like tunes like 'I'm in Love,' 'I Found a love.' Of course I have to like songs like 'Mustang Sally' and 'In the Midnight Hour.' I have a lot of fun doin' 'Land of a Thousand Dances.' But if you would really boil it down to basics, the way I can deliver my ballads pleases me very much.''

Wilson is quite pleased with the two compilations of his classic Atlantic recordings now available on Rhino, the single disc *Greatest Hits* and the more comprehensive *A Man and a Half: The Best of . . . .* Both include all the songs just mentioned, including ''I Found a Love,'' the song that started it all.

: To hear Wilson as he was first heard in the 1960s, check out the original albums still available, including *In the Midnight Hour, The Exciting . . . , I'm in Love* (with songwriting and instrumental input from Bobby Womack), and *In Philadelphia* (all Atlantic). Well worth the search are the deleted *The Wicked Pickett* and *The Sound of . . . ,* both classics.

DR. BERNICE JOHNSON REAGON (September 5, 1998)

n the ironic world of American politics, you don't often find the same people fighting for civil rights and extolling their spiritual path. One notable exception: African Americans' struggle for freedom, led and nurtured by black churches. That explains the multiple passions fueling the music of Sweet Honey in the Rock, the African-American female vocal ensemble founded by Dr. Bernice Johnson Reagon. The music itself betrays its primary roots—Reagon's experiences with twentieth century gospel music and the civil rights movement of the 1960s, as well as her love of R&B and nineteenth century African-American congregational spirituals and hymns.

Reagon got an elite education in recorded gospel via the radio in her home in Albany, Georgia. There she discovered the soulful harmonies of the Five Blind Boys of Mississippi, Dorothy Love Coates, and the Gospel Harmonettes, the Caravans, and the group that would ultimately be an important model for Sweet Honey, the Roberta Martin Singers. At age 11, Reagon joined the gospel choir, newly formed by her sister, at her family's Baptist church.

The airwaves also introduced Reagon to another form of African-American traditional music that would color Sweet Honey's sound—the blues. Late at night during her high school years, her brother would take the family radio into his room to catch a blues show, which she would overhear from her bed. ''We were supposed to be asleep,'' she remembers, ''[but] there was no other blues—old blues—on the radio except between midnight and day. . . . Straight through high school and college, I got a very strong acclimation to blues, and I knew the names and sounds of Screamin' Jay Hawkins, Lightnin' Hopkins, T-Bone Walker, B. B. King, Howlin' Wolf, Muddy Waters. I heard all of that music, but basically in my sleep."

It was during the same time that Reagon also first heard the *Staple Singers, then mainly a gospel group. The Staples would later set the standard for combining gospel, blues, and civil rights statements, along with R&B, rock, and folk. "*Mavis Staples and I are around the same age," Reagon notes "But she actually was the first young woman I heard sing bass. She was the low voice in the harmony for the Staple Singers, and her father [*Pop Staples] was the tenor."

When Reagon entered college in the early 1960s, she became active in the civil rights movement and was a founding member of the Student Non-Violent Coordinating Committee Freedom Singers. Through their music, the Freedom Singers spread the news about grassroots organizing in the South to communities nationwide. Reagon drew strength both as an activist and singer during that time from two fiercely independent African-American performers: Odetta and Nina Simone. "A lot of us would talk about being able to survive what we had to go through because we would play Odetta and Nina Simone records," Reagon recalls. "Just very, very important musicians."

Reagon, a Distinguished Professor at American University in Washington, D.C., and curator emerita of the Smithsonian Institution, would later add music straight from Mother Africa to Sweet Honey's blend. But she's also quick to credit her four companions in Sweet Honey—Aisha Kahlil, Ysaye Maria Barnwell, Nitanju Bolande Casel, and Carol Maillard—for their contributions to the group's a cappella-plus-percussion sound. "Sweet Honey in the Rock's repertoire is expanded by the different women," Reagon points out. "All of us are composers and arrangers, and all of us come in as masters of different genres. . . . So one of the things you get with me and Sweet Honey is a fascination that I have with other composers in Sweet Honey."

DR. BERNICE JOHNSON REAGON'S FAVORITE ARTISTS AND RECORDINGS

The Five Blind Boys of Mississippi—"Our Father," *The Best of . . .* (MCA), "Will My Jesus Be Waiting," and "I Wonder Do You," the latter on *My Desire/There's a God Somewhere* (Mobile Fidelity). "I think one of the earliest voices I loved as a child was Archie Brownlee, who was the leader of the Five Blind Boys from Jackson, Mississippi," Bernice recalls. "I could also sing in his key. He's a tenor, but a very high tenor, and that was very special. That's elementary school for me." The latter release combines two albums from the Peacock vaults. ●:"Our Father" can be found on *The Best of . . .* (MCA). "Will My. . ." is collected on

Father & Sons: Gospel Quartet Classics (Spirit Feel), which also includes tracks by the Sensational Nightengales and the Soul Stirrers as well as more by the Blind Boys. Another widely loved album of this group's early recordings is *The Great Lost Blind Boys Album* (Vee Jay).

Dorothy Love Coates and the Gospel Harmonettes—"Get Away Jordan" and "He's Calling Me." Bernice sang both of these songs as a teenager in the church gospel choir. ⬤: Both tunes are available on *The Best of Dorothy Love Coates and The Original Gospel Harmonettes* (Specialty).

The Roberta Martin Singers—Reagon remembers "God Specializes "from her church choir days. She considers "God is Still on the Throne" a virtuoso example of the gospel choral sound created by Martin. These are the two songs Bernice remembers best from her church choir days. ⬤: Much of Roberta Martin's material is out of print and finding these songs may prove difficult. Look for the album *The Roberta Martin Singers* (Savoy) as an introduction to the groups work.

The Caravans—"Oh Mary, Don't You Weep" on *Mary Don't You Weep* (Savoy) and"Lord Keep Me Day by Day." "The Caravans was an incredibly innovative group when you look at that sort of classical gospel music. They were led by Albertina Walker but also by Shirley Caeser, Inez Andrews, and Cassietta George, some of the great divas of the classical gospel era. 'Oh, Mary, Don't You Weep,' led by Inez Andrews, was just an incredible song in composition and performance." ⬤: Both songs are availible on *The Best of the Caravans* (Savoy). Another good introduction to the Caravans is *The Best of Shirley Caesar & the Caravans* (Savoy).

Howlin' Wolf—Reagon says Wolf was her favorite out of all the blues musicians she remembers from those late night radio shows. "And I just thought, and still think, the sound of his band is just the most powerful, energizing kind of urban blues sound that you can hear." ⬤: See Master List.

T-Bone Walker—"I really love him in terms of what he does with the electric guitar." ⬤: See Master List.

*The Staple Singers—" 'Low Is the Way" on *Uncloudy Day/Will the Circle Be Unbroken* (Vee Jay). Reagan loved this big Staple Singers hit when she was in high school. The Vee Jay CD combines two crucial early albums from their catalog, especially for anyone interested in the Staples' gospel music from the early '60s.

Tina Turner—"I heard one of the early Ike and Tina Turner songs. I don't even remember the name of the song, but I remember it was just really jukey. I was in college at the time so it was after '59, maybe '60, '61, and I followed Tina

Turner's career. I just love not only her singing, but I love the energy of Tina Turner on stage—it's very, very important." 🔘: For a survey of Ike and Tina's career from the early '60s through their big hits in the late '60s and early '70s, look for *Proud Mary: The Best of Ike and Tina Turner* (EMI). Tina's most successful solo album, commercially and artistically, has to be *Private Dancer* (Capitol). *Simply the Best* (Capitol) is a good greatest-hits package from her solo career on Capitol.

Odetta—"Joshua Fit the Battle of Jericho" on *The Essential Odetta* (Vanguard). "I really loved her music. She taught me that the songs I had learned as a child were included in the new popular folk music genre."

Nina Simone—"We called her the High Priestess. It felt like what she did was take the music that we knew and move it to another level of concert presentation. It was clearly not folk, and it was not what I would call jazz. And it was not gospel. But it seemed to just sit in the times." 🔘: *In Concert/I Put a Spell on You* (Mercury) combines two Simone albums from the '60s on a CD reissue. A rich live performance, *In Concert* contains some of her most socially conscious songs from the era of the civil rights movement.

Otis Redding—"Amazing, amazing, amazing artist. A great singer and a great band sound. The bass runs on 'I Can't Turn You Loose' put the bass in the unusual position of driving the power of the performance." 🔘: See Master List.

Ray Charles—"Drown In My Own Tears." Along with a bunch of Otis Redding hits, Reagon singles out this Charles classic as one of her favorites form the '60s. She notes that "Charles's songs like 'Lonely Avenue' [written by Doc Pomus] and 'Hit the Road Jack' [written by Percy Mayfield] became the structure for freedom songs during the 1960s sit-in movement." 🔘: "Tears" is availible on *The Best of Atlantic* (Rhino) and many other compilations.

Little Willie John—"Leave My Kitten Alone." This song was a hit for the R&B tenor, whose voice Reagon loved, and became the basis for a freedom song called "You'd Better Leave Segregation Alone." 🔘: *Fever: The Best of Little Willie John* (Rhino).

Son House—"Death Letter." "I remember the first time I heard Son House. I was singing at the Philadelphia Folk Festival. Son House was on the stage and I was up on a hill, and he started singing 'Death Letter' blues. I sat straight up because I thought they [the Delta blues singers] must all be dead . . . Hearing this bottleneck string guitar and 'Death Letter' blues and the way it sounded, I thought [she whispers] 'Oh my God! They're not all dead!' " 🔘: *The Father of the Delta Blues: the Complete 1965 Sessions* (CBS).

Pharaoh Sanders—"The Creator has a Master Plan" on *Karma* (Impulse). Leon Thomas performs the vocal on this extended composition. *Karma*, Bernice's favorite jazz record, was a minor hit when first released in 1969.

Aretha Franklin—"Never Grow Old" on *Aretha Gospel* (Chess). "It was a hymn, just a stunning rendering of that song," Reagon says of this recording Aretha made in her father's church in 1956.

Aretha Franklin and James Cleveland—*Amazing Grace* (Atlantic). "If you're going to know American music, you have to have that. It's Aretha Franklin, after she's been out there, and James Cleveland, a major force in gospel music. They got together at church and they did this double album, just an amazing, amazing album."

Various artists—*The Divas of Mali* (Shanachie). "This is the CD I'm listening to the most right now. This album includes tracks by such great Malian singers as Sonougue Kouyate and Nahawa Doumbia.

Salisu Muhammed—"He's Dagboni, Northern Ghana, and he played a gonji, and it was the first time I heard African music that sounded like blues to me. It was the relationship of his voice to his instrument. The gonji was like sort of a stringed instrument played with a bow. It was just an amazing thing to experience. And I don't know of a commercial recording that he's done." ⚫: We can't find one, either.

Various artists—*Mbuti Pygmies of the Ituri Rainforest* (Smithsonian Folkways). "It was just mind-expanding. I listened for hours to that music," Reagon says about the rich vocal and choral traditions captured on this recording.

Harry Belafonte/Miriam Makeba—*Evening with Belafonte/Makeba* (RCA). "These collaborations sort of led me into not only South African music, but the struggle against apartheid. And I was really surprised to find it so easy for me to sing South African music. The structures were so familiar to me. So I've always loved Miriam Makeba's work." Note that Harry Belafonte played a major role in Makeba's introduction to U.S. audiences.

BERNICE JOHNSON REAGON'S OWN RECORDINGS

For those just starting with Sweet Honey's music, Reagon recommends the two-CD anthology *Selections 1976–88* (Rounder), which surveys the group's first 20 years. She then suggests at least one of the single discs *Sacred Ground*, *In This Land*, or *Still on the Journey* (all Earthbeat!): "That's much more what we're doing now." She also points to her soundtrack for the PBS documentary series "Africans in America" (Rykodisc), which includes work with Sweet Honey and "more spectacularly, a major collaboration with my daughter Toshi Reagon, a singer, composer, and bandleader in her own right."Of the many adult groups making records for children and families, Sweet Honey makes some of the best. Reagon is proud of both the group's children's recordings, *All for Freedom* and *I Got Shoes* (both Music for Little People). "It was exciting for us to try to think about what we do normally, then try to think about the parents who really like what we do, and then try to develop a project that would be good for them to play for their children," she says.

: Reagon has also released solo recordings, including her *River of Life/Harmony: One* (Flying Fish), a tour de force of a capella multi-tracking. Sweet Honey explores their spiritual roots, both in the African-American church and in Liberia, on *Feel Something Drawing Me On* (Flying Fish).

JOSHUA REDMAN (January 27, 1998)

Joshua Redman was a Harvard graduate bound for Yale law school when, in 1991, he messed everything up by winning the Thelonious Monk Jazz Competition. Warner Brothers came knocking with a record contract, Joshua's debut album caused a sensation, and his subsequent discs cemented his position as one of the best players of his generation.

Of course, from another angle, Joshua simply abandoned law to enter the family business. Joshua is the son of the great avant-garde tenor player Dewey Redman, who spent seven years as a member of Ornette Coleman's band; played in Keith Jarrett's remarkable American quartet in the '70s; fronted, with Don Cherry, the Old and New Dreams band; and has released his own consistently cutting-edge solo projects.

But it's not as if Dewey taught Joshua everything he knows. Joshua's parents split up when he was a child; although he heard his father's music from the time he was an infant, the first discs that really sank in were the records his mother played around the house—an impressive, diverse collection that ranged from the timeless soul music of the 1960s to Indian classical music to the heavens-rippling jazz of John Coltrane, a massive influence on Joshua's eventual career. "*'Trane's *A Love Supreme* spent more time on the stereo than anything but the turntable pad. I literally can remember that record as far back as I can remember anything," Joshua says. "That record was probably playing in the house on the day I was born."

Another tenor giant entered the picture soon after Joshua began playing saxophone, he tells us: "I had heard of *Sonny Rollins—someone said I should check him out—so I went to the library and in the Sonny Rollins section they had a few records. One of them was called *Saxophone Colossus*, and I was like, 'Well that's a pretty impressive title. Let's check this guy out.' And it was colossal. It completely changed the way I thought, not only about the saxophone, but about jazz and about improvising. . . . [Rollins] showed me that improvisation isn't just random thoughts and ideas and emotions flying through the air. It's telling a story that has a meaning and has a beginning, middle, and end, but telling it in a very spontaneous way."

Eventually, Dad's music made its proper inpact on Joshua's musical ideas, too. As a master of free improvisation, Dewey taught Joshua the unique and difficult discipline hidden beneath the seeming anarchy of "outside" playing. Dewey's recordings also provided an avenue to the music of his former boss, Ornette Coleman. Although Joshua never lived with his father, he often saw him play with Old and New Dreams in the 1970s. "I think playing free and playing free well is one of the hardest things to do as an improviser," Joshua says of the music opened to him by that band. "I think it's one of the things people have a tendency to do very badly. True freedom doesn't mean the absence of structure, it means you're creating your structures on the spot, spontaneously. I think to do that well, you have to have more of a sense of meter and harmony and rhythm and melody than you do in any sort of already structured music. . . . I think Ornette's band and Old and New Dreams are two of the bands that played [free] very, very well."

But as much as Joshua still loves the music of the acknowledged masters, he bristles at the criticism that his generation hasn't demonstrated the same potential. "It sometimes bothers me, not only in jazz, but in pop, that people are always looking backward. They're saying, 'Oh, the best records were done thirty years ago.' That makes me mad. The bottom line is you're not going to view musicians of my generation the same way you view musicians of thirty years ago. . . . It's a different experience when you listen to music of your time. But I don't think that's a reason to think that our time isn't equally exciting and creative."

JOSHUA REDMAN'S FAVORITE ARTISTS AND RECORDINGS

John Coltrane—*A Love Supreme* (Impulse). "I don't really believe in perfection when it comes to the arts, but that record is about as close to perfection as you can get. It's so pure and so honest, yet at the same time it holds together from beginning to end. It's a true concept record. A lot of times, concept records are contrived, because they come from the mind, from theory, rather than from the soul, from emotion. This record is everything."

*Sonny Rollins—*Saxophone Colossus* (Prestige). "With Sonny Rollins, there's so much natural logic to his improvisation, the way he develops motifs, the way he gives improvisation structure and shape, and on *Saxophone Colossus*, you can hear that in just about every one of his tunes, and every one of his solos."

McCoy Tyner—*The Real McCoy* (Blue Note). "It features Joe Henderson on saxophone, who's definitely a great influence on me, Ron Carter on bass, and *Elvin Jones on drums. That was a record I loved when I discovered it sometime in high school. The compositions are beautiful, but the intensity and creativity with which those guys play really struck me. It's one of those albums that, if I really want to get riled up, if I wanna give myself a boost of energy, I'll put that record on."

Ornette Coleman—*Tomorrow is the Question* (Original Jazz Classics), *Change of the Century* (Atlantic), and *New York is Now* (Blue Note). "I think the thing that's always struck me about him was his ability to be melodic in any harmonic context. In other words, everything he played was a melody, yet [he was] playing in contexts where there was no preset harmony. Sometimes there wasn't an absence of harmony, but an absence of predetermined harmony and structure, yet he manages to play these incredible melodies without having the crutch of harmony underneath him. And as a band, that quartet [Charlie Haden, Don Cherry, and Billy Higgins] managed to create these harmonies on the spot." Note: Dewey Redman plays tenor sax on *New York Is Now*.

Old and New Dreams—*Old and New Dreams 2* (ECM). "As the title suggests, it was at once a tribute band to Ornette and also a way of carrying Ornette's ideas and innovations and extending them into the future."

Dexter Gordon—*Go!* (Blue Note). "Through the way he played on that record, I began to develop a really good sense of the bebop vocabulary."

Joe Lovano—"He's a brilliant saxophonist. I like the stuff he has done with the band with Paul Motian and [Bill] Frisell. I've heard that band live and listened to their records, and that's another example of brilliant free jazz, finding structure and meaning within freedom." ⬤: *One Time Out* (Soul Note) features the Lovano-Motian-Frisell trio.

Kenny Garrett—*Songbook* (Warner Bros.). "He's one of the most original saxophonists of the younger generation."

*Branford Marsalis—*Bloomington* (Columbia). "The level of improvisation is amazing, especially the way they play 'Everything Happens to Me' as a ballad. It's so completely improvised, but it sets a mood and keeps a mood, and tells a story within a certain emotional space. That trio [with Robert Hurst and Jeff Watts] is one of the great saxophone-led trios I've heard."

Keith Jarrett—*Birth* (Atlantic), *Death & the Flower* (Impulse), and *Silence* (GRP). Joshua rates the group on these albums—Jarrett's American Quartet, with Dewey Redman—up there with Ornette's bands and Old and New Dreams as state-of-the-art improvisers: "Those are records I come back to and they sound so fresh."

Miles Davis—*Complete Live at the Plugged Nickel* and *My Funny Valentine* (both Columbia). "I'm more partial to his playing on *My Funny Valentine*, but as a band the stuff on *Plugged Nickel* is earth-shattering. The level of empathy among the musicians, almost what I would consider telepathy: It's true spontaneity, true improvisation."

The Beatles—*Sgt. Pepper's Lonely Hearts Club Band* (Capitol). Joshua is a huge Beatles fan and calls *Sgt. Pepper* one of the greatest records ever: "It sounds so revolutionary and so groundbreaking and so modern even today, thirty years later. That's a true concept record, but the concept never gets in the way of the art."

Led Zeppelin—*Houses of the Holy* and . . . *IV* (both Swan Song). "Around the time I started playing the saxophone, I got into Led Zeppelin. I think John Bonham is definitely one of the great rock drummers of all time. His groove is so deep. What *Elvin Jones is to jazz, Bonham is to rock. He's just got this big, fat wide beat. He lays back so hard it's almost behind the beat, but yet it's still really forward moving, propulsive. The thing I really love about Led Zeppelin is the intensity and the energy, but you never feel like it's just testosterone gone wild. There's a sensitivity there, too, a lot of subtlety in their music. The kind of stuff they do with meter and time—they would write songs in these really strange time signatures. There'd be extra beats here and they'd take out beats there, but there's always a groove. It never feels like 'Oh, we're just doing this to be hip.' "

Stevie Wonder—*Songs in the Key of Life* and *Innervisions* (both Motown). "Stevie's just the man, one of my greatest idols. These are records that can stand up to any of the great creative and artistic statements of all time, of any genre. Harmonically, it's so deep. As a jazz musician, harmonic depth is something I focus on, because jazz is such a harmonically rich and deep music, and I think that some of Stevie's songs lend themselves very well to a jazz interpretation. If you can ever imagine playing those songs without Stevie singing them, which is very hard to do." Joshua considers *Innervisions* as close to a perfect record as you'll find.

Prince—*Parade* (Paisley Park). "I got into Prince around the time he did *1999* [Warner Bros.], followed him into *Purple Rain* [Warner Bros.], and *Parade* I just wore down. Like Stevie, with Prince the music is so holistic, so unified, because again the music is coming from this one person, he's playing all the instruments. I think it's got some of his best vocal work and they're just great songs, really honest. To the extent that Prince can smack of pretension a little bit, I think this album is very unpretentious."

The Police—*Ghost in the Machine* and *Synchronicity* (both A&M). "They're both great albums. I can't pick between them. The songwriting is great. The musicianship is great. They had a sound and a vision and they stuck with that and allowed it to develop."

Me'Shell NdgeOcello—*Peace Beyond Passion* and *Plantation Lullabies* (both Warner Bros.). "Two of my favorite records of the last five years."

*Public Enemy—*It Takes A Nation of Millions to Hold Us Back* (Def Jam). "I love hip-hop. It's hard for me to find hip-hop records that I can hold up against *Houses of the Holy* and *Innervisions* and *Sgt. Pepper*. But I definitely think that [this] is a great hip-hop record."

A Tribe Called Quest—*Midnight Marauders* (Jive). This is another hip-hop record that Joshua rates with the best rock and pop.

The Fugees—*The Score* (Sony). "For all the radio play it got, I still like it."

Aretha Franklin—*Lady of Soul* (Atlantic). This and the following records and artists are favorites Joshua heard via his mother's collection.

The Temptations—*Greatest Hits, Vol. 2* (Motown).

Otis Redding—*The Best of . . .* (Atlantic).

Bismillah Khan—Khan is India's most revered *shehnai* player. ⬤: *Live in London Vols. 1 and 2* (Navras).

JOSHUA REDMAN'S OWN RECORDINGS

"On a certain level, I'm satisfied with none of [my records]," says Joshua, "and that's just part of my nature. By the same token, I'm proud of every one of them, because every one of them represents me at that time." But he does have a special feeling for *Moodswing* (Warner Bros.), his third record, because it was his first disc to feature his writing exclusively. It has some of my best compositions—

not necessarily being forward-looking or revolutionary, but some of my best in terms of strong melodies and creating moods with the compositions. Plus the band that's on that record, I'm honored to play with all those musicians, because they are three of the greatest jazz musicians playing today [pianist Brad Mehldau, bassist Christian McBride, drummer Brian Blade].''

● : Not singled out by Joshua but strong testimonials to his abilities are his 1992 eponymous debut, 1993's *Wish*, and the much-praised two-CD live set, *Spirit of the Moment: Live at the Village Vanguard* (all Warner Bros.). On 1998's *Time-less Tales (for Changing Times)* (Warner Bros.), released after our interview, Joshua alternates between jazz standards and pop classics in an acoustic quartet setting, covering the Beatles, Dylan, and Joni Mitchell.

T O N Y   R I C E (October 19, 1997)

Since the mid-1960s, acoustic string music has taken several monumental leaps forward, pushed by such innovators as Clarence White, J. D. Crowe, and *David Grisman. At every one of those points, guitarist Tony Rice has leaped too, first as a listener, then as a star participant, and, for several decades now, as one of the prime shapers of the music itself.

Like the "New Acoustic" music of which he is one of the reigning masters, Tony got his start with bluegrass. His father, a devoted fan of the music, had collected a sizable stack of 78s by Bill Monroe and Flatt and Scruggs. Tony started playing guitar at four or five, showed an early knack for bluegrass picking, and, like his dad, shut almost every other form of music out.

As it turned out, bluegrass music and Tony Rice were evolving almost in lockstep. Young urban players were discovering bluegrass primarily via TV and movie themes such as Flatt and Scrugg's work on *The Beverly Hillbillies* TV show in 1963 and Earl Scruggs's "Foggy Mountain Breakdown" in the 1967 hit movie, *Bonnie and Clyde*. Southern bluegrass musicians like White and Crowe were lis-tening to urban rock, pop, jazz, and blues. Tony was riding the same train. In high school by this time, he heard jazz pianist Dave Brubeck's "Take Five" and it opened a door. "I really liked that music form a lot," Tony recalls. "I wasn't really involved in any jazz music form until many years later, but that started a period that exists to this day of listening to modern jazz, acoustic jazz primarily."

With an insatiable hunger now for new approaches to music, Tony began studying the records of progressive bluegrass guitarist Clarence White and the blues-inflected Doc Watson and finding his own style somewhere in the middle. After honing his abilities to a level few could even imagine, Tony joined J. D. Crowe and his innovative bluegrass band, the New South. He was a featured soloist, along with *Ricky Skaggs and Jerry Douglas, when the band released its revolutionary debut album of electric, eclectic bluegrass in 1975.

Next stop for Tony was the David Grisman Quintet, which was about to leapfrog over progressive bluegrass entirely and create a wholly new approach to acoustic string music. Tony, like Grisman, was a bluegrass musician who had fallen in love with jazz. But figuring that he was too deep into his career to learn a whole new musical language, he began to think about ways of fashioning an effective compromise. Meanwhile, Grisman, facing the same dilemma, conceived of a music that resembled jazz but could be played on acoustic string instruments in configurations like a bluegrass band's. He began looking around for other open-minded, highly accomplished players to help him pull it off. By this point, Tony was one of the country's acknowledged virtuosos of flat-picked guitar, with a smooth, effortless-sounding style that was a perfect fit for Grisman's vision. He got the call.

The new group played what Grisman branded "dawg music," with its jazz-like compositions and improvisation, precise ensemble playing, and harmonic nods to bluegrass and other Americana. Dawg music was just what the doctor ordered for a number of creatively frustrated country pickers, including Tony, who notes that the music "happened to coincide exactly with things I'd been hearing in my own head."

In 1980, Tony left Grisman's band to form the Tony Rice Unit and evolve his own form of improvisatory string music, "spacegrass," which edged even closer to true jazz. His recording efforts since have included several superior traditional bluegrass albums and other vocal efforts that honor his bluegrass roots, as well as "tweeners" like *Manzanita* that have a traditional veneer over some spacegrassy playing. But don't kid yourself. Wherever string music is next headed, be assured that Tony's already thinking about it.

TONY RICE'S FAVORITE ARTISTS AND RECORDINGS

J. D. Crowe—Tony not only worked with Crowe in the New South for four years but also frequently afterward, including in the superstar bluegrass group, the Bluegrass Album Band. "I learned a lot about musicianship in general from J. D. Crowe," says Tony, "and I carried that over into the music that I played with David Grisman." : From 1994, *Flashback* (Rounder) finds Crowe and company returning to traditional bluegrass but drawing material from every phase of the

New South's career and playing it with joy and drive. Other than Crowe and dobro player Phil Leadbetter, the personnel has turned over completely for 1999's *Come on Down to My World* (Rounder) but the musicianship remains first-rate on this disc, which like *Flashback* eschews the drums and pedal steel of earlier recordings for a more traditional romp. Like all great bluegrass, the grooves have a relaxed feel that perfectly complements the high-speed picking. For recommended recordings with both Crowe and Tony, see "Tony Rice's Own Recordings."

Bill Monroe—*Voice From On High* (Decca) and *Bluegrass Instrumentals* (Decca). Monroe's units and recordings featured dramatic shifts in personnel. In general, Tony prefers the band with Jimmy Martin, Rudy Lyle, and *Vassar Clements; any of the bands featuring Edd Mayfield as lead singer; and the bands with Del McCoury and Bill Keith. Tony says, "I was just blown away" by the latter's innovative banjo style. : *The Music of Bill Monroe* (MCA) is a four-CD box set covering Monroe's career from 1938 to 1994, including most of the personnel Tony mentions. *Live Recordings 1956–1959* (Smithsonian/Folkways) and *The Music of Bill Monroe* (MCA) both feature Edd Mayfield.

Flatt and Scruggs—*The Complete Mercury Sessions* (Mercury). The album Tony listened to originally was a Mercury LP titled *Country Music* but its tracks are obviously included on this classic compilation.

Jimmy Martin—*Good 'n' Country* (Decca). This 1960 album was Jimmy Martin's first as a leader.

Osborne Brothers—*Voices in Bluegrass* (Decca). Tony says this album, renowned for its augmentation of the original bluegrass style, is "really spectacular," featuring a terrific band.

Oscar Peterson—*Great Connection* (Verve). "Anybody who's ever heard Oscar Peterson would know that miraculous things happen out of him every second," Tony says. He finds Peterson's timing, phrasing, chord substitutions, and arrangements on this disc "just mind-boggling. And combine that with the bass talent of Neils Pederson—you know, magic is bound to happen and it did."

Bill Evans with Scott LaFaro—Tony loves Evans's trio recordings featuring the brilliant bassist Scott LaFaro, who was killed in an auto wreck just ten days after the latter two albums listed below were recorded. Tony particularly enjoys pianist Evans's block chord playing and LaFaro's responses to that: "Scott LaFaro played bass more like a horn player than like a bass player. And it's just amazing. . . . At any given place and time on [these albums], a few seconds of music is timeless." : *Portrait in Jazz* (Original Jazz Classics), *Explorations* (Original Jazz Classics),

Sunday at the Village Vanguard (Original Jazz Classics), and *Waltz for Debby* (Original Jazz Classics) are all superior recordings featuring the Evans/La Faro combination.

Miles Davis—*Kind of Blue*, *Four and More*, and *My Funny Valentine* (all Columbia). Davis wrote the compositions for *Kind of Blue* just hours before the band recorded the date, and the spontaneous perfection that resulted never ceases to amaze Tony, as it has countless others: "Every time I hear that album, I hear something that I've never heard before, and I've heard it hundreds of times." The latter two albums were taken from a single live concert in 1964 featuring the classic Davis rhythm section of *Herbie Hancock, Ron Carter, and Tony Williams, plus George Coleman on tenor sax. *Four* contains the uptempo material, *Valentine* the ballads. You can obtain the entire program on *The Complete Concert: 1964* (Columbia).

John Coltrane Quartet—Tony prefers Coltrane's earlier recordings featuring the quartet with McCoy Tyner, Jimmy Garrison, and *Elvin Jones: "I think one of the things that is obvious that Coltrane learned from Miles was that you could create music from nothing a lot quicker than anybody thinks. What I did learn from a lot of those albums was that music doesn't necessarily need to be discussed. Sometimes it just very simply needs to be played. And some of the best music's created that way." : See Master List.

Jean-Luc Ponty—*Sunday Walk* (BASF). "At the time, the music Jean-Luc Ponty and that quartet played had different ways of thinking about things. It kind of hit me with the impact that *Kind of Blue* hit . . . Ponty's phrasing was more like that of a horn player than a violinist. It was very unique, and the rhythm section responded accordingly. Even though that record was recorded I think in nineteen sixty-seven it's still hard to beat some of those moments that are created by the rhythm section."

Wynton Marsalis—*J Mood* (Columbia) and *Marsalis Standard Time:Volume 1* (Columbia). "The reason I love those Wynton Marsalis recordings so much is that even though they remind me of the early Miles and Coltrane recordings, there's something a little bit more precise there."

Clarence White—Tony says the best examples of White's playing are with the progressive bluegrass band White co-founded with his brother Roland, the Kentucky Colonels. : *Long Journey Home* (Vanguard) is a very fine live recording from 1964 that features several impressive duets between White and another major influence on Tony, Doc Watson. *Appalachian Swing!* (Rounder) is also excellent.

Doc Watson—Tony prefers Doc's early recordings for Vanguard. ⬤: *The Essential Doc Watson* (Vanguard) samples live performances from 1963 and 1964 and is music of spectacular grace and facility. *Doc Watson* (Vanguard), from 1964, is Watson's superb debut for the label. *Southbound* (Vanguard), also from 1964, features the first appearance of Doc's son, Merle, on second guitar, and like *Essential*, shows Watson in a state of casual mastery, both instrumentally and vocally. All three albums are highly recommended.

George Benson—*Shape of Things to Come* (A&M), *Body Talk* (CTI), and *Collaboration* (Warner Bros.), with Earl Klugh. "His phrases are his own. He doesn't sound like he stole them from anybody else. . . . You have no idea where the next phrase is going or leading."

Jerry Reed—*Jerry Reed Explores Guitar Country* (RCA). "He's the most unique guitar player out there. He's in a world of his own with his phrasing and timing and everything," Tony says. He adds that any of Reed's early albums before he became a commercial success and screen actor (*Smoky and the Bandit* and other similar films) are worth seeking out in used record stores. Most are long out of print.

Chuck Loeb—*Balance* (DMP). "It would be invaluable to a listener who was looking for something unique [in] musicianship on any instrument."

TONY RICE'S OWN RECORDINGS

Asked to name favorites of his own work, Tony laughs, "It's hard for somebody like myself to praise myself. One, I don't like to do it. Two, I get so sick of listening to that stuff by the time I'm done producing it." But he does indeed have his picks. *Manzanita* (Rounder) is a progressive folk/country album featuring Tony's Southern Comfort–smooth lead vocals and hot playing by such string masters as Darol Anger, David Grisman, Sam Bush, Ricky Skaggs, and Jerry Douglas as well as Tony. *Backwaters* (Rounder) is a jazzy "new acoustic" effort in the vein of the music he developed with the David Grisman Quintet. An all-instrumental spacegrass album like *Backwaters*, the marvelous *Devlin* (Rounder) compiles Tony's choice selections from *Still Inside* and *Mar West*, one of his favorites that is now out of print. Tony also feels especially good about the vocal albums *Me and My Guitar* (Rounder) and *Cold on the Shoulder* (Rounder), with all-star appearances from Bela Fleck, Sam Bush, *Vassar Clements, J. D. Crowe, and the late Kate Wolf. "And the last vocal album I did, which is called *Native American* (Rounder) [with Jerry Douglas and *Vassar Clements] is another one that's got moments on it that I'm particularly proud of," Tony adds. Tony has covered Gordon Lightfoot songs on several of his vocal records, but although *Native American* includes songs by several other songwriters, it has a strong Lightfoot feel throughout.

●: Fans of Tony's music should also check out his work on *David Grisman Quintet* (Kaleidoscope), the first full dawg music album, and *Tone Poems* (Acoustic Disc), a lovely duet album with Grisman. *J. D. Crowe and the New South* (Rounder) was the New South's revelatory debut, with Tony the revelatory lead guitarist. Tony not only played on but also produced the Bluegrass Album Band's records. To get into that wonderful work, start with *The Bluegrass Album, Vol. 1* and the compilations *The Bluegrass Compact Disc* and *The Bluegrass Compact Disc, Vol. 2* (all Rounder). At various times, the shifting group included Jerry Douglas and Vassar Clements besides core members Rice, Crowe, and Doyle Lawson. Tony formed this group to recreate the traditional sound established by bluegrass daddy Bill Monroe back when his band featured Lester Flatt, Earl Scruggs, Chubby Wise and Howard Watts, and it's some of the sweetest bluegrass around.

SONNY ROLLINS (November 25, 1997)

No list of influences, no bloodlines, no exceptional teachers or mentors can account for a Sonny Rollins. If Sonny had been born and raised in an isolation chamber on a barren planet, one suspects that fabulous music would still have been the result.

But not the same music. What makes the Sonny Rollins we know today is the way his unearthly gifts have been filtered through an earthly life. Sonny, widely acknowledged as jazz's greatest living soloist, was born in Harlem to parents who had emigrated from the Virgin Islands. His family lived on 137th Street. "I was surrounded by all sorts of clubs and after-hour places and etcetera," Sonny tells us by phone from his New York–area home. "So I think I absorbed a lot of jazz just by being born where I was born."

Sonny's neighborhood resonated not only with living jazz but also seminal jazz history. For instance, just a few years before six-year-old Sonny started going to the Lincoln movie theater on Saturdays to watch adventure serials, Fats Waller had been house organist there accompanying silent films and stage productions. Waller's music was played all the time in Sonny's house and was, Sonny recalls, "very much influential in making me realize the power of the music." Across the street from Sonny's elementary school stood a club that frequently booked R&B

pioneer Louis Jordan. Sonny knew and loved Jordan's music because he'd heard it at the house where his uncle and uncle's girlfriend would mind him for the day: "Coming out of school, I'd see these pictures of Louis Jordan in the window, with his saxophone and everything, so the two things came together for me. . . . I said, 'Wow, boy, that's it!' " Sonny soon quit his piano lessons and adopted the alto saxophone, Jordan's instrument.

By the age of nine, Sonny remembers, he had already taken in so much jazz that he could distinguish between the different players and what each brought to the table. With prescient taste as well, he made Coleman Hawkins, with his big tone, muscular rhythm, and bottomless musicality, his idol; at 16, he switched to Hawkins's horn, the tenor. Two other broad-toned tenor players, Ben Webster and Don Byas, made Sonny's A-list, too, and then a Byas record inadvertently led Sonny to discover Charlie Parker's bebop innovations. Sonny bought a 78 of Byas playing "How High the Moon." On the flip side was Parker's "Ko Ko."

While jazz has always been the music best suited to Sonny's abilities and inclinations, he has long incorporated elements from other forms of popular music as he saw fit. The calypso records his parents played around the house, Ray Charles's commanding soul music, Junior Walker's heated, saxy R&B—all have found their way into Sonny's many-layered style. In recent years, he has broadened his palette to include social concerns—primarily environmental ones. He announced his passion with the title of his 1998 album, *Global Warming*, named for the ominous increase of temperatures on the planet. No one seems concerned about the temperature of Sonny's music, however, although it continues to rage.

SONNY ROLLINS'S FAVORITE ARTISTS AND RECORDINGS

Thomas "Fats" Waller— : See Master List.

Louis Jordan— : See Master List.

Coleman Hawkins—"Coleman was much more of a cerebral player, and this appealed to my intellectual side, if I could say that of a boy of nine years old. . . . It was different from the elemental work of Louis Jordan, which was great. And it's not a matter of either/or, it's a matter of both/and, you know?" : *Body and Soul* (RCA Bluebird) features the Hawk in a variety of contexts from 1939 to '56. Highlights include superb smaller group tracks with Fats Navarro and J. J. Johnson and a classic performance of the title song, one of Sonny's favorites by Hawkins. Lowlight: some saccharine string arrangements, but Hawk plays terrifically in spite of them. *The High and Mighty Hawk* (London), *The Hawk Flies High* (Original Jazz Classics), and . . . *Encounters Ben Webster* (Verve) present fine small group sets. *Body and Soul Revisited* (Decca) contains "The Man I Love," another Sonny fave.

Don Byas— ⬤: Unfortunately, there is a paucity of prime Byas on available recordings. *Don Byas in Paris* (Prestige) captures him playing well with an unexceptional backing band. *On Blue Star* (Verve), also from recordings in Paris, features mainly the slow and moderate tempo material that showed him off at his best. Under Dizzy Gillespie's name, try the excellent *Complete RCA Recordings 1937–49* (2 CDs: Bluebird) with one of Sonny's favorite tracks, "Good Bait," and *Dizzy Gillespie in Paris, Vol. 2* (Vogue)—Sonny loved Byas's work with the great trumpeter.

Ben Webster—Sonny liked Webster both with Duke Ellington's great big bands in the mid-1940s and in small group configurations later on. ⬤: Four of Sonny's favorite Ellington/Webster tracks—"Cottontail," "Rain Check," "Chelsea Bridge," and "Daydream"—are on the outstanding Ellington set *The Webster-Blanton Years* (3 CDs: RCA/Bluebird). Webster made several fine records with pianist Oscar Peterson including *King of the Tenors*, *Soulville*, and . . . *Meets Oscar Peterson* (all Verve).

Charlie Parker—"[His music] sounded a lot different. It was a little bit harder for me to relate to it. Of course, in retrospect I think that had a lot to do with the fact that my ears were attuned to the tenor sound. . . . So it took me a little while." ⬤: See Master List.

Lester Young—Sonny found Young's elegant tone, which lacked the vibrato of Hawkins, Byas, and Webster, refreshing when he first heard it and his musicianship consistently inspiring. He disputes the notion that Young, depressed by the racism he experienced in the Army, was less effective after World War II: "I caught Coleman Hawkins one night when he wasn't feeling well. He couldn't play as many notes as he used to play, and he was playing far fewer notes. And it was a revelation how he sounded. So, a great artist finds a way to be great under all circumstances." ⬤: *The Complete Lester Young on Keynote* (Verve) is a superb set containing the tracks—including "Afternoon of a Basie-ite," "Sometimes I'm Happy," and "I Never Knew" with bassist Slam Stewart, pianist Johnny Guarnieri, and drummer Sid Catlett—that first engaged Sonny. Other excellent Young sets include *Classics in Swing: . . .* (Commodore), *The Complete Aladdin Sessions* (2 CDs: Blue Note), and *The Jazz Giants '56* (Verve).

Billie Holiday—"Lover Man." Sonny is a huge fan of Holiday's work in all phases of her career, but her hit version of this song tops his list. ⬤: *The Complete Decca Recordings* (2 CDs: Decca) contains the original "Lover Man" and much more terrific Holiday, backed by an orchestra and strings. For other superb Holiday discs, see Master List.

Lena Horne with Charlie Barnet—"Good-for-Nothin' Joe." "That's sort of a nostalgic record for me." 🔴: Horne's *1936–1941 Stormy Weather* (ASV).

Duke Ellington—"Sophisticated Lady," "Mood Indigo," "I Got It Bad and That Ain't Good," "Azure," and "It Don't Mean a Thing." Ellington was the first composer Sonny became interested in. These compositions were on the tip of Sonny's tongue but his love of Ellington's work goes much deeper than this. 🔴: The album *16 Most Requested Songs* (Columbia) contains all of the above-mentioned tunes except "Azure." A version of "Azure" is on . . . *1937* (Classics).

Nat King Cole Trio—"Prelude in C-sharp Minor," "Beautiful Moons Ago," "Straighten Up and Fly Right," and "Route 66." "Those were special records to me." 🔴 "Prelude" is on *The Best of Nat King Cole Trio* (Capital), a survey of Cole's great early instrumental recordings. "Beautiful" is available on *1941–1943* (Classics) and also *Trio Recordings* (5 CDs: Laserlight), a budget set that should catch the eye of anyone interested in Cole's pre-crossover career. "Route 66" and "Straighten Up" are both on the crossover compilation *Greatest Hits* (Capitol).

Ella Fitzgerald—"She's such a great artist and anything she does is great, but I must have heard a lot of things with the Chick Webb band when I was growing up. And that whole feeling of Harlem around the thirties—there's something about those songs and everything that really evokes something to me." 🔴: *The Early Years, Vol. 1* (Decca)—the material with Chick Webb's orchestra is on other labels, too, but the sound on this disc is much better.

Bunny Berigan—"I Can't Get Started." "He sings it, it's a big band, and he plays trumpet on it. It was an extremely popular record at one time [1932]." 🔴: *Portrait of Bunny Berigan* (ASV).

The Duke of Iron—Sonny honored this calypso artist by writing a tune of the same name. 🔴: *Sings Calypsos* (SOC, out of print). You can also sample the Duke on *Calypso Calaloo—Early Calypso Music in Trinidad* (Rounder), a companion CD to a book of the same title by Donald R. Hill.

Gerald Clark and his Caribbean Serenaders—Calypso artists Clark and Macbeth are two other favorites Sonny remembers from his childhood. 🔴: Clark's music is also represented with the Duke of Iron's on *Calypso Calaloo*.

Macbeth the Great— 🔴: *Calypso Holiday* (Time, out of print).

Junior Walker & the All-Stars—Walker was no jazzer but his rollicking style included more than a hint of Sonny's idol, Coleman Hawkins. ⚫: *The Ultimate Collection* (Motown).

Ray Charles—Sonny loved Charles's hits in the mid-1950s through the early 1960s—such tunes as "Georgia on My Mind," "Hallelujah, I Love Her So," "Lonely Avenue," and "I Got a Woman," many of which featured a saxophonist Sonny appreciated, David "Fathead" Newman. ⚫: *The Best of . . . : The Atlantic Years* (Rhino) is an outstanding single-disc survey of Charles's Atlantic career (1952–59). "Georgia," from 1960, is on *Greatest Hits, Vol. 1* (DCC) with many other great tracks from the '60s.

Art Tatum—This immortal pianist is one of Sonny's biggest idols. He generally prefers Tatum's solo work but trio recordings with bassist Slam Stewart are an exception. ⚫: For solo Tatum, start with . . . *Solo Masterpieces, Vols. 1–7* (Pablo, available separately). *The Complete Capitol Recordings, Vols. 1–2* (Capitol, available separately) feature the trio with Stewart and one of Sonny's favorite tunes, "Dancing in the Dark."

SONNY ROLLINS'S OWN RECORDINGS

Few soloists in jazz history have ever brought as much as Sonny does to the table. Rhythmically, he swings freely even in overdrive. Melodically, his inventiveness seems unlimited and his solos, no matter how extended, have the logic of a good novel. Harmonically, he can go anywhere. Emotionally, he is committed and cheerful. And he is disarmingly modest about all of it. Sonny cautions us that "you're going to have a hard time trying to get me to cite a record that I really like. I'm extremely self critical. As I've always said, I consider myself a work in progress . . . I'm still praying to make that record where I make the breakthrough, and I'm serious." That said, Sonny admits to liking some of his work on 1956's . . . *Plus 4* (Prestige) with the celebrated pairing of trumpeter Clifford Brown and drummer Max Roach on board; *Saxophone Colossus* (Prestige); 1957's *A Night at the Village Vanguard* (Blue Note); and 1996's *+3* (Milestone).

⚫: Excellent Sonny Rollins albums are too numerous to mention but widely acknowledged sonic feasts, besides those Sonny cites, include, from the watershed year 1956, the Prestige albums *Tenor Madness* (named for the title track's summit meeting between Sonny and John Coltrane, although the tracks with only Sonny are where the album's real value lies) and *Tour de Force* (aptly named, with several warp-speed workouts plus Sonny's magic on two romantic ballads); 1966's *East Broadway Rundown* (Impulse), on which Sonny spins out long, snaking melodic improvisations over a free-ish rhythm section of Jimmy Garrison and *Elvin Jones; 1993's *Old Flames* (Milestone), a mostly ballad session with attractive brass arrangements by Jimmy Heath; and, again, 1998's *Global Warming* (Milestone), which belies its earnest title with engaging music that is heated only in the inspirational sense. *Silver City* (2 CDs: Milestone) is a marvelous sampling of Sonny's first 25 years on the Milestone label (1972–1996). *The Complete Prestige Recordings* (7 CDs: Prestige) encompasses several of the albums mentioned above and many others that are nearly as fine.

L A E T I T I A   S A D I E R   (October 14, 1998)

Stereolab's Laetitia Sadier and beau/bandmate Tim Gane were looking for a keyboard, not bric-a-brac, when they went thrift store hopping in the early 1990s. However, their search turned up more than the equivalent in cheese— a Farfisa organ. Laetitia plunked down the funds, and Stereolab immediately adopted the organ's Krafty drone as its own. "Apart from the vocals, and kind of arranging that, I'm not directly hands-on with the sound," Laetitia admits, "[but] I did buy the Farfisa with my little savings, and it was kind of a freak thing. It just moved into the band and became very instrumental to the sound."

No less instrumental, of course, are Laetitia'a almost studiously detached vocals, which lend an otherworldly beauty to Stereolab's eccentric anti-pop. Born and raised in Paris, she brings a uniquely French pop sensibility to the group. Her singing frequently hearkens back to the outrageous 1960s hits of Serge Gainsbourg (of audio-erotic "Je T'Aime . . . Moi Non Plus" fame). But just like Stereolab's sound, Laetitia's influences are complex, reflecting a whirl of music that swept over her when she was coming of age.

As a child, Laetitia liked bright dance records. But by her early teens, she tells us, her taste had already grown complicated enough to include the gloom-tunes of Joy Division, the quirky New Wave of Young Marble Giants, and the multilayered weirdness of the Residents. Meanwhile, punk was belatedly washing up on French shores and on Laetitia as well. "Punk came in a sort of diluted version," Laetitia notes, "and after it happened in the UK, it didn't happen so brutally. It kind of bred a whole generation of musicians. Some really interesting music came out of this period in France—punk in the mind but not so much in the looks, with very good bands like Marquis de Sade or Orchestre Rouge, Metal Urbain, and Dr. Mix and the Remix. And that was a really interesting period, I would say from seventy-nine 'til eighty-five, where French people really applied themselves and they did things, you know. They weren't just intellectuals hanging around salons smoking cigars or cigarettes."

In the early 1980s, the Mitterand government deregulated the French FM radio band, setting off an explosion of alternative stations. "For three or four years it was brilliant," Laetitia remembers. It was also prophetic. Laetitia first heard, and liked, Tim Gane's band McCarthy on one of the stations. When McCarthy came to Paris, she went to a show, met Tim, and began a collaboration that has not only produced the ongoing musical experiment called Stereolab but also a baby. It may be too much to expect the kid to go into the family business someday, but we suspect it won't be many years before the first Farfisa lessons.

LAETITIA SADIER'S FAVORITE ARTISTS AND RECORDINGS

Young Marble Giants—*Colossal Youth* (Rough Trade). This 1980 album turned out to be this Welsh band's only full-length release. Laetitia says this record "was very much a focus to what I liked."

Joy Division—Laetitia was into the band and all it did. : The key albums are 1979's *Unknown Pleasure* and 1980's *Closer* (both Qwest). Much of the JD music Laetitia collected was only available on singles; many of those have been compiled on *Substance* (Qwest) along with other non-album material. The band's complete recordings have been released as *Heart & Soul* (4 CDs: London).

The Smiths—*The Smiths* (Sire). "I played it a couple of months ago, out of interest to see if I still liked it, and I still do. It was quite sophisticated but at the same time it was edgy and energetic. It had this sound, like you hear the first two notes and you know it's the Smiths. I like that about a band."

The Cure—Laetitia prefers the band's early music because "it's kind of New Wavey." : *Three Imaginary Boys* (Fiction) and *Seventeen Seconds* (Elektra) are the first two albums. Also try *Standing on a Beach: The Singles* (Elektra).

Orchestre Rouge—This band from the French punk scene was founded, ironically, by Theo Hakola of Spokane, Washington. : *Yellow Laughter* and *More Passion Fodder* (both RCA France).

Metal Urbain— : *Age d'or* (Fan Club, France) and *Les Hommes Mort* (Celluloid, France) are the only widely available albums by this French punk group. "Paris Maquis," Metal Urbain's 1978 7-inch, was the first single ever released by the Rough Trade label.

Doctor Mix and the Remix—*Wall of Noise* (Rough Trade).

France Gall—Laetitia says Gall was the first singer to impress her: "She was a French singer who started in the sixties very young, and Serge Gainsbourg wrote a couple of songs for her and they won the Eurovision song contest in nineteen sixty-five. There was a kind of youth and strength in her voice." ⬤: *Poupee de Son* (Polydor) collects most of her '60s hits. Polydor also offers a four-disc box set with the same title.

Carmel—Laetitia says this soulful English singer didn't actually inspire her because "she was a completely different genre of singing . . . [but] she shaped my desire to sing. She had a few hits—she's done some more kind of avant-garde stuff but also some more commercial stuff, even though she never had a big-time career. But she was really interesting." ⬤: *Everybody's Got a Little Soul* (ffrr) and *Live at Ronnie Scott's* (Indigo).

Brigitte Fontaine—Laetitia first heard this French singer and songwriter only two or three years ago: "It was like discovering a gold mine, trying to track down her records. There's like three periods, I'd say. . . . There's the sixties period, which you could liken to Serge Gainsbourg's early sixties stuff—very well recorded, proper sounds and all that. Then there is the seventies period which is more decomposed or deconstructed or more abstract, which is what *Sonic Youth really love. And then there's the more modern period—she's still recording now and it's still very relevant today. I mean, [her music has] not gone horribly wrong or anything, which is sometimes the case. You know, there's not just one Brigitte Fontaine. There's at least seventy-two thousand." ⬤: Shortly after our interview, Stereolab collaborated on a single with Fontaine to be released in 1999. Most of Fontaine's albums were released only in France. Via import sources, look for 1970's *Est* (Saravah France); 1971's *Comme A La Radio* (Saravah France) with Areski and the Art Ensemble of Chicago; *L'Incendie*, also from the early '70s (BYG Records, reissued on CD on Spalax France); 1974's *Fontaine 4: Je Ne Connais Pas Cet Homme* (Saravah France); and her two most recent releases, 1995's *Genre Humain* and 1997's *Les Palaces* (both Virgin France).

Lambchop—Laetitia had seen this heralded alternative country band live just prior to our interview: "They are so powerful. You know, it's a very soft, very slow kind of music, but it's very exciting. I had goose pimples . . . It's really gorgeous." ⬤: See Master List.

Blonde Redhead—"They live in New York, and they've been likened to Sonic Youth. They're in the same vein, they explore the same avenues. But they're definitely their own band—magnificent, very good songwriters, and exceptional live as well." ⬤: *Blonde Redhead* and *La Mia Vita Violenta* (both Smells Like);

Fake Can Be Just Good and *In an Expression of the Inexpressible* (both Touch & Go).

Isotope 217—*Unstable Molecule* (Thrill Jockey). "A band from Chicago which has members of Tortoise in it. We saw them in Chicago play live, many times, like in bars or casual places, and each time it was really good."

LAETITIA SADIER'S OWN RECORDINGS

In addition to albums, Stereolab's prolific output includes a blizzard of singles, B-sides, split EPs, tour singles, and other rarities released in limited quantities. The array keeps Stereolab's fans involved in an ongoing treasure hunt, but makes it difficult for Laetitia to name favorites. Plus, she says, "I've never really listened to our records, so I'm not very objective." But *Dots and Loops* [Elektra/ Duophonic] "I was able to listen to quite proudly, quite happily, quite comfortably, being able to detach myself from it." Laetitia also recommends the band's latest collection of odds and ends, *Aluminum Tunes: Switched On, Vol. 3* (2 CDs: Drag City), along with the singles "Harmonium" and "Farfisa," both of which appear on the earlier singles compilation, *Refried Ectoplasm (Switched On, Volume 2)* (Duophonic]. "And I like *'Lo-Fi* [EP, *Too Pure],*" she says, laughing, "even though Tim thinks it's a really crap record!"

: For more on Stereolab's discography, see the section on Tim Gane.

DOUG SAHM (June 21, 1995)

t's a tall order to stuff the broad cultural mix that is Texas music under one cowboy hat. But Doug Sahm has managed and made it all seem at least roughly coherent. Consider this careening résumé: A Grand Ol' Opry debut at age ten. The British Invasion–cum-Texas garage sound of his mid-1960s Sir Douglas Quintet. The James Brown–style horn accents of his second album, *Honkey Blues*. The border-roots blend of 1973's *Doug Sahm and Friends* with Bob Dylan, *Dr. John, Tex-Mex accordion icon Flaco Jimenez, and others. The country and western sweetening several 1970s releases. A return to Tex-Mex in the 1990s with the Grammy-winning Texas Tornados. A guitar style that glues Jimenez' *conjunto* rhythms to T-Bone Walker's jazzy blues and Guitar Slim and Lefty Frizzell's hard honky-tonk country. In the hands of the original space cowboy, the transitions seem as natural as chasing a jalapeno with a swig of Lone Star.

It didn't hurt, of course, that Doug was raised in a border state where blues, C&W, Western Swing, honky tonk, Tex-Mex, and Mexican music of all types live next door to each other like low-rent neighbors. Doug grew up on the Texas swing of Bob Wills and His Texas Playboys, frequented Frizzell performances as a kid, and was an early fan of both Jiminez and his father, Santiago Jimenez, Sr. On the radio, there was no escaping Hank Williams, Sr., who had already wedded blues and country.

Then, when Doug was preparing to make his own records, the British Invasion established a beachhead on American soil and Doug and his musical cohorts started marching to a new beat. His first hit, 1965's "She's About a Mover" with the Sir Douglas Quintet, sounded like an import from across the pond— entirely, he admits now, by calculation: "That was a lot of [Houston-based producer] Hughie Meaux's marketing strategy, to sound British. And you know, it worked. It's one of those things: if it works, you're a genius, and if it fails, you're a complete fuckin' idiot."

Doug soon fell under the sway of musical influences far closer to his instincts, the rootsy experimentalism of the late-1960s San Francisco scene and the electric poetics of Dylan. By the time of the next Sir Doug smash, "Mendocino" in 1969, he was again making 100 percent American music, albeit his own semi-twisted version of same. He made a series of modestly conceived but satisfying recordings in the 1970s before re-emerging in the national spotlight with *Border Wave*, featuring the re-constituted Quintet, including Augie Meyer's gloriously kitchsy Farfisa organ.

Doug made a return to full-fledged stardom in 1990 with the Texas Tornados, a Tex-Mex supergroup fronted by Flaco Jiminez, vocalist Freddy Fender, Doug, and Meyer. He's also recorded some quietly terrific discs in recent years with the Formerly Brothers, which includes simpatico roots rockers Gene Taylor (ex-keyboardist for Canned Heat and the Blasters), and Amos Garrett (ex-guitarist for Maria Muldaur and Paul Butterfield's Better Days).

In fact, it's the cracked regionalism of the latter band that seems closest to Doug's almost-humble heart. He mourns the death of the regional pop music markets of the '50s and '60s, when tunes coming from New Orleans, Dallas, and Chicago charted locally without ever making a dent nationally. "There were so many great guys," Doug recalls. "Sonny Jay out of Dallas. Johnny Owen—he was my original hero. . . . Johnny had a couple of national hits, but most of these guys had local hits. [Sonny's] 'Talk to Me,' Roy Head's 'Treat Her Right.' This scene just isn't around anymore." Wishing, of course, won't bring it back but as long as Doug Sahm and his various sidekicks stay on the road, it ain't quite dead yet.

DOUG SAHM'S FAVORITE ARTISTS AND RECORDINGS

Miles Davis—*Kind of Blue* (Columbia). Counter to his roots rock reputation, Doug listens mostly to jazz when relaxing at home. "I guess 'Kind of Blue' is the classic of all-time," he says, "Bill Evans and Miles Davis tied up with Coltrane, that's about as heavy as it gets."

Eric Dolphy—"Although he's a little out for some people, I think he was a genius." Dolphy, one of the most thoroughly original players in modern music, shone equally on alto sax, flute, and bass clarinet. ●: For a quick survey of Dolphy's career, start with the striking *Outward Bound* (Original Jazz Classics), his 1960 debut as a leader on which he is just starting to leave the solar system; proceed to *Out to Lunch* (Blue Note), an essential, revolutionary jazz recording that is the musical equvalent of, say, a Samuel Beckett play; and finish up with *Last Date* (Emarcy), not quite—as its packagers would have it—his last recording before his untimely death, but a worthy exit note with a sympathetic, precise European rhythm section.

Mose Allison—"One of my favorite vocalists, definitely a treasure." ●: For the instrumental side of Allison, whose hip world weariness colors his piano playing as distinctly as it does his singing and songwriting, try *Creek Bank* (Prestige) from the late 1950s. Also fine, *I Don't Worry About a Thing* (Rhino/Atlantic), his 1962 debut on Atlantic that includes "Your Mind is on Vacation." *Allison Wonderland* (2 CDs: Rhino) is the best compilation, covering 1957–1990.

Wes Montgomery—*Full House* (Original Jazz Classics). "He was a hero of mine, one of the hero guitar players. . . . Montgomery wasn't a huge influence on my guitar playing because I don't get to play jazz that often, but in terms of sheer velocity and skill he was head and shoulders above everybody else."

T-Bone Walker—Doug says that the smooth Walker and the gruffer Guitar Slim were his main influences on guitar. ●: See Master List.

Guitar Slim— ●: *Sufferin' Mind* (Specialty) is a generous, 26-track collection that includes Slim's great R&B hit, "The Things I Used to Do." *The Atco Sessions* (Atlantic) captures Slim's final output before his death, at 32, in 1959.

Bill Evans—Doug emphasizes his early recordings. ●: Pianist Evans catalog is one of jazz's richest in quantity and quality. Among the early trio recordings, *Sunday at the Village Vanguard* and *Waltz for Debby* (both Original Jazz Classics), recorded on the same afternoon with drummer Paul Motian and bassist Scott LaFaro, are landmarks of lyrical group interplay and sensitivity. *Portrait in Jazz* and *Explorations* (both Original Jazz Classics) are also wonderful.

Clifford Brown— ⬤ : See Master List.

Flaco Jimenez—"I love Flaco Jimenez's old stuff, and a lot of those songs his dad [Santiago Jimenez, Sr.] wrote. The Grammy-winner on the Texas Tornados record, 'Soy de San Luis'—Santiago wrote that—is a great song." ⬤ : Doug didn't specify titles, but *Viva Seguin* (FMSL) is worth the search to find it.

Lefty Frizzell—"I Love You a Thousand Ways." This hit by the country singer/ songwriter/guitarist Frizzell tore up Doug as a youngster. ⬤ : The song is included on two fine career overviews, *Columbia's Historic Edition* (Columbia), and *The Best of . . .* (Rhino).

Johnny Owen—We can't find any existing records by this artist but if you're ever in a used record shop in Texas . . .

Roy Head—"Treat Her Right." Head, like Doug an R&B–loving Texan, walked the frontier between soul and country, scoring a number of minor R&B hits in the 1960s. He left his blue-eyed soul style in the '70s and scored some hits on the country charts into the '80s. ⬤ : *Treat Her Right: The Best of . . .* (Varese Sarabande).

Sonny Jay—See Johnny Owen above.

Freddie Fender—Doug's partner in the Tornados is also one of his singing faves. ⬤ : *The Best of . . .* (MCA) covers the breadth of Fender's stylistic strands, from hard country to R&B to Cajun.

DOUG SAHM'S OWN RECORDINGS

⬤ : We interviewed Doug in the intermission between sets of his show at a club in Ashland, Oregon. He had to go back on stage before we could ask him about his own work. Early Sahm albums aren't easy to find in print, but *Doug Sahm and Band* (Atlantic) was much loved in its day and is an essential part of any Sahm collection. Besides Dylan, Jiminez, and Dr. John, the record features such tasty support players as Wayne Jackson of the Memphis Horns, guitarist David Bromberg, saxophonists David "Fathead" Newman and Mel Martin, and the ever-present Augie Meyer, and includes, besides several Sahm originals, tunes by Bob Wills, T-Bone Walker, *Willie Nelson, and Dylan. *Texas Tornados* (Reprise), the Tornados, first effort, and the follow-up, *Zone of Our Own* (Reprise), are stellar Tex-Mex plus Doug's usual twist of locoweed. The Tornados' *Hangin' on By a Thread* (Reprise) leaned even more in a Tex-Mex direction than previous albums, and the group had another hit with "A Little Bit is Better Than Nada" from 1996's *4 Aces* (Reprise). *Return of the Formerly Brothers* (Ryko), with Queen Ida guesting on a couple of zydeco numbers, is a casual set of diverse American roots music. The close-enough-for-government-work sensibility that pervades this disc is a perfect forum for Doug. Sahm has also cut several gutsy blues albums, among them the Guitar Slim tribute *Hell of a Spell* (Takoma) and *The Last Real Texas Blues Band* (Antone's). *The Best of Doug Sahm (1968–1975)* (Rhino) is a solid compilation.

DAVID SANBORN (November 24, 1998)

Versatility doesn't have the same cachet in music as it does in, say, home improvement. When it's said that a musician "can play anything," it's usually followed by descriptions like "mechanical," "lack of passion," "journeyman." But not when the subject is alto saxophonist David Sanborn. Although the masses know David best for his highly successful R&B/pop instrumental albums, even the hard-case critics praise his jazz abilities when he's had the occasion to demonstrate them. And it doesn't stop there. As he proved on his syndicated television program *Night Music* in the early 1990s, he can, well, play anything, but it always burns with the same rock 'n' soul heat he brings to his regular gig.

You don't learn that kind of emotional commitment—you feel it, or you don't. Still, as David notes when we reach him by phone before a Los Angeles show, it didn't hurt that he came up in an era when popular music was defined by the very qualities that would later define David's own career. Born in 1945, he first started paying attention to recorded music when "the music was the ultimate combination of three great strains in American music, which were to me jazz, gospel, and rhythm and blues." And no one embodied that combo better than Dave's first idol, Ray Charles. "He was like this diamond," David says, "and depending on what angle you looked at, that would be the facet that would be prevalent. But it was always this diamond that contained all the elements—jazz, gospel, rhythm and blues, pop, soul, funk. He invented it all as far as I'm concerned."

David grew up a rock 'n' roll freak, too, but that only tugged him in the direction he was already headed. In the '50s, the lead instrument in rock was saxophone, not guitar; that's basically how David ended up playing a Selmer instead of a Stratocaster. "All of the records by Fats Domino, Little Richard, and the Coasters had saxophone solos in them, so there was that really kind of roadhouse tenor sound that came out of the swing era and players like Illinois Jacquet, who really bridged the gap between swing music and early rhythm and blues," David says. It was a sound that "was like driving down the highway and seeing lights way off far in the distance. There was something goin' on and I wanted to get there.''

David would move on to appreciate the contributions of more introverted players like Cannonball Adderly and Phil Woods; soul-jazz maestros like David Newman, Hank Crawford, and Stanley Turrentine; and harmonic pioneers like Ornette Coleman. His unique vision—of a sax style that could go anywhere without cutting its soulful roots—has enabled him to work in such diverse situations over the years as the Paul Butterfield Blues Band, David Bowie's group, and arranger Gil Evans's jazz orchestras. It also made possible the groundbreaking *Night Music*, which paired strange bedfellows like *Sonny Rollins and Leonard Cohen and, hey, the Red Hot Chili Peppers plus Dave to make genre-leaping magic show after show.

There's another word for what David Sanborn represents—''openness,'' summed up by his approach to recorded music. All great records, notes David, ''say, 'Come into this world and go on this trip with me.' And you inhabit this world that this record is. And I think if you don't try to resist it, there's a lot of music that can do that to you.''

DAVID SANBORN'S FAVORITE ARTISTS AND RECORDINGS

Bill Doggett—''Honky Tonk'' on *Greatest Hits* (King). ''There was something real mysterious and scary and wonderful about that music that really moved me [as a kid]. It was dark and soulful and just kind of very sexual, although that was not in my mind at the time.''

Ray Charles— . . . *at Newport* (Atlantic) and *Genius + Soul = Jazz* (DCC). David's appreciation of Charles's catalog runs much deeper than this, but these albums rate highest with him. To David, Charles's performance of ''Night Time Is the Right Time'' on the former album is ''just one of the great moments in music.'' On the latter record, David loves the band sound (many of the players were from Count Basie's band), the arrangements by Quincy Jones and Ralph Burns, Charles's organ playing, the songs—in other words, just about everything.

Illinois Jacquet—''Flyin' Home'' on Lionel Hampton's *Flyin' Home (1942–1945)* (MCA). ''That's one of the classic solos of jazz in any genre,'' David says about Jacquet's solo on the title tune. ''Most saxophone players I know, it's like the national anthem.''

Miles Davis—*Kind of Blue* and *E.S.P.* (both Columbia). ''When I heard [*E.S.P.*], I said 'What chords are they playing? What are they doing? Where is the top of the tune?' I had no fuckin' idea what was going on, but I knew it was the greatest shit I'd ever heard in my life."

Wayne Shorter—*Speak No Evil* (Blue Note). "That's another record I would always keep with me."

Stanley Turrentine with Jimmy Smith—"I think the ultimate organ group of the later years was Jimmy Smith, Stanley Turrentine, George Benson, and Grady Tate," says Dave, who notes that Turrentine is one of his favorite saxists in any context. ⏺: Smith's *Off the Top* (Elektra) features all four players Dave mentions. Turrentine and Smith also appear on Smith's *Back at the Chicken Shack*, *Prayer Meetin'*, and *Midnight Special* (all Blue Note).

David "Fathead" Newman—*Fathead: Ray Charles Presents . . .* (Atlantic). "[The tune 'Hard Times'] had a really big influence on me, style-wise. I really wanted to play like that."

Hank Crawford—*From the Heart* (Atlantic). Dave loves the other-worldly ambiance of this album, recorded with Ray Charles's small band, Crawford told him, in the wee hours following a gig: "What Hank could do and what Hank can still do is play so slow and still make it hang together. . . . It takes real brilliance to do that." The tunes "Peeper" and "Don't Cry, Baby" are particular standouts, to his ears.

Jackie McLean—*Bluesnik* (Blue Note). "Jackie is such a great combination of bebop and just raw soul. And that record was really kind of the ultimate expression of that quality."

Phil Woods with Quincy Jones—Jones's *Quintessence* (Impulse). "That particular song, 'Quintessence'—it's a beautiful ballad and he's so expressive and his tone is so warm. . . . There was just something about his sound—the way Phil attacked notes and his phrasing was so hip. Everything he did swung."

Oliver Nelson—*Blues and the Abstract Truth* (Impulse) and *More Blues and the Abstract Truth* (Impulse). Phil Woods plays on the latter album, and Dave loves his work on it.

Ornette Coleman—*The Shape of Jazz to Come* and *Change of the Century* (both Atlantic). Despite the challenging musical concepts on these records, Coleman never distances himself from his audience or denies his R&B roots, Dave notes. He says that the music made him laugh out loud because "it was just life affirming."

Julian "Cannonball" Adderly and John Coltrane—*Cannonball and Coltrane* (Emarcy).

John Coltrane—*Impressions* (MCA) and *Live at Birdland* (Impulse). "What I always heard in his playing was even with the cascade of notes that would spin out from time to time, there was an overriding lyricism," says David. He calls 'Trane's solo on the former album's title tune "one of the great tenor solos of all time" and the performance of "Alabama" on the latter record "a towering moment in music."

Bob Dylan—*Blonde on Blonde* (Columbia). "There was just such a loose and focused quality to that record."

The Beatles—*Rubber Soul* (Capitol). David loves all the other Beatles records, as well: "It was just such great music. And it just had such a vitality and integrity to it. You listen back to those records and they hold up."

The Rolling Stones—*Between the Buttons* (ABKCO). "It's a train that you can't stop, that album. . . . Then you hear that great guitar sound on 'Miss Amanda Jones.' I mean that's a fuckin' killer sound."

Sly and the Family Stone—*There's A Riot Going On* (Epic).

Me'Shell NdgeOcello—*Peace Beyond Passion* and *Plantation Lullabies* (both Warner Bros.). "Here was somebody who was a product of the times, combining jazz, R&B, hip-hop, rap, pop, rock 'n' roll, everything, in a way that . . . has real direction and a real focus."

D'Angelo—*Brown Sugar* (Capitol). "D'Angelo's use of dynamics and nuance is so interesting. Plus, he's such a great fuckin' singer."

Bela Bartok—Concerto for Orchestra, New York Philharmonic/Leonard Bernstein (Sony). "Later, I heard the Fritz Reiner recording, which is supposed to be the definitive one. And I don't know, maybe because it's often the case that the first version you've heard of a piece may be the best for you, but may not be the best per se. I love that recording. It's still my favorite."

Giacomo Puccini—*Tosca;* Maria Callas, Giuseppe di Stefano, Tito Bobbi; Chorus & Orchestra of the Teatro alla Scala/Victor De Sabata (EMI). Dave says the Callas version of this opera "just fuckin' dropped me. And it reconnected me to lyricism. It reminded me how important melody is, and how important interpretation of melody is, and commitment to melody is."

James Brown—*Live at the Apollo* and *Star Time* (both Polydor, the latter 4 CDs). "James was so hip. These were like jazz players playing rhythm and blues. You know, Clyde Stubblefield played like a jazz drummer, had wrists like a jazz drummer. That's why that shit was so loose. And that rhythm guitar player just playin' that one single line thing, man. That was his job, but man, he played the shit out of it. . . . That music is like a Swiss watch, everything just works so well together."

DAVID SANBORN'S OWN RECORDINGS

David says that if he had to pick one favorite from his catalog, it would be 1991's *Upfront* (Elektra), a funkfest made with long-time collaborator, bassist/arranger Marcus Miller: "That was the most fun to do and the tune 'Snakes' really did it for me. It in a way it was the epitome of what I like to do." Another fave—like *Upfront*, from the *Night Music* era—is 1990's *Another Hand* (Elektra) which explores edgier territory than usual with such diverse players as NRBQ's *Terry Adams and Al Anderson; free-thinking guitarists Bill Frisell, Dave Tronzo, and Marc Ribot; jazz titans Charlie Haden and Jack DeJohnette; and connoisseur rock singer Syd Straw. In typical Sanborn style, his third pick is an even more complete change of pace, 1995's *Pearls* (Elektra), a program of standards on which David solos melodically over a string orchestra arranged by Johnny Mandel.

⊙: The quality of David's catalog is one of the most consistent in the business, so the best way to enter it is to match your taste to the style of the record. The 1981 recording *Voyeur* (Warner Bros.) marks the appearance of the tight jazz fusion arrangements that became a staple on most albums that followed; it's an approach well-suited to showing off David's succinct solo statements. The 1984 album *Straight to the Heart* (Warner Bros.) was recorded live in the studio to give the improvisations more immediacy. The 1983 disc *Backstreet* (Warner Bros.), 1988's *Close-up* (Reprise), and 1993's *Hearsay* (Elektra) feature the usual smart arrangements and compositions and expert playing by all concerned. The 1986 release *Songs from the Night Before* (Elektra) moves in more of a smooth jazz direction than most recent records. On 1999's *Inside*, David included three vocal tracks with Cassandra Wilson, Lalah Hathaway, and Sting doing the honors. Reruns of *Night Music* can be found on the BET on Jazz cable network.

BOZ SCAGGS (March 18, 1997)

Boz Scaggs has never claimed that he invented his silky soul music from whole cloth. "I have always maintained that whatever I've done has been a product of whatever the contemporary R&B scene was doing," Boz tells us unabashedly. "That was my first love—those records, that spot on the radio dial."

Born in 1944 in Ohio but raised in a small town near Dallas, Boz came along at the right time and place to grow up with R&B itself. "We had black radio in a big way," Boz says. "And not only popular rhythm and blues, but there was also sort of an archivist who had a radio show that influenced a lot of people at the time. He was really professorial and encyclopedic in his presentation every night about the roots and the history of the blues and the delta music and how it found its way up to the Midwestern and northern capitols and through Kansas City and Houston and so on."

Not that R&B and blues was the only thing filling his ears. "There was the beatnik and folk era happening. The San Francisco beat generation sort of spawned its own brand of music through the Limelighters and the Kingston Trio, and all that kind of stuff, and I was into that. This is nineteen fifty-five. I had one ear on the Top-Forty radio dial, and I had a real serious interest in folk music like Josh White and Lightnin' Hopkins." In grade school, Boz had taken up classical cello—"I was quite good at it and loved it more than anything that had ever happened to me"—but it fell by the wayside, he says, "because of my family's moving circumstances." When he started playing guitar a few years later in the midst of the folk and budding rock 'n' roll scene, he devoured every kind of guitar music he could find, venturing beyond the hip music of the day to the records of smooth country guitar virtuoso Chet Atkins, jazz guitarist George Van Eps, and flamenco guitar player Sabicas.

Boz began to focus more tightly on electric blues and rock when he left the folk trio he had started to join the Marksmen, a plugged-in unit headed by his high school classmate, Steve Miller. "The Ventures were real important [to me]," he says, "and of course Chuck Berry and all the rock 'n' roll guitar stuff. And being in that R&B capital, we had early access to Freddy King and B. B. King, and perhaps the most influential of all to us was T-Bone Walker. So it was all around, and it was available to see and to experience, and that's what we were playing."

But this was the early 1960s, when blues' sophisticated cousin, jazz, was going through a period of ferocious creativity and Boz rushed to be on the scene. At the age of 17, he went to New York and caught such icons as Miles Davis, John Coltrane, Roland Kirk, Art Blakey, and the Cannonball Adderly Septet. "Night after night, they were performing around New York, and I developed a deep passion, which remains to this day. I'm still adding to my Blue Note collection, and it became a very important part of my musical interest. That's real special," Boz says.

Inevitably, though, Boz was drawn back to the music that would dominate his career, R&B. In 1967, Boz received an invitation from Miller to join him and the fledgling Steve Miller Blues Band in San Francisco. Boz stuck around long enough to make winning contributions to the group's first two records, then left in 1968 to begin his solo career. R&B of almost any stripe turned from an interest to an obsession. The Stax sound out of Memphis. The Chicago soul music of Curtis Mayfield and the Impressions, ex-Impression Jerry Butler, and the Chi-Lites. And especially the Philly soul music being written and produced by Kenny Gamble, Leon Huff, and Thom Bell for acts such as the Stylistics. "At that time, rhythm and blues was becoming more and more sophisticated in terms of its chord structures and instrumentation was becoming more orchestral and more intricate," Boz notes. "And other musicians like myself were expanding our musical horizons and our abilities according to what those guys were doing. So, as that music became more complex, so did my attempts to do more interesting chords."

Boz has released albums only sporadically since 1980, but especially in recent years, each new Scaggs album is an event, eagerly awaited by fans and critics alike. He spends most of his time running one of San Francisco's top music clubs, Slim's, where he serves up the same tasty range of rootsy, soulful music that has defined his own career.

BOZ SCAGGS'S FAVORITE ARTISTS AND RECORDINGS

Josh White—"Where Were You, Baby?" ⊙: This tune is available on *The Best of Josh White* (Elektra, out of print). *The Legendary Josh White* (MCA) covers many of his best-known songs.

Lightnin' Hopkins—Boz doesn't remember the title of his first Hopkins album but it included one of his favorite songs, "Mister Charlie." ⊙: *Mojo Hand: The Lightnin' Hopkins Anthology* (Rhino), a fine two-CD survey of Hopkins's recordings, includes this song.

Muddy Waters—*Muddy Waters at Newport* (MCA/Chess): This album influenced many up and coming musicians in the 1960s besides Boz.

Ray Charles—*Ray Charles Live* (Atlantic). Boz calls this "one of the great albums of all time and one of the most inspiring to me." "I saw Ray Charles when I was fifteen in Dallas," he adds, "and I was probably only one of about a dozen people in an audience of three thousand that wasn't black. And that performance struck me so deeply. It was one of those momentous occasions . . . It just really made me want to play and be a part of whatever happened to me that night." Boz also devoured Charles's hit studio albums during his youth. ⊙: To sample other highlights of Charles's career, see Master List.

Chet Atkins—Boz can't remember titles but he pored over a number of Atkins records to study his smooth guitar mastery. ⬤: *Essential Chet Atkins* (RCA), a good single-disc retrospective that focuses on Atkins's instrumental numbers.

Sabicas—*Flamenco Fiesta* (Legacy).

George Van Eps— ⬤: *Seven & Seven* and *Keepin' Time* (both Concord).

T-Bone Walker—*T-Bone Blues* (Atlantic Jazz). "The definitive T-Bone Walker album."

B. B. King—Boz listened hard to B. B. during his woodshedding days, especially his work from the early and mid-1950s. He told us he wore out several copies of one B. B. album—he can't remember the title—in the process of learning from it. ⬤: The album Boz wore out is probably one of those on *Singin' the Blues/ The Blues* (Flair), an import CD that packages two King albums from the 1950s that influenced many blues guitarists and singers in subsequent years. This set includes the three B. B. tracks Boz mentioned to us—"Sweet Little Angel," "Please Love Me," and "Woke Up This Morning."

Miles Davis—*Kind of Blue* (Columbia). "I think if there was one record that I would take to my grave, it would be *Kind of Blue*."

John Coltrane—*Giant Steps* (Atlantic) and *My Favorite Things* (Atlantic).

Horace Silver—*Blowin' the Blues Away* (Blue Note). Boz bought nearly everything Silver recorded during this period from the early to mid-1960s, but *Blowin'* was his favorite.

Cannonball Adderley— ⬤: *Somethin' Else* (Blue Note). Although Boz can't remember specific titles, this was probably one of them, a Blue Note classic from 1958 featuring Miles Davis on trumpet and Art Blakey on drums. Cannonball is also a featured soloist on Davis's *Kind of Blue* (see above).

Art Blakey—*A Night at Birdland, Vols. 1–2* (Blue Note), each volume a separate disc.

Stevie Wonder—*Music Of My Mind* (Motown). "That was one of the most important records ever made, I think, to musicians who were really on the scene and listening to stuff at that time."

Curtis Mayfield and the Impressions—"This Is My Country." Mayfield wrote this black-pride message song for his group, the Impressions. It was released as a single by Mayfield's label Curtom. ⬤: *The Anthology 1961–1977* (2 CDs: MCA) combines highlights from both the Impressions and solo phases of Mayfield's work.

Curtis Mayfield—*Superfly* (Curtom). About this high-water mark from Mayfield's solo catalog, Boz says, "That was sophisticated stuff and I think it influenced a lot of people of my generation."

Chuck Berry— 🔘 : See Master List.

Freddy King— 🔘 : *Hideaway: The Best of . . .* (Rhino) is an excellent, 20-track compilation. *Just Pickin'* (Modern Blues) is a twofer that includes a pair of his most influential albums, *Let's Hide Away and Dance Away with . . .* and *. . . Gives You a Bonanza of Instrumentals.*

Isley Brothers— 🔘 : *The Isley Brothers Story, Vol. 2* (Rhino) covers the Isleys from 1968 forward, the period when they were having the biggest impact on Boz.

The Chi-Lites— 🔘 : *Greatest Hits* (Rhino).

The Stylistics— 🔘 : See Master List.

Jerry Butler— 🔘 : *Iceman: The Mercury Years* (Polygram) covers the Butler tracks produced by Gamble and Huff in Philadelphia, which again were those that most influenced Boz.

The Ventures— 🔘 : *Walk, Don't Run: The Best of . . .* (EMI America) includes all the hits and numerous album cuts among its 29 tracks.

BOZ SCAGGS'S OWN RECORDINGS

Boz's favorites among his own recordings begin with his first solo record, *Boz Scaggs* (Atlantic), a critical if not commercial success recorded in Muscle Shoals with the superb house band, plus guitarist Duane Allman. This album has a rural blues sound unlike anything Boz has done since. "We concentrated on some writing that I'd done in San Francisco just prior to that recording, and by being in Muscle Shoals itself, being such a roots, country, and basic music place and [with such rootsy] players, we just grounded ourselves in that," Boz explains.

Boz's smash album *Silk Degrees* (Columbia), featuring the hits "Lowdown" and "Lido Shuffle," "stands out to me, not only because it was a big hit, but because it was a joy to make . . . I really relished and enjoyed the success of that record. And I enjoyed the musicality of the record and my association with those players [including drummer Jeff Pocaro, keyboardist/arranger/writer David Paich, and bassist David Hungate, the studio pros who would later record as Toto]. That was a very special point in my life."

Boz is also pleased with how *Some Change* (Virgin), released in 1988 after a long hiatus from recording, turned out. Finally, Boz looks back fondly on the two records he made with the Steve Miller Band (what the band called itself after signing with Capitol), *Children of the Future* and *Sailor.* ''In putting those albums together, anything that was out there was fair game, and the musical spectrum was wide. We were working with Glynn Johns [producer for the Who and the Faces] and we recorded one of them in London. So you could take anything. You could take Beatles and Stones and everything that was out there into account.''

⚫: You can tour Boz's early roots with him on 1997's blues-oriented *Come On Home* (Virgin), which features winning covers of songs by Sonny Boy Williamson, Bobby ''Blue'' Bland, Jimmy Reed, T-Bone Walker, and others, and four sharp Boz originals in a similar vein. *My Time: A Boz Scaggs Anthology* (2 CDs: Sony) is a recent compilation.

JOHN SCOFIELD (August 18, 1998)

t's a guitar style that seems so natural—an edgy distorted rock/blues tone, the confident wiggle of funk, and the keen intelligence of jazz. Yet—quick now— how many guitar players can you name besides John Scofield who have ever pulled it off?

Maybe that's because to sound like Scofield, you have to grow up like him. John, born in 1951, began to play guitar at age 11. The era of rock guitar glory—of Cream, the Who, and Hendrix—still hadn't happened when John's dad brought home a record he thought his son would appreciate, jazz guitarist Django Reinhardt's *Djangology.* ''That was the only record, outside of rock 'n' roll and folk music, that I had,'' says John. ''And it really did show the possibilities.''

At the same time Reinhardt was sparking his interest in jazz, John was marinating in the soul music pouring out of his bedroom radio—James Brown, Aretha Franklin, and the flood of great singles issuing from Stax and Atlantic records. He was dipping into the blues of Albert and B. B. King. And, like tens of millions of other American kids at the time, his life was being saved by rock 'n' roll. But ironically, it was the potency of mid-1960s rock—specifically, Jimi Hendrix's rock—that turned John's career ambitions in another direction.

''I think Jimi Hendrix changed me in a lot of ways,'' John tells us. ''I remember hearing the song 'Fire' in my room sitting there with my little transistor radio listening to music late at night. And I'd never heard a guitarist sound like that. . . . It wasn't jazz, it was something else. But it had something too that was just blowing, like jazz . . . and then when I heard Jimi Hendrix live it made me give up being a rock guitarist because it was so good. I said, 'Why would anybody bother to play rock 'n' roll after that?' "

John began focusing more narrowly on jazz until "by the time I was eighteen, I was a jazz snob and didn't listen to anything else." He studied the recordings of the mainstream jazz guitar maestros Wes Montgomery and Jim Hall. But always nagging him was the thought that there had to be a place in jazz for the folk, blues, R&B, and rock influences that made such a difference to him early on.

Then John acquired records by Pat Martino and the Gary Burton Quartet that confirmed his intuition. With the latter band in particular, and its compositions by Carla Bley and the group's bassist, Steve Swallow, John saw the potential he had dreamed about: "[The tunes] by Carla Bley and Steve Swallow were influenced by the Beatles and Joni Mitchell and stuff like that. Very harmonic stuff as well as bluesy. But it was never, never somebody playing trite pop tunes and pandering down to the lowest common denominator. This was original music that incorporated elements of folk music and stuff into it, in a different way from any of the other jazz-rock things that came after it . . . And [guitarist Larry] Coryell really did bring in some rock elements that Jim Hall, Wes Montgomery, and those guys didn't touch. And he brought it in in a great, really tasteful way." Little did John realize that it was his own destiny to become as important as anyone in carrying this new approach forward, with one chart-topping, artistically strong album after another.

As John looks back now, part of that success owes to the fact that when he was young and his pockets were shallow, he chose his records carefully and well. "I wouldn't buy an album unless I'd heard it before at somebody else's house, or heard about it. I mean, I probably had like forty albums, and, you know, probably half of them turned out to be classics," he laughs.

JOHN SCOFIELD'S FAVORITE ARTISTS AND RECORDINGS

Django Reinhardt—*Djangology 1949* (Bluebird/BMG). "It was one of the last records he made . . . and his playing to me was even more mature and influenced by bebop than probably his most famous recordings before World War II. . . . It's a great record. I learned so much from that."

B. B. King—*Live at the Regal* (ABC/MCA). This is one of the first blues records John got into and still, in his opinion, the greatest record King has ever made.

Albert King—*Born Under a Bad Sign* (Stax). With backing by *Booker T. and the MGs and Memphis Horns, this record made a huge impact on blues and rock guitarists alike. : The CD reissue *King of the Blues Guitar* (Atlantic) contains all of 1967's *Born Under a Bad Sign* (Stax) plus assorted Stax singles.

Art Farmer with Jim Hall—*Live at the Half Note* (Atlantic). "I loved Jim's work on there and that really turned me on to his playing."

Wes Montgomery—*Smokin' at the Half Note* (Verve). John prefers live records, and this is one of the great ones. "That record killed me," says John.

Pat Martino—*El Hombre* (Original Jazz Classics). This bluesy outing by Martino "really brought me up over the top," John recalls, laughing at the memory.

John Coltrane—*Live at Birdland* (Impulse). John loved Coltrane's music and this disc, featuring the great quartet with McCoy Tyner, Jimmy Garrison, and *Elvin Jones, was his favorite.

Ornette Coleman—*The Shape of Jazz to Come* (Atlantic). John first read about this record in *Downbeat*. "The tunes are so great. I didn't know that it was free jazz or anything. I didn't realize that it was constructed differently than the jazz when they were playing on chord changes. So I just listened to it in the same way that I would listen to anything, and I loved it."

Howlin' Wolf—*Howlin' Wolf/Moanin' in the Moonlight* (MCA/Chess). This CD contains Wolf's first and second Chess LPs, the latter of which John bought in high school. Although he was in the process of becoming a jazz player, the album still cleaned his clock.

Miles Davis—*Kind of Blue* (Columbia), *Sorcerer* (Columbia), and *Bitches Brew* (Columbia). John feels that the music made by the great Davis quintet—saxophonist Wayne Shorter, pianist *Herbie Hancock, bassist Ron Carter, and drummer Tony Williams—on albums such as *Sorcerer* was even more adventurous in its way than what John Coltrane was doing in the same era, the mid- to late 1960s. John bought *Bitches Brew* when it came out in 1969 and then tried to figure how it could be the same Miles Davis who made *Kind of Blue*: "When I listened to that trumpet I realized how it was the same. . . . I loved Miles's sound."

The Gary Burton Quartet—*Duster* (Koch). This 1967 record and the unit that played on it—vibraphonist Burton, guitarist Larry Coryell, bassist Steve Swallow, and drummer Roy Haynes—made a major impact on John, especially in seeing the bridges between the different forms of music he loved. "History hasn't really remembered that record in the right light," he tells us. "The tunes are great, everybody's playing wonderful, and it's this mixture of jazz and rock, but in a different way from 'Bitches Brew' because it was very compositional."

Jimi Hendrix—*Are You Experienced?* (Reprise) and *Axis Bold as Love* (Reprise). John likes all of Hendrix's work, but "I probably like those little produced ones more than the free-flowing ones, in a way. I'd rather hear a jazz guy take a really long solo. But Hendrix in his idiom, which was this other thing—that was it!"

Bill Evans—*Sunday at the Village Vanguard* (Riverside) and *Waltz for Debby* (Riverside). "Bill Evans's music affected just about everybody, but it really got me," says John. These two legendary albums, recorded on the same day at the same gig, added an elegance to jazz, John says, much like Evans's former boss Miles Davis was doing "only it was Bill and his version of it on the piano. And his version of jazz was so personal, like Miles's was."

Paul Bley—*Footloose* (Savoy). "They're playing free-ish jazz. I had a big long period where I listened to that, wore that out. . . . [drummer] Pete LaRoca was just dealing! And he was so swinging. It made Paul, I think, dig a little harder into his bop roots. But at the same time, there was a pulling between those two guys, a tug-of-war over which way it would go, and I liked that."

Thelonious Monk—John first heard Monk on a "best-of" collection drawn from his various albums on Riverside. 🔘: *Brilliant Corners* (Riverside), *Thelonious Monk with John Coltrane*, *Monk's Music*, *Thelonious Himself*, and *Alone in San Francisco* are some of Monk's best-loved records for this label.

Medeski, Martin, and Wood—*Shack Man* (Gramavision). John liked this record by this spacey, funky organ trio "so much so that I made a record with them [1998's *A Go Go* (Verve)]."

Bill Stewart—Drummer Stewart and organist Goldings are part of John's regular band. "They're both killers," says John. 🔘: Stewart's albums as a leader are *Snide Remarks*, *Telepathy* (both Blue Note), and *Think Before You Think* (Evidence). Also check out Stewart's work on John's record *What We Do*.

Larry Goldings— 🔘: Goldings is a featured sideman on the excellent Scofield albums *Hand Jive* (Blue Note) and *Groove Elation* (Blue Note). His own stellar albums include *Light Blue* (Minor), *Awareness* (Warner Bros.), *Big Stuff* (Warner Bros.), the bossa-nova record *Caminhos* (Warner Bros.), and *Whatever It Takes* (Warner Bros.).

Joe Lovano—"I think playing with Joe Lovano in the last ten years has been one of the most rewarding things for me." 🔘: Lovano is heard to great effect on John's records *Time on My Hands* (Blue Note), *Meant to Be* (Blue Note), and *What We Do* (Blue Note) as well as Lovano's own recordings, including the superior live date, *Live at the Village Vanguard* (Blue Note).

Aretha Franklin—*Lady Soul* (Atlantic). John has been greatly influenced by certain vocalists, starting with the immortal "Lady Soul."

Ray Charles—*Crying Time* (ABC). John loves the big band arrangements on this record in addition to Charles's spectacular singing.

Frank Sinatra—*In the Wee Small Hours* (Capitol). This 1955 record is one of Sinatra's most jazz-oriented efforts.

Johann Sebastian Bach—*Goldberg Variations, BWV 988* (Sony Classical), Glenn Gould, piano. "That's as good as you can get in music."

Bela Bartok—Concerto for Orchestra. This work is widely appreciated in the jazz world. ⏺: See Master List.

Charlie Parker—*Bird At the Roost, Vols. 1–4* (Savoy). "Just the most wonderful Charlie Parker music, and it changed my life."

JOHN SCOFIELD'S OWN RECORDINGS

John's favorites from his own discography include 1978's *Rough House* (Enja) ("I think I was gettin' my own sound together around that time"); 1986's *Blue Matter* (Gramavision), which John describes as "more of a jazz-funk record"; and 1989's *Time On My Hands* (Blue Note) with a band that included Joe Lovano, Charlie Haden, and Jack DeJohnette: "And then I started playing with Lovano all the time, and a little while later we made an album called *What We Do* (Blue Note) with Bill Stewart on drums and Dennis Irwin on bass, and I think that really captures what we were about. I think that's my best kinda jazz record." His 1998 effort, *A-Go-Go* (Verve), topped the Billboard jazz charts but John's just flat-out happy with the music: "That works, man. It's just one of those things that we got in the studio and it was the right combination of people and material and it just recorded itself—it had a life of its own."

As a much-requested sideman, John has contributed to numerous albums by other jazz artists. Of that body of work, he particularly enjoys *So Near, So Far* (Verve), Joe Henderson's tribute to Miles Davis, with a terrific quartet of Joe, John, Dave Holland, and Al Foster; saxophonist Chris Potter's *Unspoken* (Concord), with John, Holland, and Jack DeJohnette backing the leader; and bassist Marc Johnson's *Bass Desires* (ECM), with drummer Peter Erskine and John and Bill Frisell on guitars. Finally, John mentions Davis's *Decoy* (Columbia), one of several albums he made with Davis in the mid-1980s, a time he considers an important period of his career.

PETE SEEGER (July 14, 1998)

Our request to interview Pete Seeger, faxed to his manager, was answered by a note in the mail from Pete himself. It stated, "Please phone me if only to confirm that in all my life, I have hardly ever listened to recorded music for pleasure. One exception—when ice skating on our home 'rink,' I listen to steel drums."

We called Pete and, sure enough, he verified that, except on the rare occasions detailed below, he has almost never played a disc to entertain himself: "I didn't listen to records as a kid. I'd prefer to do other things. Nor as a teenager—the students around me were listening to swing and saying 'Isn't that great?' And occasionally I'd listen to it. I didn't dislike it, but I had other things I preferred to do: read books, or go on hikes, or paint pictures or build something."

Still, it was a recording that Pete's musicologist father brought home of Doc Boggs playing the American five-string banjo that inspired Pete to take up the instrument himself, back in the early 1930s when Pete was in his early teens. "I thought it was from China, it was so weird," Pete recalls. "It was completely different than anything I'd ever heard."

It was also recorded music that opened Pete up to the universe of folk music, the performance and promotion of which would become his life's mission. When Pete was somewhere between 19 and 21 years old, his father began working with folklorist Alan Lomax "and I suddenly found out there were not dozens or hundreds, but thousands of extraordinary field recordings [that Lomax had made]. They were very scratchy aluminum discs, many of them. Had to be played with a cactus needle, I remember—you had to sharpen it from time to time. This was a revelation to me that this kind of music even existed."

Until he was introduced to Lomax's vast collection, Pete felt he already had a good grasp of the musical universe. He knew some classical compositions, mostly from the music played by his pianist father and violinist mother, both of whom were on the faculty at Juilliard School of Music. He knew the pop songs of the day, "which, in my opinion, were kind of foolish," and the European folk songs he was taught in school, "which seemed kind of phony to me, because the English translations were not very good. . . . So I didn't bother with 'em and all of a sudden I come across all these great songs, 'John Henry,' and 'John Hardy,' and so on, sung by people who knew them well. And performed 'em well, even as scratchy as the record was. So I started learning some of this music and in a sense I've gone on from there to try to learn as many kinds of folk music as there are different kinds of folks."

In his 80th year, Pete still keeps a full schedule that admits no time for listening to recordings (most of the artists mentioned below Pete knows more from having seen them perform live than having listened to their records). Besides, he notes, "I have music going through my head twenty-four hours a day, and I have to stop my own music to listen to something." But recorded music still plays an important part in his hopes and dreams: "All around the world, between radio and TV and recordings, the people of the world are getting acquainted with each other as never before. Words were not able to do the job as well, but music can leap the language barrier. And I think it's one of the things that will bring the human race together unless we blow ourselves apart first." Pete also dreams that recorded music will do for most listeners what it did for him as a young man. "As far I'm concerned," he says, "one of the main purposes of records is to help people decide what kind of music they want to make themselves."

PETE SEEGER'S FAVORITE ARTISTS AND RECORDINGS

Various artists—*Alan Lomax Collection Sampler* (Rounder), *Sounds of the South* (4 CDs: Atlantic), or any of the 13 volumes in *Southern Journey* (Rounder). These albums are comprised of Lomax's field recordings that so captivated Pete in his youth.

Woody Guthrie—In 1940, Pete became a close friend of Guthrie, the activist conscience of American folk music. Pete says about Guthrie and their mutual pal Leadbelly, "There's an honesty there. I think this is one of the things I find lacking in a lot of pop music and in a lot of so-called classical music. They are often trying to impress somebody." 🔘: See Master List.

Huddie Ledbetter ("Leadbelly")— "I was so impressed by Leadbelly. In the fifties, Julius Lester and I put out Folkways instructional recording called *The Twelve String Guitar as Played by Leadbelly* [Folkways is out of print and is as rare as the book of the same title published by Oak Publications] where I analyzed what he was doing with his thumb. He had a great sense of a bass line. He played chords, but not so much chords as bass notes. The bass became in many ways the most exciting part of the music, along with the melody and the words." 🔘: See Master List.

Josh White—Pete learned to play blues banjo in part by studying White's guitar technique. 🔘: *The Legendary Josh White* (MCA), *Free and Equal Blues* (Smithsonian/Folkways), and *The Complete Recorded Works, Vol 1-6* (Document).

Mississippi John Hurt—Pete first heard Hurt in 1941. "I've never been expert enough to play Mississippi John Hurt stuff. . . . I admired him tremendously." 🔘:

1928 Sessions (Yazoo) captures the original recordings made of Hurt's music. *Memorial Anthology* (Adelphi), a two-CD set of Hurt's post-"rediscovery" performances in the mid-1960s, includes a 31-minute interview of Hurt by Pete Seeger.

Joseph Spence—"I eventually met him down in Nassau," Pete says of the legendary Bahamanian guitarist. "And that's one reason I play almost always in his type of guitar tuning, where you lower the sixth string two frets. It's called 'drop-D' tuning. . . . I heard his Folkways record. I was down in Miami and I said 'I've gotta go see Joseph Spence.' He had no desire to become internationally famous. He was a carpenter by trade and liked to play music with his friends." 🔘: See Master List.

Bob Dylan—*John Wesley Harding* (Columbia). Pete normally plays only steel drum music while skating "but I remember one winter I played *John Wesley Harding* over and over while I was skating. I was very impressed by that LP."

Phil Ochs—Pete compares Ochs, as well as Dylan and Tom Paxton, to Woody Guthrie in that "there's a sense of humor at the same time there's a great seriousness of purpose. And it's this blend of humor and tragedy that I think makes a good poem and good lyrics." 🔘: *Phil Ochs in Concert* (Elektra) was actually partially or entirely recorded in the studio but is one of his finest acoustic records. *There and Now: Live in Vancouver* (Rhino) is not truly a concert record—several tracks were cut in the studio with audience noise added—but it's a fine album nonetheless. *Farewells & Fantasies* (Rhino) is a lovingly assembled three-CD box set with outstanding notes and photos.

Tom Paxton—See Phil Ochs above. 🔘: Start with *A Paxton Primer* (Pax), a best-of assembled by Paxton himself for his own label (74 East Park Place, East Hampton, NY 11937).

Joni Mitchell—"I heard 'Both Sides Now' being sung, not by her, but by some pop group, when I was trying to find out the time on the radio, and by accident, I was driving in the car and heard it. I couldn't rest until I found the song and got the words of it." 🔘: *Clouds* (Reprise) contains "Both Sides Now." *Ladies of the Canyon* (Reprise); *Blue* (Reprise), one of the most influential albums ever recorded, especially for confessional-style singer/songwriters; *For the Roses* (Asylum); and *Court and Spark* (Asylum) are other crucial Mitchell records before she took a turn toward jazz in the mid-'70s.

Cesar Franck—Violin Sonata in A. One of the few records Pete recalls making the time to listen to was a rendition of this piece, which he sought out on a friend's recommendation: "I went and borrowed the seventy-eight RPM album, this was back in thirty-seven when I was at Harvard College. I got a listening room. I lay down on the carpet for an hour and listened to it twice. It's a great piece of music." ⬤: Kyung Wha Chung, violin; Rada Lupu, piano (London); or Itzhak Perlman, violin; Vladimir Ashkenazy, piano (London).

Steel drums—"They really are just great for skating. I've always wanted to try and persuade the Ice Capades to have steel drums on ice. You could have a whole steel band skating around with steel drums playing. I tired it but I'm not very good at it. If I had another musical life to live all over, I could have led it very happily teaching steel drums to people, and playing them." ⬤: Strong steel drums recordings include *Trinidad Carnival* (Delos), live recordings from the 1989 Trinidad Carnival, and *Carnival Jump Up* (Delos), a variety of steel-bands from Trinidad and Tobago recorded live on location.

PETE SEEGER'S OWN RECORDINGS

When asked to nominate favorites in his own discography, Pete replied "I don't listen to my records ever, so I can't even tell you. I have to listen to them once, as a matter of duty."

⬤: The best introduction to Pete's music is his live recordings, which present a sample of his best-loved material and convey the special synergy he creates with his audience. There is no other artist more committed to everyday people the world over—their art and their issues—and no other artist who so intimately relates to his listeners. *We Shall Overcome: The Complete Carnegie Hall Concert* (Columbia) captures an over-two-hour concert in 1963, at the height of the folk movement explosion. *Pete Seeger Singalong* (Smithsonian/Folkways) documents a typical Seeger concert circa 1980, when he was 61.

To fully appreciate the breadth of Pete's contributions to folk music, you must delve into his social activist repertoire, on behalf of working people, the disenfranchised, the environment, and peace. The two volumes of *Broadside Ballads*, released respectively in 1963 and 1965 on Smithsonian/Folkways, present programs of topical songs originally published in *Broadsides* magazine. The 1979 release *Circles and Seasons* (Warner Bros.) showcases a set of gentle pleas for environmental caring.

"I usually put it this way," Pete says. "Some songs help you forget your troubles, and some songs occasionally help you understand your troubles. And once in a long while a song comes along that helps you do something about your troubles. Whether it's 'We Shall Overcome' or 'Yankee Doodle,' they spread widely and get people to bestir themselves in some way. My main purpose as a musician is to put songs on people's lips instead of just in their ears."

JOSEPH SHABALALA (January 28, 1998)

Joseph Shabalala, born to a poor farm family near Ladysmith township in rural South Africa, was having a modestly successful musical life when he had a dream that—blessedly—shattered everything. A singer in his youth, Joseph became a guitarist after trips to town exposed him to the pop guitar styles developing in the townships in the 1950s. He then joined a choral group called the Blacks. He had risen to become its leader and main composer when a vivid insight came to him as he slept one night in 1964. In the dream, he heard voices singing in entirely new ways. He brought the new ideas to the Blacks as a gift from God but they weren't nearly as receptive as he had hoped. In fact, the controversy led to the breakup of the group, at that time the most popular Zulu vocal ensemble.

Certain that his inspiration was valid, Joseph formed a new group, Ladysmith Black Mambazo. Recalling that moment for us, he still finds the dream experience difficult to articulate, using terms like The Spirit and The Teacher: "I was just like a person in class myself and came back to Black Mambazo with my degree. The Teacher is always with me when I am working with Black Mambazo. The guys were surprised because working with them it was something sounding in my eardrum: 'Okay, now the alto is supposed to be here, because the basses are here now. This is the key.' It was just fresh in my mind. That was the dream, and then after that it was just like a vision when I am working with them all the time."

At the same time the vision birthed Black Mambazo, it ended Joseph's guitar career. "The Spirit forced me to forget about [the guitar]," Joseph tells us, "because the harmony I was going to sing, the guitar couldn't fit in that. From the beginning to me when you talk about guitar I say 'I heard the guitar! I know the guitar! But I have this other sound.' Now I'm free."

Joseph's vision may have been Heaven sent but it still allowed some earthly influences. Traditional Zulu vocal music remains the basis of Black Mambazo's sound, although the dream rearranged the folk elements in brand new ways. And Joseph has also been inspired by American musicians. He loved Louis Armstrong's singing from the moment he first heard it on the radio. He encountered Elvis Presley when the King performed in Swaziland. And in American black gospel, he heard a crucial link with Black Mambazo's aims. "People in Africa, they were always praying with the music," Joseph notes. "Whether they were going to fight, they pray to win; whether they are going to marry one another, they pray. Their music is just like chanting, praying. [Gospel] is my favorite harmony. Now I feel like I teach everyone in South Africa about this sound."

Then there's the Paul Simon connection. Anyone familiar with Black Mambazo knows that they owe their international prominence to Simon's groundbreaking record *Graceland* (Columbia), which introduced them to the West. But Joseph tells us that the Black Mambazo/Simon link goes back farther than most people realize. In the late 1960s, when Black Mambazo was touring in southern Africa, Joseph heard Simon & Garfunkel's gospel-inspired hit "Bridge Over Troubled Water" and was intrigued. Later, he says, "my neighbor was playing a [Paul Simon] record, *One Trick Pony*, and I listened carefully and said 'I wish this man could join Black Mambazo! I love his voice.' It was a joke, but it was just like tradition that I was going to sing with him."

However, when the actual association began, it was met with distrust in South Africa. "I understand very well what they were suspecting, because in South Africa there were a lot of bad things," Joseph says. "They trusted nobody. But The Spirit was telling me that Paul Simon was a good person who was just opening the gate, especially to this tradition [in] music." Once again, the Spirit had called it right.

JOSEPH SHABALALA'S FAVORITE ARTISTS AND RECORDINGS

Paul Simon/Simon & Garfunkel— ●: Simon & Garfunkel's *Bridge Over Troubled Water* (Columbia) remains one of the most important records of the 1960s. The three-disc *Collected Works* (Columbia) includes every track from the duo's studio albums. Simon's solo debut, *Paul Simon* (Warner Bros.) is one of his finest song collections, although many feel that *There Goes Rhymin' Simon* (Warner Bros.) and *Hearts & Bones* (Warner Bros.) are near equals. *Graceland* (Warner Bros.)—essentially Simon's poetic pop sensibility superimposed on South African rhythm tracks—is one of pop's greatest albums. Some like the denser, more difficult *Rhythm of the Saints* (Warner Bros.), an Afro-Brazilian excursion, even better.

Curtis Mayfield/The Impressions—"Amen." "That song just got into my people's heart," Joseph says, and it held special significance for him as well. "That is the day I started to know that there are black people in America. I *knew* that, but the song presented me more than what I knew." He sings the chorus softly, and continues, "The day when I heard this song, it was just like 'how can we go there and bring back our people? They are lonely. They want to come back home.' Because the sound of 'Amen' is the sound we use plowing oxen on the farm. We said maybe now the spirit goes straight to them and we were all thinking 'How can we save them?' " ⬤: This song is included in a number of collections under the names Curtis Mayfield or the Impressions. One of the best is Mayfield's *The Anthology 1961–1977* (MCA).

The Winans—Ladysmith Black Mambazo has performed with this contemporary African-American gospel ensemble, and Marvin Winans sang on Black Mambazo's 1990 album *Two Worlds, One Heart* (Warner Bros.). "It was beautiful singing with this gospel group," Joseph says, "I love very much this gospel music." ⬤: *Return* or the two-disc *Live at Carnegie Hall* (both Qwest).

Louis Armstrong—"One time when I was working in Durbin, from the radio I heard this funny voice. I loved that [and thought] 'Who is this?' The radio announcer said 'Louis Armstrong,' and I talk to my guys, 'Hey this guy, I love his voice.' " Joseph mimics Armstrong's voice as he continues. "Singing just like he's talking to you or maybe he's just tickling you. That was beautiful to me." ⬤: The 1961 album *Louis Armstrong & Duke Ellington: The Complete Sessions* (Roulette) may not be prime Ellington but Armstrong is terrific.

*Bobby McFerrin—Joseph imitates McFerrin's vocals, then exclaims, "Oh that man! He has his own thing, like Black Mambazo." ⬤: See the section on McFerrin and his recordings.

Joan Baez—"We shared the stage with her in Europe. Her voice was beautiful." ⬤: Baez has a lengthy catalog of excellent releases but *Joan Baez 5* (Vanguard) contains some especially good demonstrations of her vocal prowess.

Mahlathini—"When you talk about the rhythm, you talk about Mahlathini and Soul Brothers," Joseph says emphatically. ⬤: See Master List.

Soul Brothers— ⬤: See Master List.

*Lucky Dube— ⬤: See the section on Lucky and his recordings.

JOSEPH SHABALALA'S OWN RECORDINGS

Of the thirty-odd recordings released by Black Mambazo, Joseph recommends first *Shaka Zulu* (Warner Bros.), the Grammy award–winning release produced by Paul Simon. He also likes one of the group's earliest album's, 1973's *Amabutu* (Gallo, South Africa)—the title means "warriors," he says. "But if you talk about nowadays, the record *Thuthukani Ngoxolo* (Shanachie), which means 'Let's Develop in Peace.' They used to play that record all the time when they talked about peace.''

RICKY SKAGGS (December 9, 1998)

ountry and bluegrass music fans have been known to beam with provincial pride about their favorite sounds, as if the stuff somehow sprang intact from the dirt in the Appalachian Mountains. For Ricky Skaggs, country music provides the opposite thrill. When he listens to it, he hears its roots in other cultures and faraway places. When he first came across Django Reinhardt and Stephane Grappelli's string alchemy, he understood that America's western swing was Western European born. "The fiddle, the swing, the beat, everything was just a country version of what those guys in Paris was doing twenty years before that," Ricky notes. When he listens to "father of bluegrass" Bill Monroe, he hears "a hodgepodge of Celtic music, Mississippi Delta blues with the Jimmie Rodgers influence, and almost fiery jazz somehow."

Ricky gets just as much juice from tracing roots in the opposite direction. When he plays Monroe's records from the period before he invented bluegrass, he hears a rhythm pattern that showed up years later in rockabilly, such as Bill Haley's "Rock Around the Clock." In 1963, Ricky's sister brought home a couple of Beatles 45s. "She put 'em on the turntable at home and the house just filled with a new kind of music that I'd never heard before, but yet the harmonies, the singin' structure and everything, was not something that was real foreign. I mean, it sounded like the Everly Brothers doin' the Louvin Brothers doin' the Stanley Brothers doin' the Monroe Brothers, you know." It was then that Ricky realized the hill music and bluegrass he'd grown up loving at home in Kentucky had impressed those fellas from Liverpool, too.

Ricky's cosmopolitan perspective on traditional rural music, plus his own extraordinary musicianship, has enabled him to cut a wide swath in the business. A marvelous singer and virtuosic performer on banjo, fiddle, guitar, and mandolin, he was a potent force in the progressive bluegrass movement with stints in J. D. Crowe and the New South, the Country Gentleman, and his own Boone Creek. In 1977, he began a long association with Emmylou Harris when he replaced Rodney Crowell in her Hot Band. In his stellar solo career, he has gradually moved from the updated country of the Harris-like New Traditionalists to the original bluegrass that first excited him as a kid—the idea being to make "fun music again, and not worry about charts and radio and sales and that kind of stuff."

Ricky also remains one of the most in-demand session pickers around with contributions to scores of albums by popular music's elite. But if anyone thinks they're renting a little Americana when they hire Ricky Skaggs, he's got a story to tell about that.

RICKY SKAGGS'S FAVORITE ARTISTS AND RECORDINGS

Bill Monroe—The first music to really captivate Ricky besides the early country and gospel he heard from his musician parents was the bluegrass of Monroe, Flatt & Scruggs, and the Stanley Brothers. His favorite of Monroe's countless bands was the classic lineup with Lester Flatt, Earl Scruggs, Chubby Wise, and Howard Watts. : *The Essential Bill Monroe (1945–1949)* (2 CDs: Columbia/Legacy) and *16 Gems* (Columbia/Legacy) feature that lineup playing the group's best-known material. There is overlap in material between the two but the takes are different.

Flatt & Scruggs—Ricky appeared on TV with his idols when he was just seven years old. : *The Complete Mercury Sessions* (Mercury) and *1949–1959* (4 CDs: Bear Family) encompass Ricky's favorite period of the band. He prefers the pure bluegrass sound, before they added dobroist Josh Graves in 1955, although he likes Graves's work, too.

The Stanley Brothers—Ricky points out the "high lonesome" vocal harmony style of bluegrass singing was started by this band, not Bill Monroe. Ricky loves the early Columbia recordings with Pee Wee Lambert on mandolin as well as the mid-'50s Mercury recordings, which show off Ralph and Carter Stanley's evolution as songwriters and singers. Carter died in 1966, and Ralph persisted as Ralph Stanley and the Clinch Mountain Boys. Ricky became a regular member of this band in 1969 at age 15. : *Complete Columbia Recordings* (Columbia/Legacy) and *Angel Band: The Classic Mercury Recordings* (Mercury Nashville) capture Ricky's favorite edtions of the band. Ralph Stanley and the Clinch Mountain Boys' *Bound to Ride* (Rebel) is an anthology that includes Ricky's work with the group.

The Osborne Brothers—The Osbornes used amplification, piano, drums, twin harmony banjos, steel guitar—all bluegrass innovations that expanded the music's audience in the 1960s even if it riled the purists. : There are two solid Osborne hits sets: *The Best of . . .* (Sugar Hill) and *Greatest Bluegrass Hits, Vol. 1* (CMH). For a deeper dip, go for *Bluegrass 1956–1968* and *Bluegrass 1968–1974* (both 4 CDs: both Bear Family).

The Country Gentlemen—*Folk Session Inside* (Mercury). By 1963 when this recording was made, the group had smoothed their rough edges and were at a peak, says Ricky: "They were really innovative. John Duffy was so great as a lead singer, and the harmonies between the three, Eddie [Adcock] and John and Charlie [Waller], was just really awesome." Ricky was with the group in the early 1970s. ⬤: *The Country Gentlemen Featuring Rick Skaggs* (Vanguard) is a good example of how the band sounded with Ricky on board.

The Beatles—"I loved their recordings. Everything about their music was awesome. The Beatles were a tremendous influence." ⬤: See Master List.

The Hollies—"I was a big harmony freak, so I loved the Hollies." ⬤: *All-Time Greatest Hits* (Curb) includes "Look Through Any Window," one of Ricky's favorites.

The Rolling Stones—Ricky never owned a Stones record but he ate up the singles on the radio during the British Invasion era: "I'm a big fan of their music. I think they're one of the best rock 'n' roll groups still around. They hit into a groove, and they just stay with it." ⬤: *The Singles Collection: The London Years* (ABKCO), a wonderful package, will enable you to experience the Stones much as Ricky did, although nearly every album through 1972's *Exile on Main Street* is a classic as well.

Bob Wills and the Texas Playboys—Ricky prefers the mid-1930s to late '40s recordings that feature any or all of the following: vocalist Tommy Duncan, groovemeister guitarist/arranger Eldon Shamblin, and pianist Al Stricklin: "All that stuff, it had such a danceable groove. . . . It was a country version, a poor man's version, maybe, of the big band kind of stuff . . . Instead of, you know, martinis and champagne, it was a long-necked Pearl in the back of your pocket, dancin' with some girl out in Texas." ⬤: *Bob Wills Anthology* (Columbia) covers 24 tracks from the '30s and '40s. *The Tiffany Transcriptions, Vols. 1–9* (Rhino, available separately), from 1946 to '47, come closest to capturing the group's live sound and displaying its phenomenal stylistic range.

*Vassar Clements—Under "various artists," *Hillbilly Jazz* (Flying Fish). "That whole album was just really done well."

The Nitty Gritty Dirt Band—*Will the Circle Be Unbroken* (2 CDs: EMI America). "That was a great record and it turned me on to a lot of stuff," says Ricky about this seminal recording that united the Dirt Band with an army of traditional country legends for a set of old-time classics.

Django Reinhardt and Stephane Grappelli—Ricky loves all the pre-war, Hot Club of France material: "That was awesome music." ⬤: See Master List.

Jimmie Rodgers—*The Essential* . . . (RCA). "I love to go back and listen to Jimmie Rodgers."

The Carter Family— 🔘 : See Master List.

The Chieftains—"I've just always appreciated their music and appreciate the fact that they're trying to keep the tradition alive, but yet pushing the boundaries and allowing it to grow." 🔘 : . . . *3* and . . . *4* (both Shanachie) are outstanding early '70s recordings. *Another Country* (RCA) puts the group in the company of some of country music's best, including Ricky. *Long Black Veil* (RCA) is another successful crossover effort featuring guests such as Van Morrison, Sting, the Rolling Stones, and Sinead O'Connor.

RICKY SKAGGS'S OWN RECORDINGS

Ricky feels very good about most of his solo albums, as well he should for he is widely known as one of country music's most consistent performers. He makes particular mention of 1979's *Sweet Temptation* (Sugar Hill), his solo debut that splits time between bluegrass and New Traditionalist country; 1982's *Highways and Heartaches* (Epic); 1984's *Country Boy* (Epic), with a guest appearance from Bill Monroe; 1989's *Kentucky Thunder* (Epic); 1991's *My Father's Son* (Epic); 1995's *Solid Ground* (Atlantic); 1997's *Life is a Journey* (Atlantic) and *Bluegrass Rules!* (Rounder), the latter a full-fledged, joyous return to bluegrass; and his most recent album, *Ancient Tones* (Skaggs Family), another traditional bluegrass record still in production when we speak, which Ricky predicts will "far surpass" its predecessor. (*Tones* was released in 1999.)

Ricky adds that "I love the Emmylou records that I got to be involved in," especially *Luxury Liner, Blue Kentucky Girl, Roses in the Snow, Evangeline,* and *Christmas Album (Light in the Stable)* (all Warner Bros.). *Roses* in particular showcases Ricky's instrumental prowess. Ricky also points to the well-received album he produced for Dolly Parton, *White Limousine* (CBS): "I think that really showcased her voice. . . . Comin' back to Nashville and actually doin' a real country record again was a real statement for her."

🔘 : The 1980 record *Skaggs and Rice* (Sugar Hill) pairs Ricky with master flatpicking guitarist *Tony Rice for a set of superb bluegrass duets. The 1985 release *Live in London* (Epic) is an excellent introduction to Ricky's catalog because of a virtual "greatest-hits" selection of songs and typically stunning picking. To hear the progressive bluegrass Ricky made in the late '70s with his band Boone Creek, hunt down *Boone Creek* (Sugar Hill) and especially *One Way Track* (Sugar Hill).

J O E Y   S P A M P I N A T O   (April 1, 1998)

I f NRBQ's Joey Spampinato had chosen another line of work, perhaps it would have been finish carpentry. The songs he writes are like fine furniture, sturdy enough to last decades yet also artfully wrought, every surface burnished and complete. Also like good furniture, form serves function—the romantic confections sweetly ache, the rockers rock. His bass playing blends strength and beauty in much the same way. With drummer Tom Ardolino, he nails down the beat with a punchy accuracy and decorates it with a melodic flair, making the NRBQ rhythm section one of the most respected in popular music.

Not surprisingly, Joey's biggest influences were also meticulous craftspeople, starting with the Everly Brothers and their songwriting support team of Boudleaux and Felice Bryant. "I was like nine or ten," Joey recalls. "When the Everly Brothers music came on, it was like a big open window of fresh air coming through to me. Maybe it was because they had Southern accents or something. It was just different than anything I'd ever heard. I was living in the Bronx, New York, and that experience was like a big, big thing for me. Now I can see that I learned about duet harmony from them. They were just completely perfect. They knew how to pick the right harmony to make a perfect jewel. You could not improve on it."

Like Joey, the Beatles were also huge Everly fans, so when their singles made their way to the United States, Joey's ears were already well-primed. "When they came over with 'Love Me Do,' they were doing their version of this thing that I loved so much," Joey tells us. "I think that's why I took a liking to them right from the first note."

For bass playing, Paul McCartney and Motown legend James Jamerson top Joey's list. "He's still the best at what he does," says Joey about McCartney's all-around talents. "You really listen to what he's doing on those [Beatle] records, rhythmically, he's a really precise player, he's really great. Let alone his songwriting. For someone who's so well known and respected, I think he's actually underrated as a player." As for Jamerson, Joey says that when he listened to Motown records in the mid-1960s, he locked into Jamerson's musicianship even more than the songs and singers.

Beyond these and a few other well-chosen models, Joey doesn't spend much time checking out recorded music. "I don't say 'I'm going to listen to this particular thing,' and then go search it out," he says. "Somebody might play something for me, or I might hear it on the radio, or Tom might put something on a tape that I'll hear. But I don't have an extensive record collection and study things. Lately, most of the music I've been listening to has been at my girlfriend's place. She's a musician, too, a trumpet player, and I've been hearing a lot of her Chet Baker records, which I've been loving. You miss a lot of things by not listening, so it's been good for me. I like to be open to things and you never know where or when you're going to hear something that will drive you wild."

JOEY SPAMPINATO'S FAVORITE ARTISTS AND RECORDINGS

*The Everly Brothers—Joey says the best entry to the Everlys catalog is through the greatest-hits packages. The Brothers' first recordings were for Cadence in the 1950s. About that body of work, Joey says, "It's a masterpiece, the whole thing." But he also appreciates their 1960s work for Warner Brothers. : *Cadence Classics: Their 20 Greatest Hits* (Rhino) includes all the hits plus several strong album cuts. *Walk Right Back: The Everly Brothers on Warner Brothers* (Warner Archives), a two-CD set, covers all major tracks for this label.

The Beatles—"I don't have favorites Beatles albums. It's like the Everly Brothers, I like it all, you know." But Joey would appear to have a favorite Beatle, Paul McCartney, his most obvious influence. : See Master List.

James Jamerson—Jamerson's bass playing on countless Motown recordings was a revelation to Joey as well as many other pop and rock bass players in the 1960s. : Some controversy remains about whether the late Jamerson or Carol Kaye played bass on some Motown records, even when Jamerson is credited. That is, while Jamerson indisputably played on many of the label's biggest hits, actual titles are hard to nail down. One he played on for sure is Martha and the Vandellas' "Dancing in the Street." This appears on the Vandellas' *Anthology* (Motown) among other compilations.

Marvin Gaye—Gaye was perhaps Joey's favorite artist in Motown's talented stable. : See Master List.

*Booker T. and the M.G.s—As with Motown's records, Joey focused in on the playing by the session musicians on Stax Records more than the songs themselves. And that meant the MGs—organist Booker T. Jones, guitarist *Steve Cropper, bassist Duck Dunn, and drummer Al Jackson. : See Master List.

Mary Wells—"My Guy." "The bass player is great. I really loved it just for that." Joey had heard, but couldn't confirm, that the bass player was Carol Kaye, but Carol assured us that, yes, it was her. : *Greatest Hits* (Motown).

Art Davis—"Reeds and Deeds" on Roland Kirk's *Reeds and Deeds* (Mercury): Although not really a jazz buff, Joey loved the playing by a number of bassists— Larry Gale, Butch Warren, and Reggie Workman among them—on jazz records Q bandmate *Terry Adams played for him. But this player, on this track in particular, knocked Joey flat. ⬤: The original album is out of print, but this track can be found on the collection *Verve Jazz Masters 27* (Verve).

Johnny Mercer—"You gotta go back to the old songwriters, from the thirties and forties, these guys were layin' it down," Joey urges. "It was a different style of writing, it was more sophisticated." Mercer tops Joey's list from that era. He wrote the lyrics to Gene DePaul's music for *Seven Brides for Seven Brothers* one of the first musicals Joey ever saw and still one of his favorite scores. ⬤: *Seven Brides for Seven Brothers* (Rhino) is the original motion picture soundtrack for this 1954 film.

JOEY SPAMPINATO'S OWN RECORDINGS

Like Terry Adams, Joey doesn't feel he can name favorites in NRBQ's catalog: "I think with your own music, you tend to maybe never be totally satisfied, because a recording is a snapshot of something, and then you play these songs live, and they go through changes." So he doesn't listen to his own records. But he does feel close to *You're Nice People You Are* (Rounder), a children's album that was the band's most recent recording when we spoke. He makes clear that the band didn't approach the music any differently than they would an adult album. "A lot of times people think the NRBQ thing is childlike anyway, so it's not a big stretch, by any means," he chuckles. "I don't go for the idea of talkin' down to kids. If we're doing something just silly on this record, it's a silly we would do anyway, you know what I mean?"

⬤: For our recommendations of NRBQ albums, see Terry Adams's entry.

MAVIS STAPLES (June 20, 1997)

Mavis Staples, the mighty mite lead vocalist for the Staple Singers, didn't need to listen to records for inspiration. She grew up not only hearing but knowing many of the great gospel singers of the music's Golden Age, including the remarkable Mahalia Jackson. "When I first heard Mahalia Jackson, I thought she was the queen," Mavis tells us when we meet to interview her. "We were neighbors. We got real tight. Momma would always have lots of people in the backyard for Fourth of July. And Mahalia would come over. She was my idol.

"She called me up once and told me—we were on a show in Harlem—she said, 'Halie'—she called herself Halie—'don't feel too good. I want you to help me sing this song.' My knees were knockin'. I said, 'Yes, ma'am, I'll help you. What song is it?' She said, 'Precious Lord.' Lo and behold, she wanted me to start off the song, so I did [sings opening]. Jesse Jackson—he was a youngster then—he helped her up to the mike. She started to sing, and we both sang it together."

Other notable neighbors on Chicago's 33rd Street included such budding gospel artists as Sam Cooke, Lou Rawls, Johnnie Taylor, and Curtis Mayfield, "only Curtis lived in the nice part—they had grass where he was," laughs Mavis. In the summertime, Mavis and her sisters and friends didn't have to wait for gigs to hear the great Cooke sing. Sam, along with Mavis's brother Pervis, worked on a horse-drawn watermelon truck that rolled through the neighborhood. "They'd be singing 'Watermelon, get your red ripe watermelon.' Pervis would take a turn. Sam would take a turn. People would come out of their houses just to hear them."

But Mavis was drinking in just as much music at home, from her father and the unique arrangements he created for his family band. "People didn't know what we were singing," says Mavis. "They'd say, 'I know you're singing church songs but you sound like you're singing country.' The harmonies were different— my sister's tenor would go into a lot of minors and then there was Pop with the bluesy guitar."

The blues element, in fact, got Mavis in trouble with her relatives. "I'd be walking to school and all I could hear was Buddy and Ella Johnson singing 'Since I Fell for You.' I got the worst whipping of my life for singing that song," she laughs. "The kids in school, the teachers, they knew I could sing and they pushed me on the stage in a variety show and that's what came out. [She sings, 'You made me leave my happy home.'] My uncle started coming around the side of the auditorium. He was sixteen. I thought he was coming to congratulate me. Instead, he snatched me off the stage and just walked me on home. Never did say a word to me. I didn't know what was going on. He pushed me into my grandmother's house and said 'This young lady was up at the schoolhouse singing the blues.' From that, she sent me outside to get some switchin.' 'You don't sing blues, you sing church songs in this family!' But nobody had ever told me what to sing."

Mavis owns one of the biggest voices in popular music this side of her good friend Aretha Franklin's. She says she got her vocal power from her mother but her ability to wield it came straight from Pops' side of the family: "When I started singing, there wasn't anyone I was trying to sing like. I had the bass voice. It was just a gift the Lord gave me. It's my own style. Pop would coach me, 'Mavis, you don't have to sing loud to make people feel it, just sing with feeling.' " A

Staple Singers performance these days includes a generous dose of Mavis letting that feeling all but lift her off the stage.

MAVIS STAPLES'S FAVORITE ARTISTS AND RECORDINGS

Mahalia Jackson—"Daddy had her records, seventy-eights. We couldn't touch 'em. I couldn't listen to 'em until he got home." ⬤: See Master List.

The Davis Sisters—From Philadelphia, this fabulous family gospel group was founded by Ruth "Baby Sis" Davis and included three of Ruth's sisters. ⬤: See Master List.

Dorothy Love Coates—Although not blessed with a big voice, the brilliant Coates more than compensated with an emotive, ecstatic style and heavenly swing. Mavis started listening to Coates, who also wrote and arranged for her group, as a child: "I just could see everything she would be singing . . . I love Dorothy Love. We still talk on the phone." ⬤: *The Best of Dorothy Love Coates and the Original Gospel Harmonettes* (Specialty) combines a two-volume "best-of" album set on one CD.

The Dixie Hummingbirds—This now grandfatherly seminal black gospel group is known to pop fans as the singers who backed Paul Simon on his "Loves Me Like a Rock." ⬤: See Master List.

The Sensational Nightingales—The intense lead vocals of Reverend Julius Cheeks, later replaced by the smoother Charles Johnson, helped bring this group its original acclaim. ⬤: *The Best of the Sensational Nightingales* (MCA), and *Heart and Soul/You Know Not the Hour* (Mobile Fidelity).

Albertina Walker and the Caravans—Some consider this the greatest women's gospel group of all time. Besides Walker, the Caravans included future gospel stars Shirley Caeser and Inez Andrews singing soprano. ⬤: See Master List.

The Swan Silvertones—Founded by tenor Claude Jeter, who left the group in 1965, the Silvertones also influenced a number of secular artists, including Paul Simon. ⬤: See Master List.

The Swanee Quintet— ⬤: *The Best of the . . .* (Nashboro).

Fairfield Four—One of the leading black gospel groups, the original members first came together in the 1920s. ⬤: *Angel's Watching Over Me* (P-Vine), *Standing in the Safety Zone* (Warner Bros.), and *I Couldn't Hear Nobody Pray* (Warner Bros.), which won a Grammy in '98.

Clara Ward and the Ward Singers—This group created controversy by commercializing, but Ward remains one of the most influential black gospel singers ever. : *The Clara Ward Singers* (Roulette), 22 tracks cut in 1963.

Alex Bradford—Bradford was a singer, keyboardist, songwriter, and gospel choir director whose dramatic style helped form the roots of '60s soul music. : *The Best of Alex Bradford; Rainbow in the Sky; Too Close* (all Specialty).

Mighty Clouds of Joy—This group was a later influence on Mavis after the classic gospel performers listed above. : See Master List.

Aretha Franklin—Mavis and Aretha have been close friends since they were 12 or 13. Mavis loves all of Aretha's work—gospel, soul, blues, pop, and jazz. : See Master List.

Sam Cooke and the Soul Stirrers—"Sam Cooke was the best singer in the world." : See Master List.

The Pilgrim Travelers—One of the most popular black gospel groups in the 1950s, the Travelers were also close friends of the Staples. : See Master List.

The Valentinos—Bobby Womack and his brothers (including Cecil, later of Womack and Womack) recorded two R&B hits as the Valentinos. : The revelatory *Sam Cooke's SAR Records Story* (2 CDs: ABKCO), which samples the output of Cooke's own record label, includes seven tracks with the Valentinos and three more with the brothers appearing as The Womack Brothers. The set includes such other great artists as the Soul Stirrers, Johnny Taylor, R.H. Harris, and Cooke himself. Cooke produced most tracks, gorgeously.

Bobby Womack—"Bobby Womack was like a little preacher. That boy could sing!" : *Midnight Mover* (EMI), a two-CD career retrospective of Womack's soul and R&B best, was released in 1993.

Curtis Mayfield—Like his neighbor Sam Cooke, Mayfield was a protean talent as a singer, writer, and producer. Although less noted for it, he was also a unique and influential guitarist before the accident that paralyzed him. : See Master List.

Johnny Taylor—"We used to call him Mr. Sweetness because he was just so cute. He was the best to take Sam's place [in the Soul Stirrers] because he sang more like him than anybody. But it was Johnny's stuff on Stax that was getting to me—'Who's Making Love,' 'Disco Lady.' " : See Master List.

Marvin Gaye—Mavis loves Gaye's entire catalog: "All of his albums, I must have played them for about a week after he passed, just playing records and crying.

When I met him, he was such a beautiful person." Gaye recorded many hits with Tammi Terrell, another favorite of Mavis's. : See Master List.

Marv Johnson— : See Master List.

Clyde McPhatter—"He was another one of our good friends. When he and Sam Cooke would sing, all of us girls would scream." : See Master List.

MAVIS STAPLES'S OWN RECORDINGS

: We didn't get the chance to speak to Mavis about her own catalog. We met in the afternoon before a summer evening concert in Southern Oregon, and she had to leave to ready herself for the show before we could ask her about her own music. During a long recording career with the Staple Singers, she has only occasionally stepped outside to do solo recordings. The CD reissue *Only for the Lonely* (Stax) includes two albums from the '60s, *Mavis Staples* and *Only for the Lonely*. More recently, she recorded two albums with the guy then known as Prince co-producing and performing, 1989's *Time Waits for No One* (Warner Bros.) and 1993's *The Voice* (Paisley Park). Her latest is *Spirituals & Gospel: Dedicated to Mahalia Jackson* (Polygram).

Fortunately, the Staple Singers catalog is replete with songs that showcase Mavis. A respectable Staple Singers collection begins with 1972's *Be Altitude: Respect Yourself* (Stax). The many other Staple Singers albums of note include *Uncloudy Day/Will the Circle Be Unbroken* (Vee Jay), which covers two fine albums from 1955-1960, the pre-message period for the band, on a single CD. The sound most fans associate with the group—straight-talking message songs that rocked, shook, and shimmied—came together in 1970, when Al Bell, who had played Staple Singers records on his gospel radio show in the 1950s, took over the production chores for the Staples' albums at Stax, where they had signed two years earlier. These albums include *The Staple Swingers*, with a sensational, slow-burning lead vocal by Mavis on "Give a Hand—Take a Hand" and the hits "Love is Plentiful," "Heavy Makes You Happy," and "You've Got to Earn It"; the aforementioned *Be Altitude*; *Be What You Are*, which while containing nothing as arresting as *Be Altitude*'s "Respect" and "I'll Take You There" is otherwise of a piece with it, including the charting tracks "If You're Ready," "Touch a Hand, Make a Friend," and the title song; and the re-packaged *City in the Sky*. The latter, made with the crack Muscle Shoals session players, now includes earlier hit "Oh La De De," and 1972 live versions of "Respect" and "I'll Take You There" along with the original album's hits "My Main Man" and the title song. *The Best Of . . .* (Stax) is a strong hits package.

ROEBUCK ''POP'' STAPLES (June 20, 1997)

oebuck "Pop" Staples, patriarch and leader of the Staple Singers, is not only a national musical treasure but also a phenomenon of nature. We met him in his hotel room before a 1997 performance in Jacksonville, Oregon; smooth-skinned and radiant like a stage light, he looked two decades younger than his 82 years. As if to underline the point, he was dressed decades younger, too, in a brown '70s-style Nehru suit and a large gold medallion around his neck. His electric guitar leaned against the nightstand—like Pop, ready to go to work. Pop seems to have made only one concession to age—the patience to tolerate his much younger interviewers' efforts to keep up with him.

Pop told us that he got some of his first musical cues from one of the best, Texan Blind Lemon Jefferson, who recorded in the 1920s: "Starting from there, I began to want to sing. Didn't start to think about being [a professional] artist until about 1935. I would sing at home in Mississippi with the family. We would sing gospel songs. We didn't have no radio, no television, nothing to listen to. After we got off of work in the cotton fields, we would go out in the front yard—we had a big yard—the moon was shining and we just began singing. The echoes were all over the fields and people would hear and they would come. Two or three times, [it happened that] we'd start singing . . . and it would be heard way over to the east, west, north, and south, and people would be coming across the field, come running into the yard, they'd come in singing. And at those times, that yard would just fill, there'd be twenty-five or thirty people just standing there singing. We'd just sing to good times and that's the way we amused ourselves back in those days and that's where I got bit with the bug of singing."

The guitar bug bit him when, as a young boy, he'd go to town and hear guitar-playing singers—among them fellow Mississippian Howlin' Wolf—who would travel through and sing in people's kitchens for nickels and dimes. He bought a Stella guitar for $5 from a variety store, making 25- and 50-cent payments until he was able to bring it home. He learned to play by carefully studying the local singers and recordings by national blues stars, many of whom were from his region: "I didn't know how to tune but anything I heard, I could play it. Blind Blake, Charlie Patton, all of those guys had records. I could hear them and copy."

Although Pop first modeled his guitar-playing after other musicians, he ultimately developed his own reverb-drenched style that is one of the most instantly recognizable in popular music. Pop, who started by playing blues until religion took over his life, was also apparently the man who introduced the guitar to black gospel music. "No one was playing guitar with church songs back then,"

*Mavis Staples told us later that day, "because the church people, some of them who didn't really know the Bible, they'd say 'You don't play guitar in church. That's the devil's music.' Pop had to show them in the Bible where it said, 'Praise Him with singing, praise Him with tambourines.' After that, all the gospel quartets would bring in guitars."

The Staples's vocal style also came directly from Pop. "One day it struck me. I said, 'Let's do like my family used to do,' " Pop told us. "I had four children at that time. We used to sing all together as a family, let's do that with my family." Pop didn't know the formal techniques of four-part harmonies but he experimented until "we really started to sounding good." The group sang the few songs they'd mastered at a family member's church and did well enough to be invited back. From this modest "discovery" was born a career that would carry the Staple Singers to the top of the charts.

Pop was also responding to an inner voice—as well as ugly external events—when he and the Staple Singers began performing their message songs in the mid-1960s. Mavis tells us the story behind "Why Am I Treated So Bad," occasioned by the famous 1957 incident when angry white policemen in Little Rock, Arkansas, refused to carry out a federal court order to desegregate a local high school: "Pop sat there in his reclining chair and said, 'Why are they treating [those children] like that?' That's where that song came from. 'I'm all alone as I sing my song. Hear my call. I've done nobody wrong. But I'm treated so bad.' "

Ultimately, Pop would combine forces with, and draw inspiration from, Dr. Martin Luther King to keep his messages front and center. "I called him long distance," recalls Pops. "I heard a speech of his and told him I wanted to meet with him. When I met with Dr. King, I told him what we were doing. I said, you're pitching love, peace, and happiness not just for one nationality but for all people. I told him I'd like the Staples Singers to go with him on some of his missions."

Thus began a partnership that would last through April 4, 1968, the last day of King's life, when on the balcony of King's room at the Lorraine Motel in Memphis, King asked Pop to perform his favorite Staples song, "Why Am I Treated So Bad?," for the crowds that were gathering to demonstrate and hear King speak. "I didn't know it would be the last time I would see him," says Pop. "We went on and sang the song that night and I made a record of that song for Dr. Martin Luther King."

POP STAPLES'S FAVORITE ARTISTS AND RECORDINGS

Blind Lemon Jefferson—Perhaps the first recordings that really grabbed Pop were by this massively influential blues singer-songwriter-guitarist. : *Blind Lemon*

Jefferson (Milestone) gives an excellent accounting of Jefferson's deeply personal guitar style and witty lyrics. Try also *King of the Country Blues* (Yahoo).

Howlin' Wolf—Pop loves Wolf's music—along with that of his good friend, B. B. King—more than any other. 🔘: See Master List.

B. B. King— 🔘 : See Master List.

Blind Blake— 🔘 : *Ragtime Guitar's Foremost Fingerpicker* (Yazoo) and for fanatics, the four-volume *Complete Recorded Works* (Document).

Charley Patton—This early Delta blues star was not only an influence on Pop but also an acquaintance. 🔘: See Master List.

Barbecue Bob (Robert Hicks)—This bottleneck 12-string guitar player from Atlanta died of pneumonia at 29 but made a huge impact in his short life. 🔘: *Chocolate to the Bone* (Yazoo).

Big Bill Broonzy— 🔘 : See Master List.

POP STAPLES'S OWN RECORDINGS

Of the Staple Singers recordings, Pop's favorite is the smoldering ''Respect Yourself''—''because it's saying something and I think people should listen to it.'' ''Respect Yourself'' was a major hit in 1972 on both the R&B and pop charts. Pop divides his other Staple Singers picks equally between inspirational songs—''God Can'' and the irresistible ''I'll Take You There''—and the ''message'' cut, ''Long Walk to DC,'' written by Homer Banks. ''Respect Yourself'' and ''I'll Take You There,'' along with another hit, ''This World,'' appear on *Be Altitude: Respect Yourself* (Stax), the album that most people choose as their gateway to the Staple Singers catalog. ''Long Walk to DC'' is featured on *Soul Folk in Action*, the Staple's debut on Stax. We were unable to find an existing version of ''God Can.''

Pop is also justly proud of both of his solo albums, 1992's Grammy-nominated *Peace to the Neighborhood* (Pointblank/Charisma)—with production help and musical support from Bonnie Raitt, Ry Cooder, Jackson Browne, and famed Hi Record's producer Willie Mitchell—and its Grammy-winning follow-up, *Father, Father* (Pointblank), which also includes contributions from Cooder. Pop is particularly fond of the title cut on the latter record. The Staples sing on both discs, including typically volcanic lead vocals from Mavis.

🔘: For more on the Staple Singers catalog, see Mavis Staples's entry.

J E F F   T W E E D Y   (December 5, 1997)

P atiently, Jeff Tweedy sets the record straight. Yes, he comes from a small town in Illinois' southern farm belt. Yes, he built his reputation making near-Smithsonian-worthy rural folk music with his former band Uncle Tupelo. But he grew up listening not to the Carter Family but to much the same stuff as kids raised in some ticky-tack Chicago suburb. And you can hear what he means in the alt-rock leanings of his current band, the wide-ranging Wilco. "It's somewhat rural," he says about his hometown of Belleville. But "it's more like an industrial town that had its heyday probably a century ago . . . I grew up in the initial stages of the great homogenization of America—7-Elevens and chain record stores—so I didn't really have a regional identity to rally around."

It's true that Mom played a lot of Johnny Cash around the house and Jeff is distantly related to "Cousin" Herb Henson, a well-known country DJ and TV show host during the 1950s. But the music that warmed his ears as a kid was the budget rock 'n' roll vinyl spun at home by his older brothers and sister. "They always seemed to have the cheapest album that somebody big put out," he laughs, but their low-budget collection still afforded him an elite rock education via such treasures as the Rolling Stones' *Between the Buttons*, the Beatles' second album (*With the Beatles*), and *Bob Dylan's Greatest Hits, Vol. 2*.

Infected with rock 'n' roll fever, Jeff found a record store in town where he could buy *Trouser Press* publications and *Creem* magazine and read about records he wasn't seeing in the stores. But it was the punk revolution of the mid-1970s that first gave him his own music to identify with. Jeff bought Ramones and Sex Pistols records, and then the Clash's *London Calling*, all of which laid the foundation for what would later become a pillar of Uncle Tupelo's punk-country sound.

When Jeff decided to dig into the country roots of rock 'n' roll, it was almost an academic exercise. It started "just from hanging out in record stores and finding those records and thinking they looked cool and thinking that nobody was really listening to them and hearing—like the Beatles covered 'Act Naturally,' so Buck Owens is cool," he laughs. "And I read a lot, too—I'd read about 'Stagger Lee' being on *London Calling* and how that song has probably been recorded in three thousand different variations as far back as the twenties. I'd pay attention to that stuff and try to find out [more]."

Jeff also started making determined forays through the folk music archives at the local library with co-conspirator and eventual Uncle Tupelo co-founder, Jay Farrar, a fellow punk-head he'd met at Belleville West High School. "When Jay and I started Uncle Tupelo, there was definitely at least some unwritten populist point of view in the back of our minds because we were really into folk music and field recordings and stuff like that. At the same time, we considered punk rock to be part of that tradition, [as well as] rock 'n' roll in general."

But all those musical categories matter more to others than they do to Jeff. "The more I listen to music," he says, "it's all become one thing . . . Art for its own sake to me isn't that much different than playing music for a chicken and beer dance. At the end of the day, I don't know that you can make those distinctions really bold."

JEFF TWEEDY'S FAVORITE ARTISTS AND RECORDINGS

Rolling Stones—*Between the Buttons* (ABKCO). "A big record for me. I don't think it was very big in the States. [My brothers and sister] must have gotten a deal on it."

Clash—*London Calling* (Epic). Jeff's favorite punk record, although not at first: "I didn't get it when I first listened to it. I was like thirteen years old. I kind of hated it. But for some reason, I kept playing because I paid a lot of money for it and I eventually wore it out. It's a lot to figure out when you're a kid, like this is supposedly punk rock but it was a lot of different things. It was basically the Clash in the end. I still don't think there's another record that . . . was that diverse stylistically and still coherent."

Meat Puppets—*Meat Puppets II* (SST). Starting with the Clash, Jeff developed a taste for bands with unique identities. This album fit that bill. "That's supposedly a punk rock band. It didn't sound like any punk rock bands I'd heard."

Replacements—*Let It Be* (Twin/Tone). "They came to define their era, but when their records came out and I got them, they didn't seem to fit in anywhere."

Minutemen—*Double Nickels on the Dime* (SST). "There's another band that was being rallied as an L.A. or SST punk rock band. But you buy the record and it's like jazz!"

Dinosaur Jr.—*Bug* (SST). Of both Dinosaur Jr. and Hüsker Dü, Jeff says, "Those were bands that were alive and contemporary so I got to see them live and feel a part of it."

Hüsker Dü—*Zen Arcade* (SST).

Buck Owens—*I've Got a Tiger By the Tail* (Capitol) and *Live at Carnegie Hall* (Capitol). Jeff doesn't remember the titles of all the Owens records he first listened to but these two—which many critics and fans also cite—came right to mind.

Various artists—*High Atmosphere: Ballads and Banjo Tunes from Virginia and North Carolina Collected by John Cohen in November of 1965* (Rounder). This compilation of Appalachian folk artists is one of the records that Jeff and Jay Farrar pored over at the library. Uncle Tupelo did remakes of three songs garnered from this record on their album *March 16–20*.

Various artists—*Sounds of the South* (4 CDs: Atlantic). "It's potentially all you'd need to know about music," Jeff says of this boxed set, from 1959 field recordings by Alan Lomax. The set encompasses folk tunes from the Blue Ridge Mountains, blues, black gospel, and white spirituals.

Various artists—*The Complete Stax/Volt Soul Singles, Vols. 1–3* (Stax). Each volume is a big (9–10 CDs) box set of prime Memphis soul. The volumes, in order, cover the periods 1959 to '68, 1968 to '71, and 1972 to '75. All contain much fabulous music although the classic Stax sound is best represented on Vol. 1. The company's music became smoother and more commercial from 1968 on.

Nick Drake—*Pink Moon* (Hannibal). "[This record caused me to see that] you can create your own universe with just a vocal and a guitar."

Byrds—*Sweetheart of the Rodeo* (Columbia). "That was probably as big a record as anything for Uncle Tupelo and me at the time. I would say it probably had more of an impact than the records that people [always associate with us, such as] the Flying Burrito Brothers records."

Swell Maps—"Let's Build a Car" on *Jane from Occupied Europe* (Mute). Jeff describes this group, one of his current faves, as "a deconstructed punk rock band."

Daniel Johnston—"He lives in Austin, Texas, and put out all these tapes to hand out to people and sell on the street. He eventually recorded some records—one for Atlantic, one for Shimmy Disc, and one for Homestead, which was just taken from all his tapes. All his records meant a lot to me and especially one tape called *Don't Be Scared*. [His music is] really childlike . . . He's a very troubled individual. He's been in and out of asylums his whole life. It's not for everybody [chuckles] but it' staggeringly pure music to me." : *Yip/Jump Music* (Positive), *Artistic Vice* (Shimmy Disc), *1990* (Shimmy Disc), *Continued Story* (Positive), and *Fun* (Atlantic). *Don't Be Scared* is out of print and scarce.

*Doug Sahm—*Mendocino* (Smash) and *The Best of Doug Sahm and the Sir Douglas Quintet* (Polygram). Sahm paid his admirers in Uncle Tupelo a compliment by appearing on their *March 16–20, 1992*.

Bob Dylan—*The Basement Tapes* (Columbia) and *Desire* (Columbia). "Overall, Dylan's probably my favorite of everyone. *The Basement Tapes* are something I can't get enough of and all the unofficial, unreleased basement tapes, too. *Desire* is one of my favorite records of all time."

John Cale—*1919.* "That's probably led to some changes in the way we [Wilco] record and think about things. It's John Cale with *Little Feat. It's his most re-alized and most rehearsed-sounding album, post–Velvet Underground. It's really surreal, obscure lyrics but melodically, it's amazing."

The Handsome Family—*Milk and Scissors* (Carrot Top). "I think it has some of the most beautiful lyrics of the last four or five years."

Neutral Milk Hotel—*On Avery Island* (Merge). "It's like a lo-fi version of the Kinks. A really stream-of-conscious, fresh approach to lyric-writing."

JEFF TWEEDY'S OWN RECORDINGS

Jeff feels Uncle Tupelo really hit its stride with its final two records, *March 16–20, 1992* (Rockville) and *Anodyne* (Sire): "Whatever we were doing, I don't think it was fully realized or preconceived or anything but we just started to play our own music with a certain amount of confidence. Those records stand up for me." He has the same feeling for Wilco's second effort, *Being There* (2 CDs: Warner Bros.). "It's the first step Wilco has taken to making our own music and feeling proud about it," he says.

"But I don't dislike any of the records," he adds. "I think once you make them, you just let them go and appreciate the good parts. All the records I've been a part of, I at least enjoy something about them. It's like a photo album or something."

●: Uncle Tupelo's first two records are *No Depression* and *Still Feel Gone* (both Rockville). Wilco debuted in 1995 with *A.M.* (Warner Bros.), a well-received, al-ternative country-rock record that hinted at the band's resistance to pigeonholing. Which brings us to 1999's *Summerteeth* (Reprise), a surprising but fascinating and entirely successful departure from its predecessor, *Being There*, which itself was a deliberately grubby makeover of the band that cut *A.M.* Where the lo-fi *Being There* sometimes referenced *Exile*-period Rolling Stones, *Summerteeth* with its spacey atmospheres is far more reminiscent of the Beatles and the trippy folk/pop side of Beck. But at the center of both albums, and all Jeff's work, is strong writing and melodies. On that count, in fact, *Summerteeth* underlines *Being There*'s declaration that this is a band that matters.

Speaking of which, shortly after our interview, Woody Guthrie's daughter Nora designated Billy Bragg to put music to some lyrics Guthrie had written but

never finished as songs; Bragg then asked Wilco to help. The collaborators obviously took the job as a sacred charge—the music supports Guthrie's blue-collar
poetry memorably on *Mermaid Avenue* (WEA/Elektra), one of the most highly
praised albums of 1998.

In his spare time, Jeff writes and plays with super-sideband Golden Smog,
which also features Soul Asylum's Dan Murphy and the Jayhawks' Gary Louris.
That alt-country group's well-regarded output includes 1992's *On Golden Smog*,
1995's *Down by the Old Mainstream*, and 1998's *Weird Tales* (all Rykodisc).

ADRIAN UTLEY (October 27, 1998)

W hen jazz guitarist Adrian Utley joined keyboardist Geoff Barrow and vocalist
Beth Gibbons in trip-hop band Portishead, he had to put his improvisation
abilities on the shelf. "Pretty much everything is arranged," Adrian tells
us by phone from England. "And we don't really break from that." But what
Portishead did need from Adrian was his diverse musical reference points, many
of which were foreign to Barrow and Gibbons but vital to the music Portishead
was about to make.

For one thing, Adrian, older than his bandmates, had grown up with the
music of Jimi Hendrix, which would become an important thread in Portishead's
soundscapes. Adrian also brought to the table a deep knowledge of atmospheric
jazz, beginning with one of the most deeply felt albums ever made, John Coltrane's *A Love Supreme*. "I think jazz-wise, when the sun came out and the
world lit up for me was when I heard *A Love Supreme*," Adrian recalls. "When
I first heard it, I didn't actually like it, and I remember sitting listening to it, and
one day, it was such a spiritual experience. It was the only album that I can think
of that really has ever blown me completely and absolutely away. It takes me
into another world utterly."

Adrian also knew and loved the music of Miles Davis, to which his father
had introduced him. Davis's musical values—"that sense of space," "a kind of
frugal melody," "careful statements, not overplaying," as Adrian describes
them—were precursors to the sound that Portishead would establish in the 1990s.
So was the spacious jazz made by future Davis guitarist John McLaughlin and
mates on another of Adrian's favorite records, the British jazz classic, *Extrapolation*. In addition, Adrian had spent a period delving into electronic and avant-
garde music by such innovators as Henry Cow, guitarist Fred Frith, and Gong.
That too would inform Portishead's ideas.

Meanwhile, a jazz DJ Adrian listened to in England was beginning to work hip-hop into his playlist. Through his show, Adrian discovered jazz-inflected rappers Gang Starr and especially *Public Enemy and A Tribe Called Quest. Barrow was awed by the same records, as Adrian learned when the two met. Their conversation struck sparks and Portishead soon expanded its orbit to include Adrian, just before making its debut record.

In the current Portishead division of labor, Adrian and Barrow assemble the backing tracks and Gibbons writes the lyrics. Although Adrian is the jazzbo of the crew, the group has developed a common set of influences, which besides hip-hop extends from film soundtracks to the works of classical composers Edward Elgar, Frederick Delius, and Bela Bartok to the titanic sonics of Nirvana. Adrian is pleased with the breadth of his music library, but less happy about the tonnage: "I prefer sometimes to have music in my head, which is why I've never bothered to listen to Henry Cow again and I don't own *Blow by Blow* anymore. . . . I don't want to hear them again somehow. They're in my head as a memory."

ADRIAN UTLEY'S FAVORITE ARTISTS AND RECORDINGS

Jimi Hendrix—*Axis Bold as Love* (Reprise). "That remains a favorite of mine years later, and I can still trace influences that we have from that. . . . We've used talking wah-wah sounds and screaming noise and feedback things that are kind of real references back to Jimi Hendrix."

Jeff Beck—*Blow by Blow* (Epic). Beck's influential, all-instrumental jazz-rock record—"a seminal, seminal album for me," says Adrian—was produced by ex-Beatles producer *George Martin.

Pink Floyd—*Dark Side of the Moon* (Capitol). "An intense kind of experience."

The Beatles—*Abbey Road* (Capitol).

Marc Bolan and T Rex—At the same time Adrian was taking in the classic blues and jazz records his dad introduced him to, he was devouring the wild rock guitar innovations coming down the pike one album after another in the 1970s, including Bolan's work on his glam-rock classics. ⊙: *Electric Warrior* (Reprise), *The Slider* (Relativity), and *Tanx* (Relativity).

David Bowie—*The Rise and Fall of Ziggy Stardust and the Spiders from Mars* (Rykodisc). Adrian locked into Mick Ronson's guitar playing on this prime Bowie glamfest.

Lightnin' Hopkins—Adrian mentioned an album, *Goin' to Louisiana*, Hopkins made with New Orleans session pro Earl Palmer on drums that we were unable to locate. Adrian loved the grooves on this record. ⊙: *Mojo Hand: The An-*

thology (2 CDs: Rhino), an excellent Hopkins compilation, contains some tracks with Palmer.

Muddy Waters—"The really raw kind of blues was really important to me. . . . I felt like it was real, and it had this kind of power." ●: See Master List.

White Noise—"It was strange, psychedelic, weird, electronic, quaint English music," says Adrian about this band featuring David Vorhaus. ●: *An Electric Storm* (Sammel-Lab), *White Noise* (Virgin), *White Noise III: Re Entry* (AMP), and *White Noise IV: Inferno* (AMP).

Miles Davis—*Cookin' with the Miles Davis Quintet* (Prestige), *Relaxin' with Miles* (Prestige), and *Porgy and Bess* (Columbia). Both Prestige albums feature Davis and John Coltrane with the Red Garland piano trio. Adrian also loves Davis's collaborations with arranger Gil Evans, especially *Porgy and Bess*.

John McLaughlin—*Extrapolation* (Polydor). This record, which Adrian calls a "massive" influence on him, is little known by American fans but is revered by jazz insiders as one of the best European jazz albums ever. Besides guitarist McLaughlin, the quartet featured outstanding contributions from baritone saxist John Surman and drummer Tony Oxley.

Henry Cow—*Legend* (Virgin) and *Concerts* (Caroline). "That music for me at that time was so otherworldly and strange."

Fred Frith— ●: *Guitar Solos (1974)* (ESD) and *The Technology of Tears (1987) and Other Music for Dance and Theatre* (SST).

Gong—One of the more inconsistent, but nonetheless long-lived, progressive rock bands, Gong overcame constantly shifting personnel to release over 20 albums, and they're still going. Guitarists Steve Hillage and Alan Holdsworth are among those who drifted through the band. ●: Drawing from jazz, the emerging electronic rock scene, and prog-rock, Gong probably released its best work in the mid-1970s. Look for Virgin releases of that era, including *Expresso*, *Expresso 2* and *Live, Etc.*

Hatfield and The North—*Rotter's Club* (Plan 9/Caroline). Another English prog-rock outfit to emerge from the '70s, Hatfield and the North had personnel ties to Gong and *Robert Wyatt's second band, Matching Mole. This was their second release, and the band broke up shortly after it appeared.

*Herbie Hancock—*Man Child*, *Head Hunters*, and *Sextant* (all Columbia). "*Man Child* absolutely blew me totally away when I first heard it. I just couldn't believe the groove," says Adrian, who discovered the other electronic Hancock records much later. "He's one of my absolute all-time favorites in the world, for all the stuff he's done."

James Brown—Adrian was drawn into Brown's records through "Sex Machine," a big hit in England. ⬤: See Master List.

Stevie Wonder—*Talking Book* and *Innervisions* (both Motown). "I was always a massive Stevie Wonder fan."

Barney Kessel—On Julie London's *Julie is Her Name, Vols. 1 & 2* (Liberty). Kessel's playing on vocalist London's record, from the 1950s, is widely celebrated by guitarists besides Adrian.

Frank Zappa—*Uncle Meat* (Rykodisc). Adrian loves Zappa's work in general although this instrumental album tops his list.

Eddie Henderson—*Realization* (Capricorn). Trumpeter Henderson, in Herbie Hancock's fusion band at this time (1973), recorded this well-received album in a Hancockish vein with several members of Hancock's group.

John Coltrane—*A Love Supreme* (Impulse). "I still listen to it now and still can get the same feeling from it . . . He remains completely one of my favorites, but particularly that band with *Elvin Jones, McCoy Tyner, and Jimmy Garrison."

Charlie Parker—Like many jazz fans, Adrian was mesmerized by both this alto sax giant's musicality and his execution. ⬤: See Master List.

Billy Cobham—*Spectrum* (Atlantic). As much as he loved Herbie Hancock's *Man Child*, he found this fusion record even more intriguing. It featured the late phenom, guitarist Tommy Bolin.

The Specials—*The Specials* (2 Tone/Chrysalis). "It was basically a lot of old Prince Buster tunes with new words, but with Roddy's [Radiation] kind of punk guitar over it."

The Skatalites— ⬤: See Master List.

Steel Pulse—*Handsworth Revolution* (Mango). "I just played it to death. It was another complete turning point, really."

Wes Montgomery—*Incredible Jazz Guitar* (Original Jazz Classics). "It's not the most luscious tone that he ever got, but there's just a fluidity about his playing, and a musicality about his playing."

Jimmy Smith with Wes Montgomery—Smith's *The Dynamic Duo* and *Further Adventures of Jimmy and Wes* (both Verve). Adrian loves the records the two made together, with Oliver Nelson arranging on the former as well as on a few tracks of the latter.

Grant Green—*Nigeria* (Blue Note). This marvelous album presents bluesy jazz guitarist Green with a great quartet including like-minded pianist Sonny Clark, bassist Sam Jones, and drummer Art Blakey. ⏺: For more where this comes from, pick up the uniformly excellent *The Complete Quartets with Sonny Clark* (2 CDs: Blue Note).

George Benson—*The Cookbook* (Columbia). "Fluid kind of playing, really in-touch kind of technique," Adrian observes of Benson's guitar work on this 1966 disc, featuring interplay with baritone saxist Ronnie Cuber.

Led Zeppelin—*Led Zeppelin II* (Swan Song).

A Tribe Called Quest—*The Low End Theory* (Jive). This and the Public Enemy album below were "absolutely huge for me and for Geoff as well."

*Public Enemy—*It Takes a Nation of Millions to Hold Us Back* (Def Jam).

Black Sheep—*A Wolf in Sheep's Clothing* (Mercury). This hit rap album continues to provide inspiration for Adrian and Geoff Barrow in Portishead.

Nirvana—*Nevermind* and *In Utero* (both DGC). "I just loved that intensive guitar noise, the massive dynamics they used, the passion they put into their music, and Kurt Cobain's lyrics."

Ennio Morricone—Adrian and Geoff Barrow love Morricone's older spaghetti Western and spy movie scores, both for their operatic sweep and the, uh, cheese factor. ⏺: Morricone estimates that he has scored over 600 films. Some of the more notable soundtracks, in the vein Adrian mentions, are *Hang 'Em High/Guns for San Sebastian* (CBS) (Morricone scored only the latter on this twofer); *The Good, the Bad, and the Ugly* (EMI America); *A Fistful of Dollars* (RCA); *Once Upon a Time in the West* (RCA); and *For a Few Dollars More* (RCA). *Film Music: Vols. 1–2* (Virgin, available separately), *A Fistful of Film Music* (2 CDs: Rhino), and *Legendary Italian Westerns* (RCA) are fine compilations.

John Barry—*The Ipcress File [soundtrack]* (CBS).

Roy Budd—*Get Carter [soundtrack]* (Castle).

Lalo Schifrin—*Bullitt [soundtrack]* (Warner Bros.) and *Dirty Harry [soundtrack]* (Aleph). ⏺: Schifrin's music for the Dirty Harry film series has been collected on *Dirty Harry Anthology* (Aleph).

Jerry Goldsmith—*Planet of the Apes* (Varese Sarabande). "A very favorite orchestral soundtrack of mine . . . It's intensely experimental, but there are orchestral devices in a lot of this stuff that you hear from Mahler."

ADRIAN UTLEY'S OWN RECORDINGS

Adrian's favorite records that he appears on are the ones he's made with Portishead and, of those, he's proudest of 1998's *Roseland NYC* (Polygram), recorded live with an orchestra and released both in CD and video versions. "We used thirty strings on it, and I did a lot of the arrangements with an orchestrator, so for me that was the culmination of a lot of ideas," says Adrian. The compelling Roseland video was inspired by a film of a Miles Davis/Gil Evans orchestral performance.

: Portishead's 1994 debut, *Dummy* (Polygram), was named album of the year by *Melody Maker*. It introduces the band's noir-ish mix of slow hip-hop beats, dark instrumental atmospheres, sampled accents, and gloomily sensuous vocals by Gibbons. The 1997 release *Portishead* (Go Beat!/Londo) is in a similar vein but cuts even deeper with its layered backgrounds and songwriting advances.

LOUDON WAINWRIGHT III (May 5, 1998)

You won't run up much of a phone bill talking to Loudon Wainwright III about his favorite records, as we discover when we reach him at a friend's house in the Los Angeles area. "I made a conscious decision to not listen to other people when I started to write, which was at a relatively late date," Loudon says. "I was about twenty-one or twenty-two when I wrote my first song. But that was it. I didn't listen to any more Bob Dylan records and I made a point of not listening to James Taylor. I didn't want to hear Tom Waits. I didn't want to hear David Bowie. . . . And if I was at somebody's house and they were putting on the new John Prine record, I would leave the room. So it was a bit extreme but I felt it was what I needed to do to somehow develop into my own thing."

Not that Loudon claims to have invented his style from whole cloth. By the time he decided to turn off the tap, his head had already filled with great music from his environment, starting with the musical comedy records his parents played at home during his childhood. *Guys and Dolls* made an especially strong impact with its songs by Frank Loesser. "Looking back now, I see how affected my own writing was from hearing those songs—incredibly well-constructed, clever, terrific songs," Loudon says. He also was affected by "some nuttier things that my parents listened to, like Louis Prima records. Then I stumbled on Stan Freberg and was into those kind of comedy records."

By the time Loudon began playing guitar, Bob Dylan, the Beatles, and the Rolling Stones were remaking the world, "but all this time I didn't really imagine that I was going to be a musician, so these influences were just kind of simmering away in the influence pot," Loudon recalls. "Then in sixty-eight I tried writing a song and it wasn't very good, but it was enough to kind of start me writing songs."

It was also enough to provoke his self-imposed ignorance of other songwriters' music. But influences still crept in from nonmusical sources such as literature. "I wanted to be an actor and I read a lot of plays and I was in plays," Loudon notes. "I think that the theatrical nature of my songs was affected by liking the theater and plays and things like that."

The unblinking observations that fill his songs, including observations of his own shadow side, also go back to a literary source. "I remember once in English class some teacher told us that you should be able to write about a piece of chalk," Loudon says. "I never did that, but I always liked that idea, of just describing things, and being very particular and somewhat detached, and then somehow creating an emotional effect that way. And a lot of my songs are descriptions, whether it's the event of hitting the daughter in the car ["Hitting You" on 1992's *History* (Charisma)] . . . I mean, there's nothing in that song that says 'Oh, I feel terrible about hitting my daughter in the car. It's such a bad thing to do.' It's a trick in a way, just to keep the objectivity going. So I'm writing about what I'm interested in and quite often what I'm doing is describing things." Which he does, according to plan, like no other songwriter alive.

LOUDON WAINWRIGHT III'S FAVORITE ARTISTS AND RECORDINGS

Frank Loesser—*Guys and Dolls (Original Cast)* (MCA). "I've heard some of the songs again [recently]. They're just amazing songs."

Bob Dylan—*Bringing It All Back Home*, *Highway 61 Revisited*, and *Blonde on Blonde* (all Columbia). "When he went electric, I liked that a lot. I thought that was kind of thrilling to witness, although there were people that didn't like that. For me, that was kind of a peak." : *Bob Dylan Live 1966: The "Royal Albert Hall" Concert* (Columbia) captures a famous performance during a world tour when Dylan was introducing audiences to his rock side. He meets the resistance of the folk purists with a ferocious set.

Louis Prima—*The Wildest!* (Capitol). "I like silly things, and Louis Prima's silly, but it swings pretty hard," Loudon says about Prima's music. "And you know, it's a great band, and it's theatrical." Loudon listened to this live album over and over when he was a kid: "It just had a lot of energy and . . . and of course Keely Smith [Prima's wife and the band's female vocalist] was just so amazing."

The Jim Kweskin Jug Band—"They were my favorite group . . . in a way more than Dylan. I had just about all their albums. The earliest incarnation of the band was a great incarnation, even before Maria Muldaur came in. But she certainly did add a kind of sexy, steamy quality to the proceedings." ⦿: *Greatest Hits* (Vanguard) provides a generous, 24-track introduction to the Jug Band's infectious, and often hilarious, folk music. This talented assemblage included Geoff Muldaur and banjo player Bill Keith.

The Beatles—*Rubber Soul* (Capitol). Loudon named this and the Stones album below right off the top of his head but added, "With those guys, just one record after another."

The Rolling Stones—*Aftermath* (ABKCO).

LOUDON WAINWRIGHT III'S OWN RECORDINGS

Once his records are completed, Loudon doesn't think much about them: "You work a long time on a record and you listen to it over and over and over again, and then finally it comes out. And I would never listen to it once it's out. . . . [So I don't really] have any favorites. I'm just trying to get the next one written."

⦿: The novelty song "Dead Skunk" that became Loudon's biggest hit poorly serves his reputation. Although no one in music is funnier, he rarely uses humor just for its own sake. In most of his songs, humor is just the apple juice that makes the strong medicine in his lyrics go down easier. Because Loudon is such an unflinching commentator on the changes, foibles, and failings in his own life, an intriguing way to absorb his music is to match his stage-of-life to yours (he was born in 1946). By the same token, as he gets older, he gets wiser.

That said, notable albums include 1971's *Album 2* (Atlantic); 1972's *Album III* (Columbia/Legacy); 1973's *Attempted Mustache* (Columbia); 1978's *Final Exam* (Arista); 1983's *Fame and Wealth* (Rounder); 1984's *I'm Alright* (Rounder) (on which Loudon's strong set—including an eerie mix of humor and pathos on "Not John," about the death of John Lennon—is nicely framed by a semi-acoustic band featuring guitarist Richard Thompson and violinist Ric Sanders); 1986's *More Love Songs* (Rounder) (one of our favorites, with some savage social commentary on self-absorbed country clubbers on "The Back Nine," a laugh-out-loud send-up of stoner goofiness on "The Acid Song," and a bracing look at divorce on "Your Mother and I"); 1989's *Therapy* (Silvertone); 1992's *History* (Charisma);

1995's *Grown Man* (Virgin); and 1998's *Little Ship* (Virgin). From 1979, *A Live One* (Rounder) focuses on some of Loudon's most entertaining material from the 1970s, but it's the more somber tunes such as "School Days" that really stay with you. *Career Moves* (Virgin), from 1993, is another excellent live set.

WALTER "WOLFMAN" WASHINGTON (June 25, 1997)

Port city, party town supreme, Mardi Gras, voodoo—put all that together with New Orleans' French/African/Southern culture and you get regional music like no other. Where else could you find Professor Longhair's rumba-boogie alongside Johnny Adams's smooth R&B and the Neville Brothers' second-line soul and call 'em all homebrew? Where else would you find Walter "Wolfman" Washington, master of the comfortable groove? The Wolfman's classy style combines stinging blues, jazzy R&B, simmering funk, punchy horn accents, and a second-line sway in almost genetic New Orleans fashion.

Like so many other Crescent City musicians, Walter did his earliest woodshedding in church. He began as a gospel vocalist and guitar player with his own group. As a guitarist, he developed a personal style inspired by one-time Fats Domino sideman Prince La La. "You hear a lot of guitar players who would either play chords or play scales," Walter tells us by phone from his home. "This cat didn't play like that. He mostly played what was talkin' to him inside. That's the style I play on. You might hear me run up a scale from time to time, but mostly I can't see myself playing like that. It's like saying something somebody else has already quoted instead of saying what you really feel."

After gigging around the New Orleans R&B scene for years, the Wolfman got his first break when he landed a job backing Lee Dorsey. Two years of touring gave him his fill, so he came home to work with the Soul Queen of New Orleans, Irma Thomas. Three years later, he hooked up with another of the city's legends, the late Johnny Adams. The "Tan Canary" would become Walter's most important musical connection—Walter played with Adams off and on for almost 16 years. "But you know what? It didn't seem that long," Walter says. "Because we had so much fun, and I had so much fun learning different attitudes, learning what motivates me and what motivates different band members. Johnny taught me all of that stuff. He also taught me how to sing falsetto, and how to make it plain enough. He'd take the time to show you how you can ease into certain things, to give you confidence."

Adams gave Walter the confidence to start his own group, too. "He taught me how to be a bandleader, and just look at all the things you have to deal with to be in front,'' he says. Obviously, Walter learned well. With his sidekicks, a collection of seasoned club pros called the Roadmasters, he's made a string of records that go down as easy as champagne punch but kick like bathtub gin. Smooth and greasy—that's a New Orleans thing, too. Translation for the rest of the country. It doesn't have to be in your face to shake your butt.

WALTER WASHINGTON'S FAVORITE ARTISTS AND RECORDINGS

Ray Charles—''Drown in My Own Tears.'' ''It's just the way he sings, like he wraps spirituals and blues into one.'' 💿: *Best of Atlantic* (Rhino).

Johnnie Taylor—Taylor replaced Sam Cooke in the legendary gospel group the Soul Stirrers before leaving for an R&B career. 💿: See Master List.

Prince La La— 💿: The compilation *The Best of Sue Records* (Collectibles) and the superb survey of early New Orleans rock and R&B, *Crescent City Soul: The Sound of New Orleans* (4 CDs: Capitol), both feature La La's ''She Put the Hurt on Me.''

Lee Dorsey—Walter knew Dorsey's good-time R&B from the inside out, from playing it rather than from records. 💿: *Holy Cow! Best of . . .* (Arista).

Little Willie John—Like Prince La La, fellow Crescent City R&B star John had a mostly regional following except among musicians, who have long worshipped him despite his troubled personal life. 💿: See Master List.

Irma Thomas—Thomas is another regional New Orleans star with an underground reputation nationally among those who know great soul singing. 💿: *Time Is On My Side: The Best of . . . , Vol. 1* (EMI) covers 1961 to '66, when Thomas first built her legend. Walter worked with her in the early '60s, although he doesn't appear on this collection. *Live: Simply the Best* (Rounder) is a smoking, well-recorded club date recording.

Johnny Adams— 💿: Walter and Johnny together? From the mid to late '80s, try Adams's *Room With a View of the Blues* (with *Dr. John and Duke Robillard, to boot), *From the Heart*, and *Walking on a Tightrope* (all Rounder). *Reconsider Me* (Charly) offers a good sampling of Adams's earlier work. *Man of My Word* (Rounder) was his excellent swan song.

Patti LaBelle—Patti LaBelle began her career as a founding member of the girl-group the Blue Belles back in the '60s. Renamed LaBelle and bedecked in space-funk regalia, the group was a gospel/dance hitmaking machine in the mid-'70s. Patti went solo in 1977, the better to show off her powerful, gospel-trained vocals.

: To hear Patti in her early career, go for *Over the Rainbow: The Atlantic Years* (Ichiban), which covers 1965 to '69. For a more complete survey of her work, the choice is *Lady Marmalade: The Best of Patti and LaBelle* (Epic).

Anita Baker—Walter loves Baker's sophisticated, soulful vocal style. : For Baker at her best, check out 1986's *Rapture*, plus her 1983 debut *The Songstress* (both Elektra).

Johnny "Guitar" Watson—In Walter's words one of "the hottest cats goin'," Watson began his career in blues but re-invented himself in the '70s as a funk-ateer. His mind-blowing guitar chops more than survived the transition. : Watson's early blues years are documented on *Gangster of Love* (Charly) and *Three Hours Past Midnight* (Flair). *Ain't That a Bitch* (Collectibles) was his smoldering funk debut.

Aretha Franklin— : See Master List.

B. B. King— : See Master List.

Bobby "Blue" Bland— : See Master List.

Little Milton (Campbell)— : See Master List.

WALTER WASHINGTON'S OWN RECORDINGS

Walter is most completely satisfied with 1991's *Sada* (Pointblank)— "written for my daughter," he notes. 1988's *Out of the Dark* (Rounder) is his runner-up favorite.

: Don't miss Walter's *Wolf at the Door* (Rounder), with its deeply soulful, laid-way-back cover of the Doc Pomus/Dr. John tune "Hello Stranger." The 1987 record *Wolf Tracks* (Rounder) is another typically strong example of the Wolfman's stylish music. 1998's *Funk Is In The House* (Bullseye Blues) is Walter's latest, with an accent on horn-driven New Orleans funk.

BOB WEIR (November 26, 1997)

O f the five iconoclasts who came together as the original Grateful Dead, Bob Weir's contribution is the most overlooked. Jerry Garcia was a local folk music hero, *Phil Lesh a classical and jazz sophisticate, Ron "Pigpen" McKernan a grittily authentic bluesman, and Bill Kreutzmann a versatile, experienced drummer. Weir? Bob was barely old enough to drive when he, Garcia, and Pigpen started Mother McCree's Uptown Jug Champions, the Dead's folky predecessor. He had few of the distinctive instrumental skills that would later make his contribution so important to the band's approach. And he had only occasionally performed in public. But from the beginning, Bob added a quality to the group that it could not have done without: a passion to rock. Indeed, he was the most instinctive rocker of the bunch.

Bob tells us that he probably first caught the fever from Beatles records but Chuck Berry's tunes definitely weakened his immunity: "You know, I think I was nine years old when 'Johnny B. Goode' came out, but that certainly got my attention nonetheless. That was probably the year that I learned how to dial a radio. And that was it for me, I was history. I had received and responded to the call to come hither from rock 'n' roll."

When Mother McCree plugged in and became the Warlocks and then the Dead, the band spent much of its time studying records that various members brought in for group consumption. For Bob as well as the band as a whole, some of the most crucial of those records were those lugged in by bassist Phil Lesh, including two of Bob's favorites to this day—Miles Davis's *Kind of Blue* and *Sketches of Spain*. "They were on the turntable a lot back then," Bob remembers. "They were part of the atmosphere. Those were a couple of the bricks that we built our house with." Lesh first exposed him to Karlheinz Stockhausen and John Coltrane as well, two other crucial artists for him and the band.

Although the Dead began in an almost ad hoc manner, a hallucinogen-fueled cultural scene was evolving at light speed all around them. Tight little song per-formances were out, go-with-the-flow extemporization the obvious future, so the band began to grow their ensemble and individual skills for the task. In Bob's case, that meant a considerable amount of catching up, but catch up he did. His loose, jazzy approach to the rhythm guitar helped open up the music for the Dead's sinuous improvisations, and his uniquely voiced chords helped inspire and frame Garcia's searching guitar leads. His proclivity for odd time signatures and unfamiliar harmonies fed the Dead's aura of other-worldliness. He wrote—with lyricists Robert Hunter, John Barlow, and others—much of the Dead's most enduring material. He became a compelling rock shouter and his honeyed voice was the perfect vehicle for other songs the band played. Less shy than his mates about being in the spot-light, he also helped give the Dead focus on stage.

The Dead retired after Garcia passed in 1995, but Bob wasn't exactly thrown out of work. The Dead has risen again, sort of, as The Other Ones—a group featuring Dead alums Bob, Lesh, Mickey Hart, and *Bruce Hornsby plus some elite hired help. As his primary gig, Bob leads Ratdog, an electric band that sprang from his acoustic duo tours with bassist Rob Wasserman. With *Taj Mahal, jazz saxophonist David Murray, and others, he's also developing a musical theater piece based on the life of Negro Leagues baseball legend Satchel Paige. That doesn't leave much time for keeping up with new records, but that doesn't bother Bob, he tells us, "because, you know, I still get influenced by stuff and I don't want to at my age and in my position. I just don't see where I can afford to be influenced by people. I should be hammering what I do at this point."

BOB WEIR'S FAVORITE ARTISTS AND RECORDINGS

The Beatles—*Rubber Soul* (Capitol) and *Revolver* (Capitol). "Both of those records made a huge impact on me. They to me represented the Beatles at their most fully developed before they stopped being for the most part a rock 'n' roll quartet. And I always liked them when they were a quartet. I thought their music had an incredible economy about it. And at the same time it just went about anywhere you could want music to take you."

The Rolling Stones—*The Rolling Stones (England's Newest Hit Makers)* and *12x5* (both ABKCO). Bob says that the first two Stones albums not only influenced him personally but the Grateful Dead as well. The albums included between them several songs the Dead would eventually cover including most notably Buddy Holly's "Not Fade Away" (*Hit Makers*), one of the Dead's favorite launching pads.

Chuck Berry—Bob recommends that anyone wanting to trace his path in music pick up a Berry greatest-hits package, which will contain "all the singles that wigged me out when I was a kid and made me want to play rock 'n' roll." : See Master List.

Miles Davis—*Kind of Blue* and *Sketches of Spain* (both Columbia). Bob says that *Kind of Blue* taught him "those first and important lessons about what jazz was, and what the scales were all about. . . . *Kind of Blue* was I guess what they call cool jazz, but I loved it. And then *Sketches of Spain*, he took that cool jazz and worked it in some surprising ways. His approach has always been in the back of my head and in my heart, whether I've been playing or writing."

John Coltrane—*Blue Trane* (Blue Note). This album and another one whose title Bob couldn't remember (we're guessing it's *Africa Brass* based on what Phil Lesh told us) "were a couple of Coltrane albums that also were bricks in the foundation of [the Grateful Dead's] little house," Bob says. "Not enough good could be said about Coltrane, either."

John Coltrane Quartet—Count Bob among the legions who speaks admiringly of the interplay of the Coltrane/McCoy Tyner/Jimmy Garrison/*Elvin Jones group, about which he says, "It was the way that quartet would construct a mode over a rhythm and then the way [Coltrane] would work it over the top, work that into something downright meaningful." ⬤: See Master List.

Karlheinz Stockhausen—Stockhausen Verlag (Wergo). Several versions of this piece are available but this is the original recording with Stockhausen himself and electronic performance pioneer David Tudor. The piece "Kontakte" on this disc "was real instrumental in constructing my view of what music amounted to," Bob says. "At the time it came out, it was still considered modern classical music. Electronic music hadn't achieved a niche of its own. By today's standards, it was all real crude but it sure got my attention. And you certainly have heard plenty of how that resounded in the Dead's heads over the years."

Claude Debussy—"La Mer," Columbia Symphony Orchestra/Pierre Boulez. "That's a high water mark as far as that piece is concerned. I think it's probably been recorded at least a couple dozen times since then and some of 'em are pretty good, but none of them I think amount to that particular performance. The whole orchestra is just breathing as one." ⬤: We couldn't find the recording Bob mentioned but a rendition by the New Philharmonia Orchestra conducted by Boulez (Sony) came out on Columbia Records at the time Bob said he was listening to the piece.

Bob Dylan—*The Freewheelin' Bob Dylan*, *The Times They Are A-Changin'*, and *Another Side of Bob Dylan*, *Highway 61 Revisited* (all Columbia). *"Bringin' It All Back Home* (Columbia) was a great record, too. But I think that got a lot of attention, and I thought the songs on *Highway 61*, he had more of a notion of what he was doing working with a rock 'n' roll band at that point. He had successfully made the transition from a singer/songwriter folk singer, self-accompanied, to a band musician. Great tunes like 'A Hard Rain's Gonna Fall,' or 'Blowin' in the Wind' for that matter [both on *Freewheelin'*], or 'Chimes of Freedom' [on *Another Side*] taught me a whole lot of what songwriting essentially is about: a three-way marriage of melody, harmonic progression, and lyrics. . . ."

Junior Wells—*Hoodoo Man Blues* (Delmark). Bob loves quartets, and this disc features a great one with harmonica player Wells and guitarist *Buddy Guy up front. "Once again, like the Beatles records, the economy that they exhibited in that record, working together with the various textures that they created, was eye-opening to me," Bob remembers.

Muddy Waters—*The Real Folk Blues* (MCA/Chess). In the 1960s, the Real Folk Blues compilation series on Chess introduced many folkies and rockers besides Bob to the great blues artists on Chess records. This edition features tracks from 1949 to '54.

Howlin' Wolf—*The Real Folk Blues* (MCA/Chess). The Wolf edition from this series focuses on electric tracks from 1956 to '65.

Otis Redding—*Otis Blue* (Atco). This album includes 'A Change Is Gonna Come,' 'Respect,' 'Shake,' 'I've Been Loving You Too Long,' and 'Satisfaction'—as Bob says, "a bunch of Otis's classic hits, just too many of 'em for one record, and that was real influential to me."

Aretha Franklin—*I Never Loved a Man (the Way I Love You)* (Atlantic). "That was more than I could choke down at one point," Bob laughs. "I listened to that record for years, as I've listened to the Otis Redding record."

*Taj Mahal—*Natch'l Blues* (Columbia). Another one of those agile quartet albums that Bob eats up—Taj's band at this time, with the late Jesse Ed Davis on guitar, was widely admired for its lean, balanced sound. This 1968 classic is yet to be issued on CD as of this writing.

The Who—*Who's Next* (MCA). The Who are usually thought of as a power trio-plus-singer but they often added a keyboard player so they sort of qualify as a quartet, too, Bob says. But this is a great rock record in Bob's eyes no matter how you classify the band.

*Little Feat—*Waiting for Columbus* (Warner Bros.). Bob notes that this two-CD live release "came down the pike a few years later [than the other records mentioned] but it still bent my head."

Duke Ellington—The above artists and albums were those that Bob listened to before the late '70s, "when I was most impressionable," he says. After that, "I filled in the blanks as I went on, as I started getting more appreciation for the incredible breadth and depth of the American music tradition." In particular, Bob now pores over the jazz orchestrations of Ellington, Count Basie, and Fletcher Henderson. "I wish I could say that I was listening to those folks [earlier], but we were anti-Establishment, and Duke Ellington was the stuff that we grew up with in dance class, so that was automatically out." ⊙: See Master List.

Count Basie—Basie's early bands were as raucous as Ellington's were suave—kind of like early vs. later Grateful Dead. ⊙: See Master List.

Fletcher Henderson— ⊙: . . . *1925–29* (JSP) samples a vital period for Henderson's big band, when it featured Coleman Hawkins on tenor sax and a host of other major soloists plus the outstanding charts of Don Redman.

BOB WEIR'S OWN RECORDINGS

Like so many of his peers, Bob has trouble overlooking the inevitable flaws in his recorded appearances. Despite that, certain albums stand out in his mind, starting with 1970's *Workingman's Dead* (Warner Bros.) and *American Beauty* (Warner Bros.). But he agrees with most Deadheads that both albums give a misleading picture of the Dead's live sound at that time. He calls 1977's *Terrapin Station* (Arista) "a good solid record, but it's a little overdressed. Actually some of it did sound pretty much like a rock 'n' roll band might sound live, but a lot of it was kind of fatuous, a little indulgent, I think. You know, [laughing] with the orchestra and choruses and stuff like that." From that same era and producer, he feels good about his solo album, *Heaven Help the Fool* (Arista), but again with reservations about the production. "There are a lot of good tunes on there that I wrote, I think, but once again the whole album's kind of overdressed as far as I'm concerned. If I had [that and *Terrapin*] to do over again, they'd be way more spare." The Dead finally made a studio album that worked, he says, with 1987's *In the Dark* (Arista): "That was pretty much meat 'n' potatoes Grateful Dead–style rock 'n' roll as you might hear it live. I really like that record for that."

⬤: Bob did not mention his first solo record, 1972's *Ace* (Grateful Dead), but his fans and Dead fans in general will want this one in the collection. It is virtually a Grateful Dead album—Bob co-wrote and sang all the songs, but the Dead played the music. Several of the tunes became regular parts of the Dead's concert repertoire. In the mid-'70s when the Dead were on hiatus, Bob joined the frontline of the Bay Area band Kingfish, a highly capable, roots-conscious unit more than a little reminiscent of the Dead itself. Also like the Dead, Kingfish was best experienced live; *King Biscuit Flower Hour Presents . . .* (2 CDs: King Biscuit) is a compelling document of their post-psychedelic grace, although the self-titled studio debut (Grateful Dead) is enjoyable, too. *Bobby and the Midnights* (Arista), the debut from a side band Bob led in the early '80s, presents an intriguing mix of original and cover tracks, with loads of instrumental muscle from such performers as drummer Billy Cobham, ex-Weather Report bassist Alphonse Johnson, and the late Brent Mydland, just prior to his successful audition for the Dead's keyboard chair. *Bob Weir and Rob Wasserman Live* (Grateful Dead) captures Bob and bassist extraordinaire Wasserman in the acoustic duo format they performed in before starting Ratdog.

For a comprehensive review of the Grateful Dead catalog, see Phil Lesh's entry.

LUCINDA WILLIAMS (December 28, 1998)

She titled her 1998 album *Car Wheels on a Gravel Road* but Lucinda Williams would have been justified in calling it *Last Laugh*. *Car Wheels* was released six years after its predecessor; in the interim, Lucinda became the subject of all kinds of industry jokes and uninformed speculation. Sure, it's good to be meticulous but isn't this a few miles over the line? That was the usual thinking.

Until the album came out. Tracking like a collection of closely observed short stories by one of those fine Dixie writers (Lucinda was born in Lake Charles, Louisiana), *Car Wheels* told of soured working class loves and other Southern lives gone south. The lyrics combined almost haikulike economy with rich sensory and psychological detail, and the rural rock and blues settings, not to mention the sad vulnerability in Lucinda's vocals, supported them perfectly. Although the record came out mid-year, critics immediately reserved a spot on their best-of-the-year lists—and reminded themselves that great work can take time.

Oft-covered by other artists, Lucinda has been hailed among songwriting's elite since her first album of original material came out in 1980. Although she writes sturdy, memorable melodies, what first draws your attention are the lyrics—not only their descriptive detail and stand-up honesty, but also their parsimony, the mark of a practiced writer. The literary skills evident in Lucinda's songs have more to do than you would imagine with having a poet/literature professor for a dad. Lucinda grew up around writers, she tells us from her home in Nashville, but just as important were the records her dad's college students would bring by the house. In 1965, 13-year-old Lucinda was living in Baton Rouge while her father taught at Louisiana State University. Deep into the folk music of Joan Baez, Buffy St. Marie, and Peter, Paul & Mary, she had just started taking guitar lessons when one of Miller Williams's students stopped by with a copy of *Highway 61 Revisited* under his arm. "He was just all excited about it—'This is the new Dylan album and it's just incredible!'" Lucinda recalls. "I put it on and listened to it, and of course it just immediately blew me away. I said, 'This is it, I want to strive for this.' So I set those standards for myself at a fairly young age. And I've been trying to master it ever since, because for me it's the best of both worlds: great melodies with great, introspective lyrics."

After digesting Dylan, Lucinda took the next logical steps, first investigating folk blues artists like Mississippi John Hurt and then the harder-edged blues of Robert Johnson, Muddy Waters, and Howlin' Wolf. Dad was a country music fan, and through him, Lucinda hooked into the bluesy country music of Hank Williams. "Of course, all through the '60s I was listening to all the folk-rock bands like the Byrds and Buffalo Springfield," Lucinda notes. "I was also influenced by the Doors and Cream—all the sort of blues-based rock bands. But really it all ends up coming down to the same thing, which is the blues and folk roots of it all."

All along, Lucinda has sparked off of literary sources, too—fiction writers Flannery O'Connor and Eudora Welty are particular favorites. In fact, she views her relative sparse output—four albums of original material in nearly 20 years—in primarily literary terms. "I'm not sitting here all bummed out," Lucinda says. "It's like if you don't put out a record every year they think something's wrong. . . . It's amazing to me that Bob Dylan created the stuff he did at his age, but not everybody does that. The thing is, in the writer's world you're not even considered mature until you're in your sixties. I mean, the older you get, the better you get."

LUCINDA WILLIAMS'S FAVORITE ARTISTS AND RECORDINGS

Various artists—*The Blues Project* (Elektra). Not to be confused with the band the Blues Project, this compilation featured white folk-blues artists such as Dave Van Ronk, Eric Von Schmidt, Geoff Muldaur, and Mark Spoelstra. "They were doing black delta blues music in their own way, and that influenced me, because again it was that link [between folk and blues]," says Lucinda.

Clifton Chenier— : *Zydeco Dynamite: The . . . Anthology* (2 CDs: Rhino) and *60 Minutes with the King of Zydeco* (Arhoolie), a greatest-hits package of Cheneir's work for the label, are both excellent introductions to the zydeco great's sound.

Joan Baez— *. . . 2* (Vanguard). Baez's second album, from 1961, was a major influence on Lucinda in her early teens when she was first delving into folk music.

Peter, Paul & Mary—*In the Wind* (Warner Bros.)

Simon and Garfunkel—*Parsley, Sage, Rosemary, and Thyme* (Columbia).

Leonard Cohen—*The Songs of . . .* (Columbia). This album includes the classic "Suzanne" plus "Sisters of Mercy" and "So Long Marianne."

Judy Collins—*Wildflowers* (Elektra). "I just listened to that album over and over. I still do this. When I get into a record, I just devour it. I just let it soak into my subconscious."

Nick Drake—Lucinda is one of many singer/songwriters who is enthralled with the music of this tragic folk rocker from the U.K. She likes everything Drake recorded before his death in 1974 at age 26. : See Master List.

Geoff and Maria Muldaur—*Pottery Pie* (Hannibal). "They made a couple of albums together before she got real big, after they'd left the Jim Kweskin Jug Band. [This album] had all this cool blues and folk stuff on it."

Jesse Mae Hemphill—*She Wolf* (HMG).

Bob Dylan—*Highway 61 Revisited* and *Blonde on Blonde* (both Columbia).

Mississippi John Hurt—*Today!* (Vanguard).

Robert Johnson—*The Complete Recordings* (2 CDs: Columbia/Legacy). "Once I started getting into those harder-edged artists like that, I started feeling like I don't have to sound like Judy Collins, so I quit trying to do it eventually."

Muddy Waters— : See Master List.

Howlin' Wolf— : See Master List.

*John Lee Hooker—See the section on John Lee and his recordings.

The Byrds— : See Master List.

Neil Young—*Everybody Knows This is Nowhere* (Reprise).

Buffalo Springfield—*Last Time Around* and *Retrospective* (both Atco). Lucinda got into these albums, the former the group's final release and the latter a compilation, in the late 1960s "when all that great music was coming out."

Cream—*Disraeli Gears* (Polydor). The group's second album included the massive blues-based hit, "Sunshine of Your Love."

The Doors—*The Doors* and *Strange Days* (both Elektra).

The Rolling Stones—*December's Children* and *Aftermath* (both ABKCO).

John Mayall—*The Blues Alone* (Deram).

Junior Kimbrough—*Sad Days, Lonely Nights* (Fat Possum/Capricorn). This obscure bluesman died in 1998 just when he was being discovered by a wider audience.

Ray Charles—*Modern Sounds in Country & Western Music* (Rhino). "That was that blend again of those styles [i.e. Charles's soulful interpretation of country hits]."

Hank Williams—*40 Greatest Hits* (Polydor). Lucinda says she learned to crack her voice by listening to Williams, as well as Robert Johnson.

Dinah Washington—*Take Me In Your Arms*. "It is just a classic where every single song is great. . . . It's not her earlier work. It's more sort of torch songs." : This album, which includes "Just Friends" and "Call Me Irresponsible," is apparently no longer in print but Washington was recording these songs in her last years on the Roulette label. The compilation *Dinah '63* (Blue Note) has the song "Take Me in Your Arms." *Drinking Again* (Roulette, out of print) has "Just Friends."

Memphis Minnie (Lizzie Douglas)—Lucinda says that Minnie, one of the few female blues singers to also be recorded playing guitar, was one of her greatest influences. She likes everything she's heard by her. ●: *Hoodoo Lady (1933–1937)* (Columbia) is a fine entry into Minnie's catalog. *I Ain't No Bad Girl* (Portrait) features Minnie playing electric blues in 1941. *And Kansas Joe: 1929–1934* (Document) pairs Minnie with guitarist Kansas Joe McCoy, the second of three marital/guitar partners. *Traveling Blues* (Aldabra) covers more sessions with McCoy.

Chet Baker—*Baker's Holiday: Plays and Sings Billie Holiday* (Emarcy).

Michael Hurley—*Armchair Boogie* and *Hi Fi Snock Uptown* (both Racoon/Warner Bros., cassette-only as of this writing, order on the 'Net at http://sony.inergy.com/snockonews/). Underground folk hero Hurley has been on the scene since the '60s but is exciting new interest thanks to praise by artists such as Lucinda,*Yo La Tengo, and Son Volt.

Bobbie Gentry—*Ode to Billy Joe* (Capitol). Lucinda says that this album gave her the confidence to sing, like Gentry, in a lower key rather than like her early models—Joan Baez, Judy Collins, and Joni Mitchell—whose technical assets she couldn't match. ''Eventually what you hope happens is your limitations become your advantage. . . . Instead of looking at them as limitations, you say 'Okay, I can't do this, so I'll do this other thing,' '' says Lucinda, who has so perfected her own blue country style that she's often asked to do guest vocals on other artists' albums.

Pentangle—*Basket of Light* (Edsel).

Bert Jansch—*Birthday Blues* (Demond). Then-Pentangle guitarist Jansch made this solo album in 1969 with the group's bassist, Danny Thompson, and drummer, Terry Cox.

ZZ Top—*Rio Grande Mud* and *Tres Hombres* (both Warner Bros.)

Joni Mitchell—*Blue* (Reprise).

Jefferson Airplane—*Surrealistic Pillow* (RCA).

Jesse Winchester—*Jesse Winchester* (Rhino). This terrific debut by another singer/songwriter from Louisiana had much of the feel of a Band album due to the presence of producer/guitarist Robbie Robertson and *Levon Helm.

Gordon Lightfoot—*Did She Mention My Name?* ●: This 1968 album has been reissued on CD as a two-fer with its 1968 follow-up, *Back Here on Earth* (United Artists).

Bruce Cockburn—*Joy Will Find a Way* (Columbia).

The Pretenders—*The Pretenders* (Sire).

Judee Sill—*Heart Food* and *Judee Sill* (both Asylum).

Van Morrison—*Hard Nose the Highway* (Warner Bros.)

***The Allman Brothers**—*The Allman Brothers Band* and *Idlewild South* (both Poly-dor). "All those great songs—'In Memory of Elizabeth Reed' and all that great stuff."

Dusty Springfield—*Dusty in Memphis* (Rhino). This American R&B album by the late British pop/soul queen has attained legendary status over the years.

***Gregg Allman**—*Laid Back* (Capricorn). "That's one of those that I've just been playing over and over and over."

Spirit—*Time Circle (1968–72)* (2 CDs: Sony).

LUCINDA WILLIAMS'S OWN RECORDINGS

Lucinda feels that *Car Wheels on a Gravel Road* (Mercury) is her most perfectly realized record from the standpoint of her vocal delivery, the production sound, and the playing by the musicians involved, including her longtime sideman Gurf Morlix and the great Buddy Miller. But she is also extremely proud of 1988's self-titled album on the Rough Trade label (favorite track: "Like a Rose") and 1992's *Sweet Old World* (Chameleon) (favorite moment: her cover of Nick Drake's "Which Will"). Both were lavishly praised by critics as well.

In addition, Lucinda cues her fans to not overlook her first two records, 1979's *Ramblin' on My Mind* and 1980's *Happy Woman Blues* (both Smithsonian/Folkways). The all-acoustic *Ramblin'* features Lucinda's interpretations of blues and traditional songs by such as Robert Johnson, Memphis Minnie, A. P. Carter, and Hank Williams. *Happy Woman Blues* is her first album of original songs, much folkier than the Rough Trade album but headed in that direction—the stark-but-tender country rock that is her current style as well. "People just love that first album," Lucinda notes. "I don't feel the same about it, because I see it differently. But I still think [both albums are] important, of course. You can see the roots of where I started and it all makes sense."

VICTORIA WILLIAMS (May 22, 1998)

When we reach her by phone, Victoria Williams is sitting on the porch at her remote home in California's Mojave desert, sipping mate latte tea. Her new album, *Musings of a Creekdipper*, has been garnering some of the strongest reviews of her already critically blessed career and she's excited about several self-produced projects she's working on with her husband, former Jayhawk Mark Olson. Although she still struggles with the multiple sclerosis that showed up in 1994, she seems more than content with the state of her world. Which is how it goes with her bright, quirky music, too—Victoria Williams is not about bad luck and trouble.

Victoria was born in Louisiana in 1959. Although she's largely been a Californian since 1979, the humid South still colors her folk rock songs and vocals— you can almost hear mosquitoes in the background. Her upbringing also helps explain the absence of attitude in her music. "I wasn't living in a community that was the top of the cutting edge," she says matter-of-factly. "I mostly heard things that the radio played."

But if living where she did deprived Victoria in one way, it wasn't short of compensations. "I used to listen to a lot of soul and black gospel music," she notes. "I used to watch *The Hallelujah Train* every week. It was a tri-state gospel show with local gospel bands every week, and so that was quite influential on me. All those groups, Mighty Clouds of Joy, Blind Boys of Alabama—even Al Green came on there once."

Victoria taught herself to play guitar during high school and began meeting other musical friends on the banks of a nearby river, where they'd build a fire on the sand bar and practice songs together. Some of the first things she learned to play on the guitar were Crosby, Stills, Nash & Young songs, and then Neil Young songs, she tells us. In one of those look-how-far-I've-come moments that marks a rising career, Victoria toured with Young as his opening act in 1992.

Victoria doesn't get to hear much new music these days, in part because just like her childhood days in Louisiana, there ain't a lot happening on the desert airwaves: "Out here, there's this one radio station and all it plays is like this super old stuff, like the old Sinatra and all that old stuff, and so it's kind of like we're in some strange, surreal camp. We pipe it out the windows."

VICTORIA WILLIAMS'S FAVORITE ARTISTS AND RECORDINGS

Simon & Garfunkel—*Bridge Over Troubled Water* (Columbia). "Oh gosh, it was deep yet melodic and beautiful and fanciful. It just spoke to my heart and I could sing to it."

Crosby, Stills, Nash & Young—*Four Way Street* (Atlantic). Victoria likes the vocal harmonies as well as the melodies and general songwriting on this disc. It was one of her favorites to sing along with when she first acquired it.

Neil Young—*Harvest*, *Freedom*, and *Harvest Moon* (all Reprise). Victoria named these three albums first but said "any Neil Young record I'm just crazy over."

418

Joni Mitchell—*Blue* (Reprise). "It goes deeper than you could consciously write. It's pure poetry and pure emotion and pure music."

Jesse Colin Young—Victoria especially enjoyed his song "Grey Days." ⬤: *Greatest Hits* (Award).

Poco—"A Good Feelin' to Know" on *A Good Feelin' to Know* (Epic). "It raised my spirits to put it on," Victoria says of this track, one of the more cloudlessly sunny tunes ever recorded.

Spirit—*Feedback* (Epic). This 1971 record is a nominal Spirit album because only drummer Ed Cassidy remained from the original group.

Thelonious Monk—*Alone in San Francisco* and *Monk's Music* (both Riverside). "I can always listen to Thelonious Monk. He's just a friend to have around."

Miles Davis—*Kind of Blue* and *Sketches of Spain* (both Columbia). Victoria describes early Miles as "real soul music." About *Sketches*, Victoria observes, "It has these wide open spaces, and yet it just creates a scene. For me, it's so great because you put it on and your whole world enters that scene no matter what you're doing."

Carole King—*Tapestry* (Epic). "I knew every word of that, and I was always singin' along."

Bob Dylan—*The Freewheelin' Bob Dylan*, *Blonde on Blonde*, and *New Morning* (all Columbia). "Whoooo! Early Bob Dylan, yes."

Van Morrison—*Tupelo Honey* (Warner Bros.), *No Guru, No Method, No Teacher* (Mercury), and *Poetic Champions Compose* (Mercury). "His urgency and his soulfulness" are what bond Victoria to Morrison's music. These three albums were on her mind the day we spoke but she loves a broad variety of his work in all phases of his career.

Charlie Parker—⬤: See Master List.

Wayne Shorter with Milton Nascimento—*Native Dancer* (Columbia). This gorgeous Brazilian jazz-pop record is filed under Shorter's name but Nascimento wrote five of the nine tunes and matches Shorter's soprano sax flights with his birdsonglike vocals.

Cat Stevens—*Tea for the Tillerman* and *Harold and Maude* (both A&M). *Tea* was another of Victoria's favorite records to sing along with. She also loved Stevens's work on the soundtrack of the cult film classic *Harold and Maude*.

The Mamas & the Papas—Victoria didn't really discover this group until she moved to California. She especially appreciates their vocal arrangements. ⬤: *16 Greatest Hits* (MCA) features the songs everyone most identifies with the group. *Creeque*

Alley (MCA) is a more comprehensive two-CD set that includes pre- and post-Mama work by various members among its 43 tracks. Nine tracks are from the fabulous 1966 debut album, *If You Can Believe Your Eyes and Ears* (Dunhill).

Edith Piaf—"My favorite French singer whom I just love." ⬤: *Live at Carnegie Hall* (Capitol), *The Very Best of Edith Piaf: Voice of the Sparrow* (Capitol), and *30th Anniversary Anthology* (EMI/Angel).

Allen Toussaint—*Southern Nights* (Reprise). This 1975 record by the legendary New Orleans songwriter/pianist spent a lot of time on Victoria's turntable when she was living in Louisiana.

Bobby Charles—*Bobby Charles* (Bearsville). Charles is another Southern musician who influenced Victoria. "It's got beauty, humor, and really touching, deep emotions, and a soulful feel," Victoria says about this disc.

John Prine—*John Prine* (Atlantic). Victoria appreciates the wry, biting lyric style Prine displayed on this impressive debut album.

Nusrat Fateh Ali Khan and Eddie Vedder—"The Face of Love" and "The Long Road." These haunting—and in the context, harrowing—tracks appeared in their most complete versions on *Deadman Walking: The Score* (Columbia), not the companion album subtitled "music from and inspired by the motion picture." Victoria loves the late Khan's singing in general, although she only knows his music from hearing him live. ⬤: See Master List.

Hazel (Dickens) and Alice (Gerrard)—⬤: *Pioneering Women of Bluegrass* (Smithsonian/Folkways), recorded back in the mid-1960s, featured such sidemen as Chubby Wise and *David Grisman and was one of the breakthrough albums for women singing bluegrass. *Hazel and Alice* (Rounder), from the mid-'70s, was an influential cult classic.

***The Meters**—Proto-funsters the Meters—frequently employed by Allen Toussaint on records he produced—were one of Victoria's favorite groups when she lived in Louisiana. ⬤: See Master List.

Sly and the Family Stone—Victoria loved the group's innovative rock-and-soul hits from throughout their career. ⬤: Despite some overlap, you'll need *Greatest Hits* (Epic) and *Anthology* (Epic) both to get all the prime cuts. Top single albums include *Stand!* (Epic), *There's a Riot Goin' On* (Epic), and *Fresh* (Epic), all more-than-worthy purchases on top of the hits packages.

Hank Williams—You don't have to be from the South or anywhere near to appreciate this blues cowboy's music. ⬤: See Master List.

The Drifters—This seminal R&B/doo-wop group turned over personnel quicker than a fast-food joint, but the talent remained top-notch, with such lead singers as Clyde McPhatter, Ben E. King, Johnny Moore, and Rudy Lewis. ⬤: *The Very Best of . . .* (Rhino) is the best single-disc introduction. *Let the Boogie Woogie Roll—Greatest Hits (1953–1958)* (Rhino) covers the McPhatter years, including the group's rendition of one of Victoria's favorite songs, "Suddenly There's a Valley."

The Incredible String Band—This group's brand of folk music is much in tune with Victoria's sensibility. ⬤: See Master List.

Mississippi John Hurt—"Oh, it's so good!" Victoria exclaims about Hurt's early recordings. ⬤: *1928 Sessions* (Yazoo) is the classic early album of Hurt's music.

Reverend Gary Davis—Victoria isn't sure about album titles but likes his rendition of "Twelve Gates to the City" and other religious material as well as his blues. ⬤: *Harlem Street Singer* (Prestige/Bluesville) contains "Gates" and a mix of other great blues and religious tunes such as "Samson and Delilah," "Let Us Get Together Right Down Here," "Pure Religion," and "Death Don't Have No Mercy."

Brian Blade—*Brian Blade Fellowship* (Blue Note). Jazz drummer Blade's album hadn't been released yet when we spoke to Victoria but she had heard a tape "and it's really great." Blade plays on *Musings of a Creekdipper*, has been part of Joni Mitchell's touring group, and regularly drums with *Joshua Redman, who raves about him in these pages.

Buddy Miller—*Poison Love* and *Your Love and Other Lies* (both Hightone). "He's so talented," Victoria says about her good friend, the lead guitarist for Emmylou Harris's terrific Spyboy band as well as a widely respected country-folk singer/songwriter.

Julie Miller—"Her records have meant something to me in that they would arrive at a time when I definitely needed to hear them. . . . Just set my priorities straight listenin' to them." says Victoria. Julie is Buddy Miller's wife. ⬤: *Blue Pony* (Hightone) and *Orphans and Angels* (Myrrh).

Claude Debussy—*Prelude to the Afternoon of a Faun.* Inspired by a poem by Stéphane Mallarmé, this is one of Victoria's favorite classical pieces. ⬤: See Master List.

Various artists—*Anthology of American Folk Music* (6 CDs: Smithsonian/Folkways). "The Sacred Harp Singers? Whoo! That is some nice stuff," Victoria says about this classic collection, re-issued as a CD box set in 1997. Besides the Alabama Sacred Harp Singers, the set includes Uncle Dave Macon, Blind Lemon Jefferson, Mississippi John Hurt, and the Carter Fanily.

Little Jimmy Scott—*Regal Records Live in New Orleans* (Specialty) and *All the Way* (Sire). The former was recorded early in Scott's career, the latter recently.

*Joan Armatrading—*Show Some Emotion* (A&M). "She's just somethin' else."

Gram Parsons—"Well, of course, Gram Parsons." ⊙: *GP/Grievous Angel* (Reprise) combines Parsons's two great solo albums on one CD.

Dillard and Clark—*The Fantastic Expedition of . . .* (A&M).

Rickie Lee Jones—Victoria is a big fan of Jones's whole catalog. ⊙: The 1981 release *Pirates* (Warner Bros.), 1989's *Flying Cowboys* (Geffen), and 1995's *Traffic from Paradise* (Geffen) show off the commanding artistry of this singer-songwriter's best work.

Mary Margaret O'Hara—*Miss America* (Koch). One utterly unique artist nominates another. The spacious beauty of O'Hara's songs and folk-rock arrangements is unforgettable.

*Willie Nelson—*Red Headed Stranger* (Columbia). Victoria calls this story, and storied, album a "not-to-be-missed classic."

VICTORIA WILLIAMS'S OWN RECORDINGS

Victoria seems quite content with her entire discography, starting with her 1987 debut, *Happy Come Home* (Geffen). She feels she makes better records today because she understands the recording process better, but she still enjoys the songs on *Happy* "and of course I always appreciate Van Dyke [Park]'s string arrangements on there. I just love him." She's particularly proud of 1994's *Loose* (Mammoth), to which Parks also contributed arrangements, and feels the spirited live album from the *Loose* tour, *This Moment: Live in Toronto* (Atlantic), represents her well, too. (The latter is a good introduction to her music because she highlights all her previous work in the set.) She says she always likes her most recent record, in this case *Musings of a Creekdipper* (Atlantic). And although she appears primarily as an ethereal backup vocalist, she's happy with the homemade *The Original Harmony Ridge Creek Dippers*, which features the songs and lead vocals of Mark Olson (Victoria co-wrote two tunes). This disc is an ultra-relaxed, lo-fi acoustic effort that comes off like a heartfelt gift from good friends. It also sounds like it was made by people who are very much in love. To order it or its follow-ups, *Pacific Coast Rambler* and *Zola and the Tulip Tree*, send $12 to P.O. Box 342, Joshua Tree, CA 92252.

⊙: The one album Victoria failed to mention, *Swing the Statue* (Rough Trade), should be heard by anyone who likes her other work. It was her second album and contains many of her fans' and critics' favorite songs by her.

R O B E R T   W Y A T T   (March 31, 1998)

I mmediately after its release, Robert Wyatt's 1997 album *Shleep* received glorious reviews in all the right places: *Rolling Stone*, *Spin*, *Musician*. Other media shots followed, including an adoring feature on National Public Radio's *All Things Considered*. And now we'll see what difference it makes, because Wyatt, formerly of the British jazz-rock outfit Soft Machine, has been here before. Since the early 1970s, he has made a string of impressive records that combine sharp pop hooks and melodies with sophisticated jazz touches. His lyrics can exude a Dylanesque social passion and he sings them in a fragile, almost ethereal style that has made him a hero to many of his peers. Unfortunately, the mainstream pop audience has yet to notice.

Wyatt's unique sensibilities began taking shape in a house almost devoid of popular sounds. "I was just a year before all that anybody listened to was rock music," says Robert, born in Bristol, England, in 1945. His parents weren't against pop, he says, but "they just had modern conservatory music, like Stravinsky, around the house. Then my father also remembered that he liked jazz and introduced me to that." If getting Robert's attention was Dad's purpose, it worked— particularly with one record, *Ray Charles and Betty Carter*. That album led Robert to conclude that jazz at its best "can be just as good as Bartok."

Robert started listening to jazz incessantly "whilst I should have been doing my school homework. Consequently, school was a total disaster and I had no idea what to do when I left school." After six years of slacking, he started playing drums in "beat groups" with friends. But jazz was coloring even his early pop efforts, he recalls: "When the opportunities came to do anything with a tune, even if it was a Chuck Berry tune, when you started to interpret it your own way, the ideas you'd get didn't come from listening to lots of guitar people or rock records, they came from listening to these other records, and it gradually sort of started to twist the music out of shape."

Robert and some fellow musical outsiders formed a band called the Wilde Flowers in the mid-1960s; in 1966, several of the Flowers, including Robert, founded Soft Machine, named for a William Burroughs novel. Their first single included guitar contributions from the then-largely unknown Jimi Hendrix. After Hendrix's fame exploded, Soft Machine basked briefly in its glow by opening for him on his 1968 tour. Unfortunately, the Soft's challenging marriage of psychedelia and jazz never caught on outside the rock intelligentsia, and Robert, whose ideas were expanding beyond the band's concept, left in 1971.

Robert next formed a band called Matching Mole. He and the group were planning their third album in 1973 when an accident changed everything. During a party, Robert fell from a fourth-story window and broke his back, paralyzing him from the waist down. But instead of ending his career, the accident only re-focused it. After convalescing, he released his solo debut, *Rock Bottom*, in 1974. The album thrilled critics; he then released a remake of the Monkees' "I'm a Believer," even landing on the U.K. pop charts for a time. Since then, he's toured with the Fred Frith/John Greaves avant-rock assembly, Henry Cow; contributed to Michael Mantler's arty literature and jazz projects on WATT/ECM; and continued to release occasional solo albums to a frustrating mix of critical excitement and popular neglect.

But hope abides. As we write this, the media attention showered on *Shleep* has spurred his labels, the indies Thirsty Ear (U.S.) and Hannibal (U.K.) to ready his other solo albums for reissue. Like some archeological treasure, one of the most artful careers in popular music may soon be unearthed.

ROBERT WYATT'S FAVORITE ARTISTS AND RECORDINGS

Ray Charles with Betty Carter—*Ray Charles & Betty Carter* (DCC). Robert loves the whole album, but particularly the track "Alone Together."

Charlie Parker, Dizzy Gillespie, Bud Powell, Charles Mingus, and Max Roach—*Jazz at Massey Hall* (Original Jazz Classics/Debut). "That's the first record I started drumming along to, on the table, with pencils and bits of paper. I used pencils for the sticks, or I'd roll up bits of paper and try and make brush sounds on the table surface. . . . [Drummer] Max Roach is just sizzling away, and everybody plays so well on it. I mean, [pianist] Bud Powell's solos are just searching all over the place, and every time he lands, he lands on both feet. It's quite extraordinary."

Gil Evans—*Out of the Cool* (Impulse).

Miles Davis with Gil Evans—*Porgy and Bess* (Columbia) or *The Complete Columbia Studio Sessions* (6 CDs: Columbia). The common denominator on these releases and the one above is Gil Evans as conductor/arranger. Robert enthuses, "I just think Gil Evans is wonderful. Gil Evans is very easy to listen to in the sense that he actually has harmonies suspended all the way through things, whereas on a normal jazz record they might be hinted at in little steps by a pianist and a bass player. With Gil Evans, there they are hanging there in the air." Note that the six-CD set includes the *Porgy and Bess* tracks.

Miles Davis—*The Complete Birth of the Cool* (Capitol). "If I could only buy one now, that would be the one I would buy," says Robert about this disc, to which Gil Evans also contributed arrangements along with Gerry Mulligan.

Modern Jazz Quartet—*Concorde* (Prestige). "I always stick up for them because they got some sort of flack for being too respectable and all that kind of thing. I always thought it seemed almost racist the way they were put down, as if black people are meant to be raunchy—leave the smart suits and the quiet music to us white folks. . . . So many of the tunes [leader/pianist John Lewis] wrote are so elegant—of course, he likes simple, sort of Bach-like things. And how right he is. Everyone plays immaculately." Robert advises readers to especially check out vibist Milt Jackson's performance on "All of You" on the above disc.

The Modern Jazz Quartet with Jimmy Giuffre—"I don't know if many people have heard that. I suppose it's chamber music. I think that Jimmy Giuffre hadn't had a clarinet for that long, and he said, you know, 'I'm just sort of feeling my way around the lower register.' So he plays these sort of folklike things on it." : Giuffre played with the MJQ on a couple of dates; those collaborations are included in the box set *MJQ: 40 Years* (4 CDs: Atlantic) and Mosaic's limited edition set *The Complete Capitol and Atlantic Recordings* (6 CDs). Single-disc collaborations (issued under the MJQ's name) include *Third Stream Music* (Atlantic) and *At Music Inn*, a 1959 Atlantic album reissued on the audiophile Mobile Fidelity label in '95.

Van Morrison—*Astral Weeks* (Warner Bros.). Robert says his wife Alfie turned him on to this record after criticizing his music for being too dense: "[She] said 'Don't you like the space in it, the way he just lets things ride and just lets the rhythm section breathe and leave space?' And I did listen to it, and it had a big influence on the record I made after that, *Rock Bottom*, which was altogether much more airy and less complicated than anything I did before."

Nina Simone—*I Put a Spell On You* (Mercury). "She's one of those singers, like Ray Charles, who's just monumental. When I started trying to get to grips with singing as opposed to just being a drummer, it was doing material I got from Nina Simone records. It's funny that the people I actually sing along with on records tend to have been women, whether it's Betty Carter or Dionne Warwick or whatever, because I don't have one of those deep, hairy-chested voices." : This album is currently available on the twofer *In Concert/I Put a Spell On You* (Mercury), paired with a superior live date.

Sly and the Family Stone—*Stand!* (Epic). Robert says Sly's was the music that stood out most to him when Soft Machine toured the United States in 1968: "I think it was partly because he was so open and inventive with the format and production and the sound that it was very, very far out stuff, but it was also deeply rooted in that black funk thing, and this idea that they just went together so happily. I was very knocked out by that."

El Camaron de la Isla—*Calle Real* (Philips). Of this late flamenco performer, Robert says, "He got the roots of it totally authentic, but it's modern as tomorrow at the same time. . . . Flamenco is one face of the real, long-time underground music of Europe, which is gypsy music, really, Romany music. It's the Spanish face of it. Not all flamenco singers are gypsies, just as not all blues singers are black. Nevertheless, the aristocracy, the core of it, wouldn't exist without gypsies. I would say that gypsy music is the blues of Europe, and if I was actually getting people to buy records, I would say look out for gypsy music wherever you can."

Pastora Pavon (La Niña de los Peines)—Robert found a cassette of this singer in a Spanish open-air market. Her popular name, La Nina de los Peines—"the little girl of the combs"—was given to her because, Robert says, she wears large combs in her hair: "She's just one of the great Andalusian singers, and all her CDs are compilations of seventy-eights. She was a kind of Bessie Smith figure, really, one of the women who becomes a female icon, a sort of witch-goddess. She doesn't sing *cante jondo*, she even does sort of Latin American things, but she's really a fantastic singer." ⊙: *Early Cante Flamenco—Classic Recordings from the 1930s* (Arhoolie) or *Antologia de Cantaores, Vol. 3* (EMI Spain).

Randy Crawford—"Secret Combination" on *Secret Combination* (Warner Bros). "When [my wife] Alfie's away for any length of time, there are moments where the only thing that will do, and I sit there sadly with a bottle of wine, is Randy Crawford singing sentimental songs about partners going away. And that record's it. . . . She looks after me when Alfie's away."

John Coltrane—*Africa Brass* (Impulse), *Elvin Jones, drums.

Charles Mingus—*Mingus Presents Mingus* (Candid), Danny Richmond, drums.

Ornette Coleman—*This Is Our Music* (Atlantic), Ed Blackwell, drums.

Art Blakey—*Art Blakey's Jazz Messengers with Thelonious Monk* (Atlantic), Art Blakey, drums. Robert groups these four albums together because they so strongly molded his own drumming. "They were a great inspiration to me," he says, "and in a way they meant that I could never be a really happy rock drummer. I was sort of spoiled, really, because as much as I admire the strength and simplicity of [Led Zeppelin's] John Bonham and all those sorts of people, in the back of my mind, I saw drums as sort of these seething, churning things, the way Danny Richmond played them. . . . I used a lot of rock devices, but in the end my idea of what the kit was all about, the majesty of the drum kit, the aspirations I had on the kit, I got from listening to Elvin Jones and so on."

ROBERT WYATT'S OWN RECORDINGS

Robert is quite proud of all of his solo work, starting with *Shleep* (Thirsty Ear in the United States, Hannibal in the U.K.), which sports contributions from Brian Eno, ex-

Roxy Music guitarist Phil Manzanara, Paul Weller, and Robert's wife, Alfreda Benge. He's excited about Thirsty Ear's upcoming reissue of his other solo albums, although he cautions that "there's one or two that I'm a bit anxious about that weren't recorded for posterity—for example *Nothing Can Stop Us*, which was a bunch of quickly done singles . . . I'm not convinced they make an LP." He also has some reservations about *The Animals*, a score for a film about animal abuse to which Robert and the *Talking Heads both contributed music. But as for the rest, he chuckles, "Since I didn't make any Gil Evans records, I'll have to stand by my own." The names of those releases, besides *Shleep*, are *The End of an Ear*, *Rock Bottom*, *Ruth Is Stranger than Richard*, *Old Rottenhat*, and *Dondestan*.

Robert also calls attention to a couple of albums by other artists that he contributed to, Michael Mantler's *Hapless Child* (ECM) and John Greaves's *Songs* (Resurgence). About the Mantler disc, Robert says, "He adapted some Edward Gorey verses. It was Carla Bley who got me on that session and it was the first time somebody had employed me just as a singer. I didn't have to worry about anything else, and I was just singing with this knockout rhythm section: Jack DeJohnette, Steve Swallow, and Carla Bley." The record by Greaves, on which Robert also sings, is only available in France and England, Robert says. It features Greaves's frequent partner, avant garde rocker/songwriter/cartoonist Peter Blegvad. "It could easily, and probably will, sift through the net," Robert says with more than a little empathy, "but I just think this is so good."

●:As both drummer and all-around musical personality, Robert was a driving force in the first four Soft Machine albums, which after the band's eponymous debut were simply numbered titles (*Volume 2*, *Third*, *Fourth*, etc.) All have been reissued by One Way except *Fourth*, released by Sony. Numerous live Soft Machine recordings have surfaced in the past few years, including *Virtuality* (Cunieform), recorded live in Germany in 1971. *The Druggy Jet-Propelled Photograph* (Charly), a collection of demos from 1967, shows the band focused more on psychedelic pop songs rather than the proto-fusion of later records, although jazz accents abound. Matching Mole, Robert's Soft Machine–ish interim project before his solo career, released *Matching Mole* and *Little Red Record* (both BGO) and *Live in Concert* (Windsong), taken from a BBC broadcast.

In 1999, Thirsty Ear released the 5-CD set *EPs by* . . . , containing singles and EPs never included on his albums, accompanied by Robert's own commentary.

LISTEN TO THIS!
MASTER LIST

I n the course of our interviews for *Listen to This!*, certain artists were named over and over as favorites, but without reference to any specific recordings. As always in *Listen to This!*, we endeavor to recommend recordings that will introduce you to that artist. Rather than repeat this information in the section of every interviewee who mentioned the following musicians, we have compiled it for you below.

Johnny Ace—R&B pianist/vocalist Ace died at 25 playing Russian Roulette. ●: *Johnny Ace Memorial Album* (Duke) has only 12 tracks but was the best overview available as of this writing.

Louis Armstrong—Armstrong is the most influential and innovative improviser in jazz history. ●: *Hot Fives and Sevens, Vols. 1–3* (JSP, available separately) captures Armstrong's revolutionary small group sessions in the mid-late 1920's—this music is available on other labels, too, but the sound is best on these versions.

For primo large group discs, go to the budget-priced chronological Classics series titled "Louis Armstrong & His Orchestra" over the span 1928–42.

Bad Company—This supergroup, with members from Free, King Crimson, and Mott the Hoople, achieved a number of hits from 1974 to '82 with its growling, radio-friendly hard rock. ⦿: The 1974 release *Bad Company* (Swan Song) was an arresting debut for this British arena-rock band and *10 from 6* (Swan Song) is a solid greatest-hits package.

Count Basie—A jazz institution, pianist Basie led some of the finest swing orchestras ever assembled over his near 60-year career. ⦿: *The Complete Decca Recordings* (3 CDs: GRP), one of the great collections in American music, covers 1937 to early 1939, a peak period for the band. Any of the single Classics discs from the period 1939 to '42 are also highly recommended, although recording quality is uneven from track to track.

The Beatles—This group's importance may never be equaled again in rock music. Built on a solid foundation of rock 'n' roll roots, they transcended it all with their bottomless creativity and cultural impact. ⦿: Every album is a classic but their studio creativity starts showing up in force on 1966's *Revolver* (Capitol), continuing until they retired as a band in 1970.

Chuck Berry—Though everyone knows his name, few music fans comprehend how completely Berry transformed rock with his songwriting, guitar style, and exciting stage manner. ⦿: *The Great Twenty-eight* (Chess) is a terrific compilation of Berry's Chess classics and thus a huge slice of early rock history.

Bobby "Blue" Bland—One of the greatest singers in blues and R&B, Bland's smooth but emotive style has made him one of both genres' most enduring stars and influential presences. ⦿: *The Best of Bobby "Blue" Bland* (MCA) is the best compilation to start with. *The Best of "Bobby Blue" Bland, Vol. 2* (MCA) picks up where the previous disc leaves off. For more serious fans, *I Pity the Fool/ The Duke Recordings, Vol. 1* (MCA) covers all Bland's recordings for Duke from 1952 to 1960 on two CDs. *Turn on Your Lovelight/The Duke Recordings, Vol. 2* (MCA), another two-disc set, spans the years 1961 to 1964, when the arrangements were more brass driven, as in the incendiary title cut.

Booker T. and the MGs—One of the greatest rhythm sections in soul music history, the MGs, with guitarist *Steve Cropper, backed Otis Redding, Sam and Dave, *Wilson Pickett, and so many others on many of their greatest tracks in addition to recording albums as featured artists. ⦿: To hear the back-up group at its cookin'-est, check out them out on records by any of the just-mentioned artists.

Green Onions (Atlantic) and *Very Best Of . . .* (Rhino) are excellent introductions to the group's featured-artist catalog.

Big Bill Broonzy—With his muscular style and songwriting ("Key to the Highway" among others), acoustic bluesman Broonzy, who played guitar, violin, and mandolin, is one of the foundation artists of early blues history. ●: *The Young Bill Broonzy (1928–1935)* (Yazoo) and *Do That Guitar Rag (1928–1935)* (Yazoo).

Clifford Brown—Killed in a car wreck at 26, trumpeter Brown recorded prolifically in his short time here, and most of what he left behind still stuns with its combination of virtuosity and power of exposition. With his bright tone and dense, compressed style, he stands as almost the polar opposite of Miles Davis, whose impact he rivals. ●: Check out the four-CD set *The Complete Blue Note and Pacific Jazz Recordings* (Blue Note) for some of Brown's most exciting playing. A good budget choice is *Clifford Brown and Max Roach* (Polygram), featuring Brown's memorable pairing with preeminent bebop drummer Roach. Catch Brown, Roach, and tenor sax titan *Sonny Rollins on Sonny's very fine *Plus Four*, on which both horn players solo brilliantly while Roach drives the bus.

James Brown—The Godfather of Soul's influence on popular music is incalculable. He helped invent soul music in the '60s and funk in the late '60s and '70s, and was such a dynamic and innovative bandleader that he is worshipped by jazz musicians as well. ●: The album *20 All-Time Greatest Hits* (Polydor) is a fine single-disc introduction. *Star Time* (4 CDs: Polydor) is an astounding career overview.

Bush Tetras—The Bush Tetras were a mostly female band from the New York post-punk scene that seemed to anticipate the lo-fi movement with a sound built from reggae, funk, and Afro-Caribbean rhythms. They rarely recorded. ●: *Tetrafied* (2 13 61) is a 1996 collection of rare and unreleased singles. *Better Late Than Never 1980–1983* (ROIR) is an extensive compilation.

The Byrds—The Byrds' psychedelic folk rock proved to be nearly as influential in America as the Beatles, as a quick scan of the present work reveals. More than three decades after their peak, they are vitally important to the current generation of rockers. ●: *The Byrds' Greatest Hits* (Columbia) is still a fine single-disc introduction to their best songs. *The Byrds* (Columbia) is a four-CD box set and career overview. All single albums from the 1965 debut *Mr. Tambourine Man* through 1969's *The Ballad of Easy Rider*, with the possible exception of *Dr. Byrd and Mr. Hyde* (all Columbia), are excellent.

The Carter Family—The Carter Family's music stayed close to their home in the Clinch Mountain region of Virginia and the Southern folk and spiritual music that flourished there, but looked forward rhythmically, driven by Maybelle Carter's innovative guitar style. ⬤: The Carters recorded for RCA in their prime years of 1927 to 1934; this material is available on the meticulously documented *Their Complete Victor Recordings* series (Rounder), a foundation collection for any serious fan of country music. *Country Music Hall of Fame Series* (MCA) draws from their fine Decca recordings in 1936 to '38; the CD booklet includes excellent historical documentation.

Ray Charles—Charles's gospel-charged vocal style is a foundation of '60s soul music, but his impact only begins there. As a bandleader, arranger, singer, and all-around musical visionary, he is probably the most comprehensively important figure in popular music, affecting rock, jazz, blues, pop, and even country. ⬤: *The Best of Ray Charles: The Atlantic Years* (Rhino) is a solid single-disc overview of Ray's work for Atlantic Records in the 1950s. *Greatest Hits, Vol. 1* and *Greatest Hits, Vol. 2* (Rhino) cover Charles's post-Atlantic classics. *Ray Charles Live (1958–59)* (Atlantic) and *Ray Charles—Berlin, 1962* (Pablo) are superb concert recordings. No box set of reasonable size can cover the full scope of Charles's vision but *Genius & Soul—The 50th Anniversary Collection* (5 CDs: Rhino) comes admirably close.

Nat King Cole— ⬤: *Greatest Hits* (Capitol) will introduce you to Cole's vocal classics as a crossover artist. *The Best of the Nat King Cole Trio* (Capitol) surveys his early instrumental work with his superb jazz trios.

John Coltrane Quartet—Coltrane's remarkably empathetic and able quartet, with McCoy Tyner, Jimmy Garrison, and *Elvin Jones, is one of the most admired units in music, regardless of genre. ⬤: *A Love Supreme* (Impulse) is one of jazz's most memorable albums. *Afro-Blue Impression* (2 CDs: Pablo) is a near-classic compliment drawn from the quartet's 1963 tour, with richly played staples such as "Naima," "My Favorite Things," and "Impressiions," and an especially potent "Lonnie's Lament." Surprisingly few other Coltrane albums feature the great quartet exclusively, although several have the quartet augmented by additional players. *The Classic Quartet: Complete Impulse! Studio Recordings* covers much of the group's output.

Sam Cooke and the Soul Stirrers—As a singer with the Soul Stirrers, Cooke and his colleagues created marvelous gospel during the music's Golden Age in the '50s. He smoothed out his gritty style for the pop audience and became a huge crossover success. As both a singer and songwriter, Cooke is a founding father of soul music. ⬤: *The Original Soul Stirrers Featuring Sam Cooke* (Specialty) will introduce you to Cooke's gospel work with the Soul Stirrers. *The Man and His Music* (RCA) gives a comprehensive overview of Cooke's pop career.

Celia Cruz and Johnny Pacheco—Pacheco, who moved to New York from the Dominican Republic in the late '40s, and Cuban Celia Cruz made their reputations separately but have also performed together. ⚫: For a taste of their chemistry as a duo, try *Celia and Johnny* and under Cruz's name, *Brillante* (both Vaya). From their solo catalogs, check out Pacheco's *Que Sueae la Flauta* (Alegre) and Cruz's . . . *y La Sonora Matancera* (Sony).

The Davis Sisters—Founded by Ruth Davis in Philadelphia, this gospel quintet astounded with the choruslike sound they generated from just five voices. ⚫: *The Best of the Davis Sisters* (Savoy) covers the group's best work for Savoy, where they recorded until 1962.

Manu Dibango—The Cameroonian Makossa man, with his blend of jazz and African pop, is one of Afropop's true superstars. ⚫: Start with the classic *Soul Makossa* (Unidisc)—*Makossa* refers to a Cameroonian dance groove. For a superb sample of Dibango's more recent work, listen to *Wakafrika* (Warner Bros.) with contributions from *Youssou N'Dour, *Salif Keita, Angelique Kidjo, *Ladysmith Black Mambazo, and Peter Gabriel.

The Dixie Hummingbirds—The Hummingbirds are one of the most enduring, and important, acts in gospel history, with a career stretching back to the 1930s. ⚫: *Live* (Mobile Fidelity), recorded live at a New Jersey church in 1976.

Nick Drake—This folk rocker from the U.K. died tragically in 1974 at age 26, leaving behind a recorded legacy that has been widely influential ever since. ⚫: Hannibal has reissued all of Nick Drake's albums, *Five Leaves Left, Bryter Layter, Pink Moon,* and *Time of No Reply; Fruit Tree,* a box set that includes all four; and a one-disc sampler, *Way to Blue,* the economical way in to Drake's music.

Duke Ellington—One of the great composers in American history, Ellington made just as much impact as a jazz bandleader and arranger. And he could play more than a little piano, too. ⚫: Ellington has a vast catalog of superb recordings. You might start with *The Webster-Blanton Years* (RCA/Bluebird), a three-disc set documenting one of Ellington's greatest bands between 1939 and 1942, or any of the two-disc sets from the 1940s of Ellington's *Carnegie Hall Concerts* (Prestige). *Black, Brown, and Beige* (RCA/Bluebird) and *The Far East Suite* (Bluebird) present classic extended works.

Brian Eno—A founding member of Roxy Music, Eno has since created pioneering atmospheric pop and experimental music as both a solo artist and producer. ⚫: For a good sense of Eno's poppier side, try *Another Green World* (EG), or (with John Cale) *Wrong Way Up* (Opal). To sample his important ambient music, start with *Music for Airports* (EG).

Ella Fitzgerald—Considered by many to be the greatest jazz singer ever, Fitzgerald was a true jazz artist in that she improvised like a horn player. ⏺: *Pure Ella* (MCA) pairs Ella with pianist Ellis Larkin for a wonderful standards set. She may be best remembered for her extensive catalog of recordings centered on the works of great American songwriters—Gershwin, Arlen, Porter, Kern, and so on—with orchestras led by Nelson Riddle, Billy May, and Buddy Bregman. The quality is almost uniformly terrific, so go for *Best of the Songbooks* (2 CDs: Verve), *The Complete Songbooks* (16 CDs: Verve), or any of the individual *Songbook* albums. *The Complete Ella in Berlin* (Verve) is a famous live record from 1960.

The Five Blind Boys of Mississippi—This group, led by Archie Brownlee, influenced many secular artists, including Ray Charles. ⏺: *Best of the . . . , Vol. 1* (MCA).

The Four Tops—Distinguished by the high-drama vocals of Levi Stubbs, this group cut a number of symphonic soul hits for Motown in the 1960s. ⏺: *Anthology* (2 CDs: Motown).

Aretha Franklin—Her nickname "Lady Soul" is an understatement. Her talent is unearthly but was best captured when it was matched to material and producers worthy of her, which last happened consistently almost three decades ago. ⏺: *30 Greatest Hits* (Atlantic), includes all of Franklin's stunning soul hits from the 1960s and early '70s. *Amazing Grace* (Atlantic), Aretha's 1972 gospel release, should not be overlooked by pop fans. *Queen of Soul* (4 CDs: Rhino) is a comprehensive survey of Aretha's Atlantic career, her prime work.

Lefty Frizzell—Frizzell's smooth honky-tonk singing style set the tone for traditional country vocals ever after. ⏺: *The Best of . . .* (Rhino) covers Frizzell's prime years, 1950 to '65. *Treasures Untold* (Rounder) samples his early work before a drinking problem eroded his health and career.

Marvin Gaye—Of Motown's fabulous stable of talent, Gaye may have been the best. His suave, sophisticated style worked equally well with romantic material and propulsive R&B. Once he attained creative control over his records, he made several landmark albums including the socially conscious *What's Going On.* ⏺: Good starter choices include *What's Going On* (Motown); *Anthology* (Motown), a two-CD retrospective released in 1995 (more comprehensive than the 1974 set of the same name); and *The Master 1961–1984* (4 CDs: Motown), a box set that gives the best overview of his career.

Stephane Grappelli—Grappelli's recording career spanned well over six decades and many, many fine albums as a leader, but the music that remains his most essential is that recorded with guitarist Django Reinhardt. The recordings the two made with their string band Quintet du Hot Club de France are one of the richest treasure troves in jazz. Many fans love their post-war reunion recording in Rome just as dearly. ⬤: *Souvenirs* (London) and *Swing from Paris* (ASV) are excellent introductions to the Hot Club catalog. For the Rome material, try *Djangology* (Bluebird/BMG). (Note: Many of the best recordings featuring the duo have been released under Reinhardt's name).

Woody Guthrie—A connsumate songwriting poet, Guthrie also represents the activist soul of folk music. ⬤: *Library of Congress Recordings, Vols. 1–3* (Rounder), *A Legendary Performer* (RCA), and *Dust Bowl Ballads* (Rounder).

Merle Haggard—Many considered Haggard the greatest country singer/songwriter to come along since Hank Williams when he started out, and he has sustained the reputation ever since. ⬤: *The Lonesome Fugitive: The Merle Haggard Anthology (1963–1977)* (2 CDs: Razor & Tie) is the best introductory compilation, with all of his classic hits present and most of his other best material represented.

Tim Hardin—This early singer-songwriter blended folk, blues, and jazz to write some of the most memorable songs of the 1960s. ⬤: Most of Hardin's albums contain strong material but a certain deterioration sets in after a while: Hardin died of a heroin overdose in 1980. *The Tim Hardin Memorial Album* (Polygram) and *Reason to Believe: The Best of Tim Hardin* (2 CDs: Polydor) are solid compilations that emphasize his early career, which produced such standards as ''If I Were a Carpenter,'' ''Don't Make Promises,'' and ''Reason to Believe.''

Ben Harper—Combining influences as diverse as folk music, R&B, and Led Zeppelin, Harper is widely considered one of the best of the current rockers by fellow musicians. The public has yet to catch on to that degree. ⬤: *Welcome to the Cruel World*, *Fight for Your Mind*, and *The Will to Love* (all Virgin) showcase the talented Harper's unique blend of popular sounds.

Smoky Hogg—All but forgotten today, Hogg was one of the most popular and influential blues/R&B artists of the late-'40s-early '50s. ⬤: *Angels in Harlem* (Specialty).

Billie Holiday—She didn't have a terrific voice and didn't improvise in the free manner of an Ella Fitzgerald, but from the standpoint of emotionality and sheer musicality, Billie Holiday had no peers as a jazz vocalist. Tragically, her troubled life only made her art more compelling. ⬤: *The Quintessential . . . Vols. 1–9* (Columbia, available separately) provide a solid entry into Holiday's catalog.

Lightnin' Hopkins—Hopkins, from Texas, is one of the most important country blues artists ever and, fortunately, one of the most prolifically recorded. ⬤: *Mojo*

Hand: The Anthology (Rhino) samples Hopkins's voluminous recorded catalog with 41 tracks over the course of two discs.

Howlin' Wolf (Chester Burnett)—Wolf's exuberant, gruff vocals, captured on a number of outstanding blues recordings for the Chess label primarily, are of critical importance to the development of '60s blues rock via such admirers as the Rolling Stones and the Yardbirds. 🔴: *Howlin' Wolf/Moaning in the Moonlight* (Chess), which combines Wolf's first two albums from 1959 and 1961; *The Chess Box* (Chess), a three-CD box set.

Incredible String Band—From the mid-'60s to '70s, Scotts Robin Williamson, Mike Heron, and various associates created psychedelic, fairy tale-like folk music on an eclectic assortment of stringed instruments, from guitars to ouds and sitars. 🔴: The records *5000 Spirits or the Layer of the Onion* (Elektra) and *The Hangman's Beautiful Daughter* (Hannibal) are two of the band's best single albums from the late 1960s. *Relics of the Incredible String Band* (Elektra), a compilation, draws from seven albums' worth of songs released from 1967 to '70.

Mahalia Jackson—Once the reigning queen of black gospel, Jackson sang in a deeply emotive and powerful style that won gospel many white fans when she applied it to pop material in the mid-'50s. 🔴: *Gospels, Spirituals, and Hymns* (Columbia/Legacy), *Mahalia Jackson, Vol. 2* (Columbia/Legacy), *Live at Newport* (Sony), and *How I Got Over* (Columbia).

Etta James—Her recent jazz records prove that the gospel-trained, big-voiced James, one of R&B's best, can sing just about anything. 🔴: *The Essential . . .* (2 CDs: MCA/Chess) is a fine compilation of James's years on Chess, where she recorded the tracks she's best known for, including, "Tell Mama." For a jazzy change of pace, try the superb *Mystery Lady* (Private Music), on which James remakes tunes recoreded by Billie Holiday with a terrific band.

Little Willie John (William Edgar John)—This R&B performer is still largely unknown to the listening public, but not to a host of musicians who cite his influence. 🔴: *Fever: The Best of Little Willie John* (Rhino), a single-disc anthology.

Buddy Johnson—Johnson's popular jump blues band helped pave the way for rock 'n' roll in the '40s and '50s. Johnson's wife Ella was the band's main vocalist. 🔴: *Go Ahead and Rock and Roll* (Collectibles) and *Walk'Em: Decca Sessions* (Ace) provides good single-CD introductions, but if you want to jump and boogie for a week, go for *Buddy and Ella Johnson 1953–1964* (4 CDs: Bear Family).

Marv Johnson—Johnson is a largely forgotten soul singer from the 1960s. : *You Got What It Takes: The Best of Marv Johnson* (EMI).

George Jones—Widely considered the most accomplished singer in traditional country music, Jones has performed primarily romantic material since the 1950s. ⦿: *The Best of George Jones (1955–1967)* (Rhino).

Louis Jordan—Exuberant saxophonist/singer/bandleader Jordan performed mostly novelty tunes with his group the Tympany Five, but behind the humor was a marvelous musician and band that paved the way for R&B and early rock. ⦿: *The Best of Louis Jordan* and *Five Guys Named Moe: Original Decca Recordings, Vol. 2* (both MCA).

Nusrat Fateh Ali Khan—The late Pakistani singer was the most popular exponent of the Sufi qawwalli style and as important a spiritual/musical influence on current rockers as Ravi Shankar was on the '60s scene. ⦿: *Devotional Songs* (Real World) is the album that many Khan devotees heard first. *Traditional Sufi Qawwalis* (Navras), which comes in four volumes available separately, is more like the music Khan, who often adapted his sound for popular audiences, would perform for Pakistani Muslims.

Albert King—Electric guitarist King purveyed a stinging, single-string style that won over blues purists and rockers alike during his heyday in the late '60s. ⦿: The CD reissue *King of the Blues Guitar* (Atlantic) contains all of 1967's *Born Under a Bad Sign* (Stax)—a hugely influential album for countless rock and blues guitarists—plus assorted Stax singles. Big Albert is backed by *Booker T. and the MGs and the Memphis Horns. *Ultimate Collection* (2 CDs: Rhino) is a solid compilation that focuses on King's peak years.

B. B. King—The King of the Blues, as compelling a vocalist as he is a distinctive guitar stylist, is one of the few musical superstars whose reputation is a perfect fit for his talent. ⦿: *King of the Blues* (MCA) is a 4-CD box set. *Live at the Regal* (ABC/MCA) and *Live at Cook County Jail* (MCA) are excellent concert discs.

Fela Kuti—Fela's pointed political messages coupled with his long, groove-charged songs won him huge audiences in West Africa. For his efforts, Fela was jailed and tortured by Nigeria's military government. He died in 1998 but influenced rockers for decades. ⦿: *The Best of Fela Kuti* (2 volumes: Oceana), *Original Sufferhead* (Shanachie), and *Army Arrangement* (Celluloid).

Lambchop—This alternative band plays a winking brand of Nashville country that subverts the music's cliches with dashes of indie rock attitude and irreverent humor. ⦿: Lambchop's albums include *I Hope You're Sitting Down, How I Quit Smoking, Thriller*, and *What Another Man Spills* (all Merge).

Johnny Lang—This teenage blues guitar hero is seen by many senior classmen as a savior of the form. ●: 1997's *Lie to Me* (A&M).

Huddie Ledbetter ("Leadbelly")—Although thought of largely as a folk troubador, Leadbelly was actually the first bluesman to become popular with white audiences. "Good Night Irene" and "Rock Island Line" are two of his best-known songs. ●: *Midnight Special, Gwine Dig a Hole to Put the Devil In*, and *Let It Shine* (all Rounder), although available singly, together comprise the surviving recordings of Leadbelly made by Alan Lomax for the Library of Congress between 1934 and 1942.

Liquid Liquid—Purveyors of danceable post-rock in the late '70s and early '80s, Liquid Liquid blended arty vocals and minimalist, repetitive grooves, often with a Latin carnival feel. ●: *Liquid Liquid* (Grand Royal).

Little Milton (Campbell)—Still active, bluesman Campbell has been tremendously influential since the early '60s as a singer, guitarist, and songwriter. ●: *If Walls Could Talk* (MCA/Chess) and *Grits Ain't Groceries* (Checkers) are fine albums from 1970. *Sun Masters* (Rounder) covers some of Campbell's most unrestrained moments from the early 1950s. *We're Gonna Make It/Little Milton Sings Big Blues* (MCA/Chess) is a twofer combining two of Little Milton's best from the mid-'60s.

Little Richard—Richard's flamboyance shouldn't obscure his contributions as one of the seminal early rockers, with a shouting, piano-pounding style that was equal parts gospel, New Orleans, and something entirely of his own invention. ●: *The Georgia Peach* (Specialty) includes all the big hits for the label plus other great singles.

Little Walter (Marion Walter Jacobs)—Walter made the amplified harmonica the force it now is in Chicago-style urban blues and was widely considered its greatest player as well. ●: *The Best of Little Walter* (MCA/Chess) is a superb single-disc introduction to this blues harp master. There's a second volume of the *Best of* series but a better overall strategy is to buy the two-disc *The Essential Little Walter* (MCA/Chess).

Mahlathini—Known as "the Lion of Soweto," Mahlathini is one of the biggest stars of the South African Zulu pop form *mbaqanga*, based on traditional singing styles. ●: *The Lion of Soweto* (Earthworks) is a rockin' compilation that presents the South African singer's primal vocals backed by the Mahotella Queens.

Hugh Masakela—South Africa's leading jazz trumpeter also pioneered what some now call world music, with his transcultural fusion of South African rhythms, jazz, and R&B. ⚫: His early hits, including "Grazin' in the Grass," are collected on *24 Karat Hits* (Verve). *Masakela: Introducing Hedzoleh Soundz* (Blue Thumb) is a terrifically uplifting record that sounds closer to its roots than most of today's Afropop, including current Masakela. Featuring many of the same musicians as *Hedzoleh Soundz*, *I Am Not Afraid* (Blue Thumb) introduced several Masakela songs—"In the Market Place," "African Secret Society," "Stimela"— that justifiably became much-requested parts of his regular repertoire. Unlike *Hedzoleh Soundz*, most of the songs are sung in English and are somewhat more Western-sounding overall.

Curtis Mayfield—As a singer, guitarist, songwriter, and producer, Mayfield has long been regarded by musicians as one of soul music's most protean talents. Why the public never responded quite the same way is a mystery. Paralyzed in an onstage accident in 1990, Mayfield continues to record sporadically. ⚫: *The Anthology 1961–1977* (MCA) covers both Mayfield's career with the Impressions and his best-known solo work. Import individual albums include *Curtis* (Ichiban), Mayfield's solo debut in 1970 and *Superfly* (Curtom), an ageless, groundbreaking film soundtrack released in 1972.

Clyde McPhatter—McPhatter, who did stints in both Billy Ward's Dominoes and the Drifters, is just a few steps behind Ray Charles and Sam Cooke as one of the most influential R&B vocalists from the 1950s. ⚫: *Deep Sea Ball: The Best of Clyde McPhatter* (Atlantic).

The Meters—With future Neville Brothers keyboardist Art Neville and three other crack players, the Meters were the New Orleans session-band-of-choice and recorded several albums on their own, most of which are out of print. ⚫: 1970's *Look-Ka-Py-Py* (Rounder) is one of the group's best song collections. *Funkify Your Life* (Rhino), a two-CD compilation, surveys the catalog of this band, which was making prime funk music before it was called funk.

Mighty Clouds of Joy—This Los Angeles–based gospel group made a crossover splash in the mid-'70s and has continued to record both gospel and pop. ⚫: *Live and Direct* (ABC).

Thelonious Monk—One of the great composers, in jazz or any genre, in American musical history, pianist Monk created a timeless, delightful body of work with its own rules, logic, and, at times, humor. ⚫: *Brilliant Corners* (Riverside), *Thelonious Monk with John Coltrane*, *Monk's Music*, *Thelonious Himself*, and *Alone in San Francisco* are some of Monk's best-loved records for Riverside. *The Complete Blue Note Recordings* (Blue Note), a four-CD set, presents an earlier look at this giant, with his remarkable compositional abilities already fully mature. *At the Five Spot* (Milestone) features one of Monk's better quartets with saxophonist Johnny Griffin.

Bill Monroe and the Bluegrass Boys (1945–47 version)—This unit—with guitarist Lester Flatt, banjoist Earl Scruggs, fiddler Chubby Wise, and bassist Howard Watts along with Monroe on mandolin—is the classic band against which all other traditional bluegrass is measured. ●: *The Essential Bill Monroe (1945–1949* (2 CDs: Columbia/Legacy) and *16 Gems* (Columbia/Legacy) feature that lineup playing the group's best-known material. There is overlap in songs between the two but the takes are different.

Charlie Parker—Alto saxophonist Parker, a founder of bebop, is almost without question the most important jazz artist ever on his instrument, and one of the most important on any instrument. ●: *The Complete Dial Sessions 1946–47* (Stash) is a four-CD set of astounding musical quality. *Bird: The Original Recordings of Charlie Parker* (Verve) is a good single-disc introduction to Parker's marvelous work for the Verve label. Similarly, *Charlie Parker Memorial, Vol. 1* (Savoy) contains some of his best work for Savoy in the late 1940s. *Charlie Parker with Strings: The Master Takes* (Verve) finds Parker soloing over an orchestra.

Junior Parker—An ultra-smooth stylist both as a vocalist and harmonica player, Parker was a versatile blues performer much loved by fellow blues and R&B musicians to this day. He recorded for two legendary labels, Memphis' Sun and Houston's Duke. ●: *Junior's Blues/The Duke Recordings, Vol. 1* (MCA) may be the best introduction but if you want to hear the original, pre-Elvis "Mystery Train" he cut for Sun Records in 1953, get the excellent although brief compilation *Mystery Train* (Rounder), with several tracks by James Cotton and Parker guitarist Pat Hare in addition to nine tracks under Parker's name.

Harry Partch—A true American original, Partch created unique tonal systems, performed on his beautiful homemade instruments. ●: *Delusion of the Fury* (Columbia), *The World of Harry Partch* (Columbia, out of print), or *Water! Water!* (CRI).

Charley Patton—Patton is the earliest, and one of the most rhythmically dynamic, of the Delta country blues stars. ●: *Founder of the Delta Blues* (Yazoo) and *King of the Delta Blues* (Yazoo).

Carl Perkins—A crucial link in rock history and a major influence on Beatle George Harrison among many others, Perkins combined R&B and country in his rockabilly classics for Sun Records. ●: *Original Sun Greatest Hits* (Rhino) covers

Perkins's pre-1958 career. *The Jive After Five: Best of . . . (1958–78)* (Rhino) surveys Perkins's recordings for CBS.

The Pilgrim Travelers—This was one of the most popular black gospel groups during the music's Golden Age in the 1950s. 🔊: *The Best of . . . , Vols. 1 & 2* (Specialty).

Bud Powell—A disturbed, tragic figure, Powell was, in spite of it all, one of the great pianists of the bebop era. 🔊: You'll receive a significant introduction to Powell on either volume of *The Amazing Bud Powell* (Blue Note), particularly Volume I. For a more comprehensive listen, try the four-CD *Complete Blue Note and Roost Recordings* (Blue Note).

Professor Longhair—Henry Roeland Byrd, aka Professor Longhair, cooked up a piano stew of rumba, boogie-woogie, blues, and calypso that became a foundation of the Crescent City R&B and rock 'n' roll sound. 🔊: *New Orleans Piano* (Atlantic) covers Longhair's legendary work for Atlantic in 1949 and 1953. *Fess: Professor Longhair Anthology* (Rhino) is a two-CD career overview.

Otis Redding—Killed in a plane crash when he was 26, Redding was one of the preeminent soul singers in history. 🔊: *Otis!: The Definitive Otis Redding* (4 CDs: Rhino) does the legend justice with three CDs of studio tracks and one CD of sweaty live performances. *Otis Blue* (Atco), *The Dictionary of Soul* (Atco), and *In Person at the Whiskey a Go Go* (Rhino) are the single discs to start with. There's no such thing as too much Otis.

Jimmy Reed—Reed's lazy but insistent grooves made him a major star in both the blues and R&B worlds and a primary influence on 1960s generation blues rockers. 🔊: *Speak the Lyrics to Me, Mama Reed* (Vee Jay).

Billy Lee Riley—A multi-instrumentalist and singer in the rockabilly style, Riley cut his best-known records for Memphis' Sun. 🔊: *Classic Recordings: 1956–60* (2 CDs: Bear Family) includes Riley's Sun recordings and later work in Memphis.

Django Reinhardt—See Stephane Grappelli.

Roxy Music—This arty pop group launched the careers of Brian Ferry, Brian Eno, and Phil Manzanera. 🔊: *Roxy Music* (Reprise), *For Your Pleasure* (Reprise), *Country Life* (Reprise), and *Siren* (Reprise), all released between 1972 and 1975, are the peak records.

The Skatalites—Led by the troubled Don Drummond, this ska band was composed of Jamaica's most highly accomplished musicians of their day. In 1965, just 14 months into their career, the band broke up when Drummond murdered his wife. 🔘: *Ska Authentic* (Studio One) and *Scattered Lights* (Alligator) are both strong studio collections.

Huey "Piano" Smith—This wild vocalist and R&B pianist was one of the biggest stars of New Orleans R&B in the 1950s. 🔘: *Rock and Roll Revival* (Ace) contains 16 tracks of Smith's biggest hits and best-known material.

The Soul Brothers—The Brothers are one of the most widely loved exponents of South African *mbaqanga* music. 🔘: *Jive Explosion* (Earthworks/Caroline), *Jump and Jive* (Sterns), *Born to Jive* (Sterns), *Mbaqanga* (Riverboat), and *Idlozi* (Gallo).

Joseph Spence—This Bahamanian singer/guitarist astounded folk musicians in the 1960s with his orchestra-in-his-fingertips guitar style and incandescently joyous vocals. 🔘: *The Complete Folkways Recordings (1958)* (Smithsonian Folkways) and *Happy All the Time* (Carthage).

The Stylistics—These exponents of sweet Philly soul music scored a string of hits in the 1970s. 🔘: *The Best of the Stylistics* (Amherst).

The Swan Silvertones—This gospel group was founded and led by Claude Jeter, one of gospel's greatest lead singers. 🔘: *Love Lifted Me/My Rock* (Specialty) compiles two classic LPs from the mid-1950s on one CD. *Get Right with the Swan Silvertones* (Rhino) and *Swan Silvertones/Singin' in My Soul* (Vee Jay), another single CD featuring two classic LPs, are other excellent choices.

Johnnie Taylor—Taylor replaced Sam Cooke in the gospel group the Soul Stirrers before leaving for an R&B career. 🔘: . . . *Chronicle* (Stax) compiles all Taylor's R&B hits for Stax, plus album cuts. In the superb boxed set *Sam Cooke's SAR Records Story* (2 CDs: ABKCO), Taylor can be heard singing both R&B and gospel, produced by Cooke. You'll find a much bigger dose of Taylor's gospel on the Soul Stirrers' *Heaven is My Home* (Specialty).

Thee Midniters—In East Los Angeles, this Latino R&B band was the Beatles and Stones wrapped up in one during the 1960s. 🔘: *The Best of Thee Midniters* (Rhino). The band is also represented on the three-volume *Brown-Eyed Soul* (Rhino), an anthology of East L.A. bands.

Toure Kunda—This djabadong band from Senegal now is based in France, where it has added reggae, rock, and funk to its tradition-based sound. 🔘: *E'mma Africa* (Celluloid) and *Salam* (Trama) are both fine introductions. The former record is more tradition-oriented, the latter more commercial in concept and production.

Ernest Tubb—Tubb was the first honky-tonk singer to become a major star. 🔘: *Ernest Tubb: Country Music Hall of Fame* (MCA).

Stevie Ray Vaughan—A blues guitarist of almost unfathomable ability, Vaughan was widely recognized by older blues musicians as the greatest stringbender to come along in years. His death in a helicopter crash in 1990 left a giant hole in the music. 🔘: *Greatest Hits* (Epic) is a good way to enter Vaughan's catalog since he cut a number of stunning tracks but never made a truly excellent album. The posthumous *The Sky is Crying* (Epic) gives an impressive accounting of Vaughan's stylistic versatility.

Velvet Underground—They sold very few albums when they were together but have ended up as one of the most influential rock bands ever, particularly for the current generation of disaffected rockers. 🔘: *Peel Slowly and See* (Polydor), a box set containing all four VU studio albums plus loads of unreleased tracks.

Albertina Walker and the Caravans—This group cut a number of gospel hits in the 1950s before their founder, Walker, left for a solo career in 1960. 🔘: *The Very Best of . . .* (Collectibles).

T-Bone Walker—Walker's innovative style on electric guitar came to national attention with his hit "T-Bone Blues" in 1939. His recordings over the next 15 years were crucial to the instrument's development in blues and rock. He was also an important jazz soloist. 🔘: *T-Bone Blues* (Atlantic) is a great single-disc collection of T-Bone's classic mid-'50s hits, but if you have the box bug, Mosaic has released the six-CD set *The Complete Recordings of T-Bone Walker*. A happy medium might be struck with either or both of the two-CD sets *The Complete Capitol/Black & White* Recordings (Capitol), from the 1940s, and *The Complete Imperial Recordings* (EMI), from 1950 to '54.

Thomas "Fats" Waller—One of jazz music's great entertainers, Waller was also a terrific stride pianist, wonderful composer, and jazz's first organist. 🔘: For an introduction, try any of the CDs in the Bluebird label's Fats Waller reissue series, particulary the two-CD set of piano solos *Turn On the Heat* and the group re-cordings on *Fats Waller and His Buddies*.

Muddy Waters—Born in Mississippi, Waters defines the Chicago electric blues style, which he helped invent. His importance to rock is this simple—without him, there is no Rolling Stones. In his early career, he was also blues' greatest bandleader. 🔘: Waters's three-CD *The Chess Box* (MCA/Chess), with Otis Spann on piano, Willie Dixon on bass, and alternately Little Walter Jacobs or James Cotton on harmonica, is a seminal collection. *The Best of Muddy Waters* (MCA/Chess) provides a fine, single-disc introduction to the same material.

Hank Williams—Williams is considered the father of modern country music but he was just as influenced by blues, which is at the heart of his emotional appeal.

His song catalog overflows with standards and his vocal style is still the foundation for country performers today. 🔘: *40 Greatest Hits* (2 CDs: Polydor) includes every essential track. Completists will want to invest in the eight-volume series on Polydor that presents the hits, outtakes, demos, and radio broadcasts in chronological order.

Sonny Boy Williamson II (Rice Miller)— 🔘: Sonny Boy II has an extensive catalog of great releases. *The Essential Sonny Boy Williamson* (2 CDs: Chess) is a terrific package of his Chess sides. *King Biscuit Time* (Arhoolie) captures prime early recordings from 1951.

Classical

Bela Bartok—Concerto for Orchestra. Bartok's most popular work was also the last one he completed. 🔘: For an absolutely thrilling performance of these pieces, try the 1955 recording Concerto for Orchestra and Music for Strings, Percussion, and Celeste with *Hungarian Sketches* (RCA Living Stereo), the Chicago Symphony Orchestra conducted by Fritz Reiner. Another superb version is by the Chicago Symphony, Sir Georg Solti conducting (London).

Claude Debussy—*Prelude to the Afternoon of a Faun*. This widely loved composition was inspired by a poem by Stéphane Mallarmé. 🔘: Two highly praised versions of this oft-recorded piece are the New York Philharmonic/Leonard Bernstein (with *La Mer*, *Jeux*, and Two Nocturnes, Sony) and the London Symphony Orchestra/Andre Previn (with Three *Images* for Orchestra, EMI).

Charles Ives—*Three Places in New England*. This composition, also known as First Orchestral Set, vividly illustrates Ives's remarkable ability to paint pictures with sound. 🔘: Eastman-Rochester Symphony Orchestra/Howard Hanson (Philips).

Gustav Mahler—Symphonies. 🔘: There are hundreds of recordings of the Mahler symphonies, and critical opinion diverges widely about them. We suggest you start with those conducted by Pierre Boulez. Note that a complete set of Mahler symphonies spans some 14 CDs.

APPENDIX: HOW TO FIND OBSCURE MUSIC

M any of the recordings mentioned by the artists in *Listen to This!* are rare, out of print, or at best not readily available at your local mall chain store. The resources listed in this section are good places to look for these recordings.

We encourage you, however, to start your search for any recording with your local, independent music store. Most independent stores employ knowledgeable, music-loving staff who can point you in the right direction, and who will special-order any recording currently in print. We've often found juicy, out-of-print recordings at local used music stores, too.

If your local store can't find what you're seeking, or if you don't live near an independent retailer, the following are some suggested resources for finding music. Many of these mail-order retailers are based on the World Wide Web, but wherever possible we've included phone numbers and mailing addresses for readers who don't have Web access.

A warning about the Internet: Although we have done our best to make the following information as current as possible, some of the Web addresses below may be out of date by the publication date of this book because of the rapidly evolving nature of the Internet. Also, the listing below in no way guarantees the reliability of the following sources as retailers. We have not necessarily conducted business with all of them, so *caveat emptor.*

Acoustic Sounds

PO Box 1905
Salina, KS 67402-1905
(800)716-3553
(785)825-0256 fax
www.acousticsounds.com

A good source for audiophile recordings on both vinyl and CD. You'll find some releases in audiophile editions that are out of print in their original editions. However, be prepared to pay a premium for your purchases.

Africassette Music

PO Box 24941
Detroit, MI 48224
(313)881-4108
(313)881-0260 fax
www.africassette.com
E-mail: rsteiger@africassette.com

This small company specializes in African music, both pop and folk.

Allegro Music

www.allegro-music.com

One of the largest independent importers/distributors in North America, Allegro now has a retail Web site with a searchable database. They once specialized in imports of classical music, but now distribute all kinds of music.

Amazon.com

www.amazon.com

The Internet's mail order book retailing giant also offers access to any music currently in print.

CDNow/Music Boulevard

www.cdnow.com

Another Web-based retail giant with a huge, searchable database. They can lay their hands on anything currently in print.

Collectors' Choice Music

PO Box 838
Itasca, IL 60143-0838 USA
(800)923-1122
www.ccmusic.com

A mail order firm specializing in reissues, some of which they license and compile exclusively. Everything from vintage jazz and R&B to rare '60s pop, country, and exotica. The place to go for reissues of Staff Sgt. Barry Sadler, Andy Kim, the Troggs, or Julie London. They also feature many of the monstropolous Bear Family box sets for fanatical roots music collectors with disposable income.

Compact Disc Connection

www.cdconnection.com

Another huge Web-based retailer, this is our Number One suggestion for the place to start if you have a crying music jones. CD Connection avoids the fancy graphics of the other big Web sites, so their searchable database zooms. The site includes Liquid Audio music samples.

Craig Moerer Records By Mail

PO Box 42546
Portland, OR 97242
(503)232-1735
(503) 232-1746 fax
www.records-by-mail.com/home.html

Craig Moerer boasts that he has over 800,000 pre-1985 records in stock—everything, it seems, but classical music. Searchable on-line database, too.

Cyber CD

www.cybercd.de

A huge German Web site (with an English version) where you can mail-order many obscure imports. Prices are listed in Deutsch marks and expect high shipping costs if you're ordering from the States. But if you want CDs by Brigitte Fontaine or the Blues Etilicos, they've got 'em.

Descarga

328 Flatbush Avenue, Suite 180
Brooklyn, NY 11238
(718)693-2966
(718)693-1316
(800)377-2647 (orders)
www.descarga.com
E-mail: info@descarga.com

Afro-Cuban, Caribbean, and Latin music of all kinds.

GEMM

www.gemm.com

This unusual site calls itself "an open marketplace" and its search engine polls over 1,400 discounters, importers, collectors, labels, and artists, displaying its hits in a little chart so you can get the best price. You then order through GEMM. Yes, it's sort of a virtual middleman, but we've found stuff on GEMM's Web site that we never knew existed.

Goldmine

700 E. State Street
Iola, WI 54990
(715)445-2214
www.krause.com/goldmine
E-mail: info@krause.com

Not a store, *Goldmine* is *the* magazine for music collectors. Published bi-weekly, it contains discographies, articles, and classifieds for both collectors and vendors. The classifieds can also be found on the Internet at www.collectit.net. If you absolutely can't find a rare recording anywhere else, *Goldmine*'s classified section is the place to go.

H&B Recordings Direct

PO Box 309
Waterbury Center, VT 05677
(800) 222-6872
International: (802)244-5290
(802)244-4199 fax
www.hbdirect.com
E-mail: staff@hbdirect.com

One of the largest mail order sources for classical music: That's all they sell.

Ladyslipper

(919)383-8773
(919)383-3525 fax
(800)634-6044 (orders)
www.ladyslipper.org
E-mail: orders@ladyslipper.org

A large, eclectic selection of music by women.

Midnight Records

PO Box 390, Old Chelsea Station
New York, NY 10011
(212)675-2768
(212)741-7230 fax
http://midnightrecords.com
E-mail: midnight@cerfnet.com

A legend among record collectors, Midnight specializes in rock rarities and imports, but also has rare blues, R&B, and jazz, with an on-line database.

Mobile Fidelity Sound Lab

105 Morris Street
Sebastopol, CA 95472
(800)423-5759
www.mofi.com

The pioneer in the pricey audiophile reissue market, Mobile Fidelity is often the best place to look, especially for '60s and '70s pop recordings that are now out of print in their standard pressings. But they've also reissued classic jazz and blues.

Mosaic/True Blue

35 Melrose Place
Stamford CT 06902-7533
(203)327-7111
(203)323-3526 fax
email:trueblue@ix.netcom.com
mosrec@ix.netcom.com

Mosaic Records collects and repackages meticulous limited-edition collections of jazz, blues, and R&B, specializing in classic Blue Note recordings. Their box sets are expensive, but in our opinion, worth the money for the quality sound and exhaustive liner notes. Many are available on both CD and vinyl. True Blue is a larger mail order catalog run by the same people. It also specializes in classic blues, R&B, and jazz, but with a larger selection than Mosaic. Mosaic sets are available through True Blue, also.

Music File

www.musicfile.com

A Web-based swap meet for music collectors where you can buy or sell.

Music Direct

1327 West Washington Street, Suite 102
Chicago, IL 60607
(800)449-8333
(312)433-0200 IL/International
(800)411-1280/(312)433-0011 fax
www.amusicdirect.com

Another source for audiophile recordings, with a thoughtful selection.

Public Radio Music Source

(800)75-MUSIC (inquiries and orders)
www.75music.org

A service of many of the United States' public radio stations, PRMS can deliver anything currently in print and keeps track of what's currently being played on public radio, so it's a good source if you hear something cool and obscure on *All Things Considered* or *The World Cafe*. If your local public radio station participates, the station receives a royalty for every sale coming from your community.

Roots & Rhythm

PO Box 2216
San Leandro, CA 94577
(510)614-5353
(510)614-8833 fax
(888) ROOTS-66 (orders)
www.bluesworld.com/roots.html
E-mail: roots@hooked.net

Formerly Down Home Music, Roots & Rhythm carries a comprehensive collection of blues, folk, traditional country, roots rock 'n' roll, R&B, and jazz, and is a good place to start to look for the roots recordings mentioned by artists in *Listen to This!*.

Smithsonian/Folkways

Center for Folklife Programs & Cultural Studies
955 L'Enfant Plaza, Suite 7300, MRC 953
Washington, DC 20560
(202)287-7298
(202)287-7299 fax
(800)410-9815 (orders)
www.si.edu/folkways
E-mail: folkways@aol.com

The Smithsonian now owns Moses Asch's legendary Folkways label, which released
many of the seminal recordings mentioned in *Listen to This!*, including those of
Leadbelly, Pete Seeger, Josh White, Phil Ochs, and Woody Guthrie. A great selection of
classic gospel, ethnic, and children's music, too.

Strategy Records

PO Box 517
Bethlehem, CT 06751
(800)838-7774 (USA) voice/fax
Outside USA: (203)266-7774
www.island.net/~blues/strategy.htm#

Specializes in blues, including the tremendous Document reissue series.

Tower Records

www.towerrecords.com

The on-line version of Tower Records stores, with a searchable database, music
downloads, and other juicy features.

Tunes.com

www.tunes.com

Our first choice for casual browsing, Tunes.com is loaded with audio clips of virtually
every track of every title they sell. A large collection of every kind of music, with a
searchable database. You can spend hours on this site.

Vinyl Vendors

1800 S. Robertson Boulevard, #279
Los Angeles CA 90035
(310)275-1444
(310)275-8444 fax
www.vinylvendors.com
E-mail: paul@vinylvendors.com

A great source for rare, used, and out-of-print CDs, LPs, and 45s, with a searchable
database.

Author Contact Information

Contact us via e-mail at areder@cdsnet.net and jbaxter@jeffnet.org, or by snail mail at:

Listen to This!
P.O. Box 759
Rogue River, OR 97537

Visit us on the Web at www.listentothismusic.com

Index